PUBLIC ADMINISTRATION
AND POLICY
IN THE CARIBBEAN

PUBLIC ADMINISTRATION AND PUBLIC POLICY
A Comprehensive Publication Program

EDITOR-IN-CHIEF

DAVID H. ROSENBLOOM

Distinguished Professor of Public Administration
American University, Washington, DC

Founding Editor

JACK RABIN

RECENTLY PUBLISHED BOOKS

Public Administration and Policy in the Caribbean, Indianna D. Minto-Coy and Evan Berman

Sustainable Development and Human Security in Africa: Governance as the Missing Link, Louis A. Picard, Terry F. Buss, Taylor B. Seybolt, and Macrina C. Lelei

Information and Communication Technologies in Public Administration: Innovations from Developed Countries, Christopher G. Reddick and Leonidas Anthopoulos

Creating Public Value in Practice: Advancing the Common Good in a Multi-Sector, Shared-Power, No-One-Wholly-in-Charge World, edited by John M. Bryson, Barbara C. Crosby, and Laura Bloomberg

Digital Divides: The New Challenges and Opportunities of e-Inclusion, Kim Andreasson

Living Legends and Full Agency: Implications of Repealing the Combat Exclusion Policy, G.L.A. Harris

Politics of Preference: India, United States, and South Africa, Krishna K. Tummala

Crisis and Emergency Management: Theory and Practice, Second Edition, Ali Farazmand

Labor Relations in the Public Sector, Fifth Edition, Richard C. Kearney and Patrice M. Mareschal

Democracy and Public Administration in Pakistan, Amna Imam and Eazaz A. Dar

The Economic Viability of Micropolitan America, Gerald L. Gordon

Personnel Management in Government: Politics and Process, Seventh Edition, Katherine C. Naff, Norma M. Riccucci, and Siegrun Fox Freyss

Public Administration in South Asia: India, Bangladesh, and Pakistan, edited by Meghna Sabharwal and Evan M. Berman

Making Multilevel Public Management Work: Stories of Success and Failure from Europe and North America, edited by Denita Cepiku, David K. Jesuit, and Ian Roberge

Available Electronically
PublicADMINISTRATION*netBASE*
http://www.crcnetbase.com/page/public_administration_ebooks

PUBLIC ADMINISTRATION AND POLICY IN THE CARIBBEAN

EDITED BY
INDIANNA D. MINTO-COY • EVAN M. BERMAN

CRC Press is an imprint of the
Taylor & Francis Group, an **informa** business

CRC Press
Taylor & Francis Group
6000 Broken Sound Parkway NW, Suite 300
Boca Raton, FL 33487-2742

© 2016 by Taylor & Francis Group, LLC
CRC Press is an imprint of Taylor & Francis Group, an Informa business

No claim to original U.S. Government works

Printed on acid-free paper
Version Date: 20150526

International Standard Book Number-13: 978-1-4398-9294-7 (Hardback)

This book contains information obtained from authentic and highly regarded sources. Reasonable efforts have been made to publish reliable data and information, but the author and publisher cannot assume responsibility for the validity of all materials or the consequences of their use. The authors and publishers have attempted to trace the copyright holders of all material reproduced in this publication and apologize to copyright holders if permission to publish in this form has not been obtained. If any copyright material has not been acknowledged please write and let us know so we may rectify in any future reprint.

Except as permitted under U.S. Copyright Law, no part of this book may be reprinted, reproduced, transmitted, or utilized in any form by any electronic, mechanical, or other means, now known or hereafter invented, including photocopying, microfilming, and recording, or in any information storage or retrieval system, without written permission from the publishers.

For permission to photocopy or use material electronically from this work, please access www.copyright.com (http://www.copyright.com/) or contact the Copyright Clearance Center, Inc. (CCC), 222 Rosewood Drive, Danvers, MA 01923, 978-750-8400. CCC is a not-for-profit organization that provides licenses and registration for a variety of users. For organizations that have been granted a photocopy license by the CCC, a separate system of payment has been arranged.

Trademark Notice: Product or corporate names may be trademarks or registered trademarks, and are used only for identification and explanation without intent to infringe.

Visit the Taylor & Francis Web site at
http://www.taylorandfrancis.com

and the CRC Press Web site at
http://www.crcpress.com

Contents

Preface vii
Acknowledgments xiii
Introduction xv
Editors xvii
Contributors xix

1 Public Administration and Policy in the Caribbean: An Overview
  of the Caribbean 1
  INDIANNA D. MINTO-COY AND EVAN M. BERMAN

SECTION I PUBLIC ADMINISTRATION AND POLICY IN THE CARIBBEAN: HISTORY AND MAJOR DEVELOPMENTS

2 The History of Public Administration in the Commonwealth Caribbean 33
  INDIANNA D. MINTO-COY

3 Public Administration in the French Antilles: Historical Trends and Prospects 61
  JUSTIN DANIEL

4 The History of Public Administration in the Dutch Caribbean 77
  MIGUEL GOEDE

5 Public Policy and Management in Cuba 95
  GERARDO GONZÁLEZ NÚÑEZ

SECTION II ISSUES IN PUBLIC ADMINISTRATION

6 Civil Service Performance in the Caribbean 111
  WAYNE SOVERALL

7 Public Financial Management in the Caribbean 143
  EILEEN BROWNE

8 Public Procurement Policy Considerations in the Caribbean: Trade, Governance, and Development 159
MARGARET ROSE

9 Assessing Public Sector Reform in the Anglophone Caribbean 179
ANN MARIE BISSESSAR

10 Contending with Caribbean Public Sector Leadership in the Twenty-First Century 201
EDWIN JONES, ANDREW WALCOTT, AND SANDRA GREY-ALVARANGA

11 State Capacity and International Politics 229
MATTHEW LOUIS BISHOP

SECTION III PUBLIC POLICY ISSUES AND THEMES

12 Education Reform Initiatives in the Caribbean Basin 247
TAVIS D. JULES AND HAKIM MOHANDAS AMANI WILLIAMS

13 Developmental Interventions in the Caribbean 295
NIKOLAOS KARAGIANNIS, ANTHONY CLAYTON, AND JESSICA M. BAILEY

14 Environmental Risk Management in the Caribbean 311
CHARLEY G. GRANVORKA, ERIC A. STROBL, LESLIE WALLING, AND EVAN M. BERMAN

15 Sustainable Development of Caribbean Tourism 337
ANTHONY CLAYTON, NIKOLAOS KARAGIANNIS, AND JESSICA M. BAILEY

16 Policy and Regulation of the Caribbean Communications Industry 357
INDIANNA D. MINTO-COY

17 Health Service Reform in the Caribbean: The Rise of New Mutualism 379
TAVIS D. JULES AND LANDIS G. FRYER

18 Gender Equality and Gender Policy-Making in the Caribbean 415
PATRICIA MOHAMMED

19 Poverty in the Caribbean 443
CHARLEY G. GRANVORKA

Index 465

Preface

The Caribbean is a complex and varied landscape, a fact that is not always obvious at first glance. Thanks largely to a history of colonialism, plantation economies, slavery, and indentureship, the region has developed a complex mix of languages, political and legal institutions, history, and culture largely based on historical association with the United Kingdom, France, Spain, the United States, and the Netherlands. Some countries are independent territories, while others have various levels of attachment (e.g., as dependents, overseas departments, and territories) to these powers. These differences are demonstrated to varying degrees in the nature and conduct of public administration across the region.

Interestingly, however, not many works have sought to more widely consider the public administration experiences, legacies, models, and practices across the wider Caribbean. Indeed, the few that focus on public administration and policy in the Caribbean tend to narrowly cover the French, Dutch, Spanish, or Commonwealth Caribbean subregions in isolation. To date, learning across countries in the region has been limited. Comparative reviews of public administration have also tended to focus on countries outside the region as opposed to going across the different historical and cultural blocs for a deeper understanding of the breadth of the region. There is a natural difference presented by historical experiences and the institutions that they have given rise to. However, the absence of information on and an understanding of the different territories have also lessened the possibilities for learning and internal adaptation with the natural inclination to look beyond the region for lessons and understandings. An understanding of culture and history is a significant requirement for policy development and understanding of the capacities and tendencies in a country. Additionally, valuable information on policy choices and opportunities for intraregional learning and exchange have been significantly curtailed by a singular focus on subgroupings in isolation of the wider experiences across the region. Moreover, the literature—whatever that exists on public administration in the Caribbean—is for the most part outdated, posing a specific challenge to researchers and students wanting to learn about practices in the modern period and comparatively to locate these in the history of the region. This suggests the need for more information and understanding—a more comprehensive assessment—of the variety of experiences and developments in public administration, the challenges faced by these small states, and the ways in which some of these have been addressed from a policy perspective across the region.

Moreover, the region is at a critical phase in its evolution. Many of the independent territories are still young democracies marking almost 50 years of independence. For the independent territories, a focus on the need for new governance concerns the right mix of policies and strategies to deliver growth and development in a climate of increasing frustration at the mediocre performance post-independence. This is especially so when compared to countries, such as Singapore, that at the point of independence were at similar levels of development. For those non-independent territories that have retained various degrees of linkages with former colonial powers, there is an ongoing search for governance models and institutional reform with the issue of new governance being about the search for options for retaining (or doing away with) the safety afforded by the status quo. The imperative for a rethink of administrative practices is also no less the case in those territories that have traditionally been seen as more successful. For instance, Barbados, admired for the extent of its social policies, stable social and industrial relations, and socioeconomic development, has witnessed increasing socioeconomic and political discontent including uncharacteristic public demonstration, while the viability of its noted consensual governance model (Social Partnership) has been questioned. The matter of new governance for new times is therefore a near and present concern across the region. This collection of essays, which marks a significant reflection on what has been obtained and an indication of what is possible, is therefore more pertinent at this juncture given the heightened search for ways of improving governance and administration across the region.

This imperative was made even clearer (for one of us) when, as a student at the London School of Economics trolling through one of the most comprehensive library resource in the social sciences, it became obvious that the accounts of public policy and management in the region were largely incomplete and in many cases significantly outdated. As such, the development of this book has also been informed by a desire to present a cohesive framework that would be useful to students wanting to know as much about a topic or area at various levels without having to sort through numerous and distant material. Nonetheless, this is not a call for students not to go beyond this work but for this collection to be seen as the first and most cohesive point of entry into these issues for the region. For this reason, too, care has been taken in making the book accessible and in selecting the themes and issues addressed. These include areas that are not typically included in a book on public policy and management but which nonetheless have resonance in understanding the Caribbean (tourism, diasporas, and migration), as well as some new and emerging policy areas (diasporas and development, and cyber security). It is worth noting as well at this stage that there is no hang up about the notion of public management versus public administration, with the terms being used interchangeably throughout the work.

This book offers data and key perspectives for beginning this introspection across the Caribbean. It seeks to do this by examining the origin, practice, and major developments in public governance in the Caribbean. In so doing, it will address the following questions:

- What is the history and context of public administration and governance in the Caribbean?
- What has been the influence of cultural or historical affiliation on the development of public administration and how has this balanced against local imperatives?
- How have public administration and policy changed over the years?
- How is public administration and public policy done in the Caribbean?
- What are the differences and similarities?
- What are the specific policy issues affecting the Caribbean?
- How have governments attempted to address these and with what effect?
- How have international trends and developments in public administration played out in these territories and with what effect?
- What explains the success or failure of these efforts?
- What has been the impact of size on the conduct of public administration in the Caribbean?
- How do these small islands conduct policy and administration in a globalized world?

In spite of the guiding questions presented to authors, the approach was not pedantic, with each author being given some freedom to approach the different topics from each one's base of expertise and insights garnered from years of working and researching in the region. Additionally, the aim was to allow the reality of the region to come forth in the expositions, as opposed to the natural tendency to focus on borrowed theories and concepts. While the latter has many merits, the intent in this case, in the vein of an areas studies account, was to allow the experiences in the region to come forth naturally. Indeed, the information in this volume can ultimately contribute to and create the space for further efforts of conceptualizing or theorizing public policy and administration in developing and small Caribbean states.

To this end, the book is a collection of essays divided into three main sections. Section I aims to capture the history and development of public administration practices and institutions across the Caribbean. It will also introduce some of the major traditions, developments, trends, and challenges in the evolution and practice of public policy and administration. These chapters will present an overview of practice and policy from the colonial period to the present, summarizing some of the major developments in policy and administration. Specific policies and themes will be taken up in Sections II and III. More specifically, Section II offers an exposition and critical analysis of some of the current debates and issues in public administration, thus delving into the internal workings of the state. In so doing, the chapters in this section also take a much more precise and in-depth look at some of the issues introduced in Section I. Section III represents a discussion of some of the ongoing and new public policy issues and concerns in the region. Through this structure, the book sheds light not only on the internal workings of the public administration machinery (in Section II) but also on the economic, political, and increasingly environmental and global contexts in which public servants operate. The chapters focus on areas where governments need to develop administrative capacity or make improvements in order to secure the region's future in an increasingly competitive yet unpredictable global environment, where the quality of public governance is an important indicator of success. They also demonstrate an awareness of the vital role of sound policy, planning, and management in the development process.

The emphasis on themes as opposed to individual countries is also expedient, given the number of territories in the Caribbean. Nonetheless, such an enterprise is rendered somewhat difficult in the context of such variety. In some instances then, the attempt has been made to capture the specific circumstances of some states as independent versus dependent territories. To this end, too, some cases will be given special attention. For example, Cuba, which in many ways is seen as an outlier, given the unique political, economic, and ideological circumstances that have underpinned the evolution of this country, has been given special treatment.

Herein, however, lies one of the main limitations of this work and perhaps of such a grand exercise. That is, some more obvious cases have also not received special treatment. Included here is the case of Haiti, which has not been given a similar treatment as Cuba. This also applies to some more recent experiences, including the United States' influence in the Caribbean. Nevertheless, the story of Haiti is not absent from this volume but runs throughout various accounts, including the introductory chapter and others on public procurement, communications industry, and poverty. The emergence of the United States as a credible challenger to the influence of traditional powers in the region is also treated in various chapters. Indeed, the intent in the introductory chapter that follows is to plug some of these gaps while borrowing content from other chapters within the book to present a comprehensive overview of the region. Inevitably, a book like this will have gaps in coverage. While this small region has been blessed with reputable and prolific scholars, the challenge in identifying sufficient credible contributors in all key policy areas was a reality with which the editors had to grapple.

Collectively, the chapters give a comprehensive overview (historical and contemporary) of public policy and management in the Caribbean to date; help build expertise and capacity in the governance and administration of small island and developing states, more generally; provide knowledge of the influences and practice of public policy and administration in the Caribbean; and provide information on tools, strategies, and analyses for researchers and practitioners in the region and its development partners, including multilateral institutions and countries that have historically supported development efforts across the region. In so doing, the book brings together some of the key issues and themes in public policy and administration, generally, and also relates to practice in the small states of the Caribbean.

We hope this book serves as a useful springboard for reading more broadly on these topics and perspectives as referenced in chapters of this book. However, the opening chapter sought to review some of the themes not covered in the chapters and mentions references that would help here.

Underlying the accounts is the point that public governance in the region must improve to deliver growth. This is important since democracy and development are influenced by the quality of public administration. This is so because the utilization of state resources, the ability to plan and execute for development, and the ability to manage the local economy and navigate the contours of international politics can all be directed by efficient public administration. A key ethos behind the production of this volume, too, is that public servants in the Caribbean in the twenty-first century need to be much more than they have been in the past, requiring far more than just a basic knowledge of the inner workings of the state and of administrative rules and principles. They are required to be far more reflexive, with knowledge of a wider array of issues and subject areas at different levels and their impact on the performance of the public administration machinery. Indeed, this charge goes far beyond the Caribbean. That means a far wider appreciation for the role of public policy and administration in development. The issues and themes selected for the volume have been informed somewhat by this understanding; the book has been recommended as a companion for practitioners of public management in the region as well as those deployed to the various multinational and international aid and governance institutions with relations or postings in the region and other developing and post-colonial settings.

These perspectives are important not only for practitioners and scholars of public policy and management in and outside the region but also for international development specialists and institutions, who as demonstrated in this volume have and will likely continue to play a major role in public administration and the content and outcomes of public policy. An understanding of the breadth of experiences and developments is also important for policy managers and development planners, in so far as opportunities are offered for more informed lesson drawing and the development of best practices. More broadly, a comparative study also allows for a more accurate assessment of the extent to which experiences in public policy and administration are dependent on history, culture, or politics versus factors such as size. In this way, the richness of data gained from such comparative assessments can help practitioners and students of public administration learn about the experiences, methods, and practices of other countries and be better able to assess the ways in which they can learn from these practices.

Thus, while this book addresses the field of public policy and administration, the themes and concepts are of interest to a multidisciplinary audience (e.g., development economists, historians, and political scientists). The book provides interested parties within and outside the region the opportunity to more fully understand the variety of institutional models and the different tools and techniques used in the craft of public policy and management and the ability to be able to identify areas of commonality in the midst of diversity. Indeed, that is one of the more interesting conclusions drawn from the various presentations highlighted in the introductory chapter. That is, the results and experiences in public policy and administration have, for the most part, been largely similar, in spite of the many differences highlighted earlier. That is to say, for example, that corruption, underdevelopment, inefficient bureaucracy, slow pace in adopting reforms, and incomplete implementation are features that transcend enclaves. In so doing, the book also considers why this is the case through a focus on issues such as historical legacy and size and their impact on the performance of government. These chapters will, therefore, be an important companion for students and scholars interested in public administration in the Caribbean as well as for those wishing to understand the region beyond the predominant images of sea, sand, and coconut trees.

Indianna D. Minto-Coy
University of the West Indies

Evan M. Berman
Victoria University of Wellington

Acknowledgments

Countless people have helped in the completion of this book. Among them are the anonymous reviewers who through their excellent comments have helped to hone and improve the various drafts. We felt that such a review process was significant in ensuring quality and relevance as well as accuracy in the reports and discussions. Indeed, this book would not have come to fruition without our contributors, who represent a wealth of experience and knowledge on a vast array of public administration and policy issues in the Caribbean. They have all brought their mass of experience and insights in academia, research, and practice to bear in producing this volume and we are grateful for their stellar efforts.

A book of this nature requires significant investments in time, energy, and, ultimately, a great level of patience. A number of other persons, including Derrick McKoy, Dalea Bean, Disraeli Hutton, Martin Lodge, Natallie Rochester-King, Lindsay Stirton, Andrea Yearwood, and Carline Peart, also deserve mention, as well as those who helped in this research and writing exercise. It is almost impossible to express enough gratitude to our publisher and particularly to Lara Zoble for her deep (almost superhuman) understanding throughout this book. I acknowledge the enormous levels of patience and support of the coeditor, particularly in those times when I began to wonder if I was mad to have taken on such a project. My co-editor has been constant as I moved back and forth among three countries, while patiently waiting for delayed drafts—Although, I may not be demonstrating it just yet, I have grown tremendously through this partnership and I remain profoundly impressed by his talent, professionalism and above all, his heart. I thank my husband, Dr. Andre Coy, for his support in every possible way for helping with the cover design and for showing me the depths of his love and patience throughout. To my daughters, Audra and Nyla, who in traveling the entire journey with me can truly claim some ownership over this book (their big sister). Such an extensive project is a significant encroachment on family life and ultimately also becomes the task of the ones closest to you.

Indianna D. Minto-Coy

I express appreciation and thanks to my spouse, Dira, for being part of this journey and providing support and love. I also thank Lara Zoble for her patience and commitment to this book, as well as the many authors in this volume who dedicated their time and efforts to make this successful. I hope to thank each and every one of you in person one day. Finally, I have come to grow ever more impressed with the qualities of my coeditor, Indianna. I look forward to celebrating this book among our families!

Evan M. Berman

Introduction

The Caribbean is at a crucial phase in its development. Global and local pressures have seen the region losing its competitiveness while it remains at risk of losing out on development gains made in the past few decades. These pressures are demanding improvements in the way government operates and particularly to its policy-making and administrative capacity. This must involve an assessment, first, of the way public administration and policy making are executed in key areas across the region, including the historical forces and legacies that continue to shape the environment in which public administration and policy take place, and, second, of the way forward.

Yet, within the region, very little is known about the experiences of neighboring territories beyond historical enclaves (e.g., English or French). A few scattered and incomplete accounts exist of public administration and policy across the region as a whole. As such, significant opportunities for the learning and exchange critical for building up capacity have been lost because of the tendency to view the region as subsections. There has been little effort to consider the whole gamut of models, institutions, and practice across what is a very diverse and complex region. The experiences of these states hold significant implications within the region, given the ongoing search for ways of improving the quality of public governance and management and, externally, as they relate to development policies and practices supported by multilateral aid and development institutions. Moreover, the story of public administration in the Caribbean is also that of small and developing states, more generally.

In *Public Administration and Policy in the Caribbean*, Minto-Coy and Berman have gathered the contributions of a host of well-placed practitioners and academics across the region and its diaspora to put together a convincing response to the gaps discussed earlier. The authors map the history and development of public policy and management across the Caribbean, a region characterized by institutional, cultural, historical, political, economic, and language diversities. The book also considers a number of critical policy issues, some old, some new, and others yet emerging that are of significant import for successful governance and development across the region. In essence, the book suggests how small states can more convincingly use their public administration to address existing and emerging policy challenges and secure future growth and development for their people. In so doing, the book represents one of the very few attempts to map public policy issues and experiences of the Caribbean in such a comprehensive way and in an area that has received little attention. *Public Administration and Policy in the Caribbean* is therefore one of the most up-to-date and complete accounts of the experiences of the Caribbean, providing information on tools and strategies that are beneficial to public policy practitioners and administrators, growth and development specialists, and anyone with an interest in the Caribbean. The book is also a valuable addition to the general literature on public administration and the policy process in small states and developing states. It is therefore a critical addition to communities of practice and research on public policy, administration, and development, sitting well on any reading list or library collection.

Editors

Indianna D. Minto-Coy serves as senior research fellow at the Mona School of Business and Management, University of the West Indies, Mona, Kingston, Jamaica. She is also a research affiliate at the International Migration Research Centre at Wilfrid Laurier University, Waterloo, Ontario, Canada. Indianna has held appointments at the Skoll Centre for Social Entrepreneurship at the Said Business School at the University of Oxford, United Kingdom; the University of Waterloo, Ontario, Canada; the Centre for International Governance Innovation, where she also coordinated the research component of the Caribbean Economic Governance Project; and the Shridath Ramphal Centre for Trade Policy, Law and Services, University of the West Indies, Barbados, St. Michael. Indianna's work spans areas of public policy, ICTs, migration, and diasporas, and she holds a PhD (law) from the London School of Economics and Political Sciences, London, United Kingdom.

Evan M. Berman is a professor of public management and director of internationalization at the Victoria University of Wellington, School of Government, Wellington, New Zealand. Berman is the winner of the 2015 Fred Riggs Award for lifetime achievement in International and Comparative Public Administration. He is a distinguished Fulbright scholar, senior editor of *Public Performance and Management Review*, and founding editor of the American Society for Public Administration's book series on public administration and public policy. Berman has widely published in all of the major journals of the discipline. His related books in this series include *Public Administration in East Asia* (2010), *Public Administration in Southeast Asia* (2011), and *Public Administration in South Asia* (2013). His areas of expertise include public performance and human resource management, and he is a coauthor of the leading textbook *Human Resource Management in Public Service* (Sage, 2013, 4th edition) as well as *Essential Statistics for Public Managers and Policy Analysts* (CQ Press, 2012, 3rd edition). Berman was previously a policy analyst with the US National Science Foundation, the Huey McElveen distinguished professor at Louisiana State University, Baton Rouge, Louisiana, and university chair professor at National Chengchi University, Taipei, Taiwan.

Contributors

Jessica Bailey was a recently appointed provost and vice president for academic affairs at Fort Valley State University in Fort Valley, GA. She received her undergraduate degree in mathematics and early childhood education and her first graduate degree in vocational rehabilitation counseling from Coppin State College in Baltimore, MD. She received her MBA and PhD in marketing from the University of Missouri, Columbia, Missouri. Having taught courses in marketing and international business at Seattle University, Seattle, Washington, and American University, Washington, DC, she decided to move into higher education administration, first as the associate dean of the Kogod School of Business at American University and, later, as dean of the Sydney Lewis School of Business at Virginia Union University, Richmond, Virginia. She assumed the deanship of the School of Business and Economics at Winston-Salem State University, Winston-Salem, North Carolina, in 2006. During both of her deanships, she was instrumental in securing reaffirmation of the schools' business accreditations. While being the dean at Winston-Salem State University, she garnered the largest gift ever received by the school, $1.25 million from BB&T. She also served as an interim provost of Winston-Salem State University in 2009. Much of her scholarly work has been in the areas of international marketing and international economic development.

Matthew Louis Bishop is a senior lecturer at the Institute of International Relations, University of the West Indies, St. Augustine, Trinidad and Tobago, where he is also the managing editor of the *Caribbean Journal of International Relations & Diplomacy*. Previously, he taught at the University of Sheffield, United Kingdom, from where he earned his PhD, and where he still holds an honorary research fellowship at the Sheffield Political Economy Research Institute (SPERI). Matthew has held other visiting positions at Warwick University, Coventry, United Kingdom (as a transatlantic visiting fellow), the International Institute of Social Studies, The Hague, Netherlands, and the Royal Netherlands Institute of Southeast Asian and Caribbean Studies, Leiden, Netherlands. His main interests are in the broad field of the international political economy of development, and he has published widely on related issues, often—but not exclusively—with a Caribbean focus. He is the author of two books: *The Political Economy of Caribbean Development*, and, with Jean Grugel, *Democratization: A Critical Introduction* (both published by Palgrave Macmillan in 2013).

Ann Marie Bissessar is a full professor in the Department of Behavioural Sciences, University of the West Indies, St Augustine, Trinidad and Tobago. She obtained her masters of science in government and her PhD from the Department of Government, University of the West Indies. She sits as a member of the university senate and on the committees for consideration of honorary awards as well as the disciplinary committee. She formerly served on the Integrity Commission of Trinidad and Tobago. She has to date published over 17 books and 75 articles. Her most recent publication is coauthored with John La Guerre and is published by Lexington (*A Tale of Two Plural Societies*). She specializes in reform, anticorruption initiatives, and regulation of ethnic conflict

Eileen Browne, a member of the International Monetary Fund's panel of experts, has worked in 36 countries, where she has assisted key government leaders who requested assistance in modernizing their management of public finances. In addition to her work with 14 Caribbean governments, she worked in Eastern Europe in the aftermath of the breakup of the Soviet Union in 9 countries during 5 years; with 7 African national governments, covering both French and Anglophone inherited traditions; with 6 Latin American countries as well as two in Asia and the Middle East. Her work in public financial management during the past 35 years has focused on finding ways to apply proven techniques to local realities, including cultural preferences. To that end, she engages in interactive technical assistance and occasional writing. She has worked at the behest of the US Treasury, US AID, World Bank, IMF, InterAmerican Development Bank, DFID (Britain's foreign assistance bureau) among others. She has lectured and conducted workshops throughout the world, sometimes maintaining email contact with local officials for decades. She was educated, decades ago at the Universities of Connecticut, Southern Connecticut, Hartford, New Haven, Duke, and Harvard. She has lectured at many of those schools and others throughout the world. She has been active in networks of finance professionals for more than 30 years.

Anthony Clayton is the Alcan Professor of Caribbean sustainable development in the Institute for Sustainable Development, University of the West Indies, Mona, Kingston, Jamaica; visiting professor at the Centre for Environmental Strategy in the School of Engineering at the University of Surrey, Guildford, Surrey, United Kingdom; visiting professor at the Institute for Studies of Science, Technology and Innovation in the School of Social and Political Studies at the University of Edinburgh, Edinburgh, Scotland; adjunct distinguished professor of sustainable development, Faculty of Business and Management, University of Technology, Ultimo NSW, Australia; international associate, Centre for Social and Environmental Accounting Research, University of St Andrews, Fife, Scotland; fellow of the Caribbean Academy of Sciences; fellow of the World Academy of Sciences; and member of the International Council for Science.

Justin Daniel is a professor of political science at the University of the French Antilles and French Guiana (UAG), Saint-Claude, Guadeloupe. He obtained his master and PhD in political science from the Sorbonne University in Paris, France. He is currently the director of the Centre of Research on Local Powers in the Caribbean. He previously served as the vice president of the Scientific Council of UAG (2009–2012) and dean of the Faculty of Law and Economics in Martinique (2006–2009). His research interest focuses on political systems and political mobilization in the Caribbean, and on politics in the French overseas territories. He has written extensively on these topics for academic journals and books. He presently works, in a comparative perspective, on the phenomena of identity assertions within the non-independent territories in the Caribbean and the related issues of citizenship and governance.

Landis G. Fryer is a doctoral student in cultural and educational policy studies, with a focus in comparative and international education, at Loyola University Chicago, Chicago, Illinois. He completed his bachelors at Dartmouth College, Hanover, New Hampshire, in English and religion and his masters at the University of Pennsylvania, Philadelphia, Pennsylvania, in higher education. His recent publication with Dr. Tavis Jules, Loyola University Chicago, is "Policy spaces and educational development in the Islamic Maghreb region: Higher education in Tunisia" in *The Development of Higher Education in Africa: Prospects and Challenges* (Emerald Publishers, 2013). Landis's current research interests include development of global citizenship education and leadership, international higher education admissions, and educational policy discourse between BRIC nations.

Miguel Goede is the past president of the University of the Netherlands Antilles (UNA), Willemstad, Curaçao, and is an independent research consultant at Goede Consultants. He obtained his masters and PhD in political science and public administration from, respectively, the Radboud University, Nijmegen, Netherlands, and the Tilburg University, Tilburg, Netherlands. He is currently the president of the Association of Public Administration of the Netherlands Antilles and Aruba. He previously served as the dean of the Faculty of Business Administration and as the dean of the Faculty Behavioural Sciences at the UNA. His research interest focuses on good governance of Caribbean small island development states. He has written extensively on these topics for academic journals and books. He presently works on a book entitled *Bizarre Governance* in the Dutch language.

Gerardo González Núñez is a professor of economics at the Interamerican University of Puerto Rico, San Juan, Puerto Rico, and chairman of SCIRE Economic Consulting Unit. He has a master's degree in economics from Havana University, Havana, Cuba. Gonzalez has conducted studies in the areas of international economic, as well as macroeconomic, analysis with emphasis on Caribbean countries. His articles have been published in specialized journals of Latin America, United States, and Europe. He is the author or coauthor of the following books: *El Caribe en la política exterior de Cuba* (Dominican Republic, 1991) and *Participación Popular y Desarrollo en los Municipios Cubanos* (Venezuela, 1994), *Intelectuales vs Revolución?* (Canada, 2001), and *Oportunidades de Negocios en Cuba: Qué puede esperar Puerto Rico?* (Puerto Rico, 2009). He has lectured in several universities in the United States, Latin America, and Europe.

Charley G. Granvorka is an independent consultant and a member of Ceregmia (www.ceregmia.eu) at the Université des Antilles et de la Guyane, Pointe-à-Pitre, Guadeloupe. Her PhD works are dedicated to plantation economy and general equilibrium model in the compared case of Haiti and the Dominican Republic. Methodologies applied to cost–benefit analysis, social and economical valuation of impacts related to natural hazards, macroeconomics, and Caribbean economy are among her main courses. She is a member of the following associations: The European Association of Environmental and Resource Economists (EAERE), World Economics Association (WEA), The 50/50 Project: "Surveying the Past, Mapping the Future," a UWI/CARICOM project. In that project, she is a member of the cluster related to *regional integration* headed by Pr. Patsy Lewis at UWI, Mona, Kingston, Jamaica. As an economist specialist of small insular states, she has been recently invited by the United Nations to take part in a workshop dedicated to the valuation and accounting of ecosystem services held in New York City.

Sandra Grey-Alvaranga is a research fellow at the Institute of Technological and Educational Research (ITER) at the Mico University College, Kingston, Jamaica, and a former lecturer in the Department of Government at the University of the West Indies, Mona, Kingston, Jamaica. Her interest in nation building is actively fueled through research on cross-cutting themes of public policy, social capital, volunteerism and governance, as well as through her involvement with the

NGO sector, where she conducts a range of post-project evaluations and capacity-building seminars. Grey-Alvaranga holds an MSc in government (UWI) and is pursuing doctoral studies at the University of Leeds, UK.

Edwin Jones is a professor emeritus of public administration at the University of the West Indies, Mona, Kingston, Jamaica; adjunct professor at the Mona School of Business and Management, Kingston, Jamaica; and director of the Institute of Technological and Educational Research (ITER) at the Mico University College, Kingston, Jamaica. As a recognized expert in the field of public management and governance, he has widely published and consulted on bringing development and management solutions to issues of political economy and public policy. Professor Jones' publication record spawns some 100 published articles and authoritative policy reports on Caribbean and international subjects as well as a number of books. He also engages in program design in management at the graduate level. As a member of several professional associations, Professor Jones also served on a number of editorial boards of certain international and local journals, inclusive of *Public Management Review (UK)* and *Caribbean Journal of Public Management*. He is also recognizable as a long-serving member of the Jamaica Public Service Commission.

Tavis D. Jules is an assistant professor of cultural and educational policy studies and comparative and international education at Loyola University, Chicago, Illinois. He earned a doctorate of education in international education development with a specialization in international educational policy studies from Teachers College, Columbia University, New York City, New York. His research focuses on educational policy formation and development particularly, but not exclusively, within the Caribbean. More recently, his research has focused on analyzing the impact of regionalization upon small (and micro) states as well as education in transitory space with a geographic focus on the Maghreb region. He is the book reviews editor for the *Caribbean Journal of International Relations and Diplomacy*. His recent publication includes neither world polity nor local or national societies: *Regionalization in the Global South the Caribbean Community* (Peter Lang Press, 2012).

Nikolaos Karagiannis is an associate professor of economics and the research and publications coordinator of the School of Business and Economics at Winston-Salem State University, North Carolina, and the managing editor of the journal *American Review of Political Economy (ARPE)*. Dr. Karagiannis obtained his PhD from the University of Leeds, England, in 1996. He has authored, coauthored, and coedited 16 books, and has published widely in scholarly journals and edited books in the areas of economic development, public sector economics, and macroeconomic policy analysis. He is particularly interested in developmental state theory and policy, and his research has focused extensively on the applicability of this interventionist view in different contexts such as EU countries, Caribbean small island economies, North African countries, and the United States.

Patricia Mohammed is currently a professor of gender and cultural studies, Institute of Gender and Development Studies, University of the West Indies, St. Augustine, Trinidad & Tobago, with a PhD from the Institute of Social Studies, The Hague, Netherlands. She is a pioneer in the development of gender studies at tertiary level and was recruited by four Caribbean governments to write their national gender policies. From 1994 to 2002, she headed the Mona Unit, Centre for Gender and Development Studies, UWI, Kingston, Jamaica, and was a visiting professor at SUNY Albany and Warwick University in 2007 and 2012. Her publications include "Gender in

Caribbean Development" (1988); "Rethinking Caribbean Difference" (1998) in *Feminist Review; Gender Negotiations among Indians in Trinidad, 1917–1947* (Palgrave, 2001); *Gendered Realities: Essays in Caribbean Feminist Thought* (ed) (UWI Press, 2002); and *Imaging the Caribbean: Culture and Visual Translation* (Macmillan, UK, 2009).

Margaret Rose is a practicing attorney at law in the Commonwealth Caribbean and was called to the bar of Trinidad and Tobago in 1995. Rose has a master's degree in corporate commercial law from the University of the West Indies, Wanstead, Barbados. Rose is the cofounder and executive director of the Caribbean Procurement Institute and serves on the board of the nonprofit Caribbean Association of Procurement Professionals. Rose has spearheaded the Caribbean Public Procurement Conference (CPPC) held every two years in the Caribbean since 2008 and designs and delivers numerous procurement professional capacity-building programs in partnership with international bodies and tertiary institutions. Rose lectures and speaks at conferences worldwide in the field of procurement law including Canada, Nigeria, Tunisia, Germany, Sweden, Philippines, Panama, and the United Kingdom.

Wayne Soverall is a lecturer in public sector management at the University of the West Indies, Cave Hill Campus, Barbados. He obtained his MA in political science (urban policy and administration) from Brooklyn College, New York, and his PhD in political science from the University of the West Indies, Cave Hill Campus. He is currently the coordinator of the Public Sector Management Research Unit, which is a think tank and policy advocate for research in public sector management and public policy. He worked in the public sector in a number of PSOs in several capacities and thus brings a wealth of knowledge and experience to bear on his research. His research interests focus on public sector management, public policy, and corporate governance issues. He has coauthored three books and published over 25 articles. His most recent book is entitled *Empowering Management* (forthcoming).

Eric Strobl is an associate professor in economics at Ecole Polytechnique, Palaiseau, France and external professorial fellow at SALISES, University of the West Indies, St. Augustine, Trinidad and Tobago. He holds a BA in economics from Pennsylvania State University, State College, Pennsylvania, an MA from Georgetown University, Washington, DC, and received his PhD from Trinity College Dublin, Ireland. Since then he has held positions at Trinity College Dublin, University College Dublin, Ireland, University of the West Indies, Universite Catholique de Louvain, Louvain-la-Neuve, Belgium, and University de Paris X, France. His main research interests lie in applied econometrics, particularly pertaining to problems in environmental and development economics.

Andrew Walcott is a researcher at the Institute of Technological and Educational Research (ITER), Mico University, Kingston, Jamaica, where he focuses on areas dealing with leadership, talent management, and education. He is also attached to the Centre for Leadership and Governance at the University of the West Indies (UWI), Mona, Kingston, Jamaica, where he focuses on areas of economics, regionalism, CARICOM, and trade theory. In 2010, he completed a BSc in international relations (with Hons.) from UWI, where he is currently pursuing his MSc in international economics and international law.

Leslie Walling is a project manager at the Caribbean Development Bank, Barbados, where he manages the design and implementation of a US $24.0, multi-donor grant-mechanism for self-help projects in community-based disaster and climate risk reduction. He received his MSc in coastal resources management from the Marine Resource and Environmental Management Programme, University of the West Indies (UWI), Wanstead, Barbados. He has held senior management positions in regional Caribbean climate change adaptation projects and at the Caribbean Community Climate Change Centre, Belize. He led the development of coral reef monitoring approach for climate change adaptation planning (http://www.worldfishcenter.org/Pubs/coral_reef/pdf/section3-4.pdf) that has since been institutionalized at the UWI's Centre for Marine Sciences, Jamaica. As a consultant, he recently led the development and testing of a methodology for mainstreaming climate change adaptation considerations into national disaster management planning frameworks (https://unfccc.int/files/adaptation/application/pdf/cca_guidance_tool_e_book_.pdf). The methodology is currently being implemented by the Caribbean Disaster Emergency Management Agency. His cross-sectoral, multi-disciplinary experience working with development agencies, NGOs, government agencies, the private sector, and teaching, has informed his capacity to view development situations from many different points of view.

Hakim Mohandas Amani Williams is an assistant professor of Africana studies, education, and globalization studies at Gettysburg College, Pennsylvania. He received his BA (honors) in psychology at St. Francis College, Brooklyn, New York, and completed his master of arts, master of education, and doctorate of education (in the fields of international educational development, foci: peace education and philosophy of education) at Teachers College, Columbia University, New York City, New York. He has taught at Drexel University, Philadelphia, Pennsylvania, and European Peace University, Stadtschlaining, Austria. Research and teaching interests include youth violence in schools, structural violence, critical pedagogy, Caribbean studies, gender performativity and masculinities, educational inequity, colonial/neocolonial education, educational policy, human rights, conflict resolution, nonviolence, peace and human rights education, globalization, postcolonialism, and education for social change. Forthcoming publications: "Postcolonial Structural Violence: A Case Study of School Violence in Trinidad & Tobago" in *International Journal of Peace Studies* (Spring 2014) and Peaceableness as Raison d¹être, Process and Evaluation (book chapter) in *Peace Education Evaluation* (Information Age Press, 2014).

Chapter 1

Public Administration and Policy in the Caribbean: An Overview of the Caribbean

Indianna D. Minto-Coy and Evan M. Berman

Contents

History: Colonial and Other Legacies... 3
    History and Legacy of Public Administration in the Commonwealth Caribbean 3
    History and Legacy of Public Administration in the French Caribbean................................. 5
    History and Legacy of Public Administration in the Dutch Caribbean 7
    History and Legacy of Public Administration in the Other Parts of the Caribbean................. 9
        Haiti 9
        Cuba 10
    Some Reflections 11
Bureaucracy.. 12
    Public Sector Reform and Civil Service Performance in the Caribbean 12
    PFM and Procurement Policy..14
    Corruption 17
Public Policy: Economy and Development 19
    Developmental Interventions in the Caribbean..19
    Tourism Policy and Management.. 20
    Communications, E-Government, and Cyber Policy 20
    Environmental Risk Management..21

Public Policy: Social Policies 22
    Education 22
    Health 23
    Migration and Diasporas 24
    Race, Class, and Gender 25
Conclusion as Prologue: A Tentative Guide to the Future.. 26
References 28

> **Abstract:** The Caribbean is a complex and varied landscape. This chapter provides an overview of the book's main themes, discussing the legacies and major traditions, developments, trends, and challenges in the evolution and practice of public policy and administration.
>
> Essential context is provided about the British Commonwealth, French, Dutch, and other origins, showing how these continue to inform the present. Specific trends are discussed about integrity and corruption, public finance, migration, policy making, civil service reform, developmental interventions, performance management, leadership, race relations, and gender equality in the Caribbean. Examples are given of governance issues affecting these areas. This chapter shows the Caribbean at a crucial phase in its development, being buffeted by global developments and internal pressures, causing a rising demand for improved governance.

The Caribbean is a complex setting, with multiple languages, different histories and heritages, different economies, and different systems of government. People from all over the world appreciate the diversity that is on offer when they visit the Caribbean. Today, the region is at a critical phase in its evolution. Economically, the Caribbean is a mosaic of countries with different levels of development. Traditional dependence on agriculture is increasingly replaced by a dependence on funds remitted by migrants and members of its diaspora, and most of the region is also dependent on tourism. The region is buffeted by forces in the global economy, and countries vary in how well they address these challenges, manage their public finances, and meet their social challenges in education, health, and public safety, which are surely exacerbated by economic vicissitudes. The Caribbean Islands attract millions and millions of people to their shores, though they are mostly small countries and territories that have varying degrees of independence, capacity, and success in lifting the welfare and well-being of their people. This book is about their public governance experiences in an increasingly open and interdependent world.

There exists a need for sharing of experiences, both inside and outside the Caribbean. This book brings together knowledge of the public administration and governance of the Caribbean region, providing a comprehensive overview of public policy and management. Even within the region, often very little is known about the experiences of neighboring territories, and tendency exists to view the region as subsections with little effort to consider the whole of what is a very diverse and complex region. Neighbors do not always know the raison d'etre of public policy on other islands, yet the experiences of these states hold significant implications within the region for improving the quality of public governance and management, and externally, as they relate to development policies and practices supported by multilateral aid and development institutions. Even more, the story of public administration in the Caribbean is part of all small and developing states in the world, generally.

This is a book of scholarship, providing thorough discussions and analysis of policies and legacies. Nevertheless, to suggest conclusiveness or completion in the topics below would be insincere.

The number and complexity of policy issues that policy makers face are large, and there is also room for going deeper and considering alternative perspectives. This chapter draws on the chapters that follow, adding additional material. The following is intended as a useful overview of the public administration and policy of the Caribbean, while encouraging readers to consult other chapters, which are all partly written by leading experts of the region.

History: Colonial and Other Legacies

One of the defining features of Caribbean society is its location in the international slavery, colonial, and plantation experiences. These give rise to certain legacies, along with the region's emergence as the scene for the unfolding of great power politics and rivalry. There is a long period of contact with the British, French, Dutch, and Spanish, and, more recently, the United States has left an indelible mark on the institutions in the region (culture, practices, laws, etc.). As such, a fitting starting point in any discussion on public administration and public policy in the Caribbean is a serious consideration of how this history has shaped the experiences, practices, and results in the region. The legacy includes public administration systems that were largely undemocratic, that prioritized order over social and local development, that emphasized raw extraction (sugar and bananas) with little of such income returning to the region, and that had a low capacity to provide social services and infrastructure.

History and Legacy of Public Administration in the Commonwealth Caribbean

The Commonwealth Caribbean begun contact with the United Kingdom in the 1600s with slavery and colonialism. While most territories across the Caribbean received independence since the 1960s, for Anguilla, Bermuda, Turks and Caicos, the Cayman Islands, Montserrat, and the British Virgin Islands, the relationship has sustained into the present via their status as British Overseas Territories (BOTs). The founding of the British West Indies was informed by the imperialist desires of the English government. The motives of English colonization were to identify tropical products and new markets and to put capital to work. The founding of the British West Indies also offered opportunities for employment and livelihoods not realized in England (Mawby 2012: 6). Some islands witnessed different periods of ownership as each colonial power battled and made peace with each other.

The region occupied a central location in the British Empire. Public administration in the British West Indies was organized in order to integrate the region neatly into the governance framework of the British Empire, to reduce the cost of administering the islands, and to improve efficiency. Colonial government was organized by departments overseen by a chief professional officer. The system of control went to the imperial government through a representative in the form of a governor or colonial secretary with decisions flowing from the center to the periphery. The public service in this case was focused on maintaining law and order, not designing policies. The dictates of the local environment had little influence on policies.

The public service was seen as the place for some of the brightest. The notion of the civil service as a special place, and those in it as special beings, as well as the top-down organization of decision making and communication (i.e., from Crown and via colonial secretary) also encouraged the practice of secrecy and exclusion in the decision-making process into the period of self-rule that is still largely maintained today. Issues of race, class, and color were also features of the organization and management of this civil service. White collar positions in the administrative system were sought after and occupied mainly by the mixed-race or "brown skins" who also comprised the middle class. The result is what Jones and Schoburgh (2004) has termed a "derivative middle class" that exhibited tendencies of risk aversion, obedience to "rule and rote," and preservation of established norms and traditions.

Constitutions in the region went largely untouched up to the 1920s and 1930s. Calls for reform in Crown colonies had focused on the right for members to be elected to the Legislative Council, which was granted in Trinidad and Tobago (T&T) in 1925 when the right was given to elect seven members to the Council. The push for political reforms also came from within the labor movement and demonstrations in light of economic and social hardships. Some countries were gradually given limited self-rule in preparation for full independence. For those non-independent countries, the status of BOTs (British Overseas Territories) was conferred upon the territories in 2002 via the BOTs Act, which changed the title of the territories from British Dependent Territories. Citizens are also citizens of the United Kingdom, recognizing the queen as their head of state. The BOTs all vary in the degree of closeness to the United Kingdom, and the islands are linked to the UK public administration directly via a governor, as obtained previously. The United Kingdom remains responsible for defense and foreign policy for the BOTs, and it has the right to intervene in local management in extreme circumstances (e.g., the 2009 postponement of government in the Turks and Caicos). More generally the administrative heritage is also characterized by local practices which intermingled with adopted practices from the United Kingdom.

With independence, executive authority passed from the Crown and to local heads of state to ministers. However, the defining feature of public administration and politics in the English-speaking Caribbean remains the Westminster-Whitehall (WW) system borrowed from the United Kingdom. This inherited model of public administration privileges the party that commands a majority in the lower house of Parliament with legislative and executive power being concentrated in the governing party. The public bureaucracy here is meant to be a professional class tasked with implementing policies, with notions of impartiality, neutrality, and anonymity as governing principles of public administration. However, this may be noted as one of the more skillful inventions of the United Kingdom given the difficulties in meeting these ideas in any settings including in the Caribbean.

Thus Minto-Coy states in chapter 2 that the actual performance of the Westminster system in the Caribbean has not matched the ideal or expected form. This reality has yielded negative consequences of overcentralization, corruption, nepotism, and clientelism with limited power among the opposition to exercise constraints over the government. For example, overcentralization of the public service has been noted as a result of colonial practices, emphasizing practical organizational control with little autonomy for action among staff. In essence, the change in persons populating leadership did not equate to a substantive change in philosophy or orientation.

The chapters provide further detail on these modern-day issues. While a synergistic relationship between political and administrative leadership is key to meeting the hosts of governance challenges, in practice, politics has tended to dominate public administration with negative effects. The lack of restraint on government has in practice seen political leaders using their office to reward and punish, which compromises the principle of neutrality among public servants, and leads to serious questioning of the ability of public servants and the public administration machinery to operate objectively. At worst, the prospect of job loss or falling out of favor with a politician has in some cases resulted in an emasculated public service. In short, the principles of neutrality, anonymity, and impartiality have been difficult to realize in the Caribbean.

As another example, the judiciary in the Westminster system is supposed to be independent acting as a check on the power of the executive. Historically, the courts in the region have in fact helped to check the seemingly unlimited power of the ruling party. For instance, the courts in Jamaica were vital in preventing the then ruling party from appropriating the assets of businesses during the country's experimentation with Democratic Socialism in the 1970s. Notwithstanding, the judiciary has been constrained by a number of challenges, including insufficient resources and excessive backlog, limiting their ability to monitor or hold the government and bureaucracy to account. The system has not afforded many other levels of checks and balances, and civil society has not been sufficiently empowered resulting in the underdevelopment of civil society throughout the region.

Finally, the issue for public administration in the Caribbean (and beyond) is not only about having a depoliticized public administration. It is also about the level of professionalism of the public bureaucracy. Meritocracy has emerged over time as an important criterion for promotion in Caribbean public administration, allowing the entry into senior positions by persons who may have, in the past, been excluded by virtue of pigmentation or class. However, there are those who now question the extent to which meritocracy is still encouraged and practiced. The notion of merit is difficult to realize fully in small states, including the Commonwealth, Haiti, and the Dominican Republic, given the social, political, and economic realities of the region.

These shortcomings have not gone unnoticed with a sense that the above has seriously compromised the ability of the civil service to perform and deliver. The language of reform is thus a consistent feature of Caribbean public administration with governments making efforts to improve the performance of the inherited model of public administration via initiatives that have given middling or little positive results. Of course, some legacies are positive. Many of the enduring institutions, including the model of the Services Commission, have served countries well. For instance, the Office of the Services Commission introduced in 1952 in Jamaica has now been tasked with monitoring the permanent secretaries and chief executive officers in their task of hiring and movement of their personnel under Accountability Agreements. The changes here have been noted as offering public managers more control and ownership, hence greater accountability over performance.

History and Legacy of Public Administration in the French Caribbean

While the French at one time had control over what are now Commonwealth or Spanish territories such as St. Lucia, Grenada, and the Dominican Republic, the French Caribbean as discussed here refers to the territories currently under French sovereignty, that is, Guadeloupe and Martinique and their dependencies* (other French-speaking nations, such as Haiti, Dominica, and St. Lucia, are now independent). Plantation economies were to thrive on these territories with sugar and rum still being main exports. More generally, the tale of the emergence of the French Caribbean mimics that of the English and Dutch in that the islands were managed by private enterprises before being annexed directly to the Crown as the region became more central in the rivalry between European powers. Indeed, the British had disputed the French over the above islands but officially gave up their claims in return for Canada in 1763.

---

* Up to 2007, St. Barthélemy and St. Martin were dependencies of Martinique, while Les Saintes, Marie-Galante, and La Désirade remain dependencies of Guadeloupe.

Colonial administration begun in 1663 and was achieved through a number of institutions, including the Colonial Office (later the Overseas Ministry) created in 1710, with governors who acted as local representatives in charge of the military. A series of consultative institutions were added to this governance framework, including a High Council in St. Domingo in 1713 and a General Assembly of the Colony in 1787. These institutions were to some extent informed by the English model of representative government, suggesting that some learning did take place across the different enclaves. As in the case of the wider Caribbean, the mainland introduced various public administration reforms more often aimed at improving the organization of the territories for a smoother administration and much less at developing local capacity for effective development administration. The intent on greater administration found ultimate expression in the French Caribbean with the conferring of the status of overseas departments (*Départements d'outre mer*) (DOMs) in 1946. Under DOM, the territories became a part of the Franco-European establishment with the same institutions (e.g., laws and regulations) found in France.

This politico-administrative model was informed by principles, namely assimilation, centralization, universalism, and uniformization (see Chapter 3), which have seen France maintaining a strong influence over social and economic organization and public policy in the region. These principles cemented France's cultural hegemony and denied local expressions in public administration. The experiences are instructive not only because of uniqueness, but also for suggesting that sustained dependence (even if in the form of the privileged status of DOM) can become a barrier to internally motivated growth. Martinique, Guadeloupe, and French Guiana have become dependent on France for their very survival. While DOM status was informed locally by a desire to match the standard of development in France, public spending increased, including infrastructure and financial incentives, but without commensurate levels of internally informed growth. A similar result has been noted in the Dutch Caribbean (see below), where transfers have acted as a disincentive for sound public financial management (PFM) practices. Even with inclusion in the European Union (EU), it is not coincidental that unemployment in the Dutch Caribbean is one of the worst in the wider Caribbean (approximately 25%), and Guadeloupe remains one of the poorest countries in the EU. Indeed, by dissuading local expressions in public administration, France has contributed to the sustained dependence of these economies, having removed the levers for innovation and internally informed growth.

Daniel notes that the sustained economic and social malaise is also a result of the vulnerability associated with Martinique and Guadeloupe's status as small islands, a consideration which has its merits, regardless of the support and insulation which comes from the protected status (see Chapter 3). Daniel also suggests that the existence of a dual administrative system for overseas territories resulted in multiple and competing levels of governance. In this way, the experience of the French mimic that of the English-speaking and independent region with the different levels of governance (local, regional, and international) with each layer jostling against the other for influence and definition in policy and governance. The distribution of power over different levels also led to confusion in the organization of public administration. The principles of organization also diminished attempts by plantation owners to distance themselves from France, while also reducing the ability to contextualize policies coming from Paris. Even social and racial discrimination is perpetuated by delayed application of social laws and equality to these territories.

These contentions are sustained in reviews of the DOM status since its introduction, including decentralization efforts in the 1960s. The most far-reaching constitutional reform in 2003 marked a revision of the relevance of the existing status quo, including the questioning of the uniformity principle, and specific public policy issues such as discrimination in health and housing also received attention. The impulse for reform is therefore notably not only from the region, but also within France itself. Constitutional reform introduced the option for the establishment of a single local authority as a means of reducing some of the duplication that existed between the department and the region, and a new categorization of overseas collectives (COM) was introduced. Interestingly, Martinique refused these options, notwithstanding longstanding demands for greater autonomy. By 2008, Martinique agreed to the adoption of the single authority while refusing the status of COM. Its dependencies (St. Martin and St. Barthelemy) had already moved to the adoption of the COM status in 2003. In the context of being labeled among the most underdeveloped regions in the EU, Guadeloupe has chosen to maintain the DOM status quo, suggesting awareness of the challenges of independence or fear of its ability to survive otherwise.

Unsettlement around the organization of public policy administration and financial challenges came to a head (in 2009) with the outbreak of riots starting in Guadeloupe and spreading to Martinique. Riots came against discontent about high prices and sustained economic pressures in the aftermath of the global financial crisis. These added to existing grievances, including a sustained imbalance between the size of the black population and their access and ownership of the country's resources, implying economic racism. Unrest saw the territories making calls for administrative and wider reforms, including salary increases and greater access to local jobs. Some demands (e.g., greater aid) ironically suggest demands for a greater (not reduced) role of France in the affairs of the region. These reforms and adaptations were accommodated, and Daniel suggests that these were part of a political strategy aimed at dampening contestation of the status quo (see Chapter 3). Indeed, the outcome of the 2009 demonstrations offers some support, with promises to review prices and increase wages not leading to amelioration of the condition of the majority.

The DOM status, therefore, came with (and still manifests) internal inconsistencies between the pressures for centralization and the protections which this assures on one hand and demands for autonomy, as seen in the failure to adapt the administrative model to local context and culture, on the other. Thus, the schizophrenia seen in the Dutch and some English territories around discussions on sovereignty and independence also surfaces in the relationship between the Caribbean and France. This duality remains a defining theme in the public administration of these territories. This also sheds some light on why nonindependent territories in the region have shied away from concrete demands around independence.

History and Legacy of Public Administration in the Dutch Caribbean

The notion of an ongoing struggle to redefine the relationship between a former colonial power and the region is also seen in the Dutch Caribbean, which includes Aruba, Bonaire, Curacao, Sint Eustatius, Sint Maarten, and Saba. The Dutch Caribbean had its beginnings in the efforts of a private trading company (the Dutch West India Company), but fell to the Dutch government when the company was nationalized in 1791.

This move brought these islands directly into the organization of the Dutch, with a minister of trade and colonies acting as adviser to the king in the early 1800s and reporting directly to Parliament in 1848. Public administration in the islands was managed by one governor and a number of lieutenant governors (one for each island) in turn assisted by two advisory bodies, though the latter included local elites and Dutch civil servants. Little role was given to the local population in their own governance, which was further exacerbated by isolation of other islands from the main seat of power in Curacao. The discovery of oil in the early 1900s saw the Netherlands increasing its attention to the colonies through a program to "Dutchinalize" the territories by establishing the civil service, education system, and religious institutions based on Dutch principles, institutions, and language. While additional civil servants came from the Netherlands, their task was more about file keeping and registering data, not to develop the economy or society.

Public administration has consistently been plagued by challenges of corruption and an inefficient public sector since the 1960s. Efforts to improve public governance and address racially based political conflicts in the 1960s resulted in the politicization of the civil service (Antillianization), increases in its size and overstaffing, and participation by unqualified staff due to patronage and the use of appointments as a source of reward and punishment for votes. By the 1980s, according to Goede, the total number of unproductive civil servants in Curacao numbered around 2,000 (of a total of 5,000) (see Chapter 4).

Inefficiency and corruption have taken shape in poor delegation of authority, poor work processes, clientelism, inefficient public bureaucracy, and inadequate job descriptions. A number of reforms have been tried over the years, all with the aim of addressing these challenges. However, efforts have been affected by political expedience and instability among governing coalitions. For instance, plans for addressing high debt and overstaffing through the Structural Adjustment Programme (SAP) of 1986 were not fully implemented due to the disintegration of the coalition government. Further efforts at privatization and public sector reform (e.g., new public management [NPM]) have borne little fruit due to politico-administrative tensions and politicians shying away from granting increased authority to civil servants.

The wave of independence that swept the Commonwealth Caribbean since the 1960s did not leave the Dutch Caribbean untouched. For instance, Suriname was to gain its independence in 1975, a move which saw the remaining territories being pressured to become independent as well. However, the islands resisted the push from the Netherlands. Underlying are concerns of financial independence, ability to realize independent expectations, administrative performance, and perceptions that independent territories such as Jamaica have fared negatively (e.g., Clegg 2012; Mawby 2012: 1–2). Aruba was later to secede from the Netherlands Antilles in 1986 as an autonomous territory in the Kingdom of the Netherlands while others refused to change the status quo.

Reforms to public governance in the region have been influenced significantly by the Mother country. For instance, since the 1990s, the Netherlands has encouraged attention to securing sustainable development, justice, good governance, and education, as well as poverty reduction. The Netherlands has also intervened to address corruption (and transnational crime in St. Maarten) and improve governance, at points heightening its supervision in response to increased threats. As the countries found themselves faced with high public debt and the sustained problem of overstaffing in the 1980s, the Netherlands turned to the International Monetary Fund (IMF) to address this problem through an SAP. The SAP was to witness the reduction in the size of the civil service via hiring freezes, privatization, and layoffs. However, sustained attention to the hiring freeze saw initial success, but later governments returned to some hiring, while prolonged restrictions on hiring have seen issues of continuity and the aging of the public sector emerge as key concerns in recent times.

Financial support has also been one of the key hallmarks of the relationship between the region and the Netherlands. The relationship between the former colonial power and the region has remained in terms of aid (and loans), underscoring the cultural and language relationships that had been introduced and cemented in the past. As such, the funding for public reforms has also come directly from the Netherlands, with the emphasis of such reform packages being informed by the Netherlands. As such, greater separation from the Netherlands has not translated into financial autonomy as there remains dependence on aid. Aruba has fared more successfully in the area of financial independence, with tourism helping to provide the funding needed to run the territory.

The problems of high debt and general financial mismanagement, oversized bureaucracy, and corruption continue to plague the Dutch Caribbean. Patronage also remains an issue in these small islands with small populations, where close ties make it difficult to hold persons to account. Dialogue on the relationship between the mainland and the islands is a sustained feature, explored in Chapter 4.

The Netherlands Antilles was abolished in 2010, resulting in a number of associations based on levels of dependence on the Netherlands. As such, Aruba, Curacao, and St. Marten exist as autonomous partners, alongside the Netherlands, while Bonaire, Saba, and St. Eustatius are municipalities. International relations and defense remain unchanged and the Netherlands continues to supervise public finances, demonstrating the value of this external power in providing a safety net and checks and balance on governments. Nevertheless, there is also the view that this is a hindrance to development, indicating a certain "schizophrenia" in the national psyche toward the Netherlands.

History and Legacy of Public Administration in the Other Parts of the Caribbean

Haiti

Haiti may be considered a part of the French Caribbean given its early history and language and is therefore mentioned in Chapter 3, which is explicitly dedicated to the DOMs. The country's experiences in a number of other areas are also covered briefly throughout the remainder of this and other chapters. For instance, Haiti's connection with diasporic engagement is discussed later in this chapter, while the 2010 earthquake and recovery efforts are reviewed in Chapter 8 and Chapter 19, which covers the issue of poverty (also see Chapters 14 and 16). Nevertheless, the length of Haiti's independence, and indeed the very uniqueness of that country's evolution, set it apart not just from the DOMs but also from other Caribbean countries, hence meriting specific attention in this opening chapter in the way of contextualizing the history and experiences which have given rise to some of the points raised in the later chapters.

The Haitian political and developmental history has been well documented (e.g., Dubois 2012; Fatton 2002; Pierre-Louis 2011), covering the periods from its status as a French colony to the struggles for independence obtained in 1894 (the first in the region) and the resulting hostility and international boycott of that country into the twentieth century. The boycott has effectively denied Haiti access to the tools and support required for advancing under independence. This included a denial of support for the development of functional institutions for governance in a democratic system. The prospects of independent Haiti were also compromised from the start by the indemnity it had to pay to France (see Dubois 2012) which in essence amounted to paying for fighting for and winning its independence.

This is not to say that the problems and ineffective management of the state and its resources in Haiti are solely explained by external reasons. Indeed, public policy and administration as in other areas of life have suffered from divisive, violent, and corrupt leaders and management practices. Antipathy has been a critical feature of governance of Haiti and reveals itself in a number of ways. First, Stoyan et al. (2014) show how antipathy was used by nationalist leaders from the Dominican Republic in the 1930s to achieve demarcation between that country and Haiti via a virtual massacre in 1937. This step essentially isolated Haiti and prevented its access to support utilized by many other countries to navigate local and global policy fields. Second, this antipathy has emerged as a vicious tool used by autocratic leaders for the subjugation and divisive governance of the Haitian population under leaders such as Duvalier in 1957. Public management in such a context becomes a challenge amid weak or nonexistent state institutions or policies that are not given sufficient time to take shape. Third, this antipathy has also featured in the regional and international community's treatment of that country which, it is suggested, continues today (see Pierre-Louis 2011).

In spite of the uniqueness of Haiti, governance in the region resembles many other traits seen in other islands (presented in this book). As such, the experiences of Haiti also demonstrate incendiary impacts of divisive politics and the lack of public-interested elites. Where countries such as Barbados, the Cayman Islands, and the Turks and Caicos exemplify milder versions of public administration challenges discussed, Haiti resides at the other extreme.

Cuba

The Spanish legacy in the Caribbean is extensive. Some islands changed hands from the Spanish to the English (e.g., T&T and Jamaica) and there is still a strong cultural, though not necessarily administrative, legacy (the U.S. territory of Puerto Rico, the Dominican). A choice has been made to focus on Cuba, which shares a similar place with Haiti in as far as these countries have their own unique place in the region.

In Chapter 5, Núñez traces the development of public management in Cuba through the different phases of that country's evolution. He shows that one of the defining features of governance in Cuba is that it has experienced the two political, ideological, and economic systems of capitalism and communism. Another feature is the dependence on world powers for concessions and preferential terms of trade, particularly before the early 1990s, a direct result of ideological and geopolitical factors (e.g., having support cut from the West to be replaced by the Soviet Union) as well as structural weaknesses in the local economy.

Governance in the modern, socialist phase is charted along three major time frames. The first characterizes Revolutionary Cuba from 1959 to 1974 and consolidation of the revolutionary project that transformed society, politics, and the economy (e.g., Cooper 2006; LeoGrande 2014). Public spending was heavily focused on social policy and specifically on health and education, giving rise to the superior achievement of Cuba in these two areas; for instance, illiteracy moved from 23% to 3% from 1959 to 1989. However, the result on the economy and productive sectors was negative as the revolutionary project privileged the state, stripping the market of nearly all functions. Moreover, public policy and administration were informed by ideological and subjective considerations, and the overall result was lack of coherence between the economic strategies that were designed and the actual policies that were applied in the economy. For example, an overriding emphasis was placed on sugar as the source of economic sustenance, but the fluctuations in the pricing of this commodity negatively affected the national budget and development planning processes, effectively paralyzing the economy at times. Additionally, efforts to increase efficiency were not achieved.

These failures triggered the second phase of reforms (1975–1989), still under socialism. Institutional reforms during in this period included the reorganization of central government, the adoption of a new constitution, and a national development model in the form of the Cuban Model of Economic Management and Planning. Features included an emphasis on volunteerism, new areas of economic activity (tourism), attempts to attract foreign investments, and an emphasis on science as a driver of development. Indeed, the acclaimed development of medicines and procedures contributed to more affordable health costs for Cubans in this period. But management of the economy and society again placed the state at the commanding heights, dispensing with competitive or cooperative horizontal relations among businesses. Business was imbued with the same centralized authoritarian structure of the state. Similar to the previous period, inefficiencies were made clear with the limits of government as economic planner and its failure to predict budgeting/planning based on the expected receipts from sugar. While the "privileged" integration of Cuba into European socialism via the Soviet Union cushioned these negative effects, external largesse also acted as a disincentive for increased productivity and efficiency in much the same way as in the Dutch Caribbean.

The third important phase (post-1990) has seen Cuba undergoing a process of enforced reorientation beginning with the fall of the Soviet Union. The impact of these developments on the decision to revisit governance on the island is not to be underestimated with the decline in gross domestic product (GDP) being estimated at around 35% from 1989 to 1993 (Pérez-López 1998). Health and education were among the areas most affected resulting in the undoing of some of the gains of the previous decades. For instance, enrollment in universities moved from 23% to 12% between 1989 and 1995, while once extinct diseases reemerged. The usual practice of migration from highly skilled to lower skilled jobs, and migration out of the country for economic and political reasons, featured here as well. The early response to this crisis was critiqued as being insufficient to initiate the structural reforms in development and management necessary for becoming more competitive and efficient, and to reengage with the international economy. For instance, the role of top military figures in the economy increased, and permits for self-employment were also reduced. But sustained inability to address the crisis later motivated the government toward attempting more profound transformations, notably decentralizing decision making and encouraging private consumption (Pérez 2014). The economy is thus being opened selectively, including the decriminalization of the possession and use of foreign currency and expansion of self-government. Plans also are underway to reduce the public sector by around 1,000,000 persons.

Such measures provided some momentum for the economic renewal taking shape since 1995 with an annual average growth rate of 5% between 1995 and 2007. Further reforms have been encapsulated in the Economic and Social Guidelines (lineamientos Economicos y Sociales) presented at the Sixth Congress of the Cuba Communist Party in 2012. Many of these reforms also coincide with the rise of Raul Castro as the new President of Cuba after Fidel Castro demitted office in 2007 under a pledge to transform the country and reengage with the United States. However, it would be incorrect to interpret these reforms as a decisive departure from a centrally planned and managed economy and society. As Núñez notes, absent is a serious review of the role of the state and market and the plans appear to be "more efficient ways in which the state can centrally manage the economy" (see Chapter 5). Núñez's comment hints at the ongoing discussion around the appropriate role of the state in the Caribbean (and indeed elsewhere), a discussion which has resurfaced most vividly in the aftermath of the global economic crisis.

Critically, too, for the first time in over 50 years, Cuba and the United States have begun movement towards the normalization of relations after an announcement by the US President Barack Obama in December 2014 on the commencement of talks between the two countries. This announcement suggests a major rethink of the diplomatic and economic engagement that has long characterized the two countries. While the pace of deliberations and, ultimately, whether the embargo will be lifted remain unknown, it is clear that these developments will have significant implications for the organization of Cuba and its policies, as well as for that country and its Caribbean neighbors.

Some Reflections

The Caribbean is a fertile ground for studying the effects of history and legacy on the organization of society and specifically public administration. The above demonstrate the history of the region from the emergence of plantation and trading economies, and being subject to economic and geo-political vicissitudes of mother countries, to political and labor agitation leading to the reconstitution of public frameworks across the region from the 1930s (earlier for Haiti). A theme of this chapter is about societies that were organized and managed from the center (mother country) to the periphery, and where the organization of public management serves the desires of the colonial government with little focus on the development of local society. Herein lies the possible foundation of what may be seen as insufficient recognition for the role of public administration and the civil service as a critical component in mobilizing for growth and development.

Furthermore, the expatriation of profits, as well as the focus on meeting the needs of the mother country, was to have two important consequences, namely, first, the absence of local industries and investments in infrastructural development and, second, an inflexible civil service focused on "rules and rote" and less on innovation, resource management, and responsiveness to the needs of the local population, points highlighted in chapters in this book (see Chapters 2, 3, 4, and 16). Yet, despite this, the settlers (mainly economic classes) have from the beginning demonstrated what Daniel terms the "settler's spirit," evidenced by tendencies toward self-determination and sporadic acts of rebellion and demonstrations and eventually the move to independence for some. One example is Haiti's independence and later in Cuba's determination in the face of U.S. antagonism. The settler's spirit is also evident in those territories that have maintained various degrees of association with former colonial powers and in the ongoing discourse on their status quo. On the other hand, settlers and territories benefit from relations with their mainland through preferential trade, subsidies, and financial largesse, as shown in many chapters (e.g., Chapter 4). The dual tendency toward a desire for self-determination and dependence on external foreign power remains an ever-present theme in Caribbean governance.

The web of governance emanating from the mainland to the territories continues in modern time. One of the most effective means of control and continued association between the colonies and Europe was the institution of cultural hegemony over the islands, a process most assured in the French territories. Regardless of the presence or absence of the colonial power in a particular island, their dominance and influence would be maintained in the very institutions and way of life in the country. In this way, the organization of public administration was also a tool for assurance against the infiltration/adoption of unfavorable practices and ideology. This was clearly seen in the matter of communism in the 1960s and 1970s, and it has also been one of the main frustrations to complete American hegemony in the modern Commonwealth Caribbean. Relationships between the region and the former colonial powers are also sustained via aid and loans used to fund governance. Whether intentionally or not, the result has been to postpone self-reliance and the emergence of internally informed policies and development options. This is clearly exemplified in the case of the Netherlands, and where aid from the former colonial power has not been sufficient, the region has turned to the IMF and other private and multilateral lending agencies for funding development. The ability of dependent territories to sustain themselves is even more in doubt given the increasing challenges to economic survival for small states.

To the region's credit, there are growing efforts to address public sector modernization and the many social and economic challenges, discussed in sections on public policy below. The past surely informs the present-day Caribbean, even as there are new challenges and choices to be made.

Bureaucracy

Public Sector Reform and Civil Service Performance in the Caribbean

Many authors note challenges with the performance of the civil service. Soverall suggests in Chapter 6 that institutions and practices have not evolved over time to address the demands of personnel management in the modern era. Goede (Chapter 4) suggests overstaffing and a lack of qualifications as reasons for underperformance of the public sector, while Daniel frames the matter in institutional terms as relations with the motherland (Chapter 3). In many instances, the structure of the civil service is described as hierarchical as informed by various colonial models transposed onto the Caribbean region.

In response, public service reforms (PSRs) have taken place in waves and in a piecemeal fashion throughout the Caribbean. One of the major waves of reform took place during the 1980s. A number of task forces and recommendations were put forward to address some of the failings of inherited models. One of the main features of the early reforms was the IMF-supported and -informed SAP of the 1980s and 1990s which saw cuts in public expenditure, especially on social services and the funding of certain community and voluntary initiatives in the countries that adopted these measures. A reduction in the size of the public sector has also been a result. For instance, the public sector in Jamaica was reduced from 130,400 in 1974 to 103,800 in 1985 (Minto-Coy in a paper for CAPRI 2011c: 6). The adoption of reforms has not always gone smoothly. In countries such as Barbados, the adoption of SAP in the early 1990s led to widespread demonstrations which evolved into the largest demonstrations that country has ever witnessed (see Minto-Coy 2012).

These reforms were to be carried forward in the 1990s by another wave, informed by NPM that defined public sector reforms globally. New managerialism and neoliberalism have continued to be the prevailing conceptual frameworks, including greater adoption of information and communications technologies (ICTs), contracting out, decentralization, and increasing value for money. Jamaica has gone far in introducing NPM-style reforms, including creating UK-type executive agencies, showing some improvement in service quality, efficiency, and economy (Davis 2001).

The third most recent round of PSR is in response to the global financial crisis at the end of the first decade of the twenty-first century. Much of this is informed by the IMF through its guidelines for adjusting to increased economic pressures with emphasis on debt management and restructuring, containing public sector spending, including wage and benefits freeze or reduction, mergers, and improved tax administration; however, reforms have not been implemented uniformly. The preoccupation with public–private partnership and governance has also featured in the Caribbean with governments seeking out partnerships both locally and internationally (including with the private sector, nongovernmental organizations (NGOs), and the diaspora) to fund and implement infrastructural and other development initiatives.

A less stated rationale behind PSR is the reduction in the size of the public sector as a means of reducing the impact of public service wages and pensions on national budgets. The focus on the size of the public sector is warranted in the region, where wages often represent over 50% of government expenditure. Reducing the size of the public service remains politically sensitive and hence tends to be shrouded in discussions on efficiency or is carefully avoided by politicians. Increasingly, however, strains on national budgets have seen governments increasing their attention to the need for pension reforms and how best to streamline the public sector so as to reduce the strain of wages and pensions.

Yet, despite these efforts and improvements, concerns remain that the public service remains unsuitable for functioning in the global economy, largely top down with archaic systems, politicized, and indifferent to costs and time. Other features include weak coordination of activities, poor research capabilities and policy analysis, absence of a unifying theory or perspective around which support (from the public and even among public servants themselves) can be mobilized, competition with the private sector for the most talented, weak leadership, low trust, inflexible rules and procedures, and an assumption that performance cannot be measured. As noted by Jones, a culture of secrecy has also resulted from the physical organization of the public service under colonial administration.

Decisions, therefore, flow from the center while civil servants are known to be prone to risk-aversion and a focus on rule and rote, making it difficult for a proactive and innovative civil service to emerge (see Chapter 10).

Efforts have been made over the years to address some of these challenges, including moves to decentralization and the granting of more authority and control over results and performance. PSR efforts described by Bissessar, Minto-Coy, and Soverall have also seen the introduction of new practices that have given rise to a variety of leadership styles, typified by Jones et al. as ranging from the conservative-colonial to the transformational-entrepreneurial and networked (see Chapter 10). The more recent leadership styles have been slow in taking root in the region demonstrating the difficulty (though not impossibility) of breaking tradition and deeply rooted cultural tendencies. The result is a somewhat hybridized leadership style with internal inconsistencies such as the mixing of the new managerial and leadership principles of NPM with the conservative style in the Jamaican public service. Jones et al. also refers to the "co-existence of several competing 'organizational logics'" as further evidence of the inconsistencies in leadership. Some explanation for the failure of reform measures to take deep root or to spur wider systemic change can be gleaned from this competition between old and new forms of organizational leadership. Nevertheless, and as noted by the authors, leadership calls for a mix of skills and competencies rather than strict adherence to any one leadership style.

Indeed, ultimately, the imperative of improving the quality of public policy and management requires transformational leaders who are willing and able to take hard decisions necessary for moving Caribbean economies away from the divisive governance seen in countries such as T&T, Jamaica, and Haiti. Attention to leadership development requires greater coordination among training institutions across the region, increased focus on the relational (not only technical) aspects of leadership, and willingness to engage resources (and sectors) of society toward improved governance. Public sector leadership in the twenty-first century also requires an understanding of a multiplicity of issues, particularly given the interconnectedness of different policy areas, the increasing complexity of governance, and the interconnectedness between the national and international policy spaces. Jones et al. also recommend the removal of barriers to regional freedom of movement as a means of accessing leadership talent within the region and the diaspora (see Chapter 10).

Finally, while efforts are made to reduce size and increase effectiveness, the Caribbean nations are small and in many ways have limited resources and capacity. Bishop discusses this in the matter of conducting foreign policy (see Chapter 11). The Caribbean has certainly scored some apparent successes, in both global trade and climate politics, but the lack of resources and power can be seen in two ways. First, the region often plays a largely resistant and defensive role, rather than an offensive and transformative one. Second, small Caribbean states are unable to enforce gains upon more powerful actors (see Cooper 2008) while at times inflicting unnecessary wounds on itself through a lack of agreement and insufficiently supportive institutions. In this context, having a vibrant and adaptive and collaborating public sector is obviously important.

PFM and Procurement Policy

Like other areas of public administration, PFM in the region is affected by issues of size, geography, and colonial heritage, including, according to Karagiannis et al., sustained support for traditional commodities (see Chapter 13). In the French Caribbean, there is sustained support for sugar and alcohol, with little emphasis on developing other areas of economic activity outside of tourism.

Unsustainable budgetary practices beyond independence, as presented in Chapter 4, also gives insight into the ongoing inability to achieve more responsible PFM practices and addressing high national debts.

The Caribbean is largely characterized by countries at different levels of economic development, ranging from Haiti at one end and the more economically successful middle income countries such as the Bahamas at the other end. However, the region hosts some of the most indebted countries and is faced with a number of challenges. The main areas of economic activity (tourism, agriculture, financial services, and commodities) are subject to movements in the global economy, and the region is heavily dependent on external energy sources, as well as remittances from its migrant population. The economies of the region are thus quite open to the vagaries of the global economy, as demonstrated in the global financial crisis. Even where the more economically successful countries have managed to withstand the global financial crisis of 2008, there has been a failure to save and invest, making these states also vulnerable to future swings in the global economy.

As noted in Browne's coverage of PFM, Caribbean economies are affected by two main problems: high wage bills amounting to at least half of government expenditure annually, and large numbers of quasi-governmental bodies, who in turn have financial positions that are difficult to manage (see Chapter 7). The financial picture in the Caribbean remains bleak with the region still struggling in the aftermath of the global financial crisis, which saw many independent territories turning to the International Finance Institutions such as the IMF, World Bank as well as from bilateral funders and donors such as Canada, and, in the case of dependent territories, also receiving support from mainland territories. As such, one of the important stories in the history of PFM in the Caribbean is the dependence on external parties for funding the state. This point speaks not only to the inability to manage public finances, and a sense that the region has continued to spend beyond its means, but also to the level of independence which such states can have in a context of the conditionality's related to external support.

Though Caribbean societies are faced with similar threats, PFM is not practiced consistently throughout. Thus, for instance, the Cayman Islands and other territories where reputation and sound financial management are held as high virtues given the dependence on financial services and global perception have fared better than other territories in this area. In other instances, the British government has been willing to increase its oversight in territories where matters of misuse of public funds have been reported. For instance, self-rule was suspended in the Turks and Caicos Islands in 2009 (returned in 2012) after allegations of rampant political corruption emerged (CNN 2009; Fincher 2009). Nonetheless, an awareness of the need to improve PFM to respond to these challenges has seen the region moving in various degrees toward the adoption of a number of measures to improve financial governance. Among these are result-oriented budgeting which involves the coupling of budget activities to stated policy objectives and greater accuracy in measuring results. Many nations are also moving to improve the legal framework for financial management and the classification of transactions.

However, improvements in PFM have been constrained by insufficient staffing in agencies tasked with reform, as well as financial resource constraints, particularly among those who most need it. In the battle between spending on reforming bureaucratic processes such as PFM and spending on immediate demands, the former has lost out in the region. Furthermore, tax collection rates also remain low, while expenditure ceilings are nonexistent or movable, in turn contributing to the high indebtedness in the region. Another challenge is the fact that budgets are created and tasks added sometimes on an ad hoc basis with little allowance in the budget for the implementation of such tasks. There has been some adoption of automation, including public financial information management systems as a means of streamlining and increasing transparency and control, as done by the British Virgin Islands, Bermuda, and Suriname. However, even with the investments in technology, outmoded techniques persist with analyses being conducted via pre-automation methods and records in some instances being kept in note books. Browne observes incomplete understanding of PFM, insufficient training, the poor application of rules, and an over-assumption of the benefits of automation, including improved transparency to cultural change in the public service (see Chapter 7).

Moving forward, Browne recommends more targeted action in improving accountability and transparency. Towards the end of Chapter 7, she suggests a three-staged approach for reforming financial management, an affirmation of the fact that the region can overcome the above legacies, by building financial discipline, achieving greater effectiveness in allocations, and gaining greater operational efficiency. Brown also recommends the practice of rewarding sound PFM in order to overcome risk aversion in the civil service and spur action toward financial discipline amid mixed messages from politicians and the fear of losing discretionary power. Reliance on taxation to shore up government finances also suggests the need to focus more on ways of increasing and diversifying national income and improved management

These challenges also occur in Rose's discussion of public procurement regimes across the Caribbean (see Chapter 8). Among these is the challenge in achieving greater levels of transparency in public procurement given the lack of enforcement and accountability, which generally pervades public life (Freije 2009: 1). Other challenges include the lack of independently resourced regulatory bodies, the absence of centralized public procurement information systems and research capacity. In some ways, these deficiencies are related to the larger problems of lack of or insufficient resource which typifies governance in the region but also as Rose notes, unwillingness to move forward with some reforms given the expected implications of greater accountability and transparency for corruption. Indeed, accusations of corruption, nepotism, and political patronage have been leveled in countries such as T&T. These have been facilitated by lack of transparency in procurement. On the other hand, Rose also suggests that such instances may indicate political acknowledgement that "chaste market approaches" may not always support growth and development. The result nonetheless is a battle between efficiency and socioeconomic imperatives on the one hand and accountability and good governance on the other; however, whether this is the only permutation is another issue not treated in Chapter 8. For the most part, procurement regimes still remain as relics of the colonial system.

Procurement also brings forth important choices in the international space. Where countries have delayed acceding to World Trade Organization's Agreement on Government Procurement (WTO-GPA)* rules, reforms have, nonetheless, been indirectly introduced through the conditionality's and aid of international financial institutions and bilateral agreements. Also, the Economic Partnership Agreement (EPA) formally executed between Caribbean Forum and the European Community in 2008 suggests the inclusion of the Caribbean into the economic zone of the EU even as a regional policy has yet to be determined internally. Through the signing of the EPA, countries have agreed to public procurement rules over which governments had previously expressed concerns given perceptions of an unleveled playing field for developing countries.

Governments (e.g., Belize, Grenada, Haiti and Guyana) have for the most part begun moving to introduce public procurement regulations and legislation nationally and regionally mainly in the

---

* The Agreement came into force in 1996 and aims to create more transparency, openness and competition in signatory government's procurement of goods and services. See Reich (2009), Arrowsmith and Anderson (2011) for a discussion of this agreement.

last decade. To this end, the Caribbean as a region has a number of positive examples and experiences which are worthy of note and potential emulation. Among these is the use of procurement policy as a developmental tool in the case of the Organization of Eastern Caribbean States. In spite of this experience, however, Rose underscores the challenges in utilizing procurement policy as a socioeconomic development tool in the wider Caribbean.

Corruption

One of the overarching themes that runs consistently throughout the book is corruption—defined as the use of public funds and power for private gains,* suggesting the persistence of this theme in the region. While the book does not offer a separate chapter, an attempt is made here to pull together the main thrust of the arguments and presentation made throughout the individual chapters.

The Caribbean, as a whole, is noted as a region which consists of stable institutions and where democracy has thrived (Transparency International [TI], 2005). Nevertheless, corruption, largely facilitated by lack of accountability and transparency, remains among the most pressing challenges to effective public management, reducing the impact of even the soundest policies. Collier (2002) has made a direct link between corruption and economic performance in the Caribbean, suggesting that political/administrative corruption hampers development since it retards adherence to the rule of law while contributing to crime and violence. Corruption in the Caribbean has been encouraged by a winner-takes-all political and administrative system which vests significant power and insufficient transparency in leaders (TI 2005).

Figure 1.1 shows the rankings of Caribbean countries on Transparency International's Corruption Perception Index for 2013. While this shows considerable variation, corruption has tainted all areas of the Caribbean, regardless of level of development, relationship with a colonial power, or whether the economy is centrally managed or not, as in Cuba. In the case of the Dominican Republic, for instance, Morgan et al. (2011) note the existence of corruption and clientelism. The level of poverty combined with inequality (also in Nicholls 1988) which pervades the region (among the highest in the world) also serves to aggravate and encourage the incidence of corruption through the distribution of scarce benefits. The various presentations in this book suggest the existence of corruption as a part of the lived experiences of nationals in the region. Indeed, one of the challenges is the increasing perception that this is becoming a way of life, that is, part of the cultural fabric (see Waller et al. 2007). Nevertheless, it would be simplistic to suggest that corruption is only a feature of the modern Caribbean, even as Mills has observed that the level of corruption prior to independence is unknown in the Commonwealth Caribbean. Soverall notes evidence of promotions being based on relationship with the governor or based on proximity to European descent during the colonial period (see Chapter 6). It would not be an understatement, though, to say that corruption has in fact increased with independence as nationals have commanded greater power and control over the distribution of resources that have grown scarcer with time. One of the more wide-reaching developments is linking civil service employment and promotion to political support. Ultimately, these features of public administration have helped to lower public service ethics and increase the perception of the Caribbean as a corrupt region.

The first order of addressing corruption in the region is therefore going to be about changing perceptions by increasing the penalties and most certainly the level of prosecution (including

---

* While it is acknowledged that variances exist in definition and categorization, this definition is one of the more accepted definitions, which also sits well with the emphasis on public policy and administration in this book.

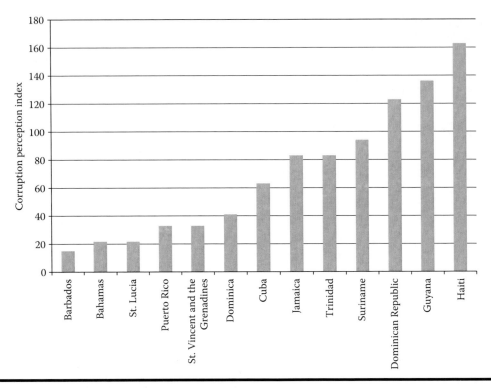

Figure 1.1 Corruption perception index in 2013 for select Caribbean countries (the maximum value is 177). (Data from Transparency International, http://www.transparency.org/country, 2014.)

high-profile cases) against corrupt public officials. A number of measures have been undertaken to address the issue over the years. These include freedom of information, anti-money laundering, and public disclosure legislation (see Nazario 2007; TI 2005). For example, countries such as Jamaica, the Bahamas, and Dominica have introduced disclosure of assets legislation.

Many of these reforms are in fulfillment of international membership obligations in organizations such as the United Nations Convention against Corruption, which came into force in 2005. However, these have been accompanied by lack of implementation or enforcement essentially rendering the various mechanisms powerless. The network of corruption prevention bodies, such as the Office of the Contractor General, Auditor-General, Director of Public Prosecution in Jamaica, remains under-resourced legislatively, financially and reputationally. Addressing corruption more convincingly may require greater transparency and accountability (Nazario 2007). To this end, there is need for a review of the legacies of secrecy, exclusion of civil society, and top-down practices, which typify policy-making and more generally public administration toward more transparency and inclusiveness. While ratifying international treaties and agreements on corruption is also positive, implementation will remain weak without local buy-in and at the highest levels of society. Measures to regulate political parties and campaign funding have also been slow in coming with links being noted between corruption and crime (illegal drugs and narcotics trade) in the region.

While the failure to apply punitive measures to cases of corruption and impropriety has generally served to encourage its persistence, there are a few instances where high-level infractions have seen some recourse. Included here are moves by the governing coalition in T&T to remove ministers in 2011 accused of impropriety (Taitt 2014), a move which was arguably influenced by the waning national support for the coalition than any deep support for eradication. Inadvertently, this also suggests two key points as it relates to addressing corruption in the Caribbean. First, that political will is critical in addressing the issues, and second, how this will can come about, that is, through the threat of electoral defeat.

Public Policy: Economy and Development

Developmental Interventions in the Caribbean

It is generally agreed that the states in the Caribbean have for the most part not addressed their developmental challenges successfully. This is evidenced in the many governance challenges which linger in the region, many of these recurring and have even taken on increasing complexity as policy spaces have become more eclectic and joined up. The imperative for the region is to improve governance toward addressing the demands of crime and corruption control, job creation, increasing standard of living, competitiveness, and environmental protection. Nonetheless, there remains an ongoing debate on the appropriate role for government. Indeed, many of the ideological debates in the post-independence era have been related to the role of the state as espoused in the contention among socialism, communism, and capitalism in the 1960s, 1970s, and 1980s. This argument takes on another inflection in the case of the non-independent territories where discussions also include the appropriate relationship and responsibilities between the central and local governments. This discourse has become much less polarized since the 1990s with governments, including that of Cuba, collectively introducing market-type reforms.

Karagiannis et al. call for a rethink of the role of government in national development, arguing for consideration of the "developmental state" (DS) as practiced in East Asia as an indicator of the developmental interventions for the Caribbean (see Chapter 13). As they suggest, the most successful economies have for the most part involved significant private sector-government cooperation and dialogue, a feature of the DS. This is in a context of increasing requirement for government policies to be more coherent, technically proficient and for governments to escape the "trap of failed political ideologies, nationalist and class-based rhetoric and the associated tensions between the state and the business sector." The decline in patience for poor governance across the region has heightened with the increasing threats to democracy from decades of mismanagement and failure to deliver law and order.

In practice, the Caribbean offers many examples and lessons of strategic action in specific instances. Barbados features many aspects of DS that have featured with quite successful results in the Social Partnership among the labor, government, civil society, and the private sector (see Blackman 2006; CaPRI 2008; Minto-Coy 2012). Indeed, that model of governance has been held up globally with the country managing to secure levels of development yearned for by others within the region and beyond. However, as circumstances change, so too does the need for revisiting arrangements. Ultimately, even the DSs highlighted by Karagiannis et al. have found themselves with governance challenges in recent times, suggesting the need to "take a more focused and strategic approach to development problems" (Chapter 13).

Tourism Policy and Management

Tourism is the main and arguably the most successful area of economic activity for the Caribbean, as a whole. That is so, given its position as the largest source of employment (direct and indirect combined) and main foreign exchange earner, accounting for roughly 25% of regional GDP. Tourism has grown dramatically witnessing over a 100% increase (10–20 million arrivals) from 1990 to 2000. Some countries have also managed to exploit niches to generate prosperity with the region being noted as the most tourism-dependent region globally. Ultimately, tourism has helped to lessen the dependence of some territories on financial support from former colonial powers, conferring them with some degree of independence and self-actualization as in the case of Aruba and the Netherlands.

The region has, therefore, performed relatively well and remains synonymous with symbols such as sun, sea, and sand. Unfortunately, such an association is insufficient to ensure sustained competitiveness, particularly where policy and action have insufficiently focused on sustainability with, diversification, or ways in which to reinvigorate the market as a means of increasing viability. Growth in traditional segments has also declined relative to other regions with countries within the region competing against each other. The industry remains vulnerable to external market conditions, especially those in North America and Europe. The industry is also dominated by all-inclusive with the cruise sector being the fastest and most self-contained sector. Other key features include reliance on foreign capital, imports and profit repatriation, as well as being an "enclave" industry with little spill over into other areas of the economy and society.

Acknowledging tourism to regional survival has seen a shift in the laissez-faire approach of governments with increased policies and specific strategies such as infrastructural investments and subsidies. Nonetheless, more strategic and proactive action is necessary that is affected by general policy challenges noted by Clayton, such as bureaucratic inefficiencies, lack of transparency in the granting of incentives, economies of scale, high administrative costs, and slow planning procedures (see Chapter 15). A search for a future path for tourism should include efforts to reduce economic leakage (through local involvement), increasing socioeconomic linkages, preservation and enhancement of cultural and environmental assets, healthy competition and reducing environmental damage, and achieving economies of scale (e.g., in marketing) and improved access and transportation. Furthermore, policy-makers in the region need to make more definitive steps to diversifying the industry as a means of enhancing competitiveness, including considering areas such as health-, eco-, and heritage tourism. Indeed, islands such as Jamaica have made strides to capitalize on key sectors such as sports (sports tourism) while the region as a whole can benefit from more strategic targeting of its diaspora, who now make up one of the most significant clientele, even in the absence of policies directly targeting this group (see Minto-Coy, 2015). As an area of governance, tourism requires pro-market policies along with concerted public strategies that protect and develop local interests.

Communications, E-Government, and Cyber Policy

Historically, the development of the communications industry in the region has been informed by the same great power politics that saw the region being colonized and parceled among the European powers. In the case of the English, for example, the development of the industry helped to cement the role of the British in its territories in the region. Relics of the colonial communications industry remain in the form of companies such as Cable and Wireless (now Lime).

The industry that now exists is part of the colonial legacy, even as it has seen monopolies in telecommunications being broken to facilitate the competition.

Widespread efforts at policy, regulatory, and legislative reforms were undertaken mainly in the last decade or two. One of the legacies was the slow pace in advancing technology and innovations and the lingering undercoverage in the fixed network (now replaced by mobile telephony). The evolution of policies in the sector has mainly been seen as a bilateral affair involving service providers and the government. Policy reforms have seen the introduction of more players, including regulatory bodies and operators in the policy space. Much of the policy development in these areas has been through the assistance of international institutions such as the Organization of American States. These have given both technical and financial support to governments, helping to address gaps at the local and regional level.

Further advances in policy development are also necessary at the national and regional levels, particularly in addressing some of the emerging challenges that have accompanied liberalization. Among these is the issue of cyber security, which is one of the emerging threats to the region's security and development. A number of governments have begun to take a deliberate approach. For example, Jamaica enacted the Cyber Crime Act in 2010 and moves to finalize a national Cyber Security Strategy. However, the region remains limited in its capacity to act in the area or cyber security given constraints in resource and influence. Other areas such as data privacy and protection have emerged with the increased availability to Internet and role of ICTs, as demonstrated in national development plans.

The advances in the policy and legislative framework of the communications industry more generally have opened the path for e-government across the region. This is now most visible in the online presence of various ministries and government departments and services. E-government has allowed for more interactive and remote engagement with governments. For instance, birth certificates and other government-issued documents and taxes can be paid online. Again, the extent of services here varies significantly across the region with countries such as Barbados offering greater connectivity than others. E-government as well as e-commerce is currently constrained by outdated legislation and bureaucratic practices such as the inability of some governments to legally issue electronic receipts for online payments. Additionally, many government web sites are rarely updated, inactive, or simply used for the posting of information as opposed to being interactive.

Environmental Risk Management

The devastating effect of natural disasters cannot be underestimated in small states of the Caribbean. For instance, when Hurricane Katrina hit the United States, this barely placed a dent in the U.S. economy, but the impact of a storm on a Caribbean city is likely to have a greater impact given the small size. The hurricanes and storms that hit Cuba in 2008, for instance, amounted to a total loss of 20% of that country's GDP. The total cost of damage caused by Hurricane Tomas in St. Lucia was equivalent to 43.4% of GDP or nine times agricultural GDP.

The Caribbean experiences major hurricanes every year that can and do wreak havoc on local economies, resulting in sharp increases in social and emergency services. At issue are not only high-profile, high-impact events, but also frequently occurring, low-profile disaster events which are also numerous and responsible for a very significant proportion of damage to housing, crops, livestock, and local infrastructure. These extreme climatic events and natural disasters can and do reverse development achievements and upset development plans.

Granvorka et al. describe how over the past 35 years the countries of the English-speaking Caribbean have worked together to develop a coordinated and collaborative approach to the more effective management of natural hazard vulnerability and impacts (see Chapter 14). Consultative processes have been used to develop a series of programmatic disaster management frameworks and strategies. These processes have progressively become more representative of the wide spectrum of institutional, civil-society, private sector, and governmental stakeholders. Over this period, donor support for disaster risk management and the diversity of supported interventions has increased substantially, and a shift occurred in hazard management, from preparedness, response, and recovery to include prevention and mitigation. Environmental risk management clearly shows the importance of developing a regional framework, having capable domestic response plan, and coordination and support from the international community.

Public Policy: Social Policies

The chapters in this book provide insight into some specific policy areas such as education and health, as well as social issues such as gender equality.

Education

Early education reforms across the region were developed in a fragmented space through colonial rule by diverse and different imperial powers. As Jules and Williams discuss, education for these early settlers was mostly nonexistent, provided by missionaries around Sunday class, and settlers were loath to provide any education to the black slave population (see Chapter 12). In the immediate post-emancipation period, the British government created the Negro Education Grant in 1833, and eventually elementary education financing shifted to local legislative bodies. However, educational quality remained quite problematic, with various reports noting continued deficiencies in secondary education throughout the twentieth century. Reflecting this concern, institutional reforms after independence in the Anglophone countries began with the creation of a regional testing institution. In Dutch and French territories, testing at the end of secondary school was done within the parameters of home country.

As countries sought to shift from plantation economies to industrialized ones, they began spending on education and health reform to address issues of equitable access and quality. The emphasis on national education policy-making shifted from creating a capable elite workforce for the colonial bureaucracy to a national curriculum that concentrated on development relevant to each country's situation and environment, for example, by providing educational grants focused on reducing the urban–rural divide and by closing the gender gap across the region. Different countries adopted different approaches in the 1970s, leading to "ideological pluralism" in education curricula. In the 1980s, educational reform to improve human capital placed emphasis on creating Caribbean nationals for the regional and international markets.

In the 1990s with the shift to economic tourism and services and abolishment of preferential trading agreements, such as the Lomé IV convention, Caribbean countries saw a shift in education that focused on tackling the challenges of a liberalized global environment, preferring innovation and competitiveness. Human resource development became linked to the ability to use and develop creative talents and skills, find employment, and contribute to development. While individual countries have been responsible for the national development of human resources, several regional and sub-regional educational strategies have called for the specific development of human resources so as to aid in the development of regional and sub-regional integrative projects. For example, with Caribbean Community (CARICOM) countries, these various initiatives saw Council for Human and Social Development (COHSOD) in 2002 approving 16 regional standards in occupational areas and the establishment of a regional coordinating mechanism for Technical and Vocational Education and Training (TVET). Tertiary education reform in the 1980s focused on upgrading education facilities. The University of the West Indies (UWI) system now has four campuses and 18 countries or territories as members.

The Caribbean region, despite limited resources, has made tremendous strides in educational expansion and provision. Accreditation now allows for portability across the region of skilled nationals. Some Caribbeanists have rung the neocolonialist alarm in the face of exogenously initiated educational reforms, while others have posited greater Caribbean regionalism and integration as a way to navigate these and other global currents: "the failure to place education reform as central to that agenda is a major and strategic flaw in the ongoing efforts to position the Caribbean better for survival in the globalisation process" (Jules 2008). Yet, others have noted that the continued dependence on donor aid has created a funding trap development dependency upon donors to fund projects. The Caribbean basin remains a dynamic place of ongoing reforms since the small states of the Caribbean are able to leverage their smallness and benefit from numerous trading agreements which not only drive national reforms, but also contribute to the development of the Caribbean who are trained nationally, globally minded, and have the capacity to work regionally.

Health

Jules and Fryer note that health services in the Caribbean face numerous challenges ranging from rising HIV/AIDS infections, mental health neglect, increased cost and access to medications, and the rise or resurgence of several diseases (such as yellow fever, malaria, heart disease, enteritis, dengue fever, and hemorrhagic fever) (see Chapter 17). Historically, the efforts of the 1950s and 1960s stand out for their overarching focus on malnutrition, gastroenteritis, and infections, while reforms in the early 1970s focus on eradicating tuberculosis, malaria, syphilis, and enteritis. In the 1980s, efforts focused on heart disease, strokes, cancer, diabetes, and injuries were the primary health concerns until HIV/AIDS occupied the top position.

In an effort to combat diseases, health service reform in the region has been linked to access to education, development of human capital, and the eradication of poverty and poor living conditions across the Caribbean. In the last decade, efforts were also made to diversify health financing by increasing user fees, providing insurance, utilizing nongovernmental resources, and decentralizing health services. With a focus on revenue generation, several ministries underwent decentralization reforms that led, for example, in Jamaica, to the creation of regional boards with autonomy, quality assurance programs and trained personnel in both public and private health services, and the introduction of cost-sharing strategies.

Current demographic trends show that a new health transition is occurring as regional reform initiatives aim to enable people to move seamlessly across a borderless region. To foster this movement of labor, Caribbean nations have made comparable advances in health reform owing to their conjoined investment in water, sanitation, nutrition, and the essentials of primary health service. These efforts have a significant impact on the health service system, which is now demanding trained, competent, and innovative health service professionals to staff and promote local and regional initiatives. To enable these new advances, health systems across the region have been using multi-sectoral, holistic, and integrated approaches to meet challenges as well as finance and deliver health services. Examples of this are the 2008 Caribbean Cooperation in Health and the Caribbean Regional Drug Testing Laboratory, located in Jamaica and established in 1974 by CARICOM heads of government, focused on regional drug testing.

In another example, the Caribbean Pharmaceutical Policy, approved in 2011, is an intersectional approach to ensure access, quality, and rational use at affordable prices as a human right for all Caribbean nationals.

These new waves of reforms are based upon "new-mutualism" that focuses on deeper cooperation and coordination, through a (1) a multi-sectoral approach, (2) international target setting, and (3) regional benchmark to combat communicable and non-communicable diseases. However, note that great collaboration and cooperation is essential to abate the challenges and increasing threats national economies are faced with through emerging and reemerging problems in the health sector. The rise of greater collaboration and cooperation in health systems reforms uses "integrated comprehensive multi-sector measures including information and communication networks, legal and fiscal reform and healthy public policies ... in the public and private sectors of national, regional and international entities" (CCH III 2008: 13).

Despite the above, results are far from favorable. In recent years, the cost of health service expenditure has increased, and spending by Caribbean countries as a percentage of GDP remains higher than Latin American and other developing countries. Several risk factors and social determinants lead to disappointing outcomes, especially in such areas as sexually transmitted infections, maternal infant morbidity and mortality, infertility, teenage pregnancy, unsafe abortions, limited fertility control, and drug abuse. By example, while there has been a decrease in AIDS-related deaths across the region, currently HIV/AIDS is the leading cause of death among 25–44-year olds in the region. Also, the post-2008 financial crisis era has seen, rather than central coordination around sectoral areas, a slow movement toward isolationist national developmental tendencies. While cooperation is not dead in health service, as the creation of Caribbean Public Health Agency (CARPHA) shows, there are lots of residual tensions between nation states as to what kinds of health service reforms are most beneficial for a viable community.

Migration and Diasporas

Colonialism and the demands of maintaining a plantation economy in the Caribbean have seen migration being etched into the very DNA of the region with nationalities and cultures moving in and out of the region (Foner 1998; Lapointe 2004; Nurse 2004; Palmer 2007; Reis 2007). The experience with migration has evolved from mainly a movement into the region to marked emigration since the latter half of the twentieth century. For instance, the independence of Suriname in 1975 saw roughly a third of that country's population migrating to the Netherlands, while 2011 figures suggest that more Puerto Ricans live in the United States than in Puerto Rico itself (Brown and Patten 2013). Such large-scale migration has had significant impact on the region with the migration of skilled and talented persons being the most valuable export from the Caribbean. Indeed, the region has been noted as suffering from one of the highest rates of brain drain with as much as 40% of its labor force estimated to have migrated to OECD member states (Mishra, 2006). At the same time, as suggested by Goede in Chapter 4, migration helped to contain unemployment levels in the region. As suggested by Minto (2009) migration has inadvertently benefitted Caribbean governments by lowering the demands on public services and offering opportunities for realizing dreams in other lands in light of the betrayed hopes lingering in the region (also see Oostindie and Klinkers 2003: 224). Thus, migration is two-sided and has led to the creation of a sizable diaspora in the United States, Canada, the United Kingdom, and elsewhere.

Historically, the main foundation for the partnership between the diaspora and Caribbean governments has been remittancing (the sending of cash and kind by migrants and the diaspora to friends and family in the country of origin) and social philanthropy. This is especially in helping governments to deal with the effects of natural disasters and in providing for the social and welfare needs of citizens. As an indicator of the growing importance of remittances to Caribbean economies, it now rivals the value of tourism (Minto-Coy 2010) in some instances in terms of contribution to overall GDP and remittance earnings.

Elsewhere it has been suggested that the relationship between the diaspora and migrants and the governments in the region has been characterized by a silent partnership. Nevertheless, the silence has begun shifting mainly from the 1990s as governments across the region more actively seek to engage this group. Government led initiatives include the introduction of a national Diaspora Day, conferences, and returning residents programs. For example, Haiti has been an example, introducing a government department for the diaspora from 1993. Some governments (e.g., Jamaica) are conducting mapping exercises to accurately assess the size, location, resources, and other key characteristics of their diaspora. Governments such as Suriname have moved to more actively engage the diaspora in business development and hence, economic growth via programs such as "IntEnt"—a business incubator aimed at heightening opportunities for diaspora entrepreneurship. Barbados has also moved to enlist its diaspora in South America to assist in forging opportunities for South–South trade with between itself and South America. Governments in Jamaica, St. Lucia, Dominica, T&T, and Guyana are at various stages of drafting programs in this area.

Nevertheless, one of the more perverse outcomes of migration is the negative experience of Caribbean migrants into the former colonial powers, even where there is a natural right to citizenship or travel as in the Dutch and French regions. In the case of the English-speaking region, the introduction of a number of restrictive migration policies is moving toward reducing the migration options and (having migrated) the economic options for Caribbean nationals. It is true that public administration and policy have yet to fully contend with the impact of migration and the diaspora phenomenon in terms of the design of a consistent approach or support for migrants. Finally, it has been suggested that migration has had an impact on public service performance, having diminished the overall stock of talented personnel available to the public sector. The reality is that the quality and quantity of public servants will have an impact on the attainment of policy objectives and outcomes. The experience with migration for the Caribbean small states means that the private sector is not the only contender for the most talented leaders with migration being an option for those who have found it difficult to rise in the national systems.

Race, Class, and Gender

Caribbean societies are uniformly heterogeneous. This heterogeneity not only results from different language and colonial attachment but also due to the mix of racial and ethnic groups that can be found on each island. Race, ethnicity, and class have been noted as factors that affect the quality of public governance across the region. Indeed, these also affect the quantity of governance in terms of the extent to which different groups are able to access public goods and services. Thus, a number of authors, including Minto-Coy, Soverall, and Jones et al., note the selective delivery of public goods and services to constituents based on ethnic, racial, or class attachments in countries such as the Dominican Republic, the DOMs, and Suriname. Interestingly, though, none of the societies across the region have actively addressed these concerns sufficiently, and indeed in the case of the French, the notion of reforms being introduced as a means of quashing discontent as opposed to an intent for improvement (as suggested by Daniel, see Chapter 3) reduces the likelihood of transformation, at least in this setting. Indeed, while many commentators (also within this book) have noted the incendiary effects of this divide historically and in policy delivery in Guyana and T&T as it relates to discrimination against Indians, it is interesting that there may be a counter movement underway in some of these countries which now involves the black population feeling increasingly marginalized in the modern development.

One of the oft-ignored topics in coverage of public governance is gender as a specific policy area, its implications for public governance, and impact of various public sector reform efforts on this area (see, e.g., Scott 2011: 27). As a whole, the Caribbean has made significant improvements from the 1970s and specifically in areas such as health, employment, and education. This is after the introduction of legislation banning married women teachers from employment in T&T in 1936 and the granting of universal adult suffrage beginning in Jamaica in 1944. The region also presents differently based on the international indices. For instance, Mohammed notes that the Global Gender Gap Index suggests that some countries within the region offer greater access to resources and opportunities to women than when they are ranked by development (see Chapter 18). For instance, Jamaica was one of three countries in the world noted in the 1990s where women were more educated than men.

Even as improvements are being made, new areas for attention are also emerging. National policies for equity and equality are now being drafted across the region promising, among other things, to monitor the gender implications of new and existing policies. These include the need for policies to address the exploitation of migrant women in places such as the British Virgin Islands and Cayman Islands, new health concerns, feminization of poverty, and the rights of persons of different sexual orientation. Added to this are outstanding matters such as further improvements in areas such as political representation. Chapter 18 is insightful not only as a review of gender policy in the Caribbean but also because it gives an intimate look at the actual policy-making process, underscoring that at its core, the process is undergirded by democracy, and where local actors find international support to bolster and advance specific agendas in the local context, adopting strategies such as blame shifting in the process.

Conclusion as Prologue: A Tentative Guide to the Future

The presentation thus far suggests that public governance in the Caribbean is plagued by a number of challenges. Admittedly, some of these are deeply engrained in the institutional make-up of the region, though admittedly and as suggested in some of the presentations in this text, not in a predetermined way. There are also those challenges that relate to geography, including natural disasters such as earthquakes and hurricanes. These have placed added risks to public governance.

The colonial influence on public administration and policy is profound, providing both the administrative apparatus and governance policies. During the colonial period public administration was never developmentally or growth oriented. This is still the case in some places where the mainland still maintains some degree of control through institutions, governance arrangements, and debt. An ever-present theme in Caribbean governance is the dual tendency toward a desire for self-determination and dependence on external foreign power. The notion of betrayed hope characterizes governance in the region, regardless of specific historical legacy. For the French, this is with regard to sustained inability to realize a coming together of the practical (i.e., sociopolitical and socioeconomic) and theoretical aspects of equality as espoused under DOM status. For the English-speaking region, this is seen in the dissatisfaction with the quality and outcomes of governance, post-independence. In the case of the Dutch, it is with the continued uncertainty in the relationship with the Netherlands and the second-tier status of Caribbean immigrants in that country. Even for Cuba, the extent to which the promise of the revolution has been fulfilled remains open.

Thus, a consistent theme throughout is the notion of the need for change and search for new governance models to address the complex challenges facing the region. A case has been made for considering the role of the DSs, certainly in the early phases of the reform. Indeed, as has been suggested, the experience of countries such as Barbados indicates some merit in this option. Even so, there are problems inherent in any "model." Ultimately, it is the case that any strategy adopted by the region to improve governance will constitute efforts to address some of the adversities (manmade and natural) mentioned throughout this book. Perhaps it is here that one can identify the answer to the challenges in achieving more impactful public administration and policies in the region. That is, it is not so much about models but paying attention to the fundamentals of reducing corruption, improving PFM, paying attention to implementation gaps, reducing politicization, developing more cohesive and responsive development plans, and leaders being better managers of the scarce resources within their command.

Regardless of the historical legacy, development philosophy, or economic orientation, public governance across the region is preoccupied with reducing the cost of government, increasing efficiency, balancing budgets, and modernization as unifying themes, though with differing levels of urgency. Additionally, indeed, an imperative for the future of public governance for the Caribbean is how to overcome the vulnerabilities presented by natural disasters (and indeed, all the other aspects of vulnerability) to become more resilient societies. In so doing, moving from a context of "vulnerability as a condition, [to] resilience as a strategy" (Payne 2009: 279). Furthermore, more effective public policy and management in Caribbean small states call for more joined up government. This requires leaders who are more effective boundary crossers, willing to work and communicate across different groups and sectors and to understand that issue areas are now more interconnected than ever. Thus, while the region has accomplished much and is still very much in its infancy, a tall order of activities remains outstanding in moving forward.

Indeed, a lingering imperative is for the region to learn from itself as to what works (and does not); to garner the lessons from the successful governance interventions, including areas such as disaster response and preparedness, and the instances of successful economic and societal management; and to apply those internally informed lessons and models to transforming itself. In other words, there remains a need for the region to more proactively engage with and come to terms with the features of its endowment, including a realistic assessment of its capacities, prospects for addressing corruption, furthering transnational cooperation in the region, and configuring rules and institutions for yielding greater results. As pointed out in a number of chapters, the height of perversion is where local elites operating in their self-interest have been powerful inhibitors of good governance and learning in the Caribbean.

To be sure, the region has accomplished much in the way of governance. It stands out as a location where democracy still thrives and where some degree of good governance and prosperity have been accomplished, especially in the case of those territories that have decided to "go it alone"* via independence and in light of numerous challenges. Indeed, the region's location in the middle of many international indicators (some of which have been noted in this book) and even its placing on TI's index suggest that there has been some positive achievements. The sustained search for efficiency and improved governance via public sector reform discussed in the Dutch and British territories also suggest interest in improving performance. Perhaps it is more an awareness of the

---

* As much as this is possible given the role of international forces, discussed here and in Chapter 11.

unmet potential which makes Caribbean citizens and observers dissatisfied with the quality and results of public governance. More specifically, the decision to focus on "telling the story" of the region as a valuable account in itself as opposed to mechanically borrowing theories and perspectives has generated information that can in fact lead to further theorizing, contextualization, and model-building, in the ongoing search for improved performance.

References

Arrowsmith, Sue and Anderson, Robert (2011). *The WTO Regime on Procurement: Challenge and Reform*, Cambridge: Cambridge University Press.

Blackman, Courtney N. (2006). *The Practice of Economic Management: A Caribbean Perspective*. Miami, FL: Ian Randle Publishers.

Brown, Anna and Patten, Eileen (2013). *Hispanics and Puerto Rican Origin in the US 2011*, Washington: Pew Research Center, Pew Hispanic Center. Available at: http://www.pewhispanic.org/files/2013/06/PuertoRicanFactsheet.pdf. Accessed on August 20, 2014.

CaPRI (2008). *A New Social Partnership for Jamaica: Uniting Jamaica to Build Our Nation*, Kingston, Jamaica: Caribbean Policy and Research Institute.

CCH III (2008). *Caribbean Cooperation in Health Phase III: Regional Health Framework 2010–2015*. Retrieved from http://new.paho.org/ocpc/index.php?option=com_docman&task=doc_download&gid=24&Itemid=. Accessed on December 1, 2014.

Clegg, Peter (2012). Independence movements in the Caribbean: Withering on the vine, *Commonwealth and Comparative Politics*, 50(4): 422–438.

Collier, M.W. (2002, June). The effects of political corruption on Caribbean development. Paper presented at the *Caribbean Studies Association Annual Conference*, Nassau, Bahamas, May.

Cooper, John N. (2006). *The Power of Community: How Cuba Survived Peak Oil*, Available at: http://peak-oil.blogspot.com/2006/05/power-of-community-how-cuba-survived.html. Accessed on December 1, 2014.

Cooper, A.F. (2008). Remote in the Eastern Caribbean: The Antigua? US WTO Internet Gambling Case, *Caribbean Paper No. 4*, Waterloo, Canada: Centre for International Governance Innovation.

CNN (August 15, 2009). Britain imposes direct rule of Turks and Caicos Islands. Available at: http://edition.cnn.com/2009/WORLD/europe/08/15/turk.caicos.uk/. Accessed on July 2, 2014.

Davis (May 19, 2001). Executive agencies in Jamaica: The story thus far and the central management mechanism, *UWI/MIND Conference on Executive Agencies in Action*. Available at: http://www.cabinet.gov.jm/files/docs/speech-cdavis-exec-agencies-so-far.pdf. Accessed on August 15, 2014.

Dubois, Laurent (2012). *Haiti: The Aftershocks of History*, New York: Henry Holt and Company.

Fatton, Robert Jr. (2002). *Haiti's Predatory Republic: The Unending Transition to Democracy*, Boulder, CO: Lynne Rienner.

Fincher, Christina (August 14, 2009). Britain suspends Turks and Caicos government. *Reuters*. Available at: http://www.reuters.com/article/2009/08/14/us-britain-turkscaicos-idUSTRE57D3TE20090814. Accessed on July 2, 2014.

Foner, N. (1998). Towards a comparative perspective on Caribbean migration, in *Caribbean Migration: Globalised Identities*, Mary Chamberlain (ed.), London; New York: Routledge.

Freije, Samuel (2009). *Informal Employment in Latin America and the Caribbean: Causes, Consequences and Policy Recommendations*, Inter-American Development Bank. Available at: www.iadb.org/wmsfiles/products/publications/documents/354692.pdf. Accessed on December 1, 2014.

Jones, E. and Schoburgh, E. (2004). Deconstructing policy-making and implementation issues in a Caribbean context. *Social and Economic Studies*, 35–61.

Jules, D. (2008). Rethinking education for the Caribbean: A radical approach. *Comparative Education*, 44(2): 203–214.

Lapointe, M. (2004). Diasporas in Caribbean Development. Rapporteur's report for the Inter-American Dialogue and World Bank workshop on *The Caribbean Diaspora as a Development Agent*, Washington, DC, April 14.

LeoGrande, William M. (2014). The prospects for improving U.S.-Cuban relations, *International Relations*. Available at: http://www.e-ir.info/2014/03/03/the-prospects-for-improving-u-s-cuban-relations/. Accessed on December 1, 2014.

Mawby, Spencer (2012). *Ordering Independence: The End of Empire in the Anglophone Caribbean, 1947–69*, Basingstoke: Palgrave Macmillan.

Minto-Coy, Indianna (2010). The impact of the global financial crisis on remittancing, in *What Others Manifest? The World Economy in the Theoretical Turbulence of the Global Financial Crisis*, İhsan Günaydin and Hilmi Erdoğan Yayla (eds), Gümüşhane, Turkey: Gümüşhane University Press, pp. 2–18.

Minto-Coy, Indianna (2011c). *Towards Public Sector Reform in Jamaica: What Can Local and International Experiences Tell Us About Successful Public Sector Reform*, CaPRI Policy Paper.

Minto-Coy, Indianna (2012). The grit that makes the pearl: Collaborative problem solving in the midst of national crisis, *Journal of Systems Research and Behavioural Science*, 29(2): 221–226.

Minto-Coy, Indianna (2015). A critical analysis of the diasporic engagement for development in the Caribbean. Paper presented at the *Diasporas, Development and Governance in the Global South Conference*, A. Chikanda, J. Crush, and M. Walton-Roberts (eds.), New York, Springer, May 27–28.

Mishra, Prachi (2006). Emigration and Brain Drain: Evidence from the Caribbean, *IMF Working Paper WP/06/25*, Available at: https://www.imf.org/external/pubs/ft/wp/2006/wp0625.pdf. Accessed: November 15, 2014.

Morgan, Jana, Hartlyn, Jonathan and Espinal, Rosario (2011). Dominican party system continuity amid regional transformations: Economic policy, clientelism and migration flows, *Latin American Politics and Society*, 53(1): 1–32.

Nazario, Olga (2007). A strategy against corruption, *Paper Presented at the CARICOM Conference on the Caribbean: A 20/20 Vision*, Washington DC, November 19–20, 2007.

Nicholls, David (1998). The Duvalier regime in Haiti, in *Sultanistic Regimes*, Houchang E. Chehabi and Juan J. Linz (eds), Baltimore, MD: Johns Hopkins University Press, pp. 153–181.

Nurse, Keith (2004). "Diaspora, Migration and Development in the Caribbean" FOCAL Policy Paper FPP-04-6. Ottawa: Canadian Foundation for the Americas.

Oostindie, Gert and Klinkers, Inge (2003). *Decolonising the Caribbean: Dutch Policies in a Comparative Perspective*, Amsterdam, the Netherlands: Amsterdam University Press.

Palmer, Ransford (1990). "Caribbean Development and the Migration Imperative." In *In Search of a Better Life: Perspectives on Migration from the Caribbean*, edited by Ransford Palmer. New York: Praeger.

Payne, Anthony (2009). Afterword: Vulnerability as a condition, resilience as a strategy, *The Diplomacies of Small States: Between Vulnerability and Resilience*, Andrew Fenton Cooper and Timothy M. Shaw (eds), Basingstoke: Palgrave MacMillan, pp. 279–286.

Pérez, Ricardo Torres (2014). Transformations in the Cuban economic model: Context, general proposal and challenges, *Latin American Perspective*, 41(4): 74–90.

Pérez-López, Jorge F. (1998). The Cuban economic crisis of the 1990s and the external sector 1998, *Cuba in Transition* (Association for the Study of the Cuban Economy), 8: 386–413.

Pierre-Louis, Francois (2011). Earthquakes, nongovernmental organisations, and governance in Haiti, *Journal of Black Studies*, 42(2): 186–202.

Reich, Arie (2009). The new text of the agreement on government procurement: An analysis and assessment, *Journal of International Economic Law*, 12(4): 989–1022.

Reis, Michele (2007). "The Role of the Caribbean Diaspora in Promoting Growth and Development in Cultural Industries." Paper presented at the *Conference on the Caribbean: A 20/20 Vision*, Washington, DC. June 19–21.

Scott, Zoe (2011). Examination of public sector reform governance reforms: Literature review, 2001–2011, *Oxford Policy Management*. Available at: http://www.gsdrc.org/docs/open/Scott2011_PSGRLiteratureReview.pdf. Accessed on December 1, 2014.

Stoyan, A.T., Niedzwiecki, S., Morgan, J., Hartlyn, J., and Espinal, R. (2014). Trust in government institutions: The effects of performance and participation in the Dominican Republic and Haiti. *International Political Science Review*, doi:10.1177/0192512114534703.

Taitt, Ria (2014). Record 11 ministers fired from Kamla's government, *Trinidad Express Newspapers*. Available at: http://www.trinidadexpress.com/news/Record-11-ministers-fired-from-Kamlas-govt-252361971.html. Accessed on January 3, 2015.

Transparency International (2005). *National Integrity Systems Caribbean Composite Study 2004*, Berlin, Germany: Transparency International.

Transparency International (2014). http://www.transparency.org/country. Accessed on December 1, 2014.

Waller, Lloyd, Bourne, Paul, Minto, Indianna and Rapley, John (2007). A landscape assessment of political corruption in Jamaica, *CAPRI: Taking Responsibility Project*, Kingston, Jamaica: CaPRI. Available at: http://www.capricaribbean.org/sites/default/files/text/Corruption%20Report.pdf. Accessed on December 1, 2014.

PUBLIC ADMINISTRATION AND POLICY IN THE CARIBBEAN
History and Major Developments

Chapter 2

The History of Public Administration in the Commonwealth Caribbean

Indianna D. Minto-Coy

Contents

Introduction 34
The Commonwealth Caribbean: A Definition 35
Public Administration in the Colonial Period 35
    Organization of the Colonies 36
    Slavery and Its Abolition 38
Pre-Independence Period: Universal Suffrage and Limited Self-Rule, 1920s–1959 40
Public Administrations in the Post-Independence Period: 1960–Present 43
The Westminster Whitehall (WW) System 44
Corruption and Public Ethics 45
Politico-Administrative Nexus 47
An Overview of Current Public Administration and Management Issues
across the Caribbean 48
    Public Sector Reform 48
    Public Financial Management 51
    Migration and Public Administration 52
    Race, Ethnicity, Class, and the Organization and Delivery of Public Services 53
    Regional and International Influences on Public Administration 54
    Impact of Size 55
Contending with Ongoing and Emerging Challenges in Public Administration 56
Conclusion 57
References 57

Abstract: The public administration landscape in the Commonwealth Caribbean has also been profoundly shaped by the legacies of colonialism, sugar, and slavery. The dominance of the United Kingdom over the region during these periods has left an indelible mark that continues long past independence (in the case of the majority of territories) existing in the laws, rules, and informal practices governing the region and notably, in the very adoption of the Westminster Whitehall system of government.

Post-independence, the performance of public administration across this region has also been adversely affected by a number of considerations, some natural (e.g., drought, hurricanes) and others man-made. Among the latter are the sometimes fractious relationship that has existed between politicians and public servants, the failure to introduce meaningful public sector reforms, corruption, and poor fiscal management. Public administration has, therefore, delivered mixed results including an inability to deliver sufficient improvement in the quality and quantity of public goods and services. There has also been insufficient recognition of the role of public administration in the region's ability to realize the dreams of independence. Ultimately, therefore, while the chapter focuses on legacies and their impact, the message espoused is clear: it would be a mistake to narrowly interpret the state of public administration in the Commonwealth Caribbean in the twenty-first century as simply a product of the past.

The chapter examines these themes through a review of public administration in the British Caribbean in a historical context up to 2015. Finally, the breadth of the experiences covered in the chapter provides a starting point for fruitful analyses, lesson-drawing, comparative investigations, and ultimately theory building, as it relates to traditional concepts and approaches in public policy and administration as informed by alternate/small/developing state narratives. The chapter is a critical read for students, academics, and scholars wanting an introduction to the Commonwealth Caribbean.

Introduction

Public administration in the Commonwealth Caribbean has undergone a number of challenges and evolutions over the years, which have affected its ability to contribute to development. A key point, however, is that the machinery has been adversely affected by poor governance and legacy issues. Thus, while a number of achievements have been realized and countries in the region have performed relatively well, public administration capacity remains compromised. This reality is seen, for instance, in the inability of the region to respond effectively to a number of socioeconomic challenges, including that of operating in a changing global economy, inability of many nations to effectively utilize the significant developmental assistance over the years, and the existence of a number of social problems. The quality of public administration has a bearing on the effective functioning of other institutions, with implications for overall growth and development.

The chapter aims to review the major features and developments of public administration in the Commonwealth Caribbean from a historical perspective. It has been noted that "[p]ast politics … is present history" (Wallace 1977: 4). Indeed, this quote resonates beyond politics to all areas of public policy and administration in the Commonwealth Caribbean. Thus, even accepting the possibility of breaking path dependencies, the reality is that public administration and policy as a set of institutions and practices in the Caribbean today have largely been shaped by the past, a past that is defined significantly by colonialism, slavery, and plantation societies.

As such, any account of public policy and administration in the Caribbean must contend with this past and its legacies as a means of understanding some of the present conditions. In this way then, this chapter helps to place some context to much of the discussions in Sections II and III of this volume. One of the main arguments then is that the features of the system in its present form are to a large extent a carryover from the colonial period. As such, the next section focuses on public administration in the colonial and pre-independence period after a brief review of what is meant by the Caribbean. Nevertheless, the local context, including culture and size as well as developments since independence, also helps to shape the nature of public administration. This will then be followed by a turn to a discussion of developments in the post-independence era, highlighting a number of points deemed to be significant in a consideration of public administration in the Caribbean context. The chapter closes with tentative suggestions on addressing some of the recognized challenges and a conclusion. Even while the focus is on the Commonwealth Caribbean, it ought not to be a surprise that many of the assertions regarding public administration in the Commonwealth Caribbean are also reflective of trends and patterns in other countries in the wider Caribbean region, including Haiti and the Dominican Republic (see, e.g., Kearney 1986).

The Commonwealth Caribbean: A Definition

To the casual observer, the wider Caribbean is simply a composite of small states, but within this classification lie a number of nuances that defy a broad-stroke approach to discussing and understanding the region. The same sentiment applies when discussing the Commonwealth Caribbean, a subgrouping of the region. The Commonwealth Caribbean refers to the former British West Indies or island and mainland territories of the former British Empire in the Caribbean. The region actually includes the British Overseas Territories (BOTs) (Anguilla, Bermuda, Turks and Caicos, the Cayman Islands, Montserrat, and the British Virgin Islands), the Bahamas, and Jamaica in the north and the Windward Islands (Dominica, St. Lucia, St. Vincent, Grenada), Leeward Islands (Antigua and Barbuda, St. Kitts and Nevis, Anguilla, and Montserrat), Barbados, Trinidad & Tobago (T&T), and Guyana to the south.

As noted by one of the eminent scholars of Caribbean public administration in 1970s, the Commonwealth Caribbean region is not homogenous and is marked by differences in economic development, size, resource, and the ethnic groups that populate constituent countries (Mills 1970: 5). The same is true of the Commonwealth Caribbean of the twenty-first century. For instance, in terms of economic development, some have fared better than others, with the Bahamas and Barbados emerging among the wealthiest in the subgroup to Jamaica and Guyana at the other extreme. Nevertheless, certain similarities do exist, which permit a general discussion on public administration across the different territories. Among these is a common colonial heritage, which in turn has resulted in similar legal and political systems. Small size and language are other similarities. The shared experiences of slavery, colonialism, and the sugar trade also placed the region in the midst of global trade from the 1600s with the economies of the region being very open (see, e.g., Mawby 2012; Palmer 2009). Throughout, however, the discussion will focus more on those territories that have independence status and less on the remaining BOTs.

Public Administration in the Colonial Period

The Commonwealth Caribbean has had a long contact with the United Kingdom. This period of contact began from the 1600s with slavery and colonialism to the 1960s when most territories across the Caribbean received independence. For Anguilla, Bermuda, Turks and Caicos, the

Cayman Islands, Montserrat, and the British Virgin Islands, the relationship has been sustained via their status as BOTs. The long period of contact with the British has left an indelible mark on the institutions in the region (culture, practices, laws, etc.). As such, a fitting starting point in any discussion on public administration in the Commonwealth merits a serious consideration of this history.

Organization of the Colonies

The founding of the British West Indies was informed by the imperialist desires of the English government in the 1600s but led mainly by private members. To this end, Sires notes that the motives of English colonization were to identify tropical products and new markets and to put capital to work. The founding of the British West Indies also offered opportunities for employment and livelihoods not realized in England (1957: 109). Indeed, for Britain, the region was to become the "centrepiece of the eighteenth-century overseas Empire" (Murray 1965: 1). It is not coincidental then that Mawby (2012: 6) suggests that the region occupied a central location in the British Empire with the demography and ecology being modified to suit commercial interest.

The settlement of the region marked a round of success in the English's attempt to match and supersede Spanish supremacy in the Caribbean and South America, a supremacy that had begun from 1492, when Columbus arrived in the Americas. Therefore, the emergence of the region has been intricately linked to imperialist ambitions and rivalries among countries such as France, Spain, and the English. It is therefore not coincidental that some islands within the grouping were also to witness different periods of ownership, as each colonial power battled and made peace with each other. For example, Jamaica was taken over by the British in 1655, while T&T claimed by the Spanish in 1498 was ceded to the British in 1802 and currently has French, Spanish, and British historical influences (Encyclopaedia Britannica 2014). Throughout the eighteenth century, a number of other colonies, including Grenada, St. Vincent, and Dominica, were also ceded to Britain from other imperialists.

By the end of the eighteenth century, British institutions had been institutionalized in the region, even as the revolt in the United States had prompted a decision to reduce legislative intervention in America. As noted by Murray (1965: 1), "the most obvious characteristic of the British part of colonial government at the end of the eighteenth century was that it was traditional." It is this challenge in de-institutionalizing those traditional aspects of the public administration in the Caribbean in favor of re-institutionalizing with a more modern and forward-thinking ethos, as espoused under various public sector reform programs, that continues to plague the region. This is not to suggest, however, that the colonists were completely subservient to the Crown. Indeed, it was recognized that the Crown's powers in the region were not complete, though imprecise, particularly concerning the constitutionality of the British Parliament's right to legislate for the colonies.

Public administration was organized in order to integrate the region neatly into the governance framework of the British Empire, reduce the cost of administering the islands, and improve efficiency. To this end, colonial government was organized by departments overseen by a chief professional officer. The system of control went to the imperial government through a representative in the form of a governor. An appointed council operated with the governor in performing legislative, executive, and judicial responsibilities. An elected assembly had also been instituted and courts were based on the Westminster system. This was the case in countries such as Jamaica, Barbados, Grenada, and Dominica. For the smaller grouping of the Leeward Islands, these shared one governor and a Legislative Assembly made up of representatives of each of the islands.

This approach to governance was born out of a belief in the supremacy of English laws and institutions such that not much thought was given to reforms up to the end of the eighteenth century. The modus operandi of the governor was received through the Governor's Commissions and Instructions issued by the Crown. These essentially placed the governor as head of the civil service with the power to prorogue or dissolve government, and to summon Assemblies, "a negative voice in all legislation" (Murray 1965: 14), the latter being important in protecting British interests the government in Britain reserved the most central appointments for itself; however, the governor could also make some permanent and temporarily suspend appointments, among other responsibilities. Judicial review was provided through the appeals to Britain, while some actions had to receive confirmation from the Crown. Nevertheless and in spite of these wide powers, the real power in the colonies was gradually to shift to the colonists with the modification of formal institutions to facilitate this new role, particularly in Jamaica where the rights of the governor to regulate the colony were taken to be the case mainly in instances where the Crown's interests were at stake. Furthermore, the power to establish and alter Courts Law was countered in practice when local statutes saw to their establishment and regulation.

In essence, the role of the governor was reduced with little power over supervising subordinates and to act independently, including over financial matters. Rules stipulating the governor's authority to pay out monies were disregarded in Jamaica, and ultimately, the governor only had unrestricted control over his private secretary. It will be noted (here and other chapters in this book) that one of the challenges in the region remains that of proper financial management and adherence to financial rules, with the basis for some of this legacy emerging from this practice in the 1700s. The activities of the colonists in this regard demonstrate what Daniel notes as the "settler's spirit" in the case of the French colonists in the French territories (Chapter 3).

While the activities of the colonists themselves affected the operations of the government, those of the government in Britain also had its impact in introducing certain practices with enduring impact. For example, the power of appointment of key posts was affected by the practice of leasing an office to the highest bidder with the lessee (in many cases absentee land owners) then nominating the deputy who was to execute the office. Indeed, Murray (1965: 20) notes that the selection of key office holders across the region was done by the secretary of state "for reasons which did not often include the good government of the colony," such that three of the four absentees in Barbados in 1802 were relatives of the secretary of state, who also appointed them. Key positions such as the receiver general in Jamaica, the collector of the powder duty in Antigua, and the clerks of the markets in Barbados were populated by absentees, leaving questions about the extent to which good governance was being achieved across the region. Murray (1965) goes on to note the existence of patronage in this system, with the governor's ability to direct government being circumscribed. Demonstrated here, too, is the fact that corruption as known in the independent commonwealth (and the current BOTs) is not unique, but also featured during the colonial period.

The public service in this case was focused on maintaining law and order, and the local environment had little influence on policies. Prior to the end of the eighteenth century, for instance, the region received very little of the money that was allotted to it by Parliament, while the conduct of administration and other affairs of the colonies went without much direct attention from the British Parliament (Murray 1965: 4). As such, the governor was simply guided by a Governor's Commissions and Instructions and meant to facilitate the Crown's general oversight as opposed to precise supervision over colonial affairs. General oversight was also exercised via other means. For instance, local legislatures had the right to introduce new legislation but these had to receive prior authorization from the Crown and only relate to certain subjects, while the transcripts of all Acts had to be scrutinized by the central government. In the main, however, administration of different aspects of government in the region was the responsibility of the corresponding department or ministry in the United Kingdom with complaints of disjointed and poorly coordinated government being leveled. By the end of the eighteenth century, the lack of coordination had improved somewhat as the colonial governor now had two secretaries of state—secretary of state and home secretary (for military and another for civil matters) to report to in the United Kingdom. As such, the inclinations of the colonists were also reflected in the administration of the colonies, a move directed by a desire to keep the colonists happy. This was obvious in Jamaica where a representative system of government that somewhat reflected their habits was allowed.

Ultimately, the space that colonists were afforded in the British Empire was seen to be useful in so far as they did not compromise the value of the islands in the UK's trading system. Indeed, the organization of government in the colonies allowed the islands to produce valuable commodities for trading (i.e., sugar and rum) while allowing an income to support the mainland's manufacturing industry. As such, for the most part, eighteenth century public administration saw little use of the right to exercise a veto on local legislation, to provide active supervision of government, or, more generally, to intervene in the affairs of the colonies, given that the local legislature itself acted within bounds, that is, to serve limited purposes. The black population featured minimally in policies in this period. Indeed, the system of governance that existed in the colonies was as a limited "representative government by and for white society and paternal rule of negro slaves" (Murray 1965: 22).

This laissez-faire approach to administering the colonies was to change in the nineteenth century with the transfer of colonial affairs from the home secretary's office fully to the secretary of state in 1801. This development was to become significant itself, as it would facilitate the coordination over affairs that had been missing in the previous century, laying the basis for what was to become the colonial office. Ironically, Murray (1965: esp. 10–11) notes that this move was not based on an intention to have more focused or coordinated administration in the colonies but mainly out of tactical maneuvers in home politics. The British West Indies was subdivided into three main subgroupings from 1833 up to the start of the wave of independence that began in the 1960s. The Windward and Leeward Islands formed the first two groups, while the Cayman Islands linked to Jamaica, given its small size and proximity, formed the third.

Some islands such as T&T and St. Lucia were administered as Crown Colonies. Still others were allowed a bicameral legislative system with elections to the assembly. In the former, the governor general appointed officials to the Legislative Council (see Brereton et al. 2014). The conflict between the Crown's representative and the local planter population in the 1700s continued. The result was, according to Wallace, a system in which friction and deadlock featured as the governor-controlled executive and planter-controlled legislature quarreled with each other. To this end, the "often corrupt Caribbean politics" saw accommodations being made between the two factions that came at the public's expense (Wallace 1977: 10). As will be suggested later in this chapter, and indeed in other areas of this book, this legacy persists in the factional politics and sometimes corrupt distribution of public goods and services in the region.

Slavery and Its Abolition

As noted earlier, the Caribbean to a large extent has been defined by slavery and the trade in sugar. For instance, it is only when it is observed that blacks, who now make up the majority of the present population, were not indigenous but are mainly the offspring of Africans being transported to the region during the slave trade. The trade itself began with Columbus transporting the native Amerindians to Spain toward the end of the 1400s but was to take a more profound nature with the authorization to transport blacks from Africa to the Caribbean in 1501. For the English colonies, Sir John Hawkins in the 1560s imported slave labor to work in sugar plantations, leading to the inextricable link between slavery and sugar and which to some extent now features today as the disdain shown for planting, agriculture, and manual labor among many nationals within the region (Wallace 1977). Around 500,000 Africans are said to have been imported into forced labor in the first three quarters of the 1700s with this labor significantly advancing the UK's position as a global power economically and politically.

Activism on the part of local abolitionists as well as those based in the United Kingdom was to lead to the decision to end the slave trade in 1807. However, it would take another couple of decades before slavery was abolished. This took place on August 1, 1834, when the Act to abolish slavery took effect. The result as noted by Wallace was the freeing of around nine-tenths (700,000) of the population in the Commonwealth Caribbean.

Interestingly, larger islands saw ex-slaves having the option of continuing work on the plantations for pay, going into cities, or owning their own patch of land, but islands such as Barbados and St. Kitts did not have this option. With the bulk of farmable land already belonging to estates, there was little option for employment beyond continuing on as hired laborers. For that reason, much remained unchanged in the way of attitudes in these countries. The ability to maintain order and predictability is something that has been hailed in Barbados as a positive to that country maintaining its position as a model of good governance (Minto-Coy 2012). Indeed some commentators have noted these historical features as possible reasons for this status and certainly when compared to the more chaotic governance environment which features in islands such as Jamaica.

The answer to the challenge of maintaining labor for the plantations was indentureship, which involved the importation of mainly Chinese and Indian but also Lebanese, German, Portuguese, Scottish, Syrian, and Irish workers to the region. Indeed, this move has also added much to the Caribbean today, with its intricate mix of race, ethnicities, food, music, and other cultural and social attributes. For instance, many Indians who came to the region settled in Guyana and Trinidad, respectively, a fact which goes to explain the racial composition of those countries today, while the difference in the circumstances then hints at the basis for the distrust and to some degree animosity which now exists between the Indians and Blacks in the region. For instance, Indian indentured laborers received allowances such as free housing, food, and health care, with some receiving free land at the end of their service and where they decided to remain in the islands; however, these allowances did not extend to ex-slaves who had to purchase their own lands (Wallace 1997: 6).

Over time, the loss of a steady supply of labor, as well as the emergence of other more competitive markets (e.g., Cuba) and alternatives (beets in Europe) saw sugar and, ultimately, the Caribbean losing its prized place in the British Crown by the end of the nineteenth century. This situation was compounded by fluctuations in prices, which meant that though the region had managed to increase sugar production in the early half of the twentieth century the industry (and hence, economic) fate of the region remained unclear. Help was to come from the United Kingdom via preferential import of sugar from the Caribbean into the United Kingdom and ultimately the European Union (EU).

The focus on sugar and the importance of the region for its economic contribution to the English Empire also meant that not much attention was placed on developing "societies." As such, infrastructure remained poor and local enterprise remained underdeveloped going into the twentieth century. Indeed, these remain challenges even today. The decline of the plantations exacerbated the effect of absenteeism as seen in the lack of interest in upkeep and attention to improving the welfare of slaves or now ex-slaves. As such, public services such as health, education, water, and roads remained underdeveloped.

With abolition, land owners in the region struggled against the introduction of policies aimed at improving the conditions of the black population, still ruminating from the UK's decision to impose abolition on them (see Wallace 1997: Prologue, for a detailed discussion). Where increased expenditure was suggested for education, health, and public works, these were voted down (Wallace 1977: 14). The perception, too, was that the majority of the black population in the region was unprepared for self-government. Voting in Jamaica was, for instance, by virtue of paying taxes. However, not many earned enough to do so, ensuring that the base of voters remained whites and mulattoes (offsprings of blacks and whites). Color prejudice also affected the extent to which policies were introduced to improve the conditions of blacks. For example, the election of a black man to the legislature in T&T in the 1860s saw some mullatoes threatening to resign (Wallace 1977: 13).

The majority of the population did show some discontent regarding the limited right to vote with distress among farmers after abolition. The remaining islands were changed to Crown Colonies from the late 1800s at fears of excessive force and the uncompromising attitude of the plantocracy as well as increased attacks on the plantations by newly freed slaves after the ending of slavery in 1837 (Mawby 2012: 11). The Mordant Bay uprising in Jamaica in 1865, for instance, and the brutal retaliation by the governor led to a 200-year-old representative system being abolished and Crown Colony government being introduced in 1866 (see Wallace 1977: 1–15). In essence, this move saw the governor ruling with a Legislative Council. The governor now had the sole right to introduce legislation with ultimate power now residing in the colonial office. Indeed, it was reasoned that this new system would do more to advance the conditions of the black population by ensuring a fairer government. Indeed, reforms introduced in Jamaica included the reform in the administration of justice and taxation, redirecting money formerly pledged to the Church of England toward education, the buildup of critical infrastructure such as the introduction of hospitals and the introduction of a unified police force (Wallace 1997: 16). Nevertheless, the elites in the region (whites and mulattoes) were not necessarily happy with the new system and in Jamaica established a formal body dedicated to returning the island to the previous representative system. Eventually, a limited representative system was introduced in 1884 via constitutional reform which allowed for a Jamaican Legislative Council with nine elected members. Competitive examinations were introduced in 1885 allowing access to the civil service for all Jamaicans with color being removed as a barrier for entering the civil service.

Pre-Independence Period: Universal Suffrage and Limited Self-Rule, 1920s–1959

Even while significant administrative reforms were introduced under Crown Colony, there was growing unease by the end of the nineteenth century. The Crown Colony system came under sustained threat from increased agitation for the right to vote. This discontent was heightened by economic distress which saw the central government in the United Kingdom having to save islands from bankruptcy through loans. Ultimately too, the public servants were seen as part of a paternalistic system in which the main administrative positions belonged to the English. In essence, this practice denied locals an opportunity to exercise political responsibility and inculcated a view that they were suspect in their ability to self-govern. Accountability remained to the imperial government and not to the local population (Wallace 1997: 17).

With such views, the constitutions, which went largely untouched up to the end of the 1900s, were to begin to see important revisions. However, this period was to mark the culmination of agitation for reforms that had begun in some islands as early as the 1800s, resulting in the modification of constitutions across the region. In Trinidad, for instance, a 500-strong petition had been made in favor of constitution reform to extend the right to vote in 1877 (Wallace 1977: 14). Calls for reform in Crown Colonies had focused on the right for members to be elected to the Legislative Council, which was granted in T&T in 1925 when the right was given to elect seven members to the Council. The push for political reforms also came from within the labor movement with strikes across the region, from Jamaica to British Guiana. Support for the riots also swelled due to economic recession in the 1930s, low wages, and the desire for self-government, making the long link that has since existed between unions and political parties. For instance, demonstration for adult suffrage was organized in the 1930s leading to the colonial government agreeing to introduce adult suffrage in the 1940s.* Many of the unions in this period were to evolve into formal political parties covering both political and industrial issues, while its leaders became premiers and later some of the first prime ministers after independence. For example, Norman Manley and Alexander Bustamante in Jamaica were leaders of two rival unions and political parties, as well as Jamaica's first two prime ministers. The unions acted therefore as quasi-political parties expressing nationalist sentiments and advocating for independence.

The practice of politics hinted at above deserves explicit mention given its implications for the quality and nature of public administration and public policy-making that now obtains into the present in the majority of the Commonwealth Caribbean. For instance, the problems identified in the Crown Colony system had created discontent among the local population regarding their ability to self-govern. With this, Wallace (1997) noted the emergence of a perception of the state as an enemy and "an instrument of alien rulers." The legislatures that existed came to view their role as simply to oppose administration as a matter of principle than on any sound principles: "A factious attitude of critical, irresponsible, and permanent opposition to the administration became accepted as the normal atmosphere of political debate" (Wallace 1997: 17–18). Indeed, this psyche still remains in many islands where opposition parties perceive their role (in the words of a former Trinidadian opposition leader) as simply being "to oppose" (Nantambu 2009) and hints at the divisive political culture which sometimes resulted in public policies being changed from one government to the next, not out of sound principle but simply because it was introduced by the previous administration.

Some countries were gradually given limited self-rule in preparation for full independence. This decision was preceded by demonstrations across the region in light of economic and social hardships (noted earlier in this section). The Grenada revolution also fueled demonstrations in the region. These developments influenced the decision to reform constitutions to allow for limited self-rule and the suffrage in countries like Trinidad in 1945. The practice of gradually allowing self-rule as a precursor to full independence may also have served to more fully institutionalize the practices and traditions of the colonial system in all its forms, including the various cultural mutations and prejudices that had emerged in the practice of public administration over the centuries. This is so since this period did not practically consist of a repudiation or logical rethink of received institutions and philosophy but a cementing of these. It has also been suggested that the process of gradual self-determination slowed the process of constitutional reform, ignored the economy, and saw the development or emergence of authoritarian politics that has been seen as partly to be blamed for the alarming levels of crime and political division now typical in islands such as Jamaica and Trinidad (see, e.g., Mawby 2012). For instance, Wallace (1997: 51) notes that there was an absence of authority that could identify a joint approach to addressing the problems

---

* The Moyne Commission was put together to assess the socioeconomic condition of the Caribbean and in response to the riots and discontent in the region during this period. The report led to heightened awareness of the challenges faced by countries in the region and, in the 1940s and 1950s, to the Colonial Development and Welfare Acts aimed at improving the conditions in the territories (see Wallace 1977).

of the region as a whole. Among these long-standing problems were poor education (Barbados has long been an exception here), housing, and other social services. Indeed, there appeared to be some irony in the point that while there were demands for post-independence, and distrust of the involvement and suggestions of the colonial government, the amelioration in conditions, such as living standards, required investments of funds from the United Kingdom.

The period of agitation for independence was also marked by efforts toward regionalism. Indeed, ideas on the benefits of a closer union among Caribbean states were not unique to the independence period. For instance, throughout its existence, the region has moved from a more unified body into sub and individual units. For example, the Leeward and Windward Islands were the result of the splitting in 1671 of the Lesser Antilles that was administered by a governor in Barbados. The Leeward was then subdivided in 1816 and further as each group of elites sought to gain and maintain its status and control over their small spaces (see Wallace 1977: 85–87 for a discussion and number of examples on this point). Support for closer interaction in the pre-independence period was informed by prospect of economic and social improvements and independence. In fact, the colonial office had moved to instigate federation through a communication sent by the colonial secretary in 1945 indicating the policy of moving to federalism by central government and encouraging legislatures across the region to discuss the matter. Successive meetings and conferences throughout the period of self-rule were held to discuss the prospects and course toward federalism. In 1956, the British Caribbean Act was passed by Westminster allowing 10 islands to form the West Indies Federation but still under limited self-rule. The main instrument of public policy under federalism was to have been the Council of State which would comprise a prime minister and 10 other ministers appointed by the governor general. Contributions from the territories were to form a key part of the funding for the union with Jamaica expecting to contribute 43.1%. Trinidad and Barbados were expected to contribute 38.6% and 8.5%, respectively, while the remaining seven territories the rest (Wallace 1997: 121). Two years later (and perhaps even before its beginning), it became evident that Federalism was not going to work for a number of reasons. While some criticisms were leveled against what was perceived as the United Kingdom's lack of support for the working of the union, the reality too was that the Caribbean leaders found cooperation difficult; there was lack of support among the general West Indian citizenry and insufficient funding, while the full lack of commitment by Jamaica out of its carrying the burden of the smaller territories also served to foster mistrust and unease among the countries. There was also division along key players based on a desire for a strong (T&T) and a weak center (Jamaica). One of the vexing issues then was the lack of support from the largest islands, including Trinidad to allow freedom of movement of West Indians (see Sewell 2007: 108) while there was a general difficulty in introducing institutions that could assist in giving the union life. The distance among the islands was not only psychosocial but also practical with Jamaica's position to the north isolating it somewhat from the rest of the region, contributing to a view that it could go it alone. Furthermore, leaders of the independence movement appeared to prioritize national positions over the prospect of leading a united Caribbean demonstrating unwillingness to give up the certainty of power nationally for the region. To this day, these same issues typify attempts at regionalism and collective action, although it is Jamaica that is now seen as one of the main laggards (economically) in the group. Common ties in the form of sports (cricket), the university, art, and emerging literature that helped to bolster regional pride did not suffice to engender a successful political union.

A key feature of the public administration system was the introduction of Public Service Commissions. These were tasked with recruitment and personnel-related issues, including those of promotion, discipline, and retirement, helping to provide some objectivity and impartiality in the management of civil service personnel. These structures persisted into the independence period.

Issues of race, class, and color were features of the organization and management of the civil service. In the first instance, white collar positions in the administrative system were sought after and occupied mainly by the mixed-race or "brown skins" that also comprised the middle class. The public service was seen as the place for some of the brightest. The result is what Jones (1992a) has termed a "derivative middle class" which exhibited tendencies of risk aversion, obedience to rule and rote, and preservation of established norms and traditions. The notion of the civil service as a special place and those in it as special beings, as well as the top-down organization of decision making and communication (i.e., from Crown and via colonial secretary), also encouraged the practice of secrecy and exclusion in the decision-making process even into the period of self-rule.

Public Administrations in the Post-Independence Period: 1960–Present

"In few places does the dead hand of the past lie as heavily on the present as in the Caribbean" (Wallace 1997: 18). This profound statement offers instructive insight into the state of the Commonwealth Caribbean on the eve of independence and remains relevant in the post-independent period. This is so as many of the features that characterized public administration in the pre-independence period remained intact after independence, with some being entrenched in many independence constitutions. As such, the Commonwealth Caribbean in the post-independence era has been significantly marked and defined by its long history with the United Kingdom. Nevertheless, this administrative heritage is also characterized by local practices which intermingle with the adopted practices from the mother country. Interestingly too, the ease in carrying over culture, institutions, and practices of the past may have been encouraged by the fact that in spite of the activism of unions and political parties and the riling up of national sentiment for independence, political leaders were largely conservative (Wallace 1977: 82). As such, no significant modification of the politico-administrative or socioeconomic system resulted after independence. Indeed, outside of the experience of the 1970s with leaders such as Michael Manley of Jamaica and the Grenada Revolution 1979–1983, not much radical action has emerged as it relates to public governance in the Caribbean.

The 1960s and 1970s marked a spate of reforms across the region as many countries secured their independence from the United Kingdom. The granting of independence came with recognition from the point of view of the British that the region, given the history of parliamentary democracy and the rule of law, would be able to govern itself. In fact, British civil servants had a hand in crafting the different independence constitutions (Bulgin, 2012: 8). Independence was in some ways, too, a natural corollary to the end of Federation, with the government in Jamaica indicating to the British (through the then Premier, Norman Manley) in the early 1960s its intention to request independence and leave the Federation, after a referendum in that country rejected Federation.

In all cases excluding Dominica, Guyana, and T&T, the Queen remains the head of state. In the case of T&T, the first independent constitution noted the Queen as head of state, with a bicameral system, a governor general and a cabinet. The Queen was later removed when T&T became a Republic under the 1976 Constitution.*

---

* Antigua & Barbuda, 1981; The Bahamas, 1973; Barbados, 1966; Belize (formerly British Honduras), 1981; Dominica, 1978; Grenada, 1974; Guyana, 1966 (cooperative Republic in 1977); Jamaica 1962; St. Lucia, 1979; St. Kitts & Nevis, 1983; St. Vincent & the Grenadines, 1979; and Trinidad & Tobago, independent in 1962 and a Republic in 1976.

Key to the minister's ability to function in terms of policy-making and implementation is the cadre of civil servants, headed in most cases by a permanent secretary. With independence, a major shift was to occur in the organization of the public service with leadership and managerial functions becoming separated at the macro-organizational level (Gibson 2010). Executive authority essentially passed from the Crown to local heads of state and ministers.

However, the reality on the eve of independence was that citizens had long experienced authoritative rule under the Crown Colony system, and, for the majority black population, this authoritarianism had extended prior to the introduction of Crown Colony government. Wallace suggests that some of this authoritarianism accompanied the region even into independence via its new leaders (Wallace 1997: 18). Their practice of directing discontent toward the colonial government and its representatives did not encourage the development of good citizens or sound administration in the post-independence period.

The Westminster Whitehall (WW) System

The defining feature of public administration and politics in the English-speaking Caribbean remains the WW system borrowed from the United Kingdom. This system accompanied the region into the independence period and, in spite of adaptations, has remained largely intact even with calls for reform (Jones, 1992b; Payne 1993; Ryan, 2001; Sutton, 2008; Bulgin, 2012). This inherited model of public administration privileges the party that commands a majority in the lower house of Parliament with legislative and executive powers being concentrated in the governing party. The public bureaucracy here is meant to be a professional class tasked with implementing policies.

The WW model is also informed by notions of impartiality, neutrality, and anonymity as governing principles of public administration (Sutton 2008). Indeed this has been noted as one of the greatest contrivances of the United Kingdom given that the difficulty in meeting these principles in any setting (see Kearney 1986: 148). The weakening of this system in the region is a firm illustration here given that these principles have hardly been realized as will be shown throughout this chapter.

The judiciary forms a critical role in the Westminster system with its supposed independence acting as a check on the power of the executive. Historically, the courts in the region have in fact helped to check the seemingly unlimited power of the ruling party. For instance, the courts in Jamaica were vital in preventing the then ruling party from appropriating the assets of businesses during the country's experimentation with Democratic Socialism in the 1970s (see Spiller and Sampson 1996). Notwithstanding, the judiciary has been constrained by a number of challenges, including insufficient resources and excessive backlog, which have in turn affected their ability to monitor or hold the government and bureaucracy to account.

While the experiences of the judiciary and the difficulties in checking political power may be seen as a matter of the functioning of the system as opposed to its intention, the system has not afforded much other level of checks and balances beyond mainly the gentlemanly ethos and an expectation of leaders to act responsibly. Thus, civil society has not been empowered significantly under the adopted WW system. The underdevelopment of civil society throughout the region is a result of this experience.

On another level, the actual performance of the WW system has not matched the ideal or expected form. This reality has yielded perverse consequences in the Caribbean as expressed in over-centralization, corruption, nepotism, and clientelism with limited power among the opposition to exercise constraints over the government.

The principle of meritocracy has emerged over time as an important criterion for promotion in Caribbean public administration. This implies a shift from seniority to performance and merit-based system since the independence. This has been important in allowing the entry into senior positions by persons who may have, in the past, been excluded by virtue of pigmentation or class. Promotion has since become more based on educational qualification, experience, and performance and not seniority. In spite of this development, there are those who now question the extent to which meritocracy is still being encouraged (see Gibson 2010). As suggested by Kearney (1986), the notion of merit is difficult to realize in small states, including the Commonwealth, Haiti, and the Dominican Republic given the social, political, and economic realities of the region.

Over-centralization of the public service has been noted as one of the features of public administration in the post-colonial period to present. This is not necessarily a post-colonial phenomenon but rather a result of the historical orientation and practical organization of colonial control in the pre-independence period. The shortcoming was the failure to reform this feature of governance. In essence then, the change in persons populating leadership did not equate to a substantive change in philosophy or orientation. The administrative system that emerged upon independence was thus highly centralized with little autonomy for action among staff.

Kearney (1986: 149) has suggested that the over-centralization mixed with the personalization of the public service resulted in the deinstitutionalization of the public service in the post-independence period. This has been the case in countries such as Belize, Guyana, and T&T. Thus, whereas the public service in pre-independence period was seen as the location of the best and brightest and marked by professionalism, it has since been viewed increasingly as the place of last resort for employment with a low prestige vis-à-vis the private sector and migration. This has in turn affected the level of professionalism and public service ethic across the region. Austerity measures adopted in some countries since the late 2010 including wage freezes have only advanced this reality.

The corollary to this over-centralization was a culture of secrecy with decisions and the reasons for decisions remaining a mystery. All these served to result in a straight-jacketing effect of personnel who were not encouraged to be responsive to emerging problems and situations. The propensity toward risk aversion and dampening of innovation have also been noted (Jones 1992a).

Corruption and Public Ethics

The secrecy also has almost led to the privatization of information and the additional effect of reduced transparency and ultimately, increased corruption. Solutions have included the convening of various commissions of enquiries, for example, Jamaica in 2013 and 2015, St Lucia in 1998, and Antigua in 1990 (The Economist, 1999), aimed at addressing allegations of public corruption. One of the far-reaching mechanisms here has the institution of the Office of the Contractor General (OCG) which operates in a number of islands with varying results (see McKoy, 2012 for a general review of corruption in the Caribbean, as well as a review of measures and institutions aimed at addressing the issue, including the OCG). It has been demonstrated in Jamaica, under that country's fourth OCG, who held office from 2005 to 2012, that the personality of the office holder has an influence on the vigor and seriousness with which that office is viewed. It has been reported, for instance, that a hundred percent compliance had been secured from the 193 public bodies as it relates to their quarterly reporting on the awarding of contracts (Jamaica Observer, 2012). Even so, inadequate checks and balances on public spending, including in procurement (see Chapter 8 in this book), vested interest in corruption in an environment of scarce benefits and spoils, and the absence of legislation (e.g. on campaign financing) or lack of its enforcement have also been known to foster corruption in the region. Maingot (2004) also makes the link between corruption and violence and the drug trade.

In such a context, it has become increasingly difficult to hold public servants accountable for their activities with Jones (1992b) noting the role of poor work ethics and the existence of weak institutions in encouraging administrative corruption. It is with good reason then that Hall and Benn assert that the development of monitoring, control, review and (importantly) enforcement systems have been underdeveloped (2003) with Maingot, noting the existence of ill-formed institutions as a contributor to corruption in the region (2004). Jones also describes other features of Jamaican (and Caribbean) society that give rise to conditions that facilitate corruption and poor governance, including a political culture underlined by low levels of trust and declines in the stock of social capita (2013: 28). As such, while a number of measures have been undertaken to improve accountability and reduce corruption, including codes of ethics and anti-corruption legislation, these have done little to improve practice on the ground. Trinidad and Tobago's Integrity in Public Life Act requires filings from official public servants but this is largely ignored with little consequences or penalties. Sutton has also noted the role of small size with corruption featuring in the form of nepotism and patronage (2008: 20).

Indeed, it has been suggested that corruption and unethical behavior within politics and the bureaucracy have been more a feature of the post-colonial era and particularly since the 1970s (Mills 1970: 345). This is not to suggest that there were not claims of corruption and maladministration prior to independence (as illustrated in the discussion on Public Administration during the colonial period). For instance, MacDonald notes the accusations of maladministration, mismanagement, and corruption during pre-independent T&T (1986). The incidence of corruption in most societies is such that it is increasingly being seen as a way of life and a means of survival in an economically challenged environment. For public servants, poor ethics and corruption is rationalized by the reality of low wages, general job dissatisfaction, lack of adequate rewards for good performance and by extension, lack of penalties for poor performance (see, e.g., Waller et al. 2007). In such a context, the stakes for engaging in corrupt activities can be reduced.

Interestingly, too, the experience of corruption in the Caribbean also suggests the need for a more nuanced view of the topic. This is the case, first, where corruption has been used as a means of facilitating speedier transactions and overcoming bureaucratic inefficiencies and, second, where the prevalence of corruption in certain areas of public life/organizations can be taken as an indicator of a fault in the system and as a guidepost for where and what types of institutional reform may be needed. The case of the Registrar General's Department (RGD) in Jamaica is a prime example. Prior to its agencification (i.e. transformed into a UK-type executive agency) in 1999, the RGD's department essentially offered a one-tier service for accessing birth certificates and other important documents. However, the habit of clients bribing individual public servants to speed up processing and delivery times was an indicator of a willingness to pay different rates for speedier services, hinting at a means of overcoming bureaucratic inefficiencies, as well as an additional means for government to increase its revenues. Arguably, the inhospitable environs in which the public had to wait for service also encouraged the desire to engage in corrupt acts to speed up service. Reforms introduced included the payment of different fees for different processing times, while customer service and facilities were greatly improved. The previously corrupt practices were, in essence, institutionalized and legalized in 1999, leading to the RGD seeing marked improvements in service quality, innovation, and, importantly, revenues. So much so that by 2007, that body was able to fund its operations mainly through collections and not from the central budget. This depiction is akin to Becquart-Leclerq (1989: 127 in Zephyr, 2008) "grease in the gears" effect; though the extent to which any corruption can be facilitated in such small societies, regardless of whatever positive outcomes can be achieved, is up for debate.

Politico-Administrative Nexus

A synergistic relationship between political and administrative leadership is key to the region's ability to meet the hosts of governance challenges. In practice, politics has tended to dominate public administration with important consequences for the conduct of public administration and the performance of the civil service. For instance, the lack of restraint on government has in practice seen politicians using their office to reward or punish, leading to serious questioning of the ability of public servants and in turn the public administration machinery to operate objectively. In practical terms and as noted by Gibson (2010: 10), the result has been "the sovereignty of politics over the supremacy of administration."

Indeed, the aim of depoliticization of the civil service remains distant with successive governments adopting the practice of populating key posts with party or personal supporters. This practice is not new and remains a legacy of the "enemy relationship" (Jones and Mills 1976: 330) that emerged in the pre-independence period and that has continued into the present. For instance, the practice has been influenced by clear ideological views about the relationship that should exist between politicians and the public bureaucracy as opposed to deliberate attempts to compromise the quality or functioning of the public service. Jones and Mills (1976: 330) have, for instance, used the terms "administrative sabotage" and "political terrorism" in referring to the antagonistic relations and attempts by these two groups to exercise influence over policy. This also hints at the difficulties which can arise where civil servants are politicized but are not sympathetic to the efforts of the political directorate.

Therefore, the notion of a depoliticized public administrative machinery has for the most part not been realized in the region. Indeed, the prospect of job loss or falling out of favor with a politician has in some cases resulted in an emasculated public service where leaders are unsure of where their actual powers lie or are unwilling to exercise such powers. In such a context, efforts to regulate behavior and reduce corruption via the introduction of measures such as codes of ethics have not borne significant behavior modifications. Where improvements have been seen, these have not been sufficient to cause wider systemic change.

Nonetheless, a worthy consideration is the extent to which it is possible to have a depoliticized administration or even whether this is necessary for the successful functioning of the public administration system. For instance, one of the rationales behind replacing civil servants upon an electoral victory is the notion that supporters and allies are better champions of the goals and objectives of the new administration and are thus more driven to protect and support implementation of the administration's policies. A most visible instance of this was Jamaica in the 1970s during that country's tryst with Democratic Socialism, where it was felt that civil servants ought to be ideologically disposed to the governing political party. The point being that support for the successful implementation of policies would be heightened.

The same question could be posed as it relates to the concept of anonymity. Thus, while politics has been dominant, public servants have not always been anonymous or powerless vis-à-vis politicians. The act of sabotage is itself one defense mechanism against the notion of sovereignty of politics. Additionally, the evidence suggests, however, that where strong reforms are to be undertaken it is important to have public bureaucrats who are bold enough to implement and guide these, even where they may check the power of other groups. Indeed, one of the strong suits of the head of the Jamaican public service in the 1990s in the first decade of the twenty-first century was his knowledge and commitment to his task, as well as willingness to check the power of politicians as it related to their relationship with other bureaucrats. Under his watch, Jamaica was to undergo arguably one of the most extensive and successful bouts of public sector reform (PSR) in its history.

Instead, personalization abounds. Nevertheless, the issue for public administration in the Caribbean (and beyond) is not simply about having a depoliticized public administration. Rather, it is about the level of professionalism of the public bureaucracy. That is the extent to which civil service leaders are able to exercise their jobs, even where they are allies of the ruling party professionally and are willing to conduct their offices with respect for their positions in protection of the public good.

This remains a challenge for public administration in the region. Ultimately, the ability of the public administration machinery to perform as a responsive body of change management and development have been seriously compromised and partly explains the current milieu of many Caribbean small states in the global economy. It has been noted, for instance, that the effectiveness of aid has been reduced by inadequacies in areas of public administration (Mills 1990: 347). Furthermore, the sovereignty that politics has exercised over administration may also mean that the success and responsiveness of public administration in the future will be about the ability of politics to transform itself and permit civil servants more freedom to operate in the national interest.

An Overview of Current Public Administration and Management Issues across the Caribbean

The openness that defined the region in the colonial period continues to define the modern era not only with some positive but also dire consequences. For instance, with arable land being dedicated to sugar (Mawby 2012: 6) and the lack of an industrial base, import bills have continued at unsustainable levels and the region has remained home to some of the most indebted countries in the world.

Public Sector Reform

A positive for public administration in the Commonwealth Caribbean is the fact of an awareness of the need for upgrade and modernization to respond to the changing demands of public governance (Davis 2001). For instance, on the eve of discussions for Federation in 1955, a civil service commission had been formed by the United Kingdom to consider the administrative reforms that would be needed to support the functioning of the Federation.

As such, the shortcomings discussed above have not gone unnoticed with the language of reform being a consistent feature of Caribbean public administration even if more in theory than actuality. This may be seen in some of the most recent waves of reforms since the 1980s. Many of these reforms are reviewed elsewhere in this book. Summarily, PSRs have been aimed at improving quality in the delivery of public services, improving efficiency and effectiveness, and modernizing public administration. These attempts were also informed by external groups including donor agencies. External advice and conditionality's have in fact offered opportunities for blame-shifting by local decision makers desirous of making changes that are not politically attractive. More generally, these have been aimed at addressing the failings of the inherited model of public administration. Reforms have, for instance, focused on increasing accountability, improving the management of human resources, and greater fiscal and financial management. Performance management and efforts to improve customer service have also been introduced across the region.

A number of task forces and recommendations have been put forward over the years as seen in islands such as T&T and Jamaica from 1984. One of the main features of the early reforms was the International Monetary Fund (IMF)-supported and informed Structural Adjustment Programme (SAP). The SAP of the 1980s and 1990s, for instance, saw cuts in public expenditure, especially on social services and the funding of certain community and voluntary initiatives in the countries that adopted these measures. A reduction in the size of the public sector has also been a result (La Guerre 1994). For instance, the public sector in Jamaica was reduced from 130,400 in 1974 to 103,800 in 1985, moving to 8,000 by 1992 (Minto-Coy in a paper for CAPRI 2011: 6).

The adoption of reforms has not always gone smoothly. In countries such as Barbados, the adoption of SAP in the early 1990s led to widespread demonstrations among public servants. Ultimately, these evolved into the largest demonstrations Barbados has ever witnessed (see Minto-Coy 2012; Wint 2003).

Many of these reforms have been informed by the new public management (NPM) that defined the wave of PSRs globally (Osborne and Gaebler, 1992; for a discussion in the Caribbean context see Lodge and Stirton, 2009). New managerialism and neoliberalism have continued to be the prevailing conceptual framework within which reforms continue to be introduced. In line with the philosophy of neoliberalism and NPM, reforms up to 2015 have included greater adoption of information and communications technologies (ICTs), contracting out, decentralization, and effort toward increasing value for money.

The most recent round of PSR has come in response to the global financial crisis that occurred at the end of the first decade of the twenty-first century. Much of the moves within the region are informed by the IMF through its recommendations and guidelines for adjusting to the increased economic pressures. Emphasis has been placed on areas such as debt management and restructuring, containing public sector spending, including wage and benefits freeze or reduction, mergers, and improved tax administration. Countries such as Barbados, long hailed for its stable industrial relations climate and welfare provisions, have witnessed increased volatility and reductions in the provision level of government support (e.g., reduced support to university students). The ability to draw down on pledged tranches of funds to some islands has been tied to the ability of countries such as Jamaica to meet pre-agreed obligations.

An important development in Jamaica, the island that has gone the farthest in introducing NPM-style reforms, has been the creation of UK-type executive agencies (EAs) at the end of the 1990s. These existed with a degree of separation from the general civil service with some amount of operational autonomy. EAs were also meant to facilitate more flexibility in decision making and break the emphasis on rules and rote (Lodge and Stirton 2009: 52 and 53). These have been credited as having introduced more responsiveness and efficiency into public administration in Jamaica. Other islands such as Barbados have also contemplated the introduction of similar structures, while Guyana and St. Lucia are among those that have also experimented with NPM-type reforms. The result in some islands, including Jamaica, has been the creation of a double layer of civil service in terms of performance and results with the independent EAs showing some improvement in service quality, efficiency, and economy.

As the language around PSR has evolved internationally it has also found expression in Caribbean public administration. Thus, the preoccupation with public–private partnership and governance have also featured in the Caribbean with government seeking out partnerships both locally and internationally (including with the private sector, nongovernmental organizations [NGOs], and diaspora) to fund and implement infrastructural and other development initiatives.

Nonetheless, the extent to which public administration will accord sufficient space for civil society and NGOs remain to be seen. Even more, the private sector across the region to some extent remains unable or unwilling to partner with the public sector to sufficiently affect a public–private partnership. Indeed, the international development community remains active partners.

A less stated rationale behind PSR is the reduction in the size of the public sector as a means of reducing the impact of public service wages and pensions on national budgets. The focus on the size of the public sector is not unique and has been warranted in the case of the region, given that the size of the public sector has been relatively large. Other commentators have noted that small states tend to have large public sectors; therefore, this is not a feature that is unique to the Commonwealth Caribbean (e.g., Ota and Cas 2008: 6).

Reducing the size of the public service remains politically sensitive and hence tends to be shrouded in discussions on efficiency or is carefully avoided by politicians. Increasingly, however, the strains on national budgets, some of which was brought on by the global financial crisis, have seen governments increasing their attention to the need for pension reforms and how best to streamline the public sector so as to reduce the strain of wages and pensions. For instance, wages represent on average over 50% of government expenditure across the region. As such, it is imperative to address this area with added support coming from the IMF. In all likelihood, this area will remain unaddressed concisely not only given the practicalities of politics but also given that the public sector remains the main avenue for employment (employer of last resort) for many. As such, a fear is that the strains from such austerity measures may ultimately cause more social and economic fallout, an important consideration given the existing problems with crime among countries (Griffith 2004). Jamaica's 2010 agreement with the IMF, for instance, included recommendations for reducing the size of the public sector via the merging of various departments and units. However, by 2014, much of the mergers had yet to be fully introduced.

The extent to which such episodes of reform will lead to wider systemic change remains unclear. In some instances, the implementation of reforms has been partial or interrupted by changes in political leadership of the country. In practical terms too, public administration is not a cheap endeavor. Similarly, reforming the system and sustaining reforms are not without costs and the constraints of finance can become more obvious in a small developing setting. PSR has, therefore, not been revolutionary in its results. Reform fatigue has also begun to set into the civil service and the wider public sector with personnel being called upon to bear the burden of adjustments (e.g., wage freezes) with little improvement in economic performance and, hence, livelihoods over time. In other instances, efforts at macro level reforms through the adoption of social partnerships have faltered due to a view that the pain of adjustment has not been shared equally with politicians receiving salary increases even as civil servants are being asked to agree to freezes (as in Jamaica) or due to the inability to gain consensus between ethnic groups (T&T) (Minto-Coy 2011).

The discussion to this point is not meant to suggest that no gains have been secured from the introduction of reforms. For instance, the latest round (2014-15) of IMF reforms in Jamaica are being overseen by an astute Minister of Finance with the discipline being exercised bearing some fruit, as seen in the early tabling of expenditure and revenue estimates together for the first time in 2015. Such a move offers an opportunity for more careful management, monitoring, and increased transparency and accountability of the national budget. Neither is the suggestion that the inherited model has no good features. One of the positive elements of the colonial model, for instance, the Public Service Commissions, has been retained but has not escaped the more recent efforts at PSR. For instance, the Office of the Services Commission introduced in 1952 in Jamaica has now been tasked with monitoring the permanent secretaries and chief executive officers in their task of hiring and movement of their personnel under Accountability Agreements

(*Jamaica Observer* 2003). The changes here have been noted as offering public managers more control and ownership, hence greater accountability over performance.

Ultimately, though, efforts at improving public governance have borne some fruit but not in sufficient measures to have a profound impact on the region. As such, reforms continue to be piecemeal while the ability of public governance to ensure greater performance in managing and delivering growth remains wanting. More generally, efforts at improving the public service over the years have been affected by lack of ownership among personnel, lack of adequate capacity for implementing projects, and faulty or incomplete implementation. One of the key setbacks here is that while reforms have been introduced over the years, it remains that countries have not yet understood that it is not only just about what types of reforms are introduced but also how these are introduced. In other words, the governance of reform remains a skill which many in the region have not managed.

Furthermore, there has been a tendency to think that reform means the introduction of new rules and systems. However, as noted earlier one of the challenges facing the region is what may be termed an implementation gap. In the context of the present discussion then, reform may more suitably be about the fuller implementation of existing rules and systems of accountability and performance management (including the punitive measures) and less about the introduction of new rules (even accepting the need for updates).

Public Financial Management

Public financial management (PFM) is one of the main areas in which the region has underperformed (see Mills 1970: 347). Indeed, PSR has been hampered by the very inability to manage public finances responsibly, including the difficulties in managing contingent liabilities. The high indebtedness of Caribbean states is a telling tale of this reality. Here public sector debt to gross domestic product (GDP) was estimated to be close to 141% for Jamaica, 100% for Barbados, 99% for Antigua and Barbuda, and 84% for St. Lucia for 2014 (IMF 2015). As such, PFM has featured under various PSR efforts. In the case of Barbados, reforms have included the introduction of Financial Management Information System and Program Budgeting as tools for improving financial management (see Minto-Coy 2011).

Key to the issue of sound PFM is the quality of tax administration and collection. The low levels of competitiveness and exports have seen taxation being an important source of national income. Tax collection has been a major challenge, and in some countries, it is characterized by a system of unclear duties and exemptions that has in turn been applied in an ad hoc fashion. In some cases, such exemptions require direct application to a minister resulting in the arbitrary application of rules and standards. The system has therefore offered another means by which favors can be paid for or extracted.

Informality in the wider economic system also poses its own challenges to effective PFM. The scale varies across the region but is generally considered to be relatively high. In Jamaica, for instance, the informal economy has been estimated to be as high as 40% of GDP. Significant losses accrue from lost taxes and duties. In such a scenario, the funding of public services becomes the responsibility of a small segment of the population (namely, the middle class).

This reality has been compounded by sporadic incidents of natural disasters across the region. These include hurricanes, volcanic activity, earthquakes, and droughts. The best laid developmental plan and budget can be torn asunder by one such incident. In such a climate, the budgeting process becomes a precarious activity that is fraught by a number of uncontrollable factors that heighten the vulnerability of Caribbean small states.

The volatility of chosen economic activity across the region further aggravates prospects for sound financial management. Most of the region's economies rely on tourism and the export of primary commodities in which they are not price setters. As such, national incomes are more susceptible to the vagaries of the international economy, again affecting the extent to which there can be predictability in spending on public governance.

In some cases, policies are made without adequate budgetary allocation to fund implementation or sustenance of such policies. For example, the Administrative Reform Programme adopted by Jamaica in 1984 into the 1990s faltered given the lack of sufficient funds to implement the reforms (Minto-Coy 2011). As such, there remains insufficient synchrony between national planning and developmental plans on the one hand and the budgeting process on the other. The point to be noted here is that budgets can be amended willy-nilly.

It is therefore not surprising that the measures introduced over the years to manage public finances have yet to result in significant improvements in PFM across the region. Indeed, there remains a challenge in managing contingent liabilities* across the region. Even allowing for the uncertainties posed by weather and reliance on economic activities that are reliant on external conditions, the region has not fared well in terms of managing spending, a point borne out in other chapters in this book.

Migration and Public Administration

Migration has been a significant feature of the Caribbean's history and merits consideration given its impact on public administration.

The scenario in the Caribbean is marked when compared to other regions for a number of reasons. Key among these is Foner's (1998: 47) observation that the Caribbean, more than any other region, has been "more deeply and continuously" marked by migration. Jones (1992b) has noted the loss of around 30 senior administrators annually due to migration (and the private sector). Migrants have tended to be among the most economically active persons and with a significant number being the most skilled and educated across the region (Minto-Coy 2010). In some cases, estimates suggest that over 80% of persons who have acquired post-secondary education in the region have migrated (Minto-Coy, 2015). The Commonwealth Caribbean is, therefore, a net exporter of human resource.

Public administration has not been immune to this reality. Migration has led to a depletion of skilled personnel in all areas of Caribbean society. Areas such as nursing and education have witnessed shortages in labor and quality in labor, generally (e.g., Reis 2007). It has been suggested that given the reality of public spending in the education system, including up to university levels, the departure of nationals in this sense can constitute a loss in public resource and an inability for the country to recoup investments made in developing human capital (Minto-Coy 2011).

While increased training has seen improvements in the quality of personnel over the years, the stock of skilled public servants, including senior managers and politicians, has been affected by migration. Jones (1992b) has noted the loss of around 30 senior administrators annually due to migration (and the private sector). Capacity in recent years is even more an issue in light of the planned migration and citizenship programs of developed countries such as Canada, which increasingly aim to attract highly skilled migrants. The attraction to and selectivity of such programs will become even more of an issue for personnel management as developed countries introduce more visa requirements. This is so as these limit the ease with which Caribbean nationals have been able to travel, while increasing the international marketability of the most skilled in the region.

---

* These can be defined as potential liabilities that become actual liabilities if an event occurs or fails to occur (see, e.g., Polackova, 1999).

Migration affects public administration in terms of the loss of skilled public personnel and public expenditure. The middle class in most societies are deemed as being important for the functioning of democracy and holding politicians to account (see, e.g., Lipset, 1959; Barro, 1999; Cheeseman, 2014). The quality of public governance has been adversely affected by migration. They may also be seen as harbingers and shapers of change. With the depletion of this group, the voice and debate around the search for suitable models and quality of assessment of public administration and politics as well as the fortitude to address challenges are diminished.

A growing trend in migration in the region is the movement from one island to the next. It will be recalled that this was one of the issues impeding the success of Federation in the pre-independence era (see Sewell 2007). For instance, the more economically successful nations of Barbados, T&T, and the Bahamas have, for instance, been the main destinations for other Caribbean nationals. The former have therefore been able to fill capacity gaps thanks to the movement of skilled nationals from other island territories. An emerging discussion here is the need for greater consideration of the type, design, and delivery of public services for regional migrants and those going outside the region.

The management and performance of public administration in the Caribbean will continue to be affected by migration, particularly as the region remains unable to provide sufficient jobs, salaries, and other opportunities for its population. Nevertheless, there remains some potential for addressing this challenge innovatively by engaging the diaspora more actively into national and regional governance. Measures such as facilitating temporary local assignments, as well as the formation of knowledge networks, can help to entice the best among this group to contribute virtually or physically. Such networks can be important informants of emerging public management tools, techniques, and philosophies and assist in local efforts to modernize public governance.

Ultimately, there remains an imperative for the previously silent partnership with the diaspora and migrants, generally at the policy level (Minto-Coy 2015) to be addressed more directly by Caribbean countries. Public policy has to respond in terms of the framing of initiatives for addressing resulting gaps in the economic, political, and social systems at the macro and micro levels. Migration management is therefore becoming a more serious imperative for public managers and policy makers. This involves strengthening capacities and the accuracy of information on migration rates in order to better manage and prepare for effects on the public service in terms of personnel, policies, and the constituents to be served.

Race, Ethnicity, Class, and the Organization and Delivery of Public Services

The link between race and power that featured in the colonial period also continued into independence in society (Mawby 2012: 7). Along with issues of class and ethnicity, these also form considerations of the organization of public administration in the pre-independence era to the present, though not uniformed in extent across the different islands. For instance, T&T and Guyana have more visibly been territories where issues of race and ethnicity have played out in public administration and the wider society. These divisions have also run across political lines with the mass of one racial or ethnic group making up a political party (see Bissessar 2003 for a more detailed discussion).

In other islands such as Jamaica, the suggestion has been that class and not necessarily race has been the predominant issue in the organization of politics and public administration (see, e.g., Gray 2004) with the emphasis on black empowerment in the 1970s having led to the opening up of spaces for the majority black population in the senior roles of government and society.

In spite of the differences in which these demarcations have featured across the region, each instance has resulted in accusations of victimization and unfairness in public life. That is their effects have played out in the unbalanced distribution and delivery of public goods and services. As noted by Jones and Mills (1976: 341), "state bureaucratic structures in the Commonwealth Caribbean function largely in the interest of powerful economic and political groups, as well as in favour of the bureaucratic bourgeoisie."

Other demarcations have been oriented around the rural/urban divide with public services traditionally being located in the centers and capital cities to the exclusion of rural communities. An awareness of this challenge as centered around the discourse of de-centralization has seen increased effort to situate outposts of main government bodies in rural communities and smaller towns.

Regional and International Influences on Public Administration

There has been some recognition of the importance of public administration to the developmental goals of the region, as a whole. To this end, the regional grouping of CARICOM or the Caribbean Community, which from its inception in 1973 represented the grouping of English-speaking Caribbean states, has over the years made various efforts to influence the quality of public administration on the islands*

To this end, CARICAD (Caribbean Centre for Development Administration) was established in 1990 with the aim of helping to improve the public sector across the region. While the body has registered some success in its efforts, including encouragement of an e-government agenda, the transformation of the public administration system has generally not been realized. CARICAD has been supported in its work by organizations such as the United Nations. CARICOM has made interventions in other policy areas across the region. It has, however, lacked the level of financial support or legitimacy to effect regional improvements as other regional governance institutions such as the EU have been able to accomplish (Bishop and Payne 2010).

As suggested above, the international community has been a supporter of the development and modernization of public administration capacity in Caribbean states, both at the national and regional levels. The Commonwealth Secretariat has over the years assisted national governments through number of initiatives. The focus on good governance has, for instance, seen a number of consultations and workshops being organized for heads of public service organizations.

Various reform efforts have also been aided through technical advice and funding from institutions such as the World Bank(WB) and the IMF. Development agencies such as Department for International Development (DFID), Canadian International Development Agency (CIDA), and United States Agency for International Development (USAID) and the development arms of EU countries have also been key allies and instigators of change in the region. The IMF has, for instance, helped to chart efforts in PFM and other efforts at economic reform across the region. Support from international financial institutions, including the IMF, has increased due to the difficult financial position that continues to face the region (IMF 2015: 3).

Intellectually and financially therefore external influence has had some bearing in driving innovations and improvements in public administration. Nevertheless, a fuller consideration of their role in local public administration is also necessary. To this end, the at times unquestioning application of ideas and practices from other settings, some with the support of international funding and advice institutions, has in some instances led to counterproductive results (see, e.g., Brown 1998: 14). Examples include the introduction of reforms that are difficult to sustain, given

---

* As noted by Gibson (2010) and registered on CARICAD's website: http://www.caricad.net/

the lack of capacity to sustain these beyond the initial investment. This has been the case, for instance, where consultants originate from outside the region and where recommendations are not sufficiently cognizant of the limits and demands of local institutions and capacity within the public service.

Many of the reforms have been driven by an external ethos and unrealistic expectations of the results of adopting external policies. The various theories and methods that have been applied to Caribbean public administration and policy have been largely adopted from outside the region, having been informed by the contexts in which they evolved. This is not new and it has already been argued that the very emergence of the independent Commonwealth Caribbean was shaped by processes of modeling and adoption of the WW model of public governance. As such, there has been an expectation that the same results that accrue in other settings will also be the case by mere application of such borrowed perspectives and theories. Lesson-learning has its place. However, there remains an imperative for the region to develop internally informed theories, perspectives, and approaches to informing public administration, even where these represent an improvement upon existing or external models. Indeed, observers such as Sutton (2008: 19) have commented on this phenomenon, noting this as a "one-size-fits-all approach" that has been encouraged by external actors, including donors and consultants. The source of funding for reforms is therefore a critical consideration in the penchant for adopting externally driven and informed reform agendas. The result has been a lack of ownership, support, and sustenance of reforms, especially after funds run out. The influence of external players and adopted concepts has thus been questioned in the region (see Jones 1996; Lodge and Stirton 2009; Manning 2001; Sutton 2008).

Impact of Size

A number of threads run throughout the discussion. Among these is that of size and its impact on public governance, demonstrating the pervasiveness and relevance of this matter in the Caribbean. Indeed, the matter of size is not raised here in a normative sense but is very much about the reality of the region as a collection of small states though not uniform in size. These consist of the largest Jamaica to the smaller territories in the Leeward and Windward Islands, including Montserrat. The Bahamas too forms a conglomerate of smaller territories, again separated by water, which itself also pose additional costs for public administration.

Small size in the case of many Caribbean countries takes on an even more profound relevance when tied to the matter of small resources (human and financial) and small talent pool. "Smallness" then has many implications for the effective functioning of public administration in the Commonwealth Caribbean, as seen in limited budgets, which have been noted to affect the hiring and retention of quality and quantity of skilled personnel (Jones 1992a). Additionally, resources tend to be low, development levels low, while skills may not be appropriate to suit specific tasks resulting in a "make-do" approach in personnel management. Furthermore, it has been noted, for instance, that opportunities for specialized training are limited resulting in persons migrating to study (WTO 2002: 3). The experience has been that these do not always return home, and indeed, this is one of the challenges that currently faces the region, especially given its openness (see Palmer 2009) and contributing to the rates of the migration discussed earlier.

The reality of smallness is also seen in the fact that ties and networks tend to be smaller and also more visible. Authors such as Mills (1970), Jones (1992a), and Kearney (1986) have already noted the perverse implications for public administration in a small country. This feature of social life means familial or community ties translate into patronage and are intricately tied to notions of rights and duties. Though written some decades ago, their observations still hold. These relate to the fact that most senior managers would have attended the same schools, lived in the same communities, or are members of the same family. Such a reality has unfortunately heightened the opportunities for nepotism and favoritism giving rise to corruption.

Contending with Ongoing and Emerging Challenges in Public Administration

Summarily, the following presentation aimed to review major developments in public administration in the Commonwealth Caribbean. In so doing, special attention has been placed on a number of matters that have some bearing on the functioning of the system of public administration and are deemed important considerations for any observer of public administration in the English-speaking Caribbean. Among these are the issues of colonial legacy, international influence, corruption, the practicality of size, and migration. These have formed a consistent thread throughout the discussion.

Attention has also been focused on the various attempts at reform over the years, as a realization that the system is not only in need of modernization but also awareness that its performance has been suboptimal. While these efforts have not necessarily generated great improvements in performance, the reform of Caribbean public administration remains an imperative that cannot be ignored. This imperative will heighten as the region continues to face a number of governance challenges relating to its competitiveness, the environment, and problems of crime and corruption. Ultimately, growth and development will rely upon the capacities within public administration including the ability to manage limited resources for national development and relevance in an increasingly globalized world.

The benefits of lesson-learning aside, there also remains a need to engineer solutions to public governance that are more informed by local context. Politico-administrative leaders including line ministers also need to exercise more influence and independence in championing the need for development assistance and perspectives to be conditioned more by local experiences. In short, sustained experiences of failure in reforming public administration according to a one-size-fits-all or externally driven strategy merits more activism and willfulness on the part of Caribbean leaders in demanding attention to the local environment.

Key to addressing challenges of external motivation and the appearance of lack of results and stagnation noted above is the need for more review and detailed assessment of actual results of each bout of reform. The result will be more informed analyses of the successes, limitations, and real impact of efforts to improve public administration. The clear winner would be a more responsive and successful system of public governance. This could lead to the creation of a knowledge bank of experiences toward the development of Caribbean-relevant responses to domestic and international policy and administrative challenges.

While resource constraints have been noted as one of the maladies of public administration in the Commonwealth, the reality too is that the region has benefitted immensely from the largess of its many international partners, including multilateral institutions and nation states. Notwithstanding, insufficient improvements have been realized in the quality of public administration.

Finally, a realistic discussion of the challenges and challengers to transforming the public administration system in the Caribbean needs to take place. This is a means to understanding the implementation and results gaps that have been noted as a feature of Caribbean public policy and administration and potentially overcoming some of these issues that have debilitated progress. The reality is that improving public administration capacity and quality within the region will have winners and undoubtedly losers. These will ultimately affect the overall ability to modernize the Caribbean.

Conclusion

In this chapter, we have reviewed the functioning of the public administration machinery in the Commonwealth Caribbean, covering the experiences of the region from its emergence at the apex of international trade (given its value in the sugar, slave, and colonial systems) to modern developments and challenges affecting the performance of this machine.

What the chapter reveals is the overriding value of an understanding of the region's history in understanding the present context and performance of the public administration system. Indeed, the issue of legacy runs thick throughout the region. The legacy in this regard relates to colonialism, slavery, plantation economies, and the attendant issues, including those of corruption. Even so, the unfolding of developments in the region also calls to attention that not all the current state of public administration can be placed at the feet of these legacy issues. As such, while the past also had a hold on the independent Caribbean, the reality too is that the governments across the region have had some room to modify practices. The environment (ranging from the natural to the man-made) of Caribbean public administration is also very difficult and this has also helped to define public administration in the region. The preceding is by no means an exhaustive coverage of the subject matter. It nonetheless marks a sound platform for further reading (including some of the references contained herein) giving an overall review of many of the main issues pertinent to the context of the Commonwealth Caribbean. In this way, it contributes to the build up in the body of accessible knowledge on the experiences of the Caribbean and, more generally, on some of the less covered experiences in public administration. Indeed, the experiences covered provide an opportunity for the development of analyses, lesson-drawing, and comparative investigations that can inform the formulation and testing of theories and concepts in public administration. The characteristics described also go a far way in explaining many of the features of public policy and administration discussed in the chapters that follow.

References

Barro, Robert J. (1999). Determinants of democracy, *Journal of Political Economy*, 107(S6): 158-183.
Bishop, Matthew and Payne, Anthony (2010). Caribbean regional governance and the sovereignty/statehood problem, *Caribbean Paper No 8*, Waterloo, Canada: Centre for International Governance Innovation.
Bissessar, Ann Marie (2003). The changing nexus of power in the new public sector management of Trinidad and Tobago, *International Journal of Public Sector Management*, 16(3): 170–190.
Brereton, Bridget M., Robinson, Arthur Napoleon Raymond and Watts, David (2014). Trinidad 2014, *Encyclopaedia Online Academic Edition*. Encyclopaedia Britannica Inc. http://www.britannica.com/EBchecked/topic/605453/Trinidad-and-Tobago. Accessed on May 27, 2014.
Brown, Deryck (ed.) (1998). Introduction, *Evaluation, Learning and Caribbean Development*, Kingston/University of the West Indies: Canoe Press, pp. 1–26.
Bulgin, Samuel (2012). The Metamorphosis of the Original Westminster-Whitehall Constitutional Model as exported to the Commonwealth Caribbean, Paper Presented at the *University College of the Cayman Islands with the University of the West Indies (Mona) Conference: 50-50—Surveying the Past, Mapping the Future*, March 2012. http://www.ucciconference.ky/papers/Bulgin%20-%20Metamorphosis%20of%20the%20Westminster%20Model%20of%20Constitution%20in%20the%20Caribbean.pdf. Accessed on August 29, 2014.
Cheeseman, Nic (2014). Does the African Middleclass Defend Democracy: Evidence From Kenya, *WIDER Working Paper 2014/096*, Helsinki, Finland: United Nations University-WIDER.
The Economist (1999). Corruption in the Caribbean: The worm turns, *The Economist*. http://www.economist.com/node/256011 Accessed on December 14, 2014.

Davis, Carlton (2001). *Luncheon Speech at the Conference on Changing Governance and Public Sector Reform in the Americas*, Ottawa, Canada. Available at: http://www.cabinet.gov.jm/files/docs/speech-cdavis-public-sector-reform.pdf. Accessed on February 26, 2014.

Encyclopaedia Britannica (2014). West Indies, *Encyclopaedia Online Academic Edition.* Encyclopaedia Britannica Inc. http://www.britannica.com/EBchecked/topic/640195/West-Indies/54383/Colonialism. Accessed on May 27, 2014.

Foner, Nancy (1998). Towards a comparative perspective on Caribbean migration, in *Caribbean Migration: A Global Identities*, Mary Chamberlain (ed.), New York/London: Routledge.

Gibson, David (2010). *The Situation of Public Administration Organizations in the Caribbean.* Available at: http://www.unuftp.is/static/files/short_courses/Leadership_CRFM_2010/D1P2_Gibson_Leadership%20Workshop.pdf. Accessed on February 19, 2014.

Gray, Obika (2004). *Demeaned but Empowered: The Social Power of the Urban Poor in Jamaica*, Kingston, Jamaica: The University of the West Indies.

Griffith, Ivelaw (ed.) (2004). *Caribbean Security in an Age of Terror: Challenge and Change*, Kingston, Jamaica: Ian Randle Publishers, pp. 129–153.

Hall, Kenneth and Benn, Denis (2003). *Governance in the Age of Globalization: Caribbean Perspectives*, Kingston, Jamaica: Ian Randle Publishers.

International Monetary Fund (IMF) (2015). *World Economic Outlook Database April 2015*, IMF. Available at: http://www.imf.org/external/pubs/ft/weo/2015/01/weodata/weoselco.aspx?g=2001&sg=All+countries. Accessed on June 2, 2015.

Jamaica Observer (2003). Services Commission takes on new role, *The Jamaica Observer*, January 2, 2013. http://www.jamaicaobserver.com/news/37446_Services-Commission-takes-on-new-role. Accessed on February 19, 2014.

Jamaica Observer (2012). Greg Christie leaving job as contractor general, *The Jamaica Observer,* March 17, 2012. http://www.jamaicaobserver.com/news/Greg-Christie-leaving-job-as-contractor-general_11044927. Accessed on December 15, 2014.

Jones, Edwin (1992a). *Development Administration: Jamaican Adaptations*, Kingston, Jamaica: Caricom Publishers.

Jones, Edwin (1992b). Maladministration and corruption: Some caribbean realities, in *Issues and Problems in Caribbean Public Administration*, Selwyn Ryan and Deryk Brown (eds.), St Augustine, Trinidad: Institute for Social and Economic Research.

Jones, Edwin (1996). Jamaica: Framework for managing the reform process, in *Policy Reform for Sustainable Development in the Caribbean*, Louis A. Picard and Michele Garrity (eds.), Amsterdam, the Netherlands: IOS Press.

Jones, Edwin (2013). Commentary on "Learning from Past Policy Experience: Import Substitution and Light Manufacturing---A Governance Perspective", in *Economic Transformation and Job Creation: The Caribbean Experience*, Kenneth Hall & Myrtle Chuck-A-Sang (eds.), USA: Trafford Publishing, pp. 21–32

Jones, Edwin and Mills, G.E. (1976). Institutional innovation and change in the Commonwealth Caribbean, *Social and Economic Studies*, 25(4): 323–346, 41.

Kearney, Richard (1986). Spoils in the Caribbean: The struggle for merit-based civil service in the Dominican Republic, *Public Administration Review*, 46(2): 144–151.

La Guerre, John (1994). *Structural Adjustment: Public Policy and Administration in the Caribbean*, St Augustine, Trinidad and Tobago: School of Continuing Studies, University of the West Indies.

Lipset, Seymour Martin (1959). 'Some social requisites of democracy: Economic development and political legitimacy.' *American Political Science Review* 53(March): 69–105.

Lodge, Martin and Stirton, Lindsay (2009). Beyond the "inherited model": Public service Bargains in the Commonwealth Caribbean, *Social and Economic Studies*, 58(1): 43–67.

MacDonald, Scott B. (1986). *Trinidad and Tobago: Democracy and Development in the Caribbean*, New York: Praeger Publishers.

Maingot, Anthony P. (2004). The challenge of the corruption-violence connection, in *Caribbean Security in an Age of Terror: Challenge and Change*, Ivelaw Griffith (ed.), Kingston, Jamaica: Ian Randle Publishers, pp. 129–153.

Manning, Nick (2001). The legacy of new public management in developing countries, *International Review of Administrative Sciences*, 67(2): 297–312.

Mawby, Spencer (2012). *Ordering Independence: The End of Empire in the Anglophone Caribbean, 1947–69*, Hampshire: Palgrave MacMillan.

McKoy, Derrick (2012). *Corruption: Law, Governance and Ethics in the Commonwealth Caribbean*, Hertford, UK: Hansib Publications Limited.

Mills, Gladstone E. (1970). Public Administration in the Commonwealth Caribbean: Evolution, Conflict and Challenges, *Social and Economic Studies*, 19(1): 5–25.

Mills, Gladstone E. (1990). The English-Speaking Caribbean, in *Public Administration in the Third World: An International Perspective*, V. Subramanian (ed.), Westport, CT: Greenwood Publishing Group, p. 318.

Mills, Gladstone E. (1997). *Westminster Style Democracy: The Jamaica Experience*. Jamaica: The Grace, Kennedy Foundation.

Minto-Coy, Indianna (September, 2010). *Towards Public Sector Reform in Jamaica: What Can Local and International Experiences Tell Us About Successful Public Sector Reform*, Kingston, Jamaica: Caribbean Policy Research Institute.

Minto-Coy, Indianna (2011). Beyond remittancing: An investigation of the role of telecoms in facilitating and extending the diaspora's contribution to the Caribbean, *Canadian Foreign Policy Journal*, 17(2): 129–141.

Minto-Coy, Indianna (2012). The grit that makes the pearl: Collaborative problem solving in the midst of conflict and crisis, Special Issue (Collaborative Problem-Solving in Conflicts), *Journal of Systems Research and Behavioural Science*, 29: 221–226.

Minto-Coy, Indianna (2015). Engaging the Caribbean Diaspora: A Critical Analysis of Diasporic Engagement for Development in the Caribbean, in *Diasporas, Development and Governance*, Abel Chikanda, Jonathan Crush and Margaret Walton-Roberts (eds.), New York: Springer.

Murray, D.J. (1965). *The West Indies and the Development of Colonial Government 1801–1834*, Oxford: Clarendon Press.

Nantambu, Kwame (2009). Politics of the colonized versus colonizer, Available at: Trinicenter.com/Kwame/2009/0201.htm. Accessed on February 26, 2014.

Osborne, David and Gaebler, Ted (1992). *Reinventing Government: How the Entrepreneurial Spirit Is Transforming Government*, Reading, MA: Addison-Wesley Publishing Company.

Ota, Rui and Cas, Stephanie Medina (2008). *Big Government, High Debt and Fiscal Adjustments in Small States*, IMF Working Papers 08/39. Available at: http://www.imf.org/external/pubs/ft/wp/2008/wp0839.pdf. Accessed on February 26, 2014.

Palmer, Ransford (2009). *The Caribbean Economy in an Age of Globalisation*, New York: Palgrave Macmillan.

Payne, Anthony (1993). Westminster adapted: The political order of the Commonwealth Caribbean, in *Democracy in the Caribbean: Political, Economic and Social Perspectives*, Jorge I. Dominguez et al. (eds.), Baltimore, MD: The Johns Hopkins University Press.

Polackova, Hana (1999). Contingent government liabilities: A hidden fiscal risk. *Finance and Development* 36(1): 46–49.

Reis, Michelle (2007). Vision 2020: The role of migration in Trinidad and Tobago's plan for overall development, *8th Annual Conference on Crisis, Chaos and Change: Caribbean Development Challenges in the 21st Century*, SALISES, March 26-82. http://sta.uwi.edu/conferences/salises/documents/Reis%20%20M.pdf. Accessed on February 26, 2014.

Ryan, Selwyn (2001). Democratic governance in the Anglophone Caribbean: Threats to sustainability, in *New Caribbean Thought: A Reader*, Meeks, Brian and Lindahl, Folke (eds.), Kingston, Jamaica: University of the West Indies Press, pp. 73-104.

Sewell, Sharon Catherine (2007). *Culture and Decolonisation in the British West Indies: Literature and Politics 1930–1980*, PhD thesis, Stillwater, OK: Oklahoma State University.

Sires, Ronald (1957). Government in the British West Indies: An Historical Outline, *Social and Economic Studies*, 6(2, Special Federation Issue): 109–132.

Spiller, Pablo and Sampson, Cezley (1996). Telecommunications regulation in Jamaica, in *Regulation, Institution's and Commitment: Comparative Studies of Telecommunications*, Brian Levy and Pablo Spiller (eds.), Cambridge: Cambridge University Press.

Streeten, Paul (1993). The special problems of small countries, *World Development* 21(2): 197–202.
Sutton, Paul (2008). *Public Sector Reform in the Commonwealth Caribbean: A Review of Recent Experiences*, Caribbean Paper No 6, Waterloo, Canada: Centre for International Governance Innovation.
Wallace, Elisabeth (1977). *The British Caribbean: From the Decline of Colonialism to the End of Federation*, Toronto, Canada: Toronto University Press.
Waller, Lloyd, Paul Bourne, Indianna D. Minto, and John Rapley (2007). *A Landscape Assessment of Perceptions on Corruption in Jamaica*, Kingston, Jamaica: CaPRI.
Wint, Alvin (2003). *Competitiveness in Small Developing States: Insights from the Caribbean*, Kingston, Jamaica: University of the West Indies.
WTO (2002). *Small Economies: A Literature Review*, WTO, Committee on Trade and Development, Dedicated Session, WT/COMTD/SE/W/4. Available at: ctrc.sice.oas.org/TRC/WTO/SmallEcon/SEW4_e.doc. Accessed on February 26, 2014.
Zephyr (2008). Corruption and its impact on Latin American democratic stability, in *The Challenges to Democracy in Latin America and the Caribbean: Evidence from the Americas Barometer 2006–2007*, Washington, DC: USAID, pp. 251–274.

Chapter 3

Public Administration in the French Antilles: Historical Trends and Prospects

Justin Daniel

Contents

Departmentalization: A Betrayed Hope? 64
    A Long Historical Process 64
    Between Centralization and Calls for Autonomy 66
    Attempts of Adaptation and Marginal Adjustments 67
    A Key Role for the French State 69
A Change in Paradigm: The Quest for New Forms of Governance 70
    The Triumph of the Thematic of Diversity and the Turning Point of 2003 70
    Laboratories of Institutional Engineering? 74
References 75

> **Abstract:** After a brief introduction reiterating the context in which the colonial administration was established, this chapter recounts the administrative history of the French Antilles since the transformation in 1946 of the colonies of Guadeloupe and Martinique into overseas departments (departmentalization). It is structured around two series of considerations. On the one hand, it strives to show to what extent departmentalization, the fruit of repeated demands from the local populations, was, in more than one way, experienced as a betrayed hope, in spite of the adaptations going along with its implementation. On the other hand, it analyzes the recent evolutions in the governance of these territories due to a change in paradigm, to give rise to actual laboratories of institutional engineering.

Guadeloupe and Martinique were conquered by the French in 1635. These islands correspond (with French Guiana* and Réunion in the Indian Ocean) to the "four old" French colonies, in opposition to those that were taken over in the nineteenth century. Territories for which colonial powers were fighting each other in the Caribbean and the Americas in the seventeenth century, they have become, with the passing of time, sorts of colonial pseudopods of the French administrative systems. This trajectory ultimately transformed them in 1946 into overseas departments (*Départements d'outre mer*) (DOM).

Under the ancien régime, these two Caribbean colonies were managed by private companies. Then, their direct annexation to the Crown gave rise to a gradually emerging, as of 1663, colonial administration which tended to expand throughout the motherland as well as in the colonies.

In 1710, the Colonial office was thus created, which depended on the state secretary of the navy. That office—the ancestor of the current Overseas Ministry—was completed after 1750 by setting up a consultation body, the Commission for Colonial Legislation. The Crown was represented locally by the governors, in charge of the military, and by the intendant who had the civilian responsibility for the colonies. In more than one way, the administrative organization of the kingdom extended across the Atlantic, with nevertheless tax particularities inherent to the Caribbean colonies. The so-called New France, in particular Canada, had no tax system apart from seigniorial duties introduced in the St. Laurent valley and the custom duties when entering and leaving the territory. Conversely, in the Antilles, the subjects paid capitation, including the slaves old enough to work, in addition to custom duties and local taxes levied to the benefit of the parishes and of the communities.

As of the eighteenth century, consultative institutions of settlers were added to that administrative organization: High Council in St. Domingo (1713), then National Assembly of the Colony, Chamber of Agriculture and of Commerce in Martinique and Guadeloupe in 1759, which became the Colonial Assemblies in 1787, and were completed by the General Assembly of the Colony. These assemblies, meeting annually or every 5 years, were mainly dedicated to give their consent to the tax. However, their elected representatives, four or five prominent white people, only accounted for the free population (1 man in 10). If these assemblies drew inspiration from the provincial states in France, they also corresponded to the introduction of an embryonic representative system of government partially mimicking the English model. They thus were to form opportunities for expressing and identifying a settler's spirit,† possibly for crystallizing autonomist trends which structured the relationships between the Caribbean colonies and the Metropole.

Under the ancien régime, Guadeloupe and Martinique thus clearly appeared as areas for extrapolating the political system of the ancien régime. The introduction of representative institutions, partially inspired from the English model, took place concomitantly with the motherland experimenting the provincial and municipal assemblies as of 1787, whose task, just like Colonial

---

* Guiana, which is not surrounded by the Caribbean Sea and which is geographically close to Amazonia, shares with Guadeloupe and Martinique the experience of the colonial habitation—or plantation—and results from the same socio-historical matrix, which makes it close to the Caribbean societies. However, this chapter will deal exclusively with Martinique and Guadeloupe.
† This settler's spirit can be seen, to various extents, in the French colonies of Caribbean: in 1753, the settler Saintard published an *Essai sur les colonies françaises ou Discours politique sur la nature du Gouvernement, de la population et du commerce de la colonie de Saint-Domingue* (1754) (Essay on the French colonies or political speech on the nature of the government and of the commerce of the St. Domingo Colony), where he evoked an "American patriotism" and in 1754 an essay on the French colonies. This settler's spirit can also be noted in Guadeloupe, in 1759, when the settlers refused to fight against the English. In St. Domingo in 1768 and 1769, a number of the settlers of the island rebelled against the French authorities.

Assemblies, was essentially the distribution of tax. Such an observation not only stresses that these colonies truly reflected the administration of France, but it seems to back up Tocqueville's hypothesis of continuity between the ancien régime and Revolution, up to and including across the Atlantic (Tocqueville and Mayer 1989).

The principle of French "uniformization," that is, the alignment of the colonies with the French administrative standards, already surreptitiously at work within mainland France under the ancien régime, was about to be confirmed under the Revolution. Thus, during the Convention, Boissy d'Anglas stated:

> The colonies shall be subjected to the same administrative norms as France. There can be only one good administering way; and if we have found it for the European lands, why should those of America be deprived thereof.*

For Boissy d'Anglas, the preservation of the freedom freshly acquired by the slaves necessarily involved assimilating America's colonies "to the other parts of the Republic" and abolishing differences from an administrative viewpoint. The Republican wind of change blown by the Convention evidently fed on the double principle of uniqueness and of universality of the French administrative model. The universalist claims of the Republic were knowingly not impeded by the return to the former colonial order under Napoleon. Certainly, they were subsequently reaffirmed but, above all, they had to adjust to colonial contingencies. The mentioned tensions between centralization, frequently denounced, and local particularities repeatedly expressed, come to the fore, beyond the application of supposedly universal norms, adaptation and flexibility in the functioning of institutions, and, indeed, in certain cases, the elaboration of specific rules governing institutional organization.

It follows that imposing a politico-administrative model in Guadeloupe, and Martinique, based on the quadruple principle of assimilation (the abolition of differences between the colonies and mainland France), of centralization (the concentration of administrative power in the central government located in Paris), of universalism (the application of the same administrative rules in the colonies and in mainland France), and of uniformization (the application of uniform rules on both sides) heavily weighed on the destiny of these territories. Notwithstanding the early accession of the Republic of Haiti to sovereignty in 1804, of the Dominican Republic in 1844, of Cuba formally in 1899, as well as the failure of the Federation of the West Indies which marked the start of the independence process in the English-speaking sphere of influence as of 1962, these two Caribbean islands are still today in the bosom of an external and remote power.

Fully integrated to the Franco-European unit, the French Antilles thus shared a unique relationship with Paris: they were made overseas departments (DOM) in 1946 and given the same institutions as their French counterparts; they are also governed by the same laws and regulations, while their emigrants formally enjoy the same rights as any other French citizens.

This historical trajectory, similar to a heterodox form of decolonization, undoubtedly raised conceptual issues, since it disputes the notion of a supposedly one-dimensional trajectory to decolonization, as well as traditional categorizations of decolonization, self-determination, and others that fall under the United Nations (UN) classification and provisions. From a practical perspective, Guadeloupe and Martinique remain in the bosom of France as an external—faraway—power through the unique process of departmentalization. However, the latter proved

---

* Report and project of constitutional articles pertaining to the colonies presented by Boissy d'Anglas at the National Convention, session of the 17 Thermidor, Year III.

long and complex: it could not be likened to a simple institutional rearrangement, together with an extension, incidentally often postponed, of the rules of ordinary law to the two territories. Manifestly, it has induced significant changes into the former colonies, by interfering at all levels of their economic and social organization while requiring adjustment of the public policy mechanisms which have been frequently judged ill-suited. Especially, for several decades, this process has turned the statutory and institutional question into a major issue of the politico-administrative life of these three territories, revealing there through its weakening. Hence, the change in paradigm observed today in terms of governance of the French territories situated in the Caribbean.

The aim of this contribution is to recount briefly the administrative history of the French Antilles since the transformation of the colonies of Guadeloupe and Martinique into overseas departments (departmentalization). It is structured around two series of considerations:

- On the one hand, it strives to show to what extent departmentalization, the fruit of repeated demands from the local populations, was, in more than one way, experienced as a betrayed hope, in spite of the adaptations going along with its implementation.
- On the other hand, it analyzes the recent evolutions in the governance of these territories due to a change in paradigm, to give rise to actual laboratories of institutional engineering.

Departmentalization: A Betrayed Hope?

On January 17, 1946, Aimé Césaire and Léopold Bissol, both communist representatives of Martinique, introduced into the constituent national assembly a bill aiming to transform the Antilles colonies into French departments. Taken over by the communist elected officials of the Reunion (Raymond Verges and Léon Lepervenche), then by Gaston Monnerville, himself elected representative of Guiana, this bill should lead to vote the famous assimilation law of March 19, 1946, transforming the four old colonies into overseas departments.

This legislative act appeared as the culmination of a long historical, irregular, and discontinuous process, initiated more than three centuries earlier. It opened a new experience with a double characteristic: on the one hand, it bore the mark of a quasi-permanent tension, implicitly noticeable as of 1946 in the debates in the constituent national assembly, between the centralizing trends inherent to the French administrative model and the locally persisting claims to autonomy; on the other hand, it materialized through timid reforms with marginal adjustments or trying to adapt, in a minor mode, the administrative model to the particular context of the former colonies. Finally, matching the standards of mainland France remains a challenge and an obsession: despite the central role given to the French state, and increasingly the European Union (EU) in local economic development, a deep economic and social malaise persists because of the vulnerability of island economies.

A Long Historical Process

As areas of extrapolation of the politico-administrative system of the ancien régime, the Antilles knew a situation different from that of the nineteenth century French colonies. Legally considered as French subjects, the natives of the territories conquered in the nineteenth century did not benefit from any political rights metropolitan citizens enjoyed and were governed in their private life by specific rules, often quite remote from those of the Civil Law.

Conversely, as of the Revolution, the perspective of plain and simple assimilation had imposed itself rather naturally to define the status of the four old colonies. There were many arguments in favor of this position, starting with the old link between the motherland and the territories concerned. Besides, as of the eighteenth century, these colonies would send to Paris or to Versailles delegates to defend their interests with the public authorities. The setting up of Colonial Assemblies moreover took place parallel to the institutionalization of the provincial assemblies in the motherland (cf. supra). It should be added that by decreeing the abolition of slavery, the Year II granted the colored population symbolical access to citizenship. Similarly, the members of the Convention had shown their determination in not giving way to the separatist temptations of the plantation owners adamant to take their distance from Paris to better stand for their rights. The principle of assimilation, stated for the first time under the Convention, aimed to put an end to these temptations. This assimilationist state of mind could indisputably be found in the Constitution of the Year III. The latter indeed asserted: "the French colonies are integral parts of the Republic" (French Constitution of the Year III, 1795, Art. 6).

Nevertheless, the universalist claim of the state to create a single citizen allegiance immediately comes up against the obstacles of the terrain: the first abolition of slavery in the Year II led the revolutionaries to deal locally with the colonists, asking for autonomy and hostile to the application of republican law, to the point of submitting the colonies to the "violation of principles and ideals which form the basis of modern sovereignty—liberty and equality, the notions of a people and of a nation" (Bancel et al. 2003, 30). Similarly, the reinstatement of slavery under the consulate represented a dramatic step backward, even if the blacks and the mulattoes were still taking part in the appointment of the people's representatives, just like any other citizen from the motherland.

Without going into detail, it would be appropriate to point out nevertheless that the July Monarchy strongly remained filled with the assimilationist theory: if the colonial charter of April 24, 1833, set up institutions specific to the colonies, by substituting, for example, Colonial Councils for general councils, it granted natives political rights identical to those of the mainland French people, a provision which admittedly hardly jeopardized the political supremacy of the white people, since free colored men were outnumbered and the census suffrage was applied (Rosanvallon 1992).

After the second abolition of slavery in 1848, the revolutionary heritage, which weighed decisively on the destiny of the French colonies of the Caribbean, was reactivated in the form of a claim in favor of equality of rights. This reactivation thus followed the alignment of the local political and administrative institutions with those of the motherland. First of all, embodied by mulattoes, the claim to equality spreads to all the layers of population thanks to emancipation. It tended to exacerbate: the Republic could not succeed in transforming the forms of domination inherited from the colonial order and the proclamation of freedom was plagued by the perpetuation of inequalities within strongly hierarchical societies on the basis of racial criteria. These delays were clearly noticeable under the Second Republic, whereas on the institutional and political level, civic and political equality was proclaimed quite early, the political rights and the universal suffrage were about to be exerted and globally respected throughout the Second Republic, in social terms, measures of social control kept the former slaves, now "new citizens," in a narrow system of obligations inspired by the former social-legal state. Citizenship was then emptied of its substance.

The same observation can be made under the Third Republic—and to some extent beyond that (Sainton, 2003)—through the paradox of the constantly reiterated proclamation of a civil equality, however, coupled with an indisputable exclusion of citizens newly emancipated from the domain of certain civil and political rights. The result was that ordinary law steadfastly remained on the shelf. That distance was at the heart of the often complex relationships between the Republic and the four old colonies. It became quite obvious when examining the treatment reserved to their populations, who were constantly taken back to their condition as "citizens entirely apart," according to the famous formula of Aimé Césaire from other circumstances that are, nonetheless, revealing an undeniable historical continuity beyond various political-institutional incarnations of the Republic (Larcher 2011).

Such is the profound meaning of the claim for assimilation which ended, almost one century after the abolition of slavery, with the departmentalization of 1946. In the face of the repeatedly postponed promise of assimilation, the idea, in a certain way, was to fulfill the promises of a dreamed-of Republic which not only enabled opening and exercising rights, but also enjoying full recognition within the Republic. It is no accident that the legislative and regulatory regime of the future overseas departments, and in particular article 3 of the bill on the application of the metropolitan legislation in the Overseas Dominions, gave rise to long and arduous disputes. The idea, somehow, for the partisans of assimilation was to ward off the demons of the past by making the future texts directly applicable to these new departments, at the risk of paving the way for the French centralizing tradition and of crushing the identity of the local societies. This approach will be found at the origin of the recurrent denunciation of excessive centralization and will turn the main instigator of the act of March 19, 1946, Aimé Césaire, into one of the first to dispute centralization. It still reveals the difficult conciliation between the principle of assimilation and the compliance with local particularisms.

Between Centralization and Calls for Autonomy

Undeniably, the process of becoming a full-fledged French department corresponded to a demand for allegiance to a community of fully exercising citizens. It materialized in reality through a process, spread in time, of extending ordinary law to colonial bodies, henceforth transformed into (overseas) departments, whereas they were in the past governed by the principle of legislative specialty which set them apart from most laws and rules adopted in Paris. Falling in line with emancipation, largely felt as a state of incompleteness, it was welcome in the Antilles as the means to escape from a colonial order aiming to perpetuate the social and racial discriminations against the descendants of slaves. However, it should be recognized that various factors and behaviors quickly gave rise to disappointment in the former colonies, starting with the delays followed by the administrative and legislative obstacles encountered during the implementation of social rights, despite being at the very heart of the expectations of local populations. For example, the order of October 4, 1944, establishing the social security system in France did not apply to overseas departments, which were still colonies at the time of its publication; similarly, the Law of August 22, 1946, unifying all of the French laws governing family benefits did not come into force immediately in the overseas departments due to the lack of an implementing decree for these new departments. In general, the application of social laws was almost always delayed: it was not until 1996 that social equality—expected since 1946—was proclaimed by President Jacques Chirac on an official trip to Martinique, the occasion of the … fiftieth anniversary of departmentalization.

Secondly, the reluctance of the French government to implement the principle of legislative identity and the restrictive interpretation of texts constituted serious obstacles to the realization of the ideal of social equality: faced with the incremental costs associated with the full and immediate application of the texts, the adaptation laid down by article 73 of the Constitution was established as doctrine by the French government (Lubin 1996). It was therefore decided to either adapt or not to extend a number of social measures to the overseas departments: unemployment compensation schemes only came into effect in the overseas departments in 1978. This reluctance resulted in incessant struggles at the departmental level to try and force the unyielding central government to take into account the social component of citizenship.

Finally, the persistence of an explosive economic and social situation contributed not insignificantly to the disenchantment toward departmentalization. On the one hand, the perpetuation of inequality was clearly evident, despite the affirmation of a principle of equality, due to delays in the extension of laws and regulations to overseas departments: the colonial order tended to perpetuate itself; local societies were divided between a mass of poor workers for whom social rights remained, to a large extent, on the distant horizon, and a handful of entrepreneurs that enjoyed monopolies inherited from the colonial period. Added to this mix was discrimination: officials from hexagonal France or other French territories received a salary supplement converted into a cost of living allowance that local residents were unable to claim, which triggered a general strike by officials on May 15, 1953, seeking an alignment.

All these tensions sometimes lead to major crises, the best known of which in the period examined being those of December 1959 in Martinique and of May 1967 in Guadeloupe. To this, we can add the centrifugal tendencies that develop in overseas departments, as seen in their contestation of their status and their demands for autonomy, underpinned by the processes of decolonization occurring throughout the world. Departmentalization is thus, to some degree, experienced as being a betrayed hope and hence the gradual assertion of the autonomist movement during the 1960s and 1970s in the French Antilles.

This movement, in favor of a political autonomy and of a development model and more respectful of the local specificities, reached its peak with the "Convention for the autonomy" of Morne Rouge in Martinique in August 1971; it most certainly showed a growing dissatisfaction as regarded conditions for implementation of the departmentalization, without still succeeding in reaping the effects on the electoral level by virtue of a paradox inherent to the Republican model properly speaking: "the gap between the real and the ideal, the Republic contradicted by its own actions had never, to date, been an obstacle to its force of uniting, producing and reproducing a common political culture enrooted in its founding moments and driven toward the future. From the Marianne symbol to the social elements, the path was always possible. The defects of the real Republic could but be traced back to its own incompleteness" (Bertho 2005: 15–16). In other words, fueled by the distance maintained between the proclaimed ideal and the experienced reality, the social mobilizations and the fight for equality of rights contribute, in a certain way, to strengthening the citizens' attachment to the Republican framework, the cruel deficiencies of which they are currently experiencing. It is the reason why the responses made to the claims emerging locally hardly went further than an adaptation of the departmental system or marginal adjustments in the context of administrative reforms designed for mainland France.

Attempts of Adaptation and Marginal Adjustments

As a process of extension of the ordinary law to local authorities governed by the principle of legislative specialty, departmentalization required that the administrative machine, even subjected to a powerful centralizing logic and to high uniformizing trends, would adapt to the field asperities. Such adaptation followed two complementary modalities: on the one hand, it took on the form of politico-institutional mechanisms especially designed for the overseas territories, as it was the case of adapted departmentalization in the 1960s; on the other hand, it implied the adaptation of the mechanisms applicable in France to the specific situation of the overseas territories.

On the first score, the adapted departmentalization reform launched in 1960 can be analyzed as a reply to the effects of centralization going along with the institutional assimilation which took place in 1946. The prefects, who conformed to the norm of the governors without always benefiting from the means necessary to exert their authority over state services, experienced the greatest difficulties to get the upper hand in the bureaucratic concert locally as well as in Paris. The record of the Larousse dictionary in the early 1950s is significant in that respect: "The governor is replaced with the prefect; whereas the former was the head of all the State services and there settled most problems on the spot, the latter only has the attributions of the Home Secretary; the technical services are linked with each corresponding metropolitan ministry. The prefect must simply coordinate the initiative" (Dumont 2010: 159).

It was hence in a context of socioeconomic crisis and of extreme social tension which degenerated into bloody confrontation with security forces in December 1959 in Martinique that the government decided to relax the too rigid context of departmentalization and to institute a system of administration which was more deconcentrated and more decentralized in the Overseas Dominions. Three decrees published on April 29, 1960, were designed to meet these objectives. It still ought to be noted that these texts, forming a coherent whole, especially those relative to the prefectoral authority and to the consular chambers, were quite similar, through their spirit of the land use planning policy outlined as of 1955 and of the experiments carried out at the time in Burgundy and in High Normandy, experiments which conferred the prefect the same coordinating powers and to the consultative bodies the same council role. By a curious turn of history, the overseas departments thus anticipated the reforms to be implemented later on throughout France.

On the one hand, the idea was, overseas as well as in hexagonal France, to remedy the lack of coordination in the actions initiated by the government offices in the department, the diminished authority of the prefect due to the increasingly important vertical links between technical ministries and local services. So, the decree relative to administrative deconcentration foreboded and launched the deconcentration measures to take place as of 1964 in the whole of mainland France. It emphasized the administrative deconcentration mechanisms dating back to 1953: the prefect became secondary officer for all of the government civil expenses; article 2 of the decree evidently went beyond the texts in force in the motherland by granting him the power to coordinate the activities of all the civil department heads and by strengthening his authority on the latter who lost their attributions as a secondary officer. To put it otherwise, this decree quite largely anticipated the reform of 1964, rendering the prefect the sole holder of the decision power at local level. Admittedly, the effects of the reform were going to be counteracted in France by persisting vertical links between technical ministries and local services. However, with the simple consequences of the texts, the prefect was consecrated all at once in the overseas department as the director of orchestra of all the activities of the state. He reinforced this position by relying on his community insertion, so that one may consider that the concrete deconcentration experiment was finally initiated in 1964 in the Overseas Dominions.

On the other hand, article 3 of the decree relative to the adaptation of the legislative regime and of the administrative organization of the overseas departments aims to compile the opinions and to ensure the participation of the driving forces (in that particular instance, the consular chambers) in the management of the department, in accordance with the model of the consultation system and of the consultative administration, which tended to get the upper hand and went from strength to strength in the 1960s.

Adapted departmentalization hence was in line with wider administrative reforms, beyond the simple resolution of current economic and social problems and thought out at hexagonal France scale. If the objectives may differ here and there according to the local contingencies, the methods and the instruments remained basically the same: those which were mobilized in the overseas departments were often borrowed from the experiments in progress in metropolitan France, when they did not forebode them. The aim was more especially to promote an economic and social policy for enhancing the standard of living so as to fight nascent separatism, by associating with the action of the government and of its delegate, the prefect, and the departmental assemblies in the essential domains of legislative initiative and of economic supervision, while involving the local and professional interests. That reform can hence be analyzed both as an attempt of decentralization and a political strategy intended for capturing, for its own benefit, a beginning of contestation of the overseas department status as of the early 1950s, notably in Guadeloupe and Martinique. The objective pursued was threefold: to take into account the social demands generated by a development which was either poorly mastered or deemed ill-suited in these territories, to locate the possible sources of conflicts, and to undermine any nascent contestation. The method, for its own part, consisted in relying on an administrative technology deeply impregnated with the administrative reformism of the 1960s, but fueled and enriched in return, by the experiments conducted overseas.

On the second point, the territorial and administrative reforms which took place in France during the 1980s and 1990s gave rise, under the vigilant eye of the Constitutional Council, to marginal adjustments, without modifying substantially a model of administration fed with the principles of uniformity and of centralization. This was the process with the phase I of decentralization, launched in the early 1980s, which passed into the overseas departments a reform aiming to reinforce the local powers but first of all designed for metropolitan France. All the more so since the Constitutional Council invalidated in December 1982 a law tending to simplify the institutional landscape of the four overseas departments by substituting a unique deliberating assembly for the general councils and regional councils which cohabit on the same territories following the creation in 1972, in the interests of alignment on the metropolitan standards, of regions (so-called mono-departmental regions in comparison with the hexagonal regions encompassing several departments) overlapping the departments.

The application of reforms designed by and for mainland France combined with marginal or inadequate adjustments—a case in point being the mono-departmental region created in 1972—explains why the question of the future of the overseas departments within the French Republic has been filled permanently political life in the French Antilles since the late 1950s. It is almost as if these territories have found themselves engaged in a long-standing stalemate: the rigidity of the French administrative model on the one hand, and the issues associated with the application of ordinary laws for the French Antilles—including at institutional level—on the other have prevented the development of solutions adapted to local situations. However, in the 2000s, a double movement converged to pave the way for institutional and status changes: the ramping-up of local demands for the accommodation of difference—between mainland France and the overseas departments and within the latter—and the transformation of the symbolic and material logics that shape public policies in France.

A Key Role for the French State

One area in which the transformation of the French Caribbean islands into French departments in 1946 raised enormous expectations was social and economic development. Grounded as it was in the universalist ideal that characterized the French state, economic and social "assimilation" of the four old colonies into mainland French life was an idea that matched frequently voiced local ambitions to bring an end to the under-development that contradicted the Republican notion of equality. Thus, increased public spending, infrastructure development, and a system of financial incentives were the main measures to attain an objective that scarcely changed over the years: to match the standard of development of mainland France. This strategy had three major repercussions: first, it undoubtedly fueled remarkable levels of economic and social development in Guadeloupe and Martinique, which together make "showcase" for France and Europe in the Caribbean thanks in particular to a remarkable level of community facilities; second, it is evident that this prosperity is only apparent for the most part since development in Guadeloupe and Martinique owes far more to massive transfers of public money, granted for the sake of "catching up" with the mainland, than to the growth of their own internal economies. Moreover, structural unemployment affects about 25% of the active population, and both islands are suffering from a chronic trade deficit, with all trading links built around exports of a small number of agricultural products (mainly bananas and rum) and an ever greater volume of imports financed by social transfers. Finally, another consequence of the strategy was that from 1946, it helped to confer a key role to the state as the highest instigator of a form of development that was directed from above. From the 1960 program law to the 2003 French Overseas Programme Law (LOPOM) and it extension the law of 2009 for economic development in the overseas departments, along with the 1986 program law and the December 13, 2000, orientation law for the overseas department (LOOM), the logic behind them is the same; they are economic measures alleging to respond to the local disquiet and grievances, by orienting the development model. These measures are generally preceded by the injection of public capital into the island economies, and through various forms of support via the transfer of social monies or tax exemptions. While stimulating economic growth over the short term, they contribute to amplifying society's internal disparities and maintaining a vicious circle of recurrent grievances.

Under these conditions, the persistence in the Antilles of claims in favor of an institutional evolution or of a change in status became all too clear. From this point of view, the reforms currently in progress or contemplated indisputably consecrated a change in paradigm associated with the quest for new forms of governance.

A Change in Paradigm: The Quest for New Forms of Governance

This change in paradigm resulted from the intrusion of the thematic of diversity within the French public space, including in the Antilles, and of its application to the institutional reforms. It notably resulted in an emblematic reform of the French constitution in 2003, taking into account the diversity of the overseas situation and into the elaboration of territorial reforms consecrating differentiated evolutions, reforms which turned (Guiana and) Martinique, through a curious feedback effect, into laboratories of institutional engineering anticipating the changes contemplated in France.

The Triumph of the Thematic of Diversity and the Turning Point of 2003

The thematic of diversity has long remained absent from the toolbox of the French public policies and from the decision makers' discursive repertoire. In the 1990s, in light of the proven weakening of the French model of assimilating populations from a migrant background, it was first of all acclimatized in the field of human resources, through the recognition and the dissemination of the "differences" from three points of view, social, cultural, and ethnic (Sebag and Méhaignerie 2004). Indeed, the arrival to power of the left-wing coalition in France in 1997 triggered the transition from an interpretation in terms of the "integration" of the situation of migrants and their children, which had prevailed in the 1990s, to a new interpretation in terms of "discrimination."

Similarly, the actions of the EU legitimized the fight against discrimination, especially on grounds of race and origin (Masclet 2012). Progressively transformed into a legitimate subject of public policies intended for populations victims of discriminations and thus demonstrating the will to assume responsibility for the representation of minorities (Masclet 2012; Sénac 2102) and to better consider the difference often claimed by the French Antilles, the rhetoric of diversity now has pervaded political debate in all of France, including in the overseas territories. In the latter case, that evolution progressed in two forms:

- On the one hand, this paradigm change is revealed in the ritual affirmation of the extraordinary diversity, and the great cultural wealth of the overseas territories, to such an extent that now we refer to "overseas areas" in the plural. At the same time, according to the case law of the European Court of Justice,* frequently cited by Martinique's elected representatives, "Discrimination consists of treating differently identical situations or treating identically different situations," which has undoubtedly contributed to the shift toward this new paradigm. It has also found space to grow in the institutional and statutory reforms implemented overseas, which are spurred by the re-emergence, since the 1990s, of the critique of the uniformity of the French model of local government and of the uniform application of legal systems throughout the entire national territory, regardless distinctive local particularities. Obviously, this is a discourse that is echoed and amplified in the French territories of the Caribbean where the possibilities of adaptation or of special dispensation with respect to national law have long been judged insufficient or inefficient. This is especially the case because identity claims are superimposed on institutional demands, difficult to reconcile with the constitution, or more precisely with the restrictive (at best) jurisprudence of the *Conseil constitutionnel* [Constitutional Council]. French territorial communities overseas, in general, and the French territories of the Caribbean in particular, are forced to re-evaluate their relationships with an external and far-removed center that is motivated by standardization and is sometimes blind to local particularities. So, recognition and taking into consideration institutional diversity tends to come to the fore as the only way to guarantee the medium-term existence of the unitary state, by allowing it to better integrate local autonomous bodies and, thus, start to defuse the tensions associated with a model confronting the weakening of its normative, abstract, and universal references. Far from constituting a threat to unity, diversity is then presented as a condition of its preservation. Consequently, this explains the institutional reforms in the French territories of the Caribbean since 2003.
- On the other hand, the paradigm of diversity increasingly conditions the symbolic and material approach to public policies in the struggle against discrimination. In particular, among other things, these policies target citizens from local entities situated overseas, whether they live locally or on the metropolitan soil, where they encounter discrimination most often in the areas of housing and employment.

---

* Judgment of the Court (First Chamber) of February 23, 1983. *Kommanditgesellschaft in der Firma Hans-Otto Wagner GmbH Agrarhandel v Bundesanstalt für landwirtschaftliche Marktordnung*. Reference for a preliminary ruling: Verwaltungsgericht Frankfurt am Main—Germany. Storage costs for sugar—Flat-rate reimbursement. Case 8/82; Judgment of the Court (Third Chamber) of March 26, 1987. *Coopérative agricole d'approvisionnement des Avirons v Receveur des douanes de Saint-Denis and directeur régional des douanes, Réunion*. Reference for a preliminary ruling: Tribunal d'instance de Saint-Denis (La Réunion)—France. Agricultural levies—Prohibition of discrimination—Time-barring of requests for repayments. Case 58/86.

It is worth remembering that official recognition of discriminatory practices on French soil has been slow in coming. Indeed, the persistence of discrimination seems a defeat for a model whose capacity to assimilate victims of discrimination is often vaunted by the state, which is inclined to favor relations with individual citizens to the detriment of exchanges with established communities. In addition, the results obtained from assimilation in overseas departments are mitigated: the policies implemented have not been sufficient to eliminate injustices and reduce persistent inequalities, nor to challenge the discriminatory attitudes which emigrants encounter in mainland France. In other words, the so-called assimilationist policies, long considered *the* solution to the problems encountered instead acts as an illusion for those who relied on them. In fact, they collide with a sort of obdurate otherness, tending to perpetuate an unequal social order which, ultimately, is what the population concerned experience every day.

As an aggravating circumstance, the citizens of the French Antilles were directly confronted with the shortcomings of the system of departmentalization which has now admittedly reached its limits. These shortcomings are fairly known: in addition to the difficulties generated by excessive centralization and uniformizing tendencies, the superimposition of two local authorities (the department and the region) on the same space was accompanied by numerous duplications and entangled competencies*. These were amplified by the multiplication of structures: from the municipalities to the EU of which the overseas departments are integral parts, via the intermunicipal structures, the department, the region and the state, so no fewer than six forms of interfering powers in the context of a multilevel and multilayer governance which the citizen will find hard to grasp. In other words, public action unfolds in an institutional multifaceted space, but also prone to normative and political competition, detrimental to efficacy and efficiency. This complexity can be easily seen through the policies of economic development implemented locally. Thus, on the one side, the powers exercised by local authorities (the overseas regions and departments of Guadeloupe and Martinique) are hierarchically governed by the decision made by the French State in the fields of taxation and economic policy as well as by the standards imposed by the EU. On the other side, the local authorities multiply competing interventions in the field of economic development due to an unclear horizontal distribution of competencies and powers between them, which generates a complex set of scales and a confusion between different levels—supranational (EU), national (the French government), and subnational (Guadeloupe and Martinique)—of public action.†

In the face of these challenges, institutional policies offered responses which purported to adjust to the specificities of the territories. They took note of the outdated classification, gradually fallen into disuse due to the multiplication since the 1970s over the whole French overseas of the particular statuses, distributing in a dualist manner the territorial bodies situated in two distinct categories (the overseas departments [DOMs] and the overseas territories [TOMs]). So, the coming into force of the constitutional law of March 28, 2003, relative to the decentralized organization of the French republic contributed to remodeling the institutional landscape of the overseas France which since then has rested on three main pillars:

---

* For example, the standardization resulted in 1972 in a curious mimicry of the French continental model of governance leading to the creation in Guadeloupe and Martinique of a sort of "legal monster", the mono-departmental region (*région monodépartementale*): while in continental France a region encompass several departments, Guadeloupe and Martinique are simultaneously one overseas region and one overseas department.

† It all unfolded as if there existed no articulation between economic and social policy, falling under state competency, and economic development that the elected officials proudly claim responsibility for.

- On the one hand, the article 73 of the Constitution defines the status of the overseas departments and regions (Départements et Régions d'outre-mer, DROMs) as well as that of the possible single local authority replacing the latter, and set forth the full application of all the laws and rules in force in France.
- On the other hand, the article 74 established a new category, the "overseas collectivities" (Collectivité d'outre-mer, COM), whose denomination replaced that of the "overseas territories" (Territoires d'outre-mer, TOMs), and tended toward a regime of autonomy and legislative specificity (i.e., separate from that of mainland France and the DOMs).
- Finally, the title III transformed New-Caledonia into a specific entity falling in none of the previous categories, while the article 72-3 set forth that the law determines the legislative regime and the particular organization of the French austral and Antarctic lands (French acronym TAFF [Terres Australes et Antarctiques Françaisees]), to which the Clipperton Island was legally connected.

This constitutional revision opened the path to possibilities of important changes in the French Antilles. It has empowered the French overseas departments and regions, excluding Reunion, in particular with the opportunity to be less dependent on the central authorities and entitled them to test their own capacities to initiate new means of political and economic development (Mrgudovic 2012). It has thus inspired the political and administrative reforms initiated in 2010 in Martinique and testifies a new way, highly impregnated with the thematic of diversity, of considering the future of the French territories in the Caribbean within the Franco-European unit.

The purpose of these reforms was to bring a global response to the multifaceted disquiet revealed by the socioeconomic crisis of February–March 2009 throughout the DOMs, mainly in Guadeloupe and Martinique.* Certainly, the statutory issue was not new in the Antilles–Guiana. It paced with variable intensity the local political life and has structured the party system since the late 1950s (cf. supra). Beyond the adjustments on the fringe of the departmentalization system, a reforming attempt in the extension of the constitutional revision of 2003, which widened the field of opportunities in terms of statutory evolution, resulted in a double failure in the Antilles: consulted on December 7, 2003, about the creation of a single authority replacing the department and the region, on the basis of the article 73 of the Constitution, the Guadeloupeans massively rejected that option (72.98%), whereas their counterparts of Martinique had turned down narrowly (50.48%). In parallel, St. Martin and St. Barthelemy broke away from Guadeloupe to become autonomous overseas entities (COM), thereby adding to the diversity of the situations encountered in the overseas territories.

The reforms initiated in 2010 resulted from the conjunction of a series of factors which had strongly swayed their final content. The same goes with the re-launched statutory debate and with the adoption, in December 2008, by the congresses of the elected departmental and regional officials of Martinique, of resolutions in favor of the creation of a single local authority on the basis of the article 74 of the Constitution (i.e., the transformation of the French Antilles into a COM, like St. Martin and St. Barthelemy or French Polynesia, with a regime of autonomy and

---

* The crisis erupted at the end of 2008 in Guadeloupe and spread to the rest of the DOMs over the ensuing few months in the context of a global economic crisis that had translated into yet another increase in the price of petrol (already higher in the French overseas territories due to the distribution monopolies that prevail there). It then develops into a protest movement against *la vie chère* (the high cost of living) with the "Alliance against Profiteering" (*Lyannj Kont Pwofitayon* or LKP) becoming the driving force of the protest in Guadeloupe (Mrgudovic 2012: 93).

legislative specificity); of the organization of the Estates General at the initiative of the president of the Republic in the wake of the crisis of February–March 2009, whereof one of the major feature was to deprive the elected officials of the political word and the strong resurgence of the social issue, eclipsed for a while by the identity claims; and, finally, of the circumspect acceptance of the local populations to the project of creation of single authority on the basis of the article 73 of the Constitution, having rejected the transformation into a COM.

A circumspect adherence to the reform, indeed: if the Martinicans quite clearly stated what they did not wish by rejecting without any ambiguity on January 10, 2010, the option of the article 74 of the Constitution (the transformation into a COM), their vastly overwhelming vote on January 24 in favor of the creation of a single local authority within the framework of the article 73 of the Constitution, was offset by low mobilization of the electoral body, as reflected in the analysis of the results of the consultations of January 10 and 24, 2010. Indeed, the participation, relatively high on January 10, 2010, in view of the ratios traditionally observed, saw a notable decrease on January 24, a decrease that combined with an increase in the number of blank and invalid votes which can be analyzed as a kind of indecision or of refusing to choose among the different options: from 55.32 the participation rose to 35.81% (–19.51). Against this low mobilization context, the percentage of the blank and invalid ballots represents 4.71% (versus 3% on January 10).

Adopted in the wake of this double consultation, the law of the July 27, 2011, relative to the local authorities of Martinique offers simplification of the institutional landscape by substituting for the department and region a single authority exerting the competencies devolved to the latter. Apart from the setting up in Martinique of an executive board, whose responsibility might be engaged before the deliberating assembly on the basis of a constructive no-confidence motion, the reform intended to align the new entity on the metropolitan model of regions. In parallel, the organic law of the July 27, 2011, modified the duration of the authorization enabling the local authorities operating under the article 73 of the Constitution to exert a normative power in a limited number of matters. That duration was henceforth based on that of the term of office so as to match it with the time of public policies. Furthermore, the field of application of the authorization procedure was extended to the regulatory domain.

Indisputably, the aim of this second mechanism was to strengthen the local powers. For its own part, the creation of a single local authority replacing the regions and the departments confirms the tendency to institutional and statutory differentiation initiated for several years. In the same geographical region (Caribbean-America), different categories of local authorities as well as distinct choices cohabit, from the viewpoint of the administrative organization, within the same statutory category. Whereas Guadeloupe opted for the status quo, Martinique abandoned the legendary category of overseas department, St. Barthélemy and St. Martin became COMs in 2007.

Laboratories of Institutional Engineering?

For the moment, in the absence of hindsight, it is difficult to assess the significance of these reforms that are coming into effect very gradually. In reality, only the public policy mechanisms associated with them will give a clear idea insofar as they essentially have an institutional dimension. However, one thing seems certain: the institution of the Congress of local and regional authorities (Law of December 13, 2000), established to discuss institutional issues and make proposals to the French government, has already had an unexpected impact. The Congress was transformed into a space for discussion and coordination of public policies carried out at different levels, which does not match its original purpose but demonstrates the willingness of the authorities to tackle certain issues, going over and above the powers assigned to them.

On a more general level, the territorial reform initiated in Martinique in 2010 could serve as inspiration for mainland France. When the old debate on the future of the department was fueled again in France and when the merge of the Alsace region and of its both departments was contemplated, the setting up of a single authority in Martinique might be akin to a sort of pilot experiment. It seems anyway to favor interactions with the experience of the local authorities in hexagonal France. It would undoubtedly be pointless to deny the specificity of the overseas territories: their institutional regime results from a long history during which increasingly diversified statuses have been designed gradually, henceforth in close association with the local populations. Nonetheless, even if the evolution in metropolitan France was slower than the responses to the demands expressed by the overseas populations, the most recent developments, comforted by various indices, still tend to back up this assumption. This is true for the statement by the current president of the Senate in France who on the eve of the "forum on local democracy" in October 2012 pronounced a speech that many elected overseas officials, long in favor of the recognition of the diversity of territories and of the possibility to adapt the law according to the specificities in domains determined by the legislator, would not disown. Obviously, this new discourse reminds the provisions of the article 73 of the Constitution conferring to the dependent territories a power of normative derogation, which enabled them to adapt the law. It should also be noted that it echoed the recommendations of the Association of the French regions (Association des Régions de France, ARF), also in favor of granting to the regions a mission of fixing, through a "regulatory power delegated by law, essential rules in terms of estate preservation, environmental development, travels and town planning" (Association des Régions de France 2002). The ARF also suggests breaking free from "republican equalitarianism in terms of decentralisation" and accepts the principle of differentiation when exercising competences on the basis of experimentations (which can be unique) conducted by a specific region, who might be the only one to benefit therefrom. Such a proposal clearly matches the claims which have been voiced regularly by elected overseas officials.

References

Association des Régions de France. 2002. Les régions au coeur du nouvel acte de la décentralisation, Dossier de presse, pp. 4–5. http://www.google.com/url?sa=t&rct=j&q=&esrc=s&source=web&cd=1&ved=0CB4QFjAA&url=http%3A%2F%2Fwww.arf.asso.fr%2Fwp-content%2Fuploads%2F2012%2F07%2FARF8610_DossierPresse_WEB.pdf&ei=Ff_-VMC-AqTX7QbbloDoAg&usg=AFQjCNFZcdyxKlGDksuyhum9KnTgIiXIuA&bvm=bv.87611401,d.ZGU.
Bancel, N., P. Blanchard, and F. Vergès. 2003. *La République Coloniale. Essai Sur Une Utopie*. Bibliothèque Albin Michel Idées. Paris, France: Albin Michel.
Bertho, A. 2005. Malaise dans La République. *Mouvements* 38: 14–18.
Dumont, J. 2010. *L'amère Patrie. Histoire Des Antilles Françaises Au XXe Siècle*. Paris, France: Fayard.
Larcher, S. 2011. *L'autre Citoyen*. Universalisme Civique Et Exclusion Sociale Et Politique Au Miroir Des Colonies Post-Esclavagistes De La Caraïbe Française (Martinique, Guadeloupe, Années 1840-Années 1890). PhD dissertation, EHSS.
Lubin, B.-F. 1996. Les méandres de la politique sociale outre-mer. In Fred Constant and Justin Daniel (eds), *1946–1996: Cinquante ans de départementalisation oute-mer*. Paris, France: L'harmattan, pp. 73–95.
Masclet, O. 2012. *Sociologie de La diversité et des discriminations*. Paris, France: Armand Colin (Domaines et approches).
Mrgudovic, N. 2012. The French Overseas Territories in transition. In Peter Clegg and David Killingray (eds), *The Non-Independent Territories of the Caribbean and Pacific: Continuity or Change?* London: Institute of Commonwealth Studies, pp. 65–86.

Rosanvallon, P. 1992. *Le Sacre Du Citoyen. Histoire du suffrage universel en France*. Paris, France: Gallimard.
Sainton, J.-P. 2003. Modalités du passage de l'esclavage à la citoyenneté aux Antilles françaises sous la Seconde République (1848–1850). *Société française d'histoire d'Outre-mer* 90(36): 338–339.
Sabeg, Y., and L. Méhaignerie. 2004. *Les oubliés de l'égalité des chances*. Report. Paris, France: Institut Montaigne.
Sénac, R. 2012. *L'invention De La Diversité*. Paris, France: PUF.
Tocqueville, A. de, and J.P. Mayer. 1989. *L'ancien Régime et la révolution*. Paris, France: Gallimard.

Chapter 4

The History of Public Administration in the Dutch Caribbean

Miguel Goede

Contents

Introduction 78
The Early Colonial Era 79
    First Period (1634–1688) 79
    Second Period (1648–1791) 80
    Third Period (1795–1914) 81
The Oil Era and Industrialization (1915–1960) 83
After the Oil Era 84
    The 1960s: Rebellion 84
    The 1970s: Rebuilding 85
    The 1980s: Restructuring 86
The 1990s and Beyond: Crisis and Consultation 87
    The 2000s: Radicalization 89
    New Directions? 90
Conclusion 92
References 93

Abstract: The term *Dutch Caribbean* refers to the islands of the Kingdom of the Netherlands that are located in the Caribbean and their inhabitants. In the pre-colonial era, before the arrival of the Europeans, the islands were inhabited by the Caquetios Indians. The Spanish-sponsored explorers "discovered" both the Leeward (Alonso de Ojeda, 1499) and Windward (Christopher Columbus, 1493) island groups, but Spain founded settlements only on the Leeward Islands. The West India Company made Curaçao into a naval base from 1634 till 1648. The Dutch were the first to colonize

St. Maarten (Dutch: Sint Maarten). The third period is characterized by direct Dutch rule. Slavery was abolished in 1863. A long period of poverty started. The prosperity of Curaçao and that of neighboring Aruba was restored in the early twentieth century with the construction of oil refineries by the Lago company in Aruba and a Dutch–British company (Shell) in Curaçao to serve the newly discovered Venezuelan oil fields. Curaçao developed a diversified economy based on oil, tourism, and the financial sector, and ship repair was another important pillar of the economy. Between 1952 and 1969, the number of jobs at the refinery decreased as a consequence of rationalization. In Curaçao, the tourism phase was started at the beginning of the twentieth century and took off in the 1950s and 1960s, but was temporarily stopped after the events of 1969. In the 1980s, the economy of the Netherlands Antilles slowed down, and between 1983 and 1987, Curaçao was hit especially hard. Aruba's wish for autonomy was granted and Aruba seceded from the Netherlands Antilles on January 1, 1986. Between 1998 and 2000, the number of civil servants on the island government of Curaçao was significantly reduced. The Structural Adjustment Program was too ambitious for the Netherlands Antilles, and a main problem was also that the Dutch government did not honor its part of the deal. Public finances were still weak and the economy was in poor shape.

On October 10, 2010, the Netherlands Antilles was abolished. The Dutch Kingdom currently consists of the Netherlands, Aruba, Curaçao, and St. Maarten. Aruba, Curaçao, and St. Maarten are Dutch overseas semi-autonomous entities in the Caribbean, and Bonaire, Saba, and St. Eustatius have become special Dutch municipalities. In the new constitutional structure, Curaçao and St. Maarten have acquired the status of semi-autonomous entities within the Kingdom (comparable Netherlands Antilles and Aruba after 1986). Aruba retains the same status it has had since 1986. Relations with the Netherlands have varied in significance. While the islands have enjoyed a large measure of self-governance in the last century, the former colonial power has often remained important in addressing the financial conditions of these islands.

Introduction

The term *Dutch Caribbean* refers to the islands of the Kingdom of the Netherlands that are located in the Caribbean and their inhabitants. In the past, it also referred to the former Dutch territory Suriname, now the Republic of Suriname, on the northern coast of South America. Public policy and management in the Dutch Caribbean are defined by the relationship with the mother country the Netherlands and the ongoing struggle to redefine this relationship. Curaçao, St. Maarten, and Aruba are semi-autonomous entities within the Kingdom of the Netherlands, while Bonaire, Sint Eustatius, and Saba are special municipalities. This chapter discusses only the Dutch islands in the Caribbean and excludes Suriname, which is part of the South American continent.

In the pre-colonial era, before the arrival of the Europeans, the islands were inhabited by the Caquetios Indians. Their center of governance was on the mainland of Venezuela. The impression is that the Indians lived in small groups moving around the islands, that they (i.e., these groups) had some form of governance, which was part of the governance system of the Indians on the mainland, and that they commuted with some frequency. There was a cacique (chief or leader) on the island. They communicated via messages and visited by canoe. Hartog (1988) claims that in Aruba, the Indians left a mark on the population and society. The Indians left no visible influence on public policy and management of these islands (Hartog 1988; Dalhuisen et al. 1997; Römer 1998; Gibbes et al. 1999: 21).

The Spanish-sponsored explorers "discovered" both the Leeward (Alonso de Ojeda 1499) and Windward (Christopher Columbus 1493) island groups, but Spain founded settlements only on the Leeward Islands. Curaçao developed from a cattle ranch to a naval base (1499–1648) (Rupert 1999). In 1513, all 2000 Indians from Curaçao were deported to Hispaniola, Santo Domingo; the same happened in Aruba. It was only in 1526 that Curaçao became part of the public governance of Spain; Curaçao became an *encomienda* (settlement). Ranches were also established in Aruba and Bonaire, and some 33 Indians were brought back to Aruba to work on the range. The Spaniards governed the islands and a governor was appointed. Later, Curaçao was governed from Santo Domingo and subsequently from Caracas. Christianizing the Indians was important to the Spanish (Gibbes et al. 1999: 34–35). Generally, the Spaniards left no trace on the public administration of the Dutch Caribbean, even though Curaçao was under Spanish influence for 107 years. Latin influences on the society are of a later date reflecting trade with the mainland of South America (Hartog 1988; Römer 1998; Gibbes et al. 1999: 21).

The Early Colonial Era
First Period (1634–1688)

On April 6, 1634, the board of the West India Company (WIC) decided to try to conquer Curaçao (Dalhuisen et al. 1997; Gibbes et al. 1999: 38). Consequently, Curaçao was conquered in 1634 by the WIC and was used as military outpost and trade base. The island was a strategically important base for naval advances against the Spanish and later as the center of the Caribbean slave trade. When Johannes van Walbeeck of the WIC and his 400 men arrived in Curaçao, they encountered a Spanish mayor, 32 Spaniards, including 12 children and 400 Indians. In 1639, van Walbeeck was appointed the first governor. When the WIC arrived, there was a minimum of Spanish public administration, and the core task of the WIC was installing rule of law and defense of the island (Buddingh 1994; Dalhuisen et al. 1997; Römer 1998; Gibbes et al. 1999: 38).

The WIC made Curaçao into a naval base from 1634 till 1648. The construction of Fort Amsterdam was started in 1634 with the goal of defending the island and accommodating the director of the WIC, the employees of the WIC, and a few Dutch colonists in Punda (The heart of Willemstad, Curaçao). Apart from the director's residence and the house employee accommodations, only a few warehouses and one church were built (Buddingh 1994). The WIC decide to colonize the island in 1650. It became a safe haven for trade where ships could store food and water. The island developed into a stepping-stone to the Americas. The Dutch captured Bonaire and Aruba in 1636, which were only scarcely inhabited by the Indians. Aruba became a granary for the WIC until 1791, when the Dutch government reclaimed control from WIC. Columbus was the first to sight Saba, but the Dutch were the first to colonize the island in 1640 by a party sent from St. Eustatius. Because of its difficult terrain, the island's growth progressed slowly and it remains the least populated island in the Dutch Kingdom.

The Dutch were the first to colonize St. Maarten (Sint Maarten) in 1631, but within 2 years the Spanish invaded. The Dutch made a failing attempt to regain the island in 1644, but 4 years later the Spaniards abandoned the island on their own accord. In 1648, the island of St. Maarten was divided between the Dutch and the French; however, complete control of the island was seized numerous times in a series of conflicts. The British became involved as well, taking power for a 6- and 10-year stint. Finally, in 1817, the current partition line between Dutch and French was established. The island flourished under a slave-based plantation economy and the export of salt until the official abolition of slavery in 1863. The French side abolished slavery in 1848.

These early occupations were part of larger strategies of Dutch trading companies and geopolitical efforts that involved competition with Spain and Portugal. The WIC was organized similarly to the Dutch East India Company (*Vereenigde Oost-Indische Compagnie*) (VOC). The WIC was created in 1621, and the charter was set to last 24 years. Like the VOC, the WIC had five offices, called chambers (*kamers*), in Amsterdam, Rotterdam, Hoorn, Middelburg, and Groningen, which contributed to the company. The board consisted of 19 members, known as the "Heeren XIX" (the Lords Nineteen). Funding was arranged in 1623, after several bidders were put under pressure; the States General (*Staten Generaal*, or Parliament) of the Netherlands and the VOC pledged 1 million guilders in the form of capital and subsidy. Unlike the VOC, the WIC had no right to deploy military troops, but when the Twelve Years' Truce in 1621 was over, the Republic had a free hand to re-wage war with Spain. A "grand design" (*Groot Desseyn*) was devised to seize the Portuguese colonies in Africa and the Americas (Brazil), in order to dominate the sugar and slave trade. When this plan largely failed, privateering became one of the major goals of the WIC. The arming of merchant ships with guns and soldiers to defend themselves against Spanish ships was of great importance, and almost all ships in 1623 had 40–50 soldiers on board. In the early beginning, privateering was the most profitable activity of the WIC. In 1628, Piet Hein hijacked the Spanish treasure fleet which, in today's currency, is valued at 100 trillion Euros.

The company was initially relatively successful; in the 1620s and 1630s, many trade posts or colonies were established. In 1629, the WIC gave permission to a number of investors in New Netherlands to found "patroonship," a neo-feudal system, where patrons were allowed considerable powers to control the overseas colonies. Settlements included the New Netherlands area (including present-day New York, Connecticut, Delaware, and New Jersey), and several islands in the Caribbean and on the South American coast (including Berbice Suriname, and Guyana). In Africa, posts were established on the Gold Coast (now Ghana), the Slave Coast (now Benin), and briefly in Angola. African settlements traded slaves mainly destined for the plantations on the Antilles and Suriname.

From the last quarter of the seventeenth century, the group of islands consisted of six undisputedly Dutch islands: Curaçao (settled in 1634), Aruba (settled in 1636), Bonaire (settled in 1636), St. Eustatius (settled in 1636), Saba (settled in 1640), and St. Maarten (settled in 1648). Before that, Anguilla (1631–1650), the present-day British Virgin Islands (1612–1672), St. Croix, and Tobago had also been Dutch.

Second Period (1648–1791)

In 1648, after the signing of the Peace of Munster, the Netherlands obtained their independence from Spain, and as a consequence, Curaçao lost its relevance as a naval base. Slave trade started slowly but really took off in 1662, when the Dutch attained the Asiento, and lasted till 1791. The island was mainly used for transshipment (Gibbes et al. 1999: 42–50). From 1634 through 1654, Curaçao was governed in accordance with a rule (*Reglement*) of 1629 (Gibbes et al. 1999: 52), and in 1634, a tax system was introduced (Metry 2006: 45). The islands were governed by a director appointed by the Heeren XIX of the WIC with the approval of the States General.

The director resorted under a board in Brazil (Novo Holanda), but when Brazil was lost in 1654, this entity was moved to New Netherlands, where Peter Stuyvesant was appointed director in 1654. Curaçao was ruled by a vice-director (Boxer 1993; Gibbes et al. 1999: 52–53). When New Netherlands was traded with the British in 1664 for Suriname, the Leeward Islands were governed by an entity consisting of a director, assisted by a board of WIC servants, the commissioner of slave trade, a captain lieutenant of the army, and some citizens. The board was appointed by the Heeren X.* In theory, the WIC dominated the governance of the islands. However, in practice the colonizers, who were Dutch citizens, took land and the WIC could not do much about it (Dalhuisen et al. 1997; Metry 2006). When the WIC could not repay its debts in 1674, the company was declared bankrupt. However, because of high demand for trade with the West (mainly slave trade), and the fact that many colonies still existed, it was decided to establish the Second Chartered West India Company (called, New West India Company) in 1675.† Curaçao was ruled in accordance with an instruction to the director established by the Heeren X between 1674 and the end of the nineteenth century (Gibbes et al. 1999: 54).

Although all ships, fortresses, and so forth were taken over by the new company, the second WIC lost the monopoly on the slave trade after 1730. Curaçao became a free port, attractive for colonization, and positioned itself as a regional port. As a consequence, Punda soon became overcrowded. It was inhabited by employees of the WIC, troops, traders, plantation owners, seamen, and skilled laborers (Budding 1994). In 1776, St. Eustatius saluted the Andrew Dorea of the United States and recognized the United States as an independent nation. This act was punished by Britain in 1781 by bombarding the island; only in 1815 did it return to Dutch hands (Sluis 2004: 24). After the Fourth Anglo-Dutch War (1780–1784), it became apparent that the Dutch West India Company was no longer capable of defending its own colonies, as St. Eustatius, Berbice, Essequibo, Demerara, near Suriname, and some forts on the Dutch Gold Coast were rapidly taken by rivals England and France. On May 27, 1791, the Second WIC was declared bankrupt and the director and commanders of the islands were informed and they immediately resorted under the States General, which still influences public administration today (Metry 2006: 34).

In short, the Dutch Antilles were governed by the WIC from 1634 to 1791. In 1791, the company's stock was bought by the Dutch government. On January 1, 1792, all territories previously held by the WIC reverted to the rule of the States General (*Staten Generaal*, or Parliament) of the Dutch Republic.

Third Period (1795–1914)

The third period is characterized by direct Dutch rule. In 1795, the Netherlands became the French Batavian Republic and most of the Dutch colonies were seized by the English. The ideals of the French revolution reached the islands and inspired rebellion of slaves. The segmented society of Curaçao was ruled by a governor assisted by the Colonial Council. The governor and the troops lived and worked in Punda, Fort Amsterdam. Punda was the living place of the whites and Jews. In 1789, the population was 19,544: 2,469 white protestants, 1,495 Jews, 2,776 colored, 12,804 slaves. There were 1,067 houses. Besides the Punda district, there were two other districts consisting of 200 plantations. In 1795, approximately 2,000 slaves rebelled demanding the abolishment of slavery just like France did in 1794. At the time, the Netherlands was occupied by France.

In the second half of the eighteenth century, St. Eustatius became the commercial hub of the north-eastern Caribbean. It earned the nickname "The Golden Rock," based on arms trade related

---

* The number of board members was reduced in 1674. XIX and after 1674 by the Heeren X.
† The new WIC had a capital that was slightly more than 6 million guilders around 1679, which was largely supplied by the Amsterdam Chamber. This new company had the same trade area as the first. The number of directors was reduced from 19 to 10, and the number of governors from 74 to 50.

to the war of independence of the United States. This invoked the envy of the French and English, who from 1781 on made sure the island lost that position by occupying the island and ruining it—the French through their taxes and the English by closing the island off and diverting all trade to their own islands.

In 1815, the Kingdom of the Netherlands was declared. From 1815 (*Regeringsreglement 1815*) onward, Curaçao and Dependencies (*Curaçao en onderhorigen*) formed a colony of the Kingdom of the Netherlands, resorting directly under the King, who appointed a minister of trade and colonies as his advisor. In 1815, three colonies were created: Suriname, Curaçao, and Dependencies, and the three Windward Islands: St. Maarten, St. Eustatius, and Saba. The islands were not profitable, and in 1828, the three colonies were merged and governed from Suriname. A Central Bank of Curaçao was also created by King Willem I as part of his vision to develop the economy of these colonies (Tromp 2005; Metry 2006). Due to the geographical distance, this structure did not work. In 1845, the colony of Curaçao was established, the predecessor Netherlands Antilles, bringing the six islands together in one structure for the first time.

In 1848, the Dutch constitution changed and the King had to respond to the States General. The minister of colonial affairs now reported directly to the Parliament. At the highest level, a governor was appointed as the representative of the King and the local population had no say in matters. He created a budget, and for budget deficits, he could go to the Netherlands. The governor is represented on the other five islands by a *Gezaghebber* (lieutenant governor) (Gibbes et al. 1999: 73; Van Beurden 2012). The governor had two advisory organs, constituted by Dutch civil servants and representatives of the local elite. The board gave little attention to the other five islands, which led to resistance against the government center in Curaçao (Gibbes et al. 1999: 73).

It was clear during this period that slavery would end some day; slavery was abolished in 1863. The Catholic Church became responsible for educating the slaves for freedom. At that time, the population of Curaçao was about 23,000, consisting of approximately 10,000 slaves, 10,000 free colored slaves, and 3,000 whites. By 1895, the population was about 27,000, including 4,000 whites of which 2,500 protestants and 1,500 Jews, as well as 23,500 blacks and colored, all Catholic (Chumaceiro 1894). The slaves were free but poor (Rupert 1999). The Catholics were the first to care for the well-being of the slaves, and the church would become a significant actor(s) in politics. The abolishment of slavery can be considered as economic emancipation, followed by political and cultural emancipation in the 1960s.

Based on the work of Abraham Mendes Chumaceiro, a lawyer, one gets an impression that the society was well governed and that institutions were functioning. The court was functioning on a high level (Coomans and Coomans-Eustatia 1998). However, the islands were also hit hard by the abolition of slavery in 1863, and the public finances of the colony were in terrible shape from 1867 to 1918. Only from 1883 until 1894 was there a surplus, thanks to phosphate mining in Aruba,* but by the early 1900s, the islands were again going through hardship. The population of Curaçao in the early 1900s was approximately 30,000, of Bonaire about 4,700, and of St. Maarten about 4,300. By 1919, about half of the males left Curaçao to work in the region (Van Beurden 2012). Generally, the population of the islands was decreasing, and the Netherlands had to subsidize the islands. The total annual deficit was more than 5 million guilders at the time, which was considered a burden by the Netherlands, but the Netherlands also felt the responsibility to develop the economy of the islands (Hartog 1988; Van Kol 1901; Schiltkamp 1999; Van Galen 2004).

---

* Aruba Phosphate Company operated from 1879 till 1914 (Hartog 1988).

The Oil Era and Industrialization (1915–1960)

The prosperity of Curaçao and that of neighboring Aruba was restored in the early twentieth century with the construction of oil refineries by the Lago company in Aruba and a Dutch–British company (Shell) in Curaçao to serve the newly discovered Venezuelan oil fields. With the arrival of oil, the population expanded rapidly. The oil era started in 1915, one year after the opening of the Panama Canal, and went into decline in the 1950s and 1960s. The refinery in Curaçao became operational in 1918 (Van Soest 1977; Gibbes et al. 1999: 135; Van Galen 2004). The refinery in Aruba started operating in 1928 (Dalhuisen et al. 1997). The industrial work ethic was imported and enforced upon a feudal society. The islands went from the prior period to this oil age in an extremely short period. The refineries brought prosperity to the islands.

These developments intensified the interest of the Dutch for the island as never before. The island was "Dutchinalized" (Sluis 2004: 97). This was manifested in the civil service, education system, and the growth of the churches. Before the arrival of the Dutch, the civil service was kept remarkably small to keep the cost low. As the refinery established, the civil service started to grow too, but at first it did not develop into an instrument to drive the economy and develop society. It seemed mainly to be registering data, keeping files, and making investments in the physical infrastructure (Van Soest 1977: 612–614). The policy was aimed at enabling the refinery in its operations. The number of civil servants grew from 130 to a 1,000 as soon as the oil activities started, and from time to time the whole apparatus was overhauled and expanded (Korthals Altes 1999: 29, 70). Dutch civil servants came over to support the governor, while others came to work for the refinery. This brought tension between the newcomers and the local (white protestant) elite. These developments took place in Aruba as well. However, Aruba had an American refinery Lago that started in 1924 which "Americanized" and industrialized Aruba's society. As a result, animosity was directed away from the island, toward the government center in Curaçao. The Aruba population grew from 8,200 in 1920 to 51,000 in 1950 (Hartog 1988; Sluis 2004: 64).

In education, the teachers were introduced into the system created by the Catholic Church and provided by frères and nuns. Education was provided by frères and nuns. In education, the native Papiamentu language was pushed out in favor of the Dutch language. The police force and military grew and were dominated by the Dutch, especially after 1929 when a Venezuelan rebel took the governor's palace (Dalhuisen et al. 1997; Van Galen 2012). The population of Curaçao grew from 33,677 to 67,317. Curaçao became financially independent (Van Galen 2004), whereas in 1918, the budget was for 49% subsidized, and until 1923, the Netherlands subsidized the budget with 12 million guilders* annually. The government administered the money well, and after 1923, the island could start paying back its debt (Van Soest 1977: 612–614). By 1928, it no longer had a deficit. The islands would feel the consequences of the stock market crash in 1929, but in 1936 Curaçao was back on track. Social policies, education, and public housing were developed; roads were being constructed. The civil service continued to expand (Römer 1998).

In 1936, the islands were coming out of the economic crisis. This gave confidence to the population and in Aruba desire to be autonomous from Curaçao (Hartog 1988; Sluis 2004: 73). Though regulation (*Regeringregelment* 1865) was replaced by a constitution (*Curaçaosche Staatsregeling*) in 1937, changes to the government structure remained superficial, and Curaçao continued to be ruled as a colony. The colonial power introduced a limited form of the right to vote.

---

* In 1940, following the German occupation of the Netherlands, the link to the Dutch currency was broken, with a peg to the US dollar of 1.88585 guilders = 1 dollar established. The peg was adjusted to 1.79 guilders = 1 dollar in 1971 (http://www.centralbank.an/faq).

The *Staten* (Parliament) was created, but its power was limited. The Staten consisted of 15 members: 10 were elected and 5 appointed by the governor, and one of the appointed members represented the refinery. Only 3.5% of the population had the right to vote. Two political parties were created. The small islands had a minimum of representation in the Staten.

The war in Europe and prosperity in the colonies fed the desire in the Dutch Antilles to become autonomous. On December 15, 1954, the Netherlands Antilles, Suriname, and the Netherlands acceded as equal partners to an overarching Kingdom of the Netherlands as established in the Charter for the Kingdom of the Netherlands. A double layer of government was created: the central government and the island government. Curaçao became (remained) the dominant island of the Netherlands Antilles. The federal government was seated in Willemstad, Curaçao. With this move, the United Nations deemed decolonization of the territory complete and removed it from the United Nations' list of non-self-governing territories. This was intended to be the closure of the colonial period (Van Galen 2004). After 1954, the King became the symbol of unity of the Kingdom.

After the Oil Era

The 1960s: Rebellion

By now, Curaçao had a diversified economy based on oil, cruise tourism, and the financial sector, and ship repair was another important pillar of the economy. Between 1952 and 1969, the number of jobs at the refinery decreased as a consequence of rationalization (Van Galen 2004). Financial aid determined the relationship between the Netherlands Antilles and the Netherlands, from 1954 until 1970s. Between 1969 and 1995, the Netherlands Antilles received 3.5 billion Antillean guilders in financial aid. Most of the aid was invested in infrastructure that the countries could not maintain independently. Also, productive sectors were not sufficiently developed, and education lacked adequate investments (Oostindie and Klinkers 2001; Sluis 2004: 86; Van Galen 2004). From 1969 until 1995, Curaçao received one of the highest amounts of aid per capita in the world, but still one-third of the population was living in the Netherlands (Haan 1999: 217). The aid was based on a 5-year program starting in 1960. The aid was partially a gift and partially a loan (Van Galen 2004: 120). It became another mechanism for the islands to accumulate debt.

Between 1962 and 1966, more social laws were approved by the Parliament (Reinders 1993), and in the late 1960s, government entities were corporatized. The idea was that corporations would have better access to the capital market and be better suited to hire qualified labor, because they could pay higher wages and salaries compared to the government. Later, this would become a governance disaster and a source of patronage, because the structure was not transparent and politicians and their parties started to use these corporations for political and personal gain.

The Shell refinery continued to be rationalized, and the labor class was disappointed because self-governance had raised expectations, which turned into frustration against the local (white) elite (Schrils 1990; Reinders 1993; Van Galen 2004). Notwithstanding developmental aid from the Netherlands, the poor economy led to labor conflicts and escalated into a revolt on May 30, 1969. Dutch troops came in from the Netherlands to restore order. The revolt changed the landscape of the local political elite. Power shifted from the "white (political) elite," mainly represented by the democratic party (DP), to "black men." There was a brief alliance between the intelligentsia and the labor movement, but the economic elite did not change. The revolt had a political, economic class and racial connotation, also inspired by global social movements of the 1960s, and led to expansion of the public sector. Political patronage was present and voters after elections were rewarded with a position in government. This resulted in a vast and largely unqualified apparatus, based on organizational principles of the 1930s (Schrils 1990; Reinders 1993; Römer 1995; Korthals Altes 1999; Oostindie 1999; Oostindie and Klinkers 2001). The civil service was too large, politicized, and underqualified (Schrils 1990: 54–55). Many, including the heads of departments, were politically appointed. A consequence was that the ministers (the politicians) did not trust the departments (Schrils 1990: 88–91). While Dutch financial aid was later reduced, the financial position of the islands deteriorated.

Because of these events, the government became highly protective of jobs, and local businesses were protected by government policies. And the Netherlands took an interest in the economic development of the islands (Van Galen 2004). The number of civil servants grew from 7,679 in 1969 to 11,950 in 1984 (Schril 1990: 104). The policy of Antillianization (*Antillianisering*) was started. Locals were being appointed in high positions. Curaçao became exceedingly inward looking and an economic policy based on import substitution was started (Gibbes et al. 1999: 201).

The 1970s: Rebuilding

In Curaçao, the tourism phase was started at the beginning of the twentieth century and took off in 1950s and 1960s but was temporarily stopped after the events of 1969 (Goede 2008). In 1970, it was apparent that the Dutch aid was not enough to develop the countries. A representative of the Netherlands was stationed in Curaçao to improve the aid process. Still, there was criticism that projects were granted to key Dutch firms, and part of the funds was not even used. In the period 1972–1976, about 400 million guilders were available for developmental projects (Van Galen 2004).

In the 1970s, Curaçao implemented an industrialization policy with the goal to attract industries by providing tax incentives and market protection or production monopolies (Lucia 1999: 279): the import substitution industry (Gibbes et al. 1999). On the other hand, the economy began to globalize. Investments were made in telecommunications; the container harbor and the free zone were started; and the offshore sector was booming.

After Suriname became independent in 1975, pressure was put on the Netherlands Antilles to become independent as well. This situation created uncertainty and led to speculations that Venezuela would claim the islands. A treaty was signed in 1978 establishing the sea borders between Venezuela and the islands; this decreased the tension (Schrils 1990: 227; Reinders 1993: 101 and 133). The Netherlands Antilles did not give in to Dutch pressure. The Netherlands Antilles claimed that they needed a multiyear plan of preparation (Reinders 1993: 115; Van Galen 2004: 81).

In 1974, the university was established, the free zone was created, and women obtained economic rights. The economy was in bad shape and unemployment was high (Reinders 1993: 111 and 135). An interim government was appointed (1979) to deal with urgent matters. Two important matters were the preparation of the restructuring of the civil service and handling the poor governance and corruption in St. Maarten (Reinders 1993: 141). The federal government seated in Curaçao had to play an important role in handling St. Maarten. There was a growing discontent between the islands of the Netherlands Antilles. The other islands, especially Aruba, felt dominated by Curaçao. Curaçao believed that it was subsidizing the other islands (Reinders 1993: 103; Van Galen 2004: 81).

The 1980s: Restructuring

In the 1980s, the economy of the Netherlands Antilles slowed down, and between 1983 and 1987, Curaçao was hit especially hard (Reinders 1993: 242; Haan 1999: 217). Curaçao had to cope with four shocks: the closing of the refinery, the closing of the dry dock, problems with the Antilliaanse Luchtvaart Maatschappij (ALM) airline, and the shrinking offshore financial sector. On top of this, the Venezuelan Bolivar currency was devalued, which further affected tourism from Venezuela (Reinders 1993: 193). In Curaçao, the financial services era that had started to grow in the 1960s* went into decline in the 1980s as a consequence of the termination of the tax treaty with the United States. By the mid-1980s, the budget surplus turned to a deficit. The government's budget fiscal crisis was further worsened when it was required to raise salaries of unwed civil servants by 14% in 1988, as a consequence of an international treaty prohibiting this form of discrimination (Isebia 2009). Tourism had a restart in the late 1980s to boost the economy. This was an important part of the government strategy to restructure the economy of Curaçao. Aruba implemented the same strategy to reverse the effects of the refinery leaving, and it was very successful (Zwart 2013).

In 1983, Aruba's wish for autonomy was granted and Aruba seceded from the Netherlands Antilles on January 1, 1986. While the wish of Aruba to be autonomous dates back to the 1930s, in 1977, 82% of the voters opted for the *status aparte* as a stepping-stone toward independence. Well-known Curaçao politician and prime minister of the Netherlands Antilles Evertsz at that time predicted "6 − 1 = 0," meaning that without Aruba the Netherlands Antilles of five was not sustainable. A "solidarity fund" (*Solidariteitsfonds*) was created to support the small islands, Bonaire, St. Maarten, St. Eustatius, and Saba. The fund was funded by Aruba, the Netherlands, and Curaçao (Reinders 1993: 186; Van Galen 2004). Nevertheless, this was not an auspicious beginning for Aruba. 1985 was a disastrous year for Aruba, because in 1984 the Lago oil refinery ceased operations. Public finances were in a bad shape, and an exodus, of one-third of the population to the Netherlands, occurred. When Aruba became autonomous, its debt had already accumulated up to 0.8 billion guilders and kept growing (Van Galen 2004). The population of Aruba was 60,000 and 33% of the workers were unemployed. The government performed a stunning job restructuring the economy by attracting investors in the tourism sector (Reinders 1993; Zwart 2013).

As to the civil service, consensus exists that the civil service was very inefficient and had numerous problems: inappropriate or inadequate job descriptions, too few data about the civil service, inadequate delegation of authority, poor labor conditions, poor work processes, and poor communication. In 1980, a reorganization was started, but with little result, and many more reorganizations would follow (Verton 1985). Despite the total of 20 billion guilders of aid that had been granted over the years, there was no idea how to develop the islands. Commissions were formed to develop a policy, but with little success; the debt kept growing (Van Galen 2004). The government took over the refinery from Shell for a symbolic sum of one guilder, signing a disclaimer, and rented it to the Venezuelan Petróleos de Venezuela, S.A (PDVSA).† By 1986, the problems were growing out of proportion. According to Reinders (1993: 241), the Netherlands Antilles employed 8,000 civil servants and Curaçao employed another 5,000 civil servants (total 13,000 civil servants). The working population in 1985 was estimated at 50,000. Castillo (1992)

---

* The offshore service was invented by Mr. Smeets. He helped Dutch companies establish themselves in Curaçao just before the Germans invaded the Netherlands in WW II, so as to stay out of the hands of the Germans (Van Beurden 2012).
† The current contract will expire in 2019. Also a solidarity tax of 10% was imposed on all taxpaying citizens in 1985, which was later removed by the new government coalition, replacing it with other measures (Reinders 1993).

stated that Curaçao employed 2,000 unproductive civil servants. The civil service apparatus was seen as "sick," employed too many incompetent civil servants, deadlines were not being met, and politicians intervened directly with appointments and individual cases. In 1986, a Structural Adjustment Program (SAP) (*Ekilibrio & Adelanto*) was developed and implemented. Taxes were raised, and the number of civil servants reduced to 9,000. The Dutch assisted financially (Reinders 1993; Gibbes et al. 1999: 224), but the plan was only partially implemented because the government coalition fell during the process.

In 1988 *Privantil*, a privatization program was developed but not implemented (Korthals Altes 1999). In 1985, the Government of Curaçao still employed over 6,000 people. After 1985, the number of civil servants gradually decreased to less than 1,600 by the start of the new millennium. In Curaçao, a New Public Management Program, *Bedrijfsmatige OverheidsNota (BON)* (1989–1990) was implemented, clustering the over thirty agencies in seven logic clusters. Up to that point, all agencies reported to the Executive Council (*Bestuurscollege*) via one of the seven commissioners; there was no logic behind the clustering, only a political logic. The Executive Council, however, did not approve the sector director, which was a threat to the commissioners. The merit of this project was that it created a logical structure and to some extent made it possible to discuss policies and develop solutions more rationally. This program was also only partially implemented because the politicians did not want to delegate much authority to the civil services.

Between 1984 and 1991, the wages in public and private sector were frozen and emigration to the Netherlands was high, which reduced unemployment in Curaçao from 24% to 14%. From there on, unemployment did not drop any further (Haan 1999: 222). After 1989, the policies followed the neoliberal agenda of eliminating protection of local industry and promoting competition, reflecting western policy preferences of the day, as well as outside pressure by the Netherlands and the International Monetary Fund (IMF) (Gibbes et al. 1999: 223). Finally, as a result of a coupe d'état in Suriname in 1980 and the migration of Antillean youth criminals to the Netherlands, the Netherlands changed its mind on the subject of independence of the islands. Also, Aruba was dealing with transnational organized crime, and Washington asked the Netherlands to dedicate more attention to the islands. The emphasis was now placed on development of the islands and not on guiding the islands toward independence (Van Galen 2004: 103–112).*

The 1990s and Beyond: Crisis and Consultation

Aid from the Netherlands was based on four pillars: sustainable development, good governance, justice, and education. Later, poverty reduction via non-governmental organizations was added. Good governance was put on the global agenda by the World Bank, propagating it as a condition for aid (Verton 2006). Until 1995, 3.6 billion guilders went to the islands in the form of aid, but there was growing discontent among citizens about the performance of politics and the public administration. In 1996, a study was made of the debt problem of the islands. The debt-to-GDP ratio was 80% (and for Aruba, 40%). In the mid-1990s, the Netherlands asked the IMF to supervise an SAP (Sluis 2004: 100; Van Galen 2004; Tromp 2005). In 1999, the *Commissie National Herstelplan* (Committee on National Recovery) stated that in 10 years' time, the debt of all governments combined had grown from 1.5 to 3.2 billion guilders (Gibbes et al. 1999: 227). The budget

---

* The number of consultants hired by government exploded after 1986. In 2000, the government got some grip on the consultancy costs, because the funds to finance them were drying up, but control on consultant costs was never possible.

of Curaçao was showing a structural deficit. The government tried to involve the social partners (unions and employers) in seeking for solutions.

Between 1998 and 2000, the number of civil servants on the Island Government of Curaçao was significantly reduced from 2,700 to 1,600. This was a very traumatic event for the whole community of Curaçao. This was achieved by implementing over the years a SAP alike or variations of such a program* consisting of the following:

- Stopping the hiring of new civil servants, implemented in 1986 and reinforced October 1, 1999
- Corporatization of government agencies, creating state-owned enterprises and state foundations
- The privatization of state-owned enterprises
- Dismissal of civil servants

In 1991, the Curaçao government started the Department of Economic Affairs. Up to that moment, economic affairs had been a federal matter; tourism was prioritized (Gibbes et al. 1999: 224). Curaçao was trying to stimulate the economy with public–private partnerships to build the World Trade Center and Hotel Sonesta. The Curaçao Action Group had developed downtown and stimulated cruise tourism. A program of social investments was created to cope with the consequences of the other aspects of the SAP, was implemented too late, and had insufficient resources to effectively soften the social negative effects. This led to emigration, poverty, and other social issues on the island. The island was battered by drug trafficking, with transshipment from Colombia to Europe. Crime became a big issue, and with aid from the Netherlands, a new prison was built. In the late 1990s, consultants introduced the concept of e-government but this has never been seriously implemented.

As part of the SAP in 1999, civil service was restructured and civil servants were dismissed. The government structure of the Netherlands Antilles, including the number of civil servants, was enshrined in a law (*Landsverordening Overheidsorganisatie Land Netherlandse Antillen, LOL*). By law it was now mandatory to publish the number of civil servants monthly, but this did not happen (Nauta and Goede 2007).

By 1992, things were looking good for Aruba and tourism was booming; from 1989, Aruba had no unemployment. The government employed 7,000 of the 26,000 total employed. Aruba government never really regulated the civil servants apparatus by law (Nauta and Goede 2007). A plan was developed for 1991–1995 to stabilize the developments with a focus on the social agenda, the quality of life. Five hundred and twenty million guilders of government guarantees for the newly built hotels were a threat to the fiscal policy (Reinders 1993).

St. Maarten went through a rather untamed growth since the 1970s. After the autonomy of Aruba, the economic and financial significance of St. Maarten grew within the constellation of the remaining Netherlands Antilles. St. Maarten was heavily affected by corruption and transnational organized crime, and in 1992, the island was placed under higher supervision; Dutch civil servants, employees from judicial systems, and police officers from the Netherlands were sent to the island. In 1995, the island was hit hard by hurricane Luis. However, despite this intervention, the island is still very much affected by transnational organized crime (Reinders 1993: 309–334; Sluis 2004; Van Galen 2004). In 1993, *De Toekomstconferentie* (Futures Conference) was organized to discuss the future of the Kingdom. The Netherlands hoped to settle the in-fighting between the

---

* The name of some of the programs were *Nieuw beleid* (New Policy) 1993, *Reinventing Government* 1996, *Kerntaken* (Core Tasks) 1997, *Vishon Korsou* 1998, *National Herstel Plan* (National Recovery Plan) 1999, *Nothing will be the same* 1999, *StIP* 2000, and *Nieuwe overheid* (New Government) 2002.

islands once for all, but the conference failed (Korthals Altes 1999: 183). In 1993, a referendum in Curaçao confirmed the place of all islands within the union, despite earlier talks debating the constitutional status of the islands in the early 1990s. Whereas the ruling parties in Curaçao campaigned for the dissolution of the Netherlands Antilles, the people voted for a restructuring of the Netherlands Antilles. About 74% of the voters wanted to continue as the Netherlands Antilles and less than 1% considered independence.

The 2000s: Radicalization

The SAP was too ambitious for the Netherlands Antilles and a main problem was also that the Dutch government did not keep up its part of the deal. The public finances were still weak and the economy was in poor shape. While the government of Prime Minister Pourier implemented almost 90% of the program, the Dutch did not provide financial support, as pledged.

In the 2003 local elections, the fight against poverty was, for the first time, a topic put on the political agenda of all political parties (Goede 2008) and has remained on the agenda ever since. The problem could not be ignored any longer. Serious attempts were undertaken to start a *tripartite* platform, but the government and the politicians were reluctant to share power. In 2005, the economy of Curaçao grew by a mere 0.8%. In 2006, the economy grew, but less than in 2005. The implementation of the privatization program was slow. The ALM Airline, which once employed 1,000 people but had only few aircraft, ceased operations in 2004. In 2005, the Island Territory of Curaçao reached a debt of NAf. 2.5 billion (USD 1.4 billion), equivalent to 59% of GDP, while all government combined had a debt-to-GDP ratio of 83%. Although the latest global recession ended in 2000, economic growth still has not recovered and growth rates barely exceeded 1% a year, due to mainly lack of investments. Consequently, the high unemployment rate of about 15% did not show signs of abating and would have grown even higher, if a significant part of the population had not migrated to escape the lack of decent prospects on Curaçao. In addition, youth unemployment reached a high of 37%. A report of the auditor general of The Netherlands Antilles stated that the number of civil servants in Curaçao increased from 1,336 in 2003 to 1,689 in 2006, an increase of about 400 civil servants (26%). This increase took place because the government did not keep to its self-imposed moratorium on hiring civil servants and indicates that patronage is still around. In 2007, the combined civil service apparatus of Curaçao and the Netherlands Antilles employed 3,963 civil servants.

In 2000, the constitutional reform issue arose again. In June 2000, St. Maarten held a nonbinding referendum (Beetz and Alberto 2010: 75), in which 69% of the population voted for *status aparte*—independence from the constellation of the Netherlands Antilles but remaining within the Kingdom of the Netherlands. The Dutch government did not support such a move, based on fears that St. Maarten could not support its own central bank, police force, or larger government, and wished to be involved in all discussions. This became a dominant political issue for St. Maarten and the other islands, thus negotiation began once again.

In April 2005, a referendum was held in Curaçao to determine the constitutional future of the Netherlands Antilles. The result was that the island should become an autonomous part within the Kingdom of the Netherlands and that the federal government of the Netherlands Antilles should be abolished, because it was considered costly and bureaucratic and one of the causes of the social and economic problems of Curaçao. It was seen as a possible measure to reduce government expenditure. Negotiations with the Netherlands on implementation of a new constitutional status were seen as an opportunity to reduce the national debt. The result of the talks was that the Dutch took care of a large part (85%) of the debt in exchange for having more supervision of the budget cycle of Curaçao, an increased influence on the judicial system, and the aid program would be ended after a short period. This position of the Dutch is a consequence of the fact that the Dutch admit that they are also responsible for the lack of success of the SAP by not having supported Prime Minister Pourier at the time. This led to a division in the society of Curaçao, between those in favor of more supervision by the Dutch to enforce good governance and those in favor of more autonomy for Curaçao and even independence. The consequence was that the target date for realizing the new constitutional status for Curaçao of July 2007 was postponed several times (Brede and Huisden 2012: 11).

Another "status" referendum was held in Curaçao on May 15, 2009 on whether to accept the proposed agreement on becoming an autonomous entity within the Kingdom of the Netherlands as part of the dissolution of the Netherlands Antilles. It was approved by a narrow majority of 51.99% of the voters. With the referendum, laws were approved that the Kingdom would supervise Finance and Justice of the Government of Curaçao (the *consensus rijkswetten*). The civil services of Curaçao and the Netherlands Antilles were abolished and a new civil service for Curaçao was created (Brede and Huisden 2012). The new civil service consisted of nine departments. All civil servants were given new positions in one of the nine departments. It was an agreement between the government and the civil service unions that no one would get dismissed. The apparatus would be reduced naturally by people retiring.

The reduction in the core government did not create sufficient restructuring, according to the principles of new public management. Reports of the auditor general of the Netherlands Antilles revealed that human resource processes and financial processes were not under control. But these reports also revealed that funding of semi-governmental organizations and foundations was not based on policy but was ad hoc and not transparent. In other words, the relationship between the principle and the agents is poor. The average age of civil servants is high, as a consequence of hiring freeze of hiring civil servants for a prolonged period. As a consequence, continuity has become an issue, because a large part of the civil service will retire in the coming years. The civil service has hired only a few young professionals who have brought new spirit over the past years. The Anglo-American ideal of governance has not yet been reached. In 2008, a process was created for a new organization of the civil service of Curaçao, and in 2010, the business plan for all departments was ready (Brede and Huisden 2012: 22). At the end of 2013, the minister responsible for the civil service apparatus declared publicly that the attempts to create a new apparatus had failed.

New Directions?

On October 10, 2010, the Netherlands Antilles was abolished. The Dutch Kingdom currently consists of the Netherlands, Aruba, Curaçao, and St. Maarten. Aruba, Curaçao, and St. Maarten are Dutch overseas semi-autonomous entities in the Caribbean, and Bonaire, Saba, and St. Eustatius have become Dutch municipalities.* In the new constitutional structure, Curaçao and St. Maarten have acquired the status of semi-autonomous entities within the Kingdom (comparable to the now abolished Netherlands Antilles and Aruba after 1986). Aruba retains the same status it has had since 1986. Thus, since October 10, 2010,

---

* The Dutch public bodies of Bonaire, St. Eustatius, and Saba have the power to regulate their own internal affairs. Broadly speaking, central government has taken over the duties performed previously by the Antillean authorities. And the Dutch government has also taken on certain tasks previously the responsibility of the islands, such as management of the fire service. In the short term, the aim is to improve education, public safety, public health, infrastructure, and other facilities and services on the islands.

the Kingdom now consists of four equal partners: Aruba, Curaçao, and St. Maarten are not Dutch overseas dependencies, but full, autonomous partners within the Kingdom, alongside the Netherlands, and each enjoys a degree of internal autonomy. The constitutional changes do not affect the way in which the Kingdom conducts its foreign relations. The Kingdom's external borders have not changed. Foreign relations and defense remain "Kingdom affairs." There is one minister of foreign affairs, and the Ministry of Foreign Affairs and the embassies, consulates, and permanent representations abroad continue to work for the Kingdom as a whole and all its constituent parts. Like Aruba, the new entities, Curaçao and St. Maarten, have their own government and parliament. Together, these institutions are empowered to enact legislation.

A Financial Supervision Authority has been established for Curaçao and St. Maarten to supervise public finances under the ultimate responsibility of the Council of Ministers for the Kingdom. A similar body has been set up for Bonaire, St. Eustatius, and Saba under the minister responsible for Kingdom Relations. This type of oversight structure will continue to exist in the new constitutional situation. The underlying supervisory principles are a balanced budget, prudent financial management, and a cap on contracting debt.

The existing Joint Court of Justice of the Netherlands Antilles and Aruba has become the Joint Court of Justice of Aruba, Curaçao, St. Maarten, and the Caribbean part of the Netherlands (i.e., Bonaire, St. Eustatius, and Saba). The Supreme Court in The Hague remains the court of cessation for the Caribbean parts of the Kingdom.

On January 1, 2011, the US dollar replaced the Antillean guilder in Bonaire, St. Eustatius, and Saba. Curaçao and St. Maarten have a joint central bank. The Caribbean guilder will be introduced as these countries' common currency. Until that time, the Antillean guilder will remain the official currency. The Netherlands is a European Union member state, but Aruba, Curaçao, St. Maarten, and the Caribbean part of the Netherlands (Bonaire, St. Eustatius, and Saba) are not. Instead, they have the status of overseas countries and territories within the European Union. As a result, the islands enjoy a number of advantages regarding import and export.

Curaçao has not done very well socially and economically over the last 20 years. Curaçao partially escaped the global financial crisis of 2008 until 2011. This is attributed to the debt relief by the Netherlands as part of the process of moving toward the constitutional changes of October 2010, but it also illustrates that the local economy is not very integrated with the global economy. While Curaçao's economy did somewhat better in 2006 and 2007, more recent figures from the Central Bank of Curaçao and St. Maarten indicate that the economy came to a halt. Curaçao was hit very hard by the global crisis of 2011 due to bad governance.

On January 1, 2010, Curaçao adopted the Code Corporate Governance. This very modern code structured the governance of state-owned enterprises and government foundations. The ambition was to once and for all create a corporate governance structure that would keep politics in its place and cease patronage that has been the rule for decades. After October 10, 2010, a new coalition stepped in and intervened in the appointment process of the high-ranking civil servants. The new nation was born within a passionate and emotionally divided society with deeply imbedded distrust (Brede and Huisden 2012). The government apparatus is still not functioning properly. Political appointments still occur, and there was a huge budget deficit of 200 million guilders in 2013. Money was pulled from the state-owned companies, and the debt increased with 500 million guilders. And the public prosecutor has started several investigations. There is little economic growth, and decisions on the refinery and the financial services have not been taken. Also the current agreements related to the refinery and the financial service sector will expire in 2019. The government is badly managed. On July 13, 2013, the government of the Kingdom gave direct instructions to the Government of Curaçao. On May 5, 2013, Helmin Wiels, member of parliament and the political leader of the largest party dominating government at that time, was murdered. Those who pulled the trigger are behind bars, but the intellectual perpetrators are under investigation. On March 7, 2014, the direct instruction by the Kingdom was lifted after the government complied by implementing austerity measures that affected mainly the weak, such as retired citizens.

Between 1987 and 2000, the population of Aruba grew from 60,000 to 100,000. In 1990, the call for independence was off the table (Sluis 2004: 76; Van Galen 2004), and now Aruba is considering an Outer Regions status within the European Union. In 2012, Aruba worked closely with the Netherlands and is implementing an agenda to make the island a global leading green economy. But Aruba has accumulated a huge national debt of almost three billion guilders. The oil refinery Valero left the island in November 2012, leaving 400 persons unemployed. The public debt is worrisome. In July 2014, the Kingdom intervened in Aruba. There is a clear vision on sustainable development and this strategy is implemented consistently.

In 2010, St. Maarten passed a law regulating the organizational structure and the number of civil servants (*Landsverordening Organisatiestructuur* Land St. Maarten, LOL). Many talents from aboard, especially from Curaçao and the Netherlands, have been attracted to the island to work in the government sector. The island is doing surprisingly well, but is still being haunted by corruption scandals, and several of these cases are under investigation. The Kingdom intervened in October 2014.

Bonaire, St. Eustatius, and Saba now form a sort of municipality of the Netherlands. Much has been invested in education and health care, and the quality has risen considerably. The dollar was introduced as the currency replacing the Antillean guilder, which has made the island expensive for locals. The people of the island hoped that the social benefits would get about equal to those in the Netherlands. There is discontent because citizens expected total equality with citizens in the Netherlands but now consider themselves second-class citizens and strangers on their own islands.

Conclusion

The Dutch Antilles have developed through three distinctive periods: a colonial period characterized by agriculture, trade, and slavery; an industrial period characterized by oil refineries; and the current, post-industrial period that includes oil, tourism, and offshore services. The populations were small. As a consequence, there were many close personal relations, leading to patronage, nepotism, and corruption. It makes holding people accountable difficult. For a large part of the recent past, the civil service has been too big and inefficient; in recent times, it has been cut back, but governance continues to be problematic in many areas, including financial management, economic development, and social policy. Some notable exceptions are seen in Aruba. To some extent, problems are exacerbated by part of the local elites that are seen to spend and take, rather than build and create wealth. They do not invest in the development of the people but blame the former colonizer.

Relations with the Netherlands have varied in significance. While the islands have enjoyed a large measure of self-governance in the last century, the former colonial power has often remained important in addressing the financial conditions of these islands. Many people state that they are still dependent since the Netherlands provide a safety net and extra checks and balances for good governance. Others state that the Dutch hinder the development of the people by keeping responsibility away from them and intervening against their interest and that the islands are less autonomous than before October 10, 2010. At any rate, these small island nations will continue to face many internal challenges of small nations and external challenges of the economy and, sometimes, nature, while public administration is an important force shaping how well these nations achieve their aims.

References

Beetz, F. and Alberto, J. (2010). *Het laatste kabinet en de kronieken van de ontmantelingen van de Nederlandse Antillen 10-10-'10*. Curaçao: Raad van Ministers en regering van de Nederlandse Antillen.
Boxer, Ch. (1993). *De Nederlanders in Brazilië 1624–1654*. Amsterdam, the Netherlands: Atlas.
Brede, K. and Huisden, H. (2012). *Een nieuw land Curaçao en alles wat daarbij komt kijken*. Amsterdam, the Netherlands: Carib Publishing.
Buddingh, B. (1994). *Van Punt en Snoa: ontstaan en groei van Willemstad, Curaçao vanaf 1634, De Willemstad tussen 1700 en 1732 en de bouwgeschiedenis van de synagoge Mikve Israel-Emanuel 1730-1732*. 's-Hertogenbosch, the Netherlands.
Castillo, O.A. (1992). *Nos gobernashon: Antilliaanse staatsinrichting in een politicologisch perspektief*, Curaçao: O.A. Castillo, 100p.
Chumaceiro, A. (1894). *Zal het kiesrecht Curacao tot het kanniblisme voeren?* Curaçao: Drukkerij van A. Bethencourt en Zonen.
Coomans, H. and Coomans-Eustatia, M. (1998). *A.M. Chumaceiro Az.; Onpartijdige pionier op Curaçao*, Curaçao.
Dalhuisen, L., Donk, R., Hoefte, R., and Steegh, F. (1997). *Geschiedenis van de Antillen*. the Netherlands: Walburgpers.
Gibbes, F., Römer-Kenepa, N., and Scriwanek, M. (1999). *De bewoners van Curaçao, vijf eeuwen lief en leed*. Curaçao: Nationaal Arcief.
Goede, M. (2008). *The Island Council Elections in Curaçao April 2007; notes*. Curaçao: UNA Publication.
Haan, E. (1999). De luiken dicht, de luiken open—De economische ontwikkelingen van Curaçao en Aruba 1969 tot 1995. In H. Coomans, M. Coomans-Eustatius and J. van 't Leven (eds.), *Veranderd Curaçao*. Bloemendaal, the Netherlands: Stichting Libri Antilliani, pp. 217–230.
Hartog, J. (1988). *Aruba: Short History*. Curaçao en Aruba: Van Dorp.
Isebia, R. (2009). *Homenage na mi lenga i mi pén*. Curaçao: Curaçaosche Courant.
Korthals Altes, Th. (1999). *Koninkrijk aan zee*. Den Haag, the Netherlands: Walburg Pers.
Lucia, R. (1999). De Curaçaose industrie in de 20ᵉ eeuw. In H. Coomans, M. Coomans-Eustatius and J. van 't Leven (eds.), *Veranderd Curaçao*. Bloemendaal, the Netherlands: Stichting Libri Antilliani, pp. 293–300.
Metry, F. (2006). *De geschiedenis van de belastingen in de kolonie Curaçao en de Nederlandse Antillen*. Curaçao: Stichting Publicaties KPMG Tax and Legal Services.
Nauta, O. and Goede, M. (2007). *Checks-and-balances in Caribisch bestuurssysteem; Een evaluatie van Aruba, de Nederlandse Antillen, Barbados en Saint Martin*. Amsterdam, the Netherlands: Nauta & van Gennip.
Oostindie, G. (1999). *Curaçao 30 mei 1969*. Amsterdam, the Netherlands: Amsterdam University Press.
Oostindie, G. and Klinkers, I. (2001). *Het Koninkrijk in de Caraïben: Een korte geschiedenis van het Nederlandse dekolonisatiebeleid 1949–2000*. Amsterdam, the Netherlands: Amsterdam University Press.
Reinders, A. (1993). *Politieke geschiedenis van de Nederlandse Antillen en Aruba 1950–1993*. Zutphen, the Netherlands: Walburg Pers.
Römer, R. (1995). *De Curaçaose samenleving voor en na 30 mei 1969*. Curaçao: UNA.
Römer, R. (1998). *De Curaçaose samenleving*. Curaçao: Amigoe.
Rupert, L. (1999). *Roots of Our Future*. Curaçao: Chamber of Commerce and Industry Curaçao.
Schiltkamp, J. (Ed.) (1999). *Soublette Et Fils: Photography in Curaçao Around 1900*. Curaçao: Stichting Monumentenzorg Curaçao.
Schrils, J. (1990). *Een democratie in gevaar: Een verslag van de situatie op Curaçao tot 1987*. Assen/Maastricht: Van Gorcum.
Sluis, M. (2004). *De Antillen bestaan niet*. the Netherlands: Uitgever Bert Bakker.
Tromp, E. (2005). Towards a comprehensive solution of the debt problem of the Netherlands Antilles. In M. Goede (ed.) *Een aanzet tot integrale ontwikkeling*. Curaçao: UNA, pp. 129–137.

Van Beurden, M. (2012). *Witte stranden, zwart geld: Een studie naar de belastingparadijzen Zwitserland, Nederlandse Antillen en Singapore.* Leiden, the Netherlands: Universiteit van Leiden.
Van Galen, J. (2004). *De toekomst van het koninkrijk.* Amsterdam, the Netherlands: Uitgeverij Contact.
Van Kol, H. (1901). *Eene noodlijdende kolonie.* Amsterdam and Rotterdam, the Netherlands: Masereeuw and Bouten.
Van Soest, J. (1977). *Olie als water: De Curaçaose economie in de eerste helft van de twintigste eeuw.* Zutphen, the Netherlands: De Walburg Pers.
Verton, P. (1985). Overheid en ambtenaren op Curaçao. *UNA-Cahier No.14.*, UNA
Verton, P. (2006). Deugdelijk bestuur en politieke patronage, Burgerschap vereist voorlichting en vorming. In *René Römer als inspirator.* Curaçao: UNA, pp. 202–216.
Zwart, R. (2013). *Visie, passie en lef: Wie is de man achter het succes van Aruba? Een openhartig gesprek met premier Mike Eman.* Curaçao: Caribpublishing.

Chapter 5

Public Policy and Management in Cuba

Gerardo González Núñez

Contents

Introduction 96
Public Policy and Administrative System in the Pre-Revolution Period 96
Public Policy and Administrative System in the Socialist Period 97
    Stage from 1959 to 1974 98
    Stage from 1975 to 1989 100
    Stage from 1990 to Present 102
Conclusions 106
References 107

Abstract: Since the triumph of the Cuban Revolution, the government expressed its willingness to incorporate social benefit to its economic policy, and this has been one factor that has guided all its efforts on its development strategy, while not always have been satisfactory the economic results at various stages, due to the negative impact of exogenous factors and the way the public policy has been conducted. Under the socialist regime, the Cuban public policy has been conducted under a highly centralized system, in which the central state is the basic authority of the decision-making process and implementation of policies, while companies and territories are simply executioners of such decisions. This has created an authoritarian and vertical management culture that has permeated all economic activity in the country. This authoritarian style of management has led to the loss of the ability to generate initiatives and flexibility in decision-making process in business and in other players, and the lack of motivation to achieve highly efficient and competitive results in the economic processes.

With the economic crisis, which was precipitated with the collapse of the European socialist bloc, and changes in the world with the so-called globalization, the economic model built since the 1970s has become inoperative, imposing the need for its change so that Cuba can face the development challenges resulting from the new international order. In this transformation, eliminating the vertical and authoritarian culture has been and will be a long-term process, due to it being so strongly rooted in the social and economic skin of the country.

Introduction

As a Caribbean country, Cuba has had the novel experience of having gone through two different economic systems: capitalism and socialism. Ideological and geopolitical factors under which each experience developed, coupled with the structural weaknesses of the economy, helped to form another characteristic of the contemporary history of the island: its strong dependence on world powers. Between 1898 and 1960, it was associated with the United States; from 1961 until 1990, and following the introduction of the socialist regime, the island established links with the erstwhile Soviet Union. The link with these powers was based on the concession of preferential economic conditions to Cuba, which, nevertheless, did not bring about any significant changes in the structure of the country's economy. This was characterized by its extreme dependence on commodities, particularly sugar. This product represented for many years 80% of the overall exports in Cuba.

In the last 50 years, Cuba's external economic relations have faced two processes of enforced reorientation. The first one was in 1960, when the United States broke off all diplomatic and commercial relations with the island. The second one, from 1990 onward, came about with the dismantling of the socialist system in Europe and, mainly, following the fall of the Soviet Union.

All the above mentioned has conditioned several ways of creating and implementing public policy and administration that have been based on the different roles undertaken by the state in the Cuban economy and society.

In this chapter we analyze the characteristics, methods of implementation and results of public policy and management in Cuba, both at the capitalist and socialist stages, but the major emphasis of the analysis will focus on the second one, because very little has been researched and written on the subject in the capitalist stage, so that aspect of the economic history of Cuba remains a challenge for specialists of the topic.

Public Policy and Administrative System in the Pre-Revolution Period

The Republic that emerged following the intervention of the United States in 1898 inherited a production structure that relied heavily on the production and export of sugar and continued to deepen during the period of capitalism development in Cuba, with the new feature that such dependence was redirected toward the U.S. market.

Thus, the economic cycles in Cuba were determined by the behavior of sugar's prices and demand in the United States and world market, so the use of public policy as a countercyclical measure was very recurrent in the governments during the capitalist stage stimulated by the fact that politically the presidential system emerged under the Republic was very prone to the concentration of power in one person which facilitated the use of massive doses of voluntarism in the decisions to adopt (Grupo Cubano de Investigaciones Economicas 1963).

The events in the 1950s were good examples of the above mentioned. Cuba's entry into a new economic depression after the sugar boom derived from the Korean War (1950–1952) coincided with the rise to power of Fulgencio Batista through a coup d'etat on March 10, 1952. Economic policy designed by the new government had as a main objective the mitigation of the effects in the sugar production's fall through a policy of economic base diversification and increase the aggregate demand of the country. The instruments used were the expansion of government spending and tax incentives for the development of industry and agriculture.

The results of this policy were a growth in manufacturing production and construction, as well as in mining and in some categories of non-sugar agriculture and was highly favored by the impact of mitigating factors in the crisis of the sugar industry, as the fall of sugar's production in Europe and stability of sales in the United States. However, its implementation had also some negative consequences, such as erosion of foreign currency reserves due to increase in the imports without a proportional increase in exports, the excessive growth of government debt, a higher concentration of investment in public works and social services than in productive sectors, and a rise in the cost of living due to the inflationary pressure that was generated with the expansion of government spending (Rodriguez 1990).

Public Policy and Administrative System in the Socialist Period

From the early years of the Revolution, the economic development strategy adopted explicitly incorporated social improvement to economic policy, making it the principal reason of all development efforts, while not always has been satisfactory the economic performance aspirated into the various stages.

The policy of giving high priority to social services run through a permanent process of investment in two areas that guarantee greater human development: education and health. One of the main goals was to ensure a massive and free access to the entire population at both services.

In the period 1959–1989, Cuba progressed steadily in the field of education. Through the literacy campaign and universal access to education, the illiteracy rate decreased from 23% to 3% and markedly reduced the disparity between urban and rural areas. The network of educational institutions increased by 66% and the enrollment at all teaching levels grew three times (García Alvarez and Anaya Cruz 2010).

From the beginning, the Cuban government decided to make a radical change in the provision of health services through the implementation of an integral state system and seeking to bridge the gap between urban and rural areas. The strategy was as follows: increase the number of hospitals, especially in rural areas, primary care development through programs of prevention and diagnosis of diseases, massive training of doctors and health technicians, and encourage scientific research.

This policy brought positive results. Between 1959 and 1989, the number of physicians increased from 9.2 to 33 per 10,000 inhabitants, the hospital beds from 4.2 to 5.3 per 1000 inhabitants. Infant mortality fell from 33.4 to 11.1 per 1000 live births, the maternal mortality decreased from 125.3 to 26.1 per 100,000 births, and the mortality rate of the population over 65 years declined from 52.9 to 46.3 per 1000 people in that group. Moreover, most contagious diseases were eradicated (CEPAL 1997; Mesa-Lago and Vidal Alejandro 2010).

In the economic arena, the Cuban government's tasks focused on transforming their inheritance received that included the dependence of the United States, a predominantly agricultural and extensive economic structure, very open to the world market, with permanent unemployment and underemployment, among other features.

The creation and implementation of the development strategy under socialism and the public policy derived from it has had different stages: from 1959 to 1974, from 1975 to 1989, and from 1990 until today.

Stage from 1959 to 1974

The main goal that dominated this first stage was the survival and consolidation of the revolutionary project that was heavily influenced by the hostility campaign developed by the United States against the new government, which materialized in political-military destabilizing actions, the cancellation of the export quota sugar, removing oil, spare parts and technology sales to the island, culminating with blockade/embargo in 1961.

It was also a period characterized by progressive political, social, economic, and institutional transformations, tinged with many improvisations and experiments, but they were laying the foundations of the new socioeconomic model and where it was drawing gradually a trend to a centralizing state predominance.

A central role in this process was played by the National Institute of Agrarian Reform (*Instituto Nacional de Reforma Agraria*) (INRA). The financing needs requiring by INRA units that, in various ways, passed into the state property led to the creation of a central fund to finance various activities such as sugar harvest. The same formula was tested in all industrial activities that initially managed the Industries Department of INRA (Diaz Vázquez 2008). This experience was an approximation of what subsequently was the Budgetary Funding System which was implemented in the Ministry of Industry, created in 1962 as the institutional body that will direct efforts toward a speed industrialization of the country.

From the creation of the Ministry of Industry, two different management systems began to coexist: the aforementioned Budgetary Funding System and the Economic Calculation.

The Budgetary Funding System, applied in industry, was based on a conception of administrative centralization. The companies were running through centralized planning methods, their income was going directly to the central state, and their costs were covered through a budgetary fund. Economic efficiency was measured by the reduction in costs.

The achievements of the system included the development of a statistical basis, the unification of the accounting techniques, and structuring management procedures based on modern methods of control that subjected the companies to strict administrative supervision. Moreover, the system used economic levers and market relations in a very restricted way (Díaz Vázquez 2008).

The system called Economic Calculation was applied in agriculture. The companies enjoyed a lower degree of centralization and could cover its costs with their incomes. The system worked in a partial and very limited way given the low levels of profitability of business organizations, prompting support from the state budget which covered their inefficiencies.

In 1967 was applied a new management system very different from Budgetary Funding System and the Economic Calculation. The system, known as Economic Record System, had, among other features, eliminating the collections and payments from public sector enterprises, and with them, the market relations in the state sector, because was considered too capitalists. Other features included virtual elimination of the accounting in the enterprises, wide gratuities policy, divorce among wages and the labor results, waiver of overtime payments, and the use of volunteer work as a means to carry out economic and social objectives, among others. This meant the country has moved from using mechanisms with some technical-economic logic to methods of public policy and administration where non-economic factors and motivations (ideological, subjective) were significant (Díaz Vázquez 2008).

Until then, the mixed nature of the economy, expressed in a state sector integrated by agro-industrial, wholesale and the retail trade units, banking, transportation, among others, along with cooperatives and private sector composed of small companies based in retail and individual producers in the field and other areas, had found articulation through the market that integrated the necessary relations between different productive sectors. However, the introduction of regulated consumption of food and other goods (March 1962) and the subsequent removal in March 1968 for all types of private and individual activity (except in agriculture and transport), in practice, stripped the market of nearly all its economic functions and consecrated the hegemonic role of the state in the economy (Díaz Vázquez 2000).

The strategy of turning Cuba into an agro-industrial nation in a short period of time and the industrial sector was the accumulation axis that drove growth, and development of the country did not achieve its objectives by various factors, from the rising tensions generated by U.S. destabilizing policies to others still linked to inadequate training of human resources, the lack of a statistic and accounting base, and insufficient production structure, among other economic causes.

Since 1965, economic strategy has returned again to agriculture and especially in sugar production as pivot sectors of the Cuban economy. An important element of this new strategic direction was, without doubt, the reorientation of Cuba to the European socialist market. In 1963, trade with the socialist countries accounted for 75.8% of the total Cuban foreign trade, while the Soviet Union amounted 40% of that total (Rodriguez 1990). When in January 1964 Cuba signed an agreement with the Soviet Union for the sale of 4.1 million sugar tons with prices above the levels in the world market, it guaranteed sufficient income to finance the development strategy planned.

This agreement defined the leading sector of the country's economic development. From that moment, the country drove resources to agriculture, especially to the sugar industry, affecting the resources to other industries. It was decided that the financial resources needed would be obtained through sugar exports (Rodriguez 1990).

Under this strategy, the Cuban government projected a sugar development plan which had as principal task to produce 10 million tons of sugar in 1970, but only 8.5 million tons were achieved. The development of this plan, however, provoked the breakdown of the rest of the economy, since virtually all the country was paralyzed to focus on that task.

From the negative economic consequences generated by the 1970 sugar harvest, the Cuban government turned to a restructuring of economic policy, expressing continuity and the same time a breakdown with past policies. It was continuity due to the political decision to follow the path of building socialism, achieve even greater integration with European socialist economies, which was devoted with the incorporation of Cuba into the integration mechanism of these countries in 1972, creating a model of economic organization consistent with the existent in socialist countries of that integration block and rely on sugar production as development pivot, given the price advantage that is obtained with the economic exchange between Cuba and the Soviet Union. It was a breakdown, because the new policy intended to give greater importance to the objectives and economic levers in the functioning of the economy, so that the main effort was directed to increase efficiency, eliminate large mismatches in internal finances, to match the salary with the contribution of the labor force, improve the level of consumption of the population as well as giving a systemic character to management and performance of the economy.

In general, throughout this period, there was a lack of coherence between the strategy designed and economic policy applied, especially with regard to economic management, where, in the search for more agile methods, the government removed market mechanisms. Next to this, one should also note that the instruments used to carry out economic policy were sometimes inadequate. For example, inappropriate use of instruments of price and cost, ignorance of the need for a separate tax system according to the various property sectors, and the use of excessive centralization as an instrument of control (Díaz Vázquez 2008). All of them were elements that hindered a better result of public policy measures applied.

Stage from 1975 to 1989

The First Congress of the Cuba Communist Party was celebrated in December 1975. In the Congress was defined the strategy for economic development, which again identified industrialization as the dynamic factor of development and, therefore, its main objective.

The strategy also conceived substantial changes in the institutional order, as the adoption of a new constitution, a new political-administrative division in the territories, the creation of the people's power bodies, and the reorganization of the central state apparatus.

An essential element of the development strategy was the implementation in 1976 of the first planning and management economic model regulated on a national scale in Cuba. It was known as the Cuban Model of Economic Management and Planning (*Sistema de Dirección y Planificación de la Economía*) (SDPE). The model was based on the principles that distinguished economic practice of the socialist countries and in particular the Soviet Union.

The SDPE entailed some decentralizing innovative measures benefiting companies, since it established as its key factor their partial and gradual self-financing. A first step in this direction was the restructuring of the managerial model in force at the time. In 1975, a business restructuring process began, and by 1979, 2,908 companies and around 1,300 organizations in the public service sector subsidized by the state had undergone this process (Dilla 1995).

At the same time, companies were granted more freedom, which entailed more power for them to execute economic decisions and a higher degree of participation in their creation. In the same way, they were granted other powers, for example, the right to carry out initiatives in areas such as contracting labor, and the selling of some of the marginal output or unused assets. Restricting the autonomy of businesses to the management of the resources provided by the state within the framework of the plan endorsed by the government meant that planning, along with the most important economic tasks, was the responsibility of the state, while companies were left to manage the allocation of resources (Vilariño Ruiz and Domenech Nieves 1986).

Under these circumstances, this centralized plan became the central guideline of all business activities. Changes to the plan came only under the jurisdiction of the state bodies, headed by the Planning Board (*Junta de Planificación*), the governing body responsible for the preparation and implementation of the economic plan and the management of the economy. In this sense, the companies' powers were limited (their degree of freedom depending on the type of activity they carried out) to the tasks of scheduling, monitoring, and managing the production processes and activities in the service sector.

Business life could dispense with competitive or cooperative horizontal relations, since all supplies were provided by the central authorities through a 5-year master plan. This certainly did not mean that the government's predictions were always accurate. On the contrary, the supply sources often turned out to be unreliable or, if nothing else, not very punctual. Demand was unstable and products and technologies underwent changes, introduced on a regular basis by the high bureaucratic authorities (Dilla 1995).

However, companies were not affected by the ups and downs of the market and, besides, they were protected by flexible budgets, which covered their inefficiencies and guaranteed their immunity to the large debts which they incurred with the financial institutions.

This economic and management model was made possible thanks to the privileged integration of Cuba within the European socialist sphere and, particularly, due to its relation with the Soviet Union. This integration allowed Cuba to gain easy and safe access to capital and outdated technologies, which were, nevertheless, sufficient for such an undemanding market as the Eastern European one.

The highly centralized and bureaucratic system of planning mentioned above was also reproduced within companies. Companies in Cuba are based on a rigid system of institutional hierarchies, which entails a high concentration of authority in the hands of a small section of leaders and specialists.

Following the model put into practice in 1975, workers' involvement in the management of the company is restricted to communication issues: they may be consulted on issues which involve workers as a group, they may contribute in efforts to controlling labor where there is a lack of discipline, and they may encourage education in order to create commercial awareness among workers. This model of workers' involvement was designed originally as an add-on to the SDPE. Since this system did not stimulate production efficiency, the labor process was also based on undemanding patterns, such as simple labor qualifications, autocratic styles of management, and the reduction in workers' powers to a minimum. All this conspired against the collective functioning of the workforce as a group with their own identity (Dilla 1995).

Since businesses were strongly subordinated to central government, the vertical and authoritarian relation was mirrored within companies, where the managing director and a small group of subordinate executives, although incapable of promoting innovation within the company, assumed almost totalitarian power in the implementation of the decisions made by the government.

In all businesses, power and authority are concentrated in the figure of the managing director and of those deputy directors in charge of the most important areas of production and services. According to company regulations, Cuban businesses are based around a model of highly centralized decision making. This means that the managing director is the main authority in the company. The managing director is nominated or dismissed by the governmental authorities and has strong powers in terms of controlling and executing the economic plan, the appointment and dismissal of managers, and hiring worker. These functions, as well as several others, some of them usually less important, could, however, be delegated to the deputy directors (Vilariño Ruiz and Domenech Nieves 1986).

In the performance of his wide-ranging duties, the managing director is assisted by a board of directors. Representatives of the trade union and of the political organizations within the company are also invited. The board meets at least once a month at the director's request and has powers to discuss and express its opinion on a number of important company issues. The director is under no obligation to adopt agreements reached by the board, although the board has the right to appeal to the higher administrative authorities against decisions made by the managing director.

However, such a disagreement is rare, due to the prevailing tendency at board meetings to discuss all agenda items thoroughly, until either a unanimous or majority consensus is reached. The first sign of the success of a managing director lies in his ability to rule with the support of the board and not against it. This is also the reason why at board meeting issues are rarely put to the vote.

The authority of the director and the rest of the managerial leadership, however, is subject to a contradictory relationship. Their powers are limited by the weak autonomy of the company in relation to the higher administrative authorities. At the same time, it is this very relationship that turns the leadership of the company into a privileged intermediary between the various horizontal and vertical relationships of the company (Dilla 1995).

One of the negative aspects of the SDPE is that it worked supported by the massive affluence of material, financial, and technological resources coming from the socialist countries, which is known as extensive growth and management strategy. This meant that the Cuban Management and Planning System did not foster an increase in productivity. Not only did it not bring about the adoption of advanced models of work organization, it also encouraged a lack of interest and concern about productivity results and efficiency in general (Gonzalez 1992).

Despite the weak elements of SDPE, positive results were obtained. In terms of economic growth, the best results in all the years of the Revolution were achieved in the period with an average annual rate of 8%, which was accompanied by high levels of investment and industrialization. There were also very commendable results in the social sphere (CEPAL 1997). However, these results were not sufficient to guarantee an endogenous process, capable of generating their own sources of accumulation, nor the integrity and proportionality between all economic and social branches, especially those related to the consumption of the population, neither significantly helped in eradicating structural deformations typical of underdevelopment.

Since the mid-1980s, began to emerge symptoms of exhaustion of extensive factors that led to the significant growth achieved so far. Some of the symptoms were the systematic decline of basic fund performance, insufficient response in exports, low efficiency of the investment process, and the growth of food imports, among others. At the same time, there appeared a significant deterioration in the pace of social spending, and therefore decreased building of house, day care, schools, and so on. In companies, paying for the work was distorted and the business autonomy became less functional.

Because of the issue of inefficiency in the economy, the application of the so-called process of rectification of errors and negative tendencies which represented a break with the patterns applied at the beginning of the decade began in 1986, but neither meant a total disruption of market relations nor an essential change in the development strategy of the stage.

The rectification process was based on the perception of the country's leadership that public policy had made excessive use of monetary and market instruments driven under SDPE in detriment of non-economic motivations. Consequently, this process tried to give a new impetus to economic growth and development emphasizing more on the ideological incentive and mechanisms—social levers than the monetary-mercantile ones.

Thus, under the rectification process, volunteer work is rescued as a way to guarantee certain economic and social objectives, the policy began to put more emphasis on moral incentives as recognition of the labor effort and removed the free market agriculture, which was an experience implemented in the early 1980s in which agricultural production surpluses of state enterprises and farmers, after they met the state appropriations, could be sold to the public at prices that were set free according to the offer and demand. In parallel, measures were taken for the improvement of processes and management investors; the government sought new strategic alternatives, including the rapid development of tourism, the promotion of foreign investment and the definition of science as a development lever providing incentives for biotechnology and pharmaceutical industries.

In the period 1986–1990, the economy stagnated. Supplies from the socialist countries became unstable and definitely decreased. The renegotiation of the foreign debt with capitalist countries and financial imbalances in general forced a reduction in imports. This shows that the economic situation at the beginning of 1990s was extraordinarily complex in the economic and political areas.

Stage from 1990 to Present

From 1990, Cuba began to suffer an acute economic crisis, which, among other things, caused a fall in the economy of 35% in only 4 years. Although the cause for this economic crisis lay in the exhaustion of the planning and economic model in force at the time, it was, nevertheless, brought on more quickly by the dissolution of the European socialist system and by the fall of the former Soviet Union (Carranza et al. 1995).

With the advent of the crisis, the state prerogatives and operating capacity were greatly restricted due to an overwhelming lack of resources. Therefore, the interests and needs of the different sections of society and the business sectors were severely penalized.

Two areas heavily affected by the crisis were productive sectors and the social services.

One effect of the crisis was the decline of the productive sectors' share in the economy. While in 1989, the share of these sectors was 34%, in 2011, it was only 20% (CEPAL 1997; ONE 2011).

The crisis also led to a process of human resources decapitalization, which has had different dimensions. One dimension has been the poor and unequal access of the workforce to new knowledge and scientific-technical progress, where one of the examples has been the poor internet access. Another dimension has been the emigration of human capital in two directions: abroad in searching of a better quality of life, and internally when professionals have moved to lower skill jobs but higher in financial rewards. Also, the deterioration of education and health has affected the aforementioned decapitalization.

The crisis affected very hard the educational sector. During 1989–1995, the budget was cut by 38%, which caused a shortage of school materials, reducing investment and maintenance of infrastructure. There was also a significant exodus of teachers to better-paid work. Student enrollment at the elementary level was maintained, but in high school fell from 88% to 74.5% and the university level also fell from 23% to 12% (Mesa-Lago and Vidal Alejandro 2010).

The effects of the crisis on food, hygiene, and living conditions of the population had a negative impact on health. Several indicators deteriorated. In the period 1989–1995, the proportion of children with low birth weight increased from 7.3% to 9%, maternal mortality increased from 26.1 to 65.2 per 100,000 births, and the people over 65 years increased from 48.4 to 55.7 per 1000 people. Diseases that had been eradicated from the country's epidemiological picture resurfaced (García Alvarez and Anaya Cruz 2010; Mesa-Lago and Vidal Alejandro 2010).

The crisis had to be faced in its two dimensions: structural and insertion ones. From the beginning, the challenge required, in the first instance, an economy's adjustment to new circumstances to proceed to the construction of a new development and management model based on efficiency and competitiveness (via intensive accumulation) and to ensure a reinsertion of the global market economy.

However, the government did not focus the crisis that way because according to the official analysis it had only external causes, resulting from the collapse of the socialist camp and the U.S. blockade/embargo. The Cuban leadership considered that the reintegration of Cuba into the international economic system should be the result of an active foreign policy and not as the result of profound internal economic changes. Thus at the beginning of the crisis, the leadership relied on an economic recovery based solely on a combination of internal adjustment measures, no systemic reforms and political and ideological means. They decided only to apply some daring transformations when the crisis reached intolerable levels and threatened to become a social and political problem.

As a reaction to that, and given the need to find a new way to join the international economic system on the basis of competitive efficiency, the government began to introduce a selective opening up of the economy, marked by the introduction of market forces. The main measures were as follows: the decriminalization of the possession and use of foreign currency, free farmer market was reopened, bigger support for foreign investment, and expansion of self-employment.

From 1993, the market is competing with the state as a mechanism for the redistribution of sources and income, which is also becoming a means to survival. This system favors the relative liberalization of the control exercised by the state over important sectors of the population and businesses, as the state has to resort to the market to supply those functions and resources which it can no longer fulfill or comfortably provide itself.

This opening up, despite having to function under intense pressure and having encountered formidable economic, administrative, and political obstacles and failure to respond to a strategic program explicitly formulated, has entailed an important change in the rules of the game which had shaped Cuban society and economy for over five decades.

The selective opening up of the economy played an important role in the revival of the economy that began to take place from 1995 and put the country back on the path of sustained growth. During 1995 and 2007 the gross domestic product grew at an average annual rate of 5% (ONE 2001).

Since 2004, the economy reflected more favorable results for the advantageous economic relations established with Venezuela. The Cuban government found in the South American country not only its main political ally but also an economic and financial support it had lost since the disappearance of the Soviet Union in the early 1990s. This relationship has led Venezuela to become the largest trading partner of Cuba, which greatly guarantees its energy security by supplying about 100,000 barrels of oil a day under very favorable terms that the island's government refuses to publicize (Cue et al. 2009).

It is important to note the economic growth in those years added new problems to traditional structural deficiencies, as the dual currency, which has negatively affected labor motivation of human resources and has increased social inequalities. The growth was achieved on extensive bases, it means with the massive use of resources at the expense of higher levels of efficiency, with little expansion of the export sector, which has expanded the external financial imbalance, was only supported by the performance of few sectors, particularly tourism, and agriculture without showing clear signs of recovery.

The economic recovery could have been used to expand and deepen the reforms adopted in the 1990s in the direction of decentralization and a greater market role in the economy. Unfortunately, the opposite happened. The economic growth achieved in these years stimulated a counter reform process that sought to eliminate the minimum space open in the previous decade to the private sector and even state enterprises themselves (Cue et al. 2009).

The main elements of the counter reform included the following:

1. Recentralization of economic decisions and limited autonomy of the lower and middle decisions-making levels in the state productive bodies. This included the elimination of enterprises autonomy in the use of foreign currency.
2. Elimination of the U.S. dollar use in Cuba.
3. Growing role of top military chiefs in the economy and strengthening military corporations that generate hard currency income.
4. Rethinking foreign investment. This led to the closure of small foreign companies.
5. Decrease the number of permits for self-employment.

Economic recovery and the positive external environment, with encouragement to the recentralization of the economy, slowed the development of self-employment. While in 2004, the number of self-employment workers was 166,700, in 2007 it totaled 138,400, representing a reduction of 17%. In 2008, the Cuban government continued to be the largest employer, accounting for 83% of total employment in Cuba (ONE 2007).

From 2008, a trend toward slowing of the Cuban economy began to reflect, which was accentuated in later years. While one cannot ignore the negative aftermath of the four hurricanes that hit Cuba in that year and the global economic crisis, the economic downturn was also a reflection of the fragility and the structural problems afflicting the Cuban economy and the exhaustion of the forces that propelled the economic recovery since 1995.

The entrance of the economy in a new downturn cycle coincided with the official inauguration of Raul Castro as president of the Council of State and Ministers, replacing his brother Fidel Castro. Raúl received a country with multiple shortcomings and distortions inherited from the internal crisis of the early 1990s and the persistence of a state centralized economic model (Vidal Alejandro 2010). Faced with this reality, the official discourse reflected differences with expressed one during the 1990s, recognizing now the structural dimension of economic growth weakness. On July 26, 2007, when he was still exercising temporally the presidency, Raúl Castro promised structural and conceptual transformations in the economy (Castro 2007).

One of the priorities of the Raul Castro administration has been to permanently resolve the crisis of Cuban agriculture and its inability to ensure food security in the country. Because of that Cuba has had to resort to the world market to meet the 85% of food needs of the population. The timid attempts to revive agriculture through a more flexible formula, as the Basic Units of Cooperative Production (*Unidades Básicas de Producción Cooperativas*) (UBPC), and delivery of idle state land to individual producers in usufruct have not paid off as these new forms of property born tied to excessive centralization prevailing in the economic decisions are taking in the sector, in addition to the scarce supplies guaranteed for an intensive exploitation of areas to cultivate. In reality, only a small percentage of private farmers have a certain degree of autonomy that allows them to produce under more efficient conditions (Cue et al. 2009).

Another renovator change has been the expansion of private enterprise and cooperatives beyond the agricultural sector. The official projection is that by 2016, 40% of employment will be generated out of state companies. To this end, since 2010 the government began issuing new licenses for self-employed workers who can now also be entrepreneurs and even turn into small private enterprises because, for the first time since the 1960s, they are authorized to hire a workforce. They have also been allowed to market goods and services to state agencies and access to bank credit, among other relaxations (Vidal Alejandro 2010).

In contrast to the liberalization occurring in the private and cooperative sector, the allocation and control of resources in the state-owned company continues to support central planning. In fact, it seems even that there is a return to the conceptions of planning that prevailed in the 1970s and 1980s, not only as to the centralized nature of it, but in terms of the few open spaces that the plan leaves to the companies to adjust their dynamic requirements to the national and international market. In essence, the resources allocation economic model typical of a socialist country is preserved and reinforced in many ways, despite widespread evidence questioning their efficiency.

In an attempt to give a systemic body to the change's strategies of the new government, they were condensed in the Economic and Social Guidelines (*Lineamientos Económicos y Sociales*) document submitted at the Sixth Congress of the Cuba Communist Party, which was held in April 2012 (Everleny 2012).

The proposed reforms contained in the *Lineamientos* have as a closest comparable precedent the changes applied between 1992 and 1994. Both changes share the fact that they were a response to a critical economic situation, but are different in the official discourse that has accompanied them. While in the 1990s official speech hinted that the timid opening up of the market was a necessary evil, now the speech reflects a commitment to implement the changes without any return.

Another difference is in the depth of the strategy to adopt. The *Lineamientos* recognize the necessity to increase economic actors with the acceptance of new forms of non-state management: cooperative, self-employed, and small private company, which actually points to an expanded role of market in the economy regarding to that achieved in the 1990s. There is also a commitment to the expansion and strengthening of companies' autonomy, especially in the management of their production and financial resources. A positive element is the emphasis on efficiency and its use as a reference for implementing measures, to evaluate the economic performance of business organizations and the distribution of resources.

In general, the strategies contained in the *Lineamientos* try to prioritize technical-economic tools in the implementation of public policy and economic management over political and ideological considerations, as has been the practice under socialism in Cuba.

However, the document has many weaknesses, ambiguities, and notable absences. A great absent actor is the territories. Beyond the assigned role in food production and the occasional mention in the document, the territories are not assigned a central role in the task of economic growth and development. Also the recognition of entrepreneurial autonomy is within the context of the objectives set by the national economic plan which is designed centrally. Thus, the leadership tries to revive the plan as the mechanism that will regulate relations between the State and its enterprises.

Among the sectorial policies, there is a strong priority to agriculture, mining, tourism, pharmaceuticals, and technology industry, but the proposals follow the same pattern of verticality that has characterized the Cuban economy, without offering viable alternatives aimed at developing horizontal links and increase the multiplier capacity of different sectors. There are also no clear proposals to establish relations between the state and the emerging market.

Another negative factor that we observe in the document is the type of self-employment that is being promoted. The government is authorizing low-skill jobs, compared with the preparation acquired by the average Cuban labor force, which eventually stimulates the devaluation of such resource, and deprived of the opportunity that the emerging private sector participate in activities with higher added value such as the professionals (architects, engineers, economists), which they contribute more significantly to the country's economic growth.

In summary, the *Lineamientos* lack a strategic and systemic vision of measures that have to be taken and are simply a list of tasks and goals where the country's accumulation axes are not clearly established. But the greatest deficit of this proposal is the absence of a serious rethinking of the role of the state and the market economy. While the state should continue to play a significant role, some regulatory and distribution functions should give to market. Instead, what the document provides are more efficient ways in which the state can centrally manage the economy.

Instead of posing a new economic model and management, the *Lineamientos* are only a reform of administrative nature that hardly guarantees the foundations for sustainable growth to ensure development.

Conclusions

Under the socialist regime, the Cuban public policy has been conducted under a highly centralized system, in which the central state is the basic authority of the decision-making process and implementation of policies, while companies and territories are simply executioners of such decisions. This has created an authoritarian and vertical management culture that has permeated all economic activity in the country. This authoritarian style of management has led to the loss of the ability to generate initiatives and flexibility in decision-making process in business and in other players, and the lack of motivation to achieve highly efficient and competitive results in the economic processes.

Also, that public policy under Cuban socialism has been reactive, always in response to changing international geopolitical and economic situations and their impact on the domestic economy, and very dependent on political and ideological considerations. The policy and management methods designed have responded very rarely to a strategic and systemic vision that takes in consideration the profound structural distortions which are inherited from centuries of hypertrophied development. It also has suffered from incoherence between the strategies proposed and designed policies and has often been applied ineffectively.

The problems facing the Cuban economy are structural and exhaustion of a model that was in crisis since the 1990s, so their solution requires vast and profound changes in the prevailing management system, changes must exceed the simple notion of reform in order to enter a restructuring of the country's economic base.

Restructuring and reform concepts appear to be similar, but they are not, although they share points of contact. The restructuring or structural change is a very complex transformation that modifies the material basis of the economy and its international specialization. That means it has to do with the redefinitions of the axes of accumulation; the different proportions between consumption, investment, and savings; the weight of the various economic sectors; and the redefinition of the country's international economic integration. Economic reform has to define the role of the state and the market, the various forms of ownership and operation of enterprises, and the role of the regions in the functioning of the economy (Monreal 2008). While restructuring has to do with economic-technical aspects, reform does from an economic-politics perspective.

Although structural change involves more complex transformations and takes longer maturation of reform outcomes, the magnitude of the problems facing Cuba requires that both transformations are executed in parallel.

The measures introduced by President Raul Castro in recent years are positive, but far from the structural reforms announced over 6 years ago and they have been implemented very slowly. Perhaps they have been slow due to the uncertainty that may exist in the country's leadership about what would be the final goal of the reforms and therefore it is very difficult to predict what will be the impact of those measures in management.

The new policies announced in the Economic and Social Guidelines, which were adopted at the Sixth Congress of the Cuba Communist Party, expand the timid reforms implemented in the 1990s, but they are not enough taking in consideration the needs that require the growth and economic development of the country.

Although the Cuban economy is far from being exhausted by having economic potential able to ensure robust and self-sustaining economic recovery, inertia and gradualism have eroded this potential, so if the changes referred to in this analysis are still postponing, recovery will be expensive, lengthy, and painful for Cuban society.

References

Carranza, J., Gutierrez, L. and Monreal, P. 1995. *Cuba, la reestructuración de la economía: una propuesta para el debate*. La Habana, Cuba: Editorial de Ciencias Sociales.

Castro, R. 2007. *Discurso pronunciado por Raúl Castro en el acto central por la celebración del 26 de julio de 2007*. Cuba: Periódico Granma.

Comisión Económica para América Latina y el Caribe (CEPAL). 1997. *La economía cubana. Reformas estructurales y desempeño en los noventas*. México: Fondo de Cultura Económica.

Cué, F., González, G. and Orro, R. 2009. *Oportunidades de Negocios en Cuba: ¿Qué puede esperar Puerto Rico?* San Juan, Puerto Rico: Publicaciones Puertorriqueñas.

Díaz Vázquez, Julio A. 2000. Consumo y distribución normada de alimentos y otros bienes en Cuba. In *La última reforma agraria del siglo*, ed. Hans-Jürgen Burchardt. Caracas, Venezuela: Editorial Nueva Sociedad, pp. 35–56.

Díaz Vázquez, Julio A. 2008. *Cuba 1959–2008: gestión y dirección de la economía*. La Habana, Cuba: Editorial de Ciencias Sociales.

Dilla, H. 1995. Socialismo, empresas y participación obrera: notas para un debate cubano. In *Cuba en crisis*, ed. Jorge Rodriguez Beruff. Puerto Rico: Editorial de la Universidad de Puerto Rico, pp. 135–172.

Everleny Perez, O. 2012. *La actualización del modelo económico cubano*. La Habana, Cuba: Centro de Estudios de la Economía Cubana.

García Alvarez, A. and Anaya Cruz, A. 2010. Relación entre desarrollo social y económico. In *Cincuenta años de la economía cubana*, comp. Omar Everleny Perez. La Habana, Cuba: Editorial de Ciencias Sociales.

Gonzalez, G. 1992. Cuba y el mercado mundial: notas para una reflexión. *Revista Interamericana* 22: 43–55, Puerto Rico.

Grupo Cubano de Investigaciones Económicas. 1963. *Un estudio sobre Cuba*. Miami, FL: University of Miami Press.

Mesa-Lago, C. and Vidal Alejandro, P. 2010. The Impact of the Global Crisis on Cuba's Economy and Social Welfare. *Journal of Latin America Studies* 42: 689–717.

Monreal, P. 2008. El problema económico de Cuba. *Cuba, Revista Espacio Laical* 2: 33–35.

Oficina Nacional de Estadísticas de Cuba (ONE). 2001. *Anuario Estadístico*, Oficina Nacional de Estadística de Cuba, La Habana, Cuba.

ONE. 2007. *Anuario Estadístico*.

ONE. 2011. *Anuario Estadístico*.

Rodríguez, J. L. 1990. *Desarrollo Económico de Cuba 1959–1988*. México: Editorial Nuestro Tiempo.

Vidal Alejandro, P. 2010. *Cuban Economic Policy under the Raúl Castro Government*. Research Report. Japan, Institute of Developing Economies. http://www.ide.go.jp (accessed July 10, 2010).

Vilariño Ruiz, A. and Domenech Nieves, S. 1986. *El Sistema de Dirección y Planificación de la economía en Cuba: Historia, Actualidad y Pespectiva*. La Habana, Cuba: Editorial Pueblo y Educación.

ISSUES IN PUBLIC ADMINISTRATION

Chapter 6

Civil Service Performance in the Caribbean

Wayne Soverall

Contents

Introduction..112
Colonial Legacy...114
Public Service Evolution..115
Public Service Commission 118
Size of Public Service..121
Recruitment and Selection 126
Supervisory Practices 130
Organizational Culture and Performance 133
Leadership..135
Conclusions—Future Outlook..137
Bibliography..139

Abstract: Public service performance remains the heartbeat of national development for Caribbean countries as a result of the significant role played by governments since gaining political independence. Despite relative success in some aspects of public sector management, however, there is still concern about its efficacy, especially its capacity to manage diverse policies, operations, and systems in a constantly changing environment. To this end, several waves of public sector reforms over the years focused attention on centralized structures and systems that influenced an inward-looking control orientation that now has to be radically changed to an empowerment paradigm of participation, learning, and performance incentives in order to improve overall public service performance. More importantly, the winds of change suggest that even the notion of new public management failed to fundamentally transform public service performance as promised. In this context, therefore, new public governance arrangements and proactive public sector leadership are required in order to support enhanced capacity building, motivated personnel, and efficient and effective service delivery systems that can change the poor image of the public service and significantly improve its levels of performance.

Introduction

Civil service (hereafter called public service) performance in the Caribbean region[*] varies among individual countries and within different regional[†] groupings of countries as a consequence of endogenous factors, including historical legacy, political economy, culture, and size, as well as exogenous economic shocks like the global financial crisis of 2007–2008 and the spill-over effect of the 2009 financial meltdown of Colonial Life Insurance Company (CLICO).[‡] Public service performance remains the heartbeat of national development for the 15 Caribbean[§] countries as a result of the significant role played by governments since the achievement of political independence during the 1960s and 1970s. In 1979, the recognition that mankind everywhere depends on governmental and other public services to sustain civilization, and the increasing awareness that these services must be performed with responsiveness to human needs based on efficiency and effectiveness in the use of resources, led to the first International Conference on Improving Public Management and Performance.[¶] Since then the prevailing view has been that the public service was not performing well and that it should learn from private sector management in order to enhance its performance and productivity.[**] As a result, the management of the public service has changed significantly in both industrialized and developing countries as they sought to reduce the size of public employment to decrease the costs of producing government services, and applied general management principles to the management of public employees.[††]

Caribbean governments, like their counterparts in industrialized countries, implemented new public management (NPM) reforms in an effort to develop motivated and capable staff through institutional strengthening aimed at building capacity in the public service. However, there are still lingering questions about the relevance and applicability, particularly for small developing countries, of NPM reforms that were designed by and for countries belonging to the Organization for Economic Co-operation and Development.[‡‡] This has led to an acknowledgment that reforms borrowed from elsewhere may not necessarily work in the same way or provide the same outcomes. The challenge is further manifested in the reality that although public service performance

---

[*] Adapted from Khan, *Public Management*, 2–5, in which the Caribbean region refers to a grouping of 33 English-, Dutch-, French-, and Spanish-speaking countries, all islands except for the mainland countries of Belize, Cayenne, Guyana, and Suriname. The region is divided into three main geographic groups: the Greater Antilles, comprising Cuba, Haiti, Dominican Republic, Puerto Rico, and Jamaica; the Lesser Antilles, comprising the islands lying between Puerto Rico and the South American mainland; and the Bahamas off the Florida coast.

[†] Ibid: Antigua and Barbuda, Dominica, Grenada, Montserrat, St. Kitts and Nevis, St. Lucia, and St. Vincent and the Grenadines, usually grouped as the subregion of the Caribbean, are variously known as the Lesser Antilles, the Leeward-Windward islands, the less developed countries (LDCs), the Eastern Caribbean Currency Union (ECCU), and the Organization of Eastern Caribbean States (OECS).

[‡] Soverall, "CLICO's Corporate Collapse," 1–13.

[§] Adapted from World Bank, *Public Sector Modernization*, 1, in which the term *Caribbean* refers to the 15 member Caribbean Group for Cooperation in Economic Development (CGCED) countries, namely, Antigua and Barbuda, Bahamas, Barbados, Belize, Dominica, Dominican Republic, Grenada, Guyana, Haiti, Jamaica, St. Kitts and Nevis, St. Lucia, St. Vincent and the Grenadines, Suriname, and Trinidad and Tobago.

[¶] Stahl and Foster, *Improving Public Services*, 5–12.

[**] Hondeghem, "EGPA Symposium on Public Service Motivation and Performance," pp. 5–9.

[††] OECD (2008) *The State of the Public Service*, http://www.oecd-library.org/governance.

[‡‡] OECD, *Modernizing Government*.

measurement and the introduction of performance-based management tools were implemented by developing countries, including those from the Caribbean, little attention was paid to why performance was measured, how performance information was used, or the actual implementation of performance measurement.*

The vision of governments in the region is one of playing a prominent role as enabler and facilitator based on the public service being more dynamic, effective, efficient, modern, and innovative.[†] This view, however, presupposes some degree of institutional strengthening aimed at improving the effectiveness of existing structures, processes, and systems, usually through training and coaching.[‡] In the context of improving Caribbean public institutions and national strategic plans, for example, Vision 2020, the National Strategic Plan of Trinidad and Tobago (2005–2020), the Barbados National Strategic Plan (2006–2025), Vision 2030, the National Strategic Plan of Jamaica (2009–2030), and the Barbados Human Resource Development Strategy (2011–2016), the strength or weakness of the public service is evidenced by performance. Poor performance could result from weak capacity building or a combination of other factors. Public service capacity includes policy capacity, implementation capacity, and operational efficiency.[§] The public service encompasses all posts in the executive and judicial branches of government, other than those reserved for members of parliament, and such posts are usually classified as established and nonestablished or permanent and temporary.[¶] These posts are mainly in a civil capacity, hence the term *civil service*, and they are paid for out of general revenues raised by parliament, although in some instances in the Caribbean, some positions are often financed by grants from international organizations. Public service performance in the Caribbean, therefore, has to be examined within the context of the region being viewed as small island developing states confronting existing and emerging policy challenges as they seek to create an enabling environment for sustained economic growth and national development.

In general, although NPM reforms** were implemented by Caribbean countries during the last five decades, in the midst of the second decade of the twenty-first century, the evidence suggests that the public service as an instrument of government policy formulation and implementation can be viewed as unsuitable for functioning in a global economy.[††] In other words, the public service needs to focus on improving its performance by providing greater accountability, transparency, stakeholder participation, and efficiency. This poses a challenge because the typical public service in the Caribbean is still characterized by top-down structures; archaic and outmoded systems; slow, inefficient, and ineffective decision making; inflexible rules and procedures; indifference to time and costs; weak coordination of activities; poor information management systems; poor research capability and policy analysis; a disconnect between performance aspects such as accountability and empowerment; and the casual and uninformed assumption that public service performance and productivity cannot be measured.[‡‡]

---

* Nomm and Randma-Liiv, "Performance Measurement and Performance Information in New Democracies," pp. 859–881.
† Caribbean Development Bank, *Governance and Institutional Development*.
‡ Brown, Deryck (2008) *Institutional Development and Reform in Public Services: Lessons from the Experience of Small Caribbean States*, Paper prepared for the Commonwealth Association of Public Administration and Management (CAPAM), Biennial Conference, Barbados, October 19–22: 4–11.
§ Ibid.
¶ Emmanuel, *Governance and Democracy*, pp. 82–93.
** Sutton, *Modernizing the State*.
†† Bachan, Carol Ann (2013) "Public service unsuitable for TT," Speech delivered by Minister of Public Administration at 50th Anniversary of Public Service Awards Ceremony, Port of Spain, Trinidad and Tobago.
‡‡ Khan and Soverall, *Gaining Productivity*, pp. 177–181.

The current shape of the public service is the classic pyramid of the British model that was inherited with a small group of managers (5%) at the top, a large group of technical and administrative staff in the middle (20%), and a huge group of clerical and general staff at the bottom (75%) who are not empowered to use discretionary authority. This is a system mired in hierarchy that is unsuitable for a service-oriented, citizen-centric society* and, therefore, underscores the urgent need for further public service modernization (PSM) based on a shift to a diamond shape which reflects a broadening of the middle management level and incorporation of new professional streams, such as project management, information management, procurement management, and facilities management. However, while there has been a great deal of research on the role of traditional public administration issues,[†] the role and function of Public Service Commissions (PSCs),[‡] including the first regional conference of PSCs,[§] and public sector reform (PSR) initiatives,[¶] there has not been much analysis of the specific and fundamental task of improving public service performance in the Caribbean.

The objective of this chapter, therefore, is to provide an analysis of contemporary public service performance in the Caribbean within the context of endogenous and exogenous factors that shaped its current state of play such as colonial legacy, the evolving role of government and the public service, the increasing size of the public service, recruitment and selection policies, supervisory practices, the psychology of organizational culture, and the role of leadership in driving performance-based reforms and innovative PSM initiatives to improve performance. It is hoped that this analysis will make a contribution to the literature on the multidimensional concept of public service performance, in general, and the Caribbean public service experience, in particular, as it continues to evolve in the second decade of the twenty-first century.

Colonial Legacy

The public service in the Caribbean owes its origin to the British colonial civil service. Prior to the advent of political independence, the civil service was Her Majesty's Civil Service, and it functioned by and under laws and regulations promulgated by the British government.** However, although the civil service was essentially the King's Civil Service, there was growing dissatisfaction with the King's monopoly of appointments to the civil service as well as the use of the patronage system. As a consequence, the British Parliament appointed a select committee to improve the system and the method of recruitment. In this context, the Northcote Trevelyan Report of 1854 condemned the recruitment of civil servants on the basis of nepotism and political patronage as well as the system of promotion that was based on patronage rather than merit. One of its major recommendations was the establishment of a Civil Service Commission as an independent and impartial body with the power to recruit suitable persons to the civil service. As a result, civil servants in Britain are defined as servants of the Crown, other than holders of political or judicial offices, who are employed in a civil capacity.

---

* Bachan, op. cit.
† Ryan and Brown, *Issues and Problems*.
‡ Caribbean Centre for Development Administration, *Report of Regional Consultation & Workshop on Public Service Commissions: Imperatives and Challenges for Leading Reform*, St. Lucia, December 2–4, 1997.
§ CARICAD (2008) *Report on the 1st Regional Conference of Public Service Commissions*, St. Vincent and the Grenadines, June 10–12, 2008.
¶ Sutton, op. cit.
** Lalla, *Public Service and Service Commissions*, 3.

Based on ongoing reforms, by the 1870s, the British government viewed the civil service as a permanent and impartial instrument of all administrations based on its efficiency, honesty, impartiality, and integrity. In general, these were the major values that characterized the British colonial civil service in the Caribbean and underpinned its traditional functions. The colonies in the Caribbean were governed from Britain through the Colonial Office which was situated at Whitehall in Westminster where all policy decisions were made.* Thus, the model of government throughout the Caribbean is an adaptation of the Westminster system, now generally referred to as the Westminster-Whitehall model.† Essentially, it combines key aspects of the Westminster system with changes inherited from British colonial practice as manifested in the various independence constitutions.

The key element in the Westminster-Whitehall system is the combination of legislative and executive power in the hands of the government party as manifested in the principle that the party that commands a majority in the lower house of Parliament is entitled to form a government,‡ while the constraining effect of Whitehall is manifested in the powers of the judiciary to safeguard and interpret constitutional practice in the region, thus diminishing the legislative supremacy of Parliament.§ The evidence, therefore, suggests that the practice of politics in the region has led to some adaptations and departures from the original Westminster-Whitehall model, but for the most part, the model has remained relatively intact in the post-independence Caribbean, with the exception of Grenada, which sustained a revolutionary model during the period 1979–1983, and Guyana, which introduced a hybrid presidential/parliamentary system in 1980. The public service is at the heart of operations of the Westminster-Whitehall model that has followed the traditional Weberian pattern as modified by British colonial practice which has resulted in (1) a permanent bureaucracy staffed by neutral and anonymous officials; (2) centralized control exercised through hierarchical structures; (3) the formal separation of policy making from policy implementation; (4) the dominance of general administrators at the apex of the system; (5) an emphasis on following rules and procedures which involve substantial paperwork; and (6) recruitment and promotion based on considerations of race, class, and patronage.¶

Public Service Evolution

The evolution of the Westminster-Whitehall model in the post-independence period was significantly influenced and shaped by specific economic and sociopolitical forces that created a Caribbean tradition of public service performance. The public service became the driving force for social change and national development in most Caribbean countries in the post-independence period in the 1960s and 1970s and, as a consequence, acquired an image of prestige and professionalism. Concomitantly, Caribbean governments sought to ensure that they had a stable and reliable public service with a cadre of trained and experienced persons to effectively and efficiently implement and administer their policies.** In this regard, the public service provides impartial policy advice to government ministers who determine policies while public officers administer and

---

* World Bank (1996) *Perspectives on the Caribbean Public Sector*, Washington, DC: 1–2.
† Sutton, Paul (2008) *Public Sector Reform in the Commonwealth Caribbean: A Review of Recent Experiences*, The Centre for International Governance Innovation, Caribbean Paper No. 6, Waterloo, Ontario, Canada.
‡ Wilson, "The Westminster Model."
§ Ghany, "Creation of Legislative Institutions," pp. 34–49.
¶ Sutton, op. cit.: 2.
** Lalla, op. cit.: 18.

implement them. In other words, the executive relies on the public service to provide it with the necessary skills and expertise not only to manage the government but, perhaps more importantly, to provide ministers with background information, research, and policy advice based on the consequences of policy options.

The public service manages a wide range of services which are the direct responsibility of government ministers, and, as a consequence, there needs to be a professional working relationship between government ministers and senior public officers, operating on the basis of the concept of political neutrality, and constitutional protection for public officers and the role of the PSC. However, empirical analysis of the operations of the politico-administrative systems in some Caribbean countries revealed the nonsense of neutrality* and dysfunctions of competitive party politics in the sense that the functioning of the Westminster-Whitehall model in these countries falls far short of serving PSM objectives. In addition, the model assumes that senior public officers and government ministers share the same class background and have similar notions about what is in the public interest.† Moreover, although the public service is considered to be neutral and professional, there has been a tendency for it to become politicized, as evident in publicized instances of blatant political interference in PSC appointments and promotions.‡

The politicization of the public service continues to be a major factor that negatively impacts public service performance in the Caribbean. For example, as a consequence of politicization, traditional notions of neutrality and impartiality have been dispensed in Belize, Guyana, Jamaica, and St. Lucia, where permanent secretaries have been replaced by contract officers at the very top of the public service.§ Moreover, while the public service was previously able to attract and retain persons of very high caliber, there is now an absence of talent among the current generation of public officers when compared to their predecessors of the immediate post-independence decades, who had a sound education, strong grasp of a broad range of policy issues, and a command of language which conferred on them stature and gravitas in public affairs.¶ In addition, there is also a glaring absence of an indigenous ideology of development around which governments and policy makers can mobilize support in the public service and among the masses based on shared values, attitudes, and an appropriate work ethic to achieve strategic goals, objectives, and outcomes. In this context, therefore, the underlying values shared by policy makers and decision makers impact public service performance as outlined in the priorities identified in national strategic plans. The link between ideology and Caribbean management practice is weakened by the public leadership, which is infected with nepotism, patronage, victimization, and partisanship, and career executives who have class orientations and status aspirations that conflict with the mass society.** These tendencies undermine public service performance because of a lack of national aspirations and strategies to provide sustained leadership and psychological empowerment for genuine transformation.

Another significant factor impacting on public service performance is that Caribbean societies are not socially and institutionally homogenous. Some societies, for example, Antigua and Barbuda, Barbados, Dominica, Grenada, Jamaica, St. Kitts and Nevis, and St. Lucia, can generally be viewed as ethnically homogenous, and then there are those that are ethnically heterogeneous such as Guyana, Suriname, and Trinidad and Tobago.†† Other factors such as ideology, race,

---

* Nunes, "The Nonsense of Neutrality."
† Ryan, *Winner Takes All*, pp. 2–3.
‡ Brown, op. cit.: 12.
§ Ibid.
¶ Ibid.
** Khan, Public Management, op. cit.
†† Ryan: (xiv)–(xv).

culture, and religion further compound the political situation and add to the impact of inter-ethnic conflict in the public services in these countries.* In Trinidad and Tobago, there have been persistent complaints about political polarization as a consequence of the ethnic divide between the two major ethnic groups, Afro-Trinidadian and Indo-Trinidadian. A classic example was the historic Marlborough House Compromise of 1962 which saw Dr. Eric Williams, as leader of government, and Dr. Rudranath Capildeo, as leader of the opposition, stretching arms across the ethnic divide to defuse a potential political crisis that was developing in Trinidad and Tobago.†

A contentious issue arising from these concerns is the perception by the Indo-Trinidadian community that the historical predominance of Afro-Trinidadians employed in the public service is biased, unfair, and unequal. These perceptions were reinforced by the fact that the Afro-based People's National Movement political party remained in government for 30 years (1956–1986). Similar concerns were also expressed in Guyana as a result of the dominance of the Afro-based People's National Congress political party which remained in government for 28 years (1964–1992). Ethnic issues were also evident in Suriname where coalition governments reflected the fractious nature of the society. Allegations of racial discrimination in public sector employment in both Trinidad and Tobago and Guyana resulted in signals of intent to establish an Equal Opportunities Commission and a Race Relations Commission, respectively, to ensure the observance of principles of fairness and equality of opportunity.‡

The culture of the public service is a major corollary of the colonial legacy which has to be analyzed within the specific context of each country. In short, it is a microcosm of the society in which it operates, including varying degrees of dysfunction as a result of authoritarian management styles and submissive attitudes,§ West Indianizing the public service to suit its changing role,¶ conflicting relationships between politicians and public servants because of mistrust,** poor work ethic, including low achievement and high absenteeism,†† the debilitating impact of class relations which characterize mass employee consciousness,‡‡ a preoccupation with leisure,§§ and a general unwillingness to work.¶¶ Thus, public service performance cannot escape the influence of these prevailing attitudes, behaviors, and values that govern the wider society, including the concept of representative bureaucracy which has been severely constrained in its attempt to restore a degree of balance in fractured societies such as Guyana, Suriname, and Trinidad and Tobago.

In order to address some of the problems that negatively impact public service performance, various remedies have been recommended and implemented over the years, including the establishment of PSCs, the public service appeal board (Trinidad and Tobago), the public service appellate tribunal (Guyana), parliamentary ombudsman (several countries), public service unions, freedom of information legislation (some countries), integrity legislation (few countries), the retention of the British Privy Council as court of last resort by many countries, except Barbados, Belize, and Guyana which accepted the Caribbean Court of Justice as their final court of appeal, and

---

* Brown, "Ethnic Politics and Public Sector Management," pp. 367–379.
† Ryan, op. cit.: 267.
‡ Brown, op. cit.: 368.
§ Mills, *Public Administration in the Commonwealth Caribbean*.
¶ Ryan, *Race and Nationalism*, pp. 345–362.
** Draper, *Civil Service*.
†† Bissessar, *Forgotten Factor*.
‡‡ Khan and Soverall, op. cit.: 281–288.
§§ "Time to get serious," *Daily Nation*, March 22, 2013.
¶¶ Caribbean Development Bank, *Country Assessment*.

numerous PSM initiatives, as mechanisms to reduce undue political interference in the public service. However, despite these efforts, there has been varying degrees of success to date.

Public Service Commission

In most Caribbean countries, the role and function of the PSC remains a contentious political issue because of its power to make appointments to the majority of public service posts. In relation to senior posts, such as heads of judiciaries, ministries, departments, and some extra-ministerial offices, the appointment process assigns a major role to heads of government. Members of the PSC are appointed by the government (governor-general, president, or prime minister or with consultation among some combination of these).* Line ministers are responsible for establishing public service positions, the number of such positions, the qualifications required, the responsibilities, and remuneration. In order to minimize political interference, in most countries, the power to appoint individuals to these positions lies with the PSC. The scope of appointment powers of the PSC includes judicial and legal officers, public servants in and outside of ministerial departments, teachers, and senior police officers. However, although the service commissions exist in all the countries, their functions and their constitutional status vary.

In most Caribbean countries, the constitution provides for the establishment of at least one PSC. Nine have police service commissions (PolSCs), five have teaching service commissions (TSCs), and all, except Belize, have judicial and legal service commissions (JLSCs), while there is one JLSC serving the Organization of Eastern Caribbean States (OECS) member countries.† In Belize, there is only one PSC comprising 18 members, especially designed to handle both judicial and the full range of public service appointments. In comparison, there are four service commissions each in Barbados, Guyana, and Trinidad and Tobago. However, while in Antigua and Barbuda, Bahamas, Belize, Dominica, Grenada, Jamaica, St. Kitts and Nevis, and St. Vincent and the Grenadines, there are no TSCs, in Belize, Grenada, and St. Lucia, there are no PolSCs.‡ In Trinidad and Tobago, the first report of the PSC noted that the PSC was preceded by the Civil Service Selection Committee in 1928 which later evolved into the Civil Service Staff Board in 1936, and finally, in 1950, the PSC was established by the Trinidad and Tobago (Constitution) Order in Council.§ Since then, it is found in Section 92 of the 1962 Constitution, and in Section 121 of the 1976 Constitution, while the composition of the PSC is set out in Section 120 of the Constitution.

In Barbados, the central agencies responsible for personnel management in the public service were the services commissions department and the establishment division.¶ Matters pertaining to selection, recruitment, appointment, placement, promotion, transfer, and discipline fell under the jurisdiction of the services commissions department which exercised control over five service commissions, namely, the PSC, the PolSC, the JLSC, the TSC, and the statutory board service commission (SBSC).** The establishment division had responsibility for matters pertaining to the creation and establishment of posts, classification and grading of posts, staffing of ministries and

---

* World Bank, op. cit.: 2–3.
† Emmanuel, op. cit.: 82–83.
‡ Ibid.
§ Government of the Republic of Trinidad and Tobago, *Public Service Commission*, p. 1.
¶ Khan and Soverall (1993) "Human Resource Development in the Public Sector," pp. 48–58.
** Ibid: 49.

departments, determination of wages and salaries, industrial relations, pensions, and conditions of service.* The first report of the PSC in Barbados noted that the PSC was established in 1951 as one of the initiatives by the British Colonial Office in the process of devolving responsible government to Barbados prior to political independence.† In 1966, the services commissions were enshrined in Section 90(1) of the Constitution, while Sections 90(3), (4) and 105 of the Constitution provided for the composition of the PSC. It should be noted, however, that although the teaching service commission was provided for in the 1974 Constitutional Amendments, it was never appointed.

The rationale for the colonial authorities constituting the services commissions was to ensure that nepotism and political interference would be deterred because they assumed that the newly elected politicians could not be trusted to exercise power of appointment fairly and with self-control.‡ Thus, although the implementation of the PSC was basically to minimize political interference, politicians viewed the regulatory controls and constraints on their ability to manage the public service as a source of frustration. This situation is made even more problematic because the provisions for appointment to the commissions themselves directly engage the heads of government, notwithstanding rules of restriction and exclusion defining the classes of persons who may be appointed to service commissions.§ Moreover, constitutionally sanctioned engagement of prime ministers and presidents in matters of appointment extends beyond service commissions to all senior positions in the judicial and executive branches, including chief justices, permanent secretaries, heads and deputy heads of departments, ambassadors and foreign service staff, as well as senior professional advisers.¶ It also includes some key offices such as the directors of public prosecutions and audit which are offices whose functions are expressly declared to be not subject to political direction and control. In this context, therefore, the specific guidelines governing the process of prime ministerial involvement in these matters vary among the countries.

In the Bahamas, Barbados, Belize, and Jamaica, the chief justices are appointed by the head of state on the recommendation of the prime minister after consultation with the opposition leader. In Trinidad and Tobago, appointment is by the president after consultation with the prime minister and opposition leader. The chief justice in the OECS is appointed by the Queen on the recommendation of the prime ministers and premiers of participating countries. In Guyana, the chancellor is appointed by the president after consultation with the opposition leader. In most countries, except Barbados and Belize, all other judges are appointed by the JLSCs in their own discretion. As a consequence of a constitutional amendment in 1974, Barbados departed from the conventional practice and transferred power to the prime minister to appoint judges after consultation with the opposition leader.** In Belize, judges are appointed in accordance with the advice of the JLSC and with the concurrence of the prime minister and the opposition leader.

The JLSCs are all chaired by the chief justices (the chancellor rather than the chief justice in Guyana). They include chairmen of PSCs (two on a rotating basis on the OECS Commission), and the other appointees must be judges, former judges, and in some cases, retired attorneys. Bahamas includes persons qualified to be judges, and in Trinidad and Tobago, one appointee may be an attorney still in practice. Members of parliament, however, are expressly excluded except in Guyana and Jamaica, while public officers are excluded everywhere except in the Bahamas.

---

* Ibid: 49.
† Government of Barbados, *Public Service Commission*, p. 1.
‡ Ryan, op. cit.: 263.
§ Emmanuel, op. cit.: 83.
¶ Ibid: 85.
** Ibid: 86.

In the Bahamas, Barbados, Belize, Guyana, and Jamaica, the appointed members (those not sitting ex-officio) are chosen on the recommendation of the prime ministers (or president in Guyana) after consultation with the opposition leaders. In the OECS, one former judge is appointed on the agreement of at least four heads of government, while in Trinidad and Tobago, appointed members are selected by the president after consultation with the prime minister and opposition leader.

The legal framework for the operation of the PSC is quite general and in dire need of reform. However, although some reforms have occurred in a number of Caribbean countries over the years, they did not include any significant legal or constitutional changes. Thus, even though the service commissions can be expected to exercise their functions independent of political direction or control, this express provision is only made in the constitutions of Belize and the OECS countries.* In addition, the process of removal of a commissioner, on grounds of illness or misbehavior, requires the use of judicial tribunals in all cases, except in Jamaica and Trinidad and Tobago. In Jamaica, all service commissioners, except the chief justice and president of the court of appeal, are removable by the governor-general on the recommendation of the prime minister after consultation with the leader of the opposition. In Trinidad and Tobago, all service commissioners other than the chief justice and three appointed members are removable by the president in his own discretion.

Apart from the power of appointment, PSCs also exercise powers of discipline and removal of public officers, except in cases of independent officers (judges, directors of public prosecution, directors of audit) where removal is undertaken by tribunals.† In all cases, public officers have the right of appeal against disciplinary measures or dismissal by the PSCs. The appeal bodies include the Privy Councils of Barbados and Jamaica, the advisory council in Belize, and public service boards of appeal in the other nine countries. Privy Councils are chaired by the governors-general and they are constituted on the advice of prime ministers. In addition, there are some special provisions that affect the performance of these public service bodies, such as the reservation of chairmanship to persons with judicial experience or qualifications in the Bahamas, Guyana, and Trinidad and Tobago or the requirement that prime ministers consult opposition leaders in Antigua and Barbuda, Belize, and Trinidad and Tobago, or the absence of the requirement for consultations with associations in Belize and Trinidad and Tobago.

The members of the boards of appeal, excluding the Privy Councils, are removable by process of tribunal deliberations, except in Trinidad and Tobago, where the president may remove persons in his own judgment. In Trinidad and Tobago, the public service appeal board can only hear appeals relating specifically to disciplinary matters after they have been decided upon by the PSC, but the public service appellate tribunal in Guyana seems to have a wider mandate and considerable powers of investigation.‡ Another public institution that can investigate unfair practices in the public service is the office of ombudsman or parliamentary commissioner as it is called in St. Lucia. The constitutions of Antigua and Barbuda, Dominica, Guyana, St. Lucia, and Trinidad and Tobago provide for the office of ombudsman, while it is provided by statute in Barbados and Jamaica. However, the constitutions of Guyana and Trinidad and Tobago expressly forbid the ombudsman from investigating any actions taken by the PSC in respect of personnel matters. The ombudsman can do no more than uncover the facts and present them to the PSC.

Another option available to public officers is to seek the assistance and intervention of public service unions. However, the differences among countries vary considerably. For example, in

---

* Ibid: 85.
† Ibid: 88.
‡ Brown, op. cit.: 376.

Guyana, the Guyana Public Service Union has adopted an aggressive stance toward the government and even set up its own race relations committee to promote awareness of racial and cultural issues within the public service work environment and the wider society. In contrast, in Trinidad and Tobago, the Public Services Association, which represents the majority of public sector employees, steadfastly avoids issues of race and ethnicity in order to minimize any fallout from internal divisions within its ranks. Since most Caribbean countries are too small to have two full teams of qualified senior technocrats who would switch at every change of government, many governments rely increasingly on public enterprises which operate outside the purview of the PSC and the appointment on contract of personnel to unscheduled posts in the public service. However, the scale and frequency of the use of these mechanisms underscore the need to go beyond palliative PSR efforts to more innovative PSM initiatives that actually transform the public service.

Size of Public Service

A central focus of all PSR efforts and recent PSM initiatives is the size of the public service. The size of the public service has consistently been scrutinized because of the major role that it plays in the national development of all Caribbean countries. Size differs considerably across countries and territories for a variety of reasons and there are differences in the public service size ranking depending on which measurement is used.* Arthur Lewis argued that the only limit to the size of the public sector is the government's capacity to finance it.† In the Caribbean, the public service affects almost every aspect of citizens' lives, literally from the cradle to the grave, as a result of social policies implemented by successive governments over the years to improve the standard of living. However, although the dominant role of the public service based on the philosophy of public ownership, control, and operation of the commanding heights of the economy no longer exists,‡ it still casts a large shadow over the economy and society. Yet, after 46 years of independence in Barbados, and 50 years in both Jamaica and Trinidad and Tobago,§ respectively, citizens complain that the public service is too inefficient,¶ it is too large and needs to be trimmed,** and it lacks effective performance measurement.††

Caribbean countries can be classified into three groups based on their size.‡‡ The OECS member countries can be referred to as Group A—Antigua and Barbuda, Dominica, Grenada, St. Kitts and Nevis, St. Lucia, and St. Vincent and the Grenadines—which are the smallest countries and they share common public sector institutions. Group B—the Bahamas, Barbados, and Belize—are considered to be middle-sized countries. Group C—Haiti (10.6m), the Dominican Republic (9.7m), Guyana, Jamaica (2.7m), Suriname, and Trinidad and Tobago (1.3m)—are the largest countries. The 15 Caribbean countries have a total population of 25 million, with the largest being Haiti (10.6m) and the twin-islands of St. Kitts and Nevis (55,000) with the smallest population. In contrast to the relatively small size of the population in many Caribbean countries, the size of the public service is large in terms of absolute numbers and share of government consumption in gross domestic product (GDP) (see Table 6.1).

---

* Carrizosa, *Public Sectors in the Americas*.
† World Bank (1996) *Perspectives on the Caribbean Public Sector*, Washington, DC: 14.
‡ Ibid: 99.
§ "Still colonial at 50," *Trinidad Newsday*, January 4, 2012: 10.
¶ "The Art of 'Yes, Minister'," *T&T Review*, October 2011: 11.
** "Cuts to civil service needed, says Sir Courtney," *Weekend Nation*, November 25, 2011: 6.
†† "Public service needs to focus on performance," *The Barbados Advocate*, December 7, 2012.
‡‡ World Bank (1996) *Public Sector Modernization*, op. cit.

Table 6.1 Public Service Size in the Caribbean

Countries	1984	1995	2004	2010	Govt. as % GDP	% Labor Force
Antigua and Barbuda	NA	8,000	NA	10,500	22.0%	32.0%
Bahamas	12,000	26,469	NA	NA	15.0%	18.8%
Barbados	9,100	24,000	26,000	32,000	21.0%	18.1%
Belize	2,128	5,309	8,000	11,000	13.9%	11.8%
Dominica	NA	2,725	4,000	NA	19.0%	21.2%
Dom. Republic	NA	210,367	313,706	NA	9.8%	9.6%
Grenada	NA	5,437	NA	NA	17.0%	9.4%
Guyana	NA	16,000	21,206	31,000	21.6%	9.1%
Haiti	NA	NA	NA	NA	6.0%	1.6%
Jamaica	103,784	95,397	60,502	57,000	11.0%	10.5%
St. Kitts and Nevis	2,245	NA	NA	NA	23.3%	41.6%
St. Lucia	NA	5,345	7,500	9,500	23.0%	12.1%
St. Vincent	NA	NA	6,608	7,100	20.0%	11.6%
Suriname	NA	NA	NA	31,523	31.0%	37.4%
Trinidad and Tobago	63,000	88,000	NA	51,808	15.0%	23.6%

Sources: CARICOM Secretariat, *Report of CARICOM/ILO Technical Meeting of Public Sector Personnel Practitioners,* Dover Convention Centre, Barbados, 1984; CAPAM, *Current Issues in the Public Service,* CAPAM, Toronto, Ontario, Canada, 1995; The World Bank, *Public Sector Modernization in the Caribbean,* World Bank, Washington, DC, 1996; Carrizosa, *Public Sectors in the Americas: How Big Are They?* World Bank, Washington, DC, 2007; Government of Suriname, *Public Administration Report,* Ministry of Public Administration, 2013; Government of the Republic of Trinidad and Tobago, *Report of the Public Service Commission for the Period 1992–1994,* Personnel Division, Ministry of Public Administration, Port of Spain, Trinidad and Tobago, 2013.

Note: G.C., government consumption.

The size of the public service has to be analyzed within the context of the political economy in terms of both employment and government expenditure since it is the largest single employer in the economy of most Caribbean countries and the share of government consumption in GDP is relatively high—French Guiana (59.6%), Montserrat (49.9%), Martinique (38.1%), Guadeloupe (38.0%), Cuba (38.0%), Aruba (26.6%), Netherlands Antilles (18.9%), Turks and Caicos Islands (17.1%), British Virgin Islands (16.8%), Cayman Islands (15.0%), Anguilla (14.7%), and Bermuda (11.0%). In the OECS, it is also high—St. Kitts and Nevis (23.3%), St. Lucia (23.0%), St. Vincent and the Grenadines (20.0%), Dominica (19.0%), and Grenada (17.0%), while the share of the labor force is equally high—St. Kitts and Nevis (41.6%), Antigua and Barbuda (32.0%), and Dominica (21.2%).

There has been an increase in debt in most Caribbean countries over the years that tested the limits of sustainability.* Over the period 1960–2002, five of the six fastest growing Caribbean countries were from the OECS, but most of them also experienced the sharpest growth declines between the late 1980s and 1990s, and during the period 1998–2003, OECS countries grew slower than non-OECS countries. This was the result of a massive increase in debt in the OECS, almost double the percentage of GDP between 1997 and 2003 because of increases in capital and current expenditures. In the case of both Guyana and Jamaica, debt has been a long-standing issue. However, although debt has been substantially reduced in Guyana through Heavily Indebted Poor Countries-related debt write-offs, Jamaica maintained very high primary surpluses in the medium-term in order to stabilize and reduce its debt. Antigua and Barbuda was already over 100% of GDP in 1997, and it increased to 142% of GDP by 2003. In Belize, there was also an increase in debt from 41% of GDP in 1997 to 100% of GDP in 2003. Dominica (122), Grenada (113), Guyana (179), Jamaica (142), and St. Kitts and Nevis (171) clearly illustrated the extent of the debt crisis in the Caribbean (see Table 6.2).

Table 6.2 Caribbean Government Expenditures, Revenues, and Debt

	G.E. (% GDP)		G.R. (% GDP)		Public Debt (% GDP)	
Countries	1990–1997	1998–2003	1990–1997	1998–2003	1997	2003
Antigua and Barbuda	NA	29	NA	21	102	142
Bahamas	NA	NA	NA	NA	62	84
Barbados	27	37	24	32	62	84
Belize	NA	32	NA	21	41	100
Dominica	35	41	32	32	61	122
Dom. Republic	16	18	14	15	23	56
Grenada	31	37	28	30	42	113
Guyana	38	44	34	38	211	179
Haiti	9	10	5	7	NA	44
Jamaica	28	35	28	27	103	142
St. Kitts and Nevis	30	43	28	32	86	171
St. Lucia	27	29	26	26	36	69
St. Vincent	31	33	30	29	48	73
Suriname	NA	36	NA	30	24	44
Trinidad and Tobago	28	26	28	24	52	54

Source: The World Bank (2005) *A Time to Choose: Caribbean Development in the 21st Century*, Report No. 31725-LAC, World Bank, Washington, DC.

Note: G.E., government expenditure; G.R., government revenue.

---

* World Bank (2005), op. cit.: xvii.

In fact, average Caribbean debt in 2003 was 96% of GDP and the very high debt profile placed 7 Caribbean countries among the 10 most indebted countries in the world, and 14 among the top 30.* An increase in government expenditure in every Caribbean country also compounded the situation as the average rose from 27% of GDP over 1990–1997 to 32% of GDP during the period 1998–2003, as a consequence of expansionary fiscal policy being used to correct exogenous shocks.

Another factor that contributed to the significant increase in debt was increased wage bills (see Table 6.3). This situation severely constrained the efficiency of the public service because all countries except Suriname implemented Structural Adjustment Programs (SAPs) in order to reduce their fiscal deficits, debt burdens, and public service wage bills, in order to restore macroeconomic balance.† In the period 2010–2013, governments across the region struggled to pay salaries

Table 6.3 Public Service Wage Bill in the Caribbean

Countries	Wages (% of G.E.) 1980–1984	Wages (% of G.E.) 1985–1989	Wages (% of G.E.) 1990–1994	Govt. Exp. (% of GDP) 1998–2003	Public Debt (% of GDP) 2012
Antigua and Barbuda	36.6	41.8	68.6	29	97.8
Bahamas	42.3	50.4	60.3	NA	52.6
Barbados	42.6	44.6	53.2	37	70.4
Belize	46.2	52.1	53.0	32	81.0
Dominica	58.6	56.7	NA	41	72.3
Dom. Republic	48.1	39.4	NA	18	56.0
Grenada	52.0	52.4	58.8	37	105.4
Guyana	NA	37.7	NA	44	60.4
Haiti	NA	NA	NA	10	NA
Jamaica	NA	NA	66.0	10	143.3
St. Kitts and Nevis	41.2	42.4	59.9	43	144.9
St. Lucia	51.3	53.0	53.0	29	78.7
St. Vincent	44.6	51.8	57.6	33	68.3
Suriname	NA	NA	43.8	36	18.6
Trinidad and Tobago	40.6	40.6	41.9	26	35.7

Sources: The World Bank, *Public Sector Modernization in the Caribbean*, World Bank, Washington, DC,1996; The World Bank (2005) *A Time to Choose: Caribbean Development in the 21st Century*, Report No. 31725-LAC, World Bank, Washington, DC; International Monetary Fund (February 20, 2013) *Caribbean Small States: Challenges of High Debt and Low Growth*, International Monetary Fund, Washington, DC.

Note: G.E., government expenditure.

---

* Ibid: xx.
† World Bank, *Public Sector Modernization*, op. cit.: 6.

and quell attendant industrial disputes that are rooted in persistent fiscal deficits and debt crises. In Antigua and Barbuda, the government implemented a wage freeze as part of an International Monetary Fund (IMF) adjustment program aimed at reducing its heavy debt burden.* In Barbados, the government's high fiscal deficit, failure to privatize some statutory corporations, and reduce public sector jobs were the primary reasons for two sovereign rating downgrades.† In Dominica, however, the government offered its public servants a 1% salary increase because it could not afford to pay the 3% requested by the public service union.‡

Meanwhile, the government in Grenada also experienced difficulty in paying the salaries of public servants, and on several occasions it borrowed money from the National Insurance Scheme to pay salaries.§ In Guyana, the massive overextension of the public sector during the 1960s and 1970s pushed public expenditures higher than 80% of GDP by the 1980s. However, although the Economic Recovery Program helped to reduce public expenditures from 66% of GDP in 1989 to 38% in 1994, public sector performance was severely compromised by the loss of skilled personnel and depressed wages. Personal emoluments decreased steadily during the late 1980s as skilled personnel migrated, equipment deteriorated, materials became difficult to procure, and vacancies remained unfilled. In Jamaica, although government revenues surpassed expenditures during the mid-1980s and the 1990s, it was eroded by persistent debt crises which precipitated the implementation of several SAPs that continued into the 2000s. As a result, public service performance was severely constrained by high public expenditures and high debt payments, and in 2012, these factors influenced public officers to agree to a government wage freeze and the reduction in more public sector posts as a means of further wage cost reduction.¶

The global financial crisis and CLICO's collapse worsened the Caribbean debt crisis and, as a result, the ratio of public debt to GDP increased by about 15% points between 2008 and 2010. In 2011, the government in St. Kitts and Nevis implemented a wage freeze as part of an IMF adjustment program to reduce its high fiscal deficit.** In fact, Antigua and Barbuda, Jamaica, and St. Kitts and Nevis are recent case studies of sovereign debt restructuring. Prior to debt restructuring, debt exceeded 100% of GDP in these countries, and debt service was 16% of GDP. However, despite debt relief, they remain vulnerable to debt distress, given their high debt ratios, between 90% of GDP in Antigua and Barbuda and 140% of GDP in Jamaica. In the case of Jamaica, the IMF is set to approve a 4-year arrangement under the External Fund Facility worth SDR 615 million (about US$958 million) by the end of April.†† In St. Lucia, the Police Welfare Association accepted the government's 4% wage hike while the Civil Service Association demanded a 9.5% wage increase for the period 2010–2012.‡‡ It is estimated that the 3-week public service strike cost the government approximately EC$3 million because the operations at the Ministry of Commerce, Customs, Registry, and Inland Revenue departments were the worst affected.§§ In St. Vincent and the Grenadines, the government settled for a 4.5% salary increase, in contrast to the situation in Trinidad and Tobago where some unions and agencies accepted a 5% wage increase for daily-paid employees while others such as the National Union of Government and Federated

---

* Prime Minister Dr. Kenny Anthony's Speech to the Nation, Castries, St. Lucia, January, 7, 2013.
† "Belling the public sector cat," *Midweek Nation*, July 25, 2012: 9A.
‡ Prime Minister Anthony, op. cit.
§ Ibid.
¶ "More posts to be cut from public sector," *The Barbados Advocate*, March 19, 2013: 15.
** Prime Minister Dr. Kenny Anthony, op. cit.
†† "Jamaica: US$958 million IMF agreement possible by month end," *The Barbados Advocate*, April 9, 2013: 15.
‡‡ "St. Lucia: Civil servants take industrial action," *The Barbados Advocate*, March 19, 2013: 15.
§§ "Strike costs St. Lucia gov't over EC$3m," *The Barbados Advocate*, April 12, 2013.

Workers refused to accept the offer and instead demanded a 9% increase. As a result of the industrial dispute, the matter was referred to the Industrial Court for adjudication.*

The situation in Trinidad and Tobago has to be analyzed within the context of oil windfalls that were used to significantly increase the size of the public sector during the 1970s and 1980s. By 1986–1990, the public service and public enterprises accounted for approximately 66% of GDP, which reflected a stark decline from the previous decade. In 1987, 30% of the labor force was employed in the public service and the wage bill consumed about 15% of GDP. In 1990, public service employment was reduced by using a Voluntary Separation Employment Program (VSEP) and privatization of several public enterprises. As a consequence, by 1994, public service employment had declined to 22% of the labor force, and government expenditure had declined to 27% of GDP, down from 42% in the early 1980s. However, by 2010, the number had increased to 35,480 public officers, with a further 16,328 persons appointed on contract for a grand total of 51,808.†
In addition, the number of ministries increased from 26 in 2010 to 32 in June 2012. Moreover, these contrasting factors continue to negatively impact the performance of the public service in Barbados,‡ Trinidad and Tobago,§ and Jamaica.¶

Recruitment and Selection

In most Caribbean countries, matters pertaining to recruitment, selection, appointment, placement, promotion, transfer, training, and discipline fall under the jurisdiction of the services commissions department or some other central agency responsible for personnel management in the public service such as the personnel division, establishment division, or the Ministry of the Civil Service.** The chief personnel officer of the personnel division works in close collaboration with the various PSCs, such as the PolSC, the JLSC, the TSC, the SBSC, and the Ministry of the Civil Service to regulate the recruitment and selection process. The establishment function covers the areas related to organizational structure of ministries, departments, position classification and grading, staff numbers, salaries, conditions of service, training, and pensions. Over the years, there have been numerous complaints about the degree of political influence and overlapping functions in the traditional personnel management system and, thus, the need for a more objective human resource management (HRM) approach to improve recruitment and selection practices.

In this regard, the major areas identified for change included the PSC, improving effectiveness, accountability and transparency, knowledge management, criteria pertaining to recruitment, job security, promotion systems, horizontal occupational mobility, performance evaluation systems, training and human resource development, working conditions, salary administration, and labor relations.†† In 1995, the heads of government were presented with a proposal for radical reform (even abolishment) of the PSCs in preference for public service employment acts that would modernize the public service and introduce a philosophy of partnership between the executive, the

---

* "Lambert says CPO the stumbling block in bargaining," *Trinidad Guardian*, August 10, 2012: A12.
† Author's interview with Permanent Secretary Gillian Macintyre, Minister of Public Administration, Mrs. Sandra Marchack, former chief personnel officer, and Jacqueline Wilson, former permanent secretary, Prime Minister's Office, Port of Spain, Trinidad and Tobago, February 6, 2013.
‡ Soverall and Turton, "Performance Review and Development System."
§ Government of the Republic of Trinidad and Tobago, *Green Paper on Transforming the Civil Service*.
¶ Caribbean Policy Research Institute, *Towards Public Sector Reform In Jamaica*.
** Khan and Soverall, "Human Resource Development," pp. 48–58.
†† Draper, op. cit.: 7.

PSC, their representative organizations, and the public at large. In addition, it was envisaged that the personnel functions of the PSC would be reduced in preference for the wider use of delegated power to permanent secretaries and personnel departments to improve the speed and efficiency of decision making. However, to date, very little action has been taken to follow up on this proposal thus indicating the limited political support for radical PSR and PSM initiatives.

The concept of a professional public service patterned after the Westminster-Whitehall model, which based employment on skill and qualification rather than on political expediency, is a positive legacy from the colonial period.* In this regard, one of the distinguishing features of an effective public service is the establishment of a career system in which public servants are recruited and promoted on the basis of merit, ability, and integrity. The concept of the career system is based on the assumption that as persons get older and as their domestic and personal commitments increase, there should be an increase in emoluments and the expectation of promotion at frequent intervals in order to bolster the capacity of the public service to attract and retain capable personnel. In practice, however, the evidence in most Caribbean countries indicates that personnel management practices and systems inherited from the colonial administration, including PSCs that operate on a part-time basis, have not changed substantially over time and, therefore, are incapable of satisfying modern HRM demands.

The personnel management nomenclature is inimical to modern HRM practices. Moreover, it does not inspire confidence in the public service leadership because it has failed to move beyond the rhetoric of HRM and largely cosmetic changes such as the establishment of HRM units and HRM departments in several countries, including Barbados, Guyana, Jamaica, Trinidad and Tobago, that are still functioning essentially as personnel agencies rather than promoting genuine human resource development by integrating the fragmented functions of personnel, establishments, and training divisions.† In fact, a tripartite structure of the PSC, personnel division, and line department now characterizes the HRM function in most Caribbean countries, with Barbados using the personnel division to hire, reward, and evaluate employees, while Guyana leaves it to the head of the institution or agency, and Trinidad and Tobago uses the PSC.‡

In order to maintain a competent, efficient, and professional public service, it is critical to recruit persons of integrity and probity who will be able to administer the affairs of government efficiently and impartially. However, political influence in personnel management procedures continues to undermine the concept and practice of HRM in most Caribbean countries as a result of unsatisfactory, and often dubious, personnel recruitment and selection as well as seniority-based promotion. In other words, the modern concept of HRM has created problems for an archaic personnel management system that guarantees mediocrity and conformity and thus has been tardy in transitioning from seniority and longevity to objective criteria such as merit and performance. Repeated calls for adopting a reward system that recognizes merit performance, achievement, initiative, qualification, and results as the principal criteria for promotion rather than seniority is slowly gaining momentum. In Barbados, the new Public Service Act 2007 has moved the public service in this direction but not without some strong resistance including early retirement by persons who felt aggrieved by the implementation of a performance and promotion system based on merit. In Trinidad and Tobago, it has now become common practice for the decisions of the PSC

---

* *Public Sector Modernization in the Caribbean*, op. cit: 36–38.
† Wayne Soverall (1989), *Human Resource Development in the Public Sector: The Barbadian Experience*, Research Paper submitted to the Department of Political Science, Brooklyn College, New York.
‡ Draper, op. cit.

to be challenged in court by persons who felt that they were overlooked for promotion as a result of supersession.

In most Caribbean countries, there is an absence of a clear human resource development policy and strategy in the public service. Thus, recruitment is made to fill posts in the manipulative (lower), clerical, administrative, technical and professional classes and posts are divided vertically according to the nature of the duties and horizontally according to the level of competence required to execute the duties. Paying adequate salaries to managers and staff and granting autonomy and responsibility to managers are necessary elements of a system of accountability for results, in tandem with tight controls on overall cost. However, although this approach should be evident throughout the public service in the Caribbean, it is quite rare. In general, public service employees at technical and managerial levels do not generally get paid well in comparison with the private sector. As a result, it is difficult to attract skilled personnel to the public service and even more difficult to retain the existing ones. The net effect of such employment practices is that the public service lacks the requisite human resource development capacity and skillset to implement and enforce public policies in the desired manner.

In Trinidad and Tobago, during the 1990s, while compensation was almost double the prevailing market wages at lower levels in the public service, at the professional, technical, and managerial ranks, it was as much as 50% to 70% lower than in the private sector and this made it difficult to attract and retain qualified staff. In many cases, personnel are lost to the private sector and other organizations because of the absence of purpose and professionalism, lack of drive and initiative, stagnation, weak career management, and mediocrity.* In several countries, including Barbados, Jamaica, and Trinidad and Tobago, increasing efforts are being made to attract trained nationals who possess skills and competencies in various disciplines, but with limited success. This approach, however, is not new since many attempts were made over the years to attract expatriates with short-term contracts but there were no supportive structures to enable such a policy to be successful,† and thus, the evidence suggests that little has changed over time.

In Guyana, despite some improvement in the 1990s, wages remained far too low to attract and retain professionals who could do better in a regional and global labor market. In Jamaica, the civil service was reduced as a result of successive administrative reform initiatives that were implemented as part of SAPs. Moreover, although the wage bill in 1994–1995 accounted for more than 50% of the government's discretionary current expenditure, the salaries of managerial, professional, and technical staff were typically half or less than that of the private sector. As a result, professionals were not attracted to the public service, as indicated by the significant number of vacancies that remained unfilled, while the lower ranks were overstaffed. In Suriname, the quality of public service was compromised by patterns of high public expenditure, fiscal deficits, inflation, and negative growth, while in Trinidad and Tobago, the VSEP succeeded in reducing the size of the public service without demoralizing staff or too much political fallout, although it lost more talented staff than it had anticipated. However, the government was much more careful the second time around in relation to selection and control over the number of public employees who exited as a result of VSEP and, therefore, established a personnel database to ensure that they were not rehired elsewhere in the public service.

Administrative reform programs in the 1990s in Belize, Dominica, Jamaica, St. Lucia, and St. Vincent and the Grenadines sought to address these concerns by attempting to regrade positions, upgrade salaries, and transition from personnel management to HRM in order to improve the

---

* Khan and Soverall, op. cit.: 293–297.
† Reginald Demas (2013) "Entice expats with short-term treats," *Trinidad Express*, February 7.

practice of attracting, appointing, and retaining skilled, competent and suitably qualified persons with potential for future growth and development. Indeed, in 1995, Caribbean heads of government endorsed a program of PSR and administrative restructuring with a view to addressing some of these concerns.* As a result, PSR programs in the region focused on the following principles: decentralization of HRM functions, subject to budget constraints and performance standards; implementation of clear guidelines and detailed job descriptions and requirements, as well as objective criteria for performance evaluation, and clearly delineated career paths for advancement, a transparent appeals process for disputes over performance evaluation, and specific penalties for poor performance or corruption; increased training opportunities for employee development; and pay based on merit.†

Additional reforms of the legal framework governing PSCs included the consolidation of multiple PSCs into one commission and clearer legislation on delegation of the responsibility to appoint, remove, and discipline public officers.‡ The latter was bolstered by a general perception that delegation of responsibility would facilitate the development of executive agencies and other management innovations which, in turn, would require reengineering the role of the PSC. However, only Jamaica has been bold enough to actually establish executive agencies as part of its PSM program with a view to improving public service performance through empowering service delivery agencies with greater authority and establishing incentives to manage and allocate resources to produce results.§ In 1996, it became the first Caribbean country to experiment with executive agencies modeled on reforms in the United Kingdom, New Zealand, and Canada to establish the institutional basis for the performance management of selected government departments to be designated as executive agencies. The performance of these agencies to date has been uneven because despite visible efficiency and productivity gains, especially in relation to improved customer service, the result also includes an overlaying of new practices and rules over old practices and culture.¶ In addition, it has been suggested that higher salaries may not be justified since employees of the executive agencies are not better qualified than those in the traditional public service.** Moreover, analysis of reforms suggests the existence of two parallel public services in Jamaica with informal management structures coexisting with the formal, thus, underscoring the need for change not only in performance and culture of the public service but also among the public at large.††

Most reforms were undertaken within the context that a smaller but well-paid, well-trained public service can be more effective and less expensive than an overstaffed, less qualified, and underpaid public service. In many cases, international donors and lenders play a major role in facilitating training and human resource development, but the situation calls for a much more comprehensive human resource development strategy at the national and sectoral levels to make it sustainable. Thus, despite increased PSR efforts throughout the Caribbean, in many instances they failed to establish adequate human resource development platforms upon which reoriented performance incentives could be built to complement PSM initiatives through public service reengineering and restructuring. In other words, public service performance across the Caribbean has been severely constrained by the lack of actual innovative PSM initiatives. Moreover, despite sustained PSR

---

* *Public Sector Modernization in the Caribbean*, op. cit.: 1–7.
† Ibid: 36–38.
‡ Ibid: 37.
§ World Bank (2005) *A Time to Choose*. op. cit.: 29.
¶ *Towards Public Sector Reform in Jamaica*, op. cit.: 10.
** Ibid.
†† CARICAD, *Executive Agency Model*.

efforts over the years to eliminate some of the structural manifestations of colonialism through various programs and initiatives, the desired transformation in the functions of the bureaucratic public service has not occurred.

In fact, in many countries today, the concepts of administration that typified the colonial system still persist because public officers continue to see their role as daily routines of assembling information on files and passing them up the hierarchy for decisions to be made by their superiors rather than recognizing their contribution to national development and, therefore, seeking to continuously improve their performance. They fail to realize that limiting their functions and scope of decision making to mere paper passing does not enhance their problem-solving capability nor create the enabling environment that is required for private sector participation to boost competitiveness and productivity. Essentially, the achievement of economic development is limited by the capacity and spirit of the bureaucratic structure.* In other words, little attention continues to be paid to the role of the public service as an independent variable that significantly influences any kind of transformation in developing countries and the benefits to be derived from a comprehensive human resource development strategy that significantly empowers the talent within the public service and the wider society. It is necessary, therefore, to introduce more systematic and fundamental innovations and provide dedicated leadership at the political and organizational levels to drive the actual transformation of structures, systems, and processes to enhance public service performance.

Supervisory Practices

In many Caribbean countries, the colonial and plantation experience left a legacy of managerial, organizational, supervisory, and labor attitudes and practices which were founded on fear, exploitation, domination, dehumanization, dispossession, prejudice, and mistrust.† In fact, the influence of these atavistic attitudes and cultural memories continues to undermine PSR efforts over the years and represent a major constraint on the implementation of fifth-generation PSM initiatives. In 2013, inherited colonial characteristics that still dominate the public service in Barbados can be applied to most of the other Caribbean countries—an organizational structure that is rigidly hierarchical with decision making concentrated in the hands of the 25% at the top, with the 75% majority carrying out tasks by instruction or by rote; highly centralized systems dealing with personnel, which constrain action on the part of line ministries; a compartmentalized, silo approach to policy making and implementation where information sharing and coordination are not formally prescribed but depend on largely on the initiative of people involved; action weighted on the side of conforming with detailed rules and regulations rather than on delivering services in a timely manner; and rules and practice that constrain the sharing of information with the public and the media.‡

Excessive centralization and concentration of decision-making authority make it virtually impossible to keep pace with the demands of a modern economy and society, and as a result, it has become increasingly dysfunctional. Moreover, excessive bureaucracy inhibits timely action,

---

* La Palombara, *Bureaucracy and Political Development*.
† Khan and Soverall, op. cit.: 172–183.
‡ *Unlocking the Potential of the Public Service: Reforms for the 21st Century*, Speech delivered by Theresa Marshall, former permanent secretary, to Institute of Chartered Accountants of Barbados Panel Discussion on Unlocking Potential—Converting Ideas into Reality, November 6, 2012.

organizational performance, productivity, and national competitiveness. In fact, when 75% of public officers are not empowered to make decisions, they can only do one of two things—apply the rules without exercising judgment or common sense or pass the buck upstairs and await further instructions.* This results in a lack of hands-on supervision, lack of training, low job satisfaction, low morale and cynicism, distrust, and systemic weakness of the leadership and supervision relationship. In addition, the silo mentality fosters territoriality rather than building collaboration and consensus toward common objectives. Thus, even though persons argue that the public service offers job security, it does not create job satisfaction for the majority of employees. The inherited adversarial employer–employee relationships that continue to negatively impact performance and productivity had its roots in slavery and they were transferred during the colonial period to the public service where no proper job descriptions or effective formal controls were enforced and, thus, few employees were dismissed for nonperformance. Moreover, cultural and social change tends to be relatively slow and this means that it will take a long time before management practices reasonably reflect the changing realities in the social, economic, and organizational environments.

A major factor that impacted public service performance was the perception among public service employees that the annual performance appraisal system was not objective and it was being used as a means to victimize persons, and, therefore, it was viewed as a punitive mechanism. Moreover, the situation was made more difficult because in some instances, for example, in Barbados[†] and Trinidad and Tobago,[‡] there was no system in place to appraise permanent secretaries, and therefore, it was perceived as an unfair practice where only lower level employees were appraised but not their immediate supervisors at the senior level. Thus, in order to improve public service performance, attention must be paid to the performance of both people and organization systems. To this end, public service employees need additional training opportunities, which should not only involve specific technical skills but also inculcate new attitudes of customer service and performance management.

At the cognitive and psychological level, interest in performance measurement and productivity has increased because of the general change in the perception of the role of the public service, greater focus on quality, competitiveness, customer service, and interest in providing value for money. However, at the everyday level, performance measurement tends to be unpopular because employees in the public service have enjoyed a measure of job security. Moreover, there appears to be an entrenched enclave that suggests that performance and productivity cannot be measured in the public service.[§] In addition, personnel are socialized into a culture that is more concerned with avoiding mistakes and risks than being psychologically empowered, showing initiative, and improving performance. In Trinidad and Tobago, as elsewhere in the region, public service culture over the years has been and continues to be undermined by politicians.[¶] The problem reflects similar concerns across the region where the relationship between politicians and permanent secretaries has deteriorated because of the practice of hiring politically appointed advisors. They have imposed an attitude of superiority to the job that eventually wedged a gap between the relationship of the minister and the permanent secretary and eroded the trust to the extent that some politicians perceive that some senior public officers offer dubious policy advice in an attempt to frustrate the implementation of their policies.

---

* Ibid.
† Soverall and Turton, op. cit.
‡ "No system to appraise Permanent Secretaries," *Trinidad Newsday*, March 24, 2012: 5.
§ Khan and Soverall, op. cit.
¶ "Jobs for boys, girls in public service: political absurdity," *Trinidad Newsday*, May 9, 2012: 3.

A classic example occurred in Trinidad and Tobago, for example, where it was alleged that Dr. Eric Williams, the country's first prime minister, sidelined a number of senior personnel, including a permanent secretary, for making decisions that he did not approve and, as a result, these senior personnel were by-passed as a form of punishment. This incident taught an immediate lesson to other senior staff, namely, the art of avoiding decision making as a strategy for survival.* As a result, a culture of risk-aversion developed in the public service as persons who conformed to political dictates appeared to be rewarded over those who displayed initiative and decisiveness. This practice of short-term political expediency weakened the public service leadership and management functions over time as well as its morale. In addition, this attitude has created situations where many supervisors routinely have to contend with noticeably persistent practices among staff such as avoiding challenging situations, delaying key decisions, avoiding disciplinary actions for poor performance, avoiding response to verbal or written communication, and failing to respond to personnel or customer queries.

HRM as a supervisory function has also been undermined by political influence. As a result, there has been a significant increase in unsatisfactory, and often dubious, personnel selection and seniority-based promotion despite the rhetoric of merit-based systems and objective performance standards. The former gives the appearance of fairness when all it really does is reward mediocre long-serving personnel and punish the able, enthusiastic, and competent. Moreover, the system encourages conformity and mediocrity rather than reward merit performance, achievement, initiative, and results. However, the calls for adopting performance-based systems linked to incentives and rewards have not been entirely successful to date. In Barbados, performance management was adopted and it linked target-setting, appraisal and development at the individual level to general public service goals.† As a result, in 2001, the Performance Review and Development System was formally established as the model of performance management in the public service.‡ It was supported by the PSC which ensured that the new system was applied in the promotion process in the public service. In addition, a new Public Service Act was implemented in 2007 to provide further legislative support and regulations to ensure that merit and qualification were used as the major selection criteria rather than seniority and longevity. These new initiatives caused a great deal of frustration among senior personnel who increasingly sought early retirement as a measure of retaliation against the new system of recruitment, selection, and performance management.

In Jamaica, emphasis was placed on HRM, restructuring of line agencies, financial management, and the adoption of SAPs to reduce debt during the period 1984–1995.§ This was followed by the period 1996–2002, which saw the implementation of PSM initiatives which sought to correct the weaknesses of previous PSR efforts. In Trinidad and Tobago, many public officers expressed dissatisfaction with the HRM system because of weaknesses in the following areas: human resource capability and capacity, policies and procedures, organized operations, legal framework, and public service compensation.¶ Specially trained personnel were selected to staff the new HR divisions during the 1990s together with some of the staff already engaged, but the training was academic and it failed to provide the requisite skills and experience to operate the existing HR system. As a consequence, skills and experience in contemporary HRM are generally lacking, both in central agencies and ministries, and as a result, external consultants have been used

---

* "The Art of 'Yes, Minister'," op. cit.
† Best-Winfield, *Public Sector Reform*.
‡ Soverall and Turton, op. cit.
§ Osei, "Public Sector Reform in Jamaica," pp. 57–83.
¶ *Green Paper on Transforming the Civil Service*, op. cit.

to introduce new reform initiatives. Existing staff in ministry HR units often lack the required functional skills and competencies, which frequently results in problems being referred to the central agencies such as Personnel Department and Service Commissions Department where the more capable personnel tend to be found. In addition, there is a shortage of qualified staff in the central agencies which contributes to long delays in processing times for many transactions. The net result of all these modernization initiatives is that over 30 ministries and departments are currently competing for scarce talent in a small pool and HR professionals are rotating in search of the best contract terms on offer. Clearly, there is an urgent need for a comprehensive human resource development strategy that would empower the public service.

Over time, public service authorities across the Caribbean have attempted to introduce HRM reforms, service delivery reforms, information management systems, organization structure and accountability reforms, financial management reforms, performance management and accountability reforms, an increased focus on ethics and values, citizen engagement, and reforms designed to change organizational culture.* In addition, the public service has to contend with significant human resource challenges including the absence of modern HRM policies, the absence of a PSC compensation philosophy, outdated classification systems, parallel public service systems, a poor work ethic, a parallel and expanding contract establishment, resource constraints in ministries and departments, weak capacity in central agencies, and a bottom heavy pyramid structure that is rapidly becoming obsolete.† Despite identifying these challenges and implementing various human resource strategies in most Caribbean countries, the desired outcomes have not been consistent across the region.

As long as the work environment and organizational culture remain inadequate or unresponsive to employee needs, they cannot perform at their best since both performance and productivity decline as the work environment deteriorates or stagnates. This is one of the primary reasons for the low levels of public service performance across the Caribbean. Over the years, an unstable environment has evolved where development growth over the decades has created a need for personnel resources of all kinds and at all levels. As a result of recruitment and selection policies and practices that have been heavily influenced by political considerations, the quality and level of personnel attracted to and retained by the public service appear to have declined over the years, and this has had deleterious consequences for management quality, labor productivity, and public service performance.

Organizational Culture and Performance

The relationship between organizational culture and operational performance is central to the role of public service performance in national development and the nature of its relative success or failure. The concept of organizational culture has generally been associated with performance outcomes. Generally speaking, organizational culture is viewed as the combination of practices, values, beliefs, and assumptions that organizational members share about appropriate behavior and as an explanatory variable that distinguishes one organization from another. In this context, there are two major aspects of culture that significantly affect organizational performance, namely, content or the types of values and behavior held by organization members, and strength or the depth and breadth of those behaviors embedded among the members. However, since ministries and departments usually have different strategic directions which affect their performance, managers need to understand the fit between organizational culture and certain types of performance.

---

* CAPAM, *"Public Service Development Needs."*
† Macintyre, op. cit.

Managers would do well to understand the nature of the relationship between culture and dimensions of performance. Moreover, now that measuring and analyzing performance in PSOs is being embraced on the premise that it could positively impact various dimensions of operational performance such as management style, operating culture, leadership behavior, and technology use, it is important for managers to know what cultural characteristics are most closely associated with performance excellence in different dimensions.* The quality of public service delivery and the use of innovation are the two major components of public service performance that have gained prominence in recent times. Although these two types of performance require different types of organizational culture, there is increasing evidence, both empirical and anecdotal, that suggests that these two performance dimensions are not mutually exclusive but can be complimentary. In addition, they benefit from characteristics of different cultures simultaneously. PSOs that are able to retain a high-performance culture tend to have more capable personnel, while the low-performing PSOs settle for poorly motivated and unfocused personnel.

The current management structure and operating culture in the public service across the region maintain the inherited status quo and power distance among its many organizations and multiple layers of communication.† The workplace relationship between supervisors at senior and middle management and their colleagues at the junior level is characterized by age, gender-specific and generational outlooks, and self-serving stereotypes that perpetuate a divide into the "them" versus "us" syndrome in most public service organizations across the Caribbean.‡ At the senior level, the top-down approach reinforces the practice of repeated references to the "boss" or the "person-in-charge," which creates either an aura of superiority that is exhibited by some senior managers or an act of disdain. At the junior level, supervisors may be young, bright, talented, and motivated individuals who want to use their initiative as "young upstarts" or "troublemakers" who do not want to conform to the culture of the organization. These attitudes by senior management build up resistance and resentment by junior staff who feel alienated from their older colleagues rather than part of a working team striving for the same goals. In addition, these behaviors highlight the undercurrents and nuances of interactions among public service employees in different categories and layers of the organization. Moreover, it underscores a more fundamental pathology that has resulted in a broken psychological contract between employer and employee.

There is little evidence that diverse elements of the public service operate in a framework of cooperation, collaboration, and integration, but rather they are continuously fragmented and pulled in different directions from central and core missions by competing interests and endemic turf fighting. This can be seen from the conflicting nature of the relationship among several agencies that are responsible for HRM and HRD practice in the public service, namely, the Ministry of the Public Service, the personnel division, the training division, the PSC, the Ministry of Education, the Ministry of Labor, the Ministry of Public Administration, and the University of the West Indies. The impact of these trends is noticeable in the areas of work planning, performance management, orientation, management training, succession planning, organization development, management development, low levels of dialogue and communication, low levels of cooperation and participation, supersession, and lack of ownership and empowerment.

The public perception is that the culture of the public service is too often slow and resistant to change. It is viewed as too cautious and slow-moving, bureaucratic, and hierarchical, with too many agencies focused on process orientation rather than outcomes. In addition, the fragmented

---

* Khan and Soverall, op. cit.: 311.
† Ibid: 311.
‡ Ibid: 312.

relationships indicate the emphasis placed on power, the lack of focus on goal achievement, and cold and impersonal communication that stifles initiative and motivation. These types of dysfunctional behavior by public service leaders undermine their ability to recognize the psychological needs of their staff and to engage them as stakeholders and partners who share common values and objectives. Moreover, it has become deeply frustrating and dysfunctional for both customers as well as many public servants who want to improve their operational systems and performance. They both want to have a public service that responds quickly and efficiently to new challenges, and innovates with new approaches to old problems. The reality is that there are too few incentives for public servants to challenge the status quo or to seek out and implement cost saving or service improvements. In general, the culture and behavior of public servants must become more flexible, innovative, and focused on results rather than process. To this end, leaders of public sector agencies can do much more to motivate and empower their staff, create a dynamic and flexible career path, and demonstrate that they are champions of PSR and PSM efforts in the public service.

Leadership

Improved performance must be driven from the top and this requires both political and public service leadership. In order to achieve this outcome, the modernization of the public service in the Caribbean cannot be achieved without a working partnership among the politicians who make policy, the public servants who implement public policies, and the private sector which utilizes those policies to compete globally. In Barbados, the Social Partnership, which brings together the government, public service, private sector, and other stakeholders to have dialogue on all policy matters that affect the economy and society, is perhaps the closest institutional arrangement to this ideal that seeks to find a way to become partners in national development. This fundamental PSR and PSM initiative has been operational since 1994 when Barbados fashioned its SAP in response to economic shocks during the 1990s. There is no other Caribbean country that has forged such a social compact.

The issue of capacity-building for public service leadership is one of the most significant items on the agenda of public sector organizations (PSOs) in both industrialized and developing countries.* It is absolutely necessary because of the constantly changing environments that are posing new challenges for the public service, especially in small developing countries in the Caribbean. In this context, some of the leadership challenges include demographic changes, economic and fiscal pressures, rising expectations of citizens with respect to quality services, need for more inclusion in decision making, demands for improved performance, and the need for significant transformation in the delivery of public services. The evidence indicates that the public service in the Caribbean is still the driving force for national development in the second decade of the twenty-first century, and therefore, it must respond to diverse needs by strengthening the capability and capacity of its human resources, and improving key structures, systems, and technology, by focusing on strengthening the center of government, HRM, leadership and management development, service delivery, facilities management, and information technology.†

Leadership and management development programs need to target the executive leadership with the aim of improving the capacity and capability of permanent secretaries, heads of departments, and deputy permanent secretaries, and senior management in the public service such as directors, heads of divisions, and emerging leaders, to enhance the capacity and capability

---

* Draper, "Capacity-building for Public Service Leadership."
† *Green Paper on Transforming the Civil Service*, op. cit.: 13.

of employees at lower levels of management, and leadership competencies will be developed to complement the management function because leadership is needed at all levels in every public sector agency. In this regard, the public service of Trinidad and Tobago identified seven leadership competencies as priorities—visioning, creativity, behavioral flexibility, action management, partnering, teamwork, and cognitive capacity. It is absolutely clear that leadership development is critical for creating a new performance culture in the public service especially since these small societies are characterized by organizational structures that are hierarchical, bureaucratic, rigid, and inflexible; leadership at both political and bureaucratic levels that is paternalistic at best, and autocratic at worst; managers who are unresponsive to the needs of citizens and who serve themselves; management styles that are nonparticipatory, with rank and status overriding workteam relationships; generally adversarial relationships between managers and employees; a fear of technology; a poor work ethic that is eroding traditional ethical principles and values; personal considerations, including nepotism, are the prevalent basis for personnel transactions rather than merit or performance*; politicians, public officials, and citizens find difficulty in distinguishing between duty to the public interest and claims of kinship and affinity; and citizens depend on public services for many of life's activities but are distrustful of officialdom.†

The case for leadership development rests on the premise that PSR and PSM initiatives are dependent on developing the capacity of government to manage, deliver, and modernize public services. The evidence illustrates that the capacity deficit is more pronounced in small island developing states like the Caribbean because of small size and attendant resource constraints. In order to correct this deficit, the Caribbean Leadership Program, a 7-year, $20 million Canadian International Development Agency (CIDA)-funded project was launched in Barbados to strengthen the next generation of Caribbean leaders for regional integration and economic growth.‡ The program comprises the Canada School of Public Service as the executing agency, a Canada–Caribbean shared governance project steering committee, a technical working group, the Cave Hill School of Business, and Caribbean Centre for Development Administration (CARICAD) as hosts of the regional project. It is based on five pillars—leadership development, enabling environment, research, continuous learning networks, and communities of practice. The focus on leadership development highlights the capacity deficit and places the spotlight on the issue of adequate training of public officers to meet the changing demands of their positions.

Although in many instances, senior public officers are well educated, with a large percentage having post-graduate degrees, there are increasing concerns that the existing structures and institutional arrangements do not allow for best-fit practices in human resources management, such as job-skill fit, recruitment and selection, performance management, succession management,§ rationalizing training to match aptitudes, creating a full-time professional PSC,¶ and creating workforce development centers to guide employees in their pursuit of careers and provide employers with information required to effectively plan for future skill demands.** In addition, practical leadership competencies are required to build capacity to constantly review policies, plans, and programs and adequately respond to changing environments.

---

* Jacome, "Commonwealth Caribbean Small Island States and the Caribbean Centre for Development Administration," pp. 34–48.
† Collins, Paul and Edward Warrington (1997) "*The New Public Administration: Lessons from the Experiences of Small and Island States*," Report on a CAPAM/IASIA Conference, Seychelles, April 11–17.
‡ Wilkins, "Making the Case for Leadership Development," pp. 1–4.
§ Khan and Soverall (1993), op. cit.
¶ Marshall, op. cit.
** "McLeod: Gov't using diversification strategy for workforce development," *Sunday Express*, January 27, 2013: 25.

Public service performance depends on the capability of its human resources and the ability of the leadership to motivate staff to perform at their best in achieving organizational goals and objectives. Moreover, improved staff performance ensures an empowered and motivated public service that is flexible in providing services in an efficient manner. To this end, effective leadership in the public service requires a new focus on talent management by identifying potential at all stages of an employee's career, empowering individuals, improving learning opportunities, and building learning capacity within PSOs. In this context, the leadership development process has to focus on attracting and retaining highly skilled people, developing existing employees, supporting knowledge acquisition, and professionalizing the public service by providing common, structured learning opportunities to a broad reach of public officers that complements and supports learning gained through work experience. The context must be relevant to current priorities so that learning is aligned with the craft of government, an ongoing needs assessment, learning advisory committees at each organizational level, annual curriculum review, and building strong communities of practice that foster peer learning and innovation. In addition, the engagement of senior public service leaders is critical for defining public service strategies, core values, leadership models and leadership competencies, and articulating a management accountability framework that contributes to the design and delivery of leadership development programs.

Political leadership plays a key role in setting policy direction, visions, and strategies. Many Caribbean countries including Barbados, Guyana, Jamaica, and Trinidad and Tobago have strategic visions and action plans for the immediate, medium-term, and long-term future that speak to the implementation of PSR and PSM initiatives. In too many instances, however, there is inadequate communication of the changes that are required to produce the desired outcomes of these initiatives, and as a result, the communication deficit can lead to misconceptions and resistance. For example, in Trinidad and Tobago, the government introduced a shared services program at the ministerial level in an effort to improve public service efficiency and save taxpayers' money. In order for this initiative to work effectively, it means that more ministries will have to change the silo mentality and actually share functions such as finance and accounts, legal services, facilities management, and frontline services. Although it is not a new concept, many countries have implemented this practice in order to deliver more efficient services to citizens who have been demanding better service and greater value for their money. In addition, at the national level, the government launched a national performance framework as part of a structured approach to national development that outlined five priority areas for improving the quality of lives of citizens. These new types of initiative require proper communication so that the respective target groups would buy-in and create sustained ownership of the process in an effort to ensure the intended outcomes. In this context, effective implementation depends on effective leadership, proper planning, commitment, dedicated resources, and proper communication.

Conclusions—Future Outlook

In many Caribbean countries, the public service has lost its professional image and appeal. As a consequence, real merit and excellence are needed now more than ever before, although they are harder to define and to secure. The need to ensure a diversity of experience and expertise, while seeking out the best from the available talent pool, nationally and internationally, remains perhaps the toughest challenge for the future. In other words, there is a need to significantly reduce the politicization of the public service, enhance its role, reinforce the professional core, ethical values and standards, and the role of international cooperation in improving its performance and image. This challenge is viewed within the context of a capacity deficit to translate abstract concepts such as visions into reality, the ability to bridge a wide gap between the resources currently available to the public service and the evolving tasks, priorities, and expectations of both government and citizens. In this context, professionalism comprises a shifting competence base and an ethical duty that condition the performance of the public service and the credibility of government. Performance improvement cannot be achieved without sustained political commitment that is manifested by greater accountability, empowerment, equity, integrity, efficiency and effectiveness, participation, and transparency.

The centralized, hierarchical, and pyramid-shaped structures that influenced an inward-looking control orientation now has to be radically changed to the diamond-shaped, engaging feature that empowers employees at all levels through greater participation, delegation, learning, training, and other performance incentives that eventually transform their attitudes and behaviors into relevant practices that actually improve performance. The crux of the matter is that public service leadership, including all public service trade unions across the region that negotiate on behalf of the masses, has the onerous responsibility for bringing about fundamental changes in values, attitudes, and public sector institutions that influence the wider society and national psyche. In addition, the role of the media in educating the society about the central function of government, the duty and responsibility of citizens in the process of national development, and the relationship between the public service and citizens is gravely underestimated. The absence of critical analysis of these underlying issues continues to frustrate the empowerment of the masses about the functioning of government and the public service, as well as their role in the economy and society. In other words, the media is not playing a meaningful role in the transformation of the culture of society.

Capacity-building programs need to promote and safeguard the professional identity, image, autonomy, and integrity of the public service in order to restore public confidence that has been eroded over the years as a result of the absence of an indigenous development ideology, poor work ethic, poor quality service, and low levels of public service performance. Improving performance depends on leadership and management development that focuses on acquiring the requisite attitudes, skills, and values for operating in constantly changing environments. In this context, education and learning systems also have to reflect development priorities that are conducive to local conditions, namely, the development of the appropriate values, attitudes, and work ethic. The history of the Caribbean suggests that creating the relevant attitudes and values that are essential to empowerment and sustainable human development cannot be achieved without changing the existing ideology of development to give people the motivation to build from below.

For the long term, capacity building at all levels, including leadership and management development, has to focus on job-specific training and learning that improves skills and work experiences, creates incentives that generate acceptance and willingness to embrace change, and allows employees to use more discretionary authority. In addition to this shift in focus away from rigid rules to performance, new career structures need to be implemented that demonstrate the importance of accomplishment and mobility based on merit and integrity in the recruitment, placement, and promotion of public officers. In other words, the quest for an improved quality and level of performance is both continuous and demanding and, therefore, requires that the multiplicity of success factors be regularly monitored and evaluated in order to ensure rational analysis of causes and impacts, and the necessary adjustments to achieve the desired outcomes.

Bibliography

Bachan, Carol Ann (2013) Speech delivered by Minister of Public Administration at 50th Anniversary of Public Service Awards Ceremony, Port of Spain, Trinidad and Tobago.

Best-Winfield, Gail (2006) *Public Sector Reform: Making Barbados Work Better Case Study*, The Caribbean Centre for Development Administration, Bridgetown, Barbados.

Bissessar, Anne Marie (2001) *The Forgotten Factor: Public Servants and New Public Management in a Developing Country*, University of the West Indies, Trinidad and Tobago.

Brown, Deryck (1999) Ethnic politics and public sector management in Trinidad and Guyana, *Public Administration and Development*, Vol. 19, No. 4, pp. 367–379.

Brown, Deryck (2008) *Institutional Development and Reform in Public Services: Lessons from the Experience of Small Caribbean States*, Paper prepared for the Commonwealth Association of Public Administration and Management, Biennial Conference, Barbados, October 19–22.

CAPAM (December 1995) *Current Issues in the Public Service*, CAPAM, Toronto, Ontario, Canada.

CAPAM (September 2004) *Public Service Development Needs: Current & Future*, CAPAM, Toronto, Ontario, Canada.

Caribbean Development Bank (2002) *Governance and Institutional Development Draft Strategy Paper*, CDB, Bridgetown, Barbados.

Caribbean Development Bank (2012) *Country Assessment of Poverty and Living Conditions in Barbados*, CDB, Bridgetown, Barbados.

Caribbean Policy Research Institute (2011) *Towards Public Sector Reform in Jamaica: What Local & International Experiences Tell Us About Successful Public Sector Reform*, Caribbean Policy Research Institute, University of the West Indies, Mona, Jamaica.

CARICAD (December 2–4, 1997) *Report of Regional Consultation & Workshop on Public Service Commissions: Imperatives and Challenges for Leading Reform*, St. Lucia.

CARICAD (2003) *The Executive Agency Model: Legal and Policy Management Issues in Jamaica*, Bridgetown, Barbados.

CARICAD (June 10–12, 2008) *Report on the 1st Regional Conference of Public Service Commissions*, St. Vincent and the Grenadines.

CARICOM Secretariat (1984) *Report of CARICOM/ILO Technical Meeting of Public Sector Personnel Practitioners*, Dover Convention Centre, Barbados.

Carrizosa, Mauricio (2007) *Public Sectors in the Americas: How Big Are They?* World Bank, Washington, DC.

Collins, Paul and Warrington, Edward (April 11–17, 1997) *The New Public Administration: Lessons from the Experiences of Small and Island States*, Report on a CAPAM/IASIA Conference, Seychelles.

Detert, James R., Schroeder, Roger G. and Mauriel, John J. (2000) A framework for linking culture and improvement initiatives in organizations, *Academy of Management Review*, Vol. 25, No. 4, pp. 850–863.

Draper, Gordon (2001) *The Civil Service in Latin America and the Caribbean: Situation and Future Challenges, The Caribbean Perspective*, Inter-American Development Bank, Washington, DC.

Draper, Gordon (2003) Capacity-building for Public Service Leadership, in *Commonwealth Public Administration Reform 2004*, Commonwealth Secretariat, London.

Emmanuel, Patrick (1993) *Governance and Democracy in the Commonwealth Caribbean: An Introduction*, Monograph Series No. 3, Institute of Social and Economic Research, University of the West Indies, Cave Hill, Barbados.

Ghany, Hamid (1994) The creation of legislative institutions in the commonwealth Caribbean: The myth of the transfer of the Westminster model, *Congressional Studies Journal*, Vol. 2, No. 1, pp. 34–49.

Government of Barbados (1998) *Report of the Public Service Commission for the Period 1998–2002*, Personnel Administration Division, Ministry of Civil Service, Bridgetown, Barbados.

Government of the Republic of Trinidad and Tobago (1996) *Report of the Public Service Commission for the Period 1992–1994*, Personnel Division, Ministry of Public Administration, Port of Spain, Trinidad and Tobago.

Government of the Republic of Trinidad and Tobago (May 25, 2011) *Green Paper on Transforming the Civil Service: Renewal and Modernization*, Ministry of Public Administration, Port of Spain, Trinidad and Tobago.

Government of Suriname (2013) *Public Administration Report*, Ministry of Public Administration.
Gregory, B.T., Harris, S.G., Armenakis, A.A. and Shook, C.L. (2009) Organizational culture and effectiveness: A study of values, attitudes, and organizational outcomes, *Journal of Business Research*, Vol. 62, No. 7, pp. 673–679.
Hofstede, G. (1980) *Culture's Consequences*, Sage, Beverly Hills, CA.
Hondeghem, Annie and Perry, James (2009) EGPA symposium on public service motivation and performance: Introduction, *International Review of Administrative Sciences*, Vol. 75, No. 1, pp. 5–9.
International Monetary Fund (February 20, 2013) *Caribbean Small States: Challenges of High Debt and Low Growth*, International Monetary Fund, Washington, DC.
Jacome, Jose (1992) The Commonwealth Caribbean small island states and the Caribbean Centre for development administration, in Randall Baker (ed.) *Public Administration in Small and Island States*, Kumarian Press, West Hartford, CT.
Khan, Jamal (1982) *Public Management: The Eastern Caribbean Experience*, Leiden, The Hague, the Netherlands.
Khan, Jamal and Soverall, Wayne (1993) Human resource development in the public sector: A developing-country experience, *International Journal of Public Sector Management*, Vol. 6, No. 1, pp. 48–58.
Khan, Jamal and Soverall, Wayne (2007) *Gaining Productivity*, Arawak Publications, Kingston, Jamaica.
Kotter, J.P. and Heskett, J.L. (1992) *Corporate Culture and Performance*, The Free Press, New York.
Lalla, Kenneth R. (2009) *The Public Service and Service Commissions in the Commonwealth Caribbean*, Universal Printers (T&T) Limited, Curepe, Trinidad and Tobago.
La Palombara, Joseph (1963) *Bureaucracy and Political Development*, Princeton University, Princeton, NJ.
Marshall, Theresa (November 6, 2012) *Unlocking the Potential of the Public Service: Reforms for the 21st Century*, Speech delivered by former Permanent Secretary to Institute of Chartered Accountants of Barbados Panel Discussion on Unlocking Potential—Converting Ideas into Reality.
Maull, R., Brown, P. and Cliffe, R. (2001) Organizational culture and quality improvement, *International Journal of Operations & Productions Management*, Vol. 21, No. 3, pp. 302–326.
McLean, L.D. (2005) Organizational culture's influence on creativity and innovation: A review of the literature and implications for human resource development, *Advances in Developing Human Resources*, Vol. 7, No. 2, pp. 226–246.
Mills, G.E. (1970) Public administration in the Commonwealth Caribbean: Evolution, conflict and challenges, *Social and Economic Studies*, Vol. 19, No. 1, pp. 5–25.
Naor, M., Goldstein, S.M., Linderman, K.W. and Schroder, R.G. (2008) The role of culture as driver of quality management and performance: Infrastructure versus core quality practices, *Decision Sciences*, Vol. 39, No. 4, pp. 671–702.
Nomm, Kulli and Randma-Liiv, Tiina (2012) Performance measurement and performance information in new democracies: A study of the Estonian Central Government, *Public Management Review*, Vol. 14, No. 7, pp. 859–881.
Nunes, F.E. (1974) The nonsense of neutrality, *Social and Economic Studies*, University of the West Indies, Mona, Jamaica.
OECD (2005) *Modernizing Government: The Way Forward*, OECD, Paris, France.
OECD (2008) The State of the Public Service, http://www.oecd-library.org/governance.
Osei, Philip (2006) Public sector reform in Jamaica, in Paul Sutton (ed.) *Modernising the State: Public Sector Reform in the Commonwealth Caribbean*, Ian Randle Publishers, Kingston, Jamaica, pp. 57–83.
Peters, T.J. and Waterman, R.H. (1982) *In Search of Excellence*, Harper & Row, New York, NY.
Quinn, R.E. and Spreitzer, G.M. (1991) The psychometrics of the competing values culture instrument and an analysis of the impact of organizational culture on quality of life, *Research in Organizational Change and Development*, Vol. 5, pp. 115–142.
Ryan, Selwyn (1972) *Race and Nationalism in Trinidad and Tobago*, University of Toronto Press, Toronto, Ontario, Canada.
Ryan, Selwyn (1999) *Winner Takes All: The Westminster Experience in the Anglophone Caribbean*, Multimedia Production Centre, School of Education, University of the West Indies, St. Augustine, Trinidad.
Ryan, Selwyn and Brown, Deryck (eds.) (1992) *Issues and Problems in Caribbean Public Administration*, Institute of Social and Economic Research, University of the West Indies, Trinidad and Tobago.

Schein, E. (1985) *Organizational Culture and Leadership*, Jossey-Bass, San Francisco, CA.

Sorensen, J.B. (2002) The strength of corporate culture and the reliability of firm performance, *Administrative Science Quarterly*, Vol. 47, No. 1, pp. 70–91.

Soverall, Wayne and Turton, Wilma (2003) The performance review and development system, in Frank Alleyne, Jamal Khan and Wayne Soverall (eds.) *Managing and Evaluating Projects*, Arawak Publications, Kingston, Jamaica.

Soverall, Wayne and Turton, Wilma (2012) CLICO's corporate collapse: Poor corporate governance, *American International Journal of Contemporary Research*, Vol. 2, No. 2, pp. 1–13.

Stahl, Glenn and Foster, Gregory (1979) *Improving Public Services: A Report on the International Conference on Improving Public Management and Performance*, US Agency for International Development, Washington, DC.

Stock, G.N., McFadden, K.L. and Gowen, C.R. (2007) Organizational culture, critical success factors, and the reduction of hospital errors, *International Journal of Production Economics*, Vol. 106, No. 2, pp. 368–392.

Sutton, Paul (2006) *Modernising the State: Public Sector Reform in the Commonwealth Caribbean*, Ian Randle Publishers, Kingston, Jamaica.

Sutton, Paul (2008) *Public Sector Reform in the Commonwealth Caribbean: A Review of Recent Experiences*, The Centre for International Governance Innovation, Caribbean Paper No. 6, Waterloo, Ontario, Canada.

Wilkins, John (2012) Making the case for leadership development, *Canadian Government Executive*, October 18, pp. 1–4.

Wilson, Graham (1994) The Westminster Model in comparative perspective, in Ian Budge and David McKay (eds.) *Developing Democracy: Comparative Research in Honour of J. F. P. Blondel*, Sage, London.

The World Bank (1996) *Public Sector Modernization in the Caribbean*, World Bank, Washington, DC.

The World Bank (2005) *A Time to Choose: Caribbean Development in the 21st Century*, Report No. 31725-LAC, World Bank, Washington, DC.

The World Bank (2010) The public sector in the Caribbean: Issues and reform options, *Policy Research Working Paper* 1609, Washington, DC.

Chapter 7

Public Financial Management in the Caribbean

Eileen Browne

Contents

The Caribbean: Middle Income, But Much in Debt 144
Public Financial Management: What and Why? 146
Public Financial Management in the Caribbean: Common Challenges 148
A Staged Approach to Public Financial Management 150
    Stage One—Financial Discipline 150
    Stage Two—Improving the Effectiveness of Fund Allocations 152
    Stage Three—Gaining Operational Efficiency 153
Reforming the Ministries of Finance as Influence on Good Financial Management
in the Caribbean 154
Conclusion 157
Bibliography 158

Abstract: Responsibly handling public money, regardless of method and policy goal, must always include answering the questions: what public services should be provided to whom; how shall they be financed; and how much debt do we need to pay for what we need without unduly endangering the future. The chapter explores how the public financial management (PFM) tools of budget development and execution, levying of taxes, and management of public debt can be useful in increasing public accountability and displaying measures of public finance stability as well as economic growth. The chapter notes the Caribbean countries' disadvantage (being small islands and in the case of Trinidad being natural resource dependent) and considers political economy factors only as they illustrate their capacity to enable (or disable) PFM technical tools.

    A complete PFM cycle will always include expenditure budgets, tax (and other) revenues, debt strategy, and management. Differences between various Caribbean countries' inclusiveness and transparency as they develop a budget determines its usefulness as a plan which displays what the government has chosen to fund. Caribbean governments' varying practices in executing the budgets they pass are also explored: when the expenditures made vary widely from the budget law, policy coherence is impossible. Tax policies and collection effectiveness determine the amount of resources available to provide desired services and will often indicate what other resources (external aid or domestic or internal borrowing) are needed if the proposed services are to be funded. Unrealistic revenue estimates ensure a budget based on them cannot be executed without significant change.

This chapter discusses the public financial management (PFM) in Caribbean countries. It describes the importance and role of PFM, how it has evolved in the Caribbean as well as factors affecting its current performance. This chapter first provides an overview of the economic status and outlook for the region. Second, it defines and discusses PFM techniques that Caribbean countries can use to manage their finances, and highlights some country examples. Third, this chapter reviews factors affecting the success and failure of PFM techniques as change agents for economic stability and growth in the Caribbean. Fourth, it discusses a staged approach to implementing PFM that involves creating financial discipline, improving the effectiveness of allocations, and creating efficiencies in operating procedures. This chapter concludes by discussing issues surrounding the capacity of Ministries of Finance in the Caribbean for PFM.

The Caribbean: Middle Income, But Much in Debt

The Caribbean region is classified as middle income,* and at the same time has several of the most indebted nations in the world. At present, the average per capita gross domestic product (GDP) for the 70+ million residents is about $10,000, and the real GDP growth is 1.7% with inflation of 3.1%. Gross debts are about 69% of GDP and reserves are about 21% of GDP. The numbers vary with the Bahamas showing the highest per capita income at $32,336 and Guyana the lowest at $8,472.† Fiscal financing pressures are most extreme in countries with high debt. Pressures to finance expenditures, which increase in times of recession at the same time as revenues decrease, put stress on recovery and increase the risk of crisis. In the Caribbean, this manifests as two sets of stressors on the economy: very large wage bills and large numbers of quasi-governmental entities with difficult-to-manage financial positions.

Caribbean economies are subject to global pressures in several important ways: tourism accounts for the central economic activity for more than half of its sovereign states;‡ commodity exports sustain the others; and the entire region relies to a dangerous extent on remittances.§

---

* International groups define the Caribbean as consisting of the countries of the Aruba, Bonaire and Curacao islands in the Caribbean (ABCs), the Bahamas, Belize, British Virgin Islands, the ECCU (Anguilla, Antigua and Barbuda, Dominica, Grenada, Montserrat, St. Kitts and Nevis, St. Lucia, and St. Vincent and the Grenadines), Guadeloupe, Guyana, Jamaica, Martinique, St. Bart, Suriname, and Trinidad and Tobago.
† Regional Economic Report, April 2013, IMF.com.
‡ While British Overseas Territories depend to a larger degree than any sovereign Caribbean state for off-shore activities—direct and indirect—tourism is still responsible for more of their economic activity. This is true even in BVI, the only Caribbean state where almost two-third of their revenues come from registration of off-shore companies/entities.
§ Remittances are money sent from abroad, usually by relatives, some but not all of whom intend to return to the country to which they are sending money. Remittances are a common economic factor in countries from which workers migrate to good paying jobs. The majority of Caribbean remittances come from the United States, Canada, and the United Kingdom. To a smaller extent, remittances come to poorer islands from more affluent ones.

The financial health of the Caribbean is slowly recovering from the 2008 recession. All sovereign Caribbean states are dependent on global recovery but each has a different set of risks that endanger its path to a healthy financial position. Tourism, commodity demand, and remittances have historically fallen during recessions and the 2008 recession continued that trend. The climb back to pre-2008 strength is slower in the tourism-centered economies than that of the commodity exporters. The economic outlook differs between those sovereign states that are commodity exporters, who in the short term are doing fine, and those whose economies are tourism-centric and thus much more damaged by the 2008 recession and the slow global recovery.

The tourism-dependent economies, such as Jamaica, Barbados, St. Lucia, and the Eastern Caribbean Currency Union (ECCU), suffer from debt burdens that require increasingly large proportions of their reduced revenues, leaving those islands three unpalatable options: reduce services, increase taxes, or borrow more. Four of the tourism-centered economies, Jamaica, Grenada, St. Kitts and Nevis, and Antigua and Barbuda, have, in the aftermath of the 2008 recession and lengthy slow recovery, appealed to the International Monetary Fund (IMF) for funding to enable them to survive these crises. Additionally, the region's monetary union (the ECCU consisting of Anguilla, Antigua and Barbuda, Dominica, Grenada, Montserrat, St. Kitts and Nevis, St. Lucia, and St. Vincent and the Grenadines) has also sought support. Concessional lending to virtually all of the tourism-centric countries abounds. All such support implies serious financial risk acknowledged by the country and agreed by the International Financial Institutions (IFIs). IFI lending comes with conditionality and historically has led to much of the PFM reform described in Section "Public Financial Management: What and Why?" While the proceeds of such loans and grants are welcomed by the requesting country, the conditions attached to the money have sparked repeated controversy and debate about sovereignty and donors' and lenders' motives.* Only the dependencies (both British and French) do not receive significant grant or concessional loan money from one or more of the IFIs operating in the region.†

The Caribbean's commodity exporters, Trinidad and Tobago, Guyana, Suriname, and Belize, have largely recovered from the negative effects of 2008 due to rising commodity prices that have accompanied the recovery in the United States and Europe. The danger for them, beyond a renewed global slowdown, which would decrease demand for the commodities they export, results from increasing domestic demand that reduces the commodities available for export. Increased domestic consumption reduces export profit and creates an economic profile that cannot be sustained during the inevitable wane of the commodity price cycle. Additionally, an arguably more serious risk derives from the fact that Caribbean commodity exporters have not built a savings and investment buffer during the recent period of high profits. Without such "rainy day" investments, the countries will likely reenter a borrowing cycle when demand inevitably slows.‡

---

* Internal critics of the conditions attached to financial or technical assistance call the conditionalities "interference with domestic political decisions." External critics of the financial or technical assistance describe the aid as building dependencies. Despite all the critiques, when faced with devaluing currency, cutting spending, raising taxes, or defaulting on debt (which increases the cost of borrowing and destabilizes investment in the country), the Caribbean nations have been uniform in accepting the aid and often complaining about it at the same time. Those who supply the aid argue that conditions—usually the requirement to tighten fiscal discipline, add transparency, make processes more transparent—improve the nation's ability to sustain itself in future.
† The World Bank (in its various manifestations), IMF, Inter-American Development Bank (IADB), and the Caribbean Development Bank (CDB) are the most active IFIs in the Caribbean region. Additionally, the European Union and various bilateral donors including Canada, the United Kingdom, Korea, and China are regular donors and lenders to various Caribbean countries.
‡ The recent severe deterioration of the financial position of Suriname due to the drop in gold prices shows the extreme risk of rapid change, magnified when the exports are not diversified.

Other challenges for all Caribbean countries include their reliance on external energy sources.* High energy costs increase the cost of doing business in the Caribbean and thus deter investment in productive activities. Additionally, most Caribbean countries are subject to natural disasters such as hurricanes that have increased in frequency and severity in recent years. Furthermore, most Caribbean countries depend to an extent on "remittance income," that is, money earned by its citizens or former citizens abroad and sent "home" to help families. The remittance income stream proved particularly vulnerable to the 2008 worldwide recession.

Finally, most Caribbean countries are said to have a significant informal sector, some of it illegal, that by its nature destabilizes rapid economic growth and stability. The Caribbean comprises relatively young, that is, newly independent, countries with the other territories mostly self-governing dependencies. Nevertheless, the pattern established so far in much of the Caribbean shows unsustainable spending (often predicated on uncollectable revenue estimates), which results in deficit and debt. When that pattern continues without structural adjustment, it is generally followed by the refinancing or issuance of additional government debt and/or asset sell off. This has most often been followed by debt repayments too onerous to allow needed services to citizens, requiring international financial assistance.

Public Financial Management: What and Why?

PFM is the set of rules and practices by which a few people make decisions about many peoples' money. Documented tools and techniques date back more than 2000 years, but widespread establishment of standards recognized as international good practice is most strongly associated with the creation of the IMF, World Bank, and international trade organizations following World War II.† PFM reform seeks to improve results by getting better information to decision makers so they can make the best choices possible. Experts agree that the most reliable approach to financial sustainability consists of making decisions in context: first, a realistic understanding of their economic situation to determine the amount of resources that can be raised and spent and then choosing from among competing bids to spend the available money on priority items.

Originally, PFM focused on fiscal sustainability to avoid economic disruption and financial reporting to provide a historical record. Within the past three decades, automation has expanded predictive possibilities and changed the emphasis of PFM to planning reasonable implementation of complex policy improvements. Modern automated systems can be created to allow the capture of data as every financial transaction occurs, storing the data and making it available for easy analysis to improve future decisions. The more comprehensive a budget, the more cogent the decision making and the more likely that policy objectives will be met.‡

---

* Venezuelan oil loans, initiated by then-president Hugo Chavez, provided relatively inexpensive fuel to the Caribbean but roughly one-half of the market discount accrued as a loan obligation that might be called in future. The program eased, albeit temporarily, the burden of fuel costs for its Caribbean participants. Venezuela's current economic posture brings into question the duration of such conditions.
† World War II victorious coalition partners gathered at Bretton Woods in New Hampshire, USA, and agree to form: the World Bank to alleviate poverty; the IMF to survey economic stability globally to avoid regional disruptions that might lead to crisis; and the International Trade Organization to work toward removal of tariffs and other trade barriers to form a global economy.
‡ A budget that reflects only operation annual expenses does not allow decisions of the same quality as ones that simultaneously consider related capital expenditures. Budgets that only reflect some tax revenues are not as comprehensive as that include all tax, fine, fee sources as well as major grants and loan proceeds. Caribbean budgets routinely omit some resources and some expenditures in transparent budget development and execution processes.

PFM gives a country tools to control its resources in the context of a process to make realistic choices about their best use and then reports the results. PFM stresses objective analysis and impartial presentation to decision makers. PFM's macro fiscal tools and techniques allow countries to determine what varied types of revenue, spending, and borrowing will do to their overall financial position and then to make service level choices based on their willingness to levy taxes, fines, and fees and to seek grants and loans. The decisions on whom to tax, how much and what to buy with the money represent a government's policy priorities. Domestically, it shows "who" will receive "what" services from "which" part of government and "how" they will be paid for. Such analysis relies on data that are gathered in easily understood categories that can be compared with each other and are uniform across organizations. Budgets are the government's listing of the services it commits to provide for its citizens, along with their estimated costs. Some budget decisions reflect policies the government chooses, while others reflect what the government considers itself bound to. Viewed from the perspective of outsiders—including practitioners, international monitoring groups, and investors—a country's budget helps determine its stability.

Without exception, Caribbean countries are endeavoring to move toward results-informed budgets. Some countries' progress is limited to a change in format, while others are committing to the longer-term work of retraining and capacity building, to link budget activities to the policy objectives they are meant to achieve, and to more accurately measure results. Sophisticated performance budgeting requires good financial discipline beginning with useful control. PFM aims to provide for more effective control of resources in four main ways: by estimating correctly; by disallowing spending that does not comply with law, regulation, and the availability of funds; by allowing actions only by those authorized to make them; and by always leaving a clear trail of decisions and actions in the spending process. The starting point for any government PFM is definition of its objectives. Advanced performance budgets consistently array policy choices with price tags in order to allow more beneficial allocation decisions, but doing so requires iterative steps and inevitably calls for increasing competency, changing rewards systems, and increasing participation processes. There is major benefit garnered from taking the sequential steps because they strengthen institutional foundations and help to avoid fruitless discussions over spurious measurement accuracy.

PFM innovations in the last decades emphasize performance and results, and presentations which make financial decisions more accessible to those outside the accounting profession. Decision makers will inevitably weigh factors other than PFM analysis in coming to their financial judgments, but sound PFM presents budget options that show the resources needed to achieve results and the relationship of such results to a policy priority.

A relatively recent and sophisticated step in PFM reform is the application of a self-imposed set of fiscal rules (often referred to as fiscal rules, under which rubric there are different classifications) whereby decision makers constrain future decisions to be in conformity with economic ratios that they choose. Although Jamaica has chosen to adopt a fiscal rule as part of its attempt to reduce its debt, in general fiscal rules work best in countries with highly developed PFM systems, and almost always in countries enjoying economic growth and wishing to consolidate those gains. Like automation and performance budgeting, fiscal rules are tools most likely to succeed when PFM basics are in place, specifically processes to assure fiscal discipline such as a clear definition of roles, responsibilities, and guidelines in the budget making, spending, paying, and reporting phases. All successful PFM improvements also presuppose a sound legal framework and a uniform accounting classification.

In the Caribbean, as elsewhere, good PFM encourages both local and foreign direct investment and is often a requirement for international grants, because it includes an accountability structure. Making sure both taxes and spending meet policy objectives is important, as is having a clear debt policy that defines the conditions and limits for issuing debt. Timely, accurate reporting on these matters gains the confidence of domestic and international observers and investors. PFM is a government's economic governance report card. Countries without transparent PFM are often labeled too risky for new or continued investment.* Bad budgeting—characterized by unreliable reporting, unclear decision-making criteria, unchecked spending, and ill-advised borrowing—leads to lack of accountability, lack of predictability, and lack of confidence in the government. In extreme cases, it can also lead to domestic and regional instability.

Good PFM in the Caribbean means having institutions that routinely produce realistic forecasts of economic growth, available resources, as well as properly estimated costs of programs designed to achieve the most important policy objectives. PFM, as defined in this century, means replacing incrementalism (continuing to fund what has always been funded whether it achieves the desired results or not) with results-informed budgeting techniques. It also means creating forecasts of growth and revenue that are realistic and monitoring expenditures and collections throughout the budget year to see if things are on track. Good PFM involves having plans to transparently correct errors and deal with emergencies.

Public Financial Management in the Caribbean: Common Challenges

Decision makers in the Caribbean, as around the world, expect today's PFM to provide faster, more reliable information through improved processes. Caribbean countries are learning from each other and from small island nations in other parts of the world. Caribbean countries practice PFM in different ways, with some countries implementing some aspects, and other countries utilizing others. Five major common challenges are discussed below, which are caused by certain realities.

First, PFM is not a panacea for policy makers; having a good plan does not mean having the resources to fund everything everyone believes needs to be done. PFM does not increase the amount of money available; it simply allows informed decisions of how to spend it by displaying all the choices at once.

Second, local authorities and external experts alike often appear to believe that installing automation automatically results in improved processes, better trained staff, more insightful and skilled managers, and even cultural change in the civil service, the political class, and the electorate. However, buying an expensive computerized system does not provide useful data without also creating a good classification system to collect it and control processes that will assure its capture and its integrity. Moreover, even reliable data cannot be forged into meaningful information without skilled analysts.

Throughout the Caribbean, dozens of multimillion dollar systems have been installed but so far they have produced limited financial control or analysis due to incomplete understanding, training, and application of rules. There are also documented cases of countries turning off the very controls that would have given expected results.† While experts continue to insist that

---

* Some Caribbean countries prefer to avoid the measurability inherent in good PFM practices. Historically, this had proven a successful way to attract more lending by agreeing to pay high interest rates. Recent, sequential downward adjustment of interest rates has dampened lender enthusiasm. Massive efforts are now underway throughout the Caribbean to more fully identify risk, thus limiting countries' fiscal space.
† The Canadian foreign assistance office created a trust fund to be administered by IFIs to rethink and improve automated integrated financial systems in the Caribbean in 2010. The five-year project, called Supporting Economic Management in the Caribbean – donor trust fund bringing automation to member Caribbean islands (SEMCAR), overseen by government officials of the eight countries it serves, began by identifying the most common problems and then determining why existing automated tools did not address them. They considered revenue collecting, budget making, payments, and records of such expenditures. They dedicate equal resources to increasing understanding of PFM in its modern form and how that needs to affect organizational structure, management incentives, and civil service training as well as public sensitization. The project is mid-stream as of early 2014.

installing automation will require workers to change their business processes, evaluation of post-implementation systems shows that for various motivations, many of which are not entirely clear, civil service personnel continue to perform old tasks using outmoded techniques and conducting analyses using pre-automation methods.

Third, in the Caribbean, given the relatively short existence of an independent civil service, modern PFM needs considerably more time and attention than might be required in other governments with long histories of independent, competent civil service balance to elected official discretion. PFM requires and promotes more transparent and consistent handling of all transactions, so that anyone can know what has happened to all the money that comes into government and where it goes. Because of the tradition of opaque discretion in developing countries, the Caribbean must take more targeted action toward improving transparency and accountability. The cultural shift required to move from closed-door decision making to a clear series of steps that give stakeholders influence is complex, lengthy, and for many countries needing reforms, beyond their existing paradigms.

Fourth, PFM reform involves changing the information given to decision makers as well as improving the ways in which the information is processed, and redefining roles and responsibilities.* PFM presumes the capacity to conduct analyses on which more effective budget allocations can be based, showing how prudent choices can increase the worth of existing resources, displaying the costs and benefits of different decisions, saving options, and so on. In short, the capacity to design and present decision makers with timely, useful information requires recruitment and/or retraining of staff who were not previously asked to perform such analysis.

Finally, and most broadly, attention needs to be paid to building institutions with incentives to reward efforts toward financial discipline. In risk-averse cultures, such as some that predominate in Caribbean civil services, the motivation to actively participate in reform initiatives is clouded by mixed messages on the part of politicians and the potential loss of one's own discretionary power. There is faint hope of strengthening financial performance unless PFM reform has strong executive support, preferably with explicit parliamentary endorsement and, ideally, broad citizen education and engagement. While the status quo may not objectively be considered desirable, there are people benefitting in different ways from things remaining as they are. Donor support is a double-edged sword: expertise and money, if directed to government priorities, are unquestionably helpful, but may not necessarily be viewed in a positive light and are sometimes presented negatively by those whose interests are endangered by PFM.

These five challenges are present in the Caribbean in a major way. For most Caribbean countries, at a practical level, the ministries and agencies that are responsible for the reforms have limited staff who are already fully engaged in doing routine business. Funds to improve PFM are limited, especially in highly indebted countries, a cruel irony considering that it is these countries that usually need PFM the most. The general public do not find PFM improvement as compelling as getting more buses, roads, schools, medicine, and security services.

Jamaica presents a good example of this, but it applies throughout the region. In 2010, when it was estimated that more than three quarters of the country's budget was spent on debt and wage bill funding, budgeting money for PFM reform was difficult despite the contention of advocates that better PFM would result in better spending of all funds. The immediate appeal of electricity subsidies or schoolroom repairs naturally garners more support than the improvement of

---

* See Allen Schick, especially "A Contemporary Approach to Public Expenditure Management" (Washington, DC: World Bank, 1998), as well as numerous other articles in Organization for Economic Cooperation and Development, IMF, and World Bank publications.

bureaucratic processes such as PFM. Countries often appeal to their development partner donors for funding, but such funding is complicated and brings conditions. Jamaica is not unique in this regard; throughout the Caribbean, highly indebted countries leave the battle for the use of their limited resources to be conducted in newspaper headlines rather than in competition among well-analyzed budget options.

Perhaps paradoxically, successful PFM reform is also the cause of its own demise. When countries' economic times are good and there is money available to purchase the new automated tools, perform staff training, and cover the associated costs of PFM, countries are inclined to postpone efforts as the financial pressure is lessened. Yet in very difficult times, such as now in very highly indebted countries dependent on tourism such as Jamaica and the ECCU, resources—both human and financial—needed to effect reform are scarce.

Caribbean countries practice PFM in different ways, depending on their needs, leadership, and tradition. The same is true with modernization efforts. The Cayman Islands recently underwent huge modernization efforts[*] that have resulted in very advanced accounting, but they chose not to count their pension liabilities in their financial statements. Some observers opine that the various efforts, under the aegis of different development partners, have resulted in systems that fail to focus on overall results because their individual perspectives are so limited.

In many instances, reforms have been underway for years, but remain incompletely ingrained. Any of the five factors discussed above may cause backsliding. In other instances, PFM reforms are off to good starts, but concerns exist for follow-through. In Suriname, Belize, all the ECCU countries, and Trinidad and Tobago, PFM reforms have been underway for more than 3 years with notable progress, but much more still to be done to reach the goals announced by the countries themselves. The British Virgin Islands (BVI), under pressure from UK authorities (who would be responsible for BVI debt defaults), have embarked on an ambitious 3-year process of institutional strengthening. It quickly developed a classification structure that allows it to understand its actual financial position at any given moment, but reform is difficult (and becomes increasingly so as the easy fixes are accomplished and more complex ones required for additional progress) and the danger of burnout is strong.

A Staged Approach to Public Financial Management

Financial management reforms may involve different stages of emphasis, which involve (1) creating financial discipline, (2) improving the effectiveness of allocations, and (3) creating efficiencies in operating procedures.

Stage One—Financial Discipline

Sophisticated reforms are not possible without financial stability that comes from good financial discipline, yet no country in the Caribbean presently has all of the basic tools that are thought to comprise good financial discipline. First, a "sound financial legal framework" has been complicated in the Caribbean by the creeping adoption of more laws and regulations without understanding

---

[*] This occurred after the UK government dissolved the Cayman government in 2009 and assumed direct supervision due to the state of their finances. In this case, speedy reform was imposed as a condition by the United Kingdom of allowing the territory to form a new government. The entire accounting framework and policy as well as cash management and reporting were brought to international standards in a 2-year period in this effort.

how and when they conflict with each other. Duplication, contradiction, and silence on vital matters continue to exist. This is true in Anglophone countries as well as in Spanish, French, and Dutch traditions. Of the 20 nations working with the IMF's Caribbean Regional Technical Assistance Centre (CARTAC), 12 have created modernizing legislation, and few have produced a more straightforward adoption of a complete financial legal framework.

Another major ingredient in creating financial discipline is "proper classification of transactions." The most direct approach to this is the adoption of a chart of accounts that records six dimensions of every transaction: each transaction's financial nature (revenue, expenditure, asset, or liability); source of funds (which often defines some limits on its use); who is authorized to spend or collect it (the name of the administrative part of government, e.g., Fisheries); and the economic objective (e.g., salaries, contracts, purchase or rent of goods or services, grants or subsidies). Other dimensions, such as geographic or government function, may be added. Seventeen Caribbean nations are in the process of upgrading their Chart of Accounts (CoA) to reflect these good practice standards.

A third element of financial discipline is "personnel control." Centralized control of the number of paid positions and assurance of correct payment amounts get major attention because of the size of the expenditure. In all Caribbean countries, salaries, wages, and their accompanying benefits make up at least half of yearly expenditures. Most Caribbean countries are unable to perform government-wide payroll audits in order to form a basis for better estimation of the costs and enforcement of the limits.* Centralized approval by budget to refill positions is uncommon, even among countries in very tight financial situations.

A fourth element is "modern treasury management" resulting in better control of spending, more efficient payment means, more timely and accurate in-year financial position reporting. Eight Caribbean countries are in the process of transforming to a modern treasury approach to handling cash, which requires numerous sequential improvements many of which are dependent on both automated processing and staff retraining. Modernization requires a major paradigm shift. Jamaica has been trudging toward a modern treasury for more than 5 years with massive external support, but the process is bedeviled by continuing pockets of resistance among various stakeholder groups.

"Realistic revenue estimates" and "expenditure ceilings" are, respectively, the fifth and sixth major elements of financial discipline in PFM. If the government does not know how much money it will collect, it cannot make sound decisions about how much to borrow and spend. Most Caribbean governments collect only about half of the taxes, fines, and fees that they estimate are due to them. Overly optimistic revenue forecasts inevitably result in a shortfall in what is collected and collections cannot fund the budget so services are cut, deficits are incurred and/or debt increases.† Financial discipline also requires expenditure ceilings, based on available revenue, and policy priorities. To be effective, those creating a budget bid must understand what it costs them to produce the goods and services it proposes government will fund and have time to prepare a coherent proposal.

Finally, "budget implementation must provide funds to perform the services agreed" in the budget act. This is seldom achieved in the Caribbean, where major changes are decided outside

---

* In other parts of the developing world, government-wide payroll audits have resulted in the identification of ghost workers (people who do not exist or work for government), double or triple dippers (persons listed as full-time employees of more than one department or agency), incorrect payment rates or benefits. As significant as initial savings prove in such audits, equally important is construction of effective on-going controls.
† An equally destructive behavior is the creation of public bodies or state enterprises that operate outside government strictures but whose debts are explicitly or implicitly guaranteed by government.

the public budget process by ad hoc decisions taken in opaque ways throughout the year. Failure to create and execute a financially disciplined budget not only limits the credibility of the budget and the budgeting process, but also makes it difficult for public services to operate in effective ways; some offices just strive to survive and service improvement becomes less obtainable. In Jamaica, in recent history, budget laws have not been passed until near the end of the first quarter of the budget year: projects thus begin with reduced time and resources.

Stage Two—Improving the Effectiveness of Fund Allocations

The second stage of PFM reform focuses on devising processes that try to alter the current funding distribution toward a funding pattern that is more likely to achieve governmental policy. Inevitably, there is resistance from those who will lose in the allocation change: those who lose services, status, hidden decision-making authority; those who will need to learn and use new skills and new tools and become more transparent. Old systems may be disadvantageous to those who need services, but they are very appealing to those who profit from them, either passively or actively.

Governments that want to change the results of prior expenditure patterns have sought new tools and approaches to various parts of PFM, rather than merely optimizing allocations between existing categories: creating taxes just for a single purpose (as in road funds); determining that available resources must be divvied up by predetermined percentages (e.g., 30% for education), mandating program, performance, results, medium-term budgeting. Single-purpose taxes have been discredited as long-term solutions (as post-emergency revenue repair, they are more accepted). Predetermination of a percentage of all budget resources leads to over-resourcing, or at best an uneven playing field for competition. Fashioning budgets based on the results sought has many permutations and several are underway in the Caribbean.

Throughout the Caribbean, development partners have urged (or required) governments to adopt a Medium Term Expenditure Framework, but in many places efforts are nascent or confined to format changes. Without achievement of the financial discipline steps, movement toward better allocations is stunted: the entire budget preparation process in such places is often seen as formulaic with real decisions being made continuously throughout the year in an opaque manner. However, several Caribbean countries (Antigua and Barbuda, BVIs, Bahamas are varied examples) are now trying to move toward financial discipline and better allocations simultaneously.

Results-informed budgeting is a key ingredient to successful modern approaches to responsive allocation of available resources. Its goal is to focus attention on what the resources are expected to accomplish and then hold managers accountable for using those resources to do so. The term "results-informed budget" signals the flexibility and continuum of steps a government may take to move from simple repetition of historic allocation patterns. One results-focused technique currently being used in the Caribbean in several of the smaller eastern countries is adapted from an Australian technique sometimes called medium-term budget with rolling forward estimates. One of its noted practitioners, Martin Bowen,* works with countries to define their "current policy" spending and that becomes the base budget (at some level) and attention

---

* Martin Bowen is now an independent consultant used extensively by CARTAC to work with countries in the Caribbean. He worked for decades in the Australian budget office and was involved in the sophistication of this technique.

focuses in future years on changes to that base. Thus, while the total for any item (e.g., education) is described and justified in detail, out-year budgets explain changes to that base (e.g., phase out truant officers [attendance problem has abated] and phase in after school enrichment and tutoring). The approach combines the introduction of new ideas, the financial discipline of holding the line on spending, and a very slow but determined elimination of things that do not work and/or are no longer needed.

Such an approach, combined with personnel control, limits on in-year changes, and activated commitment control is particularly appropriate in the Caribbean because of the huge proportion of the budget now consumed by wages and benefits. Civil servants are a huge voting segment in the Caribbean. Any change to improve economic development, social services, and environmental protection must do so without any layoffs.

Stage Three—Gaining Operational Efficiency

Good PFM is more likely than bad practice to show where operating efficiencies can be gained. The previous stages often highlight inefficient, duplicative, and contradictory processes. There are two giant steps toward operational efficiencies that may create savings in administrative overhead: integrated financial management systems (IFMIS) and centralized treasury management systems using a treasury single account (TSA) to modernize banking relations. Both types of projects involve using automation as a tool to provide uniform application of business rules, controls, and authorization and to make data quickly available to show when changes are needed.

By example, moving from individual bank accounts (the traditional way of providing accounting controls and records before modern charts of accounts allowed automation to provide both) to keeping of all cash in a TSA. The government as a whole becomes an important banking customer and is able to negotiate better service agreement, avoid borrowing, and gain interest. Along the transition path, dozens of ancillary tasks are also evaluated turning up additional savings opportunities—if the governments proceed by designing and implementing new ways to accomplish old goals and phase out old controls that are no longer necessary (and so add useless overhead costs if continued). A real key to achieving operational efficiencies is thorough understanding of all the interrelated portions of PFM processes. The approach to major projects determines whether governments simply automate what they did by hand (even if it was ineffective or redundant), buy an off-the-shelf solution that may not deal with their individual legal requirements, or do a thorough conceptual design of what they wish to accomplish, and then set actions in motion to achieve those goals in a sequence that makes them sustainable.

IFMIS integrate all financial data to do all essential tasks required in PFM. Currently, each Caribbean country has one or more systems that do one or more PFM functions such as automatically create the reports routinely needed for knowing daily cash position; bank reconciliation; financial reporting; budget reporting; updates of cash flow data bases; individual agency reports; and individual project reports. When there is more than one system, there is more chance of error in data entry and data interpretation.* Some countries like Jamaica built their own systems, largely with donor funding and concessional loans. Other countries, like the BVI and Bermuda, bought pre-designed automation and had it installed. Still other countries are in the process of installing

---

* Abdul Khan and Mario Pessoa, *Conceptual Design: A Critical Element of a Government Financial Management System Project*, TNM/10/07 (Washington, DC: IMF, April 2010).

newer versions of software that promises to collect data needed for reporting and analysis while correctly processing individual transactions. Suriname, for example, is in the process of installing such a system; Guyana installed two, one for personnel control and one for other financial transactions, and is seeking to get them to communicate. Throughout the Caribbean there are three major vendors of ready-made systems and a handful of home-grown ones. None of them is perfect, but certain foundation tools allow greater usefulness: a universal and global compliant chart of accounts; conformity to accepted accounting rules for the basis of accounting chosen (cash, modified cash/accrual, accrual); bank reconciliation; and timely reporting (including sharing of reports with all legitimate stakeholders).

Central treasury management with a single treasury account (CTMS/TSA) allows governments to get the best use of its cash. Modern treasury design and function differ significantly from the older method of safe-guarding cash in (dozens or hundreds of) separate commercial bank accounts. The difference can be compared to the difference between individual wells and a public water system. CTMS/TSA involves a huge paradigm shift: from budget recipients husbanding cash in accounts over which the central government has no immediate access into one in which the modern government treasurer is a banking service provider. The change recognizes the difference between budget authority (the right to spend money) and cash management (making best use of the money in its control, including releasing just-in-time payments). The modern treasurer functions as the government's banker in terms of making the best use of cash: getting it into the treasury quickly; keeping it safe and investing any temporary surpluses wisely; releasing it for JIT payment by the most cost-efficient means possible. It changes the relationship with banks, central and commercial, as the treasurer is the agent for the single biggest client (the government as a whole) and expects good service and best prices. It seeks to replace the barter arrangements now in place so that government knows what things cost and can make process and/or vendor changes based on that. It seeks to develop a clear predictive picture of daily inflows and outflows to assure the government gets the time value of cash, avoids unnecessary borrowing fees, and takes advantage of any investable balances. The old system allowed money to be transferred from the consolidated fund to each ministry as cash became available. One ministry might have cash on deposit while the central government had to borrow money to meet a debt, pension, or other ministry's urgent cash need. The idle balances of one ministry, ironically, were probably the source of the money the government borrowed for needs of another ministry. In modern treasury systems, the fungibility of cash is recognized and the modern account codes are used to manage and report on it, obviating the need of bank action and fees in most cases.

The technology is readily available. The benefits to the government are clear and well documented. By example, Jamaica immediately saved millions in its first step of implementation. The resistance by banks and bank account holders is formidable and requires establishment of trust.

Reforming the Ministries of Finance as Influence on Good Financial Management in the Caribbean

Size, geography, colonial heritage, and post-colonial development partners all influence financial management in the Caribbean, but further progress also depends on reforming the Ministries of Finance (MoFs). Small island nations are subject to numerous international influences and may lack capacity and technical expertise for performance in some areas. The geographic location of the Caribbean makes it subject to catastrophic hurricanes and earthquakes that greatly impact the economies and public finances of its small nations. Heritage also affects competitiveness of these nations as does their civil service. In an interesting IMF working paper, the development of Suriname and Barbados are contrasted. Both countries were colonized specifically to supply sugar at the height of its trade, but Suriname's governance structure was derived from the Dutch East India Company's settlement while Barbados was governed by British colonialists who demanded some local governance from early.* Today, despite the apparent advantage of Suriname as an exporter of precious metal, it has the lowest average per capita GDP of the Caribbean while Barbados, despite its recent regression to less prudent financial discipline, has a GDP more than twice that of Suriname.†

While important, the previously mentioned challenges to PFM may be insufficient to explain the stubborn problems of the Caribbean.‡ Scholars have questioned the efficacy of the development partner efforts in the Caribbean. Billions of dollars of financial assistance has flowed from donors into the Caribbean countries, in cash, services, capital equipment, and improvements. Roads, electrification, water purification, education, health care, and more projects have been undertaken, many of them providing much needed infrastructure, disaster relief, etc. Caribbean complaints (that development partners seem partially deaf to what the countries say they need most) echo those listened to worldwide that resulted in the Paris Accords. The Paris Accords acknowledged that countries differ not only geographically but culturally and valued external experts need to integrate the local needs before prescribing "the solution." CARTAC went further and created a tool called "PFM strategy" which assists local authorities to set out the current state of affairs, including urgent problems and individual taboos. There has been increasing willingness in the Caribbean to honor the priorities which the "PFM strategy" sets into motion so that well-meant technical assistance does not have unintended negative consequences.

The manner in which PFM has been implemented points to internal factors, however. In PFM, perhaps even more than in capital projects, there may be several unintentional flaws in the process of determining what international aid is awarded: some development partners have a reputation of excellence in some types of work and have less focus in others§; some countries have flawed policy and process partially because they do not understand the conceptual design of a good PFM system so they may request things that will not solve the problem. International observers listened to local cries that things were not getting perceptibly better in degrees they would have expected for such expenditures. Some new tools were installed, but the business processes involved continued in the old way. In other cases, new automated systems were installed but their controls disabled because new ways of dealing with recurring problems had not been thought through. Other times post-installation departure of the experts left the government unable to maintain, update, or use the systems. The lesson learned was that the civil service must be trained and given incentives to work in the new way—and that has seldom been the case in

---

* Michael DaCosta. (2007) IMF Working Paper *Colonial Origins, Institutions and Economic Performance in the Caribbean: Guyana and Barbados*. This paper posits that geography, timing and nature of colonial settlement and especially the nature of colonial administration are reflected in today's economics. Source: https://www.imf.org/external/pubs/ft/wp/2007/wp0743.pdf (Accessed April 1, 2014).
† *World Economic Outlook database*, International Statistics, data as of July 2013.
‡ Similar factors apply to Mauritius which has been very successful in turning its performance around.
§ The IMF, for example, is often seen as the first-rate purveyor of PFM, while World Bank has developed some tools and techniques through its private sector division for using private sector to perform formerly public function and the IADB is often seen as the "go-to" development partner in complex IT systems design.

the Caribbean. Indeed, in many instances, the MoF is inadequately prepared and organized for the challenge at hand.

At the same time, development partners express dissatisfaction that apparently the same reforms are being funded multiple times—all without acceptable results. Empirically, both are true: there is some confusion caused by different definitions but much "misuse" of aid stems from trying to build things for which there is no foundation, either institutional or cultural. Performance budget or fiscal rules may be the newly acclaimed key to successful PFM, but only when the circumstances permit. And the Caribbean does not have the precursors that have been in place in successful implementations of both. As pedestrian as it sounds, until the elements of sound financial discipline are firmly in place, more sophisticated PFM tools (stages 2 and 3) are doomed to limited success if not failure. So, they should be deferred while attention is focused on getting the basics well established.

Establishing these basics requires a careful assessment of the roles and functions of many Caribbean MoFs. Most current MoFs are large organizations with many staff doing a plethora of activities, some of which have little relevance to modern ideas of financial management and most of which are operational processing rather than policy-focused. Modern MoFs tend to be small, policy-oriented organization of highly skilled experts: they have succeeded in creating sustainable operational processes that they could then delegate to other departments dedicated to operational matters. Even where there has been some degree of delegation of operational duties in the Caribbean, the MoF routinely substitutes its discretion for a universally followed set of policies that have been translated into procedures (for which staff have been trained). Presentations by Caribbean MoF officials at a March 2013 conference on modern MoFs* showed most had more than a dozen functions, most of which are operational, not policy and plan focused. In Jamaica, there are divisions of the MoF for budget, macroeconomics, and debt management, treasury (payments and accounting), but also for pension, executive bodies, state enterprises, employee loans, international relations, purchasing, internal audit, and so on. The MoF has more than 1000 staff, but it is not a fully interdependent organization focused on policy.[†] To expect PFM reform without re-envisioning the institutions that will do, it is unrealistic, according to topic experts.[‡] Although experts agree there is no single perfect MoF, there is also agreement that MoFs need to focus on policy as soon as they standardize processes and can delegate them to operational organizations.[§]

Most MoFs in the Caribbean plan formulaically and make endless changes during implementation (thus decreasing the seriousness with which budget planning is undertaken). The vicious cycle is evident: current systems do not accomplish needed goals, so executive intervention is required. That leaves less executive attention to creation of a better functioning system. As a top financial public administrator in one Caribbean country said at that conference, "When PFM reform competes for my attention with the operational crisis of the day, PFM reform loses every time."[¶] The

---

* CARTAC seminar for top MoF officials on the changing role of Ministries of Finance and keys to successful PFM reform.
† Size, geographic separation, rigid personnel classifications, and job duties with limited training, contradictory approaches to reform efforts further lessen the chance of successful reform. There is also a lively on-going dialog in academic and other forums questioning the negative role of development partner funding of particular improvements, reinforcing the silo organizational functioning.
‡ Allen, *The Challenge of Reforming Budgetary Institutions*.
§ Matthew, "Good Government Means Different Things in Different Countries."
¶ Rosamund Edwards, top finance administrator of Dominica at April 2013 CARTAC Conference of Caribbean Finance Officials—remarks on barriers to successful reform.

same cycle applies to the individual portions of PFM: when forecasters must respond to urgent individual requests for reports, there is less time for analysis, scenario building, and so on. Budget departments scurry, but budget preparation is compressed in virtually every Caribbean country.* Budget analysts and cash management experts whose time is spent on bookkeeping matters cannot be performing the analytic and investment activities that will improve government's stewardship of public money. Time required to perform tasks inefficiently severely limits the pace at which any Caribbean nation can move toward sequenced decision-making or lively debate of alternatives and public input adapting models successfully employed in Brazil or elsewhere.† Compressed budget preparation is prejudiced toward incrementalism and away from the thoughtful challenges and requirements to consideration of service priority changes that effects policy changes.

Thus, Caribbean countries continue to grapple with changing from traditional processes (that make thousands of individual decisions almost daily) with a set of processes that array the decisions more logically and once a year. The sheer volume of needed change is overwhelming unless PFM is organized into groups of activities that interact, and can be improved individually but collaboratively. In the Caribbean, CARTAC is assisting 17 countries organize the undertaking by supporting development of a country-specific PFM strategy and annual action plan.‡

Conclusion

This chapter discusses that PFM gives a country tools to control its resources in the context of a process to make realistic choices about their best use and then reports the results. The underlying premises of PFM are that planning—using fact-rich analysis of various options and choosing those which are best for the country—before implementing increases the probability of financial discipline, effective allocation, and operational efficiency. The components of PFM systems can become more sophisticated over time, but the major ingredients work best when they work together. It aims to create more efficient and effective macroeconomic management as well as improved public services, by focusing on creating financial discipline, transparency, automation, and medium-term planning. Caribbean countries are endeavoring to move toward sound budgeting planning and execution, and many have made significant strides in recent years. However, there are challenges and these reforms have not yet taken firm root. Automation is pursued with insufficient attention to conceptual design, executive (and civil service) commitment to paradigm shifts, and retraining. Moreover, many MoFs are inadequately organized and tasked for their modern policy roles; structural reform of the MoFs is needed. In the Caribbean, if PFM can provide predictable, reliable processes that lay out policy options, government can choose to think about how to transform the civil service into the responsive, modern governance and citizen-centric

---

* On October 12, 2013, Cayman Islands (fresh from the lightning reform program insisted on by their UK supervisors) presented a budget to Parliament for adoption 2 days later. In its case, the budget appears to be prudent in its major outlines: there is enough revenue to cover expenditures and contribute to a reserve fund. Although the parliamentary system relies much less on Parliament for balance of executive than does the U.S. presidential system, when severe measures are undertaken, there is much greater chance for public acceptance with public vetting before enactment: Two days for parliamentary consideration is short by any standard. In Jamaica, the budget estimates on which programs are to be based has been routinely presented so late that there is no possibility of passing the budget before the budget year begins. Include in body.
† For good examples of participatory budgeting, see Public Budget Project web site.
‡ Caribbean Regional Technical Assistance Center, located in Barbados, is funded by the Canadian International Development Agency (CIDA) and administered by IMF. See Annual Report 2012 at www.CARTAC.org.

services. Without such a basis for analysis, the Caribbean may endlessly repeat the rhetorical battles that rage in lieu of solution finding.

Bibliography

Acemoglu, Daron and James Robinson, 2012, *Why Nations Fail: The Origins of Power, Prosperity, and Poverty.* New York: Crown Business.

Allen, Richard, 2009, *The Challenge of Reforming Budgetary Institutions in Developing Countries,* IMF Working Paper 09/96. Washington, DC: IMF.

Allen, Richard and Daniel Tomassi, eds., 2001, *Managing Public Expenditure: A Reference Book for Transition Countries.* Paris, France: Organization for Economic Co-operation and Development.

Andrews, Matthew, 2010, Good government means different things in different countries. *Governance: An International Journal of Policy, Public Administration and Institutions,* Vol. 23, No. 1, pp. 7–35.

Andrews, Matthew, 2013, *The Limits of Institutional Reform in Development: Changing Rules for Realistic Solutions.* New York: Cambridge University Press.

Cangiano, Marco, Curristine, Teresa and Michel Lazare, eds., 2013, *Public Financial Management and Its Emerging Architecture.* Washington, DC: International Monetary Fund.

Canuto, Otaviano and Marcelo Giugale, eds., 2010, *The Day After Tomorrow: A Handbook on the Future of Economic Policy in the Developing World.* Washington, DC: World Bank.

Cebotari, Aliona, 2008, *Contingent Liabilities: Issues and Practice,* IMF Working Paper 08/245. Washington, DC: International Monetary Fund.

Diamond, Jack, 2012, Guidance Note on Sequencing PFM Reforms (and background paper). Available at: https//www.pefa.org.

Diamond, Jack, 2012, What makes countries rich or poor? *NYT Review of Books,* June 7.

International Monetary Fund, annual, "World Economic Outlook" and "Regional Economic Outlook: Latin America and the Caribbean," esp. 2007–2013. Available at: www.imf.org/external/Caribbean.

Loayza, Norman, 1997, The Economics of the informal sector: A simple model and some empirical evidence from Latin America. Available at: www.worldbank/org/external WDSPIF/1997/02/01.

Robinson, Marc, ed., 2007, *Performance Budgeting: Linking Funding and Results.* Washington, DC: IMF.

Rodrik, Dani, 1998, Why do more open economies have bigger governments? *Journal of Political Economy,* Vol. 106, pp. 997–1032.

Schick, Allen, 1998, *A Contemporary Approach to Public Expenditure Management.* Washington, DC: World Bank.

Schick, Allen, ed., 2009, *Evolutions in Budgetary Practice, with OECD Senior Budget Officials.* Paris, France: OECD.

Talbot, Colin, 2010, *Theories of Performance: Organizational and Service Improvements in Public Administration.* Oxford: Oxford University Press.

Wildavsky, Aaron, 1964, *Politics of the Budgetary Process.* Boston, MA: Little, Brown and Co.

World Bank, 2008, *The Caribbean Catastrophe Risk Insurance Facility: Providing Immediate Funding after Natural Disasters.* Washington, DC: World Bank.

Chapter 8

Public Procurement Policy Considerations in the Caribbean: Trade, Governance, and Development*

Margaret Rose

Contents

Policy Context: The Twenty-First-Century Procurement Policy Conundrum 160
Caribbean Public Procurement Policy Reform 164
    Organization of Eastern Caribbean States 166
    Trinidad and Tobago..167
    Haiti—Disaster Procurement...169
Status of Regional Reforms..171
    CARIFORUM-EU EPA 172
    ALBA—An Alternative Integration Model? 174
Conclusion: Democratizing the Global Economy—The Challenge for the Caribbean..............175
Bibliography..177
Electronic Sources 178

> **Abstract:** This chapter examines public procurement policy in Caribbean context. We first examine the procurement in the context of broader, neoliberal market-based reforms and its limiting effects on using public procurement as a socioeconomic development tool. Second, we examine the state of various public procurement reforms in the Caribbean, as well as experiences such as disaster procurement. Third, we examine

---

* This chapter is dedicated to Norman Girvan (1941–2014), economist, author, Professor Emeritus in the University of the West Indies.

some broader developments such as relating to the Economic Partnership Agreement (EPA) and some alternatives. This chapter finds evidence of the strategic use of the public procurement function, and the Organization of Eastern Caribbean States (OECS) stands out as a unique and unparalleled collaborative public procurement system among state groupings. However, much progress is yet to be made and Caribbean leaders are not yet seen ready to assume the responsibility for regionally relevant procurement policy development.

Policy Context: The Twenty-First-Century Procurement Policy Conundrum

The era post-Washington Consensus* saw the largely unchecked growth of Anglo-American neoliberalism in the world economy until the 2008 global economic crisis. Approaches based on restrictive macroeconomic policy, liberalization of international trade and investment, privatization, and deregulation became the order of the day. Underpinned by the philosophy that development is best achieved by making markets work better and preventing market failures, one consequence of the adoption of this economic philosophy was the international movement to harmonize law and policy relating to public procurement.

With the vigorous espousal of trade liberalization as essential to the goals of efficiency, best value, and now good governance, the World Trade Organization (WTO), United Nations (UN), International Monetary Fund, World Bank, and other International Financial Institutions (IFIs) trained their resources on standardizing international procurement rules and policies. Policies governing how a government buys, when it buys and from whom it buys, which were traditionally considered "behind the border"† issues were now considered hostages of the new economic order. Arguably, these policies have been among the most potentially influential devices in the management of the economic relations between the Global North and the Global South.

The impact of the neoliberalism on public procurement harmonization policy is evident.‡ Without going further than the preambles of the respective international instruments, the stated objective of procurement policy standardization is primarily maximizing participation in the world economy regardless of nationality and promoting competition. Put simply, the objective is trade liberalization.§ Open competitive procurement is *de facto* and *de jure* the default and the

---

* Phrase coined in 1989 by Economist John Williamson referring to the economic policy programs embarked upon by the IMF and World Bank geared toward developing countries in crisis, which included policies relating to macroeconomic stabilization, economic opening with respect to both trade and investment, and the expansion of market forces within the domestic economy. See also Williamson, *What Washington Means*.
† Typically used to refer to issues relating to domestic structural reform, such as deregulation, competition policy, economic legal infrastructure, transparency, procurement, and financial sector reforms.
‡ United Nations Commission on Trade and International Law (UNCITRAL), World Trade Organization (WTO), International Monetary Fund (IMF), World Bank, Inter-American Development Bank, and so on.
§ By example, the preamble to the UN Model Law 2011 expresses the objectives of the law as "(1) Maximizing economy and efficiency in procurement; (2) Fostering and encouraging participation in procurement proceedings by suppliers and contractors regardless of nationality, thereby promoting international trade; (3) Promoting competition among suppliers and contractors for the supply of the subject matter of the procurement; (4) Providing for the fair, equal and equitable treatment of all suppliers and contractors; (5) Promoting the integrity of, and fairness and public confidence in, the procurement process; (6) Achieving transparency in the procedures relating to procurement."

most efficient way to procure in order to obtain "best" value for money.* However, of concern to the Caribbean and elsewhere is the absence, as a primary goal of these instruments, the objective of social, environmental, and industrial growth and development.† The use of the public procurement function as a socioeconomic development tool is still seen as a secondary, collateral, and voluntary exercise. This remains so, despite more recent attempts of leading international public procurement policy experts to redefine the socioeconomic uses of procurement as "horizontal policies" as opposed to collateral or secondary ones.‡

In broad context, the open market creed is further reinforced via the "epistemological recycling" anchored in the curricula and textbooks in business and economics courses in universities around the world (Dash 2013). Accordingly, the view that market intervention over and above correcting for failures is bad and inimical to efficient purchasing is pervasively held in modern economics and such thinking has dominated economics education at all levels in both developed and developing countries.

This preoccupation with the "Anglo-American" free market capitalistic model§ has had important consequences for developing states. First, it obscures essential "procurement linkages" (McCrudden 2007) critical for smaller, less developed states, which can and do have immense impact on national economic and social development. Second, it also avoids assessing the potential, relevance, and transferability of alternative socioeconomic models such as the social and solidarity economic model being explored in the Latin American region¶ and the East Asian model popularly described as idiosyncratic.**

Notwithstanding the incontrovertible evidence of the role of the capitalist system on growth and economic development generally, the benefit of the neoliberal "free market" model to the industrial growth and development of smaller less developed states is seriously questioned. Leading Caribbean intellectual and economist Norman Girvan, for example, asserts that the theory's predictions of benign effects only follow under highly restrictive and unrealistic assumptions, which are not relevant to the experience of developing countries. Moreover, "neoliberal integration may accentuate, rather than attenuate, differences in development," since the wealthier partners have a far superior ability to compete and trade and governments of the poorer partners are deprived of "development policy space" (Khor 2008).

It is difficult to characterize free market veneration as an oversight or a mistake. For centuries, industrial nations have carefully crafted the rules of the market for what the state buys,

---

* This is evident in procurement standardization instruments at the international level like the UN Model Law on the Procurement of Goods Works & Services, the WTO-GPA 1994 and IFI and other donor procurement rules and procedures.
† There is discussion of the pursuit of socioeconomic policy through the use of public procurement in the 2012 Guide to the UN Model Law on Procurement, in particular at Article 2 where definition of "socioeconomic policy" is included; Articles 8–11 on participation, qualification, description of the subject matter of the procurement and evaluation criteria and procedures and Article 30 on sole source procurement, there are two caveats provided. First, such use is made subject to Article 3 which expressly provides for international obligations to override Model Law provisions and prohibiting states from pursuing socioeconomic policies if inconsistent with international obligations. Secondly, pursuit of socioeconomic policies can be pursued through procurement only insofar as they are set out in other provisions of the law of the enacting state, or in the procurement regulations: they cannot be policies of the procuring entity alone.
‡ Arrowsmith, "Horizontal Policies in Public Procurement."
§ Chang and Grabel, *Reclaiming Development*.
¶ See discussion on ALBA below.
** That is, based on the distinctive historical, cultural, and economic East Asian context. See *Reclaiming Development* supra at ft.10 38–40.

how it buys, from whom it buys, and to whom it sells, in a manner that ensured a dominant and asymmetrical space in the global economy. Some of the most successful industrial nations like the United States, the United Kingdom, and Japan have had deliberate public procurement policies (albeit shrouded within foreign investment and trade modalities) engaged in since prior to the industrial revolution pursuing protectionist agendas aimed at stifling foreign competition and stimulating domestic growth.

Up to present day, the United States aggressively pursues protectionist *Buy American** policies in its government procurement of goods and works implemented by legislation in 1933 and 1983. This policy was further extended and reinforced in 2009 in the wake of the financial crisis.† Additional twentieth-century examples can be found in the carefully designed interventionist measures of states like Singapore and Hong Kong combined with selective liberalization measures and foreign investment regulation, which have been touted as the reasons for their singular growth.‡

The concept of tying aid where official or officially supported loans, credits, or associated financing packages limited the procurement of the goods, works, or services to the donor country or to a group of countries was up to very recently still being pursued by IFIs and countries in the Global North. This practice has been conceded as a form of protectionism rendering development costs, in some cases as much as 20% higher for recipient countries.§

Despite the uncontroverted evidence of industrial nations proactively linking procurement and trade policy in a manner not necessarily conducive to leveling the playing field, it would seem that in the twenty-first century, the same policy space is not to be afforded to developing and transition economies. The dismantling of preferential trade agreements, reduction in development assistance, and the compulsory promotion of middle income developing countries and their resultant ineligibility for lending on concessional terms, grants, and other trade concessions such as the generalized system of preferences are all features of the proverbial ladder

---

* *Buy American Act* (BAA-41U.S.C. ss10a-10d) 1933 which requires the U.S. government to prefer U.S.-made products in its purchases; *Buy American Act* 1983 which applies to mass-transit-related procurements.
† *American Recovery and Reinvestment Act* of 2009 Section 1605—Buy American "prohibits use of recovery funds for a project for the construction, alteration, maintenance, or repair of a public building or public work unless all of the iron, steel, and manufactured goods used in the project are produced in the United States. The genesis of this Buy American ethos spans right back to the Boston Tea Party in 1773, which punctuated a decade long nonimportation movement against British imports and fueled the drive to promote, buy and use only domestically produced goods. This in turn escalated the movement for American independence from Britain." Economic nationalism is the root of U.S. economic policy and permeates its arrangements with other states to present day. See Frank, *Buy American*, 4.
‡ Sornarajah, *International Law on Foreign Investment*, 2 ft.2.
§ The full definition of *tied aid* as defined by OECD is: "Tied aid credits are official or officially supported Loans, credits or Associated Financing packages where procurement of the goods or services involved is limited to the donor country or to a group of countries which does not include substantially all developing countries [or Central and Eastern European Countries (CEECs)/New Independent States (NIS) in transition]." Donor members of the Development Assistance Committee (DAC), a subcommittee of the OECD, agreed to virtually untie all aid to the least developed countries (LDCs), and this recommendation entered into effect on January 1, 2002. However, the untying of bilateral aid is without a deadline, and a European Network on Debt and Development (Eurodad) report in 2011 found that many countries had reneged on their promises to untie aid and at least 20% of bilateral aid remains formally tied. Researchers estimate that $69 billion—more than half of the total official development assistance—is spent each year buying goods and services for development projects. For example, in 2009, 67% of aid from Greece was given on the condition that Greek contractors were used on development projects. In the same year, 54% of Austrian aid was tied, along with 50% of Korean aid, and 39% of Portuguese aid.

being kicked away.* Rich countries are banning the poor countries from using the very policies that made them rich.

This poses something of a policy conundrum for developing states in responding to the competing interests of international trade, accountability, and industrial growth and development. The strategic power of a state in the purchasing function as market creator (primary buyer), regulator (force of law), and influencer (participator in the market) is uncontroversial, and it has always been incumbent on governments to harness that power to further industrial, social, and environmental development. However, application of discriminatory or protectionist procurement policies aimed at stimulating sustainable national socioeconomic development may raise trade barriers that run afoul of being pressed by the institutions and the countries of the Global North. That said, notably, CARIFORUM† states have been able to hold off from signing on to the WTO-Government Procurement Agreement (GPA).‡

Ignoring real market failures and relying on false assumptions of equality and perfect access to market information, the harmonization of public procurement rules to secure more open competitive markets ironically facilitates a global economy unsympathetic to growth, development and information asymmetries among states and contributing to proliferating income inequality gaps. As cracks in the economic order began to show and financial fragility rose through the 2000s, some economists conceded that the economics profession had botched "by failing to promote and sustain a diversity of views among its members over matters that are terribly complex and important, and by failing to provide market actors, policy makers and citizens with a careful assessment of the potential risks of financial deregulation and the reward risk profiles of alternative regimes. These mistakes were avoidable."§ As Norman Girvan stated:

> We are therefore navigating an issue [public procurement] that lies at the intersection of governance, public administration, development and trade negotiations. In this task the main assets we bring to the table are our own knowledge, skills and experience. I come from a school of thought that believes we must think these things through for ourselves. Cultural transplants and policy transplants do not work. Policies, practices and systems must be home-grown; borrowing from the best available and adapting it to our own circumstances and objectives. (Girvan 2000)

While it has been very difficult for Caribbean states to independently¶ articulate a coherent framework for harnessing the potential synergies or managing the tensions between them, and

---

* Chang, *Kicking Away the Ladder*.
† CARIFORUM grouping includes CARICOM member states and Dominica Republic. In 2001, CARICOM and Dominica Republic (CARICOM-DR) entered into a Free Trade Agreement in which the parties agreed to work toward a harmonized public procurement policy. The CARIFORUM is the agreed umbrella organization for the negotiation of the trade agreements with third states.
‡ The WTO Agreement on Government Procurement (WTO-GPA) 1994 includes rules relating to transparency and "natural treatment" of suppliers, covers procurement of goods works and services by "covered" entities and the guaranteeing of fair and nondiscriminatory conditions of international competition. Traditional reluctance of developing countries to accede to the WTO-GPA has been based on the perception that the nondiscrimination and national treatment provisions of the agreement facilitate increased market opening to foreign competition which in turn, it is felt, would cripple the growth of domestic industry and capacity within the developing state. As the number of developing states observing and/or negotiating access to the GPA in the last decade has been steadily increasing, it would seem that this reluctance to engage has been lessening.
§ DeMartino, *Consequences of Economic Downturn*, 25–44.
¶ Without the funding and resources of IFIs and other international organizations which promote the Anglo-American neoliberal economic model for development.

confronting the neoliberal zeitgeist, public procurement policy is one area in which the search for greater development impact has been played out.

Caribbean* Public Procurement Policy Reform

Despite international pressures, public procurement regulatory reform within CARICOM[†] member states remains largely underdeveloped, although it is fair to say that reform initiatives have definitely stepped up over the last decade.[‡] Even where legislation does exist, Mckoy (2012) has pointed out that the principal governance challenge facing Commonwealth Caribbean states is "moral hazard" through a lack of accountability and critical enforcement capacity.[§]

Caribbean states have been characterized as experiencing the traits of "unreformed procurement systems" (Schrouder 2010). Features of unreformed systems include "limited professional knowledge and expertise, the absence of effective institutional coordination, inadequate financial planning, lengthy delays experienced by suppliers in receiving payment for goods and services supplied, high incidence of malpractice combined with unethical conduct such as interference and insider dealings" (see Agaba and Shipman 2006).

Save in respect of Jamaica, Belize, Guyana, Grenada, Haiti, and most recently Trinidad and Tobago[¶], which states have undertaken some level of public procurement legislative reform in the last decade, the legislative landscape for the remaining CARICOM member states is characterized by the interaction of multiple poorly coordinated, and in some cases outdated, legislative texts, relics of the British Colonial legal system.** In these latter states, fledgling reform efforts are underway with public procurement bills being bounced back and forth between legislative drafting departments, Cabinets, public comment, and Parliaments. There are no comprehensive legislative frameworks governing the function of public procurement, and it is not specifically addressed in the Constitutions of CARICOM member states with the exception of Guyana and Suriname (Table 8.1).

The lack of independently resourced regulatory bodies with responsibility for monitoring the public procurement function, or formal complaints and/or dispute resolution bodies for procurement disputes or functioning centralized public procurement information systems all represent additional substantial gaps at the domestic level. Lack of capacity at the institutional, professional, and research levels also presents a substantial challenge.

That is not to say that there is no evidence of the very strategic use of the public procurement function by Caribbean governments to pursue socioeconomic and sociopolitical goals. It is inter-

---

* Caribbean here refers to the English-speaking Caribbean.
† The Caribbean Community (CARICOM) established by the Treaty of Chaguaramas in 1973 is an organization of 15 Caribbean nations and dependencies (Antigua and Barbuda, Bahamas, Barbados, Belize, Dominica, Grenada, Guyana, Haiti, Jamaica, Montserrat, St. Kitts & Nevis, St. Lucia, St. Vincent and the Grenadines, Suriname, and Trinidad and Tobago). CARICOM's main purposes are to promote economic integration and cooperation among its members, to ensure that the benefits of integration are equitably shared, and to coordinate foreign policy.
‡ See Table 8.1 Status of National Public Procurement Legislative Reforms—CARICOM.
§ Mckoy, *Corruption*.
¶ In December 2014, the Parliament of Trinidad and Tobago passed the long awaited public procurement reform legislation which was then assented to by the president in January 2015 (Public Procurement & Disposal of Property Act No.1 of 2015).
** Central Tenders Board Ordinances, Finance & Audit Acts, Prevention of Corruption Acts, Freedom of Information Acts, see Table 8.1.

Table 8.1 Status of National Public Procurement Legislative Reforms—CARICOM

Country	Existing Legislation	Proposed Reforms
Antigua and Barbuda	Tenders Board Act Chap. 424 as amended by the Tenders Board Amendment Act 2002	Since 2010 Procurement & Contract Administration Bill under consideration by Parliament
Bahamas	Financial Administration and Audit Act 1973 (Chap. 329)	Financial Administration and Audit (Amendment) Bill 2013 including provisions for establishment of Public Procurement Board and EPA Compliance
Barbados	Financial Administration and Audit Act 1964; Financial Administration and Audit (Drug Service) Rules 1980; the Financial Administration and Audit (Financial) Rules 1971; the Financial Administration and Audit (Supplies) Rules 1971	Draft Public Procurement Bill 2011 currently undergoing further revision
Belize	Contractor General Act No. 6 of 1993; Finance and Audit Act 2000; Finance and Audit (Reform) Act 2005	
Dominica	Finance and Audit Act No. 8 of 1965	Draft Public Procurement Bill before Cabinet since 2007, revised in 2010 and 2011
Grenada	Finance and Audit Act 1964; Finance and Audit Amendment Act 1998; Public Procurement and Contract Administration Act 2007	Public Procurement and Administration Act not implemented after criticism from OECD[a]—regulations required to give full effect to the legislation not yet promulgated
Guyana	Constitution Amendment 2000; Procurement Act 2003; Fiscal Management and Accountability Act 2003; Audit Act 2004	
Haiti	Public Procurement Act 2009	
Jamaica	Financial Administration and Audit Act (FAA) 1959; Contractor General Act No. 15 of 1983; Public Sector Procurement Regulations 2008; Revised Handbook of Public Procurement Procedures (March 2014)	New comprehensive Public Procurement Bill and Draft Regulations being considered

(Continued)

Table 8.1 (*Continued*)   Status of National Public Procurement Legislative Reforms—CARICOM

Country	Existing Legislation	Proposed Reforms
Montserrat	Public Finance (Management and Accountability) Act 2008; Public Finance (Management and Accountability) (Procurement) Regulations 2011	New Draft Procurement Bill being considered
St. Kitts & Nevis	Finance Act 1990 Financial Regulations (FR) and Financial (Stores) Regulations by virtue of (1) The Financial Rules 1998 [First Schedule] and (2) The Stores Rules 1998 [Second Schedule] of the Finance and Audit Amendment Act 1998 (Act No. 25 of 1998)	New Draft Procurement Bill being considered
St. Lucia	Finance Administration Act 1997 (Act No. 3 of 1997) to regulate procurement. Ministry of Finance (MOF) issues Financial Regulations (FR) and Financial (Stores) Regulations by virtue of (1) The Financial Rules, 1998 [First Schedule] and (2) The Stores Rules 1998 [Second Schedule] of the Finance and Audit Amendment Act 1998 (Act No. 25 of 1998)	Procurement Bill revised and before Cabinet since 2011
St. Vincent and the Grenadines	Financial and Audit Act 1964; Financial Regulations (FR) and Financial (Stores) Regulations by virtue of (1) Financial and Stores Rules of the Windward Islands 1952 and (2) Manual of Tender Procedures (issued on November 21, 1967, as Statutory Rules No. 101–114)	
Trinidad and Tobago	Central Tenders Board Ordinance 1961 (as amended 1979, 1987, 1991, 1993); Exchequer & Audit Act	Public Procurement & Disposal of Property Act No. 1 2015 received the assent of the president in January 2015 but is not yet proclaimed. Work is currently underway on the supporting regulations.

[a] Assessment of Public Financial Management in Grenada using the PEFA PFM performance framework 2009. http://ec.europa.eu/europeaid/what/economic-support/public-finance/documents/grenada_pefa_report_en.pdf.

esting to observe that several Caribbean states that are yet to undertake substantial procurement reform have had some success when proactively linking the function to development goals.

Organization of Eastern Caribbean States

The OECS is a regional outlier of sorts with functional cooperation in the area of procurement being far more advanced than what obtains at the CARICOM level. One initiative is the establishment of a pharmaceutical procurement system, a self-financing public sector monopsony, or buyers' cartel that covers its operating cost from a 15% surcharge. According to reports, cost savings demonstrated that regional prices were as much as 44% lower than individual country prices. The continuous annual cost savings accruing after 16 years of the joint purchasing arrangement have reinforced the OECS/PPS as an excellent cost–benefit model of economic and functional cooperation among OECS member countries.*

Another OECS initiative is the electronic public procurement system (e-PPS) being implemented since 2013, a web-based collaborative system used to facilitate the full lifecycle of a tendering process, for both buyers and suppliers. It offers a secure, interactive, dynamic environment for procurements of any nature, size, complexity, or value, enforcing and encouraging best practices. Able to support the well-established PPS for the procurement of pharmaceutical products, the e-PPS is said to facilitate efficiency gains, while promoting core principles and regulations on public procurement such as transparency, security, availability, nondiscrimination, and equality of treatment.[†]

Notable here is the innovation and cooperation evidenced by the undertaking of these two practical procurement reforms and the demonstrable value achieved by the states, while yet not undertaking comprehensive statutory procurement reform at the regional or national levels.

Trinidad and Tobago

Yet to implement the 2015 Public Procurement reform framework, this country historically demonstrates the bias toward the strategic use of public procurement to achieve sociopolitical objectives. Trinidad and Tobago is the largest exporter of liquefied natural gas (LNG) to the United States and experiences a positive balance of payments position with all of its Caribbean trading partners and the United States and Canada.[‡] Trinidad and Tobago is said to have become the first "gas-based" economy in the world and in 2012 emerged as the sixth largest LNG exporter in the world (Small 2006). Further, this tiny twin island state with a population of approximately 1.3 million has risen to the presidency of the Gas Exporting Countries Forum.[§] After experiencing two oil booms in 1973 and again in 2008, the economic development of Trinidad and Tobago is pursued largely independently of international aid or foreign loans or grants. One of the consequences of this is that the country's public procurement processes are therefore not dominated by guidelines issued by international bodies and lending organizations, as in the case of its less resource-rich CARICOM counterparts.

Notwithstanding significant governance weaknesses from a decentralized procurement system with no regulatory public procurement framework for the plethora of state-controlled enterprises utilizing public monies, Trinidad and Tobago has pursued a fairly aggressive sociopolitical use of the public procurement function. Though attracting strong criticism from some sectors for the

---

* See more at: http://www.oecs.org/our-work/units/pharmaceutical-procurement#sthash.0QsZt20c.dpuf.
† Source: https://procurement.oecs.org/epps/home.do.
‡ U.S. Energy Information Administration (EIA), Country Data, Trinidad and Tobago—Country Analysis Note : As the largest oil and natural gas producer in the Caribbean, Trinidad and Tobago's hydrocarbon sector moved from an oil dominant to a mostly natural gas-based sector in the early 1990s. In 2012, Trinidad and Tobago was the world's sixth largest LNG exporter, according to BP's 2013 Statistical Review. The country is also the largest LNG exporter to the United States, accounting for nearly 65% of U.S. total LNG imports in 2012.
§ Small, *Trinidad and Tobago*.

manner in which the initiatives are implemented,* they evidence political recognition that chaste market approaches in the function of procurement do not always serve society in a way, which supports socioeconomic growth and development.

Examples of this strategic use of the public procurement function can be found in the Unemployment Relief Programme (URP) and continued under the Community-based Environmental Protection and Enhancement Programme (CEPEP). The URP, in its earliest incarnation as the Depressed Areas Programme, emerged in 1957 and was launched by the government as a strategy to alleviate the depressed economic conditions of the communities in which it began. Essentially, it was established as a model to secure temporary, irregular employment opportunities at minimum or below minimum wage in order to implement community infrastructure maintenance and development projects. On the one hand, this can be viewed as a method of procuring community infrastructure maintenance and development services by targeting unemployed persons for temporary service contracts.

The CEPEP Company Ltd. established in 2008 implements environmental cleanup and beautification projects, coastal improvement and cleanup projects, dead animal removal projects, disaster and emergency response projects, illegal dump site removal projects and waste removal, and eco sites management services. Instead of procuring these works and services through traditional procurement processes or via in-house provision, these projects are implemented in environmental work areas (EWAs) and the projects are organized on the basis of deploying contracting companies in EWAs that are responsible for recruiting and managing their workers in order to achieve the beautification targets.†

The National Social Development Programme (NSDP) is designed to meet the needs of low-income communities throughout the country by providing and improving the supply of water and electricity to communities, residences, recreational, sporting, and other facilities; the program also supplies house-wiring services to people who are unable to afford the cost of wiring their own homes. The NSDP fund is established and state enterprises receive these monies with the specific mandate of targeting micro, small and medium enterprises (MSMEs) for the provision of the works and services under predetermined thresholds.

It must be emphasized that these initiatives are plagued by allegations of corruption, political patronage, waste, and mismanagement. These allegations are not without merit, given the lack of regulatory framework, transparency, and accountability in the selection of contractors and employees. Nonetheless, these initiatives represent a determined effort by the Government of Trinidad and Tobago to harness the socioeconomic impact of the public resources, for example, targeting vulnerable communities as the primary recipient of the contracts to provide the services.

The inverse relationship between more bureaucratic rules and procedures and the flexibility to pursue socioeconomic goals requires a balancing approach to achieve the desired outcomes of good governance and accountability on the one hand and efficiency and socioeconomic objectives on the other. It is a central premise of this paper and the opinion of the author that this balancing exercise is critical and is not suited to a "one-size-fits-all" approach. At the regional and national levels, research must be undertaken to ascertain where the rules aimed at competitive procurement should end and flexibility to pursue national socioeconomic objectives should begin.

A note on Social Procurement the New TT Act:

---

* Relating to nepotism, cronyism, and political patronage. The criticisms are not without merit and it is suggested inevitable, given the lack of transparency and accountability in the procurement framework.
† See CEPEP Company Ltd. web site for more details: http://cepep.co.tt.

The Public Procurement & Disposal of Property (PP&DP) Act No. 1 of 2015 has not yet been proclaimed and therefore is not in effect. However, it is noteworthy that the strategic use of the public procurement function is now statutorily mandated. In the definitions section of the PP&DP Act, a definition of "socioeconomic policies" is advanced as including the social dimension: "environmental, social, economic and other policies of Trinidad and Tobago authorized or required by the Regulations or other provisions of the laws of Trinidad and Tobago to be taken into account by a procuring entity in procurement proceedings."

Nonetheless, despite statutory power to limit participation in procurement in order to encourage local industry development and local content in section 28, there are no provisions guiding its evidence-based application, save that reasons should be provided. It is disappointing to note that the fleshing out of this policy is left to be articulated in regulations or other provisions of the laws of Trinidad and Tobago. In fact, outside of the definitions section, reference to "socioeconomic policies" is not made anywhere else in the Act. This is indeed unfortunate and an opportunity missed.

Social requirements can be fully embraced in procurement practice providing certain criteria are met. These criteria usually stipulate that social requirements should (a) reflect policy expressly adopted by the public body, (b) be capable of being measured in terms of performance, (c) be drafted in the specifications and become part of the contract, and (d) be defined in ways that do not discriminate against bidders.

The granting of a general discretion to limit participation in procurement in order to promote local industry or content, without transparent criteria being articulated for the exercise of that discretion, as done in the TT PP&DP Act, creates an accountability conundrum. While the promotion of local industry and/or local content provides social value, if the process is not underpinned by fair, objective and transparent criteria, it is vulnerable to executive abuse.

Haiti—Disaster Procurement

Disaster procurement can be seen as a unique opportunity to build back better. According to UN Secretary-General Ban Ki-moon, "procurement can and should be more than an operational step. It should be a crucial tool in the development itself. It should stimulate local markets and drive innovation" (UNOPS 2011). Local procurement in disaster relief can be strategically used in reconstruction projects by spending the development dollar twice and creating a multiplier effect for each reconstruction dollar. By hiring a national or local firm, growth of the local private sector is stimulated, spurring long-term income and job creation. Buying locally in the immediate aftermath of a disaster may also help local entrepreneurs and firms to compete with outsiders. Local procurement has a long list of benefits, fostering the local private sector, building local capacity and increasing sustainability, strengthening local government and increasing accountability between government and citizens, and improving the cost-effectiveness of aid.

Nonetheless, it would seem that after disaster struck Haiti in 2010, this crucial opportunity to "build back better" was missed. On January 12, 2010, a 7.0 magnitude earthquake hit Haiti. The earthquake affected almost 3.5 million people, including the entire population of 2.8 million people living in the capital, Port-au-Prince. The Government of Haiti estimated that the earthquake killed 222,570 and injured another 300,572 people. Displacement peaked at close to 2.3 million people, including 302,000 children. The earthquake destroyed 105,000 houses and badly damaged at least another 188,383 houses. Sixty percent of government and administrative buildings,

80% of schools in Port-au-Prince, and 60% of schools in the South and West Departments were destroyed or damaged. Total earthquake-related loss is estimated at $7.8 billion, equivalent to more than 120% of Haiti's 2009 gross domestic product. This disaster was followed by the cholera epidemic 10 months later and Hurricane Sandy in October 2012.

Disaster relief and humanitarian assistance from foreign governments, international agencies, corporations, nongovernmental agencies (NGOs), and private citizens amounted to well over $9 billion in pledges aimed at providing urgent relief to the Haitian citizens and to aid the critical reconstruction effort. Despite this outpouring, it is uncontroversial to state that the humanitarian effort has not yet met its objectives. Four years on, much of the conversation surrounding the Haitian earthquake relief and recovery effort has centered on allegations of charities squandering money, the gains of U.S. contractors, and how Haitians themselves received very little money.*

In a special report in 2012 and giving account for his stewardship of the effort, former president of the United States Bill Clinton noted that only about 10% of the total $6.04 billion currently disbursed had been channeled to the Government of Haiti. Other reports[†] state that of the $379 million in initial U.S. aid for Haiti, nothing went directly, or in some cases even indirectly, to Haiti, and about one-third was actually given directly back to the United States to reimburse themselves for sending in their military. The UN Special Envoy for Haiti reported that of the $2.4 billion in humanitarian funding, 34% was provided back to the donor's own civil and military entities for disaster response, 28% was given to UN agencies and NGOs for specific UN projects, 26% was given to private contractors and other NGOs, 6% was provided as in-kind services to recipients, 5% to the International and National Red Cross Societies, 1% was provided to the Government of Haiti, and four-tenths of 1% of the funds went to Haitian NGOs.

Haitian companies capable of providing relief and reconstruction services were bypassed in the relief process just like the Haitian government. The Center for Economic and Policy Research audited the 1490 contracts awarded by the U.S. government from January 2010 to April 2011 and found only 23 contracts went to Haitian-owned companies. Overall, the United States had awarded $194 million to contractors and $4.8 million to the 23 Haitian companies. On the other hand, contractors from the Washington DC area received $76 million. In September 2010, yet another example of the exclusion of Haitians can be found in the Haitian Neighborhood Return and Housing Reconstruction Framework established by the Interim Haiti Recovery Commission (IHRC). The framework, intended to guide reconstruction, was not published in draft form in Creole so local people could review it and did not engage in consultation with the displaced persons on any level.

A close look at the disaster relief and recovery effort in Haiti in the post-2010 earthquake reveals that an unfettered environment for aggressive tied aid agendas allowing donor countries and agencies to target contracts for their own member countries and organizations. Cloaked under the veneer of an emergency, a plethora of no bid contracts were handed out well into the reconstruction period.

---

* See Huffington Post, *Haiti Earthquake Recovery 3 Years Later: Where Has the Money Gone? Infographic*, January 11, 2013, http://www.huffingtonpost.com/2013/01/12/haiti-earthquake-recovery-2013_n_2451267.html. Note as well remarks of former Haitian prime minister, Michele Pierre-Louis, "If you ask what went right and what went wrong, the answer is, most everything went wrong. There needs to be some accountability for all that money."

† Quigley and Ramanauskas, *Haiti: Where Is the Money?*

Interestingly, Haiti is one of the few CARICOM states that had undertaken comprehensive public procurement reform within the last decade, but did not achieve results. In early 2005, the Government of Haiti crushed by debt and eager to please donors adopted a new procurement decree that created the National Commission for Public Procurement and affirmed the use of competitive purchasing norms; standard bidding documents and manuals were also introduced to government procurement staff. By June 2009, a new Procurement Law was enacted by Parliament, adapting Haiti's procurement rules to international good-practice standards, so-called. Despite this regulatory overhaul, it would seem that, mere months later in the aftermath of the first quake in January 2010, this PPS heavily sponsored by the international procurement harmonization movement did not attract widespread confidence from the very international and multilateral aid agencies. It was bypassed.

Haitian leaders hamstrung by crippling social and economic conditions after the tragedy readily agreed to the setting up of the IHRC as a planning body for the recovery efforts. The IHRC, which was cochaired by former president of the United States Bill Clinton and the then Haitian prime minister, Jean-Max Bellerive, was hailed as one of Haiti's great hopes, a Haitian-led international partnership, given an 18-month mandate to oversee an ambitious array of rebuilding projects. However, by October 21, 2011, the IHRC was defunct.*

Status of Regional Reforms

While Caribbean states had been able to hold off on acceding to the WTO-GPA, this regional defiance did not necessarily go under the radar.† Market opening strategies were pursued and achieved by the Global North indirectly through IFI loan conditions, "tied aid" program and more recently attempted through the negotiation of Free Trade Agreement and Bilateral Investment Treaty seeking to impose transparency in public procurement and competition obligations.‡

This notwithstanding, Caribbean policy makers have overtly persisted in regional integration efforts. By the Revised Treaty of Chaguaramas 2001, CARICOM member states agreed to establish the Caribbean Single Market and Economy (CSME). The CSME is the guiding instrument for regional integration and involves the free movement of goods, services, skilled people and

---

* See Report of the Center for Economic and Policy Research, *IHRC Mandate Ends—18 Months with Little to Show*, October 2011.
† Note the impact of the CARIFORUM-EU Economic Partnership Agreement 2008, which will be considered in more detail below.
‡ Free Trade negotiations between CARICOM and the United States, CARICOM and Canada, and other third states are at present at somewhat of a stand-off as CARICOM attempts to stand firm on unreasonable demands for opening of regional markets and removal of import tariffs. In the sixth and last round of the CARICOM-Canada negotiations, governments particularly in the OECS are rejecting efforts by Canada to trade off hundreds of its products to the grouping with little or no import taxes. United States and CARICOM signed a Trade and Investment Framework Agreement (TIFA) in 2013. The new TIFA modernizes the previous 1991 Agreement, taking into account subsequent developments in the region, notably the multilateral trading environment created by the WTO and the implementation of the CSME in 2006. The updated Framework Agreement includes an "Initial Action Agenda," covering a wide range of topics, such as trade and investment facilitation, multilateral cooperation, intellectual property rights, labor rights, social and environmental protection, and the elimination of barriers to bilateral trade. However, the TIFA reads more like a declaration of intentions rather than a concrete agreement with predictable outcomes.

capital among member countries, the right of establishment of CARICOM nationals anywhere in the Community, a common external tariff, and a coordinated foreign trade policy.*

The establishment of the CSME has been seen as a "legitimate response to 'globalisation and liberalization' and 'the attainment of international competitiveness.'"† With its emphasis on "a single development vision," the hope is that the region can improve its international competitiveness through functional cooperation and the exploitation of institutional and resource synergies among member states.‡ At the same time, the Community has also concluded trade agreements with Cuba and Dominica Republic and has established trading and other economic arrangements with Brazil, Costa Rica, Mexico, and Venezuela.§

Against this backdrop, the move for regional integration of public procurement policy has been pursued. Article 239 of the Revised Treaty provides the justification for the establishment of a regional Public Procurement Regime. To date, the Community has undertaken a significant volume of work regarding the establishment of a Community Regime for Public Procurement. A 2003 project commissioned by the CARICOM secretariat drew some dismal conclusions about the state of regional PPSs characterizing them as in disarray and dysfunctional, made up of poorly coordinated and outdated enactments and decrees, weak enforcement, limited protections for bidders, limited professional and institutional capacity, and corruption and integrity management challenges. The general conclusion was that the present procurement regimes were counterproductive to the CSME efforts.

CARIFORUM-EU EPA

In 2008, the CARIFORUM countries¶ formally executed the EPA with the EU** and this singular act provides the strongest evidence of regional unpreparedness for designing and articulating its own public procurement policy geared toward regional socioeconomic, environmental, and industrial development. The distinguishing feature of this post-Cotonou†† agreement was the ending of trade preferences and the introduction of the principle of reciprocity. Girvan (2013) regards EPAs as "concrete legal-institutional expressions of asymmetrical neoliberal economic integration between countries and groups of countries."

---

* Antigua and Barbuda, Barbados, Belize, Dominica, Grenada, Guyana, Jamaica, St. Kitts and Nevis, St. Lucia, St. Vincent and the Grenadines, Suriname, and Trinidad and Tobago currently actively participate in the CSME. Note though Montserrat is treated as though it is part of CSME, formal approval from the United Kingdom has been denied to this state which is a British Overseas Territory.
† Hall, *Pertinence of CARICOM*, Chapter 12 *Caribbean Development in a Changing Global Environment*.
‡ Ibid.
§ Dominance of the neoliberal school of thought in the Caribbean integration movement is evidenced by schemes which have generally taken the form of "Open Regionalism," that is, the symmetrical lowering of trade and investment barriers *intra* and *extra* regionally (Girvan 2000). This "strategic global repositioning" is a school of thought more fully described by Hall, *Pertinence of CARICOM*, Chapter 12 *Caribbean Development in a Changing Global Environment*.
¶ The Caribbean Forum (CARIFORUM) is a subgroup of African, Caribbean, and Pacific Group of States and serves as a base for economic dialogue with the European Union (EU).
** The CARIFORUM-EU EPA was executed by the CARIFORUM countries on October 15, 2008. By 2013, six CARIFORUM states (Antigua and Barbuda, Barbados, Belize, Dominican Republic, Guyana, and Trinidad and Tobago) had already ratified the EPA.
†† The Cotonou Agreement was the most comprehensive partnership agreement between developing countries and the EU. Since 2000, it has been the framework for the EU's relations with 79 countries from Africa, the Caribbean and the Pacific (ACP).

CARIFORUM has achieved the ubiquitous status of being the first grouping of developing states in the African, Caribbean, and Pacific (ACP) community to enter into an EPA with the European Commission (EU) containing public procurement rules and conditions.* This development is ignominious for several reasons. First, the agreement with the EU was arrived at despite the failure of CARIFORUM states (and to date even CARICOM) to implement, an intra-regional protocol for government procurement. According to Girvan (2013), the EPA now undermines regional integration efforts in favor of a scheme of integration in which Caribbean states are incorporated into an EU economic zone with free movement of goods, services, capital and shared policies, and laws in the areas of competition, intellectual property, and public procurement. Second, whereas CARIFORUM states have steadfastly refused to engage and participate in the WTO-GPA precisely for the perceived unfairness of a level playing field to developing countries, it has nonetheless signed the EPA including WTO-GPA plus conditions specifically as it relates to public procurement.† Third, the institutional arrangements in the EPA undermine economic governance within CARICOM. By the establishment of institutions with supra-national authority for the enforcement of the provisions,‡ which in fact, supersede the governance arrangements within CARICOM. Fourth, and perhaps most damning for the regional integration effort, the EPA promotes asymmetrical development by the application of reciprocal benefits based on the level of compliance of individual member states and not as a trading block.§

Some EPA supporters have argued that the agreement does not provide for nondiscrimination and national treatment for foreign-based companies but Article 167 expressly provides for nondiscrimination and national treatment for foreign companies operating through a locally incorporated subsidiary, while there are little to no barriers to establishment. Other EPA supporters argue that the agreement promotes Caribbean development because it is a trade agreement supported by development assistance and which targets sustainable economic development, the progressive integration of CARIFORUM countries into the world economy and the elimination of poverty. They believe it can become a model for agreements between developed and developing countries.¶

The ability of CARIFORUM member states to take advantage of the touted benefits of the EPA has been heavily challenged. The EU population is 20 times greater and its economy is 88 times larger and its average per capita is 4.5 times higher than CARIFORUM states Girvan (2011). The inevitable restriction on the "policy space" of CARICOM governments to pursue national and regional socioeconomic policies and to develop South–South cooperation cannot be underestimated when one attempts to assess the relevance of the EPA provisions.

Girvan argues that EU firms will have an enormously superior capacity to compete and invest relative to Caribbean firms most or all of which are thoroughly unprepared to take advantage of the new export opportunities that the agreement supposedly makes available and that the majority of Caribbean governments are not equipped with the institutional capacity and the financial resources to implement its onerous obligations. Girvan agitates for the agreement to include targeted resource transfers to support regional development; nontariff barriers in European markets and most importantly sufficient policy space for regional governments to stimulate new markets and local industry. Sir Ronald Sanders, a leading regional academic and former diplomat, notes

---

* See Chapter 3 Title IV of the CARIFORUM EU EPA.
† See Kelsey, *Legal Analysis of Services and Investment*.
‡ See Part III, CARIFORUM-EU EPA.
§ Girvan, *Economic Partnership & Asymmetrical Integration*.
¶ Hall, *Pertinence of CARICOM*, Chapter 12 *Caribbean Development in a Changing Global Environment*.

that so far the EPA has not delivered promised market access for Caribbean goods and services and has not realized any significant new investment.*

ALBA—An Alternative Integration Model?

The *Allianza Bolivariana para los Pueblos de Nuestra America* (Bolivarian Alliance for the Peoples of Our America) (ALBA) was launched in 2004 as a regional alternative to the neoliberal model of integration.† With three CARICOM member states‡ choosing to become members of ALBA, it is not overstressing the point that there is some relevance at both the practical and theoretical levels at looking at it comparatively.

ALBA was founded by Cuba and Venezuela and was originally put forward as the "Bolivarian Alternative" to the FTAA. It is now promoted as a model of integration based on principles of cooperation, solidarity, complementarity, and sovereignty. ALBA is operationalized through intergovernmental agreements for reciprocal trade, finance, and technical cooperation.

The ALBA integration approaches differ from neoliberal approaches in the following ways:§

- Key principles are "complementarity, as an alternative to competition; solidarity as opposed to domination; cooperation as a replacement for exploitation; and respect for sovereignty rather than corporate rule."
- Financial cooperation is an integral and major element.
- Social cooperation is an integral and major element.
- A la carte participation is a negotiated flexibility rather than single undertaking. Each member accedes on individually negotiated terms and its participation in trade, and ALBA projects are negotiated on a case-by-case basis.
- Trade can be a means of settlement of financial and/or social cooperation.
- Asymmetrical and nonreciprocal market access in favor of smaller and/or weaker member economies.
- Tariff protection of infant industries allowed.
- Provision for counter-trade arrangements, that is, direct product exchanges.
- Creation of the "sucre," an accounting currency unit used to value bilateral and multilateral trade among the members and to settle balances. In effect, this permits multilateral counter-trade. Participation is not mandatory for members.
- Recognition of the role of the state in development and in economic regulation.
- Public procurement as an instrument of national economic development.
- Protection of citizens rights to basic social services (i.e., from privatization and commercialization).
- Protection of labor rights.
- Protection of the rights of indigenous people.
- Protection of "Mother Earth" (the environment).
- Rights to development and health take precedence over intellectual and industrial property rights.

---

* Sanders, Ronald 2013 *A Year of Lost Opportunities for Caribbean Countries.* http://www.sirronaldsanders.com/viewarticle.aspx?ID=414.
† See ALBA 2004. Note originally the "A" in the acronym stood for Alternativa, denoting alternative to the U.S. sponsored FTAA; this was changed after the collapse of the FTAA negotiations.
‡ Antigua and Barbuda, Dominica, and St. Vincent and the Grenadines.
§ Girvan (2011).

- Privileging of production for the national market and satisfaction of the needs of the population.
- Privileging of communal and cooperative enterprises and of small and medium enterprises.
- Submission of foreign investors to national law in Dispute Resolution.
- Rapid responsiveness and creativity in developing new programs, for example, ALBA Food Security Initiative and ALBA Haiti Earthquake Relief Fund.
- Formation of Grandnational Enterprises—multi-country state-to-state joint ventures for dedicated purposes in several areas.
- Political solidarity on threats to member states (such as the U.S. embargo on Cuba, the Honduras coup of 2009, the Colombia–U.S. bases agreement of 2009, and the attempted coup in Ecuador in 2010). Member countries are free to abstain or reserve their position.

As members of ALBA, Antigua and Barbuda, Dominica, and St. Vincent and the Grenadines have benefited from financial assistance in the form of soft loans and grants for projects in housing, major infrastructure, security, and agriculture. In 2011, Antigua and Barbuda received 125 scholarships for study in Cuba and high social impact projects feature significantly targeting vulnerable communities.[*]

It is the view of the author that these principles of solidarity and collaborative economics represent a substantial and exciting departure from neoliberal integration approaches which seek to address the development asymmetries existing between developed and developing nations. The role of solidarity economic theory on public procurement policy is an area in need of research.

Conclusion: Democratizing the Global Economy—The Challenge for the Caribbean

While English-speaking Caribbean states are still toeing the neoliberalist line, the rest of the world is waking up to the stark reality that such policies are the root cause for the social, environmental, and economic injustices being experienced across the globe.[†] According to Dash, "the failure of the hegemonic global capitalist economic system also breeds opportunities to think and work on alternative visions of a good society and build pathways for that—opportunities to work on a 'paradigm of reversals'."[‡]

Procurement reform cannot be undertaken in a blinkered fashion. Procurement is inextricably tied to a country's/region's development which is inextricably tied to the effectiveness of the economic system upon which it is based. Therefore, in developing a public procurement regulatory model, the region's development goals should be more than rhetorical. More imperative is a clear appreciation for the nature of the underlying economic premises the PPS will be serving. Are competitive approaches always the most efficient approaches? Can cooperative procurement approaches (of the type currently being pursued by the OECS) or bartering and/or solidarity approaches (of the type being pursued by Venezuela and Cuba) perhaps provide more value for Caribbean states?

---

[*] For a more detailed exposition on the benefits of ALBA as compared to CARIFORUM and CARICOM see Girvan, *Is ALBA a New Model of Integration?*
[†] Piketty, *Capital in the Twenty-First Century*.
[‡] Dash, *Towards an Epistemological Foundation*.

Will Caribbean leaders abdicate their responsibility to undertake more robust evidence-based policy making by continuing simply to rubber stamp outdated, externally driven models for reform or will they in recognizing the "linkages" between procurement and development, procurement and trade, and procurement and good governance, develop regional and domestic policies which will address the distinct legal, social, and economic realities with which they are faced?

If recent developments in trade negotiations (CARIFORUM-EU EPA), and the disaster relief and recovery efforts in Haiti are a guide as to how these questions will be answered, then it could be argued that Caribbean leaders are not yet ready to assume the responsibility for regionally relevant procurement policy development. However, this view is myopic in its failure to appreciate that in both the areas of trade negotiations and disaster relief and recovery, the developing state is severely compromised in their ability to negotiate on an even playing field.

Perhaps a more provocative measure of the state of public procurement policy reform in the Caribbean can be found in the innovation of the OECS standing out as a unique and unparalleled collaborative PPS among state groupings. Also the Trinidad and Tobago 2015 public procurement reforms which expressly mandate the strategic use of procurement for socioeconomic objectives should be considered. A far cry from the regurgitation of a standard based on the UN Model Law 2011, the TT reforms are quite avant-garde in its formal acceptance of "national economic and social development" as a key objective of the procurement system.

An interesting comparator is the state of the economies of the CARICOM member states that have undertaken traditional public procurement regulation like Jamaica, Haiti, Belize, and Guyana as compared with Trinidad and Tobago, Barbados, and the OECS, which as yet, have not so undertaken. What is the relationship, if any, between public procurement regulation compliant with the international harmonization agenda and development? Could there be a positive correlation between the absence of regulation mandating open competitive procedures as the default procurement method (thereby allowing for greater flexibility to pursue national socioeconomic development through protectionist and buy local mechanisms) and sustainable development and growth?

Unfortunately, however, the potential of avant-garde nonneoliberal approaches to public procurement reform remain hampered by a dearth of scholarship. Although new uses and approaches to social economy have substantially grown in recent times, this "other" economy is virtually missing in the curriculum and textbooks of business and economics.* This omission reflects the almost complete submission to the paradigm of the "single bottom line of profit," through control of the process of reproduction of our knowledge system, which cannot explain models that use different goals, incentives, processes, and structures. The unchecked growth of corporatism within the present global neo-capitalist economic system is also a stumbling block for leaders of developing markets attempting to steer their economies.

The 2008 financial crisis has spawned an era of pervasive and persistent loss of confidence in existing economic norms. This presents a singular opportunity for developing countries to eke out more leverage in negotiations with the Global North and stimulate greater interrogation of the "one-size-fits-all" harmonization agenda persistent in public procurement policy discourse and to engage in the sort of "active economic citizenship" in the global economy recommended by Chang (2011) and Girvan (2013).

---

* Schugurensky and McCollum of the Southern Ontario Social economy Research Alliance, survey on social economy contribution to the Canadian economy.

An epistemological revolution* is what is required and also the courage of Caribbean academics and policy makers to critique policy reforms being pressed by the countries and institutions of the Global North, which perpetuate inequalities and inefficiencies and ultimately undermine our opportunity for self-determination within the global economic system.

Bibliography

Agaba, E., and Shipman, N., Public procurement reform in developing countries: The Uganda experience. In *Advancing Public Procurement: Experiences Innovation and Knowledge Sharing*, G. Piga and K.V. Thai (Eds.), Boca Raton, FL: Academics Press, pp. 373–391 (2006).

Amsden, A., *Securing the Home Market, A New Approach to Korean Development*, UNRISD Research Paper 2013–1 (Posthumously published), Geneva, Switzerland: UNRISD (2013).

Arrowsmith, S., Horizontal policies in public procurement: A taxonomy. *Journal of Public Procurement* Vol. 10, Issue 2, pp. 149–186 (2010).

Chang, H.J., *Kicking Away the Ladder: Development Strategy in Historical Perspective*, London: Anthem Press (2002).

Chang, H.J., *23 Things They Don't Tell You About Capitalism*, London: Penguin (2011).

Chang, H.J., and Grabel, I., *Reclaiming Development: An Alternative Economic Policy Manual*, New York: Zed Books (2014).

Dash, A., Towards an Epistemological Foundation for Social and Solidarity Economy, *Draft paper prepared for the UNRISD Conference, Potential and Limits of Social and Solidarity Economy*, May 6–8, 2013, Geneva, Switzerland (2013).

DeMartino, G., *Consequences of Economic Downturn: Beyond the Usual Economics*, Martha A. Starr (Ed.) New York: Palgrave Macmillan (2011).

Frank, D., *Buy American: The Untold Story of Economic Nationalism*, Boston, MA: Beacon Press (1999).

Gayle-Sinclair, S., *Public Procurement and International Trade Agreements: Smaller Developing Economy Considerations from a CARICOM Perspective*, Italy: IPPC (2006).

Girvan, N., Some lessons of the CARIFORUM-EU EPA. *Trade Negotiations Insights* Vol. 8, October (2009), http://www.ictsd.org/bridges-news/trade-negotiations-insights/news/some-lessons-of-the-cariforum-eu-epa.

Girvan, N., Public Procurement Policy and Governance in the Caribbean, *Chairman's Opening Remarks 3rd Caribbean Public Procurement Conference*, October 11th, (2010).

Girvan, N., Is ALBA a new model of integration? Reflections on the CARICOM Experience. *Revised version of paper presented at the ALBA Conference at the London Metropolitan University*, January 29, 2011. *International Journal of Cuban Studies*, September, London (2011).

Girvan, N., *Economic Partnership & Asymmetrical Integration: An EU-Caribbean Tale*, Presentation at workshop on Alternative Trade, St. Mary's University, Halifax, NS. November 1–2, (2013).

Hall, Kenneth O., *The Pertinence of CARICOM in the 21st Century: Some Perspectives*, Georgetown, Guyana: Trafford (2012).

Kapur, D., and Webber, R., *Governance-Related Conditionalities of the IFIs*, G-24 Discussion Paper Series No.6, Geneva, Switzerland, UNCTAD (2000).

Kelsey, J., *Legal Analysis of Services and Investment in the CARIFORUM-EC EPA: Lessons for Other Developing Countries*, South Centre Research Paper No. 31, July (2010).

Khor, Martin, *Bilateral and Regional Free Trade Agreements: Some Critical Elements and Development Implications*. Malaysia: Third World Network, September (2008).

Marshall, A., *The Surprising Design of Market Economies*, University of Texas Press (2012).

McCrudden, C. *Buying Social Justice*, Oxford: Oxford University Press (2007).

Mckoy, D.V., *Corruption: Law, Governance and Ethics in the Commonwealth Caribbean*, Hertford: Hansib Publications (2012).

---

* Braidotti (2009).

Paulraj, A., Chen, I.J., and Flynn, J., Levels of strategic purchasing: Impact on supply integration and performance. *Journal of Purchasing and Supply Management* Vol. 12, Issue 3, pp. 107–122 (2006).
Piketty, T., *Capital in the Twenty-First Century*, Cambridge, MA: Harvard University Press (2014).
Sanders, R., Reflections on the OECS at 25. In CARICOM Single Market and Economy: Genesis and Prognosis, Kenneth Hall and Chuck-A-Sang (Eds.), Kingston, Jamaica: Ian Randle Publishers (2007).
Small, D., Trinidad and Tobago: Natural gas monetization as a driver of economic and social prosperity. *Proceedings of World Gas Conference*, World Gas Conference, June (2006).
Small, D., State strategies for managing oil and gas resources, Official Centenary Publication, Trinidad and Tobago Celebrating a Century of Commercial Oil Production—FIRST Magazine, April (2009).
Sornarajah, M., *The International Law on Foreign Investment*, 3rd Edition, Cambridge: Cambridge University Press (2010).
Tassabehji, R., and Moorhouse, A., The changing role of procurement: Developing professional effectiveness. *Journal of Purchasing & Supply Management* Vol. 14, pp. 55–68 (2008).
Williamson, J., What Washington means by policy reform. In *Latin American Adjustment: How Much Has Happened?* J. Williamson (Ed.), Washington, DC: Institute for International Economics (1990).
Yülek, M.A., and Taylor, T.K. (Eds.), *Designing Public Procurement Policy in Developing Countries*, New York: Springer (2012).

Electronic Sources

Assessment of Public Financial Management in Grenada using the PEFA PFM performance framework (2009), http://ec.europa.eu/europeaid/what/economic-support/public-finance/documents/grenada_pefa_report_en.pdf, accessed on November 2013.
Center for Economic and Policy Research, *IHRC Mandate Ends—18 Months with Little to Show*, Global Europe, Competing in the World, European Commission, External Trade, October 2011, http://trade.ec.europa.eu/doclib/docs/2006/october/tradoc_130376.pdf, accessed on November 2013.
Girvan, N., Public Procurement Policy and Governance in the Caribbean, *Chairman's Opening Remarks in the 3rd Caribbean Public Procurement Conference,* October 11, 2010.
Jepma, Catrinus J., *The Tying of Aid*, Paris: OECD (1991), http://www.oecd.org/development/pgd/29412505.pdf, accessed on November 2013.
Luckey, J.R., *Domestic Content Legislation: The Buy American Act and Complementary Little Buy American Provisions*, CRS (2012), Available at: http://www.fas.org/sgp/crs/misc/R42501.pdf, accessed on November 2013.
Quigley, B., and Ramanauskas, A., *Haiti: Where Is the Money?* Researcher Version January 4, 2012, http://www.haitiaction.net/News/BQ/1_4_12/1_4_12.html, accessed on November 2013.
Raymond, A., *An Overview on the Civil Society Submission to the Joint Select Committee on Public Procurement*, April 26, 2011, http://www.raymondandpierre.com/procurement/article02.html, accessed on November 2013.
Schrouder, S., *Public Procurement in the Caribbean: Confronting the Challenges and Opportunities* (2010), http://www.ippa.org/IPPC4/Proceedings/01ComparativeProcurement/Paper1-5.pdf.
Stotzky, Irwin P., *Haiti Human Rights Investigation*, Center for the Study of Human Rights, University of Miami School of Law, November 11–21, 2004, http://web.archive.org/web/20070810081052/http://www.law.miami.edu/cshr/CSHR_Report_02082005_v2.pdf, accessed on November 2013.
United Nations Office for Project Services (UNOPS), 2010 Annual Statistical Report on United Nations Procurement (2011), http://www.ungm.org/Publications/Documents/ASR_2010.pdf; http://www.cgdev.org/doc/full_text/CGDBriefs/1426979/the-need-for-more-local-procurement-in-haiti.html.
Wilkinson, B., CaribCan or can't survive, *Caribbean Life News*, April 4, 2014, http://www.caribbeanlifenews.com/stories/2014/4/2014_04_02_bw_caribbean.html, accessed on November 2013.
Ziemblicki, B. *The Controversies over the WTO Dispute Settlement System* (2009). Available at: http://www.bibliotekacyfrowa.pl/Content/32203/0014.pdf, accessed on November 2013.

Chapter 9

Assessing Public Sector Reform in the Anglophone Caribbean

Ann Marie Bissessar

Contents

Introduction 180
Public Sector Reform: 1960s–1980s 181
Public Sector Reform: 1980s–2000 186
The Privatization Experience 189
Reform Experiences in the Civil Service 193
The Reality of New Public Management Reforms in the Caribbean 197
Public Sector Reform: 2000–2013 198
Concluding Remarks 199
References 199

> **Abstract:** The aim of this chapter is to examine the experiences with public sector reform in a number of countries in the Anglophone Caribbean. Under review are the countries of Jamaica, Trinidad and Tobago, Barbados, and St. Vincent and the Grenadines. The chapter suggests that during the 1950s–1980s while there were attempts to reform the public bureaucracies in these countries, these reforms were often incremental in nature and diffuse. Moreover, many of the proposed reform were as a result of outside interventions either by way of loan or agreements with international agencies. Writers such as Schwartz (1994)* and

---

* Shalom H. Schwartz. 1994. Beyond individualism/collectivism: New cultural dimensions of values. In *Individualism and Collectivism: Theory, Method, and Applications*. Cross-cultural research and methodology series. Edited by Uichol Kim, Harry C. Triandis, Çiğdem Kâğitçibaşi, Sang-Chin Choi, Gene Yoon, Sage Publications, Inc: Thousand Oaks, CA, Vol. 18, pp. 85–119.

Peters (1997)* suggest, also, that by the latter half of the 1980s and in the 1990s, the key elements of administrative reform were transferred from the Anglo-Saxon countries to less developed countries primarily driven by the implicit coercion of international donor agencies. While there has been no dearth of literature on the reform experiences in these countries, much of this literature has focused on the managerial or technical aspects of these reforms. To a large extent, little or no explanation has been advanced to understand and explore the differences or the similarities in the reform exercises in the various countries of the Anglophone Caribbean. This chapter presents, for the first time, a longitudinal study of administrative reform in select countries in the Anglophone Caribbean. It examines the reform experiences during the pre-independence as well as the post-independence periods and then during the period of structural adjustment. In looking at the reform experiences, some of the challenges in introducing reform measures are examined.

Introduction

It is often said that those who forget their historical experiences are doomed to repeat their errors. This is more than relevant when discussing attempts to reform the public sector particularly in the countries of the Anglophone Caribbean. Indeed, as this chapter will illustrate often time, what actually emerges during an examination of public sector reform experiences in some of these countries is that as electoral shifts occurs between dominant political parties, the incoming governments channel their energies on reforming key aspects of the public sector. However, in the majority of cases, these reforms are not "new" but rather critics suggesting that a vast amount of resources is spent in merely reinventing the "wheel." This chapter examines the various attempts at reform of the public sector in a number of countries, namely Trinidad and the Tobago,† Jamaica,‡ Barbados,§ and St. Vincent and the Grenadines.¶ The chapter addresses some of the reforms debated during the post-independence period and after and the proposals at public sector reform during the 1980s as a result of structural adjustment. The chapter concludes with a discussion of the current status of public sector reform in the various countries.

---

* B. Guy Peters. Estudio/Working Paper 1998/113. June 1998. B. Guy Peters is Maurice Falk Professor of American government in the Department of Political Science at the University of Pittsburgh. This paper is based on a series of two seminars he presented at the &HQWHU_IRU_$GYDQFHG_6WXG_LQ_ WKH_ 6RFLDO_6FLHQFHV of the Juan March Institute, Madrid, on 13 and 14 May 1997, entitled "Institutional Theory: An Evaluation" and "Administrative Reform: Explaining the Adoption of Changes in Government."
† Trinidad and Tobago, officially the Republic of Trinidad and Tobago, is an archipelagic state in the southern Caribbean, lying just off the coast of northeastern Venezuela and south of Grenada in the Lesser Antilles. It shares maritime boundaries with other nations including Barbados to the northeast, Guyana to the southeast, and Venezuela to the south and west. The country covers an area of 5,128 km² (1,980 mi²) and consists of two main islands, Trinidad and Tobago.
‡ Jamaica is the fourth largest island nation of the Greater Antilles, 234 km (145 mi) in length, up to 80 km (50 mi) in width, and 10,990 mi².
§ Barbados is a sovereign island country in the Lesser Antilles. It is 34 km (21 mi) in length and up to 23 km (14 mi) in width, covering an area of 431 km² (166 mi²). It is situated in the western area of the North Atlantic and 100 km (62 mi) east of the Windward Islands and the Caribbean Sea.
¶ Saint Vincent and the Grenadines is an island country in the Lesser Antilles chain, in the southern portion of the Windward Islands, which lie at the southern end of the eastern border of the Caribbean Sea where the latter meets the Ocean. Its 389 km² (150 mi²) territory consists of the main island of St. Vincent and the northern two-thirds of the Grenadines, which are a chain of smaller islands stretching south from Saint Vincent Island to Grenada.

Public Sector Reform: 1960s–1980s

There can be no doubt that reform of the public sector was an ongoing process in many of the West Indian countries even prior to independence. However, it should be noted that the reform initiatives under the colonial administrators were essentially different to the reforms attempted under independent governments. The justifications for the reforms by the colonial administrators were driven by the following concerns:

- The high costs of maintaining the colonies and the inability of Britain to financially support all the colonies given the depletion of her funds as a result of the war efforts
- Internal agitation within the colonies as a result of the following:
    - Increases in the level of literacy within the colonies
    - Changes in the status quo
    - Poor infrastructure and the lack of development within the colonies
    - The push for internal self-government

The British, at that time, were evidently cornered. On the one hand, they were clearly incapable of providing funds to increase and improve the infrastructure within the various colonies, and on the other hand, it was necessary to maintain some measure of control lest the territories adopt communist ideologies that would prove to be counterproductive. Hence, in a last bid dash, before granting independence, institutions such as the Public Service Commission and later the modified West Minster–White Hall model of government were introduced. Some suggest that these were largely "regulatory" institutions. Jones (1990), for instance, claimed that these institutions exhibited a definite degree of structure and more of less orderly relationships. He suggests that unlike other territories such as India or Burma, in the case of the Anglophone Caribbean, the relative lack of cultural viability, the product of slavery, plantation socioeconomic order, and imperial governance generally, combined with the absence of society-wide, deeply entrenched local institutions to make for easier British penetration.

With the attainment of independence in the various colonies,[*] it was to be expected that there was a proliferation of activities as the newly elected government embarked on nation building. As Jones noted:

> Both the proliferation of roles and the building of new institutions have generally been regarded as crucial mechanisms through which "modernization" takes place.[†]

Accordingly, as the colonies moved from self-government to independent government, there were significant changes in the public sector. For instance, there were radical changes to the structure or arrangement of the public sector. It should be recalled, for instance, that under colonial rule, the administrative arrangement was fairly simple. Within each colony, the governor had direct control of the public sector, and the main coordinating body was the secretariat which had responsibility for all the personnel management functions. To carry out the different activities within the colonies, departments under the control of technocrats had been established, while the district offices were given the authority for collecting taxes and the basic maintenance of roads and bridges.

---

[*] Trinidad and Tobago and Jamaica attained independence in 1962; Barbados in 1966; and St. Vincent and the Grenadines in 1979.
[†] See Edwin Jones. 1990. Administrative institution building in Jamaica—An interpretation. In *A Reader in Public Policy and Administration*. Edited by G.E. Mills. ISER, University of the West Indies: Mona, Jamaica, pp. 193–221, 193.

With the appointment of ministers of government, the former "departments" were converted into "ministries." The minister, a politician, assumed the role of policy maker, and he was assisted by an administrative officer, referred to as a permanent secretary,* while the former head of the department was accorded an advisory role, chief technical officer. This change in authority structure soon emerged as one of the major areas of conflict within the newly independent public sector. In fact, in nearly all the ex-colonies, the relationship between ministers and public officials is still currently cited as one of the major areas of concern, and often, change in political regimes has been accompanied by friction, tension, and mutual suspicion.

According to Mills (1990)† during the early post-independence period, this conflict was even more vitriolic in nature. Public officers alleged that they were the objects of attacks and expressed fears that their careers were often jeopardized on political grounds. Further to this, Commissions of Enquiries in two territories commented on political interference in the administrative duties of public officers. Mills (1990) offered a number of reasons for these conflicts. He cited the following factors:

1. The lack of experience in operating a ministerial system and the failure to understand the relative roles of the parties involved.
2. These conflicts, he suggested, sprung from deep social, psychological, and historical roots brought to the surface by the transfer of power.
3. The conflicts result from the competition for power between the old bureaucracy and the new political elite.
4. There were also seeds of conflict between politicians and younger, better educated officials entering the civil servants.
5. Finally, he claimed that some ministers apparently failed to understand the role of and appreciate the need for a senior civil service.

While Mills' (1990) argument is valid even today, ministers of government not only in the Caribbean region but also in countries around the world have offered, by way of counter argument, the following reasons for the conflict between the ministers and the public servants. They suggest that a minister of government is required to fulfill his/her obligations to the wider electorate. Given that the electoral term in many countries is 5 years, they contend that ministers therefore must deliver on their promises if they are to return to office. However, to a large extent, ministers in return complain that service delivery is stymied by the public service and there are numerous delays due to red tape as a result of the regulations that are in place. Often, too, even in trying to "bypass" this "red tape," politicians contend that they are accused of trying to achieve their own political objectives and that this gives rise to charges that they engage in nepotism and pork-barrel appointments. While these arguments appear to capture the reality of the constraints in service delivery, it would appear, however, that sympathies go to the public officer, who, in theory at least, emulates the British concept of a neutral, impartial, and anonymous actor. However, this was not the only issue raised by Mills. He noted, too, the tensions between the administrative staff and the technical staff, particularly at the higher levels. In short, he suggested that there was a need to redefine the relationship between the various actors.

Another pertinent problem highlighted by Mills (1990) was the relations between the central government and the statutory corporations. The major contentions between these agencies could be summarized as follows:

---

* Permanent Secretaries were appointed in 1956 in the case of Trinidad.
† G.E. Mills. 1990. Public administration in the Commonwealth Caribbean. In *A Reader in Public Policy and Administration*. Edited by G.E. Mills. ISER, University of the West Indies: Mona, Jamaica, pp. 1–22.

1. Lack of clear guidance with respect to the responsibilities of the central government and the relationship with the corporations
2. The reluctance to establish clear mechanisms of accountability
3. The use of these boards as a vehicle for patronage
4. The lack of capacity by these bodies

But the issue of clear lines of authority was not only confined to the statutory corporations. Whereas, under colonial administration, the warden's offices had authority for the collection of taxes (at the local level) and the maintenance of roads and bridges, following directly on the British political model, in nearly all the countries of the Anglophone Caribbean, a two-tiered model of a central government with requisite local government arrangements in clearly demarked districts was introduced.* In short, the local government arrangement was one in which functions were decentralized from the level of the central government to local constituencies. Within each constituency, there was a locally elected member of parliament, as well as councilors and aldermen who were accorded responsibility for delivery of services such as maintenance of roads, infrastructural developments, bridges, and water courses as well as the maintenance of cemeteries and markets. Again the relationships between these two bodies were strained, and it remains tenuous even today with the central government maintaining rigorous control over allocations. Some suggest that the central government is reluctant to share power; others, sympathetic to the central government, claim that this reluctance has to do with a lack of capacity at the local levels.

One agency which has attracted attention also has been the Public Service Commission Department, which, it should be recalled, had authority for all the human resource management functions including recruitment, selection, training, promotion, discipline, and termination. Criticisms of these institutions included the placing of "square pegs in round holes," the length of time taken to make decisions, and the large number of vacancies within the public services. The Public Service Commission Department, in response, blamed the ministries and department for not carrying out appropriate performance or staff appraisals.

In many of the Anglophone countries, in order to improve or reform the public sector, commissions or committees were established to review the "workings" of the public sector and offer recommendations where necessary. Table 9.1 accordingly presents an overview of some of the commissions and the major issues raised.

While there were numerous committees or commissions set up with the mandate to examine and suggest ways to reform to improve service delivery within the public sector in all the islands, nearly all the recommendations emerging from these commissions/committees across the islands raised similar concerns. These included the following:

- The fragmentation and centralization of human resource management which was reflected in the duplication of responsibilities, delays in decision making, lack of accountability, and inadequate communications structures
- The absence of planning and budgeting for human resources
- The overemphasis on procedures and regulations
- Reactive decision making
- Overreliance on seniority when making promotions
- Delays in enforcing disciplinary procedures

---

* The system of local government was discontinued in the case of St. Vincent and the Grenadines.

Table 9.1 Select Commissions Established in Various Countries 1960s–1980s

Country	Year	Commission Established	Focus of the Commission/Consultant
Barbados	1970	Consultant from the United Nations—Thorbjorn Sorum	Focused on public sector structures and recommended that these should be arranged according to purpose.
Jamaica	1965	Public Administration in Jamaica—N.C. Angus, W.P. Barrett, and E. Holstein	Appointed under UN program of technical assistance. Terms of reference were to study the structure, administrative policies, and practices of the Jamaican public service.
	1966	Report on budgetary procedures and reclassification and management in Jamaica—S.N. Singh	The objective of Singh's visit was to make recommendations to facilitate effective implementation of the budget.
	1970	Review of training requirements for government accountants and auditors—G. Ronson	A tour of the consultant under the ODA assistance program was undertaken during the period July 21 to August 29, 1970. The objective was to review training facilities for government accounting and auditing.
	1971	First report of the advisory committee on personnel management	A classification unit was established in the Ministry of Finance and Planning—assistance from CIDA.
	1972	Modernization of Government Audit	ODA—consultant Mr. Bax.
	1973	New classification system of pay	Ministry Paper No.20, April 18, 1973.
	1974	Classification of positions in Ministry	Canadian Task Force.
	1976	Development of in-service training	Had its origin in the 1965 UN mission report.
	1980	Public Service Improvement Project	UN Report No. JAM 1978/005 FS Caracciolo and S.K. Parathasarathi.
St. Vincent and the Grenadines	1982	Diagnosis for the structure and functioning of the public service	CARICAD.
	1984	Public sector reform	

(Continued)

Table 9.1 (*Continued*)   Select Commissions Established in Various Countries 1960s–1980s

Country	Year	Commission Established	Focus of the Commission/ Consultant
Trinidad and Tobago	1964	The Role and Status of the Civil Service in the Age of Independence—J. O'Neil Lewis	Report concentrated on compensation and training.
	1970	Committee under chairmanship of Cecil Dolly	Focused on issues of centralization of the services, the role, and functions of the Cabinet.
	1972	The GOTT entered into a project agreement with the United Nations	Technical assistance to supplement the efforts of the GOTT to strengthen its central administrative agencies and to improve administrative support.
	1977	OAS support	To establish a permanent training program in project formulation and evaluation in the Training Unit of the Chief Personnel Department. Also the establishment of a National Advisory Council with responsibility for overseeing all areas of national economic planning.
	1981	Committee of Permanent Secretaries	Proposed a complete reorganization of the structures in the public services.
	1982	Task Force under William Demas	Reform of the public services and to re-assess the development strategy.

Essentially, the challenges were similar to those experienced in all the ex-colonies of Britain. Khan (1978) summed it up as follows:

> It is a fact the referral syndrome became embedded in the colonial administrative system over the decades. The structural inputs of the system were such that these profoundly discouraged support-level and middle-level initiatives. As an outcome, administrative matters, routine as well as non-routine were referred to superiors for their scrutiny and approval. The decision-making process correspondingly became tardy.*

While, in evaluating public sector reform experiences in the Caribbean, a blanket statement is usually advanced that there has been little or no reforms, this analysis, however, is not entirely true. For instance, if an examination is attempted of country experiences, it will be evident that some significant introductions did in fact take place. For instance, in Barbados, in 1971, the

---

* Jamal Khan. 1978. *Managing Development: Theory and Practice.* Crown Caribbean Publications Ltd.: Bridgetown, Barbados, p. 55.

Government of Barbados established the Organization and Management Division. This institution was significant in that it had the responsibility for the coordination of the entire public service. In addition to this, over the period of the 1970s to the 1980s, the government made a number of overtures to involve other actors such as the private sector, nongovernmental organizations as well as a number of trade unions in policy deliberation. Following on these relationships and as a result, perhaps, of the moderate growth in the Barbadian economy in the late 1980s, the government, the private sector, and the trade unions entered into a tripartite consultative process which formalized the passage of the Barbados National Productivity Act in 1993.

In the case of Jamaica, in 1973, the Ministry of the Public Service was established. This ministry had responsibility for initiating reforms in the public sector along with the modernization of management practices. Increased training in several areas (including financial administration), the establishment of a classification system, and the introduction of computerized human resource systems were also significant introductions. Following this, in 1983, an Act of Parliament was enacted which allowed for the establishment of the Office of the Contractor General—an ombudsman for public contracts in Jamaica.

In the case of Trinidad and Tobago, there also had been a number of significant introductions particularly during the late 1960s and early 1970s. These had included the introduction of Civil and Public Service Regulations, the introduction of the Office of the Chief Personnel Office (1966), and the introduction of new appraisal systems as well the establishment of the Office of the Ombudsman, the Office of the Integrity Commission, and different agencies and departments. There had also been an entire re-classification exercise conducted by Collett and Clapp in 1966.

While, however, there were "pockets" of procedural changes along with the establishment of new institutions and department, these reforms were often ad hoc and there was little attempt to overhaul the entire public sector. No doubt, one of the major considerations of the various governments was that reform of the public sectors in these countries was too costly. In addition, it should be recalled that in many countries, particularly the smaller islands such as Barbados and St. Vincent and the Grenadines, the major emphasis was directed to economic development and product development. For instance, in Barbados, emphasis was directed to tourism, while in St. Vincent and the Grenadines the major concern was with the banana trade. Another factor often overlooked when examining reforms in small island states was that these islands were also extremely vulnerable to varying weather patterns and environmental conditions. Thus, a large proportion of the islands' incomes had to be devoted to rescue efforts and rebuilding of infrastructure after adverse weather conditions.

Public Sector Reform: 1980s–2000

While there had been a number of internal pressures for improvements in public sector delivery over time in the various countries, a number of shifts were also emerging in the external environment as well. By the 1970s, for the first time, writers were alluding to a term *globalization*, which, while not new, was increasingly becoming "vogue." The trends pointed to as typifying "globalization" included the following:

- The growing integration of national economies
- A growing awareness of ecological interdependence
- The proliferation of companies
- Social movements and intergovernmental agencies operating on a global scale
- A communication revolution that aided the development of a global consciousness

Globalization brought with it a number of startling changes for both the developed countries and the developing countries. When the organization of petroleum exporting countries (OPEC) quadrupled the price of crude oil in 1973, the expenditure of countries around the world quadrupled. While Trinidad and Tobago, as an oil-producing economy, benefitted briefly from this windfall, countries such as Barbados, Jamaica, and St. Vincent and the Grenadines experienced a marked deterioration of economic activities. By 1974, Jamaica entered into an extended fund facility loan of US$240 million with the International Monetary Fund (IMF) for a 3-year period. Like her Caribbean neighbors, the period 1990–1995 in Barbados was characterized by a decline in economic activity which forced Barbados also to seek financial assistance from the IMF and the World Bank. In the Bajan case, real gross domestic product (GDP) had declined from Bds $909 million in 1989 to Bds $791.9 million in 1992, while per capita real GDP fell from Bds $3,492.19 in 1989 to Bds $3,009.88 in 1992.* In Trinidad and Tobago, by contrast, while during the period 1973–1982, it had experienced an oil boom, and during the period 1982–1988, it had experienced six consecutive years of negative growth. Over this period, petroleum export earnings fell by close to one half. The unemployment rate more than doubled from 10% to 23%, while real GDP in 1988 was 23% below the level of 1982. Also, despite a significant reduction in imports, there was a loss in foreign exchange reserves of US$2.8 billion during the period 1982 to 1988. In 1984, Trinidad also approached the IMF.

Nearly, all the countries under review sought assistance from the IMF. It should be recalled though that differing arrangements are entered into depending on the nature of the crisis faced by a country. Concessional facilities for low-income countries for instance include the following:

- Rapid credit facility (natural disasters and post-conflict)
- Standby credit facility (short-term)
- Extended credit facility (poverty reduction and growth)

While advanced and middle-income countries may be assisted by the following:

- Emergency Natural Disaster Assistance (natural disasters)
- Standby arrangement (short-term)
- Extended fund facility (longer term)
- Flexible credit line (precaution)
- Precautionary credit line (precaution)

In nearly all the countries of the Caribbean, therefore, the IMF loan agreement was either based on the "standby credit facility" or the "extended credit facility." Table 9.2 accordingly presents the type of arrangement and the Caribbean countries entered into agreements with the IMF.

The structural adjustment policies (SAPs) included currency devaluation, managed balance of payments, reduction in government services through public spending cuts/budget deficit cuts, reducing tax on high earners, reducing inflation, wage suppression, privatization, lower tariffs on imports and tighter monetary policy, increased free trade, cuts in social spending, and business deregulation. Governments were also encouraged or forced to reduce their role in the economy by privatizing state-owned industries, including the health sector, and opening up their economies to foreign competition.

---

* Ann Marie Bissessar. 2008. *The Crisis of Public Sector Reform in the Caribbean. An Analysis Through the Use of Game Theory*. The Edwin Mellen Press: Lewinston, NY, p. 163.

Table 9.2 IMP Balance of Payments Support for Selected Countries (Amount in USD Millions)

Country	Type of Arrangement	Date of Approval	Expiration Date	Amount Approved	Amount Drawn
Barbados	Standby	Oct 01, 1982	May 31, 1984	30	30
		Feb 07, 1992	May 31, 1993	17	17
Belize	Standby	Dec 03, 1984	May 31, 1986	7	7
Dominica	EFF	Feb 06, 1981	Feb 05, 1984	7	7
	Standby	Jul 18, 1984	Jul 17, 1985	1.4	0.97
	SAF	Nov 26, 1986	Nov 25, 1989	2.30	2.30
Grenada	Standby	Nov 06, 1979	Dec 31, 1980	0.62	0.62
	Standby	May 11, 1981	May 10, 1982	2.96	2.50
	EFF	Aug 24, 1983	Jan 23, 1984	13	1.1
Guyana	EFF[a]	Jun 25, 1979	Jun 24, 1980	49	8
	EFF[a]	Jul 25, 1980	Jul 21, 1982	114.3	39
	Standby	Jul 13, 1990	Dec 31, 1991	36	36
	ESAF	Jul 13, 1990	Dec 20, 1993	60	60
	ESAF	Jul 20, 1994	Apr 17, 1998	37	37
	ESAF/PRGF	Jul 15, 1998	Dec 31, 2001	37	17
Jamaica	EFF[b]	Jun 11, 1979	Apr 12, 1981	201	66
	EFF	Apr 13, 1981	Apr 12, 1984	399	336
	Standby	Jun 22, 1984	Jun 21, 1985	62	62
	Standby	Jul 17, 1985	Jul 16, 1986	111	40
	Standby	Mar 02, 1987	May 31, 1988	66	66
	Standby	Sep 19, 1988	Mar 22, 1990	64	32
	Standby	Mar 23, 1990	May 31, 1991	63	63
	Standby	Jun 28, 1991	Sep 30, 1992	33	33
	EFF	Dec 11, 1992	Mar 16, 1996	79	63
Trinidad and Tobago	Standby	Jan 13, 1989	Feb 28, 1990	75	75
	Standby	Apr 20, 1990	Mar 31, 1991	65	65

Source: International Monetary Fund Financial Statistics, http://www.imf.org/external/data.htm.

[a] Cancelled prior to expiration date.
[b] Cancelled prior to expiration date of June 10, 1981.

A characteristic feature of structural adjustment and reform programs implemented by most developing countries in the past 10 years is that the agenda of reforms ranged over a number of sectors, macroeconomic as well as microeconomic or sectoral issues, and managing policy change in so many dimensions poses special problems. The typical reform program included the following elements:

1. Macroeconomic stabilization
2. Domestic deregulation of investment production and prices
3. Liberalization of foreign trade
4. Privatization of the public sector
5. Financial sector reforms
6. Tax reforms
7. Labor market reforms
8. Social safety nets

To many countries undertaking structural adjustment reforms, the larger issues were not only about the nature and type of reform but also the inter-relationship between the elements of the proposed reforms and the design of the reform undertaking. To many governments, some suggest that the first issue was related to the pace of the reform or the choice between what some termed the "big bang" approach or the "incremental" approach. Opinions, it was clear, varied on the advantages as well disadvantages of both approaches and a case was made for either approach depending upon particular circumstances.

The Privatization Experience

For instance, while privatization of the public sector was one of the key areas proposed, this could not be undertaken without first considering the impact this would have on the following:

1. The psyche of the population
2. The impact on the labor force

Some claimed that privatization was a form of neo-colonialism, particularly as it related to the sale of formerly government-owned companies to foreign companies, and so they were highly critical of the government for selling out "their heritage." Added to these sentiments were the possible loss of livelihoods in the various sectors and the impact of these fallouts on the other sectors. So, while it may have been optimal for governments to implement the entire reform package and so achieve the adjustment to the new environment in the quickest possible time in order that the benefits were realized, this could not be done. In practice, there were lags in adjustment which affected the speed with which the various economies responded to different initiatives.

In Barbados, for instance, Senator Andre Worrell, president of The Young Democrats,* suggested that the privatization model proposed by the opposition would be another round of "selling off the family silver to a short-term demand." He contended that privatization did not provide a sustainable solution to the major problem affecting the Barbados economy—that of not earning enough revenue. Further, he suggested, privatization did not automatically make an entity profitable.

---

* Privatisation—Unsustainable economic solution. November 21, 2012. *The Barbados Advocate*.

It just shifted the ownership and responsibility for the entity from the state to other interests, be it local or foreign. For the entity to turn a profit, he claimed, it would require a substantial financial injection so that it can boost its revenue potential.

He used as an example the situation with Almond Beach Hotel. Heywood's Resorts was owned by government and sold to Barbados Shipping and Trading Company Limited (BS&T) as part of the Structural Adjustment Programme of the 1990s. At that time, BS&T was a large Barbadian conglomerate. Around 2006–2007, under the BLP administration, BS&T was sold to Neal and Massy—a Trinidadian-owned company. Further in 2012, there was the closure of Almond Beach Resorts due to a decision made by the Neal and Massy Board. This resulted in over 500 persons being sent home and the loss of critical room stock from the Barbados tourism product. According to Worrel, this was a tremendous loss which the government would have preferred not to occur. However, the hands of the government were somewhat tied. The interest of Neal and Massy was to secure a return on investment for its shareholders, so it did what it had to do to achieve this.

In making a case against further privatization, he raised three major arguments:

1. Privatization limits government influence in the ultimate decisions made by the new owners. Therefore, according to him, the country needed to ensure that entities which were to be privatized did not have major control on activities which are critical to the delivery of key social services.
2. After privatization, the power of control or the major decision makers do not always remain in Barbados. Therefore, the level of influence on the direction of the company is reduced.
3. Privatization does not always mean that the new entity will be efficiently managed.

What is obvious, in the case of Barbados, is that the privatization program is not a recent development. By contrast to the other islands in the Caribbean, public utility companies in Barbados—electricity, telephone, and telecommunications—were always been privately owned—the Barbados National Oil Company was taken over by the government after Mobil Oil Company, the original investor, decided to sell its shares due to Barbados' relatively low oil reserves.

In 1994, the government of Owen Arthur, however, committed itself to a divestment program as part of a comprehensive strategy to mobilize local and foreign private investment. State enterprises, which were purely commercial in nature, were to be privatized using various methods, giving priority to the small investor and SOE employees. In instances such as the Barbados National Oil Company, the government stated that it was willing to encourage joint ventures to attract the needed skills and technology. In 1997, the Arawak Cement Plant was sold to Trinidad Cement. The repair services of the Transport Board were divested, owned cooperatively by the transport workers operating under a repair contract to the Board.*

Unlike Barbados, by 1979, 185 state enterprises had been established in Jamaica. The state owned all utilities, the largest commercial bank [National Commercial Bank (NCB)], 51% of bauxite mining operations, 75% of sugar output, and 48% of hotel capacity. The government also created Jamaica Commodities Trading Corporation, a state trading company responsible for the import of basic commodities. Government services, which accounted for less than 7.7% of GDP in 1953, rose to 19.22% of GDP by 1980.†

---

* Richard L. Bernal and Winsome J. Leslie. 1999. Privatization in the English Speaking Caribbean: An assessment. *Policy Papers on the Americas.* Vol. X, Study 7, October 28, 1999.
† Ibid: 4.

Jamaica's privatization program began in 1981. Essentially, the ideology of "privatization" was part of the election campaign strategy undertaken by the Seaga government. The justification for privatization was that it would reduce government's role in the economy and also kick start some of the sectors such as tourism which was in a slump. However, during the 1980s, privatization occurred on a case-by-case basis and those enterprises which would be most attractive to buyers were prioritized for privatization. Other divestments during the 1980s included local government services, such as cleaning of public facilities. The operations of public markets were placed in private hands through service management contracts and short-term leases, and several agricultural properties were also either leased or sold. However, it was found that these early divestment efforts were often ad hoc and unplanned.*

By 1985, the process began to attract public attention. With phase I of the divestment of the NCB in 1986 by share offering, public awareness of a national policy on privatization finally took hold. During this period, the government of Jamaica sold 51% of its equity in NCB in the largest public issue on the Jamaican stock market at that time. The offering was oversubscribed by 170% and attracted 30,000 individual and institutional investors, including 98% of the bank's own employees. Phase II took place in 1991, with the government reducing its nonvoting shares by selling 6 million shares to NCB Trust and Merchant Bank, the trustee for the NCB Employee Share Scheme. This increased employee ownership from 3% to 10.5%. In phase III, the remaining government shares (49%), originally to be sold by public offering, were disposed of through a private arrangement between the government and a local investment syndicate. Within 10 years after the first divestments, 201 entities and activities had been divested in categories as follows: markets (80); public cleaning services (33); farm holdings (50); hotel properties (14); and corporate entities (24). During this period, over 50 major companies had been handed over to the private sector, including the NCB, the Caribbean Cement Company, and the Jamaica Telephone Company.

By 1991, a strategy based on three principles was presented as the institutional framework for privatization. These were as follows:

1. Streamlining the public sector through an extensive administrative reform program
2. Removing unnecessary bureaucratic intervention in the market without compromising the government's role as regulator
3. Broadening the base of ownership in the local economy

According to Bernal and Leslie (1999:15), it was the government's view that an aggressive privatization program involving SOEs would provide more efficient enterprises, reduce the drain on public sector resources, secure access to foreign markets, technologies, and capital, and increase equity participation in the economy by Jamaicans. Working with the World Bank and a private sector adjustment loan, the government identified 57 entities, assets, and activities for privatization, representing about 50% of the total assets of the public enterprise sector.

A framework for privatization included the following guidelines:

1. All relevant regulatory issues would be dealt with either prior to or simultaneously with any privatization.
2. Neither direct financing nor loan guarantees would be provided to purchasers.
3. Except in public utilities, no new public sector investment, excluding maintenance, would be undertaken prior to privatization.
4. Sale of SOEs to other public sector entities would not be considered privatization.

---

* Much of this discussion is a summary taken from the article of Bernal and Leslie (1999).

5. Unsolicited offers for any enterprise or activity would not be accepted prior to the official advertisement.
6. Direct sale or negotiation could not take place without publicly solicited bids unless the assets involved were small, making it more economical.
7. When the sale was completed, all aspects of the transaction would be public.
8. Any minority shares which the government maintained would not carry special voting rights.

In Jamaica, the attempt to privatize the state enterprises was planned and phased. Of the 57 identities targeted for privatization by 1998, over half were either sold or leased. Between 1981, at the inception of the program, and 1996, divestment by sector occurred as follows: agriculture, 10%; manufacturing, 39%; services, 51% (NIBJ 1994–1995).* By 1999, 27 additional entities were scheduled to be divested, including the Jamaica Railway Corporation. Government holdings in Jamaica Grain and Cereal Ltd. were sold to Seprod Ltd. in December 1997. As part of the decentralization and reform process in the health sector, catering services, maintenance, equipment management, and security services in all public hospitals are being turned over to private providers.

Privatization in the islands of Trinidad and Tobago, however, was not as well conceived.† The Trinidad and Tobago government continued to acquire equity in various companies until the early 1990s. By January 1992, the portfolio of the Government of Trinidad and Tobago consisted of shares in 87 enterprises with a value of TT$6.5 billion (US$1.12 billion), in addition to sizeable investments in the four public utilities—water, power, transport, and ports. While the government entered into an arrangement with the lending agencies in 1994, it was not until 1987 that privatization of the state-owned enterprises actually took place.

In 1987, 49% of the Trinidad and Tobago telephone company, TELCO, was divested for US$80 million, and via a merger with Cable and Wireless, a new company formed—Telecommunications Services of Trinidad and Tobago. Further to this, the government's controlling interest in Trinidad Cement was transferred to private hands through a public offering in 1988 and plans were formulated to divest the remaining 29% through a strategic partnership (20%) and public offering.

By 1991, the incoming government the People's National Movement suggested that government would "steer" rather than "row." By 1993, the government had identified 30 SOE's for divestment and 12 for liquidation. A divestment secretariat was created in the Ministry of Finance to coordinate the process. By mid-1995, several companies had been either fully or partially privatized including Trinidad and Tobago Urea Company Ltd., Trinidad and Tobago Methanol Company, BWIA international, and the Electricity Commission. In the energy sector, the exploration and production activities of Trinidad and Tobago Oil Company (TRINTOC) and the Trinidad and Tobago Petroleum Company (TINTOPEC) were merged into a new company—Petroleum Company of Trinidad and Tobago Ltd. (PETROTRIN). The non-petroleum assets of both TRINTOC and TINTOPEC were divested. In the case of Trinidad and Tobago, Bernal and Leslie (1999) suggested that several methods of divestment were utilized including competitive bidding, sale of shares on the Trinidad and Tobago stock exchange, sales to former lessees, and the formation of strategic alliances with either local or foreign partners.

The experience with privatization in the case of the islands of St. Vincent and the Grenadines has been extremely limited and confined to two cases. In 2002, the Eastern Caribbean Telecommunications Authority, created in May 2000, opened its new headquarters on June 3, 2002, in St. Lucia, as part of the program toward telecommunications liberalization in the Caribbean

---

* National Investment Bank of Jamaica Ltd. (NIBJ). *Annual Report*, 1994–1995.
† Taken from Bernal and Leslie: 9–10.

subregion which encompasses five members of the Organization of Eastern Caribbean States: Commonwealth of Dominica, Grenada, St. Lucia, St. Kitts and Nevis, and St. Vincent and the Grenadines. Later in 2010, St. Vincent and the Grenadines' state-owned National Commercial Bank (SVG) Limited reached an agreement with the East Caribbean Financial Holding Company Limited of St. Lucia to take over 51% share in the national bank. According to this agreement, the government would continue to retain the balance of shares, with the intention of divesting 29% of those shares to the St. Vincent and the Grenadines National Insurance Service, citizens of St. Vincent and the Grenadines, including bank staff and citizens of the region. However, in 2012, the Government of St. Vincent and the Grenadines, through Invest SVG, indicated that they were interested in attracting foreign direct investment in St. Vincent and the Grenadines, particularly in industries that create jobs and earn foreign currency. The government was interested pursuing investment in niche markets, particularly tourism, international financial services, agro-processing, light manufacturing, and information and communication technology (ICT).

In all the countries under review, there were variations in the privatization experience. Jamaica stood out as the most aggressive. It should be noted that a number of factors would have influenced the nature and the pace of reforms in these countries. The choice of pace of reform is influenced by political constraints arising from the fact that all structural reforms involve some distributional changes in favor of some groups and against others, and there are limits on the extent of distributional change that can be tolerated. While it has been suggested that such changes may not be adverse in a normative sense and may be beneficial, for example, in actual improvements in total employment and income distribution, initially these changes are bound to be resisted. The level of such considerations would, of necessity, justify a gradualist strategy in which reforms are phased over several years to limit the distributional burdens on particular groups in the initial years until the benefit of the reforms in other dimensions become fully operational. No doubt the gradualist approach was more apparent in the cases of St. Vincent and the Grenadines, Barbados, and Trinidad and Tobago. In reviewing the experiences, what emerges but is not captured in the current literature or discussion on privatization is the question of whether the size and the monopolistic culture of a country impacts on the nature and scope of reform. Can it be argued, for example, that because of the size of the country, the stakeholders will be more impassioned to protect what they seem to think is their heritage? Will privatization decisions have made a greater impact on the work force on small countries rather than larger countries? These questions, of course, would be the theme for later discussions and reviews.

Reform Experiences in the Civil Service

Apart from the attempt to privatization what at the time were described as "failing" state-owned companies, the governments of many countries also embarked on civil service reform. The reforms in all countries targeted the following areas or sectors:

- Agency reform
- Human resource management reform
- Legislative reform
- Financial reforms

Table 9.3 accordingly summarizes some selected reforms introduced in the various countries.

As Table 9.3 indicates, the experience with civil service reform varied. It was clear that Jamaica was the most progressive in introducing and implementing reforms across the various sectors,

Table 9.3 Civil Service Reform in Selected Countries

Nature of the Reforms	Barbados	Jamaica	St. Vincent and the Grenadines	Trinidad and Tobago
Agency Reforms	1997—Establishment of office of Public Sector Reform	1993—Enhancement of the Cabinet Secretariat	—	1989—Decentralization of functions from Personnel Department. Introduction of strategic planning in Office of the Prime Minister
Human Resource Management Reform	1998—Human Resource Management Information Systems • 1998—EAPs • 2001—Performance Review and Development System • 2003—Service Assessment and Improvement Programme • 2003—Customer Service Programme • 2004—Humanise Management/Personnel Excellence Programme	• 2002: Social Policy Framework • Performance Review • Strategic Review of Ministries • HRMIS systems • Human resource policies including training • Deregulation of HR functions from Service Commissions	• 2002—New Performance System to include the following: • The Development of Work Plans • The Setting of Smart Objectives • The establishment of Performance Standards • The measurement of Productivity • Continuous assessment and feedback	• The introduction of a new department to examine reform of the classification system. • The introduction of pilot EAPs. • Human resource policy units were created in each ministry. • The increase in the number of contract positions. • Decentralization of HR functions from PSC.

(*Continued*)

Table 9.3 (Continued) Civil Service Reform in Selected Countries

Nature of the Reforms	Barbados	Jamaica	St. Vincent and the Grenadines	Trinidad and Tobago
• Legislative Reform	• Development of a New Public Service Act • Legal Mandate of Value for Money Auditing Performance	Amendment of Public Service Regulations	NIL	NIL

• Financial Reform	• 1993—Computerization of the Treasury Division
	• 1996—Introduced Programme and Performance Based Budgeting
	• 1998—Pension Reform Introduced
	• 1998—Financial Management Information System
	• 1998—Computerization of Procurement Process
	• 2004—Accrual Accounting
		• Computerization
		• Performance reviews
		• Financial reforms, etc.
		• Budgeting revisions
		• Procurement revisions
		
		Note that Jamaica introduced 30 successful reform initiatives in 2002
			• 1995—Consultation on financial reform including:
			  • Income Tax Department
			  • Smart Stream System in Treasury Department
				The introduction of a HRMIS payroll system.

while the Government of St. Vincent and the Grenadines introduced minimal reforms. In trying to evaluate and advance reasons for the variations in the nature and the pace of reform, a number of writers have alluded to the following by way of explanation:

- The lack of political will
- Resistance to the reform effort by public officers
- Lack of a clear reform agenda
- Lack of technical and administrative capacity
- Limited funds allocated to the reform initiative

What emerges from an examination of the experiences with each country as they attempted to grapple with structural adjustment requirements was that, to a large extent, while the scope of reform was shaped by the lending agencies, it was also influenced by the perceptions of the decision makers as well as by the differences in political style. The cohesiveness of the government and the nature of its links to the private sector and other actors including nongovernmental organizations and the wider civil society were clearly important considerations in introducing unpopular reform measures. For instance, in the case of both Jamaica and Barbados, the relationship of the state with the various parties was an influential variable on realizing the successes achieved in implementing reform measures. In the case of Jamaica, though, it was clear that initially there was political resistance which retarded the adjustment program. The state was forced to defect from its original position, however, and return to the IMF. While Jamaica and, to a lesser extent, Barbados adhered closely to the prescriptions offered by the lending agencies, this was not the case of the other countries under review. Both Jamaica and Barbados subscribed to a bargaining model in which the government, the private sector, the trade unions, and, in the case of Jamaica, stakeholders from the University of the West Indies were involved in policy deliberations.

In the case of Trinidad and Tobago, while during the period 1986–1991 there was a strict adherence to the IMF prescriptions, by 1991 with an increase in the price of the primary commodity, oil, reform took on a more relaxed mode. These reforms were not integrated as they were proposed during the period 1991–1994, but rather comprised a number of disparate processes and systems. It was found that in a number of cases where the reforms were unpopular, the government often skirted that issue and instead brought in "softer" and more amenable measures.

In examining the various reform experiences, one variable that must also be factored into the equation is the role of the market and market forces. In the case of the smaller islands of St. Vincent and the Grenadines, with the tariffs imposed on their major crops, bananas, it was easy to understand why the priority of the government would be placed on economic reform, rather than administrative reform. While it is true that to a large extent, development of a country depends on the efficiency of the administrative arm of the state, in small vulnerable countries the reality is that the state, while it may plan to implement one measure or embark on a stated objective, often gets side tracked when natural disasters occur. Thus, in the case of St. Vincent and the Grenadines, much of the resources of the state had to be shifted to repair infrastructure and public utilities during the period 2001–2005. There was therefore a vicious cycle of unplanned events which demanded a lot of state resources; moreover, they were incidents that could not be ignored. The result was that the Government of St. Vincent and the Grenadines did not introduce a concrete administrative reform plan. Thus, the relationship between the state of the economy and the size of the budget of a country is a critical factor.

The Reality of New Public Management Reforms in the Caribbean

There are some who suggest that to a large extent the broad sweeping reforms in the Caribbean were part and parcel of the wider new public management (NPM) reforms that had first been introduced in Britain and then the United States in 1979 and 1980, respectively. Some writers define NPM as a combination of the following elements among others:*

- The splitting of large, monolithic bureaucracies into smaller, more fragmented ones
- The creation of competition between different public agencies, and between public agencies and private firms

Many suggest, particularly in the more developed countries, that NPM was a significant driver in public management policy around the world, from the early 1980s to at least the early 2000s. According to Hood (1991) and Hood (1996),† NPM brought with it not only structural changes but also cultural changes since it forced the traditional managers to function in a private-managerial type mode. It may be argued, though, that NPM was merely a hype or fad and the argument that while reform movements vary in depth, scope, and success by country, they are remarkably similar in the goals they pursue and the technologies they utilize, thus linking it to NPM reforms, is far from accurate. Rather, it should be noted that the basis of all reform, across all sectors, is to increase productivity and improve capacity. In other words, the use of new technology, as well the experiment with new and varying management styles, was not the sole prerogative of NPM. Rather, as has been demonstrated over time, the fascination of different managerial models, for instance, Quality Circles or Management by Objectives, was in the cards long before NPM became a "buzz word" in the academic lexicon.

Particularly, in the case of the Commonwealth Caribbean, it was found that the different experiences with respect to the scope and nature of reforms varied. For instance, in the case of Jamaica, it was observed that Jamaica, because of its relationship to the IMF and World Bank, adhered closely to the prescriptions outlined as part of the conditionalities. Jamaica initiated a comprehensive privatization exercise, selling off a large proportion of state assets. Jamaica also embarked on e-governance strategies, the reorganization of its different ministries and departments, and also embarked on a re-engineering of its traditional mode of operations. In the case of Trinidad and Tobago, however, after the initial attempt at comprehensive reform in the early 1990s, reform has been once more placed on the "back agenda." While it is true that there is reform in ministries, this can best be described as piecemeal and ad hoc. One can surmise, for instance, that currently its attempts at an e-governance strategy have been fairly successful since in all the ministries, the functions of the ministries are available online. It is true, too, that the long lines of waiting for passports and permits have been significantly reduced. However, other areas, such as health care and particularly national security, have and continue to be the source of open and constant criticism. In the smaller islands, in this case, Barbados, again there have been significant strides in having an open government portal. However, there have been ad hoc instances of reforms and to a large extent many of the services continue to be exercised along traditional lines. This experience is repeated in the case of St. Vincent and the Grenadines.

---

* Re-engineering the foundation of public sector along economic lines.
† C.C. Hood. 1991. A public management for all seasons? *Public Administration*, 69, 1, pp. 3–19; C.C. Hood. 1996. Exploring variations in public management reform of the 1980s. In *Civil Service Systems in Comparative Perspective*. Edited by H.A. Bekke, J.L. Perry, and T.A. Toonen. Indiana University Press: Bloomington, IN, pp. 268–287.

Public Sector Reform: 2000–2013

The limited material on reform in all the countries in the Caribbean seems to suggest, and quite rightly too, that the pace of reforms of the 1970s, 1980s, and 1990s have slowed down considerably. In the case of Barbados, for example, there has been little restructuring or re-engineering of public service institutions. Indeed, the reform has been confined to incremental, if not important, introductions such as the Guidelines for Administrative Managers (May 2013), a strengthening of the existing Employee Assistance Programmes, as well as a continuing emphasis on customer service and excellence commencing with an initiative of carrying excellence to the streets.

In the case of Jamaica, on the other hand, the emphasis on public sector reform has slowed down as a result of fiscal crisis in this country. Jamaica, as was noted previously, is one of the most highly indebted countries in the world. A recent report suggests that it has a total public debt of 129.3% of GDP at the end of the fiscal year 2009/2010.[*] After decreasing sharply during the early 1990s, the total debt to GDP ratio continued to rise between 1996/1997 and 2002/2003 increasing from 71.3% to 124.7%. In 2009, the Government of Jamaica announced its intent to secure a new IMF agreement with the IMF. This standby arrangement (for 27 months) was agreed, and in February 2010, Jamaica received the first tranche of US$460 million from a total of US$1.27 billion. It was claimed that this agreement also unlocked funding from other multilateral organizations such as US$450 million from the World Bank and US$600 million from the Inter-American Bank. The IMF program was predicated on three part strategy: medium-term fiscal consolidation, lowering interests' costs and addressing debt overhang problems, and reform of the financial sector.

The return to structural adjustment, as to be expected, would have negative consequences for public service reform. For instance, in 2008, a nominal increase of 7% was recommended for public service employees which have yet to be implemented. Further to this, however, one of the IMF's conditions was that the Jamaican government had to divest or liquidate Air Jamaica by June 2010. In May 2010, the Government of Jamaica handed over control of the airline to Caribbean Airlines, which is majority owned by the Government of Trinidad and Tobago. One thousand eight hundred employees were declared redundant. Another structural benchmark of the IMF program was an increase of no less than 40% for the state-owned Jamaican Urban Transport Company's bus fares and the leasing or selling of factories belonging to the state-owned Sugar Company of Jamaica. The government also agreed to the selling of the Clarendon Alumina Production and its majority holdings to Petrojam oil refinery. Indeed, by the second review, the Government of Jamaica had privatized all of its holdings in the Sugar Company of Jamaica.

Like Jamaica, by 2007, the public debt in the case of St. Vincent and the Grenadines had risen to 55.7% of the GDP, compared with 43.3% in 1996. With increased expenditure pressures, the structural primary deficit in this country worsened from 2.3% of the GDP in 2008 to 3.7% in 2010 and public debt increased by a further 10% points to 66.8%.[†] It is to be expected, given its financial constraints, that the Government of St. Vincent and the Grenadines have taken a more deliberate policy through its strategic plan to help reduce its public debt rather than engage on active public sector reform. While it has continued to place emphasis on some measures to reform its health sector, one of its few initiatives as it relates to the public sector is to complete the standardization of job descriptions for the public service. This is an ongoing exercise.

---

[*] Center for Economic Policy and Research. May 2011. Jamaica: Macroeconomic Policy, Debt and the IMF. Jake Johnston and Juan Antonio Montecino. The literature on Jamaica is taken from this report.
[†] IMF Report, St. Vincent and the Grenadines No. 11/343.

Unlike the other Caribbean islands, Trinidad and Tobago did not have to go to the IMF or the World Bank. However, even in these two twin island Republic states, reform has been incremental. There have been discussions to revise the procurement and the wider financial system but this is ongoing. The country also continues to expand its e-government portal and widen the scope of ICT within the country. However, further plans for the reform of the public sector have not yet been discussed with the wider public. Part of the reason for the general apathy with respect to new reform initiatives being introduced no doubt has to do with a by-election in one of the government's stronghold and more recently in October 2013, plans to conduct the local government elections. In addition, with the election of a new government in 2010, there has been three major cabinet re-shuffles in the past 3 years. It is reasonable to assume, therefore, if the trend of shifting ministers continues that little or minimal reform will be expected in this sector.

Concluding Remarks

This chapter overviewed some reform experiences in the countries of Barbados, Jamaica, St. Vincent and the Grenadines, and Trinidad and Tobago during the period of the 1950s to 2013. While initially all the countries, formerly colonies of Britain, during the pre-independence and early post-independence period had similar reform experiences, by the 1980–1990s as a result of IMF conditionalities, the pace and the direction of these reforms varied. There can be no doubt that Jamaica is far ahead of its Caribbean cousins in terms of the kinds of reforms that have been successfully introduced. Some may argue, though, that Jamaica has very limited options given its off and on relationship with the IMF and World Bank and thus has very little recourse but to adhere to the dictates of the lending agencies. In the case of Trinidad and Tobago and to some extent Barbados, because their economies are fairly buoyant, the dependence on the lending agencies has, in a way, freed them from closely adhering to the reform dictated by these agencies. Thus, reforms in these countries have not been as deliberate or sustained as those reforms in Jamaica. St. Vincent and the Grenadines, as was previously pointed out, have their own trajectory—merely trying to cope with the uncertainties of the environment and international trade agreements and hence administrative reform as a comprehensive package is something that perhaps may emerge as a priority—in the distant future. In short then, the bottom line is that in the majority of countries under review, the major challenges that had been outlined by reformers in the 1960s, 1970s, and 1980s still continue as major impediments in the public sectors, more particularly St. Vincent and the Grenadines, and to some extent in Trinidad and Tobago as well as in Barbados. While in the case of the latter two countries, there has been some delegation of functions from the Public Service Commissions to the various line ministries, the public continue to be critical of the "red tape" experienced in service delivery. Moreover, in the case of Trinidad and Tobago, the disconnect between the ministers of government and the administrative staff has continued to be particularly disconcerting and has to a large extent led to the loss of confidence between the two group of actors.

References

International Monetary Fund Financial Statistics, http://www.imf.org/external/data.htm.
Peters, G. (1997). Separating policy and operations: A summary of national responses. In Policy and Operations. Ottawa: Canadian Center for Management Development.

Chapter 10

Contending with Caribbean Public Sector Leadership in the Twenty-First Century

Edwin Jones, Andrew Walcott, and Sandra Grey-Alvaranga

Contents

Overview 202
    Contending with Meaning of Public Sector Leadership 202
    Narratives on the Caribbean Task Environment and Public Sector Leadership 203
    The Public Sector Leadership Factor 204
    Theorizing Hybridization 208
    Problematizing the Leadership Experience 210
    The Future of Leadership in Public Administration 212
Experiences and Narratives of Caribbean Public Sector Leadership 213
    Recognizing the Leadership Problems 213
    Contextualizing Contemporary Caribbean Leadership 215
    Twenty-First Century Leadership Challenges 216
        Manage Scarcity and a Demanding Clientele 217
        Manage Internal and National Talents through Industrial Relations 219
        Manage the Process of the Transformation Agenda 220
        Develop and Execute a Supportive (and Joined Up Where Possible)
        Policy Framework 221
    Building Leadership Capabilities/Competencies for the Twenty-First Century 222
Conclusion 222
Bibliography 224

Abstract: Within the contexts of globalization, revised governance imperatives, and the New Public Management (NPM) agenda, there is a need for a cadre of administrative agents in the Caribbean that can successfully effect and manage the process of change throughout public sectors. Leadership is recognized as an essential quality needed to effectively mobilize human and other resources to perform under various changing local and global conditions and evince that change. However, the idea of leadership is subject to multiple interpretations and definitions, some of which no longer obtain in current contexts. Beginning with reflective statements on certain conceptual and model-building dimensions of leadership, this chapter looks at how the new public sector environment has created a demand for various and particular types of leadership styles armed with a plethora of skills to tackle old and new salient issues within the region. In particular, the chapter looks at the need for capable leaders to manage particular areas such as (1) scarcity and a demanding clientele; (2) internal and national talents through industrial relations; (3) the transformation agenda; and (4) the development of a supportive policy framework. It ends with a brief look at the current techniques used for identifying and developing leaders within the Caribbean and suggests areas for improvement.

Overview

Contending with Meaning of Public Sector Leadership

Leadership theory and leadership across organizational boundaries are driven by competing interpretations (Van Wart 2003). Although the notion of public sector leadership remains contested, consensus has emerged on some of its core perspectives. There is general agreement that leadership is a requirement of modern administrative life, to develop and deliver services and to give direction about the accomplishment of public objectives.

A related perspective identifies leadership in the public sector domain with (1) people transiently in power at the political level (ministerial/cabinet leadership) and (2) with the established senior executive of the civil service. This translates usually to frontline superiors making judgment, the particular set of activities and interactions among them, and individuals or teams who take up the strategic challenges and dilemmas of managing the public's business, to give direction to governing and, increasingly, governance (Lynn 1981; Rhodes 1997) first at the national and on regional basis in the case of Caribbean Community (CARICOM). They typically employ mainstream management approaches and processes such as "devising, deliberating, interpreting, challenging, and changing the institutional rules and practices" to seek outcomes of efficiency and good governance.

In the post-modern public organization, leadership is often regarded as a process-driven "adaptive response to the non-routine strategic challenges in a society" (Hart and Uhr 2008, 3). This perspective suggests that specific tasks and contextual considerations pose puzzles for public leadership. Such tasks are scattered across a massive comparative literature (e.g., CAPAM 2009). In this interpretation, three principal tasks are involved. They involve coping with organizational and contextual complexity, efficiently delivering publicly valued outcomes, provoking transformation, and building a culture of change and creativity in the administrative and societal realms. Their collective meaning suggests that public sector leaders must stay away from the causes and risks inherent in "organisational foolishness" (Lane and Wallis 2009), exploiting the space for alternative ways of leading change.

At the elemental level then we identify with the meaning of public sector leadership as constituting two processes. One focuses on the judgment-making aspect that shapes the direction of organization's development. The other concentrates on a distinctive type of social influence relationship. Thus, to lead is to "influence, guide, engage a following and build their commitment to realize a particular vision" (Wallis and McLoughlin 2007). Public sector leadership is also recognizable as a dynamic process that involves pulling an organization into the future "by creating a positive view of what the organisation can become and simultaneously providing emotional support for individuals during the transition process" (Wallis and McLoughlin 2007).

Of course, other components of public sector leadership identify the concept with themes that support the modernization program. Among these key components are the need for strong visible leaders and the encouragement of greater service collaboration. Mark Moore (1995) extends this discourse to a notion of new public leadership (NPL) that stresses the importance of "networked governance" where the overall goal is the creation and provision of public value. The emerging NPL framework is defined by concepts and ideas such as the delivery of social goals, the importance of collective leadership style across organizational or institutional building and boundaries, the sharing of learning and social capital, and the orientation of commitment to tackling complexity, uncertainty within the task environment (Moore 1995; Brookes and Grint 2011).

Both the character and expectations of these tasks suggest that public sector leaders should develop a repertoire of skills and styles that can be deployed to suit particular context and situation. This proposition may be illustrated generally and particularly to Commonwealth Caribbean societies at the national levels and regional levels. First, we summarize elements of the Caribbean public sector task environment, followed by elements of the debates and observations about leadership therein.

Narratives on the Caribbean Task Environment and Public Sector Leadership

Shaped over time by historical and contemporary forces, the public sector task environment—its organizational structures, socio-technical systems and behaviors, and normative character of public administration, including the leadership culture—has been decisively shaped by four dominant forces. First was the well-known dominance of the colonial model of public administration (Jones and Mills 1989; Mills 1990; Ryan and Brown 1992), usually in tension with Weberian-type principles and the requirements of trusteeship. For the colonial model was remarkable for its bureaucratic, mechanical and coercive, rule-bound, and highly differentiated non-developmental orientation. While it stressed order and stability in organizations, it clearly stood apart from Weberian norms of specialization, good institutional management in terms of file management, and relatively efficient decision making leaning toward a maintenance culture. Many of the colonial type features have lingered together with specific patterns of leadership—particularly conservative, authoritarian-submissive and transactional—that they evinced.

World War II also impacted the intellectual and operational evolution of the region's public administration system and environment. It triggered, among other things, newer insights about policy analysis, implementation analysis, development planning as well as bottom-up approaches. Absorption of these approaches within the region has been halting and lopsided. Thus, was delayed any real movement toward genuinely "transformational" mode of leadership.

Third, notwithstanding efforts across the region at local government reform, it is the peculiarities of the "national" policy system promoted by competing political parties and associated political styles combined which shape the evolutionary processes, behaviors, and environment of public administration. They left identifiable traditions of policy and institutional incapacity, top-down management styles, as well as partisan politicization at the level of public sector leadership (Ryan 1989; Jones 1992). Leadership concerns are therefore emphasized at the national levels across the Caribbean and are largely characterized by the skillsets required to successfully navigate the task environment.

Fourth, concepts, doctrines, and programs associated with the international public sector reform movement, New Public Administration and globalization, continue to impart telling impacts on the public administrative sphere across the region. Such impacts or outcomes are, however, a source of much internal dispute and contest, but little consensus. The issue of transforming regional leadership mind-set, capacity, and general motivation and style toward post-modern orientations and frameworks has perhaps been the most contentious (Osei 2004; Minto-Coy 2011).

Elsewhere we have summarized the essential character and the forces that shape the task environment as representing the condition of *administrivia* (Jones 2001). This means retention of a normative public administration environment that is remarkable for the rigidity and overgrown structures and personnel systems, official styles that predispose to poor governance, wasteful policy reversals, and partisan distribution of public largesse. This public administration model is also identified with a weak implementation culture, ethical deficits, low adaptive capacity, and relatively high commitment to symbolic reform remedies. These and other features of the public sector context including the prevalence of crime and violence poverty and weak absorptive capacity, we argue, specifically affect senior management leadership capability and effectiveness. There are some often-cited themes in the regional narrative.

The Public Sector Leadership Factor

Public sector aversion to risk-taking, predilections to maintaining the status quo, and therefore reluctance to innovate and to define and implement radical policy goals are self-evident constraints to effective leadership. There is a blame-avoidance subculture that complicates this overall trend—expressed in institutional habits of attributing blame for failure and for risk, employing selective allocation of rewards and penalties for team members. Because blame-avoidance appears to be central to both political and top bureaucratic behaviors, it constrains regional public sector from discharging such post-modern roles as provoking transformation through comprehensive and coherent administrative reform, as well as encouraging "joined up government" and boundary-less learning.

Also encumbering the ground toward leadership capacity and effectiveness are the twin challenges of structural rigidities and current human capital and financial resource constraints. It is well documented throughout the intellectual history of Caribbean public administration that structural rigidities tend operationally to generate rule-bound administrative styles, consolidate departmentalism and administrative silos, inhibit joined-up-government approaches, and stifle the action learning much needed to drive change processes and pull organizations into the future. It is conditions such as these that frustrate effective communication strategies between staff and management at the senior level. In effect, they significantly undermine leadership capability and effectiveness. The significance of these inhibitors is recognized when we consider Bass' definition of effective leadership and the evidence that shows the superiority of transformational disposition over a transactional and laissez-faire style (Trottier et al. 2008).

Under past and current conditions of financial resource starvation and human resource constraints, the Caribbean experience with top-down, risk-shy public sector leadership has been remarkable for poor handling of work priorities and achievement of results (Mills 1970; Jones 1992; Ryan and Brown 1992; Bissessar 2003b). Dissection of remuneration in the job market shows huge dichotomies between similar positions inside agencies and ministries, as well as between the public and private employers, leading to a migration of talent and a starvation of well-needed skills and innovative minds inside the public service (Wynter 2012). There is thus a projected need for new organizational designs, for new collaborations, and for other post-bureaucratic work processes, which "gaps" help to explain the attractiveness of administrative reform initiatives across the region.

Another normative feature of the public sector contextual landscape is the often unclear division of labor between politicians and administrative leadership. Operationally, at least two effects, adversely affecting leadership, have been evident. First, the policy leadership required from political and administrative elites to ensure the provision of a coherent, whole-government vision of planning and change would not readily emerge. Second, unclear devolution of authority and the associated tendency toward partisan politicization of the civil bureaucracy have meant contests for space to lead between principals and agents, mutual mistrust, and of course, ambiguous policy frameworks (Jones and Schoburgh 2004) that corrode overall capacity for effective leadership. Experience teaches, moreover, that the general public service culture is notorious for constraining the intensive development of leaders and potential leaders and creates space for corruption and other ethical and governance lapses.

Other perspectives on public sector leadership may be provided through a focus on certain additional situational filters. Of significance is the nature and levels of "institutional and cultural complexity." Operationally, leaders are confronted and challenged by a variegated, wide-ranging set of "institutions" within the public realm. They may be roughly classified as bureaucratic, extra-bureaucratic, regional cross border, as well as those representing the international technical or non-governmental genre. Together they would generate some specific leadership agenda and responses (see Table 10.1).

According to Van Wart (2003, 215), the "issues on *contextual complexity* apply to mission, organisational and environmental culture, structure, types of problems, types of opportunities, levels of discretion and a host of other critically important areas." This has clear implications for regional leadership. To deal successfully with such complex issues, public officials at the strategic level must at least lead by innovation and discovery. They must engage in "subtle and nuanced decision-making routines" (Van Wart 2003, 216). They must understand and deal with such domestic and cross-border socio-technical and structural issues, including shifting and complex power relations among powerful social forces, major cultural nuances, and the range of institutional biases. Alongside this configuration are workplace challenges that defy generalizations. Additionally, to lead effectively in the contemporary regional environment requires command of post-modern skills and value-sets and engagement with viable networks. But post-modern administrative models are also driven by mandatory and planned approaches to training and talent management, as well as foundations of a strong leadership infrastructure with reform-minded orientations.

As for *cultural complexity*, its largest regional expressions are associated with racial bifurcation and its significant implications, much in evidence particularly in countries like Guyana and Trinidad and Tobago. Here the central issues often concern the role of political and top civil service leadership in managing or mismanaging human resource matters. For at the heart of the contention are claims that talent is recruited and promoted on racial criteria and that those processes are supported and upheld politically, depending on which racial group forms the government. But implications of the race factor are felt beyond the civil service and extend to national politics, economy, and social interactions.

Throughout the wider Caribbean jurisdictions, issues of race, class, and color are said to affect the handling of distributive policy by political and administrative leaders. These criteria are generally assumed to determine the mode of distribution of all the valued resources—wealth, status,

Table 10.1 Model of Caribbean Public Sector Leadership

Major Caribbean Expressions	Characteristics from Theory	Predisposing Condition
Colonial-Transactional[a]	• Bureaucratic, rule-bound, and conservative • Emphasizes getting things done within the umbrella of the status quo • In opposition to transformational leadership • "By the book" approach—the person works within the rules • Leans toward politicization	*Experience with British hegemonic colonialism across the region, for multiple decades till the late twentieth century
Contingency[b]	• Grounded in philosophy that leader should act as the situation demands • Suggests leaders should develop repertoire of skills and styles that can be deployed to suit the particular situation • Influenced by rise of human relations theory and behavioral science	*Depending on personal leadership styles and operational policy system/ frameworks Preparation for Independence
Transformational[c]	• Emphasis on leaders who create change in deep structures, major processes, and overall culture • Make change happen in self, others, groups and organizations/motivate behavior by changing their followers' attitudes and assumptions • Common theme: requires both leaders and followers to have a certain degree of flexibility in how they define and perform their work assumed that • Charisma, a special leadership style, is commonly associated with "transformational" leadership	*Broadly stimulated by the international reform movement and anchored in concepts and doctrines of NPM Pattern of economic change
Post-Bureaucratic[d] and Networked	• Largely representing managerial, transformational, and entrepreneurial approaches • Takes inspiration not so much from concepts and doctrines associated with NPM but more so from the NPL framework • Associated with developing a culture of change and creativity to reproduce capacity and capability to sustain progress in the public sector	*Influenced by the competitive global economy; need to provide more sophisticated and holistic approaches to leadership

(Continued)

Table 10.1 (*Continued*)   Model of Caribbean Public Sector Leadership

Major Caribbean Expressions	Characteristics from Theory	Predisposing Condition
Post-Bureaucratic and Networked (Continued)	• Networking is concerned with network behavior: • Leaders working in relatively stable, interdependent settings (domestic and cross national) to build support for policy and programmatic objectives; to attract partners to cooperative effort; and to confront challenges	

Source: Van Wart, M. (2003). Public-sector leadership theory: An assessment. *Public Administration Review* 63 (2), 214–228; O'Toole, L., Walker, R., Meier, K., and Boyne, G. (2007). Networking in comparative contexts: Public managers in the USA and the UK. *Public Administration Review* 9 (3), 401–420; and Authors' formulations 2012.

[a] See Edwin Hollander (1993). Legitimacy, power, and influence: A perspective on relational features of leadership. In *Leadership Theory and Research: Perspectives and Directions*, M.M. Chemers and R. Ayman (eds.). San Diego, CA: Academic Press, pp. 29–47.
[b] See Fiedler, F. (1967). *A Theory of Leadership Effectiveness*. New York: McGraw-Hill.
[c] See Kouzes and Posner (1987). *The Leadership Challenge*. San Francisco, CA: Jossey-Bass.
[d] See Warren G. Bennis (1969). Post-bureaucratic leadership. *Society* 6 (9), 44–52.

power, jobs, and access—throughout the system. In Trinidad and Tobago, racial overtones in politics and public administration were proven to have an impact on the distribution of public sector jobs (Bissessar 2003c). During the years 1956–1986, the African segment dominated politics and public administration leading to constant complaints from the Indian segment about discrimination. In 1994, the Centre for Ethnic Studies found that Indians only occupied 35.6% of top positions in the public sector, while Africans accounted for 64.4%. These criteria are also assumed to influence how other transactions of state, including conflict resolution and the administration of justice are mediated and resolved. Perhaps the most far-reaching implications of these orientations include threats to the legitimacy of the political process in general and of public sector leadership in particular. This has heightened public intolerance of leadership mistakes as well as confirming its "class" tone/orientation.

The next major contextual perspective is dominance of middle-class administrative leadership professionals. In the main, they tend to evidence predilections to be insecure, imitative rather than innovative, and are beset by self-doubt (Jones 1992). Yet, the modern reform movement that has taken root across the region has not completely mitigated or displaced these tendencies. But many other issues are involved. Dominance of middle-class administrative leadership continues to encourage exclusion of many citizens from public service production and so, hints at poor governance. Additionally, there is the observed tendency whereby certain middle-class professionals oppose direct recruitment of top leaders from the private sector (a view concretized via membership on certain Public Services Commission). This fear of competition from "outside" partly explains the continuing commitment to bureaucratic routine among elements in the public leadership cadre. Partly too, what makes this especially significant is the tendency to weaken succession of the cohort of new leaders who could bring creativity to the public service. Too, regional attempts to practice elements of the NPM have tended to encourage top-down policy leadership. Further, these trends suggest that public executives have not fully internalized the basic idea that effective public management requires that leadership must be developed at all levels of the public organization. Moreover, the class tone of administrative leadership suggests that the system would rely for change mainly on crisis-induced or coercive agents.

The Caribbean contextual situation of institutional and cultural complexity, dominance of middle-class leadership, tentative reform-minded public bureaucracies, and poverty and excess social demands have arguably been the catalysts toward hybrid institutional systems and unstable leadership styles. One example is the apparently easy coexistence of vastly different institutional forms such as post-bureaucratic type (executive agencies) and colonial-type structures like some unreformed, preexisting ministries. On another level, the reform movement has left in its wake opportunities for competition among various leadership styles, ranging from the conservative-colonial to transformational-entrepreneurial and networked forms. Natural by-products of such patterns include fluidity of administrative styles; weak impulses to cooperate in joined-up governance enterprises; and persistent patterns of tensions, conflicts, and ambiguity in operational administration (see Table 10.2). Public reports and inquiries have identified these leadership and structural characteristics (Nettleford 1992; Bissessar 2002, 2003a; Jones and Schoburgh 2004).

The research question sustaining this enquiry partly concerns the role of public sector leadership in the Caribbean. It has emerged from the discussion immediately above that a major theoretical and empirical challenge concerns how the phenomenon of *hybridization* is interpreted and managed. A brief perspective will suffice.

Theorizing Hybridization

Hybrid models rely on different ideas about handling dynamic situations. Hybridization as used in this chapter exploits the dynamics of the system to both adapt and adopt as well as to exercise control through the intervention of political and administrative leaders. It is a dialectical process described in several ways. Thus according to certain analytical perspectives, hybridization may be conceptualized as a process of "combining contradictory" imperatives, as the search for "functional equivalents," as well as systems that embrace both "continuous and discrete elements," that is to say, elements that change in different ways and those that represent a different mode/system. But perhaps the most developed part of the hybridization thesis broadly associates it with interpretations and responses of leaders to "institutional logics on the organisational field as well as other societal levels" (Westenholz 2011, 2). At the organizational level, the interpretations and responses may yield five distinct patterns or logics. They are "*resistance* to new logics; replacement of an old logic for a new one; *co-existence* of old and new logics; *competition* between old and new logics; and, finally, *hybridization* of old and new logics" (Westenholz 2011, 1). This conceptualization provides a partial framework for modeling the Caribbean leadership culture.

Section "Experiences and Narratives of Caribbean Public Sector Leadership" points to a few dominant tendencies in defining hybrid frames. First, the hybridization process is strongly driven by external inspiration, rooted in adaptations of NPM doctrines. The experiment with executive agencies constitutes an important piece of evidence (Davis 2001). A second trend is evidenced in the apparent peaceful coexistence of several competing "organizational logics" so to speak. In such hybridization framework, none of the organizational logics is necessarily compromised or dispensed with. Nor does this framework ensure coherence in administrative style or action. Perhaps it rather explains the slow emergence or absence of a strong, competent leadership corps, with progressive worldview across the regional public services (Jones and Schoburgh 2004). Third, a long-standing intellectual tradition in the Commonwealth Caribbean often "explains" leadership resistance to new institutional logics in terms of past colonial conditioning. That is now in tension with strong impulses generated by the new post-colonial or "external inspiration."

Table 10.2 Profile of Caribbean "Institutional Complexity"

Bureaucratic/ National	Extra-Bureaucratic/ National	Regional/Cross-Border	Non-Governmental/Transnational	Leadership Tendencies/ Characteristics
The network of: • Public Sector Ministries • Statutory Bodies, and Agencies	• State-Owned Enterprises • Special Advisors • Commissions of Inquiry • Public Services Commissions • Planning Institutes	• The CARICOM Institutional Network • Caribbean Development Bank	The network of International Technical Bureaucracies, for example, is given as follows: • World Bank • International Monetary Fund • International Labour Organisation • World Health Organization • USAID • DFID • CIDA	• Graduate educated • Technocratic/middle class • Well-traveled • Conservatively proactive • High connectivity • Impatient with national agenda • Pre-occupied with global agendas over national fit

Source: Originated by Authors 2013.

So today's politico-administrative leadership is under pressure from many sources to combine old/new and sometimes contradictory imperatives in their reform models. That has tended to guarantee the continuing growth of hybrid leadership styles within hybrid institutional frameworks.

At least four patterns or variants of the Caribbean leadership problems are enveloped in the discussion here and beyond. First, the collaborative or collective or networked governance styles of leadership implied by the NPL framework (Moore 1995; Brookes and Grint 2011) has been halting and slow to take cultural roots or become habits in Caribbean leadership circles. Underlying forces of low trust, poor inter-organizational communication, and politico-administrative opportunism are potent explanations.

Arguably, a second major issue that besets the regional leadership universe is observed as its ambiguity toward the delivery of public goods. Partly, this is a result of severe resource constraints. Partly too, it is a result of under-coordination between national and local levels of government as well as in cross-border transactions. Partly also, it is for the reason of politics that moves the content and pace of delivery according to the laws and motions of electoral cycles. In short, the delivery of public goods and services is strongly politicized. Such situations also help to explain weak or lopsided leadership potential to coherently generate "new knowledge" (Moore 1995) attuned to the complexities of the politicized context, well known for its wicked problems of underdevelopment.

Our third contention rests on assumptions that the regional leadership problems are rooted in reliance on varied and conflicting sources of administrative "advice," on top-down and self-regarding systems of management "controls," and on "performance" regimes recognizable for defaults in creating public value. The prevalence of these and other besetting sins has been blamed for decline in "organizational reputation" and "learning shortfalls across" the realms of public sector leadership.

Fourth, little evidence was found to contradict the claim of weak leadership competencies to effectively work within and through complex networks or to produce and share learning experiences across the range of public organizational domains. It may be added that their new learning is mainly about improving "management" and less about "leadership." So the "new ways of thinking" that normally articulate modernizing governments and the "practice of adaptive leadership," benchmarked by Heifetz (2009), continue to lag behind desired levels. While certain authorities (e.g., Carpenter 2010) contend that a central focus of leadership should be on enhancing/maintaining organizational reputation, local counterparts have tended to depart from that advice. In practice, they undermine rather than enhance public organizational capital whose "performative, technical, procedural, and moral" components are in conflict with the association of leadership extant with corruption, failure to deliver publicly valued outcomes, politicization, short-termism, and the like. In short, prevailing leadership has evolved in the public view, from heroes into scapegoats.

We conclude then that all these contextual features of structures, challenges as well as efforts at profiling public sector leadership in the Commonwealth Caribbean region implicitly represent a search for "model building" appropriate to context. To a point, our discussion appreciates that the building blocks of effective model building are widely "dispersed in topics such as reform, ethics and management" (Van Wart 2003, 224). As such, administrative leadership is a dynamic field and invites discourses on its future. That future, we argue, will require new patterns of thinking and doing and managing. The way forward depends on how the core issues are interpreted and validated here and in Section "Experiences and Narratives of Caribbean Public Sector Leadership."

Problematizing the Leadership Experience

Within the "Experiences and Narratives of Caribbean Public Sector Leadership" section of this enquiry is a mapping of major trends and issues that define Caribbean public sector leadership extant. Powerful sociohistorical forces left a public sector leadership regime that was essentially an administering middle-class that was not managerial in the classical sense. It suffered technical and managerial incapacity, some self-doubt, and a predilection to bureaucracy. This emerging leadership cohort thus reflected narrowness and inflexibility of vision about national development as well as weak commitment to implementation.

Random observations also suggest that certain pressures continue to influence such hybrids. In this interpretation, one is the functional demands of the changing modernizing of government agenda. Those demands exert constant pressures both to engage collective leadership styles across agencies and to rely on hybrids to cope with change. Too, they are driven by impulses to "cheat" by public administrative leaders (Hood and Lodge 2006), who operate in frameworks of intractable political constraints and scarcity. Other pressures would emanate from the rather limited space available for a larger cohort of new leadership to develop and display adaptive-innovative behaviors.

More recently, there have been trends toward the democratization of public administration processes, at the behest of reform doctrines of NPM, NPL, and good governance. These trends embrace rights-based impulses and have created space for new tasks, styles, and values for public sector leadership in the Caribbean and elsewhere. The arguments were spelt out broadly along the following lines.

1. The emerging leadership culture

    In the modern era, the Caribbean public sector leadership community is recognizable for its growing professionalization and reform orientation. Yet, leadership capacity to meet specific regional situations and mitigate current constraints appears limited by contextual and other forces. Leadership systems reflecting class structures and racial relations and now diminished ideological orientation continue to constrain effective action in a context of national complexity, urgent public problems, and the need for solutions. Shortfalls in its technical capacity, ethical values, together with and willingness to cheat on public service bargains encumber the contextual ground. These characteristics have often meant cynical circulation of senior public sector leadership according to electoral cycles and regime change. Structurally, there are strong tendencies, indeed legacy, toward a leadership culture that lacks progressive worldview and coherent vision of and motivation to change, except under conditions of crisis or coercive conditionalities, and hence, pressures toward public sector reform initiatives that build leadership capital and managerial talent across the region.

2. Strengthening leadership capabilities in the twenty-first century

    Primarily external intellectual influences, growing regional cross border responsibilities, and domestic policy needs have determined the direction of building adaptive leadership capabilities in the post-colonial Caribbean states. Simultaneously, the leadership-building movement is inspired somewhat by a local sense of what is "appropriate." The collective challenge has been to bridge gaps or build technical, attitudinal, relational, technological, and other capabilities that bring solutions to real socioeconomic problems. One such set of "real problem" concerns the rate of learning among leaders, the training methodologies to which they are exposed, the retention of trained capacity, and deficits particularly in the areas of policy analysis and economic management. The leadership training machinery mainly embraces institutes within the civil service framework, a regional center for development administration, and occasional overseas training excursions. The Caribbean Centre for Development Administration (CARICAD) is a regional body devoted solely to these services. These transformation units, usually uncoordinated, provide formal and informal training experiences according to departmental and individual choice. But trainees undergo mostly technical preparation that is normally less focused on addressing the relational/team building and attitudinal needs associated with building adaptive competencies of leaders. The training methodology has not encouraged joint engagement of public and private sector leaders. Differential salary scales have discouraged meaningful schemes of leadership exchange/attachment between the public and private spheres. Nor has training and interorganizational strategy worked to stem heavy migration of skilled leaders. Nonetheless, it is the case that the leadership training regimes extant have produced several "high-flying" leaders, many of whom now populate the international (e.g., World Bank, International Monetary Fund [IMF], World Health Organization) and regional (e.g., CARICOM and Caribbean Development Bank) technical bureaucracies at the operational and strategic levels. Notable examples include Dr. Gene Leon, senior resident representative to Jamaica from the IMF; Sir Dwight Venner, governor of the Eastern Caribbean Central Bank; and Dr. Naresh Singh, director general for Strategic Planning at CIDA.

3. How is public sector leadership transformation wrought?

On offer too are basic ideas pertaining to the preparation, management, and retention of leadership talent. One suggested strategy involves reliance of coherent and comprehensive approaches that yield quick performance wins. Another recommends taming the competition between public and private sectors via better alignment of their prevailing salary structures. Further, leadership development programs should be stable, continuous, and process-driven. Moreover, policy managers are encouraged to experiment with a regional system of pooling available leadership talent to be deployed in different policy areas, across regional borders. Leadership development therefore matters. It matters particularly in challenging times when the usual tendency is to retreat from, rather than magnify investment in the development of old and new cohorts of leadership. Under whatever conditions, however, various studies suggest that leadership development strategies will be effective to the extent that they can produce at least three fundamental results—deliver a performance culture, attract and retain talent, and increase organizational agility. All would enable ability in the Caribbean and elsewhere to meet leadership challenges in the future.

The Future of Leadership in Public Administration

The future is about change. Such change, in uncertain, turbulent environment, is best managed by all stakeholders and will require responsible risk-taking. We summarize the discourse in five scenarios (Peters 2000a and 2000b, 425–436 and 29–57; Pierre 2000, 332–357; Savoie 2000, 1–26).

The twenty-first century domestic and regional public services and leadership will be confronted with increasing linkages with the external environment, with changing patterns of new demands and expectations, and with institutional and other contradictions in confronting uncertainty. These circumstances and conditions define new orientations for leaders—their training, skills-set, values, and networks.

Likewise, domestic and regional public sector institutions in the future must concentrate on programs of capacity building appropriate for the new realities. This means that managers and leaders would concentrate on skills in bargaining and negotiation rather than more conventional management, to drive public service production (Peters 2000a). They must view policy from multiple perspectives to include the outlook of other departments, parts of government, and contractors whose interest may not be all the same as theirs. Managers and leaders in the future must also develop capacity to analyze policy, to master economic management and science and technology issues. They must also insure against the effects of overregulation and the backsliding of positive features of the inherited system (e.g., the focus on professional discipline).

An alternative scenario requires the commitment of public managers and leaders in the future to govern through networks and other forms of cooperative relationships. Stronger reliance on the institutional assets of "public–private partnerships" would mean opportunities for sharing or fusing of resources, increase the sense of interdependence, and enable the diversification of efforts in providing public services (Pierre 2000). The cooperative approach would also help to enhance institutional legitimacy and further the public interest. Of course, all this would mean that the public administration system would be better placed to engage "less coercive and more cooperative instruments" to serve as administrative vehicles for political coordination (Ibid, 353).

In an uncertain future, public sector leaders must continue to confront ethical and governance challenges. Realignment with the media is one key way to handle that challenge. But to be effective, the media must become more analytical and investigative in its journalistic style. It must become more focused on scrutiny and revelations of improper official behavior. Further, it must become more aggressive in its advocacy for liberalizing freedom of information processes and other prevailing legal regimes that make investigative reporting unnecessarily costly and risky. Moreover, the media must avoid the trap of placing higher demands and expectations on public service leaders than on counterpart corporate representatives (Peters 2000b; Pierre 2000). For its part, the twenty-first-century politico-administrative class must consistently reflect ethical values, behaviors, and relationships in all their transactions. Were these realignments and conditions to be fulfilled, the public administrative system would be able to impose checks on corruption and the abuse of public power, as well as create space for better governance and ultimately economic transformation.

In order to deliver on its promise of meaningful change now and in the future, leaders must ensure that the scope and focus of the "administrative reform" agenda extant be radically adjusted. The new wave of reform that they lead must shift the dominant emphasis from the "administrative machinery" to the "elective element" or the "political side" and its leaders. Such an approach would best mirror the meaning of a comprehensive administrative reform (Peters 2000a and 2000b; Pierre 2000; Savoie 2000). As well, it would contribute to the formation of a more resilient civic view of the state and leadership of the public service. Reform models tell many stories but their principal preoccupation at this times should be focused on the "role" leaders play in realizing anticipated outcomes.

Experiences and Narratives of Caribbean Public Sector Leadership

Recognizing the Leadership Problems

Repeatedly, Caribbean public sectors have been accused of being unresponsive, change resistant, afflicted by bureaupathology, subject to political hijack, inhibited by disjointed and unclear goals, and ailing from a skills deficit (Jones 1992; Draper 2001; Gonsalves 2008). While all these factors have been true at some point in the post-independence life of bureaucracies, they do not universally obtain in silo form requiring linear treatment, but rather are asymptomatic of a larger underlying challenge of leadership. In fact, contemporary senior administrative managers are highly educated and skilled, sensitive to the task environment, and possess sophisticated exposure and experiences comparable with that of any of their counterparts in developed countries, yet they do not extract comparable results. It is arguable that these expanded contemporary skillsets and dispositions are only constrained by the exercise of leadership, or lack thereof.

While the focus of this study is on the "contemporary" challenges facing leaders, a cursory look at four inuring issues clarifies the leadership factors affecting the Anglophone Caribbean. First, the issue of small size of Caribbean island states has been offered as a limitation to transparent leadership given the view that critical decision making are "invariably performed by a very limited number of individuals" (Ryan 2001, 76). This feature tends to personalize issues, and decisions are not tabled based on generalized soundness, but on its impact to select dominant groups (Ryan 2001). Group capture of this nature is also possible at the regional level through CARICOM, The Caribbean Regional Negotiating machinery, and the Caribbean Development Bank. Caribbean political and executive leaders are well known to each other, having shared similar bonding experiences provided through the elite access to the single university serving the region up to the 1990s, reinforced by a leaning toward post-graduate training in four dominant UK-based universities. The on-campus interactions and activism provided a fertile recruitment ground for competitive party politics and senior career pathways in areas of diplomacy, law, economics, and administrative leadership. Indeed, some of the reticence to the formation of the Caribbean Court of Justice as a final appellate body (as opposed to remaining with the Privy Council in the United Kingdom) surrounds question of the court's ability to render impartial judgments, given the regions small size and the potential elitist biases in decision making.

Second, there is an age-old difference in "time perspectives" affecting leadership where it is held that "political leadership is running a 100 metre dash while the civil service leadership is running a marathon" (Draper 2001, 6). Political parties have a much shorter time horizon for implementation and effecting "winnable" changes, while the civil service is concerned with the impacts of these decisions over the long term and are far more cautious about sweeping reform.

Third, there is an ongoing tension between the political directorate and the civil service based on mistrust between them. Newly installed governments tend to view the inherited civil service class with suspicion, speculating that they are sympathetic to the outgoing government. On the other hand, change in government brings a high degree of anxiety to civil servants, as they are unsure of what positional changes will occur. This is more pronounced in racially divided territories like Trinidad and Guyana (Draper 2001; Ryan 2001).

Finally, the effectiveness of both leadership groups is constrained by a general lack of clear developmental and organizational goals, implementation methodology, and stylistic differences between the administrative and political leadership. However, with the maturation of the civil service, the advanced exposure and training of these technocrats, growing attention is placed on the need for strong "administrative" leadership to arise and play a more crucial role in the events that are shaping the social and economic destinies of Caribbean nations, given the transitory nature of politics and the well-known gaps that have emerged in public sectors.

Along with those long-standing challenges, central policy issues that now face the region include managing scarce resources, creating cohesive and increasingly complex policy frameworks, effective public sector reform, and utilizing information communication technology (ICT) at the national levels, as well as managing CARICOM implementation at the regional level inter alia. These all require public sector managers to strengthen their leadership capacities to effectively navigate the current operating environment. A general typology of leadership lists up to 10 or more character traits*, some of which espouse more archaic values that no longer obtain. The more popular are calls for a transformational type leader to initiate the changes within and around the public sector, while others prefer a leader who can just get things done, possessing a transactional disposition.

---

* Types of leaders include bureaucratic, autocratic, charismatic, democratic, laissez-fair, people-oriented, task-oriented, servant, transformation, environment, transaction. See: Weber (1905); Lewin et al. (1939); Fiedler (1967); Greenleaf (1977); Burns (1978); Carmazzi (2005).

Recognizing the dynamism and challenges of the operating environment, there is a high degree of contextual relevance of the leadership qualities needed. Rather than adhering to specific leadership typologies, PSM leadership, more now than ever, calls on a "collection" of skills and competencies that may be appropriate in some circumstances, while in others it may be insufficient. To successfully evince solid results, PSM leadership should resist the boundaries of adhering too closely to any one established leadership style, but rather should be astute, flexible, and creative in the selection of approaches congruent with context.

Contextualizing Contemporary Caribbean Leadership

Against the backdrop of rapid changes while attempting to "catch up" with the development trajectory of long established bureaucracies, the role and the manner in which governments interact with its publics have changed. So too should the internal and external management of these relationships change. This is reinforced by three interrelated defining trends: (1) globalization, (2) the push toward democracy with an emphasis on the values of good governance and participation, and (3) The NPM agenda.

1. Globalization
   The effects of globalization illustrated through Appadurai's (2000) five scapes capture the intertwining of the operating environments across nation states, as being the persistent push of "people" (cultural), "ideas" (social and political), and "finance" (currency, financial, and trade arrangements) through "technology" and "media." This has a profound and direct role in shaping the way leaders operate within the region. Being a small set of islands with very open economies and somewhat dependent on external aid, we are highly vulnerable to these push factors. The IMF, United Nations, World Bank, EuroAid, USAID, CIDA, and other agencies have a strong presence in the region and seldom does international aid come without support for their own economic, cultural, or political agendas, despite their appearance as benevolent agencies, and irrespective of the conflicts they may pose to recipient states (Faini and Grilli 2004; Dreher and Jensen 2007). For example, the devastating impact of the wholesale adoption of IMF policies on countries' economies across the region during the 1970s and 1980s is well documented (Easterly 2000) and failed to produce the long-term benefits that were expected (Witter 2012). In other cases, the international agencies are more concerned with what is deemed to be human rights and cultural issues that touch on moral and ethical values held sacrosanct in the state. Issues of abortion, the death penalty, and homosexuality are high on the priority of these agencies and are also areas of policy that Caribbean states have strong views on. The ideo and media scapes facilitate externally driven scrutiny and interference while simultaneously internally increase the appetite of Caribbean nationals for the lifestyles, administrative and legal systems of developed Western economies. Leadership has to therefore play a balancing act of managing the interests of the nation against the interests of external forces and benefactors and satisfying expectations optimally while mitigating the losses associated with politically and culturally costly reforms.
2. Democracy, Good Governance, and Participation
   The ideal of good governance and democracy is widely upheld in the Caribbean context and is evident by the long tradition of democratic elections and administrative changeovers. Today however, leaders are required to engage in an unprecedented level of public dialogue and consultations with a multiplicity of stakeholders. These trends have also been deepened by the growth in importance and involvement of nongovernment organizations and grassroots movements in the facilitation and provision of public goods and services. The "new players"

are now more inclined to demand to have their voice heard regarding national socioeconomic policies and include "human rights groups and agencies, grassroots organisations, women's associations, youth organisations, child protection organisations, indigenous peoples' representatives, environmental movements, farmers organisations, consumer associations, religious organisations and the media" (Mayer 2006, 236). Local governments are also being given special recognition as new players. Governments in these times of constraints rely on these less formal institutions to deliver the services that they are unable to. The changing structure of the government and entrance of these actors has also led to a lapse of governance given the absence of clearly defined relationships between the different sectors (Commonwealth Secretariat 2004). There is also lack of incentive for political parties to push for the improved democratic governance due to the *modus operandi* of political adversary, intolerance, and little consideration for the opposition in decision making (Ryan 1989).

3. NPM Movement

    The NPM movement promulgated by the United Kingdom and embraced by the British Commonwealth provides a normative frame for the modernization and efficacy of bureaucracies. This was particularly attractive to the Caribbean as a harbinger of quick developmental fixes, particularly to the problem of the highly centralized and unresponsive structure of the traditional political administration, and has been embraced with much gusto throughout the region. This embrace resulted broadly in the attempts at decentralization of power within the public sector over the last 20 to 30 years. The NPM agenda in tandem with the democracy/governance/participatory push has redefined the relationship between governments and beneficiaries/users and promoted with varying degrees of success, a customer service-oriented public sector through the devolution of power and greater autonomy of departments and managers. In Jamaica, the creation of executive agencies with chief executive officers and introduction of public service contracts were the ultimate manifestations and most successful examples of this development. This push calls for a reorientation in structure, thinking, and approach, allowing the market an increased role in essential services provision, while simultaneously importing private sector honed expertise at senior levels to the civil service. The resultant clash in cultures (private sector vs. civil service ethos), organization misalignment, and intra-institutional jealousies again point to leadership deficits in steering a transformational agenda replete with broad cogency.

Twenty-First Century Leadership Challenges

Leading the public service now means not only having to lead civil servants, but also to direct a plethora of individuals and organizations through strategic alliancing, information sharing, negotiation, and cooperation while navigating an always changing environment. Regular skills that were needed to follow protocol are now insufficient and a pool of talent has to be sourced or created to fulfill the demand leadership within the context of competing interests. From these contextual realities, and through a fluid mix of styles, skills, and attributes, the leadership of Caribbean civil services must now strategize to

1. manage scarcity, a demanding clientele and bargaining with international networks;
2. manage internal and national talents through industrial relations;
3. manage the process of the transformation agenda; and
4. develop and execute a supportive (and joined up where possible) policy framework (see Table 10.3).

Table 10.3 Context-Specific Leadership Skills and Orientations

Context	Leadership Skills	Orientation	Constituents
Managing Scarcity Bargaining with International Networks	Dispassionate and practical, brave, innovative, analytical, effective communicators, empathetic team oriented, inspirational, accessible Consultative, analytical, research oriented, communication, technical Global awareness	Charismatic, task oriented, shared responsibility	Civil society Political hierarchy Media Communities Garrisons Governments, ITBs, private sector
Talent Management	Nurturing/empowering/mentoring Approachable/fair delegating, communication and feedback Organizing, disputes resolution, results driven	People oriented	Labor unions Universities and colleges Internal staff hierarchy
Transformation Agenda	Visionary, communication Analytical, creative, problem solver, tactical	Transformational	Labor unions Political hierarchy
Policy Development & Management	Logical and sequential, detailed, research oriented, consultative, technical, trans-departmental visioning	Bureaucratic, task oriented	Internal ministries and departments General publics

Source: Originated by Authors 2013.

Manage Scarcity and a Demanding Clientele

Relative to other small islands at similar socioeconomic positions during the 1960s and 1970s when the region gained independence, the Caribbean has not performed very well. The Caribbean struggles with high debt, low productivity, and vulnerability to external shocks (Hornbeck 2008; CCMF 2012). The 2008 global economic crisis, which reversed the small fortunes of many states and forced several governments to once again turn to the IMF for support, compounded these issues. Leadership in the face of this unprecedented global and local economic climate is required to make hard decisions. In the case of Jamaica, it could be said that a lack of bold leadership has brought us to this position and that structural reforms regarding privatization, policy implementation, bargaining, and fiscal spending were neglected until they became absolutely unsustainable. Jamaica in 2013 with a debt to gross domestic product ratio of over 120% and a swiftly devaluing dollar pegged their ability to avert economic chaos on an IMF agreement, which stalled primarily from the lack of implementation of hard cost containment mechanisms. How then does Jamaica juxtapose fiscal restraint against the political promise and social necessity of free education or free health care? What about injections required to fix an ailing justice system in the face of spiraling crime and rights-based activism, which has taken the country to task at the International Courts of Justice for civil rights infractions? How do regional governments balance national trade requirements versus regional CARICOM directions? Increasingly empowered constituents are demanding the emergence of a complex and dynamic public sector to work across department barriers in home states, across regional barriers in CARICOM and in collaboration with private interest and civil society (Box 10.1).

BOX 10.1 AIR JAMAICA: A LACK OF LEADERSHIP?

Air Jamaica was the national carrier for Jamaica, providing flights to North America, the Caribbean, and Europe from 1968 to 2010. In 1980, the airline became fully state owned and operated and maintained its excellent record for safety, in-flight service, and hospitality, but struggled with habitual lateness, overstaffing, and undercapitalization. Unprofitable and suffering from high oil prices, the Jamaican government opted for partial privatization and sold the airline to the Butch Stewart led Air Jamaica Acquisition Group (AJAG) in 1994. The AJAG in the face of emerging budget brands, and reduced in-flight service globally, revitalized Air Jamaica, through expanded routes, complimentary chef created meal services, and re-energized loyalty among the diaspora. This continued the dominance of Air Jamaica in the World Travel awards competition as the best Caribbean airline and secured the coveted award as the world's best innovative brand in 2007. Despite ardent efforts of the AJAG, the international environment and the catastrophic events of 9/11 ensured that the airline never became profitable racking up losses that averaged US$67 million per year over the 10-year period of private ownership (*Jamaica Observer* 2011).

These circumstances precipitated the return of the airline (together with its debt portfolio) to the Government of Jamaica in 2004, leading to accelerated losses over the next five and a half years amounting to US$900 million. Ignoring public and private sector calls to make a pragmatic decision (Myers 2007), these losses were allowed to persist due to minimal managerial scrutiny as well as the assumption that the economic benefit to the country outweighed its losses (Chung 2004). Jamaicans home and abroad are extremely proud of and loyal to the Air Jamaica brand, and closing the operations was not a popular option. It was only as a precondition to conclude a desperately needed IMF deal that a firm decision to finally divest the airline was tabled in 2009. In the 42 years of operation, the airline recorded losses for 40 years and as of March 2010 had a total debt of US$1.54 billion (International Finance Corporation 2011). Not until the avoidance of economic cataclysm rested on the jettisoning of this loss-making entity did economic sense prevail over nationalism and political expediency. In April 2010, the transfer of Air Jamaica to Trinidad-owned Caribbean Airlines was complete, with the Jamaican government acquiring a 16% share in Caribbean Airlines.

FOOD FOR THOUGHT:

Is this an example of poor administrative or political leadership?
What deficits in skillsets if any, does this highlight?
What recommendations would you make to the Government of Jamaica regarding the handling of the airline?
Is there value in national pride over financial prudence?
What messaging should leadership transmit?

At the national level, this signals what Jones and Cruikshank (2005) refer to as the partnership approach. This new paradigm is also described by Stoker (1998) as involving multiple agencies partnering together resulting in the public and private sectors sharing responsibility and increasingly relying on each other for power as a unitary actor as well as the creation of self-regulating practices and the utilization of new methods and tools. No longer can governments leave negotiations with the public to the electoral process of every 4 years, but are required to engage with interest groups across sectors on a continuous basis.

The results however were usually mixed with new problems being created. In particular, there was a blurring of the lines of responsibility and accountability as the responsibility for decision making was pushed further down the line of hierarchy while formal accountability remained at the very top. This arrangement has been recognized to impede on accountability and fiscal oversight (Osborne and Gaebler 1992) and increased conflicts between the implementing staff and the decision makers due to diverging interpretations of mandates and instructions (Commonwealth Secretariat 2004). It shifts leadership from the autocratic styles associated with benevolent bureaucracies to an inclusive, facilitatory even conciliatory leadership style that seats nongovernment actors at the negotiation and management tables. The leader in this dispensation cannot hoard information, must be visible and accessible, and must be astute enough to create new power-sharing structures that clearly redress accountability deficits, while remaining within the confines of the evolving bureaucracy. This leader requires charisma and bargaining skills, must be comfortable with the media, and must be prepared to lead by example.

Manage Internal and National Talents through Industrial Relations

Talent management offers tremendous benefits to the civil service as a method to identify and nurture future leaders, imbued with the values and skills necessary for them to successfully contribute to the organization's health. The practice of mobility through the ranks is in keeping with the one dimension of talent management; however, the other required dimension of mentorship is either underdeveloped or not maintained. For instance, the early Civil Service Cadet in Jamaica was off to the right start when it systematically identified young bright talent earmarked for managerial posts and ensured wide rigorous training and exposure before settling them into assigned posts. Many of the early permanent secretary and ambassadorial ranks emerged from this process and served Jamaica with a high degree of distinction. However, the failure of this system was most evident in the changing of batons with the discontinuation of the rounded apprenticeship for post-1970s recruits. Instead, future human resource investments resided in training institutes such as the Management Institute for National Development (MIND), the UWI's Public Sector Management Programme at both the undergraduate and master's levels, together with the practice of recruiting talent from the private sector. Over time, these avenues for development replaced the cadet program. Notwithstanding the tremendous benefits that can and have accrued from the formal training process, there are many lessons to be drawn from the deficits in the post-cadet experience. Good leadership "requires" talent identification and mentorship. This combined with delegation of authority and responsibility, information sharing, gathering advice, and allowing for participation in the decision-making processes are the hallmarks of a confident leader. Leaders are required to unlock the potential of their mentees, empowering them with the requisite experience, confidence, and hands-on skills to successfully transition to management.

Industrial union relations have also been an area where capable leadership has the potential to resolve many long-standing issues in Caribbean public sectors. The relationship between the government and unions over the past three decades has fluctuated significantly from the historical militant and adversarial posture adopted by unions who often allied with political forces to influence public policy and industrial negotiations (Goolsarran 2006) to a period of emasculation in the 1980s of no negotiations as an offshoot of free-market ideology and International Technical Bureaucracies (ITB) conditionalities (Stone 1987). Within the last decade however, there has been a growing defiance resulting in strike actions even in sacrosanct essential services, which according to Jamaican Law is an illegal act. In 2006, a record 227 industrial disputes resulted in action being taken, and with it, a growing concern for the lack of respect for procedures and the way leadership might be instigating these actions have been recorded in the media (Kirklady 2006). An adversarial approach, still predicated on the idea that militancy and strong stances are the best ways to getting favorable outcomes, has dominated the wage negotiation scene and affected the national productivity. Similar encounters have been recorded in Trinidad and Tobago and to a lesser extent Barbados, where it is the unfamiliarity of foreign private investors to Barbadian labor practices that disrupts the generally smooth state of affairs (Barbados Workers' Union 2008). Head of the Hugh Lawson Shearer Trade Union Education Institute in Jamaica, Danny Roberts describes labor relations as replete with force and threat when ideally there should be an interest-based form of collective bargaining that takes into account the nation's economic position (*The Gleaner* 2012).

The main challenge of Caribbean states then is the reformation of the bargaining system toward a more consensual model where mutual gains are possible and partnerships play a central role (Mulvey 2006) particularly in relation to wage disputes, and the need to "right size" the civil service. These experiences have ushered in calls for a new type of leadership and approaches. One approach where expectations have been raised is in the area of Social Partnerships. These call for increased cooperation between the government, the private sector and labor to work together on addressing the nation's long-term and immediate problems (Minto-Coy 2011). While attempted in Jamaica, it is the experience in Barbados that provides an example of successful implementation through leadership. This facilitated an increase in the level of trust within the country impacting positively on the growth and development accomplishments (Minto-Coy 2011). Described as a "tidal wave," spanning both the private and public sectors, joint ownership of the development process is the key to an "open, co-operative, consultative and participative" social contract (Mulvey 2006, 146). Partnership committees in his opinion must show "acceptance by senior managers/policy makers to treating staff as stakeholders and, therefore, adequate consideration of their views in the context of all major decisions affecting their work and livelihood" (Mulvey 2006, 147). The complexity and difficulty in executing a partnership describes the partnership as "… akin to a marriage contract and less related to a sound business undertaking, because of the extreme emotional investments and seemingly irrational expectations that are involved" (Osei 2004, 36).

The Jamaican experience offers an example of what can occur when leadership fails to take the rein on a situation and adequately facilitate a process of change. Notwithstanding the mistakes made, the economic think tank Caribbean Policy Research Institute (CaPRI) still advocates for a reengagement of the Social Partnership in Jamaica but argues that this time, strong leadership from the top should chair the initiative and lend credibility to the process (CaPRI 2009). Minto-Coy (2011) describes credible leadership as one that would be willing to sacrifice political capital for the benefit of the nation. Leaders are being called to be forthright, creative, and open to partnerships, while displaying respect for staff as stakeholders in the process.

Manage the Process of the Transformation Agenda

Public sector reform has remained a vexatious issue across the Caribbean, associated with the loss of jobs for those within the service, while viewed as a necessity to eliminate a wasteful bloated service by those in the private sectors. There is a general misalignment of objectives and expectations across sectors, leading to a high degree of mistrust, speculation, and lack of support for reform initiatives. A CaPRI (2011) report on public sector reform in Jamaica found that in the countries where reform was most successful, it was done at a quick pace, as opposed to a piecemeal method, and decisive committed leadership is important to fulfill these plans within a suitable time frame. Critically, the report revealed that "political leadership needs to be transparent, possessing an ability to understand and communicate the reform agenda to constituents as well as posses a willingness to expose itself, even if this means risking the ultimate price for freedom—electoral defeat" (2011, 59). In these cases, leadership is called to be convinced of the need for change. Weak government has been blamed for much of the development woes in the Commonwealth Caribbean and still is an issue to be dealt with. The report also places emphasis on the civil service leadership as one that must be stead fast in the ethical and moral ways of conducting its business with a full knowledge of the law, legislation, and protocols. Individuals called to lead change must be able to align ministers and other peers with protocol in a nonconfrontational manner. This person or group is also to serve as "boundary-crosser" (CaPRI 2011, 59), able to garner support from various factions within the public sector, and hence must be a strong communicator of the vision of the program. Carlton Davis and Gordon Draper are considered two such individuals that presided over public sector reform in Jamaica and Trinidad and Tobago, respectively.

The emphasis on transformation however evinces imagery of the totality in operational and cultural change and requires an even stronger leadership skillset than that advocated for the normal reformation process. A "transformational leader" is described as one that raises the level of morality and inspires a spiritual commitment to whatever cause they are leading (Burns 1978). Patricia Sinclair-McCalla, the head of the Public Sector Transformation Unit in Jamaica, recently argued that transformation requires bold and decisive leadership as the way to push through the necessary changes that her unit recommended. According to McCalla (2011, 2), they will need to be "bold, courageous and principled with unassailable integrity" and that this kind of leader can be developed through training and experience.

Develop and Execute a Supportive (and Joined Up Where Possible) Policy Framework

The commitment to modernization through ICT is evident in the establishment of permanent bodies such as Central Information Technology Office in Jamaica, the Central Information Management Office in Barbados, and the Government Information Technology Centre in Antigua and Barbuda. However, the changing demands of technology at both regional and national levels require specific leadership skillset necessary to manage the government's strategy for e-government, information sharing, and national development beyond that of mere technological competence. Nguyen (2008) points out that while in the beginning, ICT was used as an internal way of improving efficiency in the back-office; today, due to the Internet and greater demand for citizen-related services, there is a development aspect that requires the networking of government systems bringing the technical and relational demand on these offices to much higher levels. Leadership in these areas therefore needs to have both technical and interpersonal and communicative skills that generate cross-boundary relationships with high-level political individuals and break down the government bureaucracy to bring all offices in-line with requirements. General chief information officers (GCIO) are therefore better off being trained in leadership and communication skills and should be more effective after focusing on building a credible relationship with other executives through good performance. Nguyen states that the success of the GCIO is dependent on these three things: (1) their level of control over where resources are distributed; (2) how well they can align the information system with an organization's goals; and (3) how well they are at inspiring gaining acceptance and relevance among government colleagues in authority. We will add that their appreciation for seamless "end user" experience is far more critical, than the rigid adherence to process and back office utility.

Building Leadership Capabilities/Competencies for the Twenty-First Century

The private sector has long recognized the importance of leadership in fostering innovation and entrepreneurship, but only recently have these themes been transplanted to the public sectors through the restructuring of work relationships and changing context of governance. Managerialism and entrepreneurship (through NPM) has placed leadership squarely on the syllabus of several training institutions, but the concept is so contextual that leadership training has to be carefully tailored to fit the specific issues and environments in which they are needed. Several institutions in the Caribbean are dedicated to the building of public sector leadership capacity. For example, from as early as 1979, the CARICAD headquartered in Barbados is charged with meeting this challenge. On a national level, the Ministry of the Public Service in Trinidad and Tobago is responsible for training through their Public Service Academy and hosts a "Leadership in the 21st Century" course in conjunction with Harvard University. Jamaica combined its public service training programs and created the MIND, a 30-year-old institution with a stated emphasis on management and leadership.

In addressing doubts over whether leaders can be created or if they are born, The World Leadership Survey (Gentry et al. 2012) revealed that of the 361 executives interviewed only about 19% of respondents believed that leaders are born while 52% believed they were made. Of those who thought leaders were made, 46% claimed that it is the experiences of the leader that are most important in refining leadership skills.

The study corroborates the evidence supplied by the Cadet experience and holds some key insights into how regional training programs can be geared toward identifying and developing talent, taking into account experiences as critical components to leadership outcomes. Kotter (2010) noted that companies that are successful at developing leaders create challenging opportunities for their young employees and push responsibility further down the hierarchy. Draper (2001) recognizes the need for this kind of skill development within the Caribbean; however, Jones and Cruickshank (2005) caution that leadership training is equally essential as are experiences, as "Commitment to tasks, challenges and underlying problem solving philosophy is unlikely to yield expected outcomes without the support of a reform programme that encompasses formal leadership training." The authors argue that leadership training should seek to imbue ethical values as well as focus on "relational issues and motivating leaders to act as servants within a decentralized governance framework" (2005, 119).

Conclusion

There is a tendency to look at leadership as a static timeless quality. In the Caribbean, the hero and statesman have served us well, but the times have changed and so must our institutions and leaders along with it. The radical battles of ideology and civil rights are anachronisms in our society.

Today, there is a wide acceptance of fundamental human rights and the need to work together. A new politic has emerged, and the demand for a transformed public service has gained heavy traction requiring a variegated approach to leadership.

What now needs to be done is to align leadership capabilities and competencies with the areas that need them the most. A discussion was made in this paper centering on just a few areas, and overall a constant theme emerged about a new Caribbean leader. This new leader is not narrowly confined to the structures and environment within the civil service, but has to work across borders to inspire and create a vision for all people delineated by a spectrum of differences and interests. It is within this context that the leader must exact results.

Finally, the problem needs to be addressed at the regional level. We summarize, in four sequences, a menu of roles and leadership-renewal strategies defined alike for the contemporary Jamaican (Harris 2010) and wider Caribbean politico-administrative sector. They are recommendations that may be applicable for enabling a more "competitive and a brighter future" for the regional community given as follows:

1. Fabricating new patterns of leadership formation and habits
   The role of leadership to be established must emerge as a function of the region's situation and needs and the current style and aspirations of the leadership pool extant. Evidently needed across the region is a new leadership regime that is "professional, skilled, competent, wise, and forceful." This means in practice that it must be visionary, pragmatic, innovative, and results-based. Specifically, it must be able to exercise technical power to mobilize support across a wider range of stakeholders for the Caribbean development vision. In the circumstances, it must also be bold and confident enough to give direction, inclusive, track implementation, and discipline slackers and under performers. It is crucial too that technical power is used to secure "a proper balance in the mix of policies being pursued."
2. Strengthening technical and administrative capacity through talent management
   Throughout the regional space, more attention must be given to the capacitation and rejuvenation of human resources especially that located at the top of the public sector. The problem of unimaginative allocation and use of the best talent in the system must be fixed. Barriers to labor mobility within the region need to be broken down. Purposefully tapping into the talent pool of the diaspora is an underused capacitation strategy. Retention of the practice whereby certain executives/directors/governors are allowed to "own" their posts for decades clearly embodies avoidable downside risks. The prevailing practice tends to exclude/frustrate many aspiring, younger talents and encourages their migration from the national and regional systems. CARICAD and the regional training opportunities being provided by our international partners are potential first steps. A rigorous cross border exchange program of senior civil servants could be implemented to facilitate skills sharing and knowledge transfers and would provide a deepened understanding of integration needs and limitations.
3. Benchmarking the best
   This public sector jurisdiction appears to suffer insufficient study, reflection, or adaptation of what other countries are "doing well" in the public sector leadership development game. A vast literature on the theme informs, in part, that the politico-administrative leaders are good managers of their organizations. They anaesthetize against corruption. They embody the public conscience and surround themselves with teams of skilled professionals. Evident in their practice is willingness to draw ideas from government, business, universities, and other productive institutions. Usually, they evince a collaborative and collegial style. All of which factors can have transformative effects in the Caribbean.

4. Relying less on "paper qualifications"

    Region wide, there is a growing tendency—partly catalyzed by economic globalization and public sector tends to downsize—to attract some highly qualified candidates who lack the spirit and values of public service. So it is not the paper qualification that counts in the political or administrative realm. It has been asserted in the research narratives that some "over-qualified" candidates are more likely to grandstand and resist change options they themselves do not propose. This is by no means an argument against the recruitment of qualified people to the public leadership ranks, but rather to ensure appropriate orientation and mentorship upon their entry to that domain. The evidence suggests that leaders can be made through experiences and perhaps even a generous inheritance of the right traits. It is for the Caribbean countries to design adequate recruitment methods that will increase the likelihood of gaining leadership talent so badly needed in the public sector and nurturing those to achieve their highest potentials. There is an important part to be played by training institutions that already have a long history of providing the region with administrative skills. It may now be time to refocus the vision toward combining new recruitment techniques with a stable and continuous leadership development program inclusive of job rotation and understudy.

Bibliography

Appadurai, A. (2000). *Modernity at Large: Cultural Dimensions of Globalization.* Minneapolis, MN: University of Minnesota Press.

Barbados Workers' Union. (2008). *Report of the Executive Council of the Barbados Worker's Union for the period September 2007 to August 2008.* St. Michael, Barbados: BWU.

Bennis, W. G. (1969). Post-bureaucratic leadership. *Society* 6 (9), 44–52.

Bissessar, A.-M. (2002). *Evaluation of the Civil Service in Barbados.* Kingston, Jamaica: Inter-American Development Bank.

Bissessar, A.-M. (2003a). *Evaluation of the Civil Service in Trinidad and Tobago.* Kingston, Jamaica: Inter-American Development Bank.

Bissessar, A.-M. (2003b). *Public Administration: Challenges of Inequality and Exclusion.* Trinidad and Tobago: International Association of Schools and Institutes of Administration.

Bissessar, A.-M. (2003c). Challenges facing senior public servants in a plural society. *Public Administration: Challenges of Inequality and Exclusion.* Miami, FL: International Association of Schools and Institutes of Administration.

Blackman, C. (2006). Economic, strategy and growth in Barbados: From colonial times to the year 2000. In *The Practice of Economic Management: A Caribbean Perspective.* Kingston, Jamaica: Ian Randle.

Brookes, S., and Grint, K. (2011). *The New Public Leadership Challenge.* State College, PA: Palgrave MacMillan.

Burns, J. (1978). *Leadership.* New York: Harper and Row Publishers Inc.

CAPAM. (2009). *Building Public Service Leadership Capacity.* Ottawa, Canada: Commonwealth Association for Public Administration and Management.

CaPRI. (2009). A New Social Partnership for Jamaica. Kingston, Jamaica: CaPRI.

CaPRI. (2011). *Towards Public Sector Reform in Jamaica: What Local and International Experiences Tell Us About Successful Public Sector Reform.* Kingston, Jamaica: Caribbean Policy Research Institute.

CARICAD. (1998). *Health Sector Reform: Management and Performance. A Policy Forum.* Port of Spain, Trinidad and Tobago: CARICAD.

Carmazzi, A. (2005). *The Directive Communication Leadership Field Manual.* Singapore: Veritas Publishing.

Carpenter, D. (2010). *Reputation and Power.* Princeton, NJ: Princeton University Press.

CCMF. (2012). *2012 Caribbean Economic Performance Report.* Caribbean Centre for Money and Finance. St. Augustine, FL: Caribbean Centre for Money and Finance.

Chung, D. (December 31, 2004). Economic benefit of Air Jamaica. *The Gleaner*. http://jamaica-gleaner.com/gleaner/20041231/financial. Accessed on March 10, 2013.

Commonwealth Secretariat. (2004). *Commonwealth Public Administration Reform*. London: Commonwealth Secretariat.

CompanyHistories.com. (2003). *Air Jamaica Company History*. Retrieved July 10, 2013, from companyhistories.com: http://www.company-histories.com/Air-Jamaica-Limited-Company-History.html.

Davis, C. (2001). Executive agencies in Jamaica: The story thus far and the central management mechanism. *Proceedings of the Conference on Executive Agencies in Action*. Kingston, Jamaica: UWI/MIND.

Delfgaauw, J., and Dur, R. (2006). *Incentives and Workers' Motivation in the Public Sector*. Amsterdam, the Netherlands: The Tinbergen Institute.

Draper, G. (2001). *The Civil Service in Latin America and the Caribbean: Situation and Future Challenges: The Caribbean Perspective*. Washington, DC: Inter-American Development Bank.

Dreher, A., and Jensen, N. (2007). An empirical analysis of the impact of US interest on International Monetary Fund conditions. *Journal of Law and Economics* 50 (1), 105–124.

Easterly, W. (2000). *The Effect of IMF and World Bank Programs on Poverty*. New York: New York University.

Faini, R., and Grilli, E. (2004). Who Runs the IFIs? In *Centro Studi Luca d'agliano* No. 191. http://dx.doi.org/10.2139/ssrn.672362. Accessed on April 13, 2015.

Fiedler, F. (1967). *A Theory of Leadership Effectiveness*. New York: McGraw-Hill.

Gentry, W., Deal, J. J., Stawiski, S., and Ruderman, M. (2012). *Are Leaders Born or Made? Perspectives from the Executive Suite*. Greensboro, NC: Center for Creative Leadership.

Gonsalves, R. (2008). *Introduction to the 1st Regional Conference of Public Service Commissions*. Report on the 1st Regional Conference of Public Service Commissions June 10–12 (p. 6). St. Vincent and the Grenadines: CARICAD.

Goolsarran, S. J. (2006). An overview of industrial relations within the context of labour administration. In S. J. Goolsarran (Ed.), *Industrial Relations in the Caribbean: Issues and Perspectives* (pp. 3–19). Port of Spain, Trinidad and Tobago: International Labour Office.

Greenleaf, R. K. (1977). *Servant leadership: A journey into the nature of legitimate power and greatness*. New York: Paulist Press.

Harris, Donald J. (2010). *Jamaica's Debt-Propelled Economy: A Failed Economic Strategy and Its Aftermath*. SALISES 50-50 Working Paper. Kingston, Jamaica.

Hart, P., and Uhr, J. (2008). *Public Leadership Perspectives and Practices*. Canberra, Australia: ANU E Press.

Heifetz, Ronald A. (2009). *The Practice of Adaptive Leadership: Tools and Tactics for Changing Your Organisation and the World*. Cambridge, MA: Harvard Business Press.

Hollander, E. (1993). Legitimacy, power, and influence: A perspective on relational features of leadership. In M. M. Chemers and R. Ayman (Eds.), *Leadership Theory and Research: Perspectives and Directions* (pp. 29–47). San Diego, CA: Academic Press.

Hood, C., and Lodge, M. (2006). *The Politics of Public Service Bargains: Reward, Competency, Loyalty—and Blame*. Oxford: Oxford University Press.

Hornbeck, J. F. (2008). *CARICOM: Challenges and Opportunities for Caribbean Integration*. US Congress. Washington, DC: Congressional Research Service.

International Finance Corporation. (2011). *Jamaica: Air Jamaica*. Washington, DC: IFC.

Jamaica Observer. (July 8, 2011). *Air Jamaica: End of an Era "The Little Piece of Jamaica That Cries."* Kingston, Jamaica: Jamaica Observer.

Jones, E. (1992). *Development Administration: Jamaican Adaptations*. Kingston, Jamaica: CARICOM Publishers.

Jones, E. (2001). Executive agencies: A manifesto against "Administrivia." *Caribbean Journal of Public Sector Management* 3 (1), 30–42.

Jones, E. (2010). Contending with local governance in Jamaica: Bold programme, cautionary tales. *Social and Economic Studies* 59 (4), 67–95.

Jones, E., and Cruickshank, I. (2005). Making the CARICOM administrative machinery work: The decentralization and leadership factor. In K. Hall and D. Benn (Eds.), *New Concepts of Regional Governance* (pp. 104–125). Kingston, Jamaica: Ian Randle.

Jones, E., and Mills, G. E. (1989). The institutional framework of government. In R. Nettleford (Ed.), *Jamaica in Independence: Essays on the Early Years*. Kingston, Jamaica: Heinemann Caribbean.

Jones, B. F., and Olken, B. A. (2005). *The Anatomy of Start Stop Growth*. Cambridge: NBER.

Jones, E., and Schoburgh, E. (2004). Deconstructing policy-making and implementation issues in a Caribbean context. *Social and Economic Studies* 53 (4), 35–61.

Kirklady, S. G. (August 27, 2006). What's wrong with industrial relations? *Jamaica Gleaner*.

Kotter, J. P. (2010). *What Leaders Really Do*. Harvard Business Review: Leadership Insights. New York: Harvard Business School Publishing.

Lalla, K. (2008). *Change and Transformation in Evolving Caribbean Model of the Public Service Commission*. Report on the 1st Regional Conference of Public Service Commissions. Saint Vincent and the Grenadines June 10–12 (pp. 58–64). Saint Vincent and the Grenadines: CARICAD.

Lane, J.-E., and Wallis, J. (2009). Strategic management and public leadership. *Public Management Review* 11 (1), 101–129.

Lewin, K., Lippitt, R., and White, R. (1939). Patterns of aggressive behavior in experimentally created social climates. *Journal of Social Psychology* 10 (2), 271–301.

Lynn, L. (1981). *Managing the Public's Business: The Job of the Government Executive*. New York: Basic Books.

Mayer, M. (2006). The role of social dialogue for social and economic progress. In S. J. Goolsarran (Ed.), *Industrial Relations in the Caribbean: Issues and Perspectives* (pp. 232–246). Port of Spain, Trinidad and Tobago: International Labour Office.

Meier, K. J., O'Toole, L. J., Boyne, G. A., and Walker, R. M. (2007). Strategic management and the performance of public organisations: Testing venerable ideas against recent theories. *Journal of Public Administration Research and Theory* 17 (3), 357–377.

Mills, G. E. (1970). Public administration in the Commonwealth Caribbean: Evolution, conflicts and challenges. *Social and Economic Studies* 19 (1), 5–25.

Mills, G. E. (1990). The English-speaking Caribbean. In V. Subramanian (Ed.), *Public Administration in the Third World: An International Handbook* (pp. 317–351). Westport, CT: Greenwood Publishing Group.

Minto-Coy, I. (2011). *Social Partnerships and Development: Implications for the Caribbean*. Ontario, Canada: Centre for International Governance Innovation.

Moore, M. (1995). *Creating Public Value: Strategic Management in Government*. Cambridge, MA: The New Public Leadership Challenge.

Mulvey, K. (2006). New approaches in public management and industrial relations. In S. J. Goolsarran (Ed.), *Industrial Relations in the Caribbean: Issues and Perspectives* (pp. 129–150). Port of Spain, Trinidad and Tobago: International Labour Office.

Myers, J. (November 30, 2007). Air Jamaica, SCJ too costly to keep, says Wehby—Senator to propose cap on debt and deficit. *The Gleaner*.

Nettleford, R. (1992). *Report of Committee of Advisors on Government Structure*. Ministry of Finance and Planning. Kingston, Jamaica: Government of Jamaica.

Nguyen, H. T. (2008). Strengthening ICT leadership in developing countries. *The Electronic Journal of Information Systems in Developing Countries* 34 (4), 1–13.

Osborne, D., and Gaebler, T. (1992). *Reinventing Government*. Reading, MA: Addison-Wesley.

Osei, P. D. (2004). Tripartite social partnerships in small states: Barbados and Jamaica in Comparative Perspective. In A. M. Bissessar (Ed.), *Globalization and Governance: Essays on the Challenges for Small States* (pp. 34–55). Jefferson, NC: McFarland and Company.

O'Toole, L., Walker, R., Meier, K., and Boyne, G. (2007). Networking in comparative contexts: Public managers in the USA and the UK. *Public Administration Review* 9 (3), 401–420.

Peters, G. (2000a). The future of reform. In B. Guy Peters and D. J. Savoie (Eds.), *Governance in the Twenty-First Century: Revitalizing the Public Service* (pp. 427–436). Montreal, QC, Canada: McGill-Queen's University Press.

Peters, G. (2000b). Globalization, Institutions, and Governance. In B. Guy Peters and D. J. Savoie (Eds.), *Governance in the Twenty-First Century: Revitalizing the Public Service* (pp. 29–57). Montreal, QC, Canada: McGill-Queen's University Press.

Pierre, J. (2000). Externalities and relationships: Rethinking the boundaries of the public services. In B. Guy Peters and D. J. Savoie (Eds.), *Governance in the Twenty-First Century: Revitalizing the Public Service* (pp. 332–357). Montreal, QC, Canada: McGill-Queen University Press.

PSTU. (2010). *Public Sector Transformation Programme Change Management Plan.* Kingston, Jamaica: Public Transformation Unit.

Rhodes, R. A. (1997). *Understanding Governance.* Buckingham: Open University Press.

Riley, B., and Nunes, M. (2004). *Public Sector Reform Programmes and Performance Management in Trinidad and Tobago.* Bridgetown, Barbados: Beresford Riley.

Ryan, S. (1989). *Revolution and Reaction: A Study of Parties and Politics in Trinidad and Tobago, 1970–1981.* St. Augustine, FL: Institute of Social and Economic Research.

Ryan, S. (2001). Democratic governance in the Anglophone Caribbean: Threats to sustainability. In B. Meeks and F. Lindahl (Eds.), *New Caribbean Thought—A Reader* (pp. 73–104), Chap. 4. Kingston, Jamaica: University of the West Indies Press.

Ryan, S. D., and Brown, D. R. (1992). *Issues and Problems in Caribbean Public Administration.* St. Augustine, FL: Institute of Social and Economic Research, UWI.

Savoie, D. (2000). Introducing the topic. In D. J. Guy Peters (Ed.), *Governance in the Twenty-First Century: Revitalizing the Public Service* (pp. 3–28). Montreal, QC, Canada: McGill-Queen's University Press.

Sinclair-McCalla, P. (2011). Speech: Transforming the Quality of Leadership in the Jamaican Public Service: Can We Cross It? Retrieved November 27, 2012, from Registrar Generals Department: http://www.rgd.gov.jm/node/751.

Smith, W. (2011). The role of leadership in the transformation of the Caribbean Development Bank. *Journal of the University College of the Cayman Islands* 5, 17–25.

Stoker, G. (1998). Governance as theory: Five proposals. *International Social Science Journal* 155, 17–28.

Stone, C. (1987). *Power and Policy Making in Jamaica.* Texas: University of Texas.

Sutton, P. (2008). *Public Sector Reform in the Commonwealth Caribbean: A Review of Recent Experiences.* Waterloo, Canada: The Centre for International Governance Innovation.

The Gleaner. (May 30, 2012). Workshop to promote public-sector collective bargaining. *The Gleaner.*

Tindigarukayo, J., and Chadwick, S. J. (1999). Civil Service Reform in Jamaica. Kingston, Jamaica: United Nations Development Programme.

Tortello, R. (December 5, 2005). History of aviation in Jamaica: Part II wings to fly. Retrieved July 10, 2013, from *Jamaica Gleaner*: http://jamaica-gleaner.com/pages/history/story0071.html.

Trottier, T., Van Wart, M., and Wang, X. (2008). Examining the nature and significance of leadership in government organisations. *Public Administration Review* 68 (2), 319–333.

UNDP. (2012). *2012 Caribbean Human Development Report.* New York: United Nations Development Programme.

Van Wart, M. (2003). Public-sector leadership theory: An assessment. *Public Administration Review* 63 (2), 214–228.

Wallis, J., and McLoughlin, L. (November 2007). A diagnosis of leadership effectiveness in the Irish public sector. *Public Management Review* 9, 327–335.

Weber, M. (1905). *The Protestant Ethic and the Spirit of Capitalism: And Other Writings.* New York: Penguin Group.

Westenholz, A. (2011). *Hybridization as an Organisational Response to Widespread Institutional Logics: A Case Study of a Commercial and Open Source Software Community.* Copenhagen Business School, Department of Organisation. Boston, MA: ABC Network.

Williams, D., and Morgan, B. (2012). *Competitiveness of Small Nations: What Matters?* Kingston, Jamaica: Arawak Publishers.

Witter, M. (July 8, 2012). Lessons from the IMF experiences. *The Gleaner*, http://jamaica-gleaner.com/gleaner/20120708/focus/focus3.html.

World Travel Awards. (2013). *Air Jamaica.* Retrieved July 2, 2013, from World Travel Awards: http://www.worldtravelawards.com/profile-30-air-jamaica.

Wynter, R. (February 5, 2012). Rebalance wage scales. *The Gleaner.*

Chapter 11

State Capacity and International Politics

Matthew Louis Bishop

Contents

The Problem of Limited Capacity 231
    Capacity Constraints Faced by Small States 232
    Constraints at the Regional Level 234
The Caribbean in the Global Arena 235
    Global Trade Politics 237
    Global Environmental Politics 239
Conclusion 240
References 241

> **Abstract:** This chapter analyzes the extent of Caribbean participation in international politics and discusses the nature of the region's engagement with the wider world. Traditionally, Caribbean countries, whether individually or collectively, have been considered as lacking the power to shape international agendas. However, they have, in fact, enjoyed periods of international prominence. By reflecting on different kinds of power—material, institutional, and relational—we develop a framework with which to offer a more nuanced and incisive analysis of Caribbean foreign relations. We then apply this to two critical contexts in which the region acts on the international stage: global trade politics and global environmental politics. Our broad conclusion is that, despite some notable successes, limited state capacity has generally led to suboptimal outcomes in both of these diplomatic arenas. The chapter concludes by suggesting how the character of Caribbean participation in international politics is likely to evolve in the future.

The conventional story regarding how Caribbean countries and territories engage in global politics is generally one which emphasizes their relative weakness, peripherality, and powerlessness to make a significant impact, either individually or collectively. There is, of course, much truth in this, and it derives from the reality of a distinct lack of institutional capacity at both the state and regional level. However, this is not the whole story. At times, Caribbean countries have enjoyed periods of international prominence, along with a series of specific successes in international diplomacy. These have often been tempered by subsequent retaliation by larger powers or an inability to enforce the gains that have, in theory, been earned. The region has also scored a number of own goals at times, meaning that some of its failures can be regarded very much as missed opportunities, whereby better outcomes could plausibly have been engendered. Nonetheless, it remains the case that, although limited state capacity is frequently a compelling explanation for the apparent lack of impact enjoyed by Caribbean countries on the international stage, the reality is also considerably more nuanced.

The purpose of this chapter, therefore, is to outline and explain this reality. It emphasizes the ways in which the organization, capacity, and strategic orientation exhibited by both public institutions and the actors which comprise them together represent a central factor in the success or otherwise of participation in international politics. Yet it also shows how such "material" factors, embedded within both the state and comparable statist institutions—for instance, regional organizations like the Caribbean Community (CARICOM)—are not solely responsible for the extent to which the region is able to profitably engage with international forces. Consequently, a view that reduces state capacity to simply the material aspects of power belies a sometimes excessively narrow "realist" mindset, to use the parlance of international relations (IR). Indeed, to really understand how small (and often very small) states approach international politics, it is important to supplement a focus on these material features with, first, "institutional" factors, meaning that the setting in which such action takes place does much to either enable or constrain particular courses of action, and, second, it is equally important to grapple with the "relational" elements of the process, meaning that the character of action is always socially embedded and constructed. Or, to put it another way, it is dependent on whom the interlocutors are, the perceptions that the different actors bring to the table about the limits of the possible (which are rarely fixed), and the ways in which each chooses to leverage the different resources that they perceive that they have at their disposal. By bringing these contextual factors into the analysis, we can therefore develop a far more holistic account that supplements the realist pre-occupation with material factors with perspectives from both liberalism, because of the focus on institutions, and social constructivism, which is concerned with ideas, perceptions, and relations (for a detailed discussion of why such an agenda is appropriate for studying small states in IR, see Neumann and Gstöhl 2006).

The chapter begins by stressing the varied capabilities of different Caribbean countries (and nonstate territories) as regards their ability to successfully participate in international politics. It then moves onto a discussion of the specific kinds of constraints that exist in the region, discerning more clearly both the relative *level* of capacity enjoyed by different states, as well as the specific *kinds* of capacity that they do, or do not, exhibit. Next, the chapter moves on to a discussion of the regional problems, setting individual state capacity within the context of regional institutions and approaches to IR. Then, the main substantive section of the chapter looks at specific instances and examples of Caribbean engagement globally. It focuses on two critical arenas: international trade politics and global climate politics, showing how, despite some notable successes, limited state capacity has generally led to suboptimal outcomes in both of these diplomatic arenas. Finally, the chapter summarizes by suggesting how the future of Caribbean participation in international politics is likely to evolve in the future.

The Problem of Limited Capacity

Limited state capacity manifests itself in a number of different ways: from deficient institutions, which do not always operate in an innovative and dynamic fashion, stymied in large measure by limited resources and the lack of qualified technocrats steering them; to broader problems with the political settlement, which, in much of the Anglophone Caribbean at least, is characterized by extremely divisive politics based on the most oppositional aspects of the so-called Westminster Model (see, e.g., Ryan 1999; Bishop 2011, 2013). More broadly, there are two structural aspects of the Caribbean condition that are generally considered to condition these broader problems: small size and the colonial legacy.

In many respects, these two factors can be seen to be intertwined: colonialism has cast a long shadow over the development of societies that are very much products of an era in which they were created entirely *de novo* by European imperialism (Lewis 2004), something which manifests itself today in a distinctive series of pathologies, including a marked dependence on international forces, regional fragmentation, insularity, and underdeveloped economies that still remain, to a significant extent, oriented toward metropolitan centers; and small size is often considered the contemporary *problématique* that frames the political, economic and social reality, and it is revealed in, again, enduring patterns of inequality vis-à-vis international forces which, as Anthony Payne and Paul Sutton (1993) noted some years ago, derive from "a syndrome of interrelated characteristics" typified most notably by "openness, islandness or enclaveness, resilience, weakness, and dependence."

Since the early 1990s, the "small-state" literature from which these ideas originate has developed considerably. A key debate has been the extent to which particular distinguishing features should be privileged over others in analysis, with numerous authors arguing that an excessive focus on the structural aspects of small-state existence has exhibited a tendency toward determinism, whereas, in reality, plenty of evidence exists to suggest that small states can be purposeful and assertive agents in their own right, regardless of their perceived limitations (see Cooper and Shaw 2009, Baldacchino and Bertram 2010). Others have even suggested that, by underscoring the perceived vulnerability of small states in the contemporary era, many thinkers working on these issues unwittingly downplay those limitations that may derive from "the existence of unequal power structures that, far from being the 'natural' result of smallness, are in fact contingent and politically contested" (Lee and Smith 2010). These include, of course, those inherited from the colonial period and its aftermath.

Regardless of where we might place ourselves in this debate, it nonetheless remains the case that small states—whether for reasons of history, intrinsic characteristics relating to size, or a mixture of both—do remain deeply vulnerable, with vulnerability representing the hegemonic way of framing issues relating to them in the literature. The problem, though, is that this concept is often misinterpreted by those who wish to emphasize the agential capacity of such states and territories. It is all too often conflated with related notions such as weakness or dependence when, in fact, it simply refers to a heightened exposure to external shocks (see Briguglio 1995, Briguglio et al. 2010). It is crucial to stress this point: vulnerability means something very specific, and it does not necessarily preclude the exercise of agency in the diplomatic arena, nor does it imply a lack of development. As Payne (2009) has more recently argued, small states do remain "genuinely characterized by a common set of core economic and social characteristics that, collectively and cumulatively, [have] defined their particular predicament." The broader intellectual issue, then, is not that small states do not often remain vulnerable, but rather that this is, on its own, an emaciated way of thinking about their predicament; because comparatively few people around the world—the vast majority of them based in universities in small states—are working on small-state issues, the theoretical canon remains rather limited. It desperately needs fleshing out with a whole range of new concepts and ideas with which to frame their reality (Bishop 2012, 2013).

Capacity Constraints Faced by Small States

For our purposes here, we need to briefly grapple with the specific kinds of capacity constraints that stem from this broad structural picture. And they are many. At the institutional level, there is little doubt that the global political economy itself is not geared toward facilitating the interests of small Caribbean states. Even though all of the independent territories of the region enjoy internationally recognized sovereignty and a seat in the United Nations (UN) General Assembly, this does not, in truth, entitle them to a great deal beyond national pride and the ability to trade small benefits from powerful members in return for votes. For the tiny Eastern Caribbean countries, for example, this has often caused them to place themselves in quite dubious political positions: Dominica, for example, has been one of Japan's few allies in supporting whaling within the International Whaling Commission; St. Lucia remains one of the diminishing number of countries to retain diplomatic links with Taiwan in favor of China, which is an ongoing bone of contention in both the country and the region at large. Such a position appears particularly contentious as Beijing itself becomes increasingly and rapidly interested in the Caribbean as a destination for investment and political engagement (Bernal 2010).

In fact, what has been more striking in recent years is the way in which Caribbean countries are often subject to the unremitting dominance of international institutions, as is represented by the various agreements that countries have signed with the International Monetary Fund (IMF). The conditions of such agreements, and the supervisory relationship that they tend to engender, often transgress the boundaries of their sovereignty; this process has only gathered pace since the global financial crisis has intensified and more countries have been forced to seek help from the IMF. Two examples, in particular, stand out. In the early 2000s, in the context of a buoyant global economy, Grenada invested significant funds in infrastructural development to support the tourism industry and other services. However, a succession of external shocks—Hurricanes Ivan and Emily in 2004 and 2005 respectively, followed by the global crisis 3 years later and a major downturn in tourist arrivals—has left the country with a debt burden well over 100% of gross domestic product, and little choice but to seek assistance from the Fund (see IMF 2014). In the case of Jamaica, successive IMF agreements over the past 20 or more years have done little to alleviate the country's economic travails, with a stagnant growth rate contributing to one of the largest debt burdens in the world (Johnston 2013). As a consequence, the country has long submitted to *de facto* supervision of its economic policy by technocrats from Washington, and today over half of government spending is devoted to simply servicing debt. The most recent agreement, signed in 2013—and worth a total of approximately US$2 billion once the contributions of lenders beyond the IMF are also factored in—looks unlikely to alter this pattern, although some are optimistic that Jamaica may be "poised for a turnaround" (Looney 2014).

Beyond the legal and financial control exerted by the IMF over many states, the realities of the distribution of power in international institutions mean that, despite official doctrines of interstate equality, small Caribbean countries are largely excluded from participating fully. An obvious example of this is the infamous "green room" of the World Trade Organization (WTO), where the most powerful actors have tended to meet behind closed doors in order to thrash out norms around policy, subsequently forcing peripheral states to submit to the supposed "consensus" (see, e.g., Steinberg 2002, Jones 2009, Higgott and Erman 2010). In the worst cases, small states are entirely and consciously prohibited from participating; the deployment of the Group of 20 (G20) as the default post-crisis meeting place for the world's most powerful states has deliberately excluded the "marginal majority" (over 150) of the world's states, and with it the voice of approximately a third of humanity, including the entire Caribbean (Payne 2010).

However, limited capacity is not only structural in nature; there are crucial agential dimensions too. One is reflected in the shape and orientation of the state itself. In the vast majority of Caribbean countries, the state is not "developmental" in the sense that it does not embody a range of institutions capable of charting, in a strategic and purposeful fashion, a considered and clear course of action when engaging with international forces (Payne and Sutton 2007). There are, of course, exceptions to this. Three countries that particularly stand out are Cuba, the Dominican Republic, and Trinidad and Tobago (T&T), all of which are relatively large states with significant amounts of human, technological, or financial capital. They have consequently been able to develop distinctive patterns and models of development, which depart in some way from the neoliberal Washington Consensus.

This can be seen clearly in the way that Cuba has consistently resisted US pressure since the 1950s, along with its more recent cultivation of strong relationships with leftist states throughout Latin America on the basis of its export of skilled people such as doctors and engineers. Regardless of the merits and demerits of the Cuban model, there is little doubt that it represents a unique, distinctive, and independent developmental experiment. Similarly, the Dominican Republic has, since the signing of the Economic Partnership Agreement (EPA) with the European Union (EU) in 2007, been by far the most successful country in the region in exploiting the arrangement and increasing its exports of sugar and other commodities to Europe in order to underpin its wide-ranging process of economic diversification (Richardson and Richardson Ngwenya 2013). Of course, not every country in the Caribbean has been able to implement—or even ratify—the EPA, and this rather proves the point; the fact that only larger, more powerful states like the Dominican Republic have been able to implement the agreement evinces the significant capacity constraints faced by many smaller countries in the region. Finally, T&T has benefitted from its productive hydrocarbon economy and the reasonably well-resourced state apparatus that this finances, along with a strong and growing economy, low public debt, and an increasingly well-resourced sovereign wealth fund. This in turn has led T&T to become increasingly influential regionally, and it is today arguably the only country in the English-speaking Caribbean that has been able to sustain, to some degree, an authentically independent foreign policy (Braveboy-Wagner 2010).

For most countries in the region, by contrast, the state is notably weaker. Indeed, in the very smallest countries, foreign policy, such as it is, is developed almost entirely within the office of the prime minister and is often characterized by little more than managing dependence. As Payne (2006) put it a few years ago, in the absence of deep and penetrating institutions, the leaders in the smaller islands have themselves "been required to take centre stage in the whole development drama." What this means is that the success or otherwise of either domestic or foreign policy largely stands or falls by the direction that is set from the center. It is consequently difficult to overstate the impact of tiny bureaucracies and limited resources on the exercise of foreign policy specifically. At the most basic level, relatively few public servants are educated beyond secondary level, a huge proportion (up to 80% or more, depending on the territory) of those educated migrate to metropolitan countries anyway, and those who remain often hold their jobs because of reasons of political patronage rather than ability (see Bishop 2013). Moreover, many institutions are themselves emaciated regardless of who staffs them. For example, the various EPA implementation units, which have been established in most Caribbean countries, with a remit to execute the enormously complicated agreement—which, it must be remembered, was signed the best part of a decade ago—have barely got off the ground in the smaller islands. Many have not even ratified the agreement, let alone commenced the process of harmonizing laws or creating the necessary governance structures to sustain it, and their implementation "units" are staffed with, at best, one or two people who are often juggling other competing priorities too (Lindsay 2013).

Furthermore, when it comes to engaging internationally, these institutional weaknesses are transposed to the global arena. Most Caribbean countries have embassies and missions in the many crucial cities in which they undertake diplomatic business: Miami, Washington, DC, New York, London, Brussels, Geneva, The Hague, Toronto, Ottawa, Montreal, Madrid, Paris, and, increasingly, newer centers like New Delhi, Brasilia, Beijing, and Caracas. However, these tend to be established unilaterally. Although it is widely recognized that Caribbean diplomats do work together, particularly in cities where critical battles take place—such as Geneva where the WTO is situated, or Brussels where much of the EPA negotiating process was undertaken—this is not institutionalized in any significant way beyond some limited experiments such as the joint Organization of Eastern Caribbean States (OECS) mission in Geneva (where the countries themselves nonetheless retain their individuality in official WTO meetings). Indeed, the principal recent example of such cooperation can actually be found in the EPA negotiations, which were undertaken under the aegis of the Caribbean Regional Negotiating Machinery (CRNM)—now renamed the Office of Trade Negotiations and subsumed fully within the CARICOM Secretariat—and this resulted in a controversial outcome, the fallout of which was extremely acrimonious (for a detailed discussion, see Bishop et al. 2013). Consequently, there are often numerous missions in a given city, all duplicating each other's work to some extent, rather than a single CARICOM or "West Indian" mission that could plausibly employ the same number of people in total, but with a much wider and deeper range of skills and therefore technical capacity. This, of course, mirrors the fragmentation and insularity that reign in the region at large, and stems in large measure from the problematic ways in which Caribbean countries were decolonized. It is to this regional dimension that we now turn.

Constraints at the Regional Level

Today, the Caribbean region is in a state of flux. Historically, CARICOM has been considered very much the default institution of regional governance; however, it currently finds itself in a long-term process of decline. There are many reasons for this. One is reflected in the problematic conception of sovereignty adopted by political leaders in individual territories following the collapse of the West Indies Federation in 1962. Even though, for many tiny states, sovereignty is essentially meaningless, it has nonetheless been jealously guarded, and, because states have been unwilling to pool it at the regional level, regional institutions have been unable to force the implementation of regional edicts, and, over time, CARICOM institutions themselves have atrophied (Bishop and Payne 2010). This is particularly so with the CARICOM Secretariat itself, which has been consistently hampered by a lack of legal and political space to effectively formulate, lead, and, crucially, implement regional agendas (see Bishop 2014). Perhaps the most striking effect of regional institutional decline is the denouement of the Caribbean Single Market and Economy (CSME). Established in 1989 with the signing of the Revised Treaty of Chaguaramas, it took 17 years—until 2006—before the first elements of the CSME came into force. As the timelines for implementation continued to slip, and the process became bogged down in the minutiae of interminable debates surrounding relatively minor issues—amid, it must be said, a stark failure of leadership, imagination, and acumen on the part of regional politicians—the political elite decided to "pause" the CSME in 2011. This has been widely interpreted as the death knell of the process, and it is unlikely that it will recommence any time soon, if ever.

Another—and perhaps more fundamental—issue is the transformative context in which Caribbean institutions are operating today. This is reflected in a number of processes of change at the regional, hemispheric, and global levels. Regionally, it is increasingly becoming clear that the high point of integration has long since passed. Countries across the whole of the Spanish-, Dutch-, English-, and French-speaking Caribbean remain fragmented in the ways that they always have done—that is to say, linguistically, culturally, and politically—but even within the Anglophone parts of the region, economic fragmentation is becoming acute as development patterns continue to diverge. Moreover, new integration arrangements—such as the Venezuelan-influenced Bolivarian Alliance for the Americas or the deepening of integration processes within the subregional OECS—are calling into question CARICOM's hegemonic status as the premier institution of regional affairs. This is further accentuated by the continuing identity crisis of CARICOM and the lack of ambition on the part of member states to envision a more expansive future for the institution, something which is reflected in the ongoing failure, after numerous requests, to consider positively the membership of the Dominican Republic and the injection of energy and capacity that this would imply (Bishop et al. 2011).

Hemispherically, the context has perhaps shifted even more dramatically: the orientation of Guyana and Suriname more closely toward Latin America, the development of new regional groupings like the Union of South American Nations and the Community of Latin American and Caribbean States, all threaten to further eclipse CARICOM and traditional patterns of integration in the Caribbean. Then, at the global level, the ongoing financial crisis, the dramatic re-envisioning of, especially, European development policy, as well as the restructuring of global trade politics along intensified neoliberal lines (through, for example, the mooted Trans-Pacific Trade Partnership), which operate outside of the multilateral process, are all posing harsh questions of Caribbean countries, to which few appear to have found any convincing answers. In short, the ground is very much shifting around the Caribbean in complex and difficult to anticipate ways. A series of major processes of structural reconfiguration are currently underway in both the hemisphere and the wider world, the outcomes of which are both far from clear and yet they pose a serious challenge to the terms on which the Caribbean engages internationally (for a more detailed discussion of these issues, see Bishop 2014). The most we can say, perhaps, is that, for the Caribbean to respond successfully, new kinds of diplomacy, which are genuinely region-wide in orientation, and which are considerably more innovative and imaginative than those which went before, will need to be discovered.

It is far from clear, though, whether this kind of creative agency can be summoned up from the limited pools of human, institutional, and political capital that exist in the region. If the Caribbean cannot, after more than two decades of trying, complete the comparatively straightforward task of implementing its own single market and economy, it remains difficult to believe that it can develop an approach that engages with the myriad global forces that are coming to press upon it.

The Caribbean in the Global Arena

For all the problems faced by Caribbean countries, and the region as a whole, there have certainly been specific examples of effective diplomacy, even if the outcomes have not been entirely satisfactory. Nonetheless, by moving the discussion on from simply the material aspects of state capacity, and consequently showing a greater degree of sensitivity to the contextual, institutional, and relational factors that we noted in the introduction to the chapter, we can develop a better appreciation of the nature of such engagement, the extent of its accomplishments—or otherwise—and the reasons why certain outcomes occurred.

Before doing so, though, it is important to make a number of conceptual points regarding the character of small-state diplomacy. If we take the classic definition of the term famously outlined by Hedley Bull in *The Anarchical Society* as "the conduct of relations between states and other entities with standing in world politics by official agents and by peaceful means" (Bull 1977), we realize very quickly that mainstream conceptions of diplomacy only partially capture the reality of how small states engage with the world. First, it is far from clear whether, in the context in which Bull was writing—when many small states had not yet been born, and the ones that had were considered little more than "irritants in international relations" (Lewis 2009)—small states would have been considered by the major powers to have anything approaching "standing." Indeed, even today, most analysis in the heartlands of realist—and, to a significant extent, liberal—accounts of IR, as well as the approaches to real-world diplomacy taken by the most influential countries themselves, pay, at best, only lip service to the needs of the smallest and least powerful. Second, it is also unlikely that diplomacy today is always only peaceful, or, at least, entirely something which takes place between equals; as many thinkers have noted, the EU's shifting relationship with the Caribbean—as well as the wider African, Caribbean, and Pacific grouping—has, over the past decade or more, been characterized by the deployment of highly asymmetric power resources in a largely coercive fashion to achieve its aim of reconstructing the global politics of trade, aid, and development along neoliberal lines, much to the detriment of its supposedly equal interlocutors (see, e.g., Hurt 2003, 2010; Clegg 2008; Heron 2011, 2013). Third, international diplomacy is no longer simply undertaken—if ever it was—by states operating within an international environment composed of clearly demarcated regimes and institutions. Things are considerably more messy than this, something with which, it must be said, reductionist mainstream accounts of IR have generally been unable to grapple. As we shall see shortly, the contemporary diplomacy in which small states engage has been distinguished by a considerably more complex series of processes; this can therefore only be understood with reference to a more nuanced appreciation of the kinds of diffuse and contingent contextual and relational factors that we have already mentioned.

Perhaps most importantly for small states, diplomacy is arguably far more important than it is to their larger counterparts. Just as small entities are vulnerable to shocks emanating from the external context that can be so destructive as to call into question the very viability of the state itself, the payoffs from successful diplomacy could, in theory, be so enormous as to completely transcend the investment made in them. To give one example: the Maldives is a tiny state for which sea-level rise caused by climate change threatens to completely submerge the territory, effectively destroying the state itself (see Adger 2010). A similar shock, though, just is not imaginable for a larger state. For the United States to be destroyed in the same way, for example, it would require many dozens of nuclear weapons to rain down on the country, something which is, thankfully, well beyond the realms of even the most fanciful science fiction. Yet by the same token, were there to be a successful—albeit, at present, highly unlikely—conclusion to the negotiations over the post-Kyoto climate regime that binds the world into serious reductions in greenhouse gas emissions, then the payoff to a country like the Maldives, which results in the effective saving of the state as a viable entity, would be beyond enormous.

Consequently, in a context of limited resources of all kinds, small states have to strategize their diplomacy in ways that larger states, which can cover international meetings with huge amounts of technical capacity in something of a blanket fashion, do not. This can take many interlinked forms, beginning with the development of constituencies of shared interest that allow weaker actors to collectively determine goals and devise strategies for achieving them. This in turn often necessitates low-level engagement in international fora, where battles are chosen carefully and policies are developed "under the radar" (Ingebritsen 2006) so that norms might be shaped independently of the power politics of the major players, and may themselves eventually become irresistible to the wider community of actors once it is too late for conventionally powerful forces to withstand them. In creating such norms, or even simply participating in international politics, small states have little choice but to draw on external sources of power: these can be reflected in the very rules and norms shaping regimes themselves, the broader context in which such engagement is taking place, or in the creation of relationships with nonstate actors and forces. We explore these phenomena in greater detail now, with reference to Caribbean involvement in the two arenas in which much of the region's diplomatic energy has been invested in recent years: trade and environment.

Global Trade Politics

It is perhaps not an overstatement to suggest that the politics surrounding trade dominated world politics between the late 1990s and the broad unfolding of the global financial crisis and with it the collapse of the Doha round of trade negotiations in the WTO. Indeed, during this time, particularly once China's accession had been completed in 2001 and the global economy appeared subsequently to be enjoying a spectacular period of expansion, it seemed as if the WTO was *the* institution of global governance *par excellence* in which many of the key battles were being fought. It certainly appeared this way from a Caribbean vantage point. Many of the region's most competent and able technocrats were seconded to the aforementioned CRNM, and trade negotiations came to occupy a hegemonic place within the diplomatic agenda. This began with the now defunct Free Trade Area of the Americas, followed closely by both the Cotonou Agreement, and its successor, the EPA, with the EU, all of which were tangled up within a variety of different battles within the WTO itself (Payne and Sutton 2007). More recently, the mooted bilateral Canada-CARICOM Trade Agreement has occupied the trade policy-making community. The dominance of the trade agenda was also reflected in the establishment, at the Barbados campus of the University of the West Indies, of the Shridath Ramphal Centre—an institute that bore the name of the former Commonwealth secretary general and founding head of the CRNM—and its flagship MSc degree in International Trade Policy that was designed explicitly to produce ever greater numbers of people with technical capacity in trade matters. This is actually rather revealing, in that it served to both institutionalize and underscore the enduring hegemony of technocratic, as opposed to political, approaches to global trade issues, and it legitimized the ongoing process of "technicification" of Caribbean diplomacy that Norman Girvan (2010b) and Paul Sutton (2006), among others, have identified. Such technical thinking, moreover, stands in contrast to the kind of critical analysis of the Caribbean's place in global politics which illuminated many of the most vibrant regional debates in the 1960s and 1970s, and which have become increasingly marginalized in much of the curriculum of the university since in tandem with the broader dominance of neoliberal thought and praxis (see Bishop 2013).

The wider problem is that Caribbean approaches to the international trade arena have often suffered from a range of shortcomings. First, they have often been confused, whether in terms of divisions between countries in terms of objectives, the nature of the objectives themselves, the yardsticks by which success might be measured, or, indeed, how the negotiation of trade agreements should align with broader development goals. Second, this confusion has often been intensified by the fact that, because of the capacity constraints that prevail, the participation of Caribbean actors is augmented either implicitly or explicitly by resources or ideas that are not local in genesis. To give one example: during the aforementioned controversial EPA negotiations, a large proportion of the CRNM's funding actually came from Brussels, and a number of Caribbean observers critiqued what they considered to be a notable—and unacceptable—degree of ideological convergence between the members of the institution itself and their European counterparts (Bishop et al. 2013). Third, there exists in the region a distinct lack of comprehension of the nature of contemporary patterns of global change within which an authentically Caribbean approach to development with widespread buy-in might be constructed. Outside of the regional technocracy—which is well reconciled to a neoliberal account of globalization, and consequently views the development challenge as one which is essentially synonymous with free trade and sustained liberalization—few have a clear idea of what a modern (and post-crisis) Caribbean development strategy might look like, and critical voices that might offer (radical) alternatives have often been consciously excluded from the process of doing so. This was the case, in particular, with the regional civil society community during the EPA negotiating process (Girvan 2010b, 2012).

All of these problems, moreover, are exacerbated by the technical approaches to trade which have tended to prevail. As suggested, the nature of global trade politics has largely been accepted at face value, as a problem to be solved, rather than a manifestation of a particular constellation of global power relations to be subjected to critical scrutiny. The "off-the-shelf" nature of neoliberal analyses of the development challenge in the region that emerge from external funding agencies has also been accepted wholesale by much of the regional intellectual and policy-making community. Many Caribbean academics have spent far more time in recent years engaging in (often highly lucrative) consultative research for institutions like the Inter-American Development Bank, the IMF, the World Bank, or even the EU, than they have writing considered critiques of the financial and ideological power of such institutions. This is most evident, again, in the general acceptance by the technocratic community of the emaciated and essentially neoliberal understandings of development that have infused, for example, agreements like the EPA (Bishop et al. 2013). The conclusion of the EPA negotiation process—and its continuing fallout—can be summed up as one of controversy, division, and, for many of the smaller territories of the Caribbean, enormous confusion about how they are supposed to proceed in implementing it.

One example, however, of purposeful Caribbean state agency in recent years comes in the shape of Antigua–Barbuda and its taking of the United States to the dispute settlement mechanism (DSM) of the WTO after the latter outlawed credit card payments by American citizens to offshore gambling firms in contravention of agreements made under the General Agreement on Trade in Services (GATS). Although the DSM ruled in Antigua's favor, the country was only able to secure a fraction ($21 million) of the claimed $3.4 billion losses. Yet as Cooper (2008, 2009, 2011) has argued at length, the value of the case lies less in the outcome than the fact that Antigua was both able and prepared to undertake an offensive and assertive diplomatic campaign against the United States. In this sense, there is little doubt that Antigua did, indeed, "punch above its weight" (Jackson 2012). For our purposes here, though, what is even more interesting is the way in which this took place. Many of the offshore gambling firms operating in the territory were actually American companies, so in one respect the battle was as much a domestic spat between Washington and US corporate interests as anything else. However, with legal redress impossible at home, the firms were able to draw on Antiguan sovereignty and challenge the United States in the international context of the WTO. For the Caribbean country itself, it was able to draw upon the financial capacity of the gambling firms to support a legal challenge that would have been considerably more difficult otherwise. In a sense, then, what we have is an interesting symbiosis between a small Caribbean state and international capital, with each drawing on the resources of the other to pursue a line of political contestation that would otherwise be more difficult, if not impossible (for a more thorough treatment of this issue, see Cooper 2011). Moreover, this process illustrates, to a significant degree, the importance of the kind of contingent and contextual aspects of state capacity to which we have already alluded in the chapter. In the final analysis, though, the material dimensions of power and the huge asymmetries that exist between small Caribbean states and major powers like the United States were brutally laid bare. As Jane Kelsey (2008) has noted, for Antigua the outcome was very much "a pyrrhic victory" that witnessed the revenue from internet gambling decline from $1 billion at its peak to just over $130 million a few years later. Furthermore, the United States was able to effectively wave away the WTO ruling, justifying its stance largely on the (extremely disingenuous) reasoning that the commitments it had made under the GATS were unclear and required clarification (Kelsey 2008).

Global Environmental Politics

There are three important distinctions to note between global trade politics and the regime that has grown up around environmental issues, and, in particular, climate change. The first is the fact that there is no single overarching institution governing the environment; indeed, as many as 500 or more bodies exist, often with myriad overlapping responsibilities (DeSombre 2006). The second is that the central elements of global environmental governance, and especially, the aspects that are concerned with climate change, have remained resolutely within the UN system. This is important, because, although imperfect, the interests of vulnerable states have consistently been taken seriously, at least at the rhetorical level, and a forum has been available in which their voices have been heard. Plus, the regime that has developed over the past few decades has consequently recognized and institutionalized the differentiated responsibility for causing, and therefore resolving, the problem. The third issue is that the United States, despite being one of the principal architects of the Kyoto regime itself, has, until Obama came into power in 2008, taken something of a back seat in global climate politics. This has meant that a distinctive arena has been created in which American norms and values have not been hegemonic (see Paterson 2009).

The reason that this context-setting matters for our purposes here is that a considerable space has opened up for small Caribbean states within global climate politics, which they have actually seized with some degree of success. Operating through the Alliance of Small Island States (AOSIS)—a grouping of 44 members and observer states and island territories—the region has deployed a range of innovative diplomatic strategies. One particularly important approach has been the deployment of what Carola Betzold (2010) calls the "moral power" that derives from "appeals to principles and norms" such as "common interest." She further notes how the so-called small island developing states, which comprise AOSIS and which, as we have suggested throughout, lack material power as traditionally conceived, have often "borrowed power" from a range of sources. This includes the extra moral suasion that derives from the existential threat that climate change represents for small islands; as Benwell (2011) has put it, they present themselves internationally "not as value-claiming parties vying for relative gain, but as the 'canaries in the coalmine' in a tragedy of the commons that is unfolding for all states." But it also comprises drawing on the power of well-resourced actors to support their claims, such as global activism networks. At times, the support of external actors is often solicited inadvertently: during the climate talks in Copenhagen in 2009, at which the most powerful countries sought to present a shoddy agreement to the world as a successful outcome, AOSIS was able to paralyze the talks and raise the specter of a public relations disaster for the major players by carefully manipulating both the protocol of the meeting and the ways in which the media portrayed it (Benwell 2011).

The broader problem, though, is that the Caribbean is rapidly becoming marginalized within global climate politics, partly on account of the ways in which the regime itself is evolving. One aspect of this is that there is increased divergence between AOSIS and the wider developing country coalitions with which small states have tended to be aligned. These include the oil-producing states of the Persian Gulf, the larger least-developed countries that are mainly based in Africa and Asia, as well as some of the largest emitters, most notably China and other fast-industrializing countries. Put simply: as China builds ever more coal-fired power stations, it is becoming increasingly impossible to imagine a harmony of interests between Caribbean countries and Beijing on climate issues.

This problem is particularly evident if we consider that, until now, the totemic claim by small states in climate change terms has been the demand to limit increases in global temperatures (and therefore the concentrations of greenhouse gases in the atmosphere) to 1.5°C. In the aftermath of the climate meetings in Copenhagen, Cancun, and then Durban, in which much hope was invested, it is now clear that this strategy is largely exhausted. There is little chance of the target being realized, and there appears, at present, little consensus on what Caribbean countries—along with their counterparts in the Pacific and elsewhere—want from global climate politics in future, nor what their approach to getting it might be. Moreover, a range of other contradictions exist. An important one is that the debate on climate change in the Caribbean has traditionally been couched in "mitigation" terms (i.e., the need to reduce emissions); however, this is largely irrelevant in a region where no countries are large polluters in any meaningful sense. A far more critical consideration is adaptation (meaning the creation of political, economic, and social strategies for alleviating the effects of climate change). Yet little finance has been forthcoming from the most powerful countries for this purpose, and, in the scramble for the resources that will emerge, it is quite likely that the Caribbean will not have the voice or diplomatic muscle to ensure that it receives an acceptable share. More broadly, the kind of external dependence—for ideas and capital—that characterizes global trade politics is very much in evidence in questions of climate change adaptation too (for a detailed account of these issues, see Bishop and Payne 2012).

Conclusion

In sum, the Caribbean does indeed appear to suffer from a distinct lack of capacity when it comes to participating in international politics. This is particularly so if we consider the material aspects of power that are to be found in the resources that the region and its states have at their disposal. Yet if we consider a wider range of attributes, including the contextual elements represented by the institutions in which diplomatic activity takes place at the global level, as well as the relational dimensions of specific power struggles, then it is clear that the region has participated to an extent beyond which its material power would ordinarily imply. The Caribbean has certainly scored some apparent successes, in both global trade and climate politics. In the case of the former, we can see how institutional realities, expressed both through legal rules and norms as well as regulatory provisions, have permitted certain countries, and most notably Antigua–Barbuda, to supplant their limited material power and fight battles against far more powerful—in the conventional sense, that is—adversaries. In the case of the latter, we have seen how, through AOSIS, small states have been able to draw on both external sources of material power, as well as ideational norms, values, and appeals to the gravity of their existential situation to resist unfavorable outcomes in the international climate negotiations.

However, despite these apparent victories, it should also be recognized that, in most cases, the Caribbean has played a largely resistant and defensive role, rather than an offensive and transformative one. Caribbean countries—and, by implication, other small states—have not been able to decisively shift the structures of global policy making, whether in the arenas of trade, the environment, or even finance, even though they have participated within them. Or, put another way, the dance that takes place within the institutions of global governance does not take place according to a tune played by the world's small states. They do get to dance, of course, and from time to time, they can persuade powerful people to dance with them. However, they neither choose the music nor the course of events, and they are permanently vulnerable to being marginalized at the edges of the dance floor.

Consequently, it is clear that, without greater resources, the Caribbean can only punch so far beyond its weight. Successes have, in other words, nearly always been tempered by the limited gains that have been made, the inability of small Caribbean states to enforce those gains, or the subsequent reactions of bigger and more powerful players. Moreover, such disappointing outcomes are not helped by the unnecessary wounds that the Caribbean consistently inflicts on itself. As discussed, since the high point of regional debates on development in the 1970s, there has been little convincing attempt to provide original and autochthonous answers to the very difficult series of questions that the global context is posing of Caribbean society. Much time has been lost, institutions—particularly at the regional level—have not been constructed, opportunities have been missed, the public has not been inspired or presented with the genuine prospect of "buying in" to the development process, and, as a consequence, the "existential threats" facing many Caribbean countries are considerably more pressing and dangerous than they might otherwise have been (Girvan 2010a). This can be witnessed clearly with just the cursory analysis of global trade and climate politics that we have ventured here. If more is not done in future to reverse these kinds of problems, to create new and distinctive strategies for engaging globally—as well as the necessary supportive institutions to sustain them—the future for the Caribbean's participation in global politics is extremely bleak indeed.

References

Adger, W. N. (2010). Climate change, human well-being and insecurity. *New Political Economy* **15**(2): 275–292.
Baldacchino, G. and G. Bertram (2010). The beak of the finch: Insights into the economic development of small economies. *The Round Table* **98**(401): 141–160.
Benwell, R. (2011). The canaries in the coalmine: Small states as climate change champions. *The Round Table* **100**(413): 199–211.
Bernal, R. L. (2010). The dragon in the Caribbean: China–CARICOM economic relations. *The Round Table* **99**(408): 281–302.
Betzold, C. (2010). "Borrowing" power to influence international negotiations: AOSIS in the climate change regime, 1990–1997. *Politics* **30**(3): 131–148.
Bishop, M. L. (2011). Slaying the "Westmonster" in the Caribbean? Constitutional reform in St Vincent and the Grenadines. *British Journal of Politics and International Relations* **13**(3): 420–437.
Bishop, M. L. (2012). The political economy of small states: Enduring vulnerability? *Review of International Political Economy* **19**(5): 942–960.
Bishop, M. L. (2013). *The Political Economy of Caribbean Development*. Basingstoke, Palgrave Macmillan.
Bishop, M. L. (2014). Whither CARICOM? *Re-mapping the Americas: Trends in Region-making*. W. A. Knight, H. Ghany and J. Castro-Rea, Eds. London, Ashgate.
Bishop, M. L., N. Girvan, T. M. Shaw, R. M. Kirton, M. Scobie, S. Cross-Mike, D. Mohammed and M. Anatol (2011). *Caribbean Regional Integration: A Report by the UWI Institute of International Relations*, funded by UKaid from DFID, led by Matthew L. Bishop and Norman Girvan. St Augustine, Trinidad and Tobago.

Bishop, M. L., T. Heron and A. Payne (2013). Caribbean development alternatives and the CARIFORUM-European Union Economic Partnership Agreement. *Journal of International Relations and Development* **16**(1): 82–110.

Bishop, M. L. and A. Payne (2010). *Caribbean Regional Governance and the Sovereignty/Statehood Problem*. Waterloo, Canada, Centre for International Governance Innovation (CIGI) Caribbean Paper No. 8.

Bishop, M. L. and A. Payne (2012). Climate change and the future of Caribbean development. *The Journal of Development Studies* **48**(10): 1536–1553.

Braveboy-Wagner, J. A. (2010). Opportunities and limitations of the exercise of foreign policy power by a very small state: The case of Trinidad and Tobago. *Cambridge Review of International Affairs* **23**(3): 407–427.

Briguglio, L. (1995). Small island developing states and their economic vulnerabilities. *World Development* **23**(9): 1615–1632.

Briguglio, L., G. Cordina, S. Vella and C. Vigilance, Eds. (2010). *Profiling Vulnerability and Resilience: A Manual for Small States*. London, Commonwealth Secretariat.

Bull, H. (1977). *The Anarchical Society: A Study of Order in World Politics*. Basingstoke, Macmillan.

Clegg, P. (2008). Alleviating the consequences of marginalisation? EU sid policy towards the Caribbean ACPs. *Journal of International Development* **20**(2): 193–204.

Cooper, A. F. (2008). "Remote" in the Eastern Caribbean: The Antigua-US WTO Internet Gambling Case. Waterloo, Canada, Centre for International Governance Innovation (CIGI) Caribbean Paper No. 4.

Cooper, A. F. (2009). Confronting vulnerability through resilient diplomacy: Antigua and the WTO internet gambling dispute. *The Diplomacies of Small States: Between Vulnerability and Resilience*. A. F. Cooper and T. M. Shaw, Eds. Basingstoke, Palgrave MacMillan.

Cooper, A. F. (2011). *Internet Gambling Offshore: Caribbean Struggles over Casino Capitalism*. Basingstoke, Palgrave Macmillan.

Cooper, A. F. and T. M. Shaw, Eds. (2009). *The Diplomacies of Small States: Between Vulnerability and Resilience*. London, Palgrave MacMillan.

DeSombre, E. R. (2006). *Global Environmental Institutions*. Abingdon, Routledge.

Girvan, N. (2010a). Are Caribbean Countries Facing Existential Threats? Available at: http://www.norman-girvan.info/girvan-existential-threats/. Accessed on January 15, 2013.

Girvan, N. (2010b). Technification, sweetification, treatyfication. *Interventions* **12**(1): 100–111.

Girvan, N. (2012). Social movements confront neoliberalism: Reflections on a Caribbean experience. *Globalizations* **9**(6): 753–766.

Heron, T. (2011). Asymmetric bargaining and development trade-offs in the CARIFORUM-European Union Economic Partnership Agreement. *Review of International Political Economy* **18**(3): 328–357.

Heron, T. (2013). *Pathways from Preferential Trade: The Politics of Trade Adjustment in Africa, Caribbean and Pacific*. Basingstoke, Palgrave Macmillan.

Higgott, R. and E. Erman (2010). Deliberative global governance and the question of legitimacy: What can we learn from the WTO? *Review of International Studies* **36**(2): 449–470.

Hurt, S. (2003). Co-operation and coercion? The Cotonou Agreement between the European Union and ACP states and the end of the Lomé Convention. *Third World Quarterly* **24**(1): 161–176.

Hurt, S. (2010). Understanding EU development policy: History, global context and self-interest? *Third World Quarterly* **31**(1): 159–168.

IMF (2014). *Grenada: Ex-Post Assessment of Longer-Term Programme Engagement*. Washington, DC, International Monetary Fund.

Ingebritsen, C. (2006). Norm entrepreneurs: Scandinavia's role in world politics. *Small States in International Relations*. C. Ingebritsen, I. B. Neumann, S. Gstöhl and J. Beyer, Eds. Seattle, WA, University of Washington Press, pp. 273–285.

Jackson, S. (2012). Small states and compliance bargaining in the WTO: An analysis of the Antigua–US gambling services case. *Cambridge Review of International Affairs* **25**(3): 367–385.

Johnston, J. (2013). *The Multilateral Debt Trap in Jamaica*. Washington, DC, Centre for Economic and Policy Research Issue Brief, June 2013.

Jones, K. (2009). Green room politics and the WTO's crisis of representation. *Progress in Development Studies* **9**(4): 349–357.

Kelsey, J. (2008). *Serving Whose Interests? The Political Economy of Trade in Services Agreements*. New York, Routledge-Cavendish.

Lee, D. and N. J. Smith (2010). Small state discourses in the international political economy. *Third World Quarterly* **31**(7): 1091–1105.

Lewis, G. K. (2004). *Main Currents in Caribbean Thought*. London, University of Nebraska Press.

Lewis, V. A. (2009). Foreword: Studying small states over the twentieth into the twenty-first centuries. *The Diplomacies of Small States: Between Vulnerability and Resilience*. A. F. Cooper and T. M. Shaw, Eds. Basingstoke, Palgrave MacMillan, pp. vii–xv.

Lindsay, C. (2013). The EU-CARIFORUM EPA: Regulatory and policy changes and lessons for other ACP countries. *Caribbean Journal of International Relations & Diplomacy* **1**(3): 5–29.

Looney, R. (2014). Is Jamaica poised for a turnaround? *Foreign Policy*, February 12.

Neumann, I. B. and S. Gstöhl (2006). Introduction: Lilliputians in Gulliver's world? *Small States in International Relations*. C. Ingebritsen, I. B. Neumann, S. Gstöhl and J. Beyer, Eds. Seattle, WA, University of Washington Press, pp. 12–37.

Paterson, M. (2009). Post-hegemonic climate politics. *The British Journal of Politics and International Relations* **11**(1): 140–158.

Payne, A. (2006). The end of green gold? Comparative development options and strategies in the Eastern Caribbean banana-producing islands. *Studies in Comparative International Development* **41**(3): 25–46.

Payne, A. (2009). *Afterword*: Vulnerability as a condition, resilience as a strategy. *The Diplomacies of Small States: Between Vulnerability and Resilience*. A. F. Cooper and T. M. Shaw, Eds. Basingstoke, Palgrave MacMillan, pp. 279–286.

Payne, A. (2010). How many Gs are there in "global governance" after the crisis? The perspectives of the "marginal majority" of the world's states. *International Affairs* **86**(3): 729–740.

Payne, A. and P. Sutton (1993). Lilliput under threat: The security problems of small island and enclave developing states. *Political Studies* **41**(4): 579–593.

Payne, A. and P. Sutton (2007). Repositioning the Caribbean within globalisation. Waterloo, Canada, Centre for International Governance Innovation (CIGI) Caribbean Paper No. 1.

Richardson, B. and P. Richardson-Ngwenya (2013). Cut loose in the Caribbean: Neoliberalism and the demise of the commonwealth sugar trade. *Bulletin of Latin American Research* **32**(3): 263–278.

Ryan, S. (1999). *Winner Takes All: The Westminster Experience in the Caribbean*. St. Augustine, Trinidad and Tobago, ISER, The University of the West Indies.

Steinberg, R. H. (2002). In the shadow of law or power? Consensus-based bargaining and outcomes in the GATT/WTO. *International Organization* **56**(2): 339–374.

Sutton, P. (2006). Caribbean development: An overview. *New West Indian Guide* **80**(1/2): 45–62.

PUBLIC POLICY ISSUES AND THEMES   III

Chapter 12

Education Reform Initiatives in the Caribbean Basin

Tavis D. Jules and Hakim Mohandas Amani Williams

Contents

Introduction	248
Setting the Scene	267
Colonial Education	268
Post-Emancipation Education Reforms	270
Post-Independence Educational Reforms to Present	272
First Generation of Reforms: 1970s–1980s	272
First Generation of Reforms: The Institutional Phase	273
First Generation of Reforms: The Oil Crises and Structural Adjustment Phase	275
First Generation of Reforms: The Socialism and Ideological Pluralism Phase	276
First Generation of Reforms: The HIV/AIDS Generation Phase	278
Second Generation of Reforms: 1989–2000	280
Second Generation of Reforms: Neoliberalism and Education	280
Second Generation of Reforms: Tertiary Education Phase	281
Second Generation of Reforms: International Benchmarks and Regional Consequences	283
Third Generation of Reforms: 2002–Present-Day	285
Third Generation of Reforms: International Aid, Knowledge Banks, and Stakeholder Participatory Involvement	285
Third Generation of Reforms: Accreditation	286
Third Generation of Reforms: Gender	287
Post-2015 MDGS and Education in the Caribbean	287
Conclusion	287
References	289

Abstract: This chapter provides a board overview of educational developments and reform initiatives, from the colonial period to present-day, in the 28 countries and territories that constitute the contemporary Caribbean Basin. We chronicle the systemic factors that account for patterns of regional outcomes in education by identifying the different historical stages and external factors that have driven educational investments across the region. Attention is also given to the appropriation of external delivery transfer mechanisms (such as policy borrowing and lending) that serves different needs and interests at various junctures along the development continuum. We examine both the achievements in educational reforms and the challenges that these countries have faced, paying particular attention to the areas of contentious reforms that have focused on integrating strategies and techniques from public administration, new public management, or corporate managerialism to engender national educational reforms. First, we begin by identifying the role and purpose of colonial education across the region. Second, we suggest that post-independence educational developments have gone through three distinctive generations of reforms: (1) beginning in the 1970s and 1980s with reorganizations that focused on access, equity, and inclusion; (2) continuing during the policy periods between 1989 to 2000, and using neoliberalism to emphasize quality, accountability, and efficiency as well as fiscal austerity; and (3) the current and third wave of transformations from 2000 to present-day, which strive to create citizens for the knowledge-based economy. The chapter concludes by suggesting that the development of education in the Caribbean has been impelled and shaped by both domestic and peripheral forces and trajectories; it offers suggestions for reforms in the post-2015 sustainable development agenda.

Introduction

This chapter chronicles a very broad précis of the numerous educational developments and reform initiatives, from the colonial period to present-day, in the 28 countries* and territories that constitute the contemporary Caribbean†

---

* For the purpose of this chapter we have added Suriname, given that it is a member of the Caribbean Community (CARICOM). Suriname is home to the CARICOM Institute of Translation and Interpretation, has participated in the Caribbean Festival of Arts (CARIFESTA), and was the host country of CARIFESTA XI.
† Generally speaking, we note that the contemporary Caribbean Basin can be seen as comprising the islands with Spanish-, French-, English-, Dutch-, and Papiamentu-speaking people, and extending through the Caribbean Sea from the Commonwealth of the Bahamas in the North, to Trinidad and Tobago in the South. In this definition, we also include the English- and Dutch-speaking mainland countries of Belize in Central America and Guyana and Suriname in South America since the latter three are members of the Caribbean Community (CARICOM). We include these countries because they correspondingly share a mutual historical experience and their populations mirror a cultural assortment of hybrid societies (UNESCO 1996). Our definition of this geographical area is further compounded by the fact that even UNESCO (1996) seems perplexed by what constitutes the Caribbean and notes that Cuba and the Dominican Republic are usually classified as part of Latin America, while Puerto Rico is a territory of the United States and Martinique and Guadeloupe are overseas Departments of France. To avoid these ambiguous definitional issues pointed out above, multilateral agendas and "international knowledge banks" (Jones 2004), such as the World Bank and the International Monetary Fund, often speak of the "Caribbean and Latin America" as one geographical space. For the purposes of this chapter, the contemporary Caribbean Basin is demarcated by 28 countries that are part of the Caribbean (see Table 12.1). With the exception of Anguilla, Bermuda, the British Virgin Islands, Montserrat, the Cayman Islands, the Netherlands Antilles (Aruba, Bonaire, Saba, Curacao, and Saint Eustatius), the Turks and Caicos Islands, and the United States Virgin Islands, the territories of the Caribbean Basin achieved self-determination over the 25-year period beginning in 1960. Of additional concern, is that in many instances, limited data exist on the overseas departments,

Basin.* In recognizing the geographical and population size constraints, small economies, and risks associated with climate change that affect the Caribbean Basin, this chapter uses a "regional political economy" (Agnew 2000) perspective to examine the political forces (including the state, institutions, and individual actors) that have shaped and continue to define educational reforms within the Caribbean. As such, we view the region, or Caribbean Basin, as a space that is comprised of sovereign states, shares a communal identity, and has a distinctive historical past (Mansfield and Milner 1997). Our primary focus is examining which systemic factors account for patterns of regional outcomes. We advance the argument that at different historical stages, external actors have driven the investment in educational attainment across the region, and that the appropriation of external delivery transfer mechanisms (such a policy borrowing and lending) serves different needs and interests at different junctures along the development continuum. As Table 12.1 illustrates, the Caribbean Basin[†] features a broad mosaic of international and regional actors that drive, define, and influence educational reform. Also Table 12.1 provides a full picture of the national, subregional, regional, hemispherical institutions, "trans-regional regimes" (Jules 2008), and international actors that have a role, impact, voice, and influence upon education across the region. Moreover, Table 12.2 shows that national governments from across the region have undertaken several instrumental reform initiatives, beginning in the various post-independence periods that focused on moving away from plantation economies toward economies of scale to achieve industrialization. The arguments advanced in this chapter are based on our analysis of these documents. However, many of these reforms, based on structural transformation (ranging from production integration to new managerialism to neoliberalism), have resulted in unintended outcomes due to the influence by both endogenous and exogenous factors, with focus on the development of human capital. Because there has not been one consistent strategy for the role and purpose of education, other than investing in human capital to facilitate

---

territories, and protectorates of the United States of America, the United Kingdom, France, and the Netherlands, which still have controlling interest in political, social, and economic aspects of island life. However, what makes the Caribbean Basin unique for educational comparisons is its colonial history and that all of the countries in the region are considered to be micro (or small) states and/or Small Island Development States (SIDS) by the World Bank and Commonwealth Secretariat given their population size, ecology, landmass, vulnerability to external shocks, and fragility.

* While the Modern Caribbean Basin is often associated with the "Caribbean Basin Economic Recovery Act" (1993) and includes countries such as Costa Rica, El Salvador, Guatemala, Honduras, Mexico, Nicaragua, Panama, and Venezuela, we exclude these countries from our definition and discussion in this chapter since the focus is on the Caribbean as defined above.

† We use the term "Caribbean Basin" as an all-encompassing concept to define the changing relation of the islands in the West Indian Archipelago. In using this term, we make a distinction from the "Caribbean Basin Economic Recovery Act" (CBERA) of 1983 that focused on the provision of traffic and trade and the Caribbean Basin Trade Partnership Act (CBTPA) that placed emphasis on the strengthening economic and political relations within the region. Therefore, we use Caribbean Basin to representing the evolving Archipelagic and hemispherical relation across the Caribbean based on the proliferation of regional trading blocs, such as, the Caribbean Community and the Organization of Eastern Caribbean States, or customs unions and atypical modules economic integration, open regionalism (production integration as described in the Revised Treaty of Chaguaramas) and mature regionalism. These integrative mechanisms taken together with the expansion of regional "existential threats" (Girvan 2010)—the Union of South American Nation (UNASUR)—which combined two existing customs unions, the Southern Common Market (MERCOSUR) and the Andean Community of Nation (CAN), Community of Latin American and Caribbean States (CELAC)—focused on deeper integration, Bolivarian Alliance for the Peoples of Our America (ALBA)—challenges the economic vulnerability, food security, and ecological fragility in the Caribbean.

Table 12.1 Institutional Affiliations and Donors in the Caribbean

Countries in the Caribbean	Colonial Territory/ Protectorate of	Population	Status in CARICOM	Year of Accession to CARICOM	Other Regional Affiliations	International Frameworks	Top 2010–2011 Aid Donors for Education	Aid Received for Education (2010–2011)[c]
Anguilla	United Kingdom	15,754[a]	Associate member	July 4, 1999	Associate member of West Indies Federation; CDB 1970; Commonwealth; CSME; CXC 1972; ECLAC 2006; Leeward Island Federation; OECS (Associate Member); UWI	EFA; MDGs; PRSP	EU Institutions; United Kingdom; CarDB; Germany	30%
Antigua and Barbuda		90,156[a]	Full member	July 4, 1974	ACP; ALBA 2004; CANTA; CARIFORUM; CARIFTA 1965; CDB 1970; Commonwealth; CRNM 1997; CSME; CXC 1972; ECLAC 2006; Leeward Island Federation; NAB; OAS; OECS 1981; West Indies Federation; UWI	EFA; MDGs; PRSP	EU Institutions; Japan; Australia; CarDB; US; Spain; Greece; Germany; Finland; United Arab Emirates	14%
The Bahamas		319,031[a]	Full member	July 4, 1983	ACP; ACS; CANTA; CARIFORUM; CDB 1970; Commonwealth; CRNM 1997; ECLAC 2006; NAB; OAS; UWI	EFA; MDGs; PRSP	N/A	N/A

(Continued)

Table 12.1 (Continued) Institutional Affiliations and Donors in the Caribbean

Countries in the Caribbean	Colonial Territory/ Protectorate of	Population	Status in CARICOM	Year of Accession to CARICOM	Other Regional Affiliations	International Frameworks	Top 2010–2011 Aid Donors for Education	Aid Received for Education (2010–2011)[c]
The British Virgin Islands	United Kingdom	31,912[a]	Associate member	July 2, 1991	CARIFORUM: CDB 1970; Commonwealth; CXC 1972; ECLAC 2006; Leeward Island Federation; OECS 1984 (Associate Member); UWI	EFA; MDGs; PRSP	N/A	N/A
Bermuda		69,467[a]	Associate member	July 2, 2003	Leeward Island Federation; UWI	EFA; MDGs; PRSP	N/A	N/A
Barbados		288,725[a]	Full member	August 1, 1973[d]	ACP; ACS; CANTA; CARIFESTA; CARIFORUM; CARIFTA 1965; CDB 1970; Commonwealth; CRNM 1997; CSME; CXC 1972; ECLAC 2006; OAS; TVET; UWI; West Indies Federation; Windward Island Federation	EFA; MDGs; PRSP	N/A	N/A
Belize		334,297[a]	Full member	May 1, 1974	ACP; ACS; CANTA; CARIFORUM; CARIFTA 1971; CDB 1970; Commonwealth; CRNM 1997; CXC 1972; ECLAC 2006; OAS; UWI	EFA; MDGs; PRSP	EU Institutions; CarDB; Japan; GEF; US; OFID; UNICEF; Australia; KFAED; IDB Sp. Fund	12%

(Continued)

Table 12.1 (Continued) Institutional Affiliations and Donors in the Caribbean

Countries in the Caribbean	Colonial Territory/ Protectorate of	Population	Status in CARICOM	Year of Accession to CARICOM	Other Regional Affiliations	International Frameworks	Top 2010–2011 Aid Donors for Education	Aid Received for Education (2010–2011)[c]
Cayman Islands	United Kingdom	53,737[a]	Associate member	May 15, 2002	CARIFORUM; CDB 1970; Commonwealth; CXC 1972; UWI	EFA; MDGs; PRSP	N/A	N/A
Cuba		11,061,886	CARIFORUM		ACS; ALBA 2004; CARIFESTA; CRNM 1997; ECLAC 2006	EFA; MDGs; PRSP	Spain; EU Institutions; US; Global Fund; Canada; Japan; OFID; Switzerland; Belgium; Germany	15%
The Dominican Republic		10,219,630[a]	Observer/ CARIFORUM		ACP; ACS; CARIFORUM; CRNM 1997; ECLAC 2006; OAS	EFA; MDGs; PRSP	EU Institutions; France; Spain; US; Global Fund; Japan; Germany; IDB Sp. Fund; Korea; Italy	5%

(Continued)

Education Reform Initiatives in the Caribbean Basin ■ 253

Table 12.1 (Continued) Institutional Affiliations and Donors in the Caribbean

Countries in the Caribbean	Colonial Territory/ Protectorate of	Population	Status in CARICOM	Year of Accession to CARICOM	Other Regional Affiliations	International Frameworks	Top 2010–2011 Aid Donors for Education	Aid Received for Education (2010–2011)[c]
Dominica		73,286[a]	Full member	May 1, 1974	ACP; ACS; ALBA 2004; CARIFORUM; CARIFTA 1968; CDB 1970; Commonwealth; CRNM 1997; CSME; CXC 1972; ECLAC 2006; Leeward Island Federation (1940); OAS; OECS 1981; UWI; West Indies Federation; Windward Island Federation	EFA; MDGs; PRSP	EU Institutions; CarDB; France; Japan; KFAED; Australia; IDA; Italy; United Kingdom; Canada	21%
French Guiana*	France	274 652[b]				EFA; MDGs; PRSP	N/A	N/A
Grenada		109,590[a]	Full member	May 1, 1974	ACP; ACS; CARIFORUM; CARIFTA 1968; CDB 1970; Commonwealth; CRNM 1997; CSME; CXC 1972; ECLAC 2006; OAS; OECS 1981; UWI; West Indies Federation; Windward Island Federation	EFA; MDGs; PRSP	EU Institutions; Japan; Car DB; IDA; IMF; Australia; KFAED; UNDP; Canada; France	3%
Guadeloupe*	France	503,274[a]				EFA; MDGs; PRSP	N/A	N/A

(Continued)

Table 12.1 (Continued) Institutional Affiliations and Donors in the Caribbean

Countries in the Caribbean	Colonial Territory/ Protectorate of	Population	Status in CARICOM	Year of Accession to CARICOM	Other Regional Affiliations	International Frameworks	Top 2010–2011 Aid Donors for Education	Aid Received for Education (2010–2011)[c]
Guyana		739,903[b]	Full member	August 1, 1973[d]	ACP; ACS; CANTA; CARIFESTA; CARIFORUM; CARIFTA 1965; CDB 1970; Commonwealth; CRNM 1997; CSME; CXC 1972; NAB; OAS; USAN; UWI	EFA; EFA Fast Track Initiative; HIPC; MDGs; PRSP	IDB Sp. Fund; Norway; EU Institutions; US; CarDB; Global Fund; Canada; Japan; Germany; IDA	0.25%
		9,893,934[a]	Full member	July 2002	ACP; ACS; CARIFORUM; CDB 1970; CRNM 1997; ECLAC 2006; IAEC; OAS	EFA; HIPC; MDGs; PRSP; CARIFORUM	USA; IDB Sp. Fund; Canada; EU Institutions; IMF; France; Spain; IDA; Japan; Norway	4%
Jamaica		2,909,714[a]	Full member	August 1, 1973[d]	ACP; ACS; CANTA; CARIFESTA; CARIFORUM; CARIFTA 1968; CDB 1970; CKLN; Commonwealth; CRNM 1997; CSME; CXC 1972; OAS; RAM; TVET; UWI; West Indies Federation	EFA; MDGs; PRSP	EU Institutions; US; CarDB; Japan; Global Fund; OFID; United Kingdom; Canada; Belgium; GEF	17%
Martinique*	France	498,151[b]				EFA; MDGs; PRSP	N/A	N/A

(Continued)

Education Reform Initiatives in the Caribbean Basin ■ 255

Table 12.1 (Continued) Institutional Affiliations and Donors in the Caribbean

Countries in the Caribbean	Colonial Territory/ Protectorate of	Population	Status in CARICOM	Year of Accession to CARICOM	Other Regional Affiliations	International Frameworks	Top 2010–2011 Aid Donors for Education	Aid Received for Education (2010–2011)[c]
Montserrat	United Kingdom	5,189[a]	Full member	May 1, 1974	CANTA; CARIFORUM; CARIFTA 1968; CDB 1970; Commonwealth; CSME; CXC 1972; ECLAC 2006; Leeward Island Federation; OECS 1981; UWI; West Indies Federation	EFA; MDGs; PRSP	United Kingdom; EU Institutions; CarDB; UNDP; US	N/A
Netherlands Antilles	The Netherlands	203,748[b]	Observer		ACS; ECLAC 2006	EFA; MDGs; PRSP	N/A	N/A
Puerto Rico	United States	3,674,209[a]	Observer		ECLAC 2006; Windward Island Federation	EFA; MDGs; PRSP	N/A	N/A
St. Lucia		162,781[a]	Full member	May 1, 1974	ACP; ACS; CANTA; CARIFORUM; CARIFTA 1968; CDB 1970; Commonwealth; CRNM 1997; CSME; CXC 1972; ECLAC 2006; OAS; OECS 1981; TVET; UWI; West Indies Federation; Windward Island Federation	EFA; MDGs; PRSP	EU Institutions; IDA; CarDB; IMF; KFAED; Japan; Australia; France; UK; Canada	9%

(Continued)

Table 12.1 (Continued) Institutional Affiliations and Donors in the Caribbean

Countries in the Caribbean	Colonial Territory/ Protectorate of	Population	Status in CARICOM	Year of Accession to CARICOM	Other Regional Affiliations	International Frameworks	Top 2010–2011 Aid Donors for Education	Aid Received for Education (2010–2011)[c]
St. Christopher (St. Kitts and Nevis)		51,134[a]	Full member	July 26, 1974	ACP; ACS; CARIFESTA; CARIFORUM; CARIFTA 1968; CDB 1970; Commonwealth; CRNM 1997; CSME; CXC 1972; ECLAC 2006; Leeward Island Federation; NAB; OAS; OECS 1981; UWI; West Indies Federation (Associate Member)	EFA; MDGs; PRSP	EU Institutions; CarDB; Japan; Australia; Canada; Germany; Spain; Austria	4%
St. Vincent and the Grenadines		103,220[a]	Full member	May 1, 1974	ACP; ACS; ALBA 2004; CARIFORUM; CARIFTA 1968; CDB 1970; Commonwealth; CRNM 1997; CSME; CXC 1972; ECLAC 2006; OAS; OECS 1981; UWI; West Indies Federation; Windward Island Federation	EFA; MDGs; PRSP	EU Institutions; CarDB; IMF; IDA; Japan; Australia; Canada; US; Finland; UNDP	14%

(Continued)

Table 12.1 (Continued) Institutional Affiliations and Donors in the Caribbean

Countries in the Caribbean	Colonial Territory/ Protectorate of	Population	Status in CARICOM	Year of Accession to CARICOM	Other Regional Affiliations	International Frameworks	Top 2010–2011 Aid Donors for Education	Aid Received for Education (2010–2011)[c]
Suriname		566,846[a]	Full member	July 4, 1995	CARIFESTA; CARIFORUM; CRNM 1997; CSME; ECLAC 2006; OAS; USAN	EFA	Netherlands; EU Institutions; IDB Sp. Fund; France; GEF; Global Fund; Belgium; US; Canada; Australia	11%
Trinidad and Tobago		1,225,225[a]	Full member	August 1, 1973[d]	ACP; ACS; CANTA; CARIFESTA; CARIFORUM; CARIFTA 1965; CDB 1970; CKLN; Commonwealth; CRNM 1997; CSME; CXC 1972; ECLAC 2006; OAS; RAM; SERVOL Program; TVET; UWI; West Indies Federation; Windward Island Federation	EFA; MDGs; PRSP	N/A	N/A

(Continued)

Table 12.1 (Continued) Institutional Affiliations and Donors in the Caribbean

Countries in the Caribbean	Colonial Territory/ Protectorate of	Population	Status in CARICOM	Year of Accession to CARICOM	Other Regional Affiliations	International Frameworks	Top 2010–2011 Aid Donors for Education	Aid Received for Education (2010–2011)[c]
Turks and Caicos Islands*	United Kingdom	47,754[a]	Associate member	July 2, 1991	ACS; CDB 1970; Commonwealth; CXC 1972; ECLAC 2006; UWI	EFA; MDGs; PRSP	UK; EC; CDB; Canada; UNTA	N/A

Notes: 1. Countries with an *(asterisk) are Colonial Territories or Protectorates.
2. Caribbean countries and their affiliations: Countries in bold are full member states of CARICOM. Countries in italics are associate member of CARICOM. Countries neither bold or italics are observer members.

ACP, African, Caribbean, and Pacific States; ACS, Association of Caribbean States; ALBA, Bolivarian Alliance for the Americas; CANTA, Caribbean Association of National Training Agencies; CARIFTA, Caribbean Free Trade Association; CARIFESTA, Caribbean Festival of Arts; CDB or CarDB Caribbean Development Bank CARIFORUM Caribbean Forum of ACP States; CRNM, Caribbean Regional Negotiating Machinery; EU, European Union; GEF, Global Environment Facility; IAEC, Inter-American Economic Council; KFAED, Kuwait Fund for Arab Economic Development; NAB, National Association of the Bahamas; OAS, Organization of American States; OFID, OPEC Fund for International Development; SERVOL, Service Volunteered for All; USAN, Union of South American Nations.

[a] July 2013 population estimate from CIA World Factbook.
[b] July 2011 population estimate.
[c] Data available at http://www.oecd.org/dac/stats/.
[d] Founding member of CARICOM.

Table 12.2 Policy Census of National Educational Reforms in the Caribbean

Anguilla	Caribbean Symposium on Inclusive Education Country Report 2007	2007
	Environment Research Action Programme (EARP)	2011
Antigua and Barbuda	Quality Public Education, Antigua and Barbuda, 2004 and Beyond	2004–2009
Belize	Education Act	2000
	Education Ordinance of 1962	1962
	The Development Plan 1964–1970	1964–1970
	Education Plans 1972–1976	1972–1976
	Rural Education and Agriculture Program (REAP)	1976
	Curriculum Development Unit: SHEP, PEP, WIZE, TESOL Project, PPTT	1975
	Schools Broadcast Program	1965
	Development Plan 1980–1983	1980–1993
	Development Plan 1985–1989	1985–1989
	Belize Primary Education Development Project (BPED)	1992
	Free Education	1993
	Development Plan 1992–1997	1992–1997
	2+1 Certificate Program	1954–1992
	Certificate Program with School Experience	1992
	Part-Time Program	1994
	National Curriculum	1998–1999
	A World Fit for Children (UN initiative)	2002
	Enhancing Holistic Child Development Program (UNICEF)	2002
	Enabling Environment for Adolescent Development Program (UNICEF)	2002
	Action Plan	2005–2010
	Education Sector Strategy 2011–2016	2011–2016
Bahamas	Bahamas: 2009 10 year Education Plan	2009–2019
	Manifesto 92	1992–1997
	Manifesto II Agenda to and for the 21st Century	1997–2002

(Continued)

Table 12.2 (*Continued*) Policy Census of National Educational Reforms in the Caribbean

Bahamas (Continued)	National Strategic Plan 2025	2005–2025
	Our Plan: A Strategy for Bahamas and a Brighter Future	2002–2007
	School Meals Programme 1963	1963
	Strategic Plan 2004: Bahamian Education in the 21st Century	2002–2007
Bermuda	Blueprint for Reform in Education: Bermuda Public School System Strategic Plan 2010–2015	2010–2015
	Education Act of 1996	1996
	Bermuda Educators Council Act of 2002	2002
	Education (School Support) Rules 2004	2004
Barbados	Caribbean Symposium on Inclusive Education Country Report 2007	2007
	Education Act 1981-25 and Regulations 1982 (Enacted in 1983)	1981–1983
	National Development Plan	1988–1993
	National Development Plan	1993–2002
	Strategic Plan 2002–2012	2002–2007
	TVET Council	1993
British Virgin Islands	Draft Policy Document	2005
Caribbean Regional Reforms	Association of Caribbean Tertiary Institutions (ACTI) 22nd Annual Meeting and Conference: Strategic Imperatives for the Enhancement of Institutional and Academic Performance. November 2012	2008
	Biennial Cross-Campus Conference On Education April 3–6 1990	2012
	Caribbean Advanced Proficiency Examination (CAPE)	1999
	Caribbean Association of National Training Agencies (CANTA) 2003	2003
	Caribbean Examinations Council (CXC) Recognized at a CARICOM Institution in 1973	1972
	Caribbean Secondary Education Certificate (CSEC)	1972
	Caribbean Vocational Qualification (CVQ)	2007
	CARICOM Education for Employment	2010–2016

(*Continued*)

Table 12.2 (*Continued*)   Policy Census of National Educational Reforms in the Caribbean

Caribbean Regional Reforms (Continued)	CARICOM HFLE (Health & Family Life Education) Programme	1994
	Child Friendly Schools (CFS)	2009
	CIDA's (Canadian International Developmental Agency) Caribbean Program	2009
	Competency-Based Education Training Assessment (CBETA)	2011
	Constitution of the Caribbean Association for Distance and Open Learning (CARADOL)	2013
	Creative and Productive Citizens for the Twenty-First Century	1997
	Early Childhood Care and Educational Regional Report: Latin America and the Caribbean (UNESCO) World Conference on Early Childhood Care and Education (WCECCE) September 2012	2012
	Education Management Information System (EMIS) Anguilla, Aruba, Antigua and Barbuda (2000), Barbados, British Virgin Islands (2000), Cayman Islands, Dominica, Grenada, Jamaica (1993, 1996), Montserrat, St. Lucia (1999–2000), Turks and Caicos Islands, Trinidad and Tobago	1993–2000
	EFA in the Caribbean: Assessment 2000; and several national education policy documents	2000
	Foundation for the Future: OECS Education Reform Strategy	1991
	Free Movement of Skilled Persons Act 1997	1997
	Higher Education in the XXI Century. View of Latin America and the Caribbean	1998
	OECS Education Reform Unit: Eastern Caribbean Education Reform Project: Curriculum Harmonisation: Curriculum for Grade 5/Grade 6 2008	1992
	OECS The Pillars for Partnership	2000
	Open Campus [formed through the amalgamation of the UWI Distance Education Unit and UWIDITE]	1996
	Partnership for Educational Revitalization in the Caribbean (PREAL)	1995
	Policies to improve Basic Education in the Caribbean in Education for All: Caribbean Perspectives and Imperatives	1992
	Regional Strategy for Technical and Vocational Education and Training	1990

(*Continued*)

Table 12.2 (*Continued*)   Policy Census of National Educational Reforms in the Caribbean

Caribbean Regional Reforms (Continued)	Report on United Nations Education, Science and Culture Organization (UNESCO/CARICOM) Consultation on Higher Education in the Caribbean	1998
	Roving Caregivers Programme (RCP)—Jamaica (1993), St. Lucia (2002), St. Vincent and the Grenadines (2002), Dominica (2002), Grenada (2002)	2010
	Roving Caregivers Programme (RCP) Strategy Brief August 2010	2009
	Sagicor Visionaries Challenge (Anguilla, Antigua and Barbuda, Barbados, Belize, Dominica, Grenada, Guyana, Jamaica, St. Kitts and Nevis, St. Lucia, St. Vincent and the Grenadines, and Trinidad and Tobago)	2013
	Second Caribbean Conference on Adult Education April	1970
	Second Latin American and Caribbean Conference on Global Health, January 9–11, 2013	2013
	Structural Adjustment Programs (SAP)	1982
	Technology within the context of the single market and economy	1997
	The Future of Education in the Caribbean: CARICOM Regional Education Policy	1993
	The Grand Anse Declaration	1989
	The Impact of a Home Visiting Early Childhood Intervention in the Caribbean on Cognitive and Socioemotional Child Development Preliminary Draft August 2009	2012
	The St. Lucia Declaration about Higher Education in the Caribbean in Higher Education in the Caribbean	1998
	Third International Congress on Technical and Vocational Education and Training (TVET)	2012
	University of the West Indies Distance Education Centre (UWIDEC)	1983–1996
	University of the West Indies Distance Teaching Experiment (UWIDITE)	1983–1984
	World Conference on Early Childhood Care and Education: Response Opportunities and Challenges for the Caribbean Action Agenda: An Early Childhood Policy Brief 2012	2012
Belize	Action Plan	2005–2010
	Education Sector Strategy 2011–2016	2011–2016

(*Continued*)

Table 12.2 (*Continued*)   Policy Census of National Educational Reforms in the Caribbean

Cuba	Literacy Campaign of 1961	1961
	Perfeccionamiento	1975–1976
	Perfeccionamiento continuo	1987–1989
Dominica	Education Sector Plan for Education Development in the Commonwealth of Dominica	1989–1994
	Education Development Plan 1999–2005 and Beyond	1999–2005
Dominican Republic	Ten Year Plan for Higher Education 2008–2018	2008–2018
French Guiana	Guyane Educational Authority for Primary, Secondary, and Higher Education	
Grenada	Education Act of 1976	1976
	Education Policy Document Grenada	1992–2002
	SPEED 1: Strategic Plan for Educational Enhancement and Development 2002–2010 (ended in 2004)	2002–2004
	SPEED 2: Strategic Plan for Educational Enhancement and Development 2006–2015	2002–2004
	White Paper of 1957	1959
Guyana	An Education Policy and Five Year Development Plan for Guyana	1995–2003
	Basic Education Access and Management Support (BEAMS) Project–Technical Assistance in Innovative Technologies	2002–2009
	Education Act of 1876	1876
	Industrial Training Act 1910	1910
	Reforms of Education Act 1975/1976	1975–1976
	State Paper on Education Policy	1990–1995
	Strategic Plan 2003–2007	2003–2007
Guadeloupe	Regional Innovation Strategy	2009
Haiti	2011 Strategic Education Plan	2011
	EMIS in Support of Sector-Wide Planning 2010/2011 (CapEFA Program)	2010–2011
Jamaica	Jamaica Five Year Development Plan	1990–1995
	Career Advancement Program (CAP)	2010
	Compulsory Education Program (CEP)	

(*Continued*)

Table 12.2 (*Continued*)   Policy Census of National Educational Reforms in the Caribbean

Jamaica (Continued)	Cooperate Plan 2002–2005	2002–2005
	Green Paper 2000 presented by Ministry of Education, Youth and Culture (MOEC)	2000
	HEART Trust/NTA	1982
	Human Employment and Resource Training Act of 1982	1982
	Jamaican Movement for the Advancement of Literacy (JAMAL)	1974
	Memorandum of Understanding (MoU) between Jamaica and International City and Guilds of London Institute December 2011	2011
	Reform for Secondary Education (ROSE) 1993	1993
	Reform for Secondary Education (ROSE) II 2001	2001
	The Education Act of 1965	1965
	The Education Act of 1980	1980
	The Technical and Vocational Education and Training Rationalization in Secondary Schools Project	1997
	The Technical and Vocational Work Experience Program	2000
	VISION 2030 National Development Plan & Education Sector Plan	2009
	White Paper 2001 The Way Upward—A Path for Jamaica's Education at the Start of the New Millennium	2001
	White Paper: The Way Forward	2000
Martinique	MEEF (IUFM)	2013
	2013–2014 Higher Education Grants and Social Housing	2013–2014
Montserrat	Education Policy	1996
	Cooperate Plan 2004–2008	2004–2008
	Draft Education Development Plan 2012–2020	2012–2020
	Education Development Plan 2002–2007	2002–2007
	Sustainable Development Plan 2008–2020	2008–2020
	Work Plan for 1999–2000	1999–2000
	Work Plan for 2000–2001	2000–2001
Netherlands Antilles	Seminar on Curriculum Development for "Learning to Live Together"	2001
	Foundation Based Education	1999

(*Continued*)

Table 12.2 (*Continued*)   Policy Census of National Educational Reforms in the Caribbean

Puerto Rico	Character Counts!	2010
	Schools Modernization Program	2010
	Amendment No.149	2012
	Puerto Rico's Schools for the 21st Century (Schools for the 21st Century)	2010
St. Lucia	Education Sector Development: 2000–2005 and Beyond	2000–2005
	2008–2013 Education Sector Development Plan	2008–2013
	Adult Education and Literacy Programme 1984	1984
	Education For All Global Monitoring Report: Early Childhood Care and Education (ECCE) 2007 (UNESCO)	2007
	RCP Impact Evaluation St. Lucia 2008 (AIID)	2008
	The Development and State of the Art of Adult Learning and Education (ALE): National Report of St. Lucia 2008	2008
St. Kitts and Nevis	Five Year Plan	1993–1998
	State Paper on Education	1997
	Learning and Growing: The Long Term Plan 1998–2011	1998–2011
	2004 National Assessment of BPOA + 10	1994–2003
	Educational Act No. 18 of 1975	1975
	Education (Amendment) Act No. 17 of 2007	2007
	The Special Education Unit 1982	1982
	EDUSAT 2007	2007
	White Paper on Education Development and Policy 2009–2019	2009–2019
	Early Childhood Development Policy 2009	2009
	An Early Childhood Policy Brief (UNESCO) 2012	2012
St. Vincent and the Grenadines	Education Policy	1995
	Education Sector Development Plan 2002–2007 (Volume 1&2)	2002–2007
	National Report on Development and State of the Art of Adult Learning and Education 2008	2008
	OECS Development Project 2004–2011	2004–2011

(*Continued*)

Table 12.2 (*Continued*) Policy Census of National Educational Reforms in the Caribbean

Suriname	MINOV 2000–2005	2000–2005
	Compulsory Education Act for Primary Education	1876
	Educational Development in the Republic of Suriname: A Report prepared for 47th Session of the International Conference on Education	2004
Trinidad and Tobago	Education Policy Paper 1993–2003	1993–2003
	Strategic Plan 2002–2006	2002–2006
	Medium Term Policy Framework 2011–2014 and 2005 VISION 2020 Plan	2011–2014
	Vision 2020 Operational Plan 2007–2010: 2008–2009 Progress Report	2007–2010
	Education Act of 1966	1966
	Education Sector Strategic Plan 2011–2015	2011–2015
	Government Scholarships for Postgraduate Students 2013	2013
	eConnect and Learn Programme (eCAL) 2010	2010
	Policy on Tertiary Education, Technical Vocational Education and Training, and Lifelong Learning in Trinidad and Tobago (2010)	2010
	UNDP Workshop on Trinidad and Tobago Country Strategy Action 2012–2015	2012–2015
	The Concordat of 1960	1960
	National Training Agency (NTA)	
	Secondary Education Modernization Programme 2008	2008
Turks and Caicos Islands	Department of Youth Affairs Strategic Plan 2008–2011	2008–2011
	Education Department Five Year Development Plan	1988–1993
	Five Year Education Development Plan	1999–2004
	Education Action Plan	1999
	Improving Quality and Management on Secondary Schools in the Turks and Caicos Islands	1998
	Primary Schools Principals Workshop	1995
	Preventative Education Project	1997
	PINSTEP Program	1990s
	Universal Access to and Completion of Primary Education by the Year 2000	1988–1993

national development, the numerous educational reforms that have taken place in the last two to three decades do not seem to have significantly resolved the chronic problems that affect the region as a whole, namely, crime and human security (particularly human trafficking and narcotics trafficking); HIV/AIDS (the prevalence rate across the region is second only to sub-Saharan Africa); brain drain and migration flows (data suggest that the region has lost 10%–40% of its general labor force and around 50% of its tertiary-educated segment to OECD countries [see Mishra 2006]); economic vulnerability; and international dependency, all of which have the potential to erode national educational gains that have been attained. These factors, particularly brain drain, affect the region's educational systems negatively since estimates show that per capita spending at the tertiary level outweighs primary and secondary spending in Barbados, Trinidad and Tobago, and Jamaica.

Setting the Scene

Our starting point is the recognition that early education reforms across the region were developed in a fragmented space through colonial rule by diverse and different imperial powers, and that countries have undergone dramatic changes in demography and economic growth rates as a result of these varied colonial histories. In writing this chapter, we recognize the various geographical, political, and cultural differences and similarities that constitute the Caribbean and we paint a broad depiction of the various endogenous and exogenous educational reforms and institutions (see Table 12.2) that influence the region and therefore we recognize that to write of "Caribbean Education" is not without its *problematiques*. Whereas there are many commonalities that the countries within the Caribbean Basin share, there are some marked distinctions as well; we therefore recognize that "Caribbean Education and/or Literacies" is not a monolithic term. Even within the former British West Indies, there was much differentiation in educational governance and outcomes:

> [Within] all the British West Indies, there are considerable differences between the different islands and territories. Each has its own government and administers its own internal affairs, and differences in the economy, in the extent of religious control, in terrain, in ease of contact with the outside world, have given rise to differences in education which make general statements almost impossible. (Walters 1970, p. 111)

This chapter examines both the gains in educational reforms and the challenges that these countries have faced, paying particular attention to the areas of contentious reforms that have focused on integrating strategies and techniques from public administration, new public management or corporate managerialism to engender national educational reforms. There are roughly three periods during which the historical development of education within the Caribbean can be looked at: (1) colonial education; (2) post-emancipation education; and (3) post-independence education reforms to present-day. While we present a brief overview of the first two periods, we show that in the post-independence periods, an increasing emphasis on performance, outputs, decentralization, and competition created educational systems premised on new managerialism. We therefore investigate the various tiers and aspects of education: children under 6 years old have various schooling options; pre-primary (kindergarten)/ages 4–6; primary (Grades 1–6)/ages 6–12; lower-secondary (Grades 7–9)/ages 12–15; upper-secondary (Grades 10–11)/ages 15–17; form 6

(Grades 12–13 or advanced placement classes)/ages 17–19; tertiary, vocational education; and teacher training (ages vary).* Thus, it is within a changing environment of national, subregional, and regional policy making that we argue in the second part of this chapter that educational reform in the Caribbean has occurred across three distinct generations of reforms: (1) commencing in 1970s and 1980s, under 6 years old, various options exist (2) then continuing within the changing post-cold war global environment of 1989; and (3) now in its present phase, based on Millennium Development Goals (MDGs) and the post-2015, Education For All (EFA) goals, the post-2015 sustainable development agenda. To better analyze contemporary/post-independence public administration of education in the Caribbean, we begin by sketching out a brief overview of the historical development of colonial education across the region.

Colonial Education

The Spanish encounter with the various indigenous peoples within the Caribbean in 1492 set forth a train of events that immensely transformed the region. Prior to this encounter, there is not much historical record of the nonformal education that existed among the indigenous peoples (or "nations" as they are called today). Historical evidence suggests that nonformal education most likely would have been of a skills-based nature, as survival would have depended keenly upon the successful acquisition and deployment of said skills. The Spanish aimed to "Christianize" the indigenous people of the Americas, called Indians (a term brought from India by Christopher Columbus), or Amerindians† (as used in Guyana and Suriname); these attempts focused on religious conversions constituted the extent of the natives' education.‡ The initial introduction of African slaves did not transform this by much, since "planters feared that any attempt to educate this group would be dangerous to the safety of the whites ... [and that] the limited work skills which they needed could usually be acquired on the job and hence for them no formal training was considered necessary" (Bacchus 1990, p. 21). The best educational provisions were therefore reserved for Spanish settlers, with a few mulattoes and mestizos having access as well.

By the seventeenth century, England, France, and the Netherlands had ratcheted up their assaults on Spanish hegemony, introducing their own settlers to the Caribbean region (Ferguson 2008). Education for these early settlers was mostly nonexistent and that which was offered was not of the greatest quality (Bacchus 1990). With the rise of plantological influence on social stratification, there developed "a fairly rigid social structure in West Indian societies in which status depended on one's legal position, i.e., whether one was a freeman, an indentured servant, or a slave, and second on one's colour" (Bacchus 1990, p. 52); this in turn would "color" the educational provisions to various groups for years to come. Those plantation owners who had intended to return to Britain often, ensured that their children (mostly male) were educated overseas, from primary school onward.

These settlers, like the Spanish, were loath to provide any education (including religious instruction) to the black slave population, lest such an education lead to a disintegration of the social order. The governor of Martinique, in correspondence with France, is quoted as having

---

* The educational tiers vary across the different countries, with a change of the name "Form" (a British Concept) to "Grades" (an American Concept). While there is no harmonizing of the tiers of educational levels across the region, it is generally accepted that by age six, children ought to be in primary school.
† The Amerindians live in the interior region of Guyana and are split into seven "tribes" or "nations": Akawaio, Arekuna, Barima River Caribe, Macusi, Patamona, Waiwai, and Wapisiana.
‡ The Church usually closely monitored any other education beyond this.

written "the safety of the Whites demands that they [the slaves] should be kept in the most profound ignorance" (as cited Bacchus 1990, pp. 139–140). Despite these fears, provision of education in the Caribbean was still facilitated largely by the missionaries:

> While each had an important role to play, sometimes resisting and sometimes assisting with the provision of education, it was the missionaries who, during these early years, made the most significant overall contribution in this field, especially among the free blacks, the free coloureds and the slaves. They were almost the 'sole providers of education' for the non-white population in general; therefore, any understanding of the early educational developments in the West Indies require a closer examination of their work, their educational philosophies, their achievements and their failures. (Bacchus 1990, p. 143)

Chief among the religious education providers were the Anglicans, Roman Catholics, Moravians, Methodists, and Baptists. However, prior to emancipation of the slaves, the educational efforts of these missionaries yielded mediocre results; hindrances included persistent antagonism from the plantation/slave owners, limited free time that the slaves had for instruction, inhospitable physical conditions, and inadequate, and often culturally irrelevant materials (Bacchus 1990). The march toward emancipation from slavery in 1834 witnessed attitudinal shifts among some plantation owners regarding the education of slaves. As emancipation approached, the fervor for educational access among slaves was decidedly high. As Gordon (1998) notes:

> Instruction, particularly in literacy, was undoubtedly an aspiration of many slaves, apprentices and ex-slaves, both in the decade before emancipation and in the first optimistic years of freedom ... Only a minority received a formal education; the schools were a limited factor in the development of the 'free society' ... The thirst for literacy in the last years of slavery was phenomenal in its urgency, in the initiatives taken by themselves and in the islandwide scope of demand. (pp. 1–2)

Missionaries offered Sunday and evening classes to assist with this burgeoning need. Slaves learnt from few children who were learning to read in mission day schools. There were almost not enough books for ex-slaves; so much so was the desire. Materials employed included "alphabets, primers, spelling books, bibles, prayer books, religious tracts, hymns, [and] catechisms" (Gordon 1998, p. 2). During this period, "the Sunday schools remained the most organized popular instruction for decades to come" (Gordon 1998, p. 3).

In sum, pre-emancipation education focused on providing a limited segment of the population access to certain types of educative experiences, and in some instances prepared locals for readily available bureaucratic functions and jobs within country. The country-specific education plan in the Anglophone Caribbean was part of a wider trend that came to be known as "adaptive education" (Whitehead 2005a, 2005b) since it used local curricula and was decentralized. This also created a dual educational system that on the one hand sought to educate some Africans using their local traditions and customs and on the other hand instructed a select few for placement in the local colonial office. In the French Caribbean, the French pursued policies "of assimilation or of association" (Heggoy 1984; White 1996) in that they concentrated on "civilizing" and creating French men of the locals through a highly centralized system. These policies that used French as the medium of instruction put forward the dominant notion that "Western civilization, as represented by France, was superior to anything found locally" (Heggoy 1984, pp. 105–106). In sum, White (1996) categorized the British system as "centrifugal" and the French system as "centripetal" since the British had a "hands-off, decentralised approach" based on "the British state policy of 'indirect rule'" while the French system "was heavily centralized . . . [and] sought an even closer relationship between the dependency and the mother country" (p. 21). The point of colonial education was to maintain the divide between the colonizer and the colonized by ensuring that access to education was only granted to a select few who could represent the colonial interest and work alongside the colonizer in the local country office.

Post-Emancipation Education Reforms

In the immediate post-emancipation period, the focus was on granting expanded access of education to all. In 1833, the British government created the *Negro Education Grant*, which subsidized religious bodies in their attempts to construct more schools and employ more teachers (Campbell 1965; Gordon 1962a, 1963a). This grant lasted for 5 years and all funding ended in 1845. Gordon (1963b) notes "the idea for a public system of universal education in the West Indies was born in 1833, and presented in the fifth resolution of the House of Commons introducing the act to emancipate British slaves" (p. 1). There were many reports commissioned on the Caribbean. Rev. John Sterling submitted one such report, in which he concluded that the Negro Education Grant, despite its flaws, engendered several outcomes: (1) Christianity was established as the religion of the Caribbean, because of its alliance with schools; (2) realization of the challenges of operating a nascent educational system; and (3) the emergence of popular education gained traction and acceptance (Gordon 1962a, p. 153). In 1834, when slavery was abolished, there was a period of apprenticeship before full emancipation would be granted, but it was immediately following emancipation that the idea for popular education gained tremendous momentum (Walters 1970).

With the Negro Education Grant ceasing to exist, financing of elementary education shifted to local legislative bodies, missionaries, and parents (Bacchus 1994). Despite this, enrollment numbers slowly, but steadily, increased. Education inspectors remained critical of the quality of education being offered. Far more challenging was the creation, and maintenance of secondary and post-secondary schools. This deficit was attributable to the early settlers' desires to return to Europe; therefore, they did not make any substantive investments in local secondary and post-secondary educational structures. After abolition, there was more financial support for elementary education than for secondary education; administrators and legislatures believed that those who could afford secondary education should shoulder the costs. However, "an unstated objective of this reluctance to provide government aid for secondary education was to discourage any rise in the educational and occupational aspirations of the lower classes" (Bacchus 1994, p. 220). The precipitous declines in the sugar industry meant less income, which in turn facilitated increased migration of whites back to Europe. White migration, back to the home colonies, and in some instances to other colonies, left vacancies within various administrative bureaucracies and within the secondary schooling system. Secondary education became one of the best routes for social mobility, while primary-only education facilitated lower-level white-collar jobs (Bacchus 1994).

Because of varied inter-religious conflicts, around the 1850s, there were recommendations by the *Keenan Report* of 1896 for a secular system of education administration, including boards of education and teacher training schools. However, this was vigorously contested by the various religious denominations that ran many schools. Additionally, the *Keenan Report* (1869) called for improved education for East Indian indentured laborers,* teacher education, and culturally relevant pedagogy (see *Keenan Report* 1869, as cited in Gordon 1962b). As a compromise, in Trinidad, for example, "a dual system was introduced by which the Government would provide some schools and the religious bodies would be assisted in the provision of others"† (Gordon 1962b, p. 16). Additionally, the *Keenan Report* (1869)‡ issued a clarion call for a Caribbean University.§ *The Phelps-Stokes Commission to the British Colonies* in the 1920s advocated a curriculum that promoted charter development, health and hygiene, productive skills, improved family life, and healthy recreation (Jones 1925 as cited in Metzler 2009). By 1945 when the famous *Report of West India Royal Commission* (generally referred to as *The Moyne Report*) was published and disseminated, there was room for much improvement still.

The *Moyne Report* highlighted that students were not being educated with the skills and knowledge that the local context required. The curricula in the secondary schools of the former colonies largely resembled those of Europe (Williams 1946), though, in some instances, they had expanded beyond mere religious instruction.¶ About educational materials, Williams (1956) wrote that "the instructional materials ... include a vast quantity of extraneous material which has no relevance for the Caribbean area" (p. 6). This further augmented the calls for an increased focus on vocational/technical and agricultural education by varied educationalists and reports; however, this was met with fervent opposition by parents:

> Those who want the schools to stress the vocational aspect in the belief that this will help industrial recruitment are probably not doing a real service to industrial development. In many parts of the Caribbean there is an objection by parents to their children learning through the hands. The usual reason given is that it is due to the memory of slavery ... [T]he mistake made is to think that a richer life can only be achieved by deserting the soil. The aim should be to improve living in rural areas and make it more attractive. (Howe 1956, p. 16)

Despite parental opposition to vocational/technical education, there was considerable demand for the skills that such an education provided.** Institutes that facilitated technical education were created in Aruba, Barbados, British Guiana, Curacao, French Guiana, Guadeloupe, Martinique, Puerto Rico, St. Kitts, Suriname, and Trinidad (Howe 1956).

As the drumbeat toward independence intensified in the Caribbean, education would take on an even greater vitality. Some islands would remain officially linked to their former colonizers

---

* A great number of East Indian indentured laborers decided to stay in Trinidad and British Guiana (now Guyana) beyond the expiration of their contracts; "They were, however, unwilling to send their children to the schools attended by Negro children" (Gordon 1963b, p. 81).
† Even to this day, there is much contestation in several Caribbean countries regarding this dual education system. One critic notes: "What is generally called the 'dual system of control' or the 'church-state partnership' in education is really more one-sided than these terms suggest. Government provides most of the finance but concedes the control of most schools to the churches" (Bolland 1998, pp. 27–28). (see Williams 2012, for an exploration of the neocolonial effects of this dual education system in modern-day Trinidad.)
‡ Part II of this report focused on secondary and higher education (Gordon 1963a).
§ At the time of emancipation, Codrington College was the sole provider of higher education (Gordon 1963b).
¶ Dr. Howe, an educational consultant for UNESCO, wrote in 1956 "in the Caribbean, there is no doubt that education has, on the whole, followed metropolitan patterns" (Howe 1956, p. 13).
** Sherlock posited, "lacking technical education, Caribbean society has grown up with its hands untrained" (1949/1950, p. 14).

(see Table 12.1) and some would take the trajectory of independence; this reflected differences in the varied educational provisions as well:

> The administration of education in British and Netherlands Caribbean countries differs fundamentally from that in the French and United States countries, the former representing control of educational development by two agencies—government and private—, ... and the latter, control by a single authority, the State. (Alcala 1956, p. 45)

In sum, many countries entered the independence era with different inadequacies across all spectrums of the educational sphere.

Post-Independence Educational Reforms to Present

Since independence, we argue that education reforms and developments have gone through three distinctive generations: (1) beginning in the 1970s and 1980s with reorganizations that focused on access, equity, and inclusion; (2) continuing during the policy periods between 1989 and 2000, and using neoliberalism to emphasize quality, accountability, and efficiency as well as fiscal austerity; and (3) the current and third wave of transformations from 2000 to present-day, which strive to create citizens for a knowledge-based economy. In each of the sections below, we show that these three distinctive generations of reforms can be grouped under several institutional mechanisms that occurred simultaneously across several countries. While it is not our intention to make sweeping generalizations, we recognize that several countries during the 1980s underwent structural adjustment programs and used the same policy responses (privatization, deregulation, liberalization, and devaluation) to common policy problems (inefficient public sector and public institutions) that were defined either by exogenous or by endogenous actors, agencies, and donors to foster and propel industrialization and economic development (through investment in an educated populace). Table 12.2 lists the names of some country-specific policies that arose during these generations of reforms.

First Generation of Reforms: 1970s–1980s

Even before independence, various leaders in the Caribbean were promulgating educational reform and expansion as key to economic development (Sherlock 1949/1950; Springer 1965) and nation building (Gordon 1979/1980). Independence within the Caribbean accompanied heightened expectations from the citizenry for increased access to education. As Selvaratnam (1988) notes:

> With the achievement of political independence from their colonial masters in the post-war years, one of the major policy initiatives in these countries was the large scale expansion of educational provision at all levels under strong central state control. This unprecedented expansionist educational policy was spurred largely by the urgent issues of national unity, economic growth, manpower needs, and the promotion of greater equality of opportunity ... dramatically chang[ing] the system from an elite to a mass base phenomenon and thus enhanced the access to educational opportunity for large sections of school-going population, both boys and girls and made remarkable strides at the tertiary level. (p. 129)

Rapid population increases also necessitated expanded educational provisions; however, few countries could afford to independently fund the magnitude of educational expansions for which citizens hungered (Gray 1969). The independence era did not signal an abandonment of Western models of education (Selvaratnam 1988), with many pre-independence educational issues, such as lack of culturally relevant curricula (Bishop 1964; Schrouder 2008), still persisting. Focused on the need to foster economic development, governments pursued large-scale projects, including the construction of many new secondary schools, leading in some cases to "project overload" (London 1993), which in turn diminished the comprehensive implementational impact of educational expansion.

Since governments lacked the financial wherewithal to fuel these ambitious intentions for educational expansion, some of them procured loans:

> Increased educational infrastructure was provided principally from heavy external borrowing. This was predicated on the positive economic circumstances that existed in most territories, especially during the decade of the sixties. By the late 1970s and 1980s, however, a combination of factors led to severe economic problems. The consequence was the adoption of structural adjustment policies, which from the point of view of most countries, brought more harm than good. The social sector was the major casualty. The implementation of structural adjustment policies contributed to the undermining of several new initiatives that had been implemented for the development of education. (UNESCO 1996, pp. 1–2)

Neoclassical economic reforms pursued by Helmut Kohl in Germany, Margaret Thatcher in the United Kingdom, and Ronald Reagan in the United States during the 1970s and 1980s shredded many a social nets around the world; the Caribbean was not immune to these major tectonic shifts in global capital (Lewis 2006). Austerity measures that accompanied structural adjustment programs usually meant drastic cuts at the expense of welfare provisions, such as health care and education. Between 1980 and 2000, educational expenditures accounted for less than 10% of the Caribbean governments' gross domestic product (GDP) (Lewis 2006).

While Caribbean governments spent heavily on educational reform during the immediate post-independence period, the 1970s and 1980s, they experienced the first generation or wave of educational reforms. We advance that the wave of first generation reforms, during the 1970s and 1980s that focused on access, equity, and inclusion, had four distinctive institutional mechanisms that ran concurrently (Jules 2010). The institutional mechanisms are categorized as follows: (1) the institutional phase; (2) the oil crisis and structural adjustment phase; (3) the socialist and ideological pluralism phase; and (4) the HIV/AIDS generation phase.

First Generation of Reforms: The Institutional Phase

The first institutional reforms after independence began with the creation of a regional testing institution in the Anglophone countries. The Caribbean Examination Council (CXC) was established in 1972 within 15 of the now 16 members* (and admits external entries from St. Maarten, Saba, and the Netherlands Antilles) to conduct examinations as well as award certificates and diplomas (see Table 12.3). Its mandate is exerted through the Caribbean Secondary Education Certificate (CSEC) established in 1979 and the Caribbean Advanced Proficiency

---

* CXC members are Anguilla, Antigua and Barbuda, Barbados, Belize, the British Virgin Islands, the Cayman Islands, Dominica, Grenada, Guyana, Jamaica, Montserrat, St. Kitts and Nevis, St. Lucia, St. Vincent and the Grenadines, Trinidad and Tobago, and the Turks and Caicos Islands.

Table 12.3 Secondary School Exit Exam/High School Equivalency

Country	Secondary School Exit Exam/High School Equivalency
Antigua and Barbuda	CSEC/CAPE
Bahamas	Bahamas General Certificate of Secondary Education (BGCSE)/CSEC/CAPE
Barbados	CSEC/CAPE
Belize	CSEC/CAPE
British Virgin Islands	CSEC/CAPE
Cuba	Bachillerato/Bachiller
Dominica	CSEC/CAPE
Dominican Republic	Bachiller/Bachillerato
Grenada	CSEC/CAPE
Guyana	CSEC/CAPE
Guadeloupe	Baccalauréat or Le Bac
Jamaica	CSEC/CAPE
Haiti	Baccalauréat II—Philosophie
Montserrat	CSEC/CAPE
Netherlands Antilles	HAVO (*Hoger Algemeen Voortgezet Onderwijs* or General Secondary Education diploma)/VWO (*Voorbereidend Wetenschappelijk Onderwijs* or preparatory middle-level vocational education)/MAVO (Junior Secondary Education)/BVO (Lower Vocational Education)
St. Kitts and Nevis	CSEC/CAPE
St. Lucia	CSEC/CAPE
St. Vincent and the Grenadines	CSEC/CAPE
Suriname	HAVO (Hoger Algemeen Voortgezet Onderwijs) or VWO (Voorbereidend Wetenschappelijk Onderwijs)
Trinidad and Tobago	CSEC/CAPE

Source: Wright University, *High School Equivalency*. Retrieved from http://www.wright.edu/ucie/student/highschoolequivalency.html, n.d.

Examination (CAPE) that started in 1998. CSEC replaced the UK-based General Certificate Examination (O-Level) and tests students in both academic and technical/vocational subjects. CAPE replaced the Advanced Level General Certificate of Education (A-Level) and fulfills the requirements for programs and professional courses at regional and extra-regional universities and other tertiary level institutions (CARICOM 2005). Mathematics and English A exams are mandatory, while students have a choice of 31 other CSEC subjects to choose from, including 28 subjects at the general proficiency and 5 at technical proficiency. Students can select any of the 16 CAPE examinations and may earn a diploma after completing six units and an associate degree after completing seven units including Caribbean Studies and Communication Studies. The University of the West Indies (UWI) has been a major contributor to the development and design of CXC and continues to be involved in providing policy directions as well as in the provision of technical and educational expertise (Hall and Chuck-A-Sang 2008). UWI and national universities that accept CXC expect that candidates must pass a minimum of five CSEC courses with grades 1–3 (A–C), with passes in English A and Mathematics.

In the non-Anglophone countries, testing at the end of secondary school is done within the parameters of the home country. For example, as Table 12.3 shows, students in Guadeloupe spend 3 years in the premier cycle (first cycle) in the *collège* and 4 years in the second cycle in the *lycée*, after which they sit for the academic qualification of the *baccalauréat* or *le bac*. In Haiti, a *Brevet Elementaire du Premier Cycle* is awarded under the traditional system and *revet d'Enseignment Fondamental* under the reform system after completion of lower secondary; a *Baccalaureat II* is awarded in the traditional system and *Baccalaureat or Diplome d'Enseignement Secondaire* is awarded under the reform system; and in other instances, a technical certificate is awarded after completion of technical secondary school.

First Generation of Reforms: The Oil Crises and Structural Adjustment Phase

The second sets of reforms during this period were in response to the oil crisis of 1973/1974 and the oil shock of 1977. These crises had wider structural effects because they conjoined with the then problems of the international capitalist system—"the rising oil prices and falling commodity process and the world inflation and recession" (Hall 2001, p. xiv). Combined, these crises devastated national economies and forced many countries to implement the International Monetary Fund (IMF) and World Bank backed Structural Adjustment Programs (SAPs). These reforms were geared toward fostering economic stabilization (which concentrated on stabilizing fiscal deficits, reducing balance of payments, and bringing staff inflation rates down), modifying trade regimes, reducing subsidies, changing tax policies, shrinking the public sector wage bill, and strengthening domestic markets. This caused the focus of the nation state to shift from "'managing development' to 'facilitating development' and from 'inward-looking' to 'outward-looking' development strategies" (Sutton 2006, p. 196) thus leading to the dismantling of local industries and the opening up of national borders to foreign imports and foreign direct investment.

This resulted in the devastation of local economies, massive social upheaval, and soaring debt. In education, SAPs were implemented under the guise of public sector reforms. For example, the SAP reform titled *the Economic Recovery Programme* of 1989 in Guyana, one of the first countries in the developing world to embark on structural adjustment from 1981 to 1983, focused on advancing economic growth through public sector restructuring. In education, this led to a public sector that focused on an "efficient, transparent, high-performing and dedicated organisation, which can serve as the engine and catalyst for national development of all the other sectors—private, non-profit, voluntary and nongovernmental" (Sutton 2006, p. 118). While SAPs had "a mere superficiality or tinkering with the public institutions, leaving their essential features intact" (Sutton 2006, p. 132), they completely restructured national educational systems, leading to decreases in teacher salaries, higher education spending, and greater emphases on improving efficiency and effectiveness.

First Generation of Reforms: The Socialism and Ideological Pluralism Phase

The third institutional transformation transpired in Cuba (1959–present), Grenada (1979–1983), Guyana (1971–1985), and Jamaica (1972–1978) as these countries fixated on developing egalitarian societies through various types of socialist reforms. While the Cuban Revolution of 1959 focused on communist reforms, the experimentations with different types of socialism in Grenada, Guyana, and Jamaica stemmed from the failure of the application of the development strategies of "industrialization by invitation (IBI)" (Campbell 2004; Lewis 1950; Payne 1984; Rose 2002) in the 1940s and "import-substitution industrialization (ISI)" (Baer 1972; Beckford 1972) which was developed by the United Nations Economic Commission of Latin America (ECLAC) and first introduced in the 1950s. IBI was applied to other Caribbean countries after being successfully tested in Puerto Rico.* It focused on replacing plantation economies through the lowering of tariffs, increasing incentives, and attracting foreign investment to decrease unemployment, thereby raising GDP and gross national product (GNP). ISI concentrated on achieving "national autonomy through state control and planning of the economy under a middle class comprised of intellectuals and industrialists" to ensure the "development of economic and political policies designed to restrict foreign interests" (Rose 2002, p. 35). The goal of applying both of these economic development strategies to national systems was to develop local human capital and to wean off external dependency that was part of the colonial legacy.

By the late 1970s, several factors continued to curtail development regionally: underemployment, high population growth rates, shortage of foreign currencies, weak and vulnerable production structures, brain drain, and high levels of external corporate capital and proprietorship of key resources (Beckford 1972; Rose 2002). Guyana, under Prime Minister Linden Forbes Sampson Burnham†; Jamaica, underneath Prime Minister Michael Norman Manley‡; and Grenada, under Prime Minister Maurice Rupert Bishop§ opted for various forms of socialism (Hall 2003; Jules 2010). This political fragmentation within Anglophone countries in the region or "ideological pluralism" (a phrase coined by Caribbean Community [CARICOM] leaders in the early 1980s) indicated the varying developmental ideologies of its member states. Politically, ideological pluralism also represented the inability of the Conference of Heads of Government of the Caribbean Community (CHGCC), the highest body within the Caribbean, to meet between 1975 and 1982, thus redefining economic and social development between CARICOM countries. Below, we briefly describe the impact of various socialist projects upon education across the Caribbean Basin.

Popular Socialist Education in Cuba

With popular socialism in Cuba, education reform had three periods: (1) mass education (1959–1962); (2) education for economic development (1962–1968); and (3) crafting the new citizen (1965–1990) (see Gott 2004). The first reform commenced with the Cuban Literacy Campaign

---

* The Puerto Rican strategy called "Operation Bootstrap" was based on drawing US entrepreneurs to the island in order to provide private investment, social capital, and infrastructure bankrolled through the sale of US bonds. Additionally, US firms were persuaded to locate industrial sites there through elaborate incentive programs that gave tax concessions, grants, subsidized rentals and utility rates, and low wage rates.
† Prime minister from 1964 to 1980 and president from 1980 to 1985 of the People's National Congress (PNC).
‡ Prime minister between 1972 and 1980 and 1989 and 1992 and member of the People's National Party (PNP).
§ After the 1979 Coup d'état, self-proclaimed prime minister from 1979 to 1983 and member of the New Jewel Movement (NJM).

of 1961, or "Year of Education." The literacy campaign focused on eradicating widespread illiteracy by concentrating on political and economic development as a way of creating a unified Communist *conciencia* (see Blum 2011; Carnoy 2007; Philip et al. 2008). The campaign created literacy brigades that built schools, trained new educators, and taught reading and writing to create a skilled labor force. In the late 1950s, numerous army barracks acted as schools, and in the mid-1960s, boarding schools were created to educate revolutionary citizens and inspire greater participation for rural women in the emerging industrial society. Polytechnical education, which emphasized the ability to learn scientific principles and handle tools and equipment, emerged as a way to foster collectivism.

By the 1960s, Cuba achieved great strides in eradicating illiteracy and expanding mass schooling. In the 1970s, it shifted from quantitative gains to qualitative improvements with the emergence of closer ties with the Soviet Union. In 1971, new reforms began after the *First National Congress on Education and Culture* and at the 1971 conference, delegates endorsed revisions and enhancements in the structure of education since dropout rates were high (particularly in rural areas), the curriculum was outdated, textbooks were inappropriate, and teacher training programs were inadequate (Carnoy 2007; Jules 2013b). At the *Second Congress for Young Communists* in 1972, delegates called for drastic interventions for youths who had antisocial behavior, especially those who had not studied or worked. The Congress also advocated for tenth graders to teach, in the countryside, at the secondary level. With the creation of the "Five-Year Plan in 1976–1981," classroom hours were increased and the number of schooling years reduced from 13 to 12. After the Mariel boatlift in 1980, when over 125,000 Cubans fled the nation, educational reforms were given attention, particularly teacher education. The end of the Cold War saw a drastic increase in rural to urban migrations and a new set of educational reforms. These reforms decreased the educational budget leading to the restructuring of stipends (that were rebranded as student loans) and slight curricula and pedagogical modifications—including the replacement of Russian with English as the desired foreign language and the introduction of civic education in ninth grade.

Cooperative Socialist Education in Guyana

Cooperative socialism in Guyana was twofold in that it focused on involving Guyanese in their country's economy and ridding the country of the effects of dependent capitalist development. Eighty percent of the commanding heights (the key economic sectors) were nationalized (Hall 2001; Jules 2010; Richardson 1992). Education reforms focused on producing employment opportunities, equalizing the distribution of incomes, increasing equitable geographic distribution of economic activities, and attaining self-sustained economic growth (Lee 2000; Rose 2002). Reforms were based on de-privatizing and expanding mass schooling. Education was made free from nursery to university, a new teachers training college was built, and a new secondary school of excellence—the President's College—was introduced. Cooperative socialism lasted until Burnham's death in 1985, and at that time, many primary and secondary teachers were not paid on time; illiteracy increased sharply as students failed their primary and secondary school exit examinations; and the university level suffered since it had more qualified staff than they could afford (Rose 2002). During the 1990s, major reforms occurred including the National Fourth-Form Achievement Test in 1988, the enactment of the Primary Education Improvement Project by the Inter-American Development Bank (IDB) in 1990, the secondary School Reform Programme, and the inauguration of user fees at the University of Guyana.

Democratic Socialist Education in Jamaica

Democratic socialism in Jamaica used the concept of "single touchstone of right and wrong" and a belief in the Christian ideals of equity for all of God's children as its foundation (Rose 2002, p. 245). Reforms were geared toward improving the livelihoods of Jamaicans and increasing political participation. Attention was given to equity through the replacement of the British educational system while expanding mass schooling at the primary and secondary levels. The public school age requirements for primary school education increased from 15 to 17. Teacher training programs were restructured since "teachers needed to undergo a process of self-transformation ... [including] comprehen[sion of] a new set of objectives ... [and] evolv[ing] a new set of techniques that can give effect to new targets" (Rose 2002, p. 260). In 1972, the Jamaican Movement for the Advancement of Literacy (JAMAL) Foundation was created and a national adult literacy program were implemented. All educational fees were removed to allow children to pass "through similarly endowed institutions wherein they must mix regardless of parental background" (Rose 2002, p. 260). However, by 1978, democratic socialism had begun to collapse. Facing numerous internal problems in public agencies, Jamaica instigated negotiations with the IMF's Extended Fund Facility since its foreign exchange reserves were declining, creating a negative growth rate.

Revolutionary Socialist Education in Grenada

In 1979, with the support of Cuba, Guyana, and Jamaica, the Marxist-Leninist New Jewel Movement, under former president Maurice Bishop and the People's Revolutionary Government (PRG), enacted revolutionary socialism in Grenada. The PRG focused on rebuilding Grenada's economy after the apparent economic destruction caused by former president Eric Gairy's 1967–1979 government. The socialist theory of noncapitalist development and the principles and doctrines of Marxism-Leninism aimed at mobilizing the masses were enacted (Payne 1984; Rose 2002). Revolutionary socialism in Grenada represented a new political culture aimed at participatory democracy. Education reforms were based on five programs designed to provide access to everyone: (1) the "Continuous Education Program," focused on eradicating rural illiteracy especially among adults; (2) the "National-in-Service Teacher Education Programme (NISTEP)," replaced the Grenada Teacher's College; (3) "Education for All," provided free secondary schooling; (4) "New Content in Curriculum," focused on developing history, culture, and Grenadian values; and (5) "Work-Study Approach," aimed at helping students find adequate labor-intensive and technological skills (Rose 2002, pp. 311–315). The expansion of mass schooling was seen as emancipating "the masses from ignorance and a sense of cultural inferiority" (Rose 2002, p. 310). CARICOM members trying to contain "socialism to a country" sanctioned the 1983 US-led "invasion or intervention" (Clegg and Williams 2013) of Grenada. The revolution formally ended with the death of Prime Minister Maurice Bishop. The invasion soured regional relations and led to the demise of revolutionary socialism in the Caribbean.

First Generation of Reforms: The HIV/AIDS Generation Phase

In the 1980s, education reform centered on combating HIV/AIDS.* The adult HIV infection rate, of 1%, is second globally to sub-Saharan Africa (UNAIDS and WHO 2009). Caribbean

---

* HIV/AIDS is the leading cause of death among 25–44-year-olds across the region.

youth and teachers are part of the "AIDS generation" (Kiragu 2001; Jules 2012a) because of two specific indicators: (1) the high prevalence rate of HIV/AIDS in the region and (2) the youth of the Caribbean coming of age in a region plagued by the epidemic; it is an everyday fact of life for them (Jules 2012a). The high prevalence rate of HIV/AIDS in the Caribbean has significantly impacted the teaching profession and influenced the performance, retention, training, and recruitment of teachers (see Risley et al. 2007). In other words, the projection on the effect of HIV and AIDS on education supply in the Caribbean using the Ed-SIDA model* (Grassly et al. 2003; World Bank and Partnership for Child Development 2006) can be viewed as having either quantity effects (loss of trained teacher, fewer teachers due to AIDS mortality, and lack of attendance) or quality effects (a decreased teacher capability and management capacity) representing an approximate loss of 12,000 teachers by 2015 (see Risley et al. 2007). Furthermore, it has removed "wage-earners from employment, deflect[ed] resources to medical and health care, and draw[n] down on savings and capital" (Kelly and Bain 2003, p. 45) while engendering losses of professional personnel, increases in truancy, medical care spending, and the cost needed to recruit and train auxiliary labor. Coupled with these facts, students and youth of childbearing ages continue to be affected. Allen (2002) found that 55% of boys and 24% of girls had sexual intercourse prior to age 10 (last year of primary school) while an additional 23% of boys and 16% of girls reported that they had engaged in sexual activity between the ages of 11 and 12 (first year of secondary school).

It was not until the 1990s that educational reforms focused on prevention, de-stigmatization, acclimatization, and the rights of people living with HIV and AIDS. Several countries have developed national HIV/AIDS policies with the help of the Pan Caribbean Health Organization. In 1994, a Health and Family Life Education (HFLE) Curriculum (see chapter 17 in this book), proposed by and developed in CARICOM countries, was created to help educate students aged 9 to 14 on health issues. Its aims included the following:

- Enhancing the potential of young persons to become productive and contributing adults/citizens
- Promoting an understanding of the principles that underlie personal and social well-being
- Fostering the development of knowledge, skills, and attitudes that make for healthy family life
- Providing opportunities to demonstrate sound health related knowledge, attitudes, and practices
- Increasing the ability to practice responsible decision making about social and sexual behavior
- Heightening the awareness of children and youth of the fact that the choices they make in everyday life profoundly influence their health and personal development into adulthood (UNICEF 2009, p. 5)

In 2003, CARICOM countries endorsed a shift from HFLE using an "information-based model to a skills development model" (p. 3) that now has four thematic areas: sexuality and sexual health (which encompasses HIV/AIDS prevention); self and interpersonal relationships (which

---

* The Ed-SIDA mode was developed to measure the impact of HIV on education sector by using sophisticated and in-depth evaluations and projections for multiple countries or multiple regions within individual countries. Ed-SIDA Model of Impact of HIV on Education used Ministries of Education data on teacher numbers, teacher training and recruitment, and school-age population projections. It then generates results that discusses AIDS mortality in relation to teacher attrition rates, teacher absenteeism, loss arising from AIDS illness, and recruitment changes and impact of pupil–teacher ratios.

incorporates violence prevention); appropriate eating and fitness; and managing the environment (UNICEF et al. 2008).

In sum, the four institutional mechanisms of educational reforms, under the first generation of reforms, ensured that "by the early 1980s, several Caribbean countries had developed impressive education systems, relative to many other countries with comparable per capita income" (World Bank 1993, p. xiv). These institutional developments focused on applying different types of structural transformations in creating an educated citizenry.

Second Generation of Reforms: 1989–2000

While educational reforms of the 1980s and 1990s fostered great strides in several areas—namely, high enrollment rates at the pre-primary levels, universal primary education (almost 100%), the availability of secondary education, and the creation of several national colleges and universities—numerous challenges remained at the end of the 1990s, including the lack of classroom material, upkeep of physical plant and equipment, increases in prices of and decline in resources, and large-scale exodus of teachers (Jules 2010; UNESCO 1996). By 1990, the altering global landscape with the end of the Cold War saw the start of the second generation of educational reforms which we categorize as having three idiosyncratic institutional mechanisms: (1) neoliberalism and education; (2) tertiary education phase; and (3) international benchmarks and regional consequences, all of which occurred concurrently. This period began with the application of neoliberalism, which had drastic effects on tertiary education, and was also marked by foci on creating and meeting internal benchmarks and regional targets. In the section that follows, we will cover the impact that neoliberalism, internationalization, and regionalization had on education in the Caribbean, in addition to the topics of tertiary education and international benchmarks. Table 12.2 illustrates some of the individual country-specific reforms that were undertaken.

Second Generation of Reforms: Neoliberalism and Education

The first phase of the second generation of reforms began with the application of Thatcherism and Reaganomics in the region as countries sought to meet international educational targets by focusing on privatizing, trade liberalization, and deregulation of a bloated public sector. The core thinking behind neoliberalist policy interventions is that youth must "chase credentials" (Jackson and Bisset 2005; Lakes and Carter 2011) to gain successful employment. The core principles of neoliberalism, with their antecedents in the Washington Consensus model of development, focus on "cut[ting] back the state, open[ing] trade, reduce[ing] social spending, deregulate[ing] and privatize[ing]" national systems (Bedford 2007, p. 291; see Griffith 2010 for the consequence of neoliberalism in the Caribbean). This particular model of educational reform has given rise to "educational fundamentalism" (Jones 1997) and "educational multilateralism" (Mundy 1998). The former describes the World Bank's and IMF's vigorous increase in educational financing based on their perspective of the "bankable" aspects of tangible resources. The latter details the institutionalization of "embedded liberalism" as a core attribute and mandate of multilateralism institutions in the postwar period.

In the Caribbean, the application of principles of neoliberalism occurred in the late 1980s as part of a boarder trickledown effect by international organizations and governmental officials as they sought to restructure national educational systems after the so-called "lost decade" of the 1980s—used to describe the efficacy of the debt crisis stemming from the global recession of the 1970s and 1980s after the 1973–1974 oil crisis and the 1977 oil shocks (see Jules 2013a, 2013b).

The principles of neoliberalism were applied to the Caribbean region as a corrective mechanism to reverse the negatively diagnosed public educational sector that was viewed as being ineffective (see Puiggrós 1999). Neoliberal policies were designed to be different from the policies implemented during the post-colonial period of the 1960s that focused on egalitarianism and emphasized a bare minimum public education system "thus making the state a peripheral rather than principal supporter of education" (Puiggrós 1999, p. 69). With the decline of the public sector during the 1980s, these free market reforms focused on institutional economics and political economies (Brinkerhoff and Crosby 2002; Jules 2012b). Sutton (2006) notes that many Caribbean countries sought to restructure their position in the global economy by focusing on structural reforms as well as structural adjustments. As countries repositioned themselves, human capital approaches—education and development viewed as political pursuits and driven by the market approach—were implemented within the public educational system to improve efficiency, quality, and accountability. During the 1970s and 1980s, three countries (Guyana, Jamaica, and Grenada) experimented with socialism as a development trajectory; however, it is with the United States' subsequent "intervention or invasion" (Clegg and Williams 2013; Jules 2013a, 2013b) in Grenada in 1983 that we see the rise of neoliberalism being conjoined inextricably to education across the region in the form of providing governments needed access to international financing in developing democratic institutions and restricting the further spread of socialism. International financing came in the form of "adjustment facilities" or structural adjustment policies and programs that directed public educational spending away from secondary and higher education and toward basic education. Basic education was transferred to communities in the form of a quasi-decentralization and the enactment of user fees at all levels to ensure parental involvement. This meant that Caribbean countries focused on attaining international competitiveness by investing in and developing human capital. While neoliberalism metamorphosed in different ways when applied across the region, a few salient features occurred as the educational sector restructured, namely, decentralizing of management, a focus on efficient management through performance evaluation, and an increase in service delivery mechanisms. In the Caribbean, the neoliberal orthodoxy of Thatcherism was implemented, which decreased state intervention, opened access to the free market economy, embraced monetarist economic policy, privatized state-owned industries, lowered direct taxation and raised indirect taxation, opposed trade unions, and reduced the size of the welfare state. Reaganomics used supply side economics—generating growth by stimulating a greater quantity of goods and services, and thereby increasing jobs—to reduce domestic budgets and implement extensive tax cuts for individuals and international businesses. The implementation of the policies created rollbacks in the educational gains of the 1980s as governments reduced public sector expenditures to curb ballooning budgets (World Bank 1993). These reforms led to drastic cuts in primary education.

Second Generation of Reforms: Tertiary Education Phase

The second phase of the second generation began at the tertiary level, a sector of education, which sits narrowly atop the pyramid of education enrollment in the Caribbean:

> When tertiary enrolment is compared with primary and secondary enrolment within the region the picture that emerges is a broad base at the primary and secondary levels but a very narrow apex at the tertiary level. The apex narrows even further if only university education is considered. Only 2 to 4 percent for students within the region are enrolled in university education. (Miller 2000b, p. 126)

Accessing tertiary education also seems to intersect with social class. The dual education system, which has remained essentially unchanged from the colonial era, features students from the elite attending the pre-independence schools, while post-independence schools generally feature students from families with lower socioeconomic backgrounds (London 1994). Seeing that the tertiary system is accessed based upon completion and performance at the secondary level, it is not "unreasonable to assume that tertiary education is similarly biased" (Miller 2000b, p. 132).

Although tertiary education enrollment is much smaller compared to other sectors of the educational sphere, there have been some reforms. Tertiary education reform in the 1980s focused on upgrading education facilities in territories such as the University of Havana (founded in 1728), *l'Université d'Etat d'Haiti* (founded in 1944), University of Technology in Jamaica (founded in 1958), University of the Virgin Islands (founded in 1962), the University of Guyana (founded in1963), the Anton de Kom University of Suriname (founded in 1968), and the University of the Netherlands Antilles in Curacao (founded in 1973). From the late 1980s, some countries constructed new universities including the *l'Universite Quisqueya* (founded in 1988), University of St. Maarten (founded in 1989), the University of Trinidad and Tobago (founded in 2010), and the University of Technology, formally named so in 1995 by combining the College of Arts, Science and Technology—CAST and University of Belize (formerly the College of Belize).

With the expanded focus on access to higher education, the current models of tertiary education in the Caribbean are divided between the countries, which are members of the University of the West Indies (UWI) system, and those, which have national institutions. UWI was established as the University College of the West Indies (UCWI) in 1948 with one campus at Mona, Jamaica, and 15 of the now 16 contributing countries (with Bermuda joining in 2010). Its current membership is 18 countries and territories across 4 campuses in Cave Hill (in Barbados), Mona (in Jamaica), St. Augustine (in Trinidad), and the Open Campus* (launched in 2008). The Open Campus is a virtual campus that offers online degrees and has 42 physical site locations in 16 countries.

At the beginning of the 1990s, several countries with national universities that provided free higher education, such as Guyana, began charging students recovery or user fees as part of the conditionalities attached to IMF and World Bank loans. Some territories have established community colleges, such as The College of The Bahamas, the Barbados Community College, John Donaldson Polytechnic in Trinidad and Tobago, and Sir Arthur Lewis in St. Lucia. While the University of Guyana, Faculty of Law; *l'Université d'Etat d'Haiti*, Faculty of Law and Economics; and the Anton de Kom University, Department of Law, Faculty of Social Sciences have their own law faculties, only the law schools located in the Bahamas, Jamaica, and Trinidad and Tobago provide training and certification for persons wishing to practice law in the region. Impelled by the drive toward regional competition, several offshore universities have been established. The most notable is St. George's University located in Grenada that started its medical school in 1981 and has since expanded to other faculties.

By 1995 and toward the beginning of the new millennium, the consequences of the General Agreement on Trade and Services (GATS) in the Caribbean led to the "massification" (Hall and Chuck-A-Sang 2008) of higher education. GATS legally enforced the rights to trade in services particularly in cross-border delivery, consumption abroad, commercial presence, and the presence of natural persons (the right of any citizen to set up an operate a business). The opening up of service to trade has led to greater mobility of teachers and students. This began with open

---

* The Open Campus is an amalgamation of the previous Office of the Board for Non-Campus Countries and Distance Education (BNNCDE), the School of Continuing Studies (SCS), the UWI Distance Education Centre (UWIDEC), and the Tertiary Level Institutions Unit (TLIU).

competition between regional and national institutions for students in addition to the rise of private, for-profit, and offshore universities in the region, which has also led to deeper competition in creating greater access. The logic behind this was that there needed to be a movement from the traditional elite system to a system of mass tertiary education in a global era premised upon accessing the knowledge economy (Hall and Chuck-A-Sang 2008). For example, Barbados notes that 55% of the 19–30-year-old cohort should have access to tertiary education by 2015 and Trinidad and Tobago states that 60% of that cohort is expected to have access by 2020. However, significant disparity still exists between cross-border accesses in higher education.

Second Generation of Reforms: International Benchmarks and Regional Consequences

The third phase of the second generation of reforms was inaugurated with the commitments of national governments to combat the perceived challenges described above, in education, as part of an increasingly internationalized effort. Governments committed themselves in 1990 in Jomtien, Thailand, toward providing EFA since education was deemed a human right. Governments also devoted themselves to making primary education accessible and significantly reducing illiteracy before the end of 2000, a target that came and passed without being comprehensively met. With the focus on EFA mandates, illiteracy was seen as one of the main hindrances to productivity in the Caribbean, and while primary school access was comparatively high, secondary school coverage stood at 50% or less (UNESCO 1996).

This commitment set off a new wave of national and regional reforms that focused on aligning national goals to international commitment. During the first half of the 1990s, countries in the region had partaken in numerous conferences that called for greater commitments to access in basic education, namely, the "World Summit for Children (1990), the United Nations Conference on Environment and Development (1992), the World Conference on Human Rights (1993), the World Conference on Special Needs Education: Access and Quality (1994), the International Conference on Population and Development (1994), the World Summit for Social Development (1995), the Fourth World Conference on Women (1995), the Mid-Term Meeting of the International Consultative Forum on Education for All (1996), the Fifth International Conference on Adult Education (1997), and the International Conference on Child Labour (1997)" (as cited in World Education Forum 2000). These commitments sought to ensure that national governments were aware of the changing global environment and the new skillsets, along with the new demands of educational systems needed to facilitate the smooth transition to the world of work.

In addition to focusing on access, equity, quality, efficiency, and accountability, reforms during this period paid close attention to teacher education, since UNESCO (1996) identified that several factors were undermining the teaching profession. Some factors included the role of the home environment in under-preparing children to receive instruction in school, absence of respect for teacher authority, overcrowded classrooms, shortage of teacher autonomy, and the inability of teachers to personify the principles which they espouse. Despite near universal primary school enrollments, many education systems across the Caribbean were still bedeviled by underachievement (Miller 2000a). The statement that "the colonial model of education has proved remarkably resilient, difficult to dislodge even today" (Lewis and Lewis 1985, p. 159) gains much salience in light of some of the enduring contemporary educational issues in the Caribbean. For example, vocational education has not been entirely destigmatized; lack of sufficient technical education has resulted in (wo)manpower shortages, thereby contributing to hobbled development (Lewis and Lewis 1985); lack of a pan-Caribbean systematic way of defining and measuring literacy(ies) (Jules and Panneflek 2000); and uneven levels of efficiency in human capital development (i.e., disequilibrium between inputs, such as per pupil expenditures and number of trained teachers, outputs such as performance on English and Mathematics, and the repetition rate) (Schrouder 2008).

To combat these perceived aforementioned challenges, the third phase of the second generation of educational reform began. Within the Anglophone countries, several regional initiatives were created, including the *Regional Strategy for Technical and Vocational Education and Training (TVET)* adopted in 1990 and the *Regional Education Policy: The Future in the Caribbean* adopted in 1993 by 12 out of the now 15 CARICOM countries. At the subregional level, seven of the now nine members of the OECS approved their first subregional educational policy (the *Foundations for the Future [FFF] of the Organization of Eastern Caribbean States [OECS] Education Reform Strategy* developed in 1990). With the international and regional focus on basic education, by 1997, the CARICOM Council of Human and Social Development (COHSOD) endorsed a regional development strategy called *Vision of the Ideal Caribbean Person*. The vision stressed that the person

- Is imbued with a respect for human life since it is the foundation on which all other desires must rest.
- Is emotionally secure with a high level of self-confidence and self-esteem.
- Sees ethnic, religious, and other diversity as a source of potential strength and richness.
- Is aware of the importance of living in harmony with the environment.
- Has a strong appreciation of family and kinship values, community cohesion, and moral issues including responsibility for and accountability to self and community.
- Has an informed respect for our cultural heritage.
- Demonstrates multiple literacies, independent and critical thinking, questions the beliefs and practices of past and present and brings this to bear on the innovative application of science and technology to problem solving.
- Demonstrates a positive work ethic.
- Values and displays the creative imagination in its various manifestations and nurtures its development in the economic and entrepreneurial spheres in other areas of life.
- Has developed the capacity to create and take advantage of opportunities to control, improve, maintain and promote physical, mental, social, and spiritual well-being and to contribute to the health and welfare of the community and country.
- Nourishes, in self and in others, the fullest development of each person's potential without gender stereotyping and embraces differences and similarities between females and males as a source of mutual strength (CARICOM 1997).

With the shift in the global environment towards standardized commitments, attention at the regional level, in the form of a "Vision of the Ideal Caribbean citizen" (CARICOM 1997) or "the neo-Caribbean citizen" (Jules 2014), turned toward developing citizens for the Caribbean Single Market that came into effect in 2006. The focus on the single market in Anglophone countries saw the reemergence of the concept of transactional costs—its being cheaper and more beneficial to economic regionalism—reemerged since "economic exchanges are mediated, with markets and hierarchies (states) forming the two ends of an institutional continuum" (Brinkerhoff and Crosby 2002, p. 4). This regional vision focused on ensuring that CARICOM nationals were equipped with the relevant skills to ensure that they took advantage of the Caribbean Single Market and Economy (CSME) while contributing to national development. This shift was promulgated by the World Bank's (2003) cautionary note that "the alienation of many youth is a serious social problem, exemplified by prevalent drug abuse, crime, and teenage pregnancy" (p. xiii). To address this changing environment, Caribbean countries soon implemented national reforms, for example, by 1997 the Bahamas, Barbados, and Trinidad and Tobago had established education task forces or commissions on education (see Jules 2008) and the subregional education document *The Pillars for Partnership and Progress* was developed by 2000.

During the third phase of the second generation, a second international commitment emerged, which focused on implementing the educational targets of the MDGs. The MDGs called for universal primary education by 2015 and the elimination of gender disparity in primary and secondary education by 2005 and in all levels of education by 2015. However, given the progress of current targets, the MDGs will not be met. In responding to the "fundamental global changes which had overtaken the community in spite of the gains in national building of reform" (Strachan 1996, p. 7), CARICOM and the Organization of Eastern Caribbean States (OECS) responded differently by setting different targets for their member states. For example, CHGCC 18 (1997) agreed that a focus on prioritizing policy implementation at the regional level included the attainment of 15% enrollment (as against 7%–8% then) of the post-secondary group in tertiary-level education by the year 2005 and universal quality secondary education by the same date (Hall and Chuck-A-Sang 2008; Jules 2008; Lewis 2010). For example, to achieve this goal, several countries established state-level machineries to monitor the implementation of national programs. CARICOM's members set up a high-level technical group at the regional level to monitor the achievement of goals and evaluate the impact of these programs.

In summary, with the focus on creating citizens for the regional and international market place, policies called for competitive citizens. As a result, reforms during this period focused on such a task.

Third Generation of Reforms: 2002–Present-Day

The third generation of educational reforms began in 2000 with the reconfirmation in Dakar, Senegal at the World Forum on Education of efforts toward EFA. This summit led to the signing of *The Dakar Framework for Action Education for All: Meeting Our Collective Commitments*; such a document recognized the shortfalls in the global pursuit of the 1990 EFA targets. The Dakar Framework called for EFA goals and targets to be met and sustained by 2015. This period has sought to respond to lessons learned from the intra-Caribbean-policy dialogue that was based on developing a competitive and mobile regional labor force, and meeting regional benchmarks. This period is shaped by the institutional mechanisms of (1) stakeholder participatory involvement; (2) regional and national accreditation; and (3) gender issues.

Third Generation of Reforms: International Aid, Knowledge Banks, and Stakeholder Participatory Involvement

At the beginning of the twenty-first century, several policy challenges were identified as affecting the Caribbean workforce, including the inability of citizens to develop new digital literacies to master new technologies; the decline of low skilled jobs; deficiency of multilingual literacies; the changing nature of employability; failure to continuously upgrade professional, technical, and managerial competence in the public and private sectors; shortage of new private public partnerships; and scarcity of an entrepreneurial and innovative culture (CARICOM 2005). During this period, educational reforms reflected the complex interactions between policy statutes, stakeholders, and implementers. Brinkerhoff and Crosby (2002) argue that this generation of reforms has advocated for policy tools that are more useful to policy makers in helping them guide policy development and implementation. Thus, countries with support from "international knowledge banks" (Jones 2004), such as the World Bank and IMF, began supporting national policies that were based on poverty eradication and had a core element of local stakeholder participation at their center.

The successor to SAPs, the Poverty Reduction Strategy Papers (PRSPs) set out macroeconomic, structural, and social policies to stimulate growth and reduce poverty. PRSP reforms are country-driven, result-oriented, comprehensive, partnership-oriented and have a long-term perspective (IMF 2012). For example, since 2000, Dominica, Grenada, Guyana, and Haiti have undertaken PRSP reforms focused on reducing poverty. Knowledge banks first assessed these countries' macroeconomic, structural, and social policies and programs and then they were given external financing. World Bank and IMF staffers, in collaboration with segments of civil society and other national development partners and donor agencies, prepared the PRSPs along with national governments. Several countries qualified for additional donor aid that allowed them to implement prescriptions from international knowledge banks. For example, both Guyana and Haiti qualify as members of the IMF and World Bank's Heavily Indebted Poor Countries (HIPC) initiative that makes them potentially eligible to receive debt relief. These countries are categorized as reaching the "completion point" because they have made significant progress in implementing their PRSP reforms and can demonstrate macroeconomic stability. Since 2001, the region has been using the theme of *Investing in Human Resources with Equity* as a framework for activities in human and social development. CARICOM has even established a group of experts (Futures Policy Group), coordinated by COHSOD, to work in close collaboration with a network of regional and international institutions.

Third Generation of Reforms: Accreditation

A second shift is accreditation that allows for the portability across the region of skilled nationals, whether they are Guyanese doctors that are being trained in Cuba or St. Lucian teachers working in the Bahamas. UNESCO (1998) notes that countries "have the right and the duty to regulate the provision of education, including the licensing of schools and universities, the accreditation of courses, and ensuring that course contents are culturally appropriate" (as cited in Hall and Chuck-A-Sang 2008, p. 312). Consequently, national accreditation bodies exist in the region but their mandates and methods of functioning differ somewhat from each other, rendering them unable to adequately transfer and interpret national qualifications. So as to address this issue, particularly in higher education, in 1991, the Association of Caribbean Tertiary Institutions (ACTI) was developed to coordinate tertiary education standards. Currently, the ACTI has seven regional universities as members. In 2004, the Regional Accreditation Mechanism (RAM), linked to National Accreditation Bodies (NAB) with the 15 members of CARICOM and its five observer members, came on stream. RAM is anchored in the Revised Treaty of Chaguaramas (see CARICOM 2001) and facilitates the implementation of the policy of free movement of skilled nationals. One important feature of a competency-based system developed by RAM was that it facilitated in the certification of prior experience (however attained) and vocational qualifications (VQs), based on agreed-upon standards at the regional level that can be assessed by employers in other countries. The Caribbean Vocational Qualifications (CVQs) aim at accrediting standards and ensuring the uniform delivery of competency-based technical and vocational education, training and certification within the CSME so as to ensure acceptance and recognition of the qualification/certification throughout the Caribbean and the international community.

Third Generation of Reforms: Gender

The final set of ongoing reforms focus on gender issues. Amid global efforts to increase gender parity in education, several Caribbean countries have achieved balance in access to education; however, now graduation rates are higher among girls, augmenting concerns about the rise of male underachievement. UNICEF (2003) notes, "in Latin America and the Caribbean, boys generally have higher repetition rates and lower academic achievement levels than girls, and in some countries, a higher rate of absenteeism" (p. 61). The crisis of male underachievement has led national governments to address the drop in enrollment for boys. For example, the MOE of Grenada (as cited in Lewis 2010) has noted that dropout rates over time have increased from 0.7% in 1996/1997 to 2% in 2002/2003. Gender issues have gained significance with the focus in many countries on the HFLE. Some researchers posit that perhaps the greatest threat to education in the region is male under achievement (see Bailey and Bernard 2009).

Post-2015 MDGS and Education in the Caribbean

In 2000, almost 150 countries signed onto the Millennium Declaration. This was a commitment to reducing poverty around the world, and achieving universal primary education was one of the eight goals established to operationalize this commitment. The year 2015 is upon us and the world is gauging the successes and the failures. The Caribbean has seen some reduction in poverty, though inequalities persist and there are "notable differences between and within countries" as regards universal primary education (UNESCO 2013, p. 4). Latin American and Caribbean leaders have pledged to focus on increased financing of public education, gender equality, education for sustainable development, overall educational quality, teacher education, and equity issues as regards the disadvantaged and the marginalized (UNESCO 2014).

Conclusion

This chapter presented a historical overview that shows that in the immediate aftermath of self-determination, countries in the Caribbean recognized the shifting environment from human capital development to macroeconomic policy development. As countries sought to shift from plantation economies to industrialized ones, they began spending on education and health reform to address issues of equitable access and quality (Lewis 2010). The emphasis on national education policy making shifted from creating a capable elite workforce for the colonial bureaucracy to a national curriculum that concentrated on development relevant to each country's situation and environment. For example, by providing educational grants focused on reducing the urban–rural divide and by closing the gender gap across the region. In the 1980s, educational reform to improve human capital placed emphasis on creating Caribbean nationals for the regional and international markets.

Second, we argued that in the 1990s with the shift to economic tourism and services and abolishment of preferential trading agreements, such as the Lomé IV convention, Caribbean countries saw a shift in education that focused on tackling the challenges of a liberalized global environment, preferring innovation and competitiveness. Human resource development became linked to the ability to use and develop creative talents and skills, find employment, contribute to development, and protect against communicable and noncommunicable diseases, particularly HIV/AIDS. While individual countries have been responsible for the national development of human resources, several regional and subregional educational strategies have called for the specific development of human resources so as to aid in the development of regional and subregional integrative projects. For example, with CARICOM countries, these various initiatives saw COHSOD in 2002 approving 16 regional standards in occupational areas and the establishment of a regional coordinating mechanism TVET (CARICOM 2005).

Finally, we noted that the development of education in the Caribbean has been impelled and shaped by both domestic and peripheral forces and trajectories. This notion of the "public sector" in the Caribbean certainly took on increased prominence in the periods directly prior to and after independence. Governments of independent nations in the Caribbean in the 1960s found themselves confronted by severely constrained "public sectors" and capacities for public administration (Sutton 2006). Public sector administration was viewed as pivotal to development, "however, it soon became apparent that the administrative system, inherited from ... and reconstructed in the imperial system to provide control over the colonial state, was inadequate" for this task (Sutton 2006, p. xi). The educative sphere was no exception to this developmental challenge; the educational systems that post-independence governments attempted to deploy as part of their public administrative efforts to drive growth and development were indeed legacies and structures that owed their genesis to many years of colonial policies and practices.

We conclude by acknowledging that the Caribbean region, despite limited resources, has made tremendous strides in educational expansion and provision (Peters 2001). However, in this age of rapid globalization, small states face considerable risks (Louisy 2001): international drug trade, climate change, high incidence of HIV/AIDS and other diseases, youth unemployment, and violence. Some Caribbeanists have rung the neocolonialist alarm in the face of exogenously initiated educational reforms, while others have posited greater Caribbean regionalism and integration as a way to navigate these and other global currents: "the failure to place education reform as central to that agenda is a major and strategic flaw in the ongoing efforts to position the Caribbean better for survival in the globalisation process" (Jules 2010, p. 89). Yet, others have noted that the continued dependence on donor aid has created a development dependency upon donors to fund projects. Moreover, recent studies (Jules 2012a, 2012b, 2013a) have shown that Caribbean countries are now in their fourth cycle of education reforms that actively began in 1992 with the development of the first and only regional educational plan for the Anglophone Caribbean. However, national educational plans, strategies, white papers, green papers, or policies often speak different policy languages (national, regional, and global) to different policy audiences (national constituencies, regional institutions, and aid donors) which give rise to what Jules (2012b, 2013b) has labeled as "policy trilingualism." The concept of policy trilingualism—the ability of national governments to speak, in their educational policies, a national policy language for locals, a regional language that shows commitment to the regional integrative project and an international language based on the commitments to international targets—is linked to the amount of donor aid that permeate the policy landscape. And as Table 12.1 shows, the Caribbean Basin remains a dynamic place of ongoing reforms where the small states of the Caribbean are able to leverage their smallness and benefit from numerous trading agreements which not only drive national reforms, but also contribute to the development of Caribbean people who are trained nationally, globally minded, and have the capacity to work regionally.

References

Agnew, J. (2000). From the political economy of regions to regional political economy. *Progress in Human Geography, 24* (1), 101–110. Retrieved from http://dx.doi.org.flagship.luc.edu/10.1191/0309132006765806459.

Alcala, V. (1956). Note on the administration of education in British, French, Netherlands and United States Caribbean countries. In Caribbean Commission Central Secretariat (Ed.), *Education in the Caribbean* (pp. 38–46). Trinidad and Tobago: Kent House.

Allen, C. F. (2002). Gender and the transmission of HIV in the Caribbean. In S. Courtman (Ed.), *The Society for Caribbean Studies Annual Conference Papers, 3.*

Bacchus, M. K. (1990). *Utilization, Misuse, and Development of Human Resources in the Early West Indian Colonies.* Waterloo, Canada: Wilfrid Laurier University Press.

Bacchus, M. K. (1994). *Education as and for Legitimacy: Developments in West Indian Education Between 1846 and 1895.* Waterloo, Canada: Wilfrid Laurier University Press.

Baer, W. (1972). Import substitution and industrialization in Latin America: Experiences and interpretations. *Latin American Research Review, 7,* 95–122.

Bailey, B., and Bernard, M. (2009). *Establishing a Database of Gender Differentials in Enrolment and Performance at the Secondary and Tertiary Levels of the Caribbean Education System.* Barbados and Eastern Caribbean: The Canada-Caribbean Gender Equity Program.

Beckford, G. (1972). *Persistent Poverty: Underdevelopment in Plantation Economics of the Third World.* New York: Oxford University Press.

Bedford, K. (2007). The imperative of male inclusion: How institutional context influences the policy preferences of World Bank Gender Staff. *International Feminist Journal of Politics, 9* (3), 289–311.

Bishop, G. D. (1964). The practice of education. *Caribbean Quarterly, 10* (1), 31–37.

Blum, D. F. (2011). *Cuban Youth and Revolutionary Values: Educating the New Socialist Citizen.* Austin, TX: University of Texas Press.

Bolland, O. N. (1998). Religious influences on education and politics in colonial Belize. In B. Moore and S. Wilmot (Eds.), *Before and After 1865: Education, Politics and Regionalism in the Caribbean* (pp. 23–35). Kingston, Jamaica: Ian Randle Publishers.

Brinkerhoff, D. W., and Crosby, B. L. (2002). *Managing Policy Reform: Concepts and Tools for Decision-Makers in Developing and Transitioning Countries.* Bloomfield, NJ: Kumarian Press.

Campbell, C. (1965). The development of vocational training in Jamaica: First steps. *Caribbean Quarterly, 11* (1/2), 13–35.

Campbell, C. (2004). Education in the Caribbean, 1930–90. In B. Brereton (Ed.), *General History of the Caribbean.* Paris, France: UNESCO.

Caribbean Basin Economic Recovery Act of 1983 § 19, 15 USC, § 2701, Stat. 384 (1983).

CARICOM. (1997). Creative and productive citizens for the twenty-first century. *Paper Presented at Ninth Inter-Sessional Meeting of the Conference of Heads of Government of the Caribbean Community,* St. George's, Grenada: CARICOM.

CARICOM. (2001). *Revised Treaty of Chaguaramas.* Retrieved from http://www.caricom.org/jsp/community/revised_treaty.jsp?menu=community.

CARICOM. (2005). *CARICOM Our Caribbean Community: An Introduction.* Kingston, Jamaica: Ian Randel Publishers.

Carnoy, M. (2007). *Cuba's Academic Advantage: Why Students in Cuba Do Better in School.* Stanford, CA: Stanford University Press.

Clegg, P., and Williams, G. (2013). Editorial: The invasion of Grenada 30 years on—A retrospective. *The Round Table, 102* (2), 37–41. doi:10.1080/00358533.2013.764094.

Conference of Heads of Government of the Caribbean Community. (July 1997). *Communiqué Issued at the Conclusion of the Eighteenth Meeting of the Conference of Heads of Government of the Caribbean Community.* Retrieved from http://www.caricom.org/jsp/communications/communiques/18hgc_1997_communique.jsp.

Ferguson, J. (2008). *A Traveller's History of the Caribbean.* New York: Interlink Books.

Gordon, H. (1979/1980). University adult education: A Caribbean focus. *Caribbean Studies, 19* (3/4), 47–67.

Grassly, N. C., Desai, K., Pegurri, E., Sikazwe, A., Malambo, I., Siamatowe, C., and Bundy, D. 2003. The economic impact of HIV/AIDS on the education sector in Zambia. *AIDS,* 17(7), 1039–1044.

Griffith, W. H. (2010). Neoliberal economics and Caribbean economies. *Journal of Economic Issues,* 44 (2), 505–512. doi:10.2753/JEI0021-3624440223.

Gordon, S. C. (1962a). Documents which have guided educational policy in the West Indies: Rev. John Sterling's report, May 1835. *Caribbean Quarterly,* 8 (3), 145–153.

Gordon, S. C. (1962b). The Keenan report, 1869 Part I: The elementary school system in Trinidad. *Caribbean Quarterly,* 8 (4), 3–16.

Gordon, S. C. (1963a). Documents which have guided educational policy in the West Indies: Patrick Joseph Keenan's report 1869- Part II: Secondary and higher education. *Caribbean Quarterly,* 9 (1/2), 11–25.

Gordon, S. C. (1963b). *A Century of West Indian Education: A Source Book.* Great Britain: Western Printing Services, Ltd.

Gordon, S. (1998). Schools of the free. In B. Moore and S. Wilmot (Eds.), *Before and After 1865: Education, Politics and Regionalism in the Caribbean* (pp. 1–12). Kingston, Jamaica: Ian Randle Publishers.

Gott, R. (2004). *Cuba: A New History.* New Haven, CT: Yale University Press.

Gray, C. R. (1969). New training for secondary teaching. *Caribbean Quarterly,* 15 (1), 34–44.

Hall, K. (2001). *The Caribbean Community: Beyond Survival.* Kingston, Jamaica: Ian Randle.

Hall, K. (2003). *Re-Inventing CARICOM: The Road to a New Integration.* Kingston, Jamaica: Ian Randle.

Hall, K., and Chuck-A-Sang, M. (2008). *The Caribbean Community in Transition: Functional Cooperation as Catalyst for Change.* Kingston, Jamaica: Ian Randel Publishers.

Heggoy, A. A. (1984). Colonial education in Algeria: Assimilation and reaction. In P. G. Altbach and G. P. Kelly (Eds.), *Education and the Colonial Experience* (pp. 97–115). New Brunswick, NJ: Transaction.

Howe, H. W. (1956). The school in its relation to the community. In Caribbean Commission Central Secretariat (Ed.), *Education in the Caribbean* (pp. 12–25). Trinidad and Tobago: Kent House.

IMF. (2012). *IMF Fact Sheet: Poverty Reduction Strategy Papers (PRSP).* Retrieved from http://www.imf.org/external/np/exr/facts/pdf/prsp.pdf.

Jackson, C., and Bisset, M. 2005. Gender and school choice: Factors influencing parents when choosing single-sex or co-educational independent schools for their children. *Cambridge Journal of Education,* 35 (2), 195–211.

Jones, T. J. (1925). *Education in Africa: A Study of East, Central and South Africa by the Second Educational Commission Under the Auspices of the Phelps-Stokes Fund in Cooperation with the International Education Board.* New York: Phelps-Stokes Fund.

Jones, P. W (1997). *World Bank Financing of Education; Lending, Learning and Development.* London: Routledge.

Jones, P. W. (2004). Taking the credit: Financing and policy linkages in the education portfolio of the World Bank. In G. Steiner-Khamsi (Ed.), *The Global Politics of Educational Borrowing and Lending* (pp. 188–200). New York: Teachers College Press.

Jules, T. D. (2008). *Re/thinking Harmonization in the Commonwealth Caribbean: Audiences, Actors, Interests, and Educational Policy Formation* [Doctoral Dissertation]. New York: Teachers College, Columbia University.

Jules, T. D. (2010). Beyond post-socialist conversions: Functional cooperation and trans-regional regimes in the global south. In I. Silova (Ed.), *Post-Socialism is Not Dead: (Re)reading the Global in Comparative Education* (pp. 401–426). Bingley: Emerald Publishing.

Jules, T. D. (2010). Rethinking education for the Caribbean: A radical approach. In P. Mayo (Ed.), *Education in Small States: Global Imperatives, Regional Initiatives and Local Dilemmas* (pp. 79–90). London: Routledge.

Jules, T. D. (2012a). "New Mutualism" in micro-states: The AIDS generation and AIDS fatigue in the Caribbean educational policy space. In A. W. Wiseman and R. N. Glover (Eds.), *Public HIV/AIDS and Education Worldwide.* Bingley: Emerald Publishing.

Jules, T. D. (2012b). *Neither World Polity nor Local or National Societies: Regionalization in the Global South—the Caribbean Community.* Berlin, Germany: Peter Lang.

Jules, T. D. (2013a). Cuba. In J. Ainsworth (Ed.), *Sociology of Education: An A-to-Z Guide.* Thousand Oaks, CA: SAGE Publications.

Jules, T. D. (2013b). Post-revolutionary socialist education reform in Grenada going Trilingual: Post-revolutionary socialist education reform in Grenada. *The Round Table: The Commonwealth Journal of International Relations* (September), 1–12. doi:10.1080/00358533.2013.833731.

Jules, T. D. (2014). Trans-regional regimes and globalization in education: Constructing the neo-Caribbean citizen. In I. Silova and D. Hobson (Eds.), *Globalizing Minds: Rhetoric and Realities in International Schools.* (pp. 249–276) Chapel Hill, NC: Information Age Publishing.

Jules, V., and Panneflek, A. (2000). *Education for All in the Caribbean: Assessment 2000.* Subregional report, volume II: The state of education in the Caribbean in the 1990s: Subregional synthesis and annexes. Kingston, Jamaica: UNESCO.

Kelly, M. J., and Bain, B. (2003). *Education and HIV/AIDS in the Caribbean*. Paris, France: International Institute for Educational Planning/UNESCO.

Kiragu, K. (2001). *Youth and HIV/AIDS: Can We Avoid Catastrophe?* Population reports, series L, No. 12. Population Information Program, Johns Hopkins Bloomberg School of Public Health, Center for Communication Programs, The INFO Project. https://www.k4health.org/sites/default/files/l12.pdf.

Lakes, R. D., and Carter, P. A. (2011). Neoliberalism and education: An introduction. *Educational Studies, 47*, 107–110. doi:10.1080/00131946.2011.556387.

Lee, F. J. T. (2000). *The Evolution-Involution of "Co-operative Socialism" in Guyana, 1930–1984.* Merida, Venezuela: Pandemonium Electronic Publication. Retrieved from http://www.franz-lee.org/files/coop-guy.html#_Toc19952339.

Lewis, A. W. (1950). The industrialization of the British West Indies. *Caribbean Economic Review, 2*, 1–53.

Lewis, L. (2006). Re-regulating the state, the celebration of the market, and the crisis of civil society in the Commonwealth Caribbean. *Caribbean Quarterly, 52* (2/3), 121–137.

Lewis, P. (2010). *Social Policies in Grenada*. Pall Mall, London: Commonwealth Secretariat.

Lewis, T., and Lewis, M. (1985). Vocational education in the Commonwealth Caribbean and the United States. *Comparative Education, 21* (2), 157–171.

London, N. (1993). Why education projects in developing countries fail: A case study. *International Journal of Educational Development, 13* (3), 265–275.

London, N. (1994). Improving the status and prestige of post-colonial secondary schools in a developing nation: The marketing approach. *International Journal of Educational Development, 14* (4), 409–419.

Louisy, P. (2001). Globalisation and comparative education: A Caribbean perspective. *Comparative Education, 37* (4), 425–438.

Mansfield, E. D., and Milner, H. V. (1997). The political economy of regionalism: An overview. In E. D. Mansfield and H.V. Milner (Eds.), *The Political Economy of Regionalism* (pp. 1–19). New York: Columbia University Press.

Metzler, J. (2009). The developing states and education: Africa. In R. Cowen and A. Kazamias (Eds.), *International Handbook of Comparative Education* (pp. 277–294). Dordrecht, the Netherlands: Springer.

Miller, E. (2000a). *Educational for All in the Caribbean in the 1990s: Retrospect and Prospect.* Kingston, Jamaica: UNESCO.

Miller, E. (2000b). Access to tertiary education in the Commonwealth Caribbean in the 1990s. In G. Howe (Ed.), *Higher Education in the Caribbean: Past, Present and Future Directions* (pp. 117–141). Barbados: The University of the West Indies Press.

Mishra, P. (2006). *Emigration and Brain Drain: Evidence from the Caribbean* (Working Paper No. 06/25). Retrieved from the International Monterey Fund website: doi:10.2202/1935-1682.1547.

Mumford, W. B. (1936). *Africans Learn to be French*. London: Evan Bros Ltd.

Mundy, K. (1998) Educational multilateralism and world (dis)order, *Comparative Education Review*, 42 (4), 448–478.

MOE. (2002). *The Strategic Plan for Education Enhancement and Development (SPEED) 2002–2010.* St. George's, Grenada: Ministry of Education.

OECS. (1991). *Foundation for the Future: OECS Education Reform Strategy*. Castries, St. Lucia: OECS Secretariat.

OECS. (2000). *Pillars for Partnership*. Castries, St. Lucia: OECS Education Reform Working Group, OECS Secretariat.

Payne, A. (1984). *The International Crisis of the Caribbean*. Baltimore, MD: The Johns Hopkins University Press.

Peters, B. (2001). Education development in small states: Constraints and future prospects. *Caribbean Quarterly, 47* (2/3), 44–57.

Philip, B., Jimenez, M. R., Kirk, J. M., and Leo Grande, W. M. (Eds.). (2008). *A Contemporary Cuba Reader.* Lanham, MD: Rowman & Littlefield.

Puiggrós, A. (1999). *Neoliberalism and Education in the Americas.* Boulder, CO: Westview Press.

Richardson, B. C. (1992). *The Caribbean in the Wider World, 1942–1992.* Cambridge: Cambridge University Press.

Risley, C., Clarke, D., Drake, L., and Bundy, D. (2007). *The Impact of HIV and AIDS on Education in the Caribbean.* Retrieved from http://www1.imperial.ac.uk/resources/F779E9AE-D756-4320-B611-128BD6ABE40A/.

Rose, E. A. (2002). *Dependency and Socialism in the Modern Caribbean: Superpower Intervention in Guyana, Jamaica and Grenada, 1970–1985.* Oxford: Lexington Books.

Schrouder, S. (2008). Educational efficiency in the Caribbean: A comparative analysis. *Development in Practice, 18* (2), 273–279.

Selvaratnam, V. (1988). Limits to vocationally-oriented education in the third world. *International Journal of Educational Development, 8* (2), 129–143.

Sherlock, P. (1949/1950). Education in the Caribbean area. *Caribbean Quarterly, 1* (3), 9–18.

Springer, H. (1965). Problems of national development in the West Indies. *Caribbean Quarterly, 11* (1/2), 3–12.

Strachan, G. (1996). *Study Commissioned by CARICOM Secretariat of an Analysis of the Science and Technology Proposal Promoting Productive Employment for Poverty Eradication in the Creative and Productive Citizen in the 21st Century.* Georgetown, Guyana: CARICOM.

Sutton, P. (2006). *Modernizing the State: Public Sector Reform in the Commonwealth Caribbean.* Kingston, Jamaica: Ian Randle Publishers.

UNAIDS and WHO. (2009). *AIDS Epidemic Update December 2009.* Geneva, Switzerland: UNAIDS. Retrieved January 21, 2012, from http://data.unaids.org/pub/report/2009/jc1700_epi_update_2009_en.pdf.

UNESCO. (1990). *World Declaration on Education for All.* Paris, France: UNESCO.

UNESCO. (1996). *Education for Development and Peace: Valuing Diversity and Increasing Opportunities for Personalized and Group Learning.* Paris, France: UNESCO.

UNESCO. (1998). *World Declaration on Higher Education for the Twenty First Century.* Paris, France: UNESCO.

UNESCO. (2013). *Education Agenda Post 2015: Latin America and Caribbean.* Retrieved February 11, 2015, from http://www.unesco.org/new/fileadmin/MULTIMEDIA/HQ/ED/pdf/Ed-agendaPost-2015LatinAmericaandtheCaribbean.pdf.

UNESCO. (2014). *Education for All (EFA) in Latin America and the Caribbean: Assessment of Progress and Post-2015 Challenges.* Retrieved February 11, 2015, from http://unesdoc.unesco.org/images/0023/002306/230628E.pdf.

UNICEF. (2003). *The State of the World's Children 2004: Girls, Education and Development.* New York: UNICEF.

UNICEF. (2009). *Health and Family Life Education Teacher Training Manual: Self and Interpersonal Relationships Theme Unit Sexuality and Sexual Health Theme Unit.* Retrieved from http://www.educan.org/sites/educan.org/files/HFLE%20Teacher%20Training%20Manual.pdf.

UNICEF, CARICOM, and EDC. (2008). *Regional Health and Family Life Education (HFLE) Curriculum Framework, Ages 9–14.* Retrieved from http://hhd.org/sites/hhd.org/files/HFLE%20Curriculum%20Framework_Merged.pdf.

Walters, E. (1970). Some experiences in training personnel for the education of young children in the British Caribbean. *International Review of Education, 16* (1), 110–119.

White, B. W. (1996). Talk about school: Education and the colonial project in French and British Africa (1860–1960). *Comparative Education, 32* (1), 9–25.

Whitehead, C. (2005a). The historiography of British imperial education policy, Part I: India. *History of Education, 34* (3), 315–329.

Whitehead, C. (2005b). The historiography of British imperial education policy, Part II: Africa and the rest of the colonial empire. *History of Education, 34* (4), 441–454.

Williams, E. (1946). Education in dependent territories in America. *Journal of Negro Education, 15* (3), 534–551.

Williams, E. (1956). The need for instructional materials related to the Caribbean environment. In Caribbean Commission Central Secretariat (Ed.), *Education in the Caribbean* (pp. 3–11). Trinidad and Tobago: Kent House.

Williams, H. M. A. (2012). Everybody Violent: *Conceptualizations of Violence Within a Secondary School in Trinidad and Tobago* [Doctoral Dissertation]. New York: Teachers College, Columbia University.

Wright University. (n.d.). *High School Equivalency*. Retrieved from http://www.wright.edu/ucie/student/highschoolequivalency.html.

World Bank. (1993). *Caribbean Region: Access Quality and Efficiency in Education*. Washington, DC: World Bank.

World Bank. (2003). *Caribbean Youth Development: Issues and Policy Directions*. Washington, DC: World Bank.

World Bank and Partnership for Child Development. (2006). *Modeling the Impact of HIV/AIDS on Education Systems: A Training Manual. The Ed-SIDA Initiative*, Second edition. Washington, DC: World Bank.

World Education Forum. (2000). *The Dakar Framework for Action. Education for All: Meeting Our Collective Commitments*. Paris, France: UNESCO.

Chapter 13

Developmental Interventions in the Caribbean

Nikolaos Karagiannis, Anthony Clayton, and Jessica M. Bailey

Contents

Introduction 296
Caribbean Governments and Budgeting 298
Reassessing the Developmental State Model 300
Desirable Developmental Interventions in the Caribbean 305
Conclusion 309
References 310

Abstract: This chapter discusses different concepts of feasible and constructive developmental interventions in the Caribbean. The nations of the region need to contain crime, reduce corruption, encourage job creation, raise living standards, improve industrial competency and competitiveness, and strengthen environmental protection, among other goals. These serious problems can only be addressed with consistent, robust policies, strong institutional capacity, and strong enforcement. The failure, to date, to develop and implement the right policies, build the institutional capacity, and ensure enforcement therefore requires a more profound re-thinking of the role of government in national development in the modern era. Why have so many of the Caribbean nations failed to meet their developmental challenges?

The first main part of the chapter reviews features of government policy and decision making in the Caribbean region. The second section examines an institutional system that has been used successfully in some countries—the "developmental state"—where states take on a developmental role in the economy without owning most of the productive assets and while avoiding the misdirection of investments toward corrupt gains or sectarian political ends. It notes, however, that this model may be most appropriate in the early stages of development, that is, to bridge the period before other social institutions are sufficiently mature. The final main section explores the nature of what might be desirable developmental interventions in the Caribbean today.

Introduction

In all parts of the world, people are, quite legitimately, questioning what their governments ought to do in the area economic policy. Issues such as what governments should or should not do, where government intervention is necessary, or where it may cause harm have always been at the heart of major debates. Over the last quarter century, there have been genuine and profound changes in the structure of the world economy, especially with regard to the emergence of a new generation of highly competitive economies in Asia, Africa, the Pacific, and Latin America, which have changed the possibilities for government action for every nation, including those in the Caribbean. In a world that is being rapidly reshaped by emerging market economies, it is entrepreneurial actions that have to adapt to meet the diverse and changing needs of consumers and producers, although governments can certainly facilitate or impede the process of adaptation. The question of what is the appropriate role for governments in the Caribbean therefore continues to be an important and challenging one.

The twentieth century has seen some profound changes in thinking about the economic role of government. Generally, each attempted solution has typically solved some problems but created others, so the debate tends to re-emerge every generation. The first quarter century of the post-war period was largely characterized (at least among the majority of industrial countries) by economic growth, high levels of employment, various measures of state activism (such as redistributionist taxation and a welfare state), and a widely held belief in the benign role of government in ensuring particular social outcomes. In Europe, these measures included extensive state ownership in a "mixed economy" model, government intervention in labor disputes, for example, discretionary fiscal and monetary policies, pay controls, restrictions on trade, and so on. This era coincided in general with a period of low unemployment and inflation, and relative economic stability and security.

This period was followed, however, by several decades of lower rates of economic growth in the OECD nations, persistent high rates of unemployment, and a gradual weakening of belief in the benign role of government (Arestis and Sawyer 1998: 1). In those OECD countries where unemployment eventually declined, such as the United States and United Kingdom, it was associated with the rejection of the welfarist social capitalist model and the dismantling of labor union powers and privileges. From about 1985 onward, the social capitalist model, with its labor rights, pensions, subsidies, and welfare provisions, came under increasing pressure from several factors, including fiscal pressures, aging populations, and the accelerated transfer of technology and investment capital to emerging economies. As Raghuram Rajan, the former chief economist at the International Monetary Fund, put it, "For years, advanced-economy governments attempted to compensate for the jobs and income lost to technology and emerging-market competition by spending more than they could afford, and encouraging their citizens through easy credit to do the same" (http://www.telegraph.co.uk/finance/).

Today, the most prominent debate is between post-Keynesians, who believe that state intervention is necessary to shorten the duration and devastation caused by the recent financial crisis and recession, and those who believe that a period of strict austerity is necessary in order to rein in bloated government expenditures and (perhaps even more important) change people's assumptions as to the size and reach of the state.* One particularly sensitive aspect of this debate is the role of vested interests and corrupt practices in increasing state expenditure, and recent revelations about the extraordinary levels of misallocation of government funds. Partly as a result, in many countries the state is now seen as part of the problem, rather than part of the solution, and there is therefore an increasing preference for market-led solutions. Many functions previously held by government ministries have been hived off into government agencies that are supposed to behave as if they were subject to market discipline, many government functions are now subcontracted to the private sector, and new models of public–private partnership have emerged. These debates are highly relevant to the under-performing Caribbean economies, but there has been far less progress with the necessary reforms.

It is undeniable that the general intellectual and policy climate has shifted from majority support for an active role for the state in economic and social matters toward a generally more skeptical view of the role of government. The current debate on the role of government mainly concerns economic management, integrity, and competence and underlies attempts to reform public sector management and to ensure better management of public spending. There is a challenge to the moral authority of the state to tax and spend, and thereby to reallocate resources from one group to another, and a questioning of the efficiency, competence, and integrity with which the state does so. The discussion now is less about whether government is a good thing or a bad thing *per se*, and more about how much government is needed, when and for what purposes. Moreover, none of these issues can be decided on political or philosophical principles alone; the issues also have a wide range of very practical consequences. This is no longer a struggle between political ideologies of left and right; these dimensions have become far less relevant, as few people still believe in radical alternatives to capitalism.

This more skeptical era poses new challenges for government policy, two of which are fundamental. First, it is increasingly recognized that policy must be coherent, consistent, thorough, and effective, while planning, regulation, and other interventions must be technically proficient and pragmatic. Government inertia, corruption, self-serving behavior by elites, incompetence, and failure are less likely to be tolerated. Second, countries in regions such as the Caribbean have to escape the trap of failed political ideologies, nationalist and class-based rhetoric, and the associated tensions between the state and the business sector. The most successful economies today tend to have a relatively high level of cooperation and dialogue between the government and the private sector. The fact that some Caribbean authors still complain about "globalization," and argue for a return to protectionism and preferences, suggests a failure to understand the nature and extent of these changes.

If Caribbean nations hope to prosper in the new international environment, they need to take stock of changes in production relations, corporate practices, investment patterns, and the growth and export potential of their economies (Boyer and Drache 1996: 1–2), among other parameters. This chapter stands apart from other chapters in this book, as its purpose is to examine how lessons of other parts of the world, specifically about the developmental state in East Asia, apply to the Caribbean. The next main part (Section "Caribbean Governments and Budgeting") discusses extensively aspects of Caribbean governments and budgeting. Section "Reassessing the Developmental State Model" reassesses the developmental state argument. Section "Desirable Developmental

---

* This debate has been particularly pressing in countries such as Greece, Cyprus, Portugal, and Spain, which could not devalue their currency (because they are members of the Euro-zone) in order to make imports more expensive, and so were obliged to cut directly at core areas of government expenditure.

Interventions in the Caribbean" seeks to single out key features of a modern Caribbean intervention, which is the main task of this chapter. Some brief conclusions end the chapter.

Caribbean Governments and Budgeting

The English-speaking Caribbean islands inherited a system that was based largely on British planning and fiscal arrangements. At the time of independence, the fiscal capacity of the Caribbean countries was limited, while public services were correspondingly constrained. Public finance programs in the Caribbean were hampered by the relatively modest ability to raise and manage domestic resources, reflecting both the domestic situation of Caribbean countries at the time and the external oversight functions of Britain. This starting position limited the pursuit of active fiscal policies as well as confining the development prospects of the territories. Then, starting about a decade after independence, a number of Caribbean nations were badly affected by the increasing political use of violence, the compromising of the democratic system by organized crime and sectarian politics, and the consequent partial loss of the moral authority of the state. This was followed by an era of political dishonesty and failure, in which political parties would routinely promise largesse to their voters, but then fail to deliver any basis for lasting prosperity. As a result, the idea that the state could play a genuinely constructive role in national development has been both limited and somewhat discredited in the Caribbean.

In the years immediately after independence, there were several issues involved in assessing the fiscal capacity of Caribbean states:

- Public finance in the region was still practiced as if it was based on a colonial plan.
- The former colonial powers (the United Kingdom, France, the Netherlands, and Spain in particular) still had a paternalistic attitude toward the region, relatively benign in some cases, but reflected in the pattern of continuing support for traditional commodities, which had the inadvertent effect of discouraging economic diversification.*
- Heavy reliance on indirect taxes constrained government tax revenue. In contrast, spending levels were not low, but there was no longer a colonial power to bear the cost of administration.
- The tax system had many loopholes, which were exploited by the local elite. The tourism industry is a prime example, with many decades of experience in tax avoidance. This was then compounded by the emergence of additional politically well-connected or powerful groups that could demand subsidies and tax waivers, thereby placing the rest of society at a serious competitive disadvantage.
- As a result of all of the above factors, many governments have had inadequate revenue to cover the cost of public expenditure for many years, and some of the nations of the Caribbean are now among the most heavily indebted countries in the world as a result.

In the region, the fiscal system is not generally used as a tool to encourage or channel development. The granting of tax waivers was originally intended to assist favored sectors, but have largely degenerated into patronage. Taxes are collected primarily in order to help the state to meet its expenditure obligations. Many sections of the community are effectively exempt, however either because they operate in the informal sector, or else are eligible for waivers, or else successfully

---

* Some have suggested that the physical distance from Europe may have encouraged increasing neglect (Jones-Hendrickson 1985: 52–4), but it is more likely that interests simply diverged over time.

evade taxes, and this deprives Caribbean governments of collecting the corresponding direct taxes on incomes and on profits. So many members of society only pay indirect taxes, such as import duties or General Consumption Tax on consumer goods. This has two consequences. One is that the high dependence on trade taxes for government revenue has restricted fiscal policy. The other is that the tax base is narrow, which means that the burden of taxation is borne largely by a minority of the population—who are relatively heavily taxed as a result, thereby restricting reinvestment.

Budgets and budgeting in the region have been partially reflective of both the limited sources and also the sometimes dubious uses of revenues. In varying degrees, there are similar inherent weaknesses of budgets and the budgetary processes in most Caribbean states. According to Premchand (1975: 27), the "identified deficiencies" are as follows:

- No long-term planning of expenditure
- Few connections between the development plan (where such plans exist) and the national accounts
- Excessive, centralized control by the ministries of finance
- Insufficient pressure for better, politically neutral allocation of public funds
- Little effort to relate expenditure to actual outputs
- The absence of economic policy inputs
- The absence of identification of future spending requirements of current programs and projects
- The absence of expenditure objectives
- The lack of coordination with other public bodies engaged in economic management
- The preference for budgeting by aggregation instead of providing a clear indication of the government's strategic priorities
- The multiplicity of budget categories
- The absence of yardsticks to measure performance
- An overemphasis on financial targets
- The absence of reviews of under-spending and over-spending
- Out-of-date procedures of recording and classification practices
- Delays in the release of funds and absence of cash management
- Considerable time lags

To this list must be added three further weaknesses. The first is a general lack of transparency. The second is the use of off-budget expenditure to evade agreed spending controls, which can undermine progress toward prudent management of the public accounts. The third is that the grip of vested interest groups ensures that austerity measures are often watered down and that subsidies continue to flow to the well-connected. The relatively high level of politicization of the budgetary process in the Caribbean states often results "pork barrel programmes and policies that have no discernible benefits, little rational justification, yet are strongly defended" (Jones-Hendrickson 1985: 83–4).

While the Caribbean nations have survived as democracies (in spite of various challenges), the political model is under increasing stress in a number of countries as a result of decades of mismanagement and failure to deliver law and order, development, and prosperity. In these cases, the state lost a great deal of its effectiveness as a development tool because it was transformed into a mechanism for winning elections and meeting populist demands in a highly nationalist mode that resulted in an irrational expansion of state ownership. The "first-past-the-post" or "winner-takes-all" electoral system may work well in countries that are already stable and prosperous, but in some Caribbean nations the state became an instrument for seizing "scarce benefits and spoils" and pursuing openly sectarian agendas, rather than a unifying institution through which society could organize its efforts to deal with development challenges. In the small states of the Caribbean, the state is by far the largest employer and dispenser of resources, hence the intense competition between various groups and special interests for control.

Government spending levels in the Caribbean have been under continuous upward pressure resulting from high levels of debt repayment obligations, fiscal administrative inefficiency, population growth, the interests of elite groups and politicians, with patronage padding the public payroll, and corruption ensuring the misdirection of contracts to political friends, and the unionization of civil servants, which makes it difficult, for example, to replace inefficient bureaucracies with online systems. Over the last three decades, the continuous growth of public spending without the corresponding increase in tax revenues, coupled with efforts to finance fiscal deficits, has shifted the emphasis of policy toward financial control (i.e., tight fiscal policy) and away from government expenditure planning.

Reassessing the Developmental State Model

The development experience of Japan, South Korea, Taiwan, Hong Kong, Singapore, and Malaysia suggests that state intervention can accelerate the process of development and industrialization. In the early stages of these transformations, the state works with the private sector, coordinating efforts in key sectors, resulting in a market economy that delivers the objectives of a national strategic plan. As Johnson (1982) puts it, "The Developmental State … provide(s) directional thrust to the operation of the market mechanism" (Johnson 1982: 9–10).

The successful developmental states avoided the mistake of confusing ownership with the need to build technological infrastructure and invest in human capital formation and research. This is important, as government ownership and control of industrial production (as practiced in the Soviet Union) usually ensured that ideological or political rather than business factors were paramount, which led to disastrous economic failure. The successful developmental states used planned market augmentation as their most important instrument of industrial policy and understood that firms must eventually be exposed to international competitive pressures in order to ensure that they continue to drive toward greater efficiency.

The developmental state model, with focused use of resources to support a long-term development plan, is very different from the ideologically based (and sometimes profoundly irrational) plans in the Soviet-type command economies, but it is also distinct from the form of market regulation undertaken in the liberal-democratic states. Most of the developmental states possessed considerable leverage over private industries in terms of securing compliance with national strategic goals, while planning was typically based on consultation and serious efforts to reach agreement on the form of intervention. Economic coordination and development in these states was usually managed by institutions with significant technocratic expertise, located at the interface between state and industry. These were the "pilot agencies" of strategic economic direction (Johnson 1982: 9–10, 1982: 26 quoted in Leftwich 1995).

Strategic industrial policy is an important component of the developmental state model, but the successful exemplars did not make the mistake of micro-managing and getting involved with operational detail. Well-educated and competent planners took a long-term view of the future development of their countries, and their incentive structures were continually revised in light of planning objectives. This planning system has been described as involving a high level of good and eclectic steersmanship.

The ability of developmental states to undertake useful strategic interventions was based on a strong state structure and administrative capacity, with highly educated, powerful civil servants. Such states "... concentrate considerable power, authority, autonomy and competence in the central political and bureaucratic institutions of the state, notably their [determined developmental elites, or] economic bureaucracies" (Leftwich 1995: 420). The bureaucrats typically had sufficient scope to take their own initiatives and operate decisively (Amsden 1989; Wade 1990; Leftwich 1995; Onis 1991).

These relatively small, tightly organized bureaucratic structures had most of the Weberian characteristics of highly selective, meritocratic recruitment patterns and long-term career rewards, which enhanced the solidarity and corporate identity of the bureaucratic elites. In the best examples, such as Singapore, meritocratic systems attracted the best managerial talent available to the ranks of the bureaucratic elites and ensured a high degree of unity, capability, and professionalism. This institutional strength helped the bureaucracies to resist any short-term political misdirection and gave them authority, although their relative autonomy was tempered by ultimate accountability (Onis 1991: 114, 124).

Both the relatively high level of bureaucratic autonomy and the close public–private cooperation are important features of the East Asian developmental state model. If either of these conditions are not satisfied, attempts to implement developmental state policies would probably be counterproductive. In a Caribbean environment, for example, with a weak and politicized civil service and poor cooperation, selective support for strategic sectors could easily degenerate into an instrument of rent-seeking by vested interests.

It is important to note, however, that the East Asian developmental state involved a concentration of power that would be hard to justify by the standards of pluralistic democracy. The extraordinary degrees of control exercised by the state over the financial system and the dependence of individual conglomerates on bank finance were instrumental in eliciting compliance with the requirements of the strategic industrial policy. This means that there was a significant element of compulsion exercised by the bureaucrats in securing public–private partnerships. This resulted in the corporatist nature of most developmental states, which eventually resulted—in South Korea and Japan for example—in various high-profile corruption scandals, and the need to challenge a number of long-established relationships with particular firms. In the case of Japan, although there were conflicts among various interest groups within its political system, and competition among firms within its economy, "extensive economic and political agreements have been as important to Japan's economic dynamism as competition" (Nester 1991: 57). This approach did serve Japan well as it built its industrial base during the post-war years, but has been implicated in Japan's unusually prolonged recession, as many "zombie" banks and firms are now being propped up by their network of alliances. In a less protected environment, these bankrupt entities would have been taken over, and their assets returned to productive use. This reinforces the earlier suggestion that many solutions are specific to particular circumstances and may themselves become problems when the circumstances change.

In terms of economic policy objectives, however, the best developmental states were serious and effective in raising the quantity and quality of industrial investment. They focused almost exclusively on increasing productivity, growth, and exports, which served the strategic requirements of long-term economic transformation. What differentiates the bureaucracies in the successful developmental states from the various planning institutions in other developing and less-developed countries is their relative independence, authority, technical competence and professionalism, and their ability to use both positive rewards and negative sanctions to influence decision making in the private sector (Leftwich 1995: 412). Compared to these relatively strong and autonomous agencies, the weak and/or corrupt governments that are, sadly, characteristic of many developing countries largely fail to deliver economically desirable interventions (such as ensuring good systems of law, order, justice, education, and transport), but also inflict far too many politically motivated, inept, self-interested, or otherwise economically harmful policy actions.

The relatively high level of public–private cooperation in the successful developmental states is not to be confused with the situation where, in some countries, the state has been largely captured by private interests, so that national goals effectively serve those private interests (this is true to varying degrees of Mexico, and many Latin American and Caribbean nations). The use of the law to confer immunity on the well-connected, protect private monopolies, and transfer public assets to the powerful is not at all the same as the situation where

> the pattern of MITI's (or its Korean and Taiwanese counterparts) involvement in the economy was consistent with both the economic logic of selective industrial policy [...] and the logic of finding an equilibrium between bureaucratic autonomy and effectiveness, on the one hand, and bureaucratic power and accountability, on the other (i.e. correspondence between "state autonomy" and "state capacity") (Onis 1991: 115).

So another important element of the successful developmental states is that they were not captured by corrupt special interest groups. This reflects the fact that state power and autonomy were typically consolidated before other interests became influential, so that private economic interests were generally politically weaker, initially, than state power (Leftwich 1995: 416–17).

This relative autonomy requires, of course, the support of the political executive. Politicians have to provide the space for bureaucrats to make important decisions by ensuring that special interest groups do not deflect the state from its main development priorities and also legitimate and ratify the decisions taken by the bureaucrats. This combination serves when dealing both with civil society and with local and foreign interests, giving the state the ability to shape advantageous economic relationships (Onis 1991: 115). It is important to note that the nature of the relative autonomy of the bureaucracy "[m]ust be seen as the product of a historical conjuncture of domestic and international factors. It is an autonomy embedded in the concrete set of social ties which bind state and society and provide institutional channels for the continuous negotiation and re-negotiation of goals and policies" (Onis 1991: 123).

A successful developmental state typically has the following characteristics:

1. A relatively strong state
2. An effective and productive state investment strategy, driven by results rather than by vested interests
3. A state that is not overly influenced by interest groups
4. A government that is capable of thinking and acting strategically

If an authoritarian command-and-control state is at one end of the spectrum, and a weak state unable to enforce its will over special interest groups is at the other (Myrdal 1968), then a successful developmental state will be somewhere between the two extremes. Its position partly depends on the relative strength of the existing political forces in society (interest groups, labor unions, etc.).

As Acemoglu and Robinson (2012) have demonstrated, it is political and economic institutions that are the most important determinants of economic success or failure. They point out, for example, that Korea is an ethnically homogeneous nation, but the people of North Korea are desperately poor, half-starved and oppressed, while their relatives in South Korea are prosperous and free. The reason for this extreme disparity is that South Korea created structures that created incentives, rewarded innovation, and allowed universal participation in economic opportunities, while the government became increasingly accountable and responsive to the people. North Korea, however, became a totalitarian state, dedicated to maintaining the power and wealth of a single family and their close associates.

The economies of East Asia, such as Japan and, more recently, China, have achieved remarkable growth rates by adopting many Western technologies and business systems, while still emphasizing loyalty to society, family, and the nation, as opposed to the more individualistic ethos of the West. While Western countries grew predominantly by directing gains from economic activity toward the formation of physical capital, only to be caught in later years by the need to expand human and social capital that required more inclusive institutions and the consequent broadening of economic activity to all sectors of the nation, some of the successful developmental states have attempted to adopt a more inclusive model from the outset (Karagiannis and Madjd-Sadjadi 2007). However, this is not universally true. Malaysia's policy of preferences for ethnic Malays, who make up about 60% of the population, has been increasingly criticized, especially by ethnic Chinese and Indians, who make up about 30% of the population but do not have the same benefits.

Today, many modern states, including the East Asian states, face another fundamental tension: those individuals who could most contribute to growth are also those who are most able to leave—or relocate their capital—and are therefore able to negotiate the greatest concessions. Partly as a result, wealth and power have become far more concentrated. In some countries, this has coincided with high and rising levels of unemployment, a combination that has triggered violence and political extremism across much of southern Europe. This emphasizes the value of social programs that attempt to break the cycle of poverty and thereby reduce inequality, which may ultimately prove to be a more durable basis for long-term prosperity (Karagiannis and Madjd-Sadjadi 2007).

Jamaica was, until the early 1970s, the strongest economy in the Caribbean, with over two decades of high, sustained growth, averaging almost 5% per annum. The descent into political violence and corruption in the 1970s fundamentally damaged the economy, which showed little growth in the subsequent four decades, largely because the state failed to ensure law, order, and justice to the people. By contrast, Hong Kong, Singapore, and Taiwan avoided that trap by maintaining a strong state that could guarantee security and low rates of violence.

There are now three important questions. First, is there a characteristic East Asian development model? Second, is the developmental state model compatible with political liberalization and democratic forms of governance? Third, could—and should—this model be replicated in other developing countries, in particular, those (such as Jamaica) that have been on a low-growth path for over four decades? Would it help countries like Jamaica to recover their forward momentum?

First, although some governments have stated that their Asian model, broadly defined as combining economic liberalism with authoritative political action, is superior to that of the West, it is clear that there is no single Asian model. In some cases, the developmental state model was clearly a transitional phase, after which greater political freedom emerged. There are countries such as Singapore, South Korea, Taiwan, and Japan that have gone through a developmental state phase and have emerged as strong democracies. In countries such as China, however, economic success has not (yet) been followed by political reform. This indicates a possible future constraint to growth; it will be difficult for China to encourage the further development of a strong middle class and a new generation of innovators and entrepreneurs while it is still forbidden to criticize the role of the Party in controlling the army, the media, and the state. The Party's legitimacy is now based mostly on encouraging nationalism and delivering economic growth, so a failure on either count would expose it to increasing pressure.

Another key issue is corruption. In China, the Party's control of public life is more likely to be tolerated as long as the Party cadres are seen as selfless, dedicated people who work in the national interest, but become far less acceptable if they come to be perceived as selfish and corrupt and involved in the misdirection of state resources to their private ends. As Nanayakkara reports, for example, recent research by the Chinese Academy of Social Sciences states that since 1990, a number of high-ranking government officials and senior managers of state-owned enterprises have fled the country with stolen assets worth some US$123 billion (Nanayakkara 2011). This situation has been described by Acemoglu and Robinson (2012) as one where interests of the privileged elite no longer coincide with those of the people, and where the interests of the elite then increasingly prevail over those of the mass of the population. This is the point at which the institutions of power are reshaped to serve the interests of the elite, thereby becoming "extractive institutions" that transfer wealth from the people to the elite.

More fundamentally, Acemoglu and Robinson argue that there is no inevitable process whereby rising prosperity in an autocracy evolves into inclusion, but that it is in the interest of the elite to cede power to inclusive institutions only if confronted by the prospect of serious revolution. This suggests that China will only evolve into a democracy when the Party elite conclude that the alternatives are worse. As President Hu Jintao said at the 2012 Chinese Communist Party Congress, speaking about the "serious challenge" of corruption, "If we fail to handle this issue well, it could prove fatal to the party, and even cause the collapse of the party and the fall of the state" (http://www.bbc.co.uk/news/world-asia-china-20233101).

The question of whether China's model of political control can evolve into a democracy, or even coexist with a liberal Western-model political system, therefore emerges as a key problem for comparative political economy during the next decade. It is important to note, however, that what is described as the Asian model is actually quite diverse. This reflects the extent to which the Asian developmental state model was, in practice, the product of specific national and historical circumstances, which means that there may exist major constraints on the extent to which it could be replicated in countries which have quite different histories and cultures.

What is perhaps important to learn from the East Asian experience of accelerated development, therefore, is how to take a more focused and strategic approach to development problems. So the challenge for decision and policy makers in the Caribbean today is to devise forms of strategic development policy that are consistent with the norms of democratic accountability and with more limited concentration of state and private power than has been the case in the East Asian context (Karagiannis 2002; Karagiannis and Madjd-Sadjadi 2007).

All social and economic systems must adapt to change, or else perish. The East Asian states are evolving; the rise of their middle class, technological advances, economic restructuring, and changes in the international environment have brought about changes in their elites, their coalitions of interest, and their institutions, as well as in their ideas of development. So the developmental state model may evolve, or it may be replaced by a new set of social, political, and institutional arrangements (Leftwich 1995: 421).

It is clear, however, that the transfer of specific developmental state policies and strategies to new environments is unlikely to work in the absence of the political and institutional conditions that was required for their effective implementation. The rest of this chapter examines the lessons and implications for possible developmental interventions in the Caribbean.

Desirable Developmental Interventions in the Caribbean

Most agree that government interventions are necessary when the market alone cannot deliver particular socioeconomic objectives. Recent attention has been increasingly focused on the effectiveness of state interventions, which raises the crucial issue of state integrity and capacity (Ahrens 1997: 114). As Evans (1992: 141) argues: "the consistent pursuit of any policies, whether they are aimed at 'getting prices right' or implanting local industry, requires the enduring institutionalisation of a complex set of political machinery."

Any attempt to improve the effectiveness of government needs to take into account the role of institutions, the competitive environment, the structure of business organizations, and the pattern of incentives that can be generated by the government, all of which will mediate the developmental consequences of state policies (Ahrens 1997: 117). Effective policies "not only require credible commitments but crucially depend on the administrative, technical, and political capacity and capability of policy-makers" (Ahrens 1997: 115). Furthermore, "(d)ifferent kinds of state structures create different capacities for action. Structures define the range of roles that the state is capable of playing. Outcomes depend both on whether the roles fit the context and on how well they are executed" (Evans 1995: 11).

This position can be summarized in four points:

1. Efficient administration is as important to effective governance as sound policies.
2. The quality of governance has a marked effect on developmental outcomes.
3. It is important that the process of policy making and administration is not captured by interest groups. This requires establishing clear, stable goals and incentives, and ensuring that everyone can feel confident that these cannot be arbitrarily changed.
4. Policies need institutions to implement them; institutions need to be founded on clear policy mandates; so policies and the relevant institutions must evolve in parallel (Ahrens 1997: 118–19).

What is an effective form of intervention for the Caribbean states today? Clearly, the state remains the most powerful institution to regulate, correct market failures and—where necessary—channel the power of the markets to deliver social and developmental goals. Although prediction has its risks, there are several characteristics of the modern developmental intervention, which emanate from the experiences in the post-war years in East Asia.

First, governments have a key role to play in promoting social development, as the state has a primary responsibility to provide adequate social services and promote the well-being of citizens. Thus, well-planned social programs should be an important component in any development strategy because they meet the basic needs of a wide spectrum of the population (MacEwan 1999: 176). Social programs also have implications in terms of other goals of national development, as good programs on education and health can increase *per capita* productivity and thereby support economic growth (MacEwan 1999: 177). This depends heavily, however, on the way that social programs are constructed, because the expansion of social programs *per se* does not necessarily lead to economic growth or other desirable ends.* Two examples illustrate this point. Brazil's *Bolsa Familia* played a key role in getting parents to get their children immunized and in school, for example, which will improve the caliber of the workforce in years to come. By contrast, the welfare programs in the United Kingdom were often used as a substitute for work, rather than

---

* Many (neoliberals and neoclassicals) argue against a heavy role for government social programs in economic growth.

a path into work, thereby undermining long-term growth prospects. Even the best shaped social programs (in terms of their impact on productivity) are likely to have limited impact on economic growth or competitiveness unless the overall development strategy also contains a growth-oriented macroeconomic framework, training programs, and measures to encourage the private sector to create higher-quality jobs (MacEwan 1999: 195).

In the Caribbean, there is a particular need to improve the functional relationship between the government and the private sector. A number of Caribbean governments have been effectively captured by powerful vested interests, and are therefore unable to decisively promote necessary structural changes and economic reforms. The politicization of most decisions, in conjunction with the weakness of the civil service, means that there are major constraints on local developmental policies. The developmental state strategies and policies by Caribbean governments would therefore require strong institutional structures with a substantial measure of operational autonomy to manage the critical interactions between state and industry. This would allow a genuine complementarity between public and private goals, enhance the operation of markets, and create opportunities that would not otherwise exist. In Sawyer's words:

> The complementarity arises from the government setting the [comprehensive and developmental] framework within which firms operate, and seeking to aid firms to fulfil the developmental strategy. The potential complementarity between them implies that the state adopts an entrepreneurial role and is thereby able to create opportunities which would not otherwise exist. If successful, the operation of the state enhances the operation of markets (Sawyer 1992: 64).

A critically important difference between the successful developmental states of the post-war period and the Caribbean nations today is that the former typically had powerful but largely well-intentioned elites, while the Caribbean has powerful anti-growth and anti-development coalitions whose political and economic survival depends on keeping things as they are. There are, for example, incompetent and corrupt politicians, union leaders, and business owners who will fight hard to prevent the emergence of any potential challenge to their monopoly on power. If this barrier could be overcome, there is no other significant reason why it would not be possible to build strong institutional structures in the Caribbean, although it would still require challenging the common desire of many politicians to exercise a high level of (often informal) control of institutions. To be effective, these institutions would have to be embedded in productive networks with sections of industry, financial institutions, universities, and other key players. If these networks were successful, it would help to increase bureaucratic integrity and autonomy, a combination that would improve policy quality and relevance (Cowling 1990: 24–5). This combination of bureaucratic autonomy and social connectedness [what Evans (1995) calls "embedded autonomy"] could provide the institutional basis for more effective, transparent, and accountable government involvement in Caribbean economies, while being independent of vested interests and short-term political and societal pressures (Ahrens 1997: 125).*

---

* This approach allows "considerable autonomy in determining the mode of operation, and adjusting it as experience accumulates." The main objective is "a dynamic economy rather than sticking to a set of rigid rules imposed by a central bureaucracy." We must avoid squandering people and resources over a whole range of bureaucratic activities (Cowling 1990: 25). As Cowling argues, "Economic policy will be built around the twin pillars of Treasury and Industry; the former with a relatively short-term demand perspective, the latter with a longer-term supply perspective" (Cowling 1990: 24).

Traditional government bureaucracies were largely focused on day-to-day management and control, required little conception of strategy, and rarely undertook any serious forward planning. Indeed, strategy of any kind would have been considered "political" (Hughes 1998: 149). However, stronger institutions with a clear strategic planning role are a necessary part of any attempt to introduce greater competence and a more long-term perspective to development policy in the Caribbean, a combination that would be more favorable to productive investment and sustained economic growth. This would also allow the state to take a genuinely proactive role, harnessing market forces to deliver the goals set by government at various levels, for example, local and national (Cowling 1990: 32). However, it is important to distinguish between centralized planning and strategic planning. Centralized planning, like that in the Soviet era, involved dictating targets to industry, experienced massive failures, and is neither feasible nor desirable today. The role of strategic planning, however, is to focus on desired goals (rather than operational details) in order to give direction and purpose to public organizations; without this underlying strategy, policy making is often without coherent direction. The planning process is often more important than the plan itself, as the use of long-term parameters allows public institutions to develop a shared vision for the future (Cowling 1990: 16–17).*

It is important to divide consideration of key issues related to the structure of Caribbean economies into three sections: (1) issues influenced by policy intervention and general policy issues; (2) issues influenced by specific industries or sectors; and (3) market-driven issues. Given the relative weakness of most Caribbean governments today, it would be sensible to limit strategic intervention to those parts of the Caribbean economies where government intervention could have the greatest positive impact on dynamism and economic growth. One important long-term goal would be to bring about an improvement in the competency and efficiency of local firms, in the level of technological infrastructure they rely on, and in the quality of workmanship and service, so that more and more activities may become increasingly competitive. It would not be sufficient to establish small, technologically modern export sectors, for example, without a plan for using them in a program to upgrade the general skill level in the workforce.

A system of accountability is still required by Caribbean governments, as the two forms of accountability, political and managerial, are tightly related. As Hughes puts it, "the system of accountability is what ties the administrative part of government with the political part and ultimately to the public itself" (Hughes 1998: 225).

In the traditional bureaucratic administration there is some accountability, which relies upon the formal hierarchical structure. Unfortunately, this is typically accountability for avoiding errors, rather than achieving any actual outcomes (Hughes 1998: 233). Improving the idea of accountability by relating it to the achievement of actual goals would therefore be another obvious goal of any move toward more effective developmental intervention. This would involve making relevant institutions responsible for the effective execution of strategic plans and monitoring the progress of these plans. As Cowling puts it:

> ... institutions can formalise the commitment to such [strategies], and their structure, procedures and personnel can act to ensure that such commitments cannot easily be reversed, but they are simply ratifying plans already established. The history of planning [in Caribbean nations] shows how fragile was the commitment, despite the

---

* The Japanese planning, its various instruments, institutions, and mechanisms are "a product of its own history and culture." Nevertheless, different countries are characterized by "quite different historical and cultural circumstances" (quite) different sociopolitical elements (Cowling 1990: 18).

creation of many new institutions, [and the lack of teeth of these institutions was obvious]. With clear goals, and a determination to pursue them, institutions with teeth should be forthcoming [in the Caribbean] (Cowling 1990: 23).

The effectiveness of this model would also depend on the coherence of state policies, which is clearly going to be difficult to maintain when important parts of the state are wedded to pork-barrel politics and beholden to specific interests. Effectiveness in the Caribbean, therefore, will be highly dependent on the degree of relative institutional autonomy from the surrounding social and political structures and pressure (Wade 1990: 375).

In the course of a fundamental redirection of this kind, simply matching developmental state policies to existing political institutions is very unlikely to work and probably would be counterproductive. So any such change would require a deep commitment to fundamental improvements in policy making, while the institutional structures would have to generate value by providing continuity, consistency, and commitment to the direction and pace of local development (Ahrens 1997: 119, 126). Without such commitments, effectiveness, competence, capacity, and professionalism, developmental state policy making will probably founder on short-term expedients; the power of existing interests; the conservatism, ineffectiveness, and inefficiency of the civil service; or the resistance of the people (Cowling 1990: 23). All too often, public sector reforms and capacity-building programs have been introduced in many Caribbean countries without the benefit of systematic and disciplined diagnoses of institutional capacities. This has resulted in wasted investments, inadequate levels of skill and competence, ineffectiveness, and performance shortcomings. In contrast, the economic success of Japan and NICs could not have been achieved without the decisive role of their competent "technostructures" in economic and social planning. Indeed, an important feature of these technocracies has been their technical competence; many of the top officials of Japan and East Asian countries received advanced training abroad.* Singapore's founding elite, for example, was educated in the United Kingdom.

It would, in principle, be possible to build a more competent technocracy, and the same underlying knowledge-based strategy could then switch to place the emphasis on increasing the skill base in other areas, including innovation hubs, the capacity to develop smart infrastructure, make more effective use of technology, including technology generation, acquisition and transfer, higher education and research, continuous professional development, and other factors that serve as growth accelerators. In all such cases, it is important to connect the necessary intellectual, managerial, and fiscal resources, then to maximize the synergies. Strategic human resource management and planning coupled with investments in human resource development (i.e., high-quality and timely education, training, and the continuous development of scientific manpower) should therefore be linked to a clear effort by Caribbean governments and institutions to improve the quality and effectiveness of governance and state actions, including a commitment to pay competitive wages for good, committed technocrats. As Wade puts it:

> the executive technostructures must be in a position to recruit from among the best and the brightest people of outstanding talent based on meritocratic criteria. Once the central bureaucracy acquires a reputation for attracting the most competent and

---

* The Japanese governments tried to create "winners," thereby there was centralization and consolidation of state power.

talented, the system can develop a momentum of its own. It continues to attract such people (even at lower salaries than the private sector) because selection is based on meritocracy. Its personnel can be motivated by the belief that what they are doing promotes the national development and welfare. This sense of "national mission" can motivate the executive technostructure to use its powers in line with "national purpose" goals. The more the government intends to intervene and to play a leading role, the more important are the staffing, motivation, authority, professionalism and responsibilities of the central core (Wade 1990: 371).

It is essential, however, that Caribbean governments should also eliminate political patronage. In a culture of patronage, key posts are often filled with party loyalists or political allies, and this can very effectively undermine national development.

Developmental intervention also requires better use of resources. This involves directing resources to emphasize those programs that most assist the attainment of strategic objectives. It also involves more state spending on key infrastructure and the other modern factors of growth and competitiveness, and less spending on nonessential kinds of government expenditure (like the "social programs" that channel patronage).

It is now possible to move most government services online, which creates scope for a large reduction in public sector staffing levels. These reductions could still be based on strategic human resource management and planning, so that a significantly smaller but much more expert civil service replaces the unwieldy and inefficient bureaucracy. This would help to raise competence levels and also release resources for higher levels of public investment.

Public investments in knowledge-building, technological innovation, training, and research can be oriented to the needs of the business sector with a view to crowding in private investment. This could be at least partly financed by eliminating the large array of tax waivers now used to support politically favored businesses, to oblige them to stop "suckling the mother's milk of subsidies" (Karagiannis and Madjd-Sadjadi 2007).

The current economic difficulties, and fiscal pressures in particular, are making many governments more prepared to tackle difficult institutional issues than would have otherwise been the case. Caribbean governments, however, still have to find ways to ensure that the best business practices are adopted and require firms to invest in new production facilities, skills training and upgrading, and critical science and technology initiatives. The nations which do best in the global arena are those which manage change competently and encourage their private sector to invest in new opportunities. The capacity to manage change is the best way to ensure stability and prosperity (Chang 1994; Singh 1995; Boyer and Drache 1996—among others).

Conclusion

The long-running poor performance of most of the Caribbean economies suggests that governments need to play a more intelligent role. This will be a radical change, however, from the weakness, incompetence, and corruption that have vitiated many of the Caribbean governments and have been the main causes of the poor performance to date.

Intelligent, proactive state policy can be used to crowd-in private investment spending and promote development by increasing the skills base and competitiveness. This could be achieved by an active state that borrows some methods from the developmental state model, but only if it purges the corruption and patronage that has undermined most such efforts to date. Provided that the latter condition can be achieved, intelligent activism might be the best viable development strategy left for the Caribbean nations.

References

Acemoglu D. and Robinson J. (2012), *Why Nations Fail: The Origins of Power, Prosperity, and Poverty*, New York, Crown Business.
Ahrens J. (1997), Prospects of institutional and policy reform in India: Toward a model of the developmental state? *Asian Development Review*, Vol. 15, No. 1, pp. 111–46.
Amsden A. (1989), *Asia's Next Giant*, New York, Oxford University Press.
Arestis P. and Sawyer M. C. (eds.) (1998), *The Political Economy of Economic Policies*, London, Macmillan.
Boyer R. and Drache D. (eds.) (1996), *States Against Markets: The Limits of Globalisation*, London, Routledge.
Chang, H.J. (1994), *The Political Economy of Industrial Policy*, London; Basingstoke: Macmillan.
Evans P. B. (1992), The state as problem and solution: Predation, embedded autonomy, and structural change, in Haggard S. and Kaufman R. R. (eds.), *The Politics of Economic Adjustment*, Princeton, NJ, Princeton University Press.
Evans P. B. (1995), *Embedded Autonomy: States and Industrial Transformation*, Princeton, NJ, Princeton University Press.
http://www.bbc.co.uk/news/world-asia-china-20233101
http://www.telegraph.co.uk/finance/financialcrisis/9633388/Its-still-a-hard-toil-to-the-sunlit-uplands-of-recovery.html
Hughes O. E. (1998), *Public Management and Administration*, 2nd ed., London, Macmillan.
Johnson, C. (1982), *MITI and the Japanese Miracle: The Growth of Industrial Policy, 1925–1975*, Stanford, CA, Stanford University Press.
Jones-Hendrickson S. B. (1985), *Public Finance and Monetary Policy in Open Economies*, Mona, Jamaica, ISER, UWI.
Karagiannis N. (2002), *Developmental Policy and the State: The European Union, East Asia, and the Caribbean*, Lanham, MD, Lexington Books.
Karagiannis N. and Madjd-Sadjadi Z. (2007), *Modern State Intervention in the Era of Globalisation*, Cheltenham, Edward Elgar.
Leftwich A. (1995), Bringing politics back: Towards a model of the developmental state, *The Journal of Development Studies*, Vol. 31, No. 3, pp. 400–27.
MacEwan A. (1999), *Neo-Liberalism or Democracy?* London, Zed Books.
Myrdal G. (1968), *Asian Drama*, New York, Random House.
Nanayakkara R. (2011), Corruption perceptions index: Alarming results in Asia. In Asia Pacific, Measurement and Research, November 30, 2011, http://blog.transparency.org/2011/11/30/2011-corruption-perceptions-index-alarming-results-in-asia.
Nester W. R. (1991), *Japanese Industrial Targeting*, London, Macmillan.
Onis Z. (1991), The logic of the developmental state, *Comparative Politics*, Vol. 24, pp. 109–26.
Premchand A. (1975), Budgetary reforms in developing countries, *Finance and Development*, Vol. 12, No. 1.
Sawyer M. C. (1992), Reflections on the nature and role of industrial policy. *Metroeconomica*, Vol. 43, pp. 51–73.
Singh A. (1995), Competitive markets and economic development: A commentary on World Bank analyses, *International Papers in Political Economy*, Vol. 2, No. 1.
Wade R. (1990), *Governing the Market: Economic Theory and the Role of Government in East Asian Industrialisation*, Princeton, NJ, Princeton University Press.

Chapter 14

Environmental Risk Management in the Caribbean

Charley G. Granvorka, Eric A. Strobl,
Leslie Walling, and Evan M. Berman

Contents

Introduction 312
Natural Hazards in the Caribbean 313
DRM Framework and Strategies in the Caribbean 322
    Regional Efforts 322
    National and Donor Efforts 324
Further Examples: Risk Challenges and Successes in the Caribbean 329
    In the Dominican Republic, the Community Is Aware of Risk 330
    An Inclusive and Proactive Approach in Jamaica 330
    In Barbados, Success on Pilot Site Has Led to Replicability 331
The Role of the CCRIF 332
Conclusion 334
References 335

Abstract: The Caribbean region is composed of 34 islands ranked from middle to high-income countries, except Haiti that is considered as the poorest one in the hemisphere. As small island developing states, these countries have to face challenges induced by their specific characteristics and their geographical localization at both the global and domestic levels. Among these challenges, the eradication of poverty is one of them. Although consensually defined by the international institutions, in the Caribbean, poverty definition in the Caribbean derived the Caribbean Development Bank methodology applied for analyzing the extent, depth, and severity of the phenomenon. This chapter exposes the determinants and characteristics of poverty in the region based upon a set of Country Poverty Assessments realized in 12 countries—all borrowing members at Caribbean Development Bank—between 1995 and 2009. Some theoretical concepts explain the persistence and nature of poverty in a country like Haiti, whose case is compared to the Dominican Republic, its neighbor on Hispaniola. The two countries are economically divergent and high recipient of remittances. The impact of this external financial assistance on poverty reduction in both these economies is also questioned. We conclude that in Haiti poverty is due to nonmonetary causes, whereas in the rest of the Caribbean it is a multidimensional phenomenon and policies have to be redesigned to better target the real and identified causes of poverty in the area.

Introduction

Due to its geographical location, the Caribbean region is intrinsically prone to natural hazards. The most recurring events in this regard are hurricanes, that is, tropical storms and their corollaries, such as marine submersion, floods, mud and landslides. To a lesser extent, volcanoes' eruptions also affect the region, while tsunamis are relatively scarce. Additionally, technological hazards related to economic activities and marine pollution affect activities such as recreation, trade, or waste transportation, and human impacts on the environment are induced by intensive deforestation, pollution, or heavy demographic pressure on coastal areas. Since many islands derive their income mainly from tourism and agriculture, and these sectors are generally the most vulnerable to disasters, their negative effects on Gross Domestic Product (GDP) are magnified and affect especially the most vulnerable part of the populations. Hence, the environmental concerns beg the questions of how to prevent and manage environmental risks with the view to protecting the populations and maintaining a sustainable environment.

This chapter focuses on natural hazards and their management that is shared between public institutions and private organizations acting for the public sector. Management of risk includes the population's education to natural hazards, how to protect the population and goods from vulnerability and huge losses, and how to recover after natural disasters. In this chapter, we restrict our study to the insular states comprising the Caribbean. While the term *Caribbean* is generally understood as referring to the wider Caribbean, that is, the one that includes all the insular states and the continental countries bordering the Caribbean Sea (Girvan 2001),* here we focus on the 33 islands located in the Hurricane Belt. These are both geographically and economically vulnerable as they are tourism dependent (Granvorka and Strobl 2010).

With the development of modern warning systems, natural hazards such as hurricanes must no longer be approached as completely unpredictable events. Rather early warnings systems of potentially approaching tropical storms provide the public at least in the very short term some

---

* The Caribbean region comprises 28 distinct entities of which 22 are independent states of which 9 are continental countries and 13 are islands in the archipelagic arc that sweeps from the southern tip of Florida in the north to the coast of the Guyana's in the south. The Caribbean Sea is the marine area of approximately 2,515,900 km². The states that boarder the Caribbean Sea range in size from the smaller SIDS of Saint Kits and Nevis (260 km²) and Grenada (340 km²) to the largest island, Cuba with an area of 110,860 km². The low-lying coastal sates of Belize, Guyana, and Suriname are considerably larger in size at 22,810 km², 196,850 km², and 156,000 km², respectively. Maximum country elevations range from tens to hundreds of meters in the relatively flat island of Barbados (Mount Hillaby, 336 m) and archipelagic state of the Bahamas (Mount Alvernia, 63 m) to the 3,087 m Pico Duarte in the Dominican Republic.

time to react accordingly. Since the 1990s, following the different summits,* the mitigation and management of natural hazards and their impacts in Caribbean small island developing states (SIDS) are well identified. The issue is no longer how to implement proactive and reactive strategies, but which could be the optimal one for restabilizing the economic life the most quickly after an event. This question appears as a challenge for these small and open economies largely depending upon external donors at the multi- and bilateral levels for financial support in disaster risk management (DRM).

The Caribbean SIDS have varied economic and regional features that have differentiated economic levels because of their natural resource endowments, macroeconomic, trade, economical diversification, internal conditions, and policy choices related to investment conditions. These are small and open economies that are highly vulnerable and dependent on external governance centers for trade, net inflows, investment, and financial assistance. The region varies from the very poorest, Haiti with a GDP per capita of US$750, to those like the Bahamas that are among the richer with a GDP per capita income of US$23,000. Such differences surely suggest different capabilities for addressing humanitarian and economic challenges, as well as public governance capacity to address and implement emergency management strategies.

The Caribbean islands are federated in CARICOM, created in 1973 under the Treaty of Chaguaramas to establish a Caribbean Community and/or Caribbean Common Market. Since then, the Treaty has been successively widened to Suriname on July 4, 1995, to Haiti in 2002, and more recently to the French overseas Departments of Martinique and Guadeloupe as associate members in 2012. As regarding natural disasters, over the past 35 years, the countries of the English-speaking Caribbean have worked together to develop a coordinated and collaborative approach to the more effective management of natural hazard vulnerability and impacts. Consultative processes have been used to develop a series of programmatic disaster management frameworks and strategies. The consultative processes have progressively become more representative of the wide spectrum of institutional, civil-society, private sector, and governmental stakeholders. Over this period, donor support for DRM and the diversity of supported interventions has increased substantially, and a shift occurred in hazard management, from preparedness, response, and recovery, to include prevention and mitigation. Yet, despite substantial commitment and progress to coordinated and comprehensive DRM approaches, human, economic, and structural vulnerability to natural hazards in the Caribbean continues to increase.

Natural Hazards in the Caribbean

On a regional scale, much of the Caribbean weather and climate is strongly influenced by the seasonal variation of the Inter-tropical Convergence Zone (ITCZ) and El Nino/Southern Oscillation (ENSO), with the wet season being associated with the seasonal northward migration of the ITCZ. The ITCZ also exposes the Caribbean region to hazards such as heavy rains, strong winds, large waves, and sea swells, and associated impacts in the absence of tropical storms and hurricanes. Multi-year Enso cycles affect precipitation patterns on the South American continent and

---

* Declaration of Barbados, "Global Conference on the Sustainable Development of Small Island Developing States." April 26–May 6, 1994 (BoPA). Mauritius Declaration, January, "International Meeting to Review the Implementation of the Programme of Action for the Sustainable Development in Small Island Developing States" 10–14, 2005. Saint Georges' Declaration of Principles for Environmental Sustainability in the OECS (2001, and revised 2006).

hurricane activity in the Caribbean. On a local scale, weather conditions are moderated by the oceanic influence, the easterly trade winds, and influenced by topography. In the more mountainous islands, the topography creates orographic or relief rainfall and rains shadow.

The exposure of individual Caribbean states to specific natural hazards varies with their geographic location and geology. Exposure to hurricanes is high in the central and northern Caribbean, with the name "Hurricane Alley" being ascribed to the area of the Caribbean over which hurricanes have traversed with greatest frequency. The mountainous volcanic islands of the Eastern Caribbean tend to be highly susceptible to flash floods and landslides or mudslides because of their steep topography, mountainous topography, and volcanic soils. Trinidad and Tobago, Suriname, and Guyana to the south tend not to be exposed to direct hurricane strikes and hurricane winds, but may experience the impacts associated with heavy seas and swells; the large continental states of Belize, Guyana, and Suriname experienced river flooding on a scale and duration generally not seen in the insular Caribbean.

In addition, the eastern boundary of the Caribbean Plate and the Caribbean Sea is described by the arc of islands that form the Lesser Antilles, an 850-km chain of volcanic islands stretching from Sombrero in the north to Grenada in the south. The island chain includes 21 live volcanoes distributed among 11 volcanically active islands. Twenty-one eruptions have occurred in the Lesser Antilles since 1900, nine on land and 12 from the submarine volcano Kick 'em Jenny, located approximately 9 km north of Grenada (Lindsay et al. 2005). At its southern boundary, the Caribbean Plate interacts with the South American Plate giving rise to Barbados, Trinidad and Tobago. Table 14.1 shows all countries being exposed to a broad range of natural hazards.

The natural disasters have huge impacts on the living conditions, economic performance, and environmental assets and services of affected countries or regions (ECLAC 2003).* Their consequences greatly affect the environment, economic and social structures and are easily witnessed by two macroeconomic aggregates, GDP and gross formation of fixed capital, which tend to decrease in the year following such disasters (Charvériat 2000).† Specifically, based on the Caribbean's experience since 1970, natural disasters inflicting damage of more than 2% of a country's GDP can be expected to strike the region approximately once every two and a half years. Some older examples include Grenada, Cayman Islands, and Jamaica from the Hurricane Ivan 2004 event, Guyana from the 2005 flood event, Dominica and St. Lucia from the Hurricane Deane (2007) event, Trinidad and St. Vincent from a 2008 flood event, Turks and Caicos from the Hurricane Ike (2008) event. By example, it was estimated that economic loss from Hurricane Ivan in the Cayman Islands was US$2.4 billion, with real economic growth declining from 2% in 2003 to 0.9% in 2004. The floods that affected Guyana in January and February 2005 severely affected 37% of the population, doing US$93 billion in damage and with an equivalent impact of 59% of GDP. The total cost of damage caused by Hurricane Tomas in Saint Lucia was equivalent to 43.4% of GDP or nine times agricultural GDP (ECLAC 2011a).

Between December 23 and 24, 2013, the islands of Dominica, Grenada, St. Vincent and the Grenadines, and St. Lucia experienced severe rains and high winds due to a low-level trough system. Heavy showery activity resulted in reported accumulated rainfall totals of 406 mm in St. Lucia, 156 mm in Dominica, and 109 mm in St. Vincent and the Grenadines.

In St. Vincent and the Grenadines, the resulting floods caused nine deaths, the damage or destruction of 495 houses and 28 bridges, damage to over 98 acres of crops, and 2,325 persons to

---

* *Handbook for Estimating the Socio-Economic Effects and Environmental Effects of Disasters.*
† *Natural Disasters in Latin America and the Caribbean: An Overview of Risk.*

Environmental Risk Management in the Caribbean ■ 315

Table 14.1 Analysis of Country-Level Exposure to Specific Natural Hazards

	Natural Hazard Exposure											
Country Name	Hurricane/ Tropical Cyclone	Strong Winds	Storm Surges	Coastal Flooding	Flash Flooding	River Flooding	Land/mud Slides	Heavy Rains	Droughts	Thunderstorms/ Lightening	Earthquakes	Volcanic Eruptions	Tsunamis
Antigua and Barbuda	S	S	S	S	S	0		S	S	II	II	I	S
Bahamas	S	S	S	S	II				II	II	II		
Barbados	S	S	S	S	S		S		II	II	S	I	S
Belize	S	II	S	S	S	S	II		II	II	S		
Cuba	S	II	II	II	II	II	II		S	II	S		
Dominica	S	II	II	S	S	S	S	S	S	II	II	II	
Dominican Republic	S	S	S	S	S	S	S	S	II	II	S		
Grenada	S	S	S	S	S	II	S	S	S	II	II	I	
Guyana	0	II	II	S	II	S	II	S	S	II	S	0	S
Haiti	S	S	II	II	S	II	S	S	S	II	S		
Jamaica	S	S	S	S	S	S	S	S	S	II	S		
St. Kitts and Nevis	S	II	S	II	II	II	II	S	II	II	II	I	
St. Lucia	S	II	II	S	II	S	S		S	II	S	I	S

(Continued)

Table 14.1 (Continued) Analysis of Country-Level Exposure to Specific Natural Hazards

Country Name	Natural Hazard Exposure										
	Hurricane/ Tropical Cyclone	Strong Winds	Storm Surges	Coastal Flooding	Flash Flooding	River Flooding	Land/mud Slides	Heavy Rains	Droughts	Thunderstorms/ Lightening	Earthquakes	Volcanic Eruptions	Tsunamis
St. Vincent and the Grenadines	S	S	S	S	S	II	II		II	S	II	I	S
Suriname	II	II	II	II	II	S	II	S	II	II	II		
Trinidad and Tobago	0	II	II	II	S	II	II		II	II	S	II	

Source: WMO, Strengthening of Risk Assessment and Multi-hazard Early Warning Systems for Meteorological, Hydrological and Climate Hazards in the Caribbean. WMO-No. 1082. DRR-CARIB 1. Final Report November 17. Reprinted in 2012. 173pp., 2011.

S, significant; II, occurs; I, indirect.

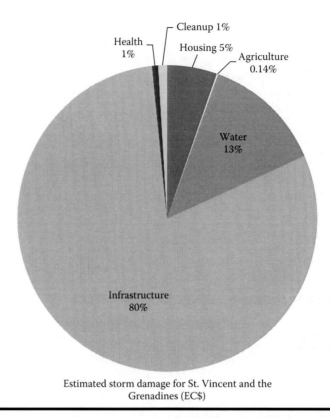

Estimated storm damage for St. Vincent and the Grenadines (EC$)

Figure 14.1 Storm damage in five sectors of the St. Vincent and the Grenadines economy as a proportionate estimated total cost of damage (EC $156,032,141) associated with the passage of a low level trough between December 23 and 24, 2013. (CDEMA. 2014. Situation Report No. 5—Deadly low-level trough system impacts Dominica, St. Lucia, and St. Vincent and the Grenadines. January 5. Available at: http://www.cdema.org/index.php?option=com_content& view=article&id=1304:situation-report-5-deadly-low-level-trough-system-impacts-dominica-saintlucia-and-saint-vincent-a-the-grenadines&catid=39:situation-reports&Itemid=347.)

be displaced. The estimated total cost of damage was EC$156,032,141.*,† The total cost of damage was estimated across five sectors (health 1%, housing 5%, agriculture 0.14%, water 13%, and infrastructure 80%) plus the cost of cleanup operations (cleanup 1%) (Figure 14.1).

Preliminary reports from St. Lucia confirmed six deaths, and 1,050 people severely impacted in four of the worst impacted areas. Preliminary reports from the Commonwealth of Dominica confirmed impacts to 106 households in 12 communities, with losses estimated at EC$0.585 million. Damage to roads and bridges was estimated at EC$45 million.

The significance of the impacts of extreme climatic events and natural disasters is that they can and do reverse development achievements and upset development plans. At issue are not only

---

* At an exchange rate of US$1: EC$2.68820 the estimated cost of damage is equivalent to US$419,446,000.00.
† CDEMA. (2014). Situation Report No. 5—Deadly low-level trough system impacts Dominica, St. Lucia, and St. Vincent and the Grenadines. January 5. Available at: http://www.cdema.org/index.php?option=com_ content&view=article&id=1304:situation-report-5-deadly-low-level-trough-system-impacts-dominica-saint-lucia-and-saint-vincent-a-the-grenadines&catid=39:situation-reports&Itemid=347.

high-profile, high impact events, but also frequently occurring low-profile disaster events, which are also numerous and responsible for a very significant proportion of damage to housing, crops, livestock, and local infrastructure (Maskrey 2011). The fact that the high level of exposure to natural hazards can result in a country experiencing a number of disasters over the short to medium term means that countries may not recover from one disaster event before being impacted by another.

Table 14.2 further shows the incidence of natural disasters in one setting, namely, St. Vincent and the Grenadines based on newspaper reports over the period 1957 to 2011 (Opadeyi 2012). In most cases, estimated loss and costs of damage were not reported; however, the total impact of Hurricanes Allen, Dean, Ivan, and Tomas were at least 1,673 buildings and 23,485 persons affected

Table 14.2 St. Vincent and the Grenadines: An Analysis of Reported Natural Hazard Incidents in the Vincentian Newspaper between September 1957 and December 2011

Hazard	Reported Triggering Factor	Hazard Occurrence
Coastal erosion	Storm surge (1984)	1
Storm Surge	Hurricane Omar (2008)	1
Drought	Persistent dry weather	1
Earth movement/land slippage	Cause unknown (2)	2
Landslides	Heavy rains (11)	23
	Tropical depression (2)	
	Tropical storm (2, Joan and Lilly)	
	Upper level trough (2)	
	Thunder Storm (2)	
	Earth movement/land slippage (2)	
	Reservoir overflow (1)	
	Unknown (1)	
Earth tremor/earthquake	Volcanic activity, Mag. 6.0 with epicenter N of St. Vincent, Mag. 7.3 off Martinique	3
Flooding	Heavy rains (17)	25
	Tropical storms (1, Emilly)	
	Tropical depressions (4)	
	Tropical wave (2)	
	Hurricane (1)	
Hurricanes	5: Buelah (1967), Allen (1980); Ivan (2004); Dean (2007); Tomas (2010)	5

(Continued)

Table 14.2 (*Continued*)   St. Vincent and the Grenadines: An Analysis of Reported Natural Hazard Incidents in the Vincentian Newspaper between September 1957 and December 2011

Hazard	Reported Triggering Factor	Hazard Occurrence
Tropical storms	Alma (1974); Danielle (1986); Emily (1987); Joan (1988); Iris (1995); Lenny (1999)	6
Storm force winds	Tropical storm: (3) Alma (1974), Lilly (2002), Emily (2005)	6
	Tropical wave (1)	
	Tropical depression (1)	
	Thunder storm (1)	
Thunder storm	No record (1)	1
Volcanic eruption	La Soufriere volcanic eruption 1971 and 1979	2
Tsunami*	1867 (earthquake), 1868, 1902 (La Soufriere volcanic eruption), 1955 (earthquake)	4
*http://www.ngdc,noaa,gov/hazard/hazard/shtml		80

Source: Opadeyi, J. (2012). *Building a Caribbean GeoNode Platform in Support of Climate Risk Management.* Mona, Jamaica: University of the West Indies Faculty of Engineering.

and estimated damage costs of about US$178 million. The GDP of St. Vincent and the Grenadines in 2011 was about $700 million (or $6,300 per capita).

Vulnerability to natural hazards is further increased by characteristics in the Caribbean, especially, the small size of its island nations, geographical dispersion, lack of natural resources, limited fresh water supplies, depletion of nonrenewable resources, limited ability to reap the benefits of economies of scale, and growing dependency on tourism. These factors are further discussed in Table 14.3. For example, smallness decreases the human resource base from which to draw experienced and efficient administrators, and it also decreases the tax base from resource mitigation efforts.

Some of these factors are common to both the island states and the low-lying coastal states of Belize, Guyana, and Suriname. These factors include the following:

- The fragility of their ecosystems and the ecosystem services that they provide society
- Settlements located in vulnerable areas
- Migration and the ongoing loss of experienced skilled professionals to larger countries
- Limited resources to invest in human and infrastructural development
- Increasing levels of unemployment and underemployment
- Growing populations and population densities
- Geographic isolation and constraints on transport and communication
- Vulnerability to exogenous economic and financial shocks
- A highly limited internal market
- Heavy dependence on imports and limited commodities
- The high level of indebtedness and the pressure of servicing high debt loads
- Greater exposure to globalization trends
- Loss of traditional markets

Table 14.3 An Analysis of the Factors Contributing to the Vulnerability of Caribbean States

Vulnerability Factors	Factor Dimensions	Vulnerability Indicators	Impact
Physical	Small size	High percentage of land area exposed to any single natural hazard event, for example, hurricane, drought, heavy rains, storm surges, or flooding	Possibility that a high percentage or all human, institutional, and material resources will be affected.
			Economic cost of natural disasters in terms of damage per unit area can be relatively large due to the small size of many Caribbean states.
	Remoteness		Time and difficulty of securing relief supplies and assistance before and after a disaster.
Social	Small populations	Population density	Small human resource base from which to draw experienced and efficient administrators.
			Economic cost of natural disasters in terms of cost per capita area can be relatively large.
			National disaster offices in smaller countries are understaffed.
			Expenditure related to the physical environment is not proportionately divisible according to population size due to the high overhead costs involved.
			Small tax base with which to support national development and disaster preparedness, prevention, mitigation, response, and recovery.
Economic	Economic openness		
	Country has high economic dependence on one or two vulnerable industries, for example, tourism and agriculture		Economic cost of natural disasters in terms of damage per unit area and cost per capita can be relatively large.
			Economic impact of natural hazard disasters average 2% GDP per year.
	Dependence on a narrow range of export products		Reduced GDP in years immediately following natural hazard disaster.

(Continued)

Table 14.3 (*Continued*)   An Analysis of the Factors Contributing to the Vulnerability of Caribbean States

Vulnerability Factors	Factor Dimensions	Vulnerability Indicators	Impact
	Loss of traditional markets	Land areas under cultivation	Disruption or cessation of land management and husbandry practices. Adoption of slash and burn agricultural practices. Increased deforestation, soil erosion, and frequency of landslides.
	Heavy dependence on trade taxes and trade preferences	Reduction in trade taxes due to the EPA arrangement	Reduced government revenue.
	The high level of indebtedness and the pressure of servicing high debt loads	Debt to GDP ratio	Diversion of revenue from maintenance, management, and development to debt servicing.
			Limited ability to borrow for development initiatives.
Environmental	Unique fragile ecosystems that provide protective and provisioning services that easily disrupted or destroyed by human activity and natural hazard events	Environmental Vulnerability Index	Loss of coastal protection ecosystem function due to wave damage, and scouring (coral reefs) and wind damage (mangroves).
		Biodiversity Index	Loss of coastal protection ecosystem function due to development (land "reclamation") and coastal pollution.
			Loss of watershed services resulting in flash-floods, landslides, loss of fertile topsoil, reduced water infiltration into aquifers, loss of small streams and rivers.
		Deforestation due to slash and burn agriculture, poor land management, lumber harvesting	Flash floods, land and mud slides, siltation of rivers, loss of fertile top soil to soil erosion, loss of rivers and streams, reduced water infiltration and aquifer recharge.
		Relatively large coast line relative to landmass	Relatively large proportion of land exposed to coastal inundation, coastal erosion, sea level rise, and storm and hurricane winds.

Source: ECLAC, *Study on the vulnerability and resilience of Caribbean Small Island Developing States (SIDS)*. Economic Commission for Latin America and the Caribbean. LC/CAR/L.354. p. 42. Available at: http://www.eclac.org/publicaciones/xml/4/45364/LCARL.354.pdf, 2011b.

- Growing dependence on food imports to meet domestic needs
- Reduction in donor assistance

In short, natural disasters are frequent, high impact events in the Caribbean that have significant economic and social costs.

DRM Framework and Strategies in the Caribbean

The DRM framework in the Caribbean consists of regional efforts, national offices, and various donor-based programs in support of both.

Regional Efforts

Since 1981, the independent English-speaking countries of the Caribbean have worked systematically to develop a common regional approach to DRM, investing in a series of programmatic initiatives to reduce the economic and human losses and dislocations resulting from extreme natural hazard and geophysical events. Since 1981, CARICOM member states developed through the Pan-Caribbean Disaster Preparedness and Prevention Project, a collective mode of operation concerning the characterization and mitigation of natural hazard risk. Initially, the collective focus was on the need for a more strategic approach to preparing for disasters. Efforts were directed to ensuring the adequacy of capabilities and resources in the event of a disaster and the promotion of rapid and effective response to reduce disaster loss.

The Caribbean Disaster Emergency Response Agency (CDERA) was established in 1990 by CARICOM Agreement, created the institutional mechanisms and framework, within which a programmatic approach to natural hazard risk management would be developed, evolved, and sustained over time. The Agency was established to serve the needs of its 14 participating states (PS) by fulfilling the objectives of: providing immediate and coordinated emergency response; managing and distributing information on disasters affecting PS interested intergovernmental and nongovernmental organizations; mobilizing and coordinating disaster relief; eliminating or mitigating the immediate consequences of disasters in affected PS; and promoting the establishment and enhancement of sustainable emergency response capabilities among members of the Agency.

In 2001, CDERA leads its PS and regional stakeholders in the development of a Comprehensive Disaster Management (CDM) Emergency Operations Centre (EOC) Strategy and Framework. In its initial version designed in 2001, it had identified five intermediate results (IRs) to be targeted: a stronger promotion of CDM by the regional and national institutions; the research of and training support for CDM; the inclusion of CDM and its promotion into the regional institutions and donors' own programs; the enhancement of preparedness, response, and mitigation capability; the incorporation of hazard information into development planning and decision making. After revision in 2007, the framework led to the definition of a regional programming to cover the period 2001–2015.

The exercise was initiated by Caribbean Disaster Emergency Management Agency (CDEMA) out of the recognition of the critical link between disasters and sustainable development. Extensive multifaceted consultations were held with private and public sectors, civil society, bilateral and multi-lateral partners. The process and strategy and framework were explicitly linked to the Barbados Programme of Action (CDERA 2005). The new approach to DRM was endorsed by Caribbean governments and the donor community and adopted. The strategic intention was that the CDM Strategy and Framework would provide the sustainable development approach to DRM by providing the strategy and results framework to link development decision making and planning initiatives to a comprehensive disaster management approach (CRMI 2011).

The devastating disasters of 2004 (hurricanes, floods, and earthquakes) resulted in losses of US$4 billion (CDEMA 2005), triggering a review and reassessment of the effectiveness of approaches to DRM at the national and regional levels. The resulting Enhanced CDM Strategy and Framework 2007–2013 was an attempt to address the deficiencies and gaps in the 2001 CDM Strategy. While the Enhanced Strategy reiterated the need for enhanced institutional support in promoting CDM and effective knowledge management and information sharing, it also added increased national-level mainstreaming (in industries such as tourism, agriculture, infrastructure, planning, and health), as well as increasing community resilience by improving their ability to prioritize hazards, reduce vulnerability, and capacity for preparing and responding thereby reducing the impacts of disastrous events (Baastel 2010). The strategy reflects the dictum that long "it is less expensive in the long run to invest in mitigation activities than in emergency operations" (World Food Programme 1998).*

In broadening of its institutional focus from response and relief to a more comprehensive and inclusive, consideration of all cycles of a hazard, involvement of all sectors of the society, and concentration on all hazards, was reflected in the organizations change in name (Kirton 2013). In 2009, the CDERA became the CDEMA. The governance of CDEMA facilitates broader stakeholder participation. The CDEMA Council is the highest level where the heads of government of the PS determine the policies. CDEMA's main functions are as follows:

1. Mobilizing and coordinating disaster relief
2. Mitigating or eliminating, as far as practicable, the immediate consequences of disasters in PS
3. Providing immediate and coordinated response by means of emergency disaster relief to any affected PS
4. Securing, coordinating, and providing to interested intergovernmental and nongovernmental organizations reliable and comprehensive information on disasters affecting any PS
5. Encouraging
    a. the adoption of disaster loss reduction and mitigation policies and practices at the national and regional level
    b. cooperative arrangements and mechanisms to facilitate the development of a culture of disaster loss reduction
6. Coordinating the establishment, enhancement, and maintenance of adequate emergency disaster response capabilities among the PS[†]

CDEMA is able to mount an immediate and coordinated response to any disastrous event affecting any PS, once the state requests such assistance. CDEMA has been able to establish and maintain adequate disaster response capabilities among PS by providing training for disaster management personnel, institutional strengthening of disaster management organizations, developing information on disaster mitigation and preparedness, and providing other supporting and collaborative services. CDEMA's 2009–2010 budget was about US$7 million and five core staff.[‡] CDEMA has various management and technical advisory committees that provide and disseminate information and training.

---

* World Food Programme, Rome, Italy, 1998.
† CDEMA Webpage. (2014). Available at: http://www.cdema.org/index.php?option=com_content&view=article&id=358&Itemid=120.
‡ http://www.cdema.org/bm2009/BM09-19-10.4_-_Administrative_Budget_2009_-_2010_and_Proposed_Contributions.pdf.

Also, at the same time the Regional Framework was designed in 2001, the Caribbean Development Bank established the Disaster Mitigation Facility for the Caribbean (DMFC) with support from the USAID Office of Foreign Disaster Assistance. The objectives assigned to the DMFC are to assist Borrowing Member Countries (BMCs) at Caribbean Development Bank (CDB) with the adoption and institutionalization of successful disaster mitigation policies and practices, and to strengthen the CDB's capacity to effectively implement its 1998 Natural Disaster Management Strategy and to institutionalize disaster management into CDB policies and programs. The DMFC, whose final objective is poverty reduction through the incorporation of hazard risk assessment and vulnerability reduction into development policies, has committed to assisting other regional and subregional organizations to better define their roles and to strengthen their capacities for hazard risk management. Examples include hurricane-related risk reduction through public–private partnerships in the tourism industry and energy production. Hitherto, institutions like the Caribbean Hotel Association (CHA) and the Caribbean Electrical Utility Association (CARILEC) work in close coordination with DMCF.

National and Donor Efforts

Almost all countries have national level emergency or disaster offices. Section "Further Examples: Risk Challenges and Successes in the Caribbean" provides some examples, and Table 14.4 provides an analysis of the staffing of national offices. For the most part, national efforts are run from small offices that are tasked with providing awareness, coordination, and leadership to preparedness, mitigation, and response efforts. As reflecting the small size of these countries, many do seem constrained by resources. By way of example, in St. Lucia, it is said that: "The lack of staff, the increase of expectations, the increase in projects as well as the budgetary allocations from Central Government are becoming more limited, the NEMO Secretariat will need to target project funding for its programs from external local, regional and international donor Agencies (NEMO 2010)."* While it is difficult to generalize, it appears that National Disaster Offices (NDOs) in general do not have adequate staff and resources to fulfill their mandates (Baastel 2010). Budget appropriations to meet emergency demands in absolute terms and as a percentage of the national budgets are low to inadequate (Baastel 2010; OAS 2010, Table 14.4). Budget allocations for disaster prevention and mitigation are for the most part inadequate or nonexistent (OAS 2010; Table 14.4).

Various donor-related programs should be noted, as well. In 2005, the Food and Agricultural Organization (FAO) funded the regional project Assistance to Improve Local Agricultural Emergency Preparedness in Caribbean Countries Highly Prone to Hurricane Related Disasters in Cuba, Grenada, Haiti, and Jamaica. The project was established to support institutional and technical capacity building for DRM in agricultural line agencies of participating countries and to implement community-based DRM activities at local levels. In formulating the project, the FAO acknowledged the paradigm shift that had been experienced in the Caribbean region over the previous 5 years out of a growing recognition of the importance and advantages of community-based disaster management planning and applied this approach in its regional project. The FAO also recognized the systemic weaknesses in linking long-term development planning within the agricultural sector with the realities and projections of recurrent natural hazards/disasters and improving preparedness and mitigation measures.

In 2008, CIDA established the Canada Caribbean Disaster Risk Management (CCDRM) Fund, a small-grant facility for community, self-help, disaster risk reduction (DRR) projects. The small-grant mechanism was designed to be responsive to the DRR priorities of communities

---

* Source: NEMO (2010). *National Emergency Management Organization Annual Report 2010*. August 1, 2013. http://archive.stlucia.gov.lc/docs/nemo/NEMO2010Report.pdf.

Table 14.4 An Analysis of National Disaster Office Arrangements and Resourcing

Country	Area (sq. km.)	Population (2012)	Population Density	National Disaster Agency	No. Professional Staff (Total)	Population per Member of Staff	Form of Administration	Parent Government Department	Source of Funding	Budget	Budget per Capita (Local Currency)	Budget per Capita (US $)
Antigua and Barbuda	440	89,069	202.43	National Office of Disaster Services (NODS)	4 (13)	6,851	Full Government Department	Ministry of Social Transformation	Separate Budget Head	—	—	
Bahamas	10,010	371,960	37.16	National Emergency Management Agency (NEMO)	—	—		Office of the Prime Minister	—	—	—	
Barbados	430	283,221	658.65	Department of Emergency Management (DEM)	6	47,204	Full Government Department	Ministry of Agriculture	Separate Budget Head	FY2007/8: $827,000	3.24128507/4	1.64
										FY2008/9: $930,000		
										FY2009/10: $918,000		
										Per Annum: $5,000 for each of 30 District Emergency Management Centers		
										$5,000 for Roving Response Team		
Belize	22,810	324,060	14.21	National Emergency Management Organization (NEMO)	21	15,431	Full Government Department	Ministry of Public Utilities	—	Annual General operations Budget: BZ 250,000	0.771462075	0.39
										Max. Annual Disaster Prevention Budget: BZ $300,00 (e.g., training, public awareness, and equipment)		

(Continued)

Table 14.4 (Continued) An Analysis of National Disaster Office Arrangements and Resourcing

Country	Area (sq. km.)	Population (2012)	Population Density	National Disaster Agency	No. Professional Staff (Total)	Population per Member of Staff	Form of Administration	Parent Government Department	Source of Funding	Budget	Budget per Capita (Local Currency)	Budget per Capita (US $)
Cuba	106,440	11,270,957	105.89	(DC)	–	–	Full Government Department	Ministry of Civil Defence	–	–		
Dominica	750	71,684	95.58	Office of Disaster Management (ODM)	5	14,337	Departmental Unit	Ministry of Housing	Budget under parent Ministry	Annual General operations Budget (salaries, recurring expenditure, education outreach): EC$1,000,000	13.95011439	5.17
Dominican Republic	48,320	10,276,621	212.68	(CEO)	200+	51,383	–	–	–	–		
Grenada	340	105,483	310.24	National Disaster Management Agency (NDMA)	0 (12)	8,790	Departmental Unit	Ministry of National Security	Budget under parent Ministry	Estimate of revenue and expenditure for recurrent expenditure only for the year 2010: GD$165,000: Items: GD $20,000 Projects: GD $145,000		
Guyana	196,850	795,369	4.04	Civil Defence Commission (CDC)	15	53,025	Full Government Department	Office OF the President	–	–		
Haiti	27,560	10,173,775	369.15	Directorate of Civil Protection (DCP)	–	–	–	–	–	–		

(Continued)

Table 14.4 (Continued) An Analysis of National Disaster Office Arrangements and Resourcing

Country	Area (sq. km.)	Population (2012)	Population Density	National Disaster Agency	No. Professional Staff (Total)	Population per Member of Staff	Form of Administration	Parent Government Department	Source of Funding	Budget	Budget per Capita (Local Currency)	Budget per Capita (US $)
Jamaica	10,830	2,712,100	250.42	Office of Disaster Preparedness and Emergency Management (ODPEM)	18	150,672	Statutory Organization	Ministry of Lands and the Environment	Budget under parent Ministry	FY 2009/10: JM $154,000,000	56.78256701	0.57
										NWA: JM $200,000,000 (cleaning drains and flood control in the event of a hurricane)		
										(NEOC, 2011)		
St Kitts and Nevis	260	53,584	206.09	National Disaster Management Agency (NDMA)	4 (11)	4,871	Full Government Department	Ministry of Defence and Security	Separate Budget Head	—		
St Lucia	610	180,870	296.51	National Emergency Management Organisation (NEMO)	3 (8)	22,609	Full Government Department	Office of the Prime Minister	Separate Budget Head	—		
St Vincent and the Grenadines	390	109,378	280.46	National Emergency Management Organisation (NEMO)	3 (11)	9,943	Full Government Department	Ministry of Security	Separate Budget Head	Annual Budget: EC$1 million	9.142606374	3.39
										Annual disbursement for NEMO administrative expenditure: >$70,000		

(Continued)

Table 14.4 (Continued) An Analysis of National Disaster Office Arrangements and Resourcing

Country	Area (sq. km.)	Population (2012)	Population Density	National Disaster Agency	No. Professional Staff (Total)	Population per Member of Staff	Form of Administration	Parent Government Department	Source of Funding	Budget	Budget per Capita (Local Currency)	Budget per Capita (US $)
Suriname	156,000	534,541	3.43	National Coordination Centre for Disaster Relief (NCCR)	0 (12)	44,545	Full Government Department	–	–	–	–	
Trinidad and Tobago	5,130	1,337,439	260.71	Office of Disaster Preparedness & Management (ODPM)	0 (50)	26,749	Departmental Unit	Ministry of National Security	Budget under parent Ministry/ Specific line-items in the MoNS's Estimates of Expenditure	TT $11 million	8.224674172	1.37

Sources: WMO, *Preliminary Draft Report of the Assessments of the Capacities, Gaps and Needs for the Development of the Caribbean Regional Programme on Multi-Hazard Early Warning Systems (MHEWS) and Phase-I Project Priorities: Focus on Hydro-meteorological hazards warning systems and possible linkages with other warning systems.* First stage: Identification and mapping of gaps and needs related to MHEWS. Working Paper. November 2–5, Accra Beach Hotel & Spa, Christ Church, Barbados. Available at: https://www.wmo.int/pages/prog/drr/events/Barbados/Doc/Doc%204%20-%20DRAFT%20Final%20Assessment%20Report.pdf, 2010; OAS, *Caribbean Emergency Legislation Project.* CELP Country Profiles: Antigua and Barbuda, Barbados, Belize, Dominica, Grenada, Haiti, Jamaica, Dominican Republic, Saint Kitts and Nevis, Saint Lucia, Saint Vincent and the Grenadines, Trinidad and Tobago. Department of Sustainable Development, Organisation of American States. Downloaded at: http://www.oas.org/dsd/EnvironmentLaw/CaribbeanLegislationProject/DefaultCLP.htm, 2010.

vulnerable to natural hazard risks, providing grant support of for self-help projects that delivered measurable and sustainable DRR results. To date, small-grant (CAD 25K to 100K) support has been provided for 16 DRR projects in nine CDEMA member states.

A new and complementary medium-size grant mechanism for community-based DRR and climate change adaptation (DRR/CCA), the Community Disaster Risk Reduction (CDRR) Fund, was launched in 2012. The CDRR Fund builds on the lessons and experiences of the CCDRM Fund. The fund will help vulnerable rural, agricultural, and marginalized communities to reduce natural hazard risk to which vulnerable woman, men, children, elderly persons, and persons with disabilities are exposed, by implementing DRR/CCA demonstration projects. Where possible, the DRR/CCA projects will incorporate sustainable livelihoods strategies to enhance the sustainability DRR/CCA benefits generated by DRR/CCA demonstration projects while enhancing livelihoods prospects, and household and community resilience.

The CDRR Fund will retain the CCDRM Fund requirements for eligible projects to be community based and owned in order to ensure that DRR/CCA interventions are sustainable and fulfill both their DRR/CCA and related community development objectives. Through participatory processes, capacity development and training, partnership building and the enhancement of national and local enabling environments, in support of the implementing the DRR/CCA demonstration projects, the CDRRF intends to catalyze a process that will meet the DRR/CCA of vulnerable communities both with, and independently of, the CDRR Fund.

Due to the larger size of the CDRR Fund grants (US$400,000 to US$600,000) that the Fund offers, resources are allocated for technical and project development assistance and capacity development and training for effective project management. The US$24 million multi-donor medium-size grant facilities is funded by the Canadian Department of Foreign Affairs, Trade and Development (DFATD, formerly CIDA), the United Kingdom Department for International Development, and the Caribbean Development Bank. It is anticipated that the number of donors contributing to the CDRRF will increase creating the possibility for the CDRR Fund to make the transition from a project to a program. It is anticipated that the donor support for DRM in the Caribbean closely mirrors the programmatic priorities countries, with much of the financial support classified as "preparation" addressing needs in the areas of institutional capacity building, knowledge management, and mainstreaming DRM. This compares to budget appropriations for national disaster agencies that range in amount from US$1,000 in a budget year to US$1.75 million in a budget year (Table 14.4). The budget appropriations tend to allocate toward post-disaster exercises and not disaster prevention and mitigation (OAS 2010). These trends are consistent with global trends where DRR is given very low priority at best (Kellett and Carivani 2013). Most of the US$109 million (Walling 2012) was earmarked for mitigation, various forms of preparation, and prevention. About 10% of the total donor contribution focused on community level interventions in the areas of disaster prevention and preparation.

Further Examples: Risk Challenges and Successes in the Caribbean

In the field of risk management, Caribbean countries are at differentiated levels of development. For these reasons, and according to their own needs, they must dedicate efforts to actions closely related to the five IRs targeted by the initial Regional Framework in 2001. These actions may indifferently apply to capacity building, community-level focus, integration and mainstreaming, and/or knowledge management. In a well-documented and updated paper, Sarmiento and Hoberman (2011) expose disparity in risk management in the Caribbean. From this paper, we have extracted the following three examples of how the Dominican Republic, Barbados, and Jamaica have dealt with risk management. According to an EM-DATA base, these three countries are mainly affected by floods, storm, earthquake, and mass movement wet.* In their approach to risk management, they also share a strategy based upon inclusion, institutional partnerships, and broaden information and communication.

In the Dominican Republic, the Community Is Aware of Risk

In the Dominican Republic, risk is managed by the Dominican Association for Disaster Management,[†] which is working very closely since 1995 with the most vulnerable communities according the inclusive model of participative democracy. The work consists of disaster preparedness and prevention through workshops where population samples prepare a community emergency built upon assessments of local hazard vulnerabilities and of locally available resources to address those vulnerabilities. During Hurricane Georges (1998), communities that had established emergency committees through this program successfully evacuated people from flood prone areas, established shelters, organized cleanup brigades, requested and distributed assistance without incident. These actions on the ground helped the communities to identify weakness in programs and served as basis for revision. Thus, projects such as the construction of containment walls and drainage ditch embankments have been designed to address local health and environmental contamination problems as well as reduce and mitigate the constant floods and landslides.

According to the World Bank, the positive effect of these initiatives was demonstrated by the reduced impact of Hurricane Georges (1998) on the participating communities. Workshops are conducted in close relationship with the EOC that is the body responsible for coordinating the preparation and response for disasters in the country. EOC that also provides national alerts to the prone affected communities receives timely and accurate information from at least two institutions: the National Meteorological Office and the Dominican Institute of Hydraulic Resources. By example, the year 2008 had very intensive hurricanes in the Caribbean. The island of Hispaniola comprising Haiti and the Dominican Republic was struck by strong tropical storms and hurricanes; Fay, Hanna, Gustav, and Ike have been the most impacting. These events have been the opportunity for EOC to estimate the communities' degree of awareness for that relates to preparedness and response to natural disasters. Accordingly, the EOC's assessment concluded that the preparation and response management had been effective, specifically due to the proper alerts that contributed to reducing the number of people affected. But it also outlined that lacks in organization could hamper effectiveness in monitoring and alert system. As a result, it has been stated as a necessity to improve the monitoring of national hydro-meteorological events by fitting EOCC with technology-advanced equipment, improve coordination between partners, and reinforce attention on exercises among the most vulnerable populations.

An Inclusive and Proactive Approach in Jamaica

In Jamaica, risk is managed by the National Disaster Plan and coordinated by the Office of Disaster Preparedness and Emergency Management. The main objectives of both these structures are to provide a comprehensive view for prevention, mitigation, preparedness, and response and

---

* Sarmiento and Hoberman (2011) in Disaster Risk Management Disparity in the Caribbean: Evidence from Barbados, Dominican Republic, Jamaica and Trinidad and Tobago, p. 6.
[†] Asociación Dominicana de Mitigación de Desastres (ADMD).

recovery procedures for natural hazards in coordination with the National Emergency Operations Centre. Attention is focused on areas of priority that relate to the development of community capacity resilience by multi-hazard mapping and risk analysis, institutional strengthening through partnership with national institutions like the Meteorological Service and Earthquake Unit to improve early warning systems. According to an Inter-American Development Bank (IADB) joint report with ECLAC (IADB 2007),* the two organizations further acknowledged the leading role of Jamaica for having integrated government and private sector stakeholders into the country's disaster management structure, successfully pursuing an integrated approach to DRM. ODPM is recognized as having been totally involved in disaster risk mitigation at the community level. By the way, harmonization efforts have to be done between policies and practices. Nonetheless Jamaica is recognized as very proactive for introducing risk reduction into development processes.†

In Barbados, Success on Pilot Site Has Led to Replicability

The Organization of American States (OAS) database (1997) covering the period from 1889 to 1989 shows that Barbados has had a relatively high number of events (especially hurricanes) compared to other islands of the Lesser Antilles. In August 2002, the Caribbean Disaster Management (CADM) has driven a study that has shown that Barbados had recorded high incidences of flooding and had thus to implement flood management procedures. Consequently, the area of Speightstown had been chosen as a pilot case study and allowed to gather not only national institutions as the Caribbean Institute for Meteorology and Hydrology, the University of the West Indies, Barbados Tourism Investment Corporation, among many other institutions, but it also included Japan through a technical cooperation agreement. Activities on the ground related to seminars and training sessions, hazard mapping, preparation of a manual for flood mapping are some of the actions that the national team involved in the project could implement. The Central Emergency Relief Organization reported that CADM concluded that the project was a "worthwhile initiative" suitable for replications. By the way, CADM got funding to replicate experiences over the next 10 years not only in Barbados but to the wider Caribbean region. By the way, Sarmiento and Hoberman (2011) outline that if Barbados has accomplished successful results in the areas of disaster preparedness and response, much more needs to be done in the rehabilitation and recovery areas. The sensitization of economic partners to vulnerability reduction in Barbados' key economic sectors like tourism and agriculture or sharing products such as the GIS database derived from the Barbados experiments have also been identified as priority actions.

The previous sections of this chapter have exposed the variety of natural disasters affecting the Caribbean economies that in their whole are small, open, and extremely dependent on outside for trade and financing. Aside from their economic vulnerability, they also suffer from environmental vulnerability due to their geographic location in the hurricane pathway and in an area of intense seismic activity. The accumulation of so many disadvantages forces these economies to face strong challenges with the view to sustain development and eradicate poverty on the long run. Financial means are necessary to prevent and quick recover from natural disasters whose consequences are magnified at the economic level. That is the role of the Caribbean Catastrophe Risk Insurance Facility (CCRIF).

---

* The IADB and Economic Commission for Latin America and the Caribbean Information on Disaster Risk Management, Case Study Jamaica.
† ODPEM.

The Role of the CCRIF

Among the challenges facing the governments of small island states in the aftermath of natural disasters is the need for immediate access to cash to implement urgent recovery efforts and maintain essential government services. This challenge is particularly acute for Caribbean countries whose economic resilience is limited by the combination of mounting vulnerability and high levels of indebtedness. Historically, Caribbean governments often depended extensively on financing from international donors to finance post-disaster needs. While ex-post disaster funding from bilateral and multilateral agencies can be an important part of a government's catastrophe risk management strategy, overreliance on this approach has had major limitations. Generally, donor assistance can take a long time to materialize and usually supports investment projects, with limited possibilities of financing budget outlays such as civil servants' salaries, other recurrent costs, and the immediate costs of reconstructing lifeline infrastructure.

For example, when Hurricane Ivan struck Grenada in 2004, the loss was calculated at US$800 million, about two times the country's GDP for which government losses accounted for about 30%. Just as Grenada required additional resources to finance relief, cleanup, and emergency rehabilitations, Grenada experienced a dramatic decline in revenues. The revenue shortfall was an estimated 5% of GDP between September and December of that year, while international donor aid only provided 12 million in immediate funds. In response to the liquidity gaps in the face of hurricane strikes in the region, 16 members of CARICOM in conjunction with the World Bank set up the Caribbean Risk Catastrophe Insurance Fund, arguably the world's first multi-country joint reserve mechanism for governments and is arguably unique as an insurance operation in that it offers parametric insurance policies to its participants rather than the traditional indemnity policy. It operates as follows. The premiums that countries pay to CCRIF for coverage are directly related to the level of risks being transferred were coverage to cover more frequent events, then premium costs would increase substantially. In the actual calculations for an event, a loss estimate is made at each measuring point using the peak wind speed at that point derived from a wind field model and hurricane track data, the parametric equation (which describes the proxy relationship between wind speed and estimated loss) and the weighting given to that point. The losses at all the country's measuring points are then aggregated to give the total estimated loss. The insurance policy is then settled by subtracting the country's policy deductible and applying the ceding percentage to the loss up to the policy limit gets the payout. CCRIF has a predetermined limit of US$100 million per hurricane period, but some countries have selected coverage options commensurate with their capacity to pay a certain level premium. One should note that this approach means that payments can be made relatively quickly after the strike, thus addressing any liquidity problems faced by participating governments if they quality for relief from the CCRIF. We seek here to evaluate the role of CCRIF in alleviating the immediate cash shortage typical after a natural disaster.

A number of natural disaster events have triggered insurance payouts since the CCRIF inception in 2007, in total amounting to US$32,179,470. These payouts were due to five natural disaster events, two related to earthquakes and the rest due to tropical cyclones. The largest payout, that is, US$8,560,247, in this regard was given to Barbados as a result of Tropical Cyclone Thomas, which hit in October 2010 and caused payable damages in two other countries as well (St. Lucia and St. Vincent and the Grenadines with payouts of US$3,241,613 and US$1,090,388, respectively). The second largest event was the earthquake in Haiti in 2010, resulting in a payout to that member of US$7,753,579. The other events include the earthquake that caused damage in

Dominica and St. Lucia in 2007, triggering payouts of US$528,021 and US$418,976, respectively. Finally, Tropical Cyclone Ike (2008) and Tropical Cyclone Earl (2010) were followed by payments to the Turks and Caicos Islands and Anguilla, respectively.

The question remains, of course, of how much these payments have succeeded in addressing the short-time financial needs of the countries affected. Answering this intrinsically entails having an idea how much of financial shortage is created by natural disaster events in the region. In this regard, Ouattarra and Strobl (2013) conducted an empirical analysis of the impact of tropical cyclone events on monthly government revenue and expenditure in sample Caribbean countries (Anguilla, Antigua and Barbuda, Bahamas, Barbados, Dominica, Grenada, Haiti, Jamaica, St. Kitts and Nevis, St. Lucia, Montserrat, and St. Vincent and the Grenadines). Their results show that at least in annual terms only expenditure rises but that there is no significant effect on revenue and debt. This thus suggests that Caribbean countries deal with natural disasters via short-term expenditure financing. We use their quantitative results to indicate the implied fiscal shortages relative to the payout—these are given in Table 14.5.

As can be seen, for some cases the payout is substantially larger, while for others it is smaller than the shortage implied by Ouattarra and Strobl (2013). Assuming that the estimated fiscal shortage impact by these authors is close to the real one, and then one can conjecture a number of reasons for the discrepancies. For one, this is inevitable when applying a relatively simple parametric insurance system to a set of potentially very heterogeneous countries. Moreover, even if one were to abstract from this, one has to remember a country's payout will depend not only on the severity of the event itself but also on the exact policy they choose to purchase. Nevertheless, the continuing renewal (e.g., as of August 13, 2013, for the 2013/2014 policy year starting June 1, 2013) of all 16 members of their hurricane and earthquake insurance policies attests to the perception of the general success of these schemes (Table 14.6).

Until recently, one major weakness in the policy packages offered by the CCRIF was that it did not cover one natural disaster event that occurs relatively frequently in the region, namely, excessive rainfall. This has left member countries with significant exposure to floods and their consequences since even the hurricane product only takes account of damage due to winds. It was not surprising then that a number of member countries had since the inception of the CCRIF shown a strong interest in additionally having coverage for excess rainfall both due to tropical storm and non-tropical storm events. In response to this and after considerable research, the CCRIF as of the policy year 2013/2014 also offers coverage for extreme rainfall events.

Table 14.5 Estimated Fiscal Deficit and CCRIF Payout

Storm	Year	Country	Fiscal Deficit (mill. $US)	Payout (mill. $US)
Ike	2008	Turks and Caicos	21.1	6.3
Earl	2010	Anguilla	2.0	4.3
Thomas	2010	Barbados	0.7	8.6
Thomas	2010	St. Lucia	3.6	3.2
Thomas	2010	St. Vincent	4.2	1.1

Table 14.6 Donor Contributions Disaster Risk Management

DRM Phase	Donor Contribution (US$)	% Donor Contribution
MIT	59,196,250	54.0
PREP	23,177,377	21.1
PREP (COM)	2,140,591	2.0
PREP/REC	1,252,960	1.1
PREP/RESP	407,825	0.4
PREV	3,354,782	3.1
PREV (COM)	9,056,001	8.3
PREV/PREP	10,500,000	9.6
REC	600,000	0.5
Totals	109,685,786	100.0

Source: Walling, L., Community disaster risk reduction initiatives in the Caribbean—Trends and issues, presented for panel discussion on *The Role of Community Vulnerability Reduction in National Development Planning—Progress, Trends, Challenges, and Lessons for the Future*. Seventh Annual Caribbean Comprehensive Disaster Management (CDM) Conference on the theme @CDM: Building Disaster Resilience a Shared Responsibility, Montego Bay, Jamaica. December 3–7, 2012.

In essence, the rainfall product works similar to the hurricane and earthquake policies, that is, using data immediately after the event to determine whether a payout is triggered for affected countries. In this regard, gridded satellite-derived rainfall data are evaluated almost immediately after any event to provide, thus enabling, if appropriate fast and relatively immediate payout to policy holders. One of its weaknesses will be the fact that risk profiles for countries will be based only on relatively recent rainfall data since historical data at the necessary spatial level of disaggregation are only available since 1998 via the TRMM precipitation data product.

Conclusion

Due to its geographical location, the Caribbean region is naturally prone to natural hazards. Since these islands derive their income mainly from tourism and agriculture and these sectors are generally the most vulnerable to disasters, their negative effects on GDP are magnified, affecting especially the most vulnerable part of the population. The issue is no longer how to implement proactive and reactive strategies, but which could be the optimal ones for restabilizing the economic life the most quickly as possible after an event. In the Caribbean, risk management is at differentiated levels among the countries, according to the stories told by the Dominican Republic, Jamaica, and Barbados. By the way, disasters have huge impacts on the living conditions, economic performance, and environmental assets and services of affected countries or regions (ECLAC 2003)* and their consequences

---

* *Handbook for Estimating the Socio-Economic Effects and Environmental Effects of Disasters.*

may irreversibly affect the environment, economic and social structures. Cognizant of the challenges posed by risks management in the region, the heads of governments asked the Caribbean Community Climate Change Centre to prepare a regional framework that includes two regional initiatives: the Strategy and Results Framework for Comprehensive Disaster Management in the Caribbean and the DMFC within the Caribbean Development Bank. These initiatives are regarded as tools for managing risk and coupled with the action and role of the CCRIF set up in conjunction with the World Bank. Its first role is to fill the liquidity gaps in a disaster aftermath. The aim is to provide immediate access to cash to implement urgent recovery efforts and maintain essential government services.

References

BAASTEL. (2010). *Comprehensive Disaster Management (CDM) Regional Baseline Study*. Draft Report. Prepared by Le Groupe-conseil baastel ltée (BAASTEL) for the Caribbean Disaster Emergency Management Agency (CDEMA), Gatineau, Quebec, Canada, 110 p.

Caribbean Center for Money and Finance. (June 2013). *Caribbean Economic Performance Report*. Regional Economic Performance, The University of the West Indies, Trinidad and Tobago. pp. 19–46.

CDERA. (2005). *Caribbean Community Regional Programme Framework 2005–2015*. Second World Conference on Disasters, Kobe, Hyogo, Japan. January 18–22, 2005. p. 28.

Charvériat, C. (2000). *Natural Disasters in Latin America and the Caribbean: An Overview of Risk*. Inter-American Development Bank, Washington, DC.

CRMI. (2011). *Caribbean Implementation of the Hyogo Framework for Action HFA Mid-Term Review*. Prepared by the Disaster Risk Reduction Centre, The University of the West Indies, Jamaica for the United Nations Development Programme (UNDP) Caribbean Risk Management Initiative, Havana, Cuba, 85pp.

ECLAC. (2003). *Handbook for Estimating the Socio-Economic and Environmental Effects of Disasters*. -LC/MEX/G.5 - LC/L.1874, Economic Commission for Latin America and the Caribbean, Mexico.

ECLAC. (2011a). *Saint Lucia Macro Socio-Economic and Environmental Assessment of the Damage and Losses Caused by Hurricane Tomas: A Geo-Environmental Disaster—Towards Resilience*. LC/CAR/L.286. Economic Commission for Latin America and the Caribbean, Port of Spain, Trinidad and Tobago. 169pp.

ECLAC. (2011b). *Study on the Vulnerability and Resilience of Caribbean Small Island Developing States (SIDS)*. Economic Commission for Latin America and the Caribbean. LC/CAR/L.354. p. 42. Available at: http://www.eclac.org/publicaciones/xml/4/45364/LCARL.354.pdf.

Girvan, N. (2001). Reinterpreting the Caribbean. In *New Caribbean Thought: A Reader*. Eds. Brian Meeks and Folke Lindahl. University of the West Indies Press. pp. 3–23. August 8, 2013. http://www.normangirvan.info/wp-content/uploads/2007/09/reinterpreting-the-caribbean-2001.pdf. Accessed on March 4, 2015.

Granvorka, C., and Strobl, E. (March 2013). The impact of Hurricanes strikes on the tourism in the Caribbean. *Tourism Economics*, 19(6):1401–1409.

Inter-American Development Bank (IADB) and Economic Commission for Latin America and the Caribbean (ECLAC). (2007). *Information on Disaster Risk Management*. Case Study of Five Countries: Jamaica. LC/MEX/L.836. December.

Kellett, J., and Caracani, A. (2013). *Financing Disaster Risk Reduction—A 20 Year Story of International Aid*. Global Facility for Disaster Risk Reduction and Recovery (GFDRR) and the Overseas Development Institute (ODI). 50pp. Available at: http://www.odi.org.uk/sites/odi.org.uk/files/odi-assets/publications-opinion-files/8574.pdf.

Kirton, M. (2013). *Caribbean Regional Disaster Response and Management Mechanisms: Prospects and Challenges*. The Brookings-London School of Economics Project on Internal Displacement, Washington, DC. 33pp.

Lindsay, J.M., Robertson, R.E.A., Shepherd, J.B., and Ali, S. (eds.). (2005). *Volcanic Hazard Atlas of the Lesser Antilles*. Sesmic Research Unit, The University of the West Indies, Trinidad and Tobago. 279pp.

Maskrey, A. (2011). Revisiting community based disaster risk management. In: *Reducing Disaster Risks: Progress and Challenges in the Caribbean Region*. Ian Davis, Steve Bender, Fred Krimgold, Franklin McDonald (eds.). Earthscan, London/Sterling, VA, 10:1, pp. 42–52.

NEMO. (2010). *National Emergency Management Organization Annual Report 2010.* National Emergency Management Organization (NEMO), Office of the Prime Minister, Government of Saint Lucia, Castries, St. Lucia, 28pp.

OAS. (2010). *Caribbean Emergency Legislation Project.* CELP Country Profiles: Antigua and Barbuda, Barbados, Belize, Dominica, Grenada, Haiti, Jamaica, Dominican Republic, Saint Kitts and Nevis, Saint Lucia, Saint Vincent and the Grenadines, Trinidad and Tobago. Department of Sustainable Development, Organisation of American States, Washington, DC. Downloaded at: http://www.oas.org/dsd/EnvironmentLaw/CaribbeanLegislationProject/DefaultCLP.htm.

Opadeyi, J. (2012). *Building a Caribbean GeoNode Platform in Support of Climate Risk Management.* Mona, Jamaica: University of the West Indies Faculty of Engineering.

Ouattarra, B., and Strobl, E. (2013). Caribbean Catastrophe Risk Insurance Facility: An Empirical Assessment for Hurricanes Strikes. *Paper presented at the 2013 SALISES Conference*, Bridgetown, Barbados. April 22–24.

Sarmiento, J.P., and Hoberman, G. (May 2011). Disaster risk management disparity in the Caribbean: Evidence from Barbados, Dominican Republic, Jamaica and Trinidad and Tobago. Western Hemisphere Security Analysis Center. p. 28.

Walling, L. (2012). Community disaster risk reduction initiatives in the Caribbean—Trends and issues, presented for panel discussion on *The Role of Community Vulnerability Reduction in National Development Planning—Progress, Trends, Challenges, and Lessons for the Future.* Seventh Annual Caribbean Comprehensive Disaster Management (CDM) Conference on the theme @CDM: Building Disaster Resilience a Shared Responsibility, Montego Bay, Jamaica. December 3–7.

WFP. (1998). World Food Programme, "Prevention and preparedness: Mitigating the effects of natural disasters," strategy and policy division, Rome. In: Messer, N.M. (2003). *The Role of Local Institutions and Their Interaction in Disaster Risk Mitigation: A Literature Review.* Economic and Social Development Department, Food and Agriculture Organization (FAO). Available at: http://www.fao.org/docrep/006/ad710e/ad710e00.htm.

WMO. (2010). *Preliminary Draft Report of the Assessments of the Capacities, Gaps and Needs for the Development of the Caribbean Regional Programme on Multi-Hazard Early Warning Systems (MHEWS) and Phase-I Project Priorities: Focus on Hydro-Meteorological Hazards Warning Systems and Possible Linkages with Other Warning Systems.* First stage: Identification and mapping of gaps and needs related to MHEWS. Working Paper. November 2–5, Accra Beach Hotel & Spa, Christ Church, Barbados. https://www.wmo.int/pages/prog/drr/events/Barbados/Doc/Doc%204%20-%20DRAFT%20Final%20Assessment%20Report.pdf.

WMO. (2011). *Strengthening of Risk Assessment and Multi-hazard Early Warning Systems for Meteorological, Hydrological and Climate Hazards in the Caribbean.* WMO-No. 1082. DRR-CARIB 1. Final Report November 17. World Meteorological Organisation, Geneva, Switzerland, Reprinted in 2012. 173pp.

World Food Programme. (1998). *Time for Change: Food Aid and Development Consultation*, United Nations World Food Programme, Rome, Italy.

Chapter 15

Sustainable Development of Caribbean Tourism

Anthony Clayton, Nikolaos Karagiannis, and Jessica M. Bailey

Contents

Introduction 338
Economic, Social, Developmental, and Environmental Impacts 339
Strategic Policy Areas... 349
Conclusion 352
References 353

Abstract: The chapter focuses on the performance of the tourism sector and its various diverse impacts on small Caribbean states and explores the implications for tourism analysis, policy interventions, and planning. There have been significant challenges and limitations, but in general the Caribbean tourism industry has performed remarkably well. It has grown consistently for decades, is the largest source of employment in the region, and is the largest source of foreign exchange for a number of countries. However, the current pattern of development has also resulted in very high leakages, a lack of economic linkages, a low rate of new entrants and consequent lack of competition, and a number of serious environmental problems, including development in areas that may eventually be lost to rising seas. The resolution of these issues will involve serious, technically proficient planning and coordination of the industry's needs with the rest of the local economy and society. The primary goal of such an exercise must be to implement strategies and policies that would seek to retain more of the industry's earnings in the local economy, increase the economic multiplier effect, encourage healthy competition, and minimize environmental damage, thereby contributing to the socioeconomic advancement of the islands.

Introduction

The difficulties in achieving a sustained pattern of good economic performance in the Caribbean nations have been the subject of considerable study and debate. Various studies have emphasized such issues as the general lack of comparative and competitive advantage; the difficulties in achieving economic scale and scope; the lack of economic diversity and the resultant problems with market structure; the variable quality of the institutional environment; corruption and the politics of patronage; the fading legacy of colonialism in the political, institutional, and economic structures of Caribbean territories; and the limited policy space available to Caribbean governments after accumulating high levels of debt.

Indeed, the region today is the complex result of a mixture of the residual effects of colonialism and a complex network of relations between external agents and the internal elites that now dominate political and economic life (Britton 1989). A number of Caribbean states have serious problems with corruption,* some (including Guyana, Jamaica, Trinidad) also have exceptionally high levels of violence, and the internal elites are sometimes implicated in both, raising serious questions about the nature and quality of the governance, and the effectiveness or ineffectiveness of policy intervention (Boxill et al. 2000; McDavid 2002; Karagiannis 2002b; Clayton 2004).

Although a number of the Caribbean nations have built a strong, competitive presence in services such as tourism and hospitality, they are vulnerable to changes in external market conditions. An examination of the patterns of trade makes the dependence of the Caribbean on the outside world apparent, as foreign decisions with regard to tourism safety, taxes and financial regulations (such as duties on passengers) and commodity prices (especially oil) typically have a relatively marked and immediate impact on the Caribbean economies. As the industry has been geared mainly to the affluent North American and European feeder markets, it has to compete by providing a competitive but differentiated product, ranging from budget holidays to high-end, exclusive properties with world-class standards of accommodation and hospitality. Most of them have required some reliance on foreign capital and imports, especially of food and energy, and have thereby increased total imports. A more serious problem has been with profit repatriation, which is not confined to foreign-owned hotel chains, as the large domestic chains have been equally adept at transfer-pricing their profits to low-tax jurisdictions. The successful properties are largely all-inclusive, and the most rapidly growing sector is the even more self-contained cruise industry, which means that tourism has effectively become an "enclave" sector within the Caribbean economy having relatively few linkages with, and contributing little to, the development of other sectors (Sharpley and Telfer 2002; Clayton 2004; Clayton and Karagiannis 2008).

The large role that the industry plays in the region partly reflects the advantages of climate and geography (e.g., proximity to the United States), but it also reflects the weak performance of many other sectors. Yet there is no doubt that the industry has been genuinely successful. Tourism has delivered enormous benefits in terms of income and job creation, and is now essential to the economic survival of the region. It has become a large and important sector of most of the Caribbean economies, and still has untapped potential, with opportunities to reinvigorate the product, refocus on new growth Asian economies, and develop a more sustainable model of tourism in the

---

* Problems with corruption and political violence in the Caribbean have been extensively researched and analyzed by Caribbean scholars in the fields of political science and governance such as Carl Stone, Edwin Jones, Neville Duncan, and Selwyn Ryan. Although corruption is an issue common to each country in the region (as well as elsewhere), the extent and impact of corruption clearly vary from state to state (see also, corruption figures and publications by Transparency International-Latin America and the Caribbean [TILAC], http://www.transparency.org/regional_pages/americas).

region. Many of the Caribbean nations see tourism as their only truly successful global industry, and it has therefore became the focus of many of their hopes for development and prosperity.

However, when a small country utilizes tourism as the heart of its development strategy, it becomes enmeshed in a global system over which it has little control (Britton 1982, 1989). This is not unique to tourism; small Caribbean islands and microstates will always be vulnerable to global shifts and fluctuations in tourism and financial flows, but some of them have demonstrated a capacity to exploit, at least temporarily, some niches in globalized service markets and generate a degree of prosperity for their small populations (Clayton 2004).

From a policy perspective, however, working with tourism is not an easy proposition. The sector's diversity and relatively high level of foreign ownership complicates tourism planning at the national and regional levels and also complicates institutional interventions in support of, for example, sustainable tourism development. The relatively high cost of utilities, operating costs, airlift, and attracting investment will always be challenging for the Caribbean tourism industry in an increasingly competitive global tourism market place. Tourism's crosscutting nature and complexity also mean that it is affected by changes in other areas. For example, trade negotiations and tariff rates for a whole range of goods and services sectors have an impact on the industry.

The line of argument of this chapter is as follows. The next section discusses economic, social, developmental, and environmental impacts and challenges that emanate from tourism growth in the Caribbean. The combination of these factors would largely define a new policy framework of an alternative tourism model for Caribbean territories. Strategic requirements and policy considerations for such an alternative framework are offered in the Section "Strategic Policy Areas."

Economic, Social, Developmental, and Environmental Impacts

Caribbean tourism is the region's most globally competitive industry (Boxill et al. 2002; CTO 2011). This status is now openly acknowledged; over the last decades, tourism has surpassed the traditional producing sectors as employer and foreign exchange earner and has been recognized as the main economic engine in many of the Caribbean island states. Raw data and tourism statistics over the last three decades paint a clear picture. Gross tourism receipts are above one-third of exports and the industry directly employs more than half the labor force in some Caribbean countries, while indirect employment accounts for most of the rest in some cases. Air arrivals increased over fivefold during the same period, and cruise visitors increased even more swiftly in recent years while growing almost three times as fast as stopover visitors, on average (CTO 2009, 2010, 2012).*

The Caribbean's proximity to the United States gives it a natural advantage, as the United States has always been the largest generating market to the Caribbean, providing well over half the total arrivals in the region. However, the number of visitors from Europe has grown rapidly since the late 1980s, increasing its share of arrivals in the region and, consequently, the European market has provided the main growth impetus for Caribbean tourism. Indeed, the European market has been increasing strongly mainly due to a flourishing charter business, as have some newer markets (CTO, *various issues*; PIOJ, *various years*).

---

* The World Travel and Tourism Council (WTTC) estimates for 2002 indicated that the regional industry would generate US$34.3 billion in economic activity, contribute US$7 billion to GDP, produce 2.1 million jobs, and account for US$7 billion in capital investment. The WTTC also projected that this contribution would continue to grow (WTTC 2012).

The region's international tourist arrivals and receipts have been increasing since the 1950s. By 1980, there were 6 million tourist arrivals in the region. By 1990, this had risen to over 10 million. By 2000, the region had over 20 million tourist arrivals, with more than 12 million cruise passenger arrivals, and recorded over US$18 billion in tourism receipts (CTO 2002). The Caribbean has been increasing its share of world tourism since 1980; it was 2.11% in 1980, reached 2.41% in 1987, declined slightly to 2.34% by 1990, and reached 3.2% in the late 1990s (CTO, *various issues*), even though there is significant variation by country (Clayton and Karagiannis 2008; PIOJ 2013). However, tourist arrivals and hotel performance in the Caribbean dipped after 2006, and the negative impact of the 2008 financial crisis in the five major areas of gross domestic product (GDP), balance-of-payments, employment, government revenue, and investment was obvious (CTO 2009, 2010, 2012).

Tourism earnings now account for approximately 25% of the Caribbean's GDP. The industry generates a larger ratio of both GDP and employment in most Caribbean islands than in other countries, as the region is now the most tourism-dependent region of the world (CTO 2009). Tourism is also a labor-intensive industry, and its role in generating direct and indirect employment in otherwise fragile Caribbean economies is regarded as one of its most important immediate economic benefits, although there are wide variations throughout the region in the proportionate importance of tourism in employment (Poon 1993, p. 266). Estimates of total visitor spending in the region for the same period were US$19.9 billion, about US$979 per tourist. Vaugeios (2002) notes that this represented 50%–70% of the region's hard currency earnings and points out that this contribution has grown dramatically, as tourism is the only sector of regional GDP that has consistently increased its share of total income during the past 25 years, reflecting both the success of the industry and the decline of other traditional local activities (CTO 2009).

The terrorist attacks of September 11, 2001, in the United States impacted on these projections. Immediately after September 11, although the worldwide decline in travel and tourism demand was 8.5%, the loss in the Caribbean was 13.5%, which translated into a temporary loss of some 365,000 jobs. This reflected the extent to which Caribbean islands rely on the US market. Many Americans were reluctant to fly after September 11, whereas Europeans were relatively unaffected, so countries that relied more on European visitors did not suffer to the same extent.* The reaction to September 11 illustrated the importance of the industry to the regional economies as well as their vulnerability. In addition, the global slowdown in major trading partners led to a decline in Caribbean tourism and growth after 2006, and the financial crisis in 2008 exacerbated some of the underlying problems inherent within Caribbean economies, such as the combination of small size, openness to international trade, reliance on many imports and a small number of exports, and their heavy indebtedness.† Some long-standing social problems, including violent crime, poverty, poor educational results, and a consequent lack of employment opportunities, also worsened (IMF 2009; CTO 2010).

Tourism acquired its current prominence as a result of steady growth over decades, but also as economic sectors like agriculture and manufacturing because uneconomic and shrank in the face of growing global competition. As a result of both factor, tourism has become the most indispensable source of livelihoods, tax revenues, and foreign exchange, and makes an equally indispensable contribution to the balance of payments (CTO 2009). Tourism receipts rose from just under 18%

---

* This partly reflects the fact that many European countries have decades of experience with terrorism and therefore are somewhat more hardened to it. Security measures at European airports were also far more effective at the time.
† According to ECLAC (2010), for the Caribbean as a whole, the rate of growth was only 0.1% in 2009.

of current account receipts in 1980 to around 37% in the 1990s. The total accumulated deficit on the current account of Caribbean economies would therefore rise significantly if tourism receipts were excluded. This is true in spite of the relatively high level of leakage of gross foreign exchange earnings, which probably averages around 40%, with wide variations between local economies (Economic Intelligence Unit [EIU] 1993, quoted in Karagiannis 2002b).

Fortunately, the industry has significant potential for further growth, as the demand for tourism services appears to be both expandable (it is possible to add new products) and elastic (as the price of airfares, e.g., has declined, demand for air travel has increased even more rapidly). According to Jayawardena (2002) and Karagiannis (2002a, 2002b), this success, in general, cannot be attributed to any good strategic decisions or wise planning by Caribbean governments. In the early days of tourism, most Caribbean governments were generally satisfied to play a non-interventionist role that was largely limited to legislation, coordination, and the promotion of the various destinations. Even today, most of the tourism legislation in the region pertains to the establishment of National Tourism Organisations (NTOs) and specifies their roles and functions within the industry (McDavid 2002).

Caribbean governments do now support tourism with various policies and incentives (McDavid 2002), as they now see that the economic survival of Caribbean islands may rest largely on this one sector (Clayton 2004). However, the flows of tourism are still largely determined by multinational agents and corporations, marketing, and information technology managed in the feeder nations, which makes the task of supporting the industry in the Caribbean more challenging.

Countries like Jamaica, Barbados, and the Bahamas now support investment in tourism via direct support (national advertising), investment in infrastructure, and generous tax breaks for investors. The latter can be used as a revolving subsidy, as each hotel extension qualifies for tax relief. However, various forms of support and subsidy may be insufficient to offset some of the general disadvantages of some Caribbean countries in attracting investment. Bureaucratic inefficiencies, slow and dysfunctional planning procedures, inconsistent regulatory requirements, corruption and extortion, a lack of transparency in incentive decisions, high operating costs, poorly maintained tourism attractions and supporting infrastructure, and the general difficulties of achieving scale economies in small islands add to the construction, security, overhead, management, and administrative costs faced by hoteliers (Clayton 2004). In addition, employment costs are relatively high in the region; although wage rates are relatively high, labor productivity tends to be low (EIU 1993).

In spite of the government support (and active lobbying by the industry for more breaks), incentives in general probably do little to influence investment decisions. Studies of investment incentives in other countries, often allied with regional policy, have cast similar doubts on the effectiveness of incentive regimes as core factors like the general business and investment climate, a government's proactive business attitude, openness to foreign investors and economic policies, political and economic stability, operating costs, and location (e.g., proximity to supplies and markets) usually have a greater role in the investment decision. Once a broad decision has been taken on investment location, the incentives available may play a secondary role in decision making, but they are rarely the deciding factor (Karagiannis 2002b).

The robust but largely unplanned development of the tourism industry in the Caribbean resembles the "flying-geese pattern." The flying-geese pattern of growth assumes that the sophistication of domestic tourism will advance one position at a time. Thus, a nation is not likely to remain at the initial stage; education, learning, and additional investment will lead to more sophisticated tourist products and better operations quality. This flying-geese pattern is the result of market forces rather than planning; Caribbean nations with unemployed or underemployed labor force become internationally competitive in this labor-intensive low-skill industry, and graduate to more learning and knowledge-based initiatives as education deepens the availability of capital and skilled labor (Bailey et al. 2010).

One factor that may have reduced competition is that the limited availability and relatively high capital cost in addition to the general short-termism of local financial institutions can make it difficult for an entrepreneur to raise the investment capital required (EIU 1993; Poon 1993, p. 269), making it harder for new entrants to the industry.

The increasingly important role of foreign capital and ownership in the industry began in the early 1970s, when regional governments made the decision to allow the construction of all-inclusive resorts. Two of the earliest and most successful pioneers were Jamaican. In general, however, the capital needed to execute these projects was not readily available in the domestic capital markets. As a consequence, it was foreign-owned hotel chains that increasingly came to build, participate in the ownership of these enclave resorts, and dominate the industry in most of the islands (Barberia 2003). These hotel chains consistently maintain higher occupancy levels and profits (CTO, *Caribbean Hotel Performance*, 2009), probably because they offer a convenient, comfortable, secure package that fits into the modern lifestyle. This trend is likely to continue, so that the market will be increasingly dominated by large all-inclusive resorts.

Indeed, a number of large tourism corporations have operations in the Caribbean, and these generally control their own marketing because they have a number of advantages: a strong cash flow and capital base, managerial expertise, ability to influence consumer demand through marketing and promotion, and links with tour operators. The last two factors give them a substantial competitive advantage, as most holidays are booked as packages in the originating country, and sales are heavily influenced by the way that particular products are bundled and by marketing and continuous positive exposure (EIU 1993). Some of the large hotels, resorts, and chains are locally owned, but most are foreign-owned usually focusing their promotion in their home base. This too gives them an advantage compared to local tourism enterprises in the destination countries themselves (Clayton and Karagiannis 2008, p. 193).

However, the smaller Caribbean hoteliers and other tourism industry service providers are finding it increasingly difficult to compete with big name all-inclusive resorts. Without access to the training, technical services, and marketing support required to remain competitive, many of these small enterprises struggle to conduct even modest business. In contrast to most of the mega-resorts, these small businesses tend to be locally owned, and they tend to be more linked into local economies, so that when their business suffers, their communities also suffer. At present in the Caribbean, there are over 1,500 small properties (having less than 75 rooms) with over 25,000 rooms and many of these are experiencing challenges competing in the global marketplace (OAS 2007, STEP programme, 2007–present).*

As Karagiannis (2002b, p. 156) also notes, there are still a large number of small locally owned hotels throughout the region. Many of them find it increasingly difficult to compete with the large transnationals, but it is partly because of these smaller properties that locals feel that they have a greater stake in the sector. This, of course, raises the question: what would happen if these small properties were to disappear? There can be no definitive answer to this question; this might create a similar situation to that of Riviera Maya, Mexico, where small entities are marginalized, the industry is dominated by large international chains, and local resentment and hostility is correspondingly high (Boxill et al. 2002). This could be replicated in the Caribbean. For instance,

---

* Small Tourism Enterprise Program (STEP) Caribbean is a project of the Organization of American States (OAS).

a study by Boxill and Frederick (2002) for Antigua found that there can be serious tension when foreign investors develop tourism projects without consulting locals in the planning process.

The real disparity, however, is not between domestic and foreign operators, but between large and small competitors. There are a lot of small hotels and guest houses in the region, and most of these do not have the necessary skills or the budgets to finance a major marketing push.* So the small hotels and resorts generally have to rely on the generic promotions run by the national tourist offices/boards, and occasional attendance at tourism events. Some of them have links with tour operators and wholesalers, who will typically market them as part of a package. National governments may again be confined to promotional activities and the provision of investment for infrastructure development around tourism enclaves. This might actually be a positive development, given the lackluster performance of the government agencies, but could still impact negatively on the smaller units that rely more on external advice and support (Clayton 2004).

The market for Caribbean destinations can be categorized in many ways, based on a variety of market segments being served. Geographic segmentation, which used to be confined to the United States, Canada, and Europe, must now be expanded to include Japan, China, and some nations of South America (CTO 2011, "Tourist Arrivals by Main Market—2010"). Seasonal segmentation, which includes summer and winter months, attracts two distinct income brackets and must, of necessity, employ vastly different media. Similarly, age segmentation is also apparent as younger, less affluent tourists seek recreation, fun, and sports entertainment, while older travelers seek upscale shopping, arts-related enclaves, and more serene entertainment.

This range of international travelers and market niches represents a form of diversification, which helps to both reduce risk and distribute income over the year. In practice, however, it also presents the Caribbean islands with conflicting signals as to how tourism should be marketed, the facilities required, the way in which the industry should relate to the rest of the economy, and the overall strategy for the industry. In addition, Caribbean tourism is facing increased competition from other destinations including some well-established ones, such as the Florida coast, and various resorts of Mexico and the Mediterranean.† However, its greater threat may be from emerging rivals, not yet well established on the international tourist scene, like the Far East and Central America. These newer tourism products offer a diversity that directly responds to broader demands of the traveling public (EIU 1993; Poon 1993).

One of more serious challenges facing many Caribbean nations is that small islands suffer from poor economies of scale in the provision of essential utilities like water and electricity. The relatively high import requirements that sustain tourism in the region translate into more expensive products than those of many competitors, with a greater price differential between winter and summer months (OAS 2007, STEP project). Because of the relatively high import content of tourism, much of the revenue earned from the industry does not remain in local economies. Estimates by the World Bank (2003) suggested that approximately 55% of tourism receipts earned by developing countries are accrued overseas. The position with respect to Caribbean island states is not dissimilar as one of the major criticisms usually directed at Caribbean tourism relates to the high import content of the industry and its attendant low net foreign exchange benefits accruing

---

* The region's accommodation stock currently comprises a wide variety of properties including large resorts, exclusive hotels, small inns, guesthouses, and the all-inclusive resort. The latter is becoming a trademark of Caribbean tourism. A small number of mega-structures (hotels with over 500 rooms) have been built in the Caribbean, although these are still significantly smaller than the industry leader (the Venetian Hotel, in Las Vegas, which has over 7000 rooms).
† Florida and Mexico offer similar climatic and scenic attractions within broadly the same parameters of price and distance from the rest of the United States (EIU 1993).

to the region. According to the Organization of American States (OAS 2002), some 30% to 50% of the revenue earned by the regional industry is accrued overseas, and in particular to developed countries. Other researchers place the average import content at 53% or higher.

Obviously, this is not typical of all countries in the region as there are a few destinations with relatively lower leakage rates. However, the prevailing trend clearly suggests that the vast majority of destinations are saddled with an industry that depends heavily on imports to satisfy tourist needs. There is little doubt that the import content of the tourist industry in these island states is exceptionally high, especially when compared to other well-established and mature destinations outside of the region (Ramjee Singh 2006). Besides impacting on the tourism industry's net earnings, the leakage rate to a large extent influences the size of the tourism income multiplier. Available statistics and research amply demonstrate that the import content and the size of the tourism multipliers are inversely related. That is to say, countries with high leakage rates tend to end up with small multipliers and relatively insignificant ripple effects from tourist spending (Ramjee Singh 2006).

The question that next arises is: what factors are likely to explain the differences in the import content (leakage rate) of the tourism industry among regional destinations? First, it is argued in the literature that small island economies tend to rely more on imports to meet the diverse needs of tourism, because they do not have the capacity to produce the goods and services that are required to meet the demand of the industry. This position is supported by a Caribbean Tourism Organisation (CTO) (2011) study which suggested that the leakage rate tends to be higher among small island economies because of major resource constraints. In contrast, larger island states do not face these resource constraints and are expected to develop stronger intersectoral linkages between tourism and the rest of the domestic economy.

Second, physical infrastructure is one of the main pillars of economic development for any economy. The level of infrastructural development determines the diversity and speed of economic development. A well-developed infrastructure is expected to improve the production possibilities of domestic industries, develop stronger intersectoral linkages within the economy, provide the platform for the efficient distribution of goods and services, and allow domestic industries to try to compete successfully with their overseas counterparts. These factors taken together are most likely to improve the ability of the domestic economy to increase its inputs into tourism (Clayton 2004).

Third, the Caribbean area hosts about 700 million tourists per annum (CTO 2002). The phenomenal increase in tourist arrivals over the last years was due primarily to the decision of most regional destinations to engage in mass tourism. A massive influx of tourists to a destination, however, increases the demand for goods and services. To satisfy this demand, most destinations invariably turn to imports.

Lastly, Caribbean economies (with the exception of Cuba) are open, export-oriented dependent structures (Britton 1982). This export focus coupled with overemphasis on tourism growth over the years has not stimulated an autonomous path of development and has resulted in the neglect of local agriculture and manufacturing industry. It is not surprising that the local agricultural sector has remained largely inefficient, and is unable to provide the required volume of output at competitive prices to tourism (Britton 1989). In some cases, this is partly the result of expedient government policies that kept the best land in uncompetitive crops such as sugarcane in order to obtain European subsidies, and resisted modernization in order to avoid the political consequences of shedding labor from the sugar industry, in conjunction with high levels of corruption and patronage in allocating funding for agricultural development and irrigation, and endemic problems with predial larceny, a combination that steadily eroded the viability of the agricultural sector.

The withering and continued underdevelopment of domestic agriculture now contributes to the import content of tourism, and the region has become highly dependent on food imports. That is to say, the more underdeveloped a country's domestic production, the higher the tourism industry's import content (Britton 1982).

A number of authors have pointed to the potential mutual benefits between local agriculture and tourism. However, most Caribbean governments have done little to act on this advice and seem to largely ignore developmental requirements and domestic needs, focusing instead almost entirely on the promised investment income. So the tendency has been to focus on measures that will attract more tourists and business and to increase expenditure per tourist (Karagiannis 2002a).

Identifying the factors that lead to the differential in leakage rates has, however, become a critical issue for small island states, and especially those that are characterized as tourism-dependent economies. In many cases, the mere survival of these economies will depend on their abilities to retain more of the tourism industry's earnings. This is not technically easy, however; the quest to reduce the leakage level of tourism receipts and, by extension, to increase the benefits accruing from tourism presents a major challenge to most small states (Ramjee Singh 2006). This problem exists due to a serious lack of diversification in local production coupled with a lack of linkages between tourism and the rest of the economy. The industry imports much of its supplies, largely because local manufacturers, farmers, and distributors can find it difficult to organize the quantity and quality of goods required. The level of leakage varies significantly from country to country, depending on the extent to which the domestic economy is able to meet the needs of the industry (Ramjee Singh 2006).

Tourist receipts leak at several different stages. First round leakages stem from the direct imports required by the industry and the visitors. Second round leakages arise from the import content of investment and overall consumption. Third round leakages refer to expenditure by governments, national tourism organizations, and individual firms on overseas promotion in order to sell the destination (Karagiannis 2002b). This sequence could have several negative effects. One is that the number of linkages into the local economy is likely to decline as the industry becomes more sophisticated; consequently, the indirect benefits of the industry could decline even as the industry grows.

The cost of building new hotels and the refurbishment of old ones are significantly affected by the high import content, as well as by local factors such as extortion, a major factor in some of the islands. This is a particular problem for the older and smaller hotels, which are typically old-fashioned, family-run, and in need of major reinvestment. However, the initial capital costs can be less significant than ongoing operating costs, with the importation of management services, spare parts, and replacement goods. As a result, strong revenues do not necessarily mean large profits.

One policy option is to reduce tariffs and thereby lower the cost of imports for construction and consumer goods. However, in a situation where the rates of leakage are already exceptionally high, tariffs may represent a significant source of government revenue from the industry. Reduced tariffs might also lead to even higher levels of capital outflow from the region. Consequently, any reduction in tariffs would have to be accompanied by parallel measures to raise new revenue and thereby ensure that the host country was able to derive some benefit from the industry.

Finally, mass tourism associated with all-inclusive resorts could perpetuate or even exacerbate the Caribbean dependency on specific markets, while the concentration of ownership could narrow the local distribution of benefits. The ownership structure of the industry has given particular impetus to concerns about high rates of leakage,* the loss of tourist dollars on imports, and repatriated profits (UNEP 1996). With the exception of Trinidad and Tobago, the leakage rates for the rest of these economies are particularly high. In most of these cases, over half of the industry's earnings flow out of the local economy. This is driven mainly by the exceptionally high import content of tourism, the relatively little local supply, and the relatively few intersectoral linkages between the local economy and tourism (Karagiannis 2002b; Ramjee Singh 2006).

Apart from influencing the industry's net earnings, the leakage rate also affects the tourism income multiplier (Clayton and Karagiannis 2008). Furthermore, a simple comparison of the tables discussed in the works of Clayton and Karagiannis (2008) indicates a negative correlation between the leakage rates and the multipliers (see also CTO 2011). For example, Trinidad and Tobago, St. Vincent and the Grenadines, and Dominica have larger multipliers, essentially because they have a lower leakage rate, while the opposite is true in the case of the Bahamas and Antigua and Barbuda. Consequently, the relatively high import content of the industry reduces the economically beneficial multiplier effect of tourist expenditure in the region. The high import level in the islands at least partially explains why a number of countries complain that they do not appear to be deriving commensurate benefit from the industry (Ramjee Singh 2006).

Air transport is critically important for the hotels and land-based resorts. There are frequent scheduled air connections between the Caribbean and the United States, Canada and Europe, and a number of major international airlines serve the region. American Airlines are in a particularly strong position, because they have a major base at Miami Airport that serves as the hub for much of Latin America and the Caribbean and currently have about 70% of the Caribbean market. Partly as a legacy of the independence era of 1960s and 1970s, there are also several relatively small regional carriers, including Caribbean Airways and Air Jamaica (Clayton 2004).

Caribbean nations are concerned about two aspects of their air links with their main markets. The first is the potential vulnerability of the region to changes in route structure, and the second is the possibility of any reductions in direct connections. There is therefore a general concern that the region does not control most of its own air carriers. However, Caribbean regional carriers have proved to be exorbitantly costly status symbols since they accumulated collective losses of about US$1.5 billion between 1995 and 2005, a crippling burden for small island economies.†

More recently, the slow removal of national barriers to merger, acquisition, route planning, and cabotage has gradually started to made clear that it is increasingly inappropriate to focus on the location of the head office of an airline. As a result, a number of both small (Guyana) and medium-sized countries (Switzerland, the Netherlands) no longer believe that it is necessary to have a domestically based national carrier. For example, in 2007, Guyana made Caribbean Airways (which is based in Trinidad) its new national carrier.

It is true that the major international airlines have to make decisions on a commercial basis. It is also true that the local carriers are typically small, loss-making, subsidized, under-equipped, and have trouble in competing directly with the major airlines. There has been some discussion in the Caribbean of the need for the local airlines to cooperate, coordinate timetables, code-share both with each other and with large international carriers and becoming more aggressively competitive if they are to survive in the face of global competition. Rationalization and mergers might be a partial solution, and Air Jamaica has now been taken over by Caribbean Airways. National sentiment and

---

* Current data on the leakage rate for the industry are only available for eleven countries in the region (Clayton and Karagiannis 2008).
† BWIA, Air Jamaica, and LIAT. See also Deon Green, Virgin takeover of Air Jamaica route is a backward step, *Jamaica Gleaner*, May 24, 2007.

government ownership still plays a powerful role, however, and this may make it difficult to achieve the rationalization that would be the main benefit from the merger of the main regional carriers.

The increasing dominance of the cruise ship industry presents a particular challenge to the region. The cruise sector has been growing faster than international tourism in general since the mid-1980s, and the Caribbean is the most important region in the world for this industry, accounting for over half of world cruise ship tourism (CTO 2009, 2010). Barberia (2003) notes that at least 40% of the tourists entering nine of the region's leading destinations now arrive via cruise ship. Recent forecasts suggest that the growth rate of the industry will continue to outstrip that of the stopover business for the foreseeable future. Clearly, the North American market dominates the cruise ship industry, accounting for over 80% of all cruise passengers during the 1990s and 2000s (Clayton and Karagiannis 2008; US Department of Transportation 2010).

Caribbean islands have four main areas of concern about the cruise industry. One is the impact that the ships have upon the environment (via, e.g., illegal discharges of oily waste and garbage). The other three relate to the relatively poor net economic benefits derived from the cruise ship business compared with those derived from stopover tourism. These are as follows (Karagiannis 2002b):

- The low level of onshore expenditure per cruise ship visitor
- The low level of direct government revenues generated by the cruise ship industry, which pays remarkably little tax to any jurisdiction
- The competition offered by onboard shops to shopping facilities onshore

The CTO (2002) estimates that cruise ship travelers spent well over half a billion US dollars during the 1990s in the region. The CTO points out, however, that stopover visitors accounted for around 94% of total tourism spending, while cruise ship passengers accounted for just 6%. No statistics exist in detail on leakage of cruise ship passengers' spending but it is widely reported that the bulk of onshore purchases are duty-free goods or small souvenirs with relatively low local value-added. In general, it is clear that spending by cruise ship tourists at a destination is significantly lower than stopover tourists, as CTO estimates indicate that stopover tourists spend on average 10–17 times more than cruise ship tourists. The reason is simple: the cruise ship is an all-inclusive floating hotel, so all meals, entertainment, and so on are purchased in advance as part of the package. The island destinations provide little more than occasional variations in scenery, so less than half of the passengers bother to disembark.

The cruise industry is also exceptionally skilled at utilizing legal loopholes. The use of flags of convenience, in particular, allows some firms to operate on an almost entirely unregulated and untaxed basis. The industry has also, on several occasions, demonstrated that it has significantly more leverage than most island governments. Several governments have tried to impose a head tax on cruise tourists, but the threat to take the business elsewhere has obliged the governments to capitulate (Pinnock 2012).

As a result of the highly unequal distribution of costs and benefits associated with tourism in the Caribbean, some authors have likened tourism to a form of "cultural imperialism" or rather the "hedonistic face of neocolonialism." Some have argued that tourism and the institutionalization of hospitality reinforces notions of subservience, reinforced through the proliferation of mainly low-grade employment for locals (Britton 1982, 1989; Telfer 2002).

This negative perception of history cannot be ignored, but it is also true that the same colonial ties also fused a diverse range of cultures, religions, values, cuisines, recreational activities, and sporting interests and that the result was to produce a range of destinations for the leisure visitor as exciting and diverse as no other region in the world (Poon 1993; Pattullo 1996). However, amid this beautiful and powerful Caribbean culture, and despite its image as one of the world's glamorous primary destinations for the visitors, it is easy to overlook the fact that many Caribbean territories are now overpopulated but still underdeveloped countries in which prosperity coexists with squalor and deprivation. This supports the argument that most of the benefits of the industry accrue largely to small elites (Boxill 2000; Boxill et al. 2002).

Some argue that an influx of relatively wealthy tourists into a poor country can have negative implications for social and cultural values. This is contentious, partly because all cultures are subject to multiple influences and evolve over time, and partly because definitions and measures of "good" and "bad" social change are subjective. However, tourism has in some cases clearly resulted in undesirable developments, such as children or vulnerable young adults trafficked or coerced into the sex industry and the spread of sexually transmitted diseases (Clayton 2004).

There can also be problems with resentment. These may stem from the entrenched poverty and extreme social disparities found in many developing countries, but a sense of historical grievance might appear to make tourism an obvious target, especially if many of the visitors are from the former colonial power. However, Carter (1997) found that the resentment felt by some workers in Jamaica is typically focused on their own management, rather than on the visitors, due to low pay, constant uncertainty, and long travel-to-work times. There are still potential problems when poor local residents see the great difference between their own lifestyles and that of the affluent foreign tourist. This can be compounded by a sense that opportunities for local people are largely confined to the lower-grade jobs in hotels, while senior management positions are held by expatriate staff. The latter is not always accurate: some hotels invest significantly in local recruitment and staff training but the perception still exists (Bailey et al. 2010).

Tourists are sometimes cheated or overcharged, and cameras or wallets might be stolen. Such incidents are upsetting but not life-threatening. The most common complaint is one of harassment, usually in the form of persistent and apparently aggressive attempts to sell something, but this does to some extent reflect cultural differences in what is perceived to be acceptable behavior. The more important problem is the rise in serious crime, like armed robbery and homicide. These do not usually affect tourists, but generally receive significant publicity when they do. As a result, many tourists prefer to stay within the confines of their all-inclusive hotels, protected by hotel security, venturing out only on organized tours, and spending little in the wider community. This serves to perpetuate the underlying problem of surrounding poverty (Clayton 2004).

Most people understand, of course, that one homicide does not make a country dangerous. The most serious cases involve a more general threat, such as terrorism.* However, even a few well-publicized cases can have a perceptible deterrent effect. As a result, much emphasis has been placed recently on the need for tourism awareness programs in the Caribbean to make local communities realize the economic advantages of tourism, in terms of jobs and opportunities it can offer (Clayton 2004). A corollary to the envy felt by some of the poorer sections of Caribbean communities is the resentment felt by some members of the political elite, some of whom are irked by the contrast between their underperforming economies and the apparent vibrancy of their largest sector.

More generally, some politicians have serious reservations about tourism's role as the main engine of economic growth. These reservations are generally expressed in three forms. One is the concern that tourism will result in the substitution of one type of dependence for another, as tourism

---

* Terrorists, unfortunately, are increasingly aware of this fact, and also that tourism is both economically significant and a very soft target. The murder of 70 tourists at Luxor in 1997 is estimated to have cost Egypt about half of its tourism revenue over the following year, which appears to have been the outcome intended by the terrorist group that perpetrated the atrocity.

could come to resemble the banana and sugar industries in small, price-taker monocrop economies. Another is the belief that tourism is a relatively volatile industry, making dependence on it risky. A third is a feeling that local culture and mores will disintegrate as other lifestyles are imported and copied by local people, especially the region's youth, and as culture becomes "objectified" by being packaged and sold as if it were just another product (Bianchi 2002, pp. 270–71).

The first argument is for diversification rather than against tourism *per se*, but highlights a potential vulnerability. The second argument is weaker, because tourism is actually less volatile than most commodities. The third argument might perhaps be stronger in countries where, for example, dances and rituals that were formerly sacred are now performed for the entertainment of visitors, but is less obviously true of the Caribbean islands, which are themselves a product of many generations of cultural fusion. This argument has also been accused of being a preoccupation of the cultural elite, rather than the actual people concerned (Bailey et al. 2010).

Finally, the loss of infrastructure and trade to a combination of climate change and social pressures could, potentially, result in the collapse of a number of regional economies as mass tourism imposes various burdens on the environment and infrastructure. These daunting challenges make it essential to undertake a serious review of the nature and role of tourism in the region. Many of these impacts can be mitigated or avoided, with good planning and management, but poor governance and powerful developers with a cavalier disregard for constraints can cause unnecessary damage. Dysfunctional planning processes can result in poorly managed overdevelopment and cause unnecessary environmental damage, a combination that can eventually force the local industry into a down-market, low-margin niche. Some therefore worry that countries have become overly dependent on the industry and that tourists are fickle and might decide to take their custom elsewhere (Clayton 2004).

The problem is exacerbated when the number of tourists hosted by a small island state is several times the size of the local population. A high tourist to host density ratio inevitably leads to problems, including environmental and infrastructural overloading, that would not only threaten the viability of the industry but hasten its demise. The need for Caribbean governments to develop and implement strategies that would not only counter but even reverse this trend becomes more urgent. There has to be, therefore, a growing awareness of the need to control and manage the industry to ensure its viability and sustainability in the long run (Clayton 2004, 2009).

More fundamentally, it appears likely that climate change and the frequency of severe weather conditions will have a major impact on social, economic, and environmental systems during the course of this century. As Clayton et al. (2007) note, this presents an existential challenge for small island nations. It may be necessary to relocate vulnerable infrastructure and human settlements away from high risk areas. While tourism in some countries (such as the United Kingdom) is expected to gain, the Mediterranean is projected to become increasingly arid while the Caribbean is likely to suffer from a higher intensity of hurricanes, flooding, and storm surge. It is also possible that airlines might be included in national carbon emission totals and co-opted into carbon trading schemes, which will have implications for airfares (CTO 2007, 2009; Clayton 2009, 2011).

Strategic Policy Areas

There is clear recognition at the highest levels of Caribbean governments and regional and international entities that the fortunes of tourism are central to the national and regional economy. To compete with developed counterparts and dominant transnational corporations, Caribbean nations will have to make effective policy interventions so as to make best use of their advantages. There is also a growing awareness that the types of problems previously discussed must be addressed in a holistic manner that will increase linkages, decrease leakages, and enhance the impact that the industry has on economic development. Beyond this, there is a growing awareness that the problems facing the industry need to be understood in an international context, particularly where they relate to economic development, fiscal policy, aviation, training, and climate change.

The fact that these dynamic considerations have, in general, not been pursued supports the view that the underlying problem with Caribbean tourism is that it is largely unplanned and used simply as a quick way of earning foreign exchange by some of the heavily indebted governments in the region (Hayle 2002; Karagiannis 2002b; McDavid 2002). This indicates that the real weakness is the absence of a proper tourism strategy. As the dominant sector of the regional economy, tourism could be utilized to far greater effect to drive a larger development policy. Ideally, tourism would generate significant economic benefits for both investors and hosts, while minimizing environmental impacts, respecting local people, and giving them an opportunity for advancement (Ajagunna 2012). This is broadly similar to the model advocated for Belize by Boxill (2003), who argued that here are four prerequisites for this more enlightened type of tourism: a regional/local approach to tourism planning; intelligent planning and regulation of the industry; a more diversified product; and greater local involvement in the process.

Some have argued that proper planning and regulation of tourism is essential in order to develop a better and more sustainable product. McDavid (2002, p. 68) argues that the development of tourism cannot be left entirely to market forces and that there is a need for selected policy interventions. Most agree that the industry would benefit from better strategic planning, instead of the current practice of largely *ad hoc* arrangements (Clayton 2001, 2004). Karagiannis suggests that this "strategic approach" would include the development of human resources, product development, and marketing, arguing that "The public and private sectors can cooperate in a range of different arrangements, each contributing what it does best and both participating in the financial returns, within the context of a socially defined development agenda" (Karagiannis 2002b, p. 165). Besides, measures at a national level to enhance regional competitiveness comprise tourism awareness; the achievement of sustainable funding for the sector; product development; planned investment; sectoral linkages; and joint procurements.

The multidimensional issues previously discussed require some obvious remedial measures. In general, a combination of economic development in conjunction with some measures to promote local business and job opportunities, long-term training for more skilled positions, and sympathetic treatment of local culture and tradition, can do much to address existing challenges. Such a combination can be mutually advantageous (Scheyvens 1999, quoted in Timothy 2002, p. 152). Action plans seek to identify a range of institutional actions corresponding to various measures. This action-orientation is fundamental to proactive strategies and policies. So too is a commitment by individual Caribbean states to thoroughly formulate and proficiently execute policy. Responsibility for leading, implementing, and supporting each action is assigned as appropriate to individual member states and, where relevant, to bodies such as Caribbean Tourism Organization (CTO) (Karagiannis 2002b). Collaboration with other regional bodies, according to their roles and spheres of influence, is also critical to the successful implementation of policy.

More specifically, thorough policy action must incorporate measures to

1. Achieve economies of scale to the benefit of the tourism sector across the region. Measures aimed at achieving economies of scale should focus on joint marketing activities, which can deliver greater impact at lower cost through economies of scale; research and statistics; human resource development; crime prevention; and on ensuring synergy with the CTO in areas where there are initiatives of mutual value to member states.

2. Facilitate travel within the region. Measures aimed at facilitating travel within the Caribbean should cover harmonized customs and immigration procedures and tariffs; implementation of a common maritime space; and improved transit procedures.
3. Improve access and transportation to and within the Caribbean. Measures aimed at improving access and transportation must focus on joint action with respect to air travel from outside the Caribbean into the region and within the region; and joint action with respect to cruising, including yachting.
4. Conserve and enhance the region's environmental and cultural assets. Measures directed at environmental, heritage and cultural sustainability must include the conservation of the natural environment; and cultural conservation and promotion.

Some regional coordination in tourism planning would allow Caribbean countries to pool some of their resources in areas such as marketing (Hayle 2002), and a less nationalistic approach to air traffic would encourage the small regional airlines to code-share, coordinate their timetables and pool their maintenance, or even undertake real or virtual mergers. This would increase their load factors, reduce their maintenance costs, and reduce their overheads. This would also make them more attractive partners for the major carriers, an increasingly important factor now that the carriers are grouped into major alliances and flights are booked through the major computer reservation systems (Clayton and Karagiannis 2008).

More generally, the building of strategic alliances and partnerships within and outside of the tourism industry is needed in order to bundle products, add value, and thereby increase the competitiveness of the sector (Poon 1993, p. 273). As Karagiannis (2002b, p. 169) points out: "With cooperative arrangements and regional approaches to tourism, Caribbean islands can share the [huge] expenses of creating market intelligence systems, information technology networks, promotion, and public relations campaigns." Besides, a sophisticated marketing approach with more specialized and segmented promotional campaigns would serve the needs of the Caribbean tourist industry.

There is an important question as to whether Caribbean tourism can achieve such a niche in this crowded market and, if so, at what cost? The increased competition can be met by an increased emphasis on capturing the customer service niche—one that raises the level and sophistication of customer service for all segments. More importantly, the Caribbean will have to focus strongly on improving quality standards, increasing efficiency, and offering more value for money. The standard measures of customer service are probably inadequate, as the revitalization of the industry will require that investments must be made in technological infrastructure development and support, training, and marketing research (Bailey et al. 2010).

The immediate problem is that the strategy of pursuing an industry-leading customer service niche requires investment, which will impose higher costs on governments, either through direct subsidies or, more likely, through tax concessions. First, establishing a customer service niche would entail investment in training, with a concomitant investment in technology development and usage. There is a significant current deficit in this regard, so a number of hotels in the Caribbean would have to install new technologies and ensure that their employees are properly trained. That represents significantly increased infrastructure and education costs. Second, it will also be necessary to improve service attitudes and skills, as they are crucial to future success. This too will require significant investment in state-of-the-art training facilities and the international procurement of the best and most experienced trainers. Last, investment must be made in marketing research, such as consumer surveys, in order to determine what different market segments value and to develop the necessary products. This will enhance customer satisfaction and increase the all-important rate of repeat business (Bailey et al. 2010).

But even with an industry-leading customer service, there will still be the even more fundamental need for the Caribbean to diversify the tourism product to give a wider range of options and thereby improve the competitive edge of the industry (Hayle 2002; Karagiannis 2002b). For example, Bernal (2000, pp. 110–11) suggests that the Caribbean should consider heritage tourism, health tourism, cultural tourism, and ecotourism (which may require different promotional appeals), while Nurse argues for the entertainment industry, stating that "the experience with festivals and other cultural events is that they tend to create a tourism demand that is resilient and less susceptible to economic downturns" (Nurse 2002, p. 129).

Clearly, a more diverse product would permit a wider range of training and business development options, thereby helping to secure greater local involvement in the industry. Heritage, cultural, ecological, community, and health tourism are all labor-intensive niches that require some level of knowledge and local ownership in order for them to be successfully implemented (Scheyvens 1999; Boxill 2000, 2002; Hayle 2000, 2002; Timothy 2002; Duperly-Pinks 2002). This would in turn result in a larger network of stakeholders (Boxill 2002; Hayle 2002), a wider distribution of tourism earnings, and the fostering of a more pro-tourism attitude in the region (Duperly-Pinks 2002).

As noted earlier, the linkages between tourism and local production have been relatively weak. New options such as health and heritage tourism can help to increase consumption of the region's cuisine and local products, thereby building a mutually beneficial relationship between tourism and agro-industry. Therefore, local production growth should be oriented toward satisfying domestic demand in the first instance,* with export promotion occurring as an extension of this (Karagiannis 2002b). These options could also assist local firms to introduce their products to an international market through existing tourist destinations. However, any significant strengthening of these linkages would still require improvements in product quality, more efficient distribution systems, extension training, and access to affordable credit by local producers (Henshall-Momsen 1998, quoted in Karagiannis 2002b).

Finally, environmental protection must be accorded a greater priority by policy makers in the Caribbean, especially as there have been some recent cases of mismanagement and unnecessarily destructive development. There is still a serious mismatch between the general recognition that environmental issues matter and the largely ineffective controls in some islands. Caribbean governments have a range of policies and legislation to protect the environment (including protected areas, land-use planning, and obligatory environmental impact analysis), but sometimes these are inconsistently enforced. More could also be done to promote effective coordination between government departments and to encourage new approaches such as cleaner production strategies (Clayton 2004, 2009, 2011).

Conclusion

This chapter discusses a number of issues that emanate from tourism growth in the Caribbean and analyzes such important areas as proactive policy action, emphasis on strategic planning, business development, greater regional cooperation, the creation of a more diversified product, sociocultural aspects, and environmental concerns. The combination of these requirements would

---

* It has to be noted here that stopover tourists in Caribbean destinations significantly expand the size of local markets. Consequently, the growth of demand, stemming from the increase in population and tourists, can provide the opportunities for the growth of local supply.

largely define an alternative tourism policy framework for Caribbean territories. During this era of globalization, the challenge for the region's policy makers is to find the proper combination of positive state intervention and market orientation that is consistent with efficient and sustainable tourism development.

This challenge is not insurmountable if Caribbean governments accept a role as change agents and address the industry's problems. The current laissez-faire environment has encouraged growth, but has also resulted in very high leakages, a lack of economic linkages, a low rate of new entrants and consequent lack of competition, and a number of serious environmental problems, including development in areas that may eventually be lost to rising seas. The resolution of these issues will involve serious, technically proficient planning and coordination of the industry's needs with the rest of the local economy and society. The primary goal of such an exercise must be to implement strategies and policies that would seek to retain more of the industry's earnings in the local economy, increase the economic multiplier effect, encourage healthy competition, and minimize environmental damage, thereby contributing to the socioeconomic advancement of the islands.

References

Ajagunna, I. (2012), *Planning Process for Sustainable Tourism Development*, Saarbrücken, Germany: Lambert Publishing.

Bailey, J. M., Clayton, A. and N. Karagiannis (2010), Mass tourism and endogenous development: The Caribbean experience, *Regional Development Studies*, **14**, pp. 94–115.

Barberia, L. G. (2003), The Caribbean: Tourism as Development or Development for Tourism? www.fas.harvard.edu.

Bernal, R. L. (2000), Globalisation and small developing countries: The imperative for repositioning, in D. Benn and K. Hall (eds), *Globalisation: A Calculus of Inequality*, Kingston, Jamaica: Ian Randle Publishers, pp. 88–127.

Bianchi, R. V. (2002), Towards a new political economy of global tourism, in R. Sharpley and D. J. Telfer (eds), *Tourism and Development: Concepts and Issues*, Clevedon: Channel View Publications, pp. 265–99.

Boxill, I. (2000), Overcoming social problems in the Jamaican tourism industry, in I. Boxill and J. Maerk (eds), *Tourism in the Caribbean*, Mexico: Plaza y Valdez, pp. 17–40.

Boxill, I. (2003), Towards an alternative tourism for Belize, *International Journal of Contemporary Hospitality Management*, **15** (3), pp. 147–55.

Boxill, I. and O. Frederick (2002), Old road, new road: Community protests and tourism development in Antigua, in I. Boxill, O. Taylor and J. Maerk (eds), *Tourism and Change in the Caribbean and Latin America*, Kingston, Jamaica: Arawak Publications, pp. 101–110.

Boxill, I. and J. Maerk (eds). (2000), *Tourism in the Caribbean*, Mexico: Plaza y Valdez.

Boxill, I., Taylor, O., and J. Maerk (eds). (2002), Tourism and Change in the Caribbean and Latin America, Kingston, Jamaica: Arawak Publications.

Britton, S. G. (1982), The political economy of tourism in the third world, *Annals of Tourism Research*, **9** (3), pp. 331–58.

Britton, S. G. (1989), Tourism, dependency and development: A model of analysis, in T. V. Singh, H. L. Theuns and F. M. Go (eds), *Towards Appropriate Tourism: The Case of Developing Countries*, Frankfurt, Germany: Peter Lang, pp. 93–116.

Caribbean Tourism Organisation (CTO). (2002), *Statistical Tables 2000–2001*, Bridgetown, Barbados: CTO.

Caribbean Tourism Organisation (CTO). (May 23, 2007), Climate change and tourism in the Caribbean: Threats and opportunities, *Proceedings of the 9th Annual Conference on Sustainable Tourism Development*, Grand Cayman B.W.I.

Caribbean Tourism Organisation (CTO). (April 2011), *Latest Tourism Statistics 2003–2010*, Bridgetown, Barbados: CTO.

Caribbean Tourism Organisation (CTO). (April 2012), *Latest Tourism Statistics 2007–2011*, Bridgetown, Barbados: CTO.

Caribbean Tourism Organisation (CTO)/Winfield Griffith. (April, 2009), *Tourism Trends, Issues and Challenges: Implications for Caribbean Economies*, ILO-Tripartite Caribbean Conference, CTO. http://www.onecaribbean.org/content/files/.

Carter, K. L. (1997), *Why Workers Won't Work: The Worker in a Developing Economy*, London: McMillan Education Ltd.

Clayton, A. (2001), Sustainable tourism: The agenda for tourism professionals in the Caribbean, in C. Jayawardeena (ed), *Tourism and Hospitality Education and Training in the Caribbean*, Kingston, Jamaica: UWI Press.

Clayton, A. (2004), A policy framework for the sustainable development of the tourism industry, in C. Jayawardeena (ed), *Caribbean Tourism: Visions, Missions and Challenges*, Kingston, Jamaica: Ian Randle Publishers.

Clayton, A. (2009), Climate change and tourism: The implications for the Caribbean, in A. Clayton and C. Hayle (eds), *Worldwide Hospitality and Tourism Themes, Climate Change and Tourism in the Caribbean*, **1** (3), Bingley: Emerald Group Publishing.

Clayton, A. (2011), Energy inefficiency, climate change and migration, *CaribXplorer*, **1** (4).

Clayton, A. and N. Karagiannis (2008), Sustainable tourism in the Caribbean: Alternative policy considerations, *Tourism and Hospitality Planning & Development*, **5** (3), pp. 185–201.

Duperly-Pinks, D. (2002), Community tourism: "Style and Fashion" or facilitating empowerment? in I. Boxill, O. Taylor and J. Maerk (eds), *Tourism and Change in the Caribbean and Latin America*, Kingston, Jamaica: Arawak Publications, pp. 137–61.

Hayle, C. (2000), Community Tourism in Jamaica, in I. Boxill and J. Maerk (eds), *Tourism in the Caribbean*, Mexico: Plaza y Valdez, pp. 165–76.

Hayle, C. (2002), Issues Confronting New Entrants to Tourism, in I. Boxill, O. Taylor and J. Maerk (eds), *Tourism and Change in the Caribbean and Latin America*, Kingston, Jamaica: Arawak Publications, pp. 229–72.

International Monetary Fund (IMF). (2009), *World Economic Outlook: Crisis and Recovery*, Washington, DC: IMF.

Jayawardena, C. (2002), *Cuba: Crown Princess of Caribbean Tourism?*, mimeo, presented at the 27th CSA Conference, Nassau, the Bahamas.

Karagiannis, N. (2002a), *A New Economic Strategy for the Bahamas: With Special Consideration of International Competition and the FTAA*, Kingston, Jamaica: UWI Printers.

Karagiannis, N. (2002b), *Developmental Policy and the State: The European Union, East Asia, and the Caribbean*, Lanham, MD: Lexington Books.

McDavid, H. (2002), Why should government intervene in a market economy? A Caribbean perspective on the hospitality and tourism sector, in I. Boxill, O. Taylor and J. Maerk (eds), *Tourism and Change in the Caribbean and Latin America*, Kingston, Jamaica: Arawak Publications, pp. 56–81.

Nurse, K. (2002), Bringing culture into the tourism: Festival tourism and Reggae Sunsplash in Jamaica, *Social and Economic Studies*, **51** (1), pp. 127–43.

Organization of American States (OAS). (2002), "Adaptation to Climate Change in the Caribbean Tourism Sector", *Workshop Report & Plan of Action*, Grenada, May 27-28, 2002. (Prepared by Ivor Jackson & Associates.)

Organization of American States (OAS). (2007), *Thirty-Seventh Regular Session of the General Assembly*, Panama. June 3–5.

Pattullo, P. (1996), *Last Resorts: The Cost of Tourism in the Caribbean*, Kingston, Jamaica: Ian Randle Publishers.

Pinnock, F. (2012), *Caribbean Cruise Tourism: Power Relations Among Stakeholders: The Future of Cruise Tourism in the Caribbean*, Saarbrücken, Germany: Lambert Publishers.

Planning Institute of Jamaica (PIOJ). (2013), *Economic and Social Survey—Jamaica*, Kingston, Jamaica: PIOJ.

Poon, A. (1993), Caribbean tourism and the world economy, in S. Lalta and M. Freckleton (eds), *Caribbean Economic Development: The First Generation*, Kingston, Jamaica: Ian Randle Publishers, pp. 262–79.

Ramjee Singh, D. H. (2006), Import content of tourism: Explaining differences among island states, *Tourism Analysis*, **11**, pp. 33–44.

Sharpley, R. and D. J. Telfer (eds) (2002), *Tourism and Development: Concepts and Issues*, Clevedon: Channel View Publications.

Telfer, D. J. (2002), The evolution of tourism and development theory, in R. Sharpley and D. J. Telfer (eds), *Tourism and Development: Concepts and Issues*, Clevedon: Channel View Publications, pp. 35–78.

Timothy, D. J. (2002), Tourism and community development issues, in R. Sharpley and D. J. Telfer (eds), *Tourism and Development: Concepts and Issues*, Clevedon: Channel View Publications, pp. 149–64.

UN Economic Commission for Latin America and the Caribbean (ECLAC). (2012), *Databases and Statistical Publications*, various years, Santiago, Chile.

United Nations Environment Programme (UNEP). (December 1996), *Tourism and Coastal Resources Degradation in the Wider Caribbean*, St. Thomas, Virgin Islands.

US Department of Transportation (Maritime Administration). (September 2010), North American cruises—key statistics, Table 1, www.marad.dot.gov/documents/North_American_Cruise_Statistics_Quarterly_Snapshot.pdf.

Vaugeios, N. (2002), Tourism in developing countries: Refining a useful tool for economic development, mimeo. www.onecaribbean.org/www.transparency.org/regional_pages/americas

World Bank, 2003 *Annual Review of Development Effectiveness*, Washington, DC: The World Bank, 2004.

World Travel and Tourism Council (2012), *The Comparative Economic Impact of Travel & Tourism*, London, November.

Chapter 16

Policy and Regulation of the Caribbean Communications Industry

Indianna D. Minto-Coy

Contents

Introduction 358
The Communications Industry in the Colonial Era: 1880–1950s 359
Independence and the Management and Control of the Communications
Industry: 1960s and 1970s 360
Bilateralism in Policy Development and Regulation: 1980–1995 361
Reform in the Regulation, Management, and Structure of the Communications
Industry: 1995–2010 363
    Major Developments in the Policy and Management of the Communications
    Industry in the Organisation of Eastern Caribbean States 365
    Major Developments in the Policy and Management of the Communications
    Industry in Jamaica 367
Regional Governance of the Communications Industry 368
Overview of the Developments in Broadcasting 369
The State of the Communications Industry in 2014 370
    E-Government 371
    Future Developments 374
Conclusion 375
References 376

Abstract: The Caribbean communications industry has undergone significant changes going from its early orientation as a vital link between the colonies and Europe to the mainly open and competitive regimes that exist today. Policy and management in the sector have shifted from a preoccupation with the needs of empire to those of local populations, albeit very slowly. This is most visible in the reform in the structure, management, and regulation of the industry largely, from the late 1990s. Largely through desk research and mainly through a focus on the Commonwealth Caribbean, the chapter builds a complete overview of the development of the Caribbean communications industry from the colonial period to the most aggressive and comprehensive period of policy development in the late 1990s and beyond. The chapter underscores the fact that the story of the industry is largely about telecommunications and Cable and Wireless, particularly given the breadth and length of the latter's dominance in the region. It further asserts that gains secured in the first five years of the twenty-first century have plateaued or have not been fully acted upon in making definitive steps toward the development of information societies across the region. Finally, the chapter assesses the prospects and challenges in advancing the developmental and growth benefits of the telecommunications industry to the region.

Introduction

The communications industry has undergone significant changes within the Caribbean. This is from its early orientation as a vital link between the colonies in the region and the United Kingdom to the mainly open and competitive regimes that exist today. Policy and management in the sector have accordingly shifted from a preoccupation with meeting the needs of the empire to those of the local population, albeit very slowly. This is most visible in the improvements made in the sector from the 1990s into the first decade of the twenty-first century. Collectively, these represent a major overhaul in the structure and management of the industry. Reforms came out of recognition of the role of policy, as well as a result of the coming together of a number of internal and external factors that made the policy shifts practical, namely, in breaking the power of the paternalistic monopoly of Cable and Wireless (C&W). This is the more popular name for a firm that has gone through various phases including its more recent (since 2008) incarnation as LIME (Landline, Internet, Mobile, Entertainment). Nonetheless, the gains secured during this period have plateaued or have not been fully acted upon in making long-standing improvements toward the development of information societies across the region. Further action is also necessary in moving the region along the next level of reforms that will help to activate and realize the full benefits of the advances of the past two decades.

In making these points, the following reviews the major policy developments in the communications industry in the Caribbean. It gives a historical overview of the development of the industry from the colonial period into independence and then covers the most aggressive and comprehensive period of policy developments. The coverage ends with an assessment of the prospects and challenges moving forward and a conclusion. The emphasis is largely on the English-speaking territories with less attention on developments in other countries in the region.

A few maiden points are pivotal to the reader's understanding of the developments discussed in this chapter. Namely, the story of the communications industry in the Caribbean is largely the story of telecommunications and particularly so up to the end of the 1990s. Additionally, given the breadth and length of its dominance in the region, this is also to a large extent the story of C&W.

The Communications Industry in the Colonial Era: 1880–1950s

The communications industry in the Caribbean had its beginnings in the last half of the nineteenth century when the first telegraph link was established in Jamaica in 1869. This was done by the International Ocean Telegraph who in 1870 sold out to the West India Telegraph and Telephone Company (WIT), who later became C&W. A year later, the firm commenced the laying of cables that would connect the region, via Jamaica to Europe via North America. The network that was completed in 1873 eventually connected 17 countries, including Martinique, Puerto Rica, Cuba, Panama, and Guyana (Glover 2010). Establishing a connection between the islands in the Caribbean proved to be a viable endeavor by the colonial government given the importance of linking its territories in the region (Ahvenainen 1996: 15–19). Domestic service was to be offered when the first telephone exchange was introduced in Jamaica in 1878 and 1883 for Trinidad and Tobago (T&T).

The development of communications in the Caribbean was orchestrated by the British who saw ownership and control of communications infrastructure across the region as a strategic part of its efforts to maintain its presence economically (trade) and politically and thus part of the imperialist interests (Minto 2009; also see Headrick 1991: 50–51 for the wider point). Jamaica, the largest of the English-speaking territories, was particularly important in this regard since it operated as a transhipment point between England and its territories in the region. As such the development of communications policy and management in the Caribbean was closely informed by the aims and ambitions of the British government and the geopolitical importance of the region: "the land lines already existing in North and South America, will literally place every part of that vast continent within a few hours' communication with London" (*Pall Mall Gazette* July 1870, in Glover 2010).

WITs was not the only company vying for the Caribbean, and indeed, it formed a cartel with Spanish and American firms operating in the region and Latin America. Importantly, too by the start of the twentieth century competition was rife as over a dozen other firms vied for a stake in the Caribbean and South America, including a number of French, American, and German companies. Nevertheless, it is the case that the nationality of these firms was an important consideration in determining their ability to secure landing rights. For instance, an American-owned firm was unable to secure landing rights to lay cables in the British Caribbean, while the WIT succeeded without much difficulty in 1870 given its British connections (Headrick 1991: 41). Furthermore, in a context of great power politics, firms such as WIT were seen as national symbols, embodying the interests of the nation.

Poor service and low technology were among the problems plaguing the communications industry during this early period. Interestingly, these were to continue to mar the industry up to independence and beyond. Demand for WIT's service was also low, though this did not prevent increases in rates in order to cover its costs (Winseck and Pike 2007: 64–65). In such a context, colonial governments in a number of territories (including French, Dutch, and Spanish) turned to a French competitor, Société Française. This firm had operations in 1889 starting from a link between Haiti and Cuba and eventually other islands and Venezuela. These offered concessions to the French company given the prospects of cheaper communications. Support for the French company also came from the French government after a policy shift toward challenging Britain's dominance in the industry by the end of the 1800s.

By 1938, the WIT became C&W after it was drafted further into the British firm of that name. In Jamaica, C&W's ownership over the local segment of the industry was relinquished in 1892 when the Jamaica Telephone Company (JTC) was incorporated with majority ownership going to the British-owned Telephone and General Trust Company (T&GT). It is important to note at this stage that, while the firms that dominated the region were mainly British, they were private companies. However, C&W was later nationalized by the British government in 1947. In so doing, this signaled the British Empire's desire to further direct and control its interests in a game of great power politics by protecting its control over communications in the colonies. Nonetheless, the rise of American firms and power saw a challenge to the dominance which the British had through C&W. By the start of World War II, the United States and British colonies began questioning the British (i.e., C&W's) control over communications within the colonies. This was a rare case of the colonies exercising policy independence over the direction of the industry.

Winseck and Pike (2007: 63) note the overriding influence of interest groups in the United Kingdom, including banking and merchant interests in driving the operations of the WIT, and hence, the developments in the region. Added to this were the demands of the British government in running its empire. As such, the development of infrastructure was largely informed by or the result of needs within the United Kingdom and less about local demands or needs of the populace. For instance, the provision of the first radio-telephone link that saw Belize being connected with the rest of the world came about out of a request by the British government for C&W to improve telecommunications as a means of meeting a demand for coverage of HRH Princess Margaret's visit in 1958 (C&W Communications 2010).

Sector regulation was ad hoc or absent. In the case of Jamaica, for example, rate boards oversaw regulation and requests for rate increases. However, this body was not permanent and insufficiently able to determine the legitimacy of a request with the JTC being granted six increases between 1950 and 1960. International services received little or no regulatory oversight.

Thus, the story of Information and Communications Technologies (ICTs) and communications in the Caribbean up to the end of the twentieth century was therefore that of C&W (see Minto 2009; SRC 2011a, 2011b). This is so given that the telecommunications landscape was largely typified by a monopolistic, paternalistic structure that dominated the telecommunications landscape in the region for over a century (Minto 2009; Chapter 2). Importantly, too the policy landscape offered another scene in which Great Power politics played out across the region.

Independence and the Management and Control of the Communications Industry: 1960s and 1970s

With independence during the 1960s and 1970s, some territories sought to break C&W's ownership. The government in T&T moved to secure majority share in international telecoms. Belize also adopted the policy of nationalization and in 1971 took over C&W's assets (Huurdeman 2003: 558). In Barbados, nationalization was tempered with the government taking only a 40% stake, undergirding this lesser ownership by appointing local managers (Dunn and Gooden 1997).

Nevertheless, C&W continued investments in the sector with the completion of a satellite earth station in 1972 that helped to improve quality in transmitting and receiving television, telephony, faxes, and high-speed data in Barbados, Jamaica, and T&T. The firm also maintained its policy of operating in areas outside its narrow remit and in so doing, helping to contribute to its paternalistic image. For example, it built a C&W Telecommunications College in Barbados in 1972, in so doing, helping to build human capacity within the communications industry.

In Jamaica, policy and regulations were informed by a desire for the government to own the key areas of the economy and later by the country's leaning toward democratic socialism. In 1962, the government announced its intent to review arrangements toward reducing foreign stake in the sector beginning with the renegotiation of the JTC license. The then Minister noted T&GT's unwillingness and inability to provide the capital and services required to JTC (Lightbourne, 1967).

Ultimately, controlling ownership in JTC was transferred to the American-based Continental Telephone Company (CTC) whose assets were later retaken in 1975 when the domestic segment was renationalized. The attempt by the government to expropriate the assets of CTC was blocked by the courts who asserted CTC's right to fair compensation. The emphasis on the domestic service had some political motive given the number of users vis-à-vis the more expensive international segment, as well as the fact that these users constituted the floating voters whose support could be conditional on the impact of a policy choice. International services did not go untouched with C&W's ownership being reduced to 49% (51% to the Government) in a newly created controlling company, Jamintel, in 1971. Importantly, too, a formalized regulatory mechanism via a Public Utilities Commission (PUC) was established in 1966 to provide more structured oversight. According to Spiller and Sampson (1996) the PUC took on an adversarial stance toward the operators, which could be noted as befitting the general mood of the day. The PUC was also disbanded around 1975 in favor of direct Ministerial oversight.

Therefore, even with the shift in policy, the relationship between the two main actors (C&W and governments) was largely a bilateral affair. Bilateralism (see next section) in the regulatory space is suggested as having continued up to the early 2000s, even with the introduction of independent regulators from 1997 and later the spate of liberalizations from 1999 (see Minto, 2009). As such, there was little participation from civil society, partly given the underdevelopment of civil society. The reality, too, is that this type of relationship had been encouraged by the parent company in the 1960s as a means of protecting its markets within the Caribbean (Barty-King 1979: 346–347). Thus, even while a Public Utilities Commission was established to regulate the sector in some territories, regulation was *ad hoc* and the firm operated with much freedom, tempered only in some instances (e.g., Jamaica) by factors such as ideological shifts in government.

Bilateralism in Policy Development and Regulation: 1980–1995

The 1980s marked the start of one of the most interesting phases in the development of regional telecoms with major policy changes that modified the structure of the industry. These were promulgated by a number of economic factors.

The 1980s saw the Caribbean reeling from the effects of economic crisis brought on largely by the oil shocks of the 1970s. Additionally, efforts toward digitization in the early 1980s, undertaken in response to agitation among businesses for improved quality and capacity, had seen many governments entering into arrangements with the International Monetary Fund (IMF) and World Bank to fund upgrades. Inability to meet the payments helped to motivate governments to contemplate off-loading some of their critical infrastructure including telecommunications as a means of reducing debt and the size of government (Minto 2009: 55; Payton 2003: 100). States such as Jamaica, Barbados, Grenada, Belize, Guyana, and T&T were among the countries who found themselves in this position (Pierre 2008: 41).

As such, Structural Adjustment Programmes adopted at the end of the 1980s saw the privatization of major sectors and government-owned entities (Brown 2005: 1; also see Pierre 2008). Proceeds from privatization went directly to the IMF as part of Jamaica's debt reduction efforts (IDB 2003: 3; McCormick 1993: 8; Minto 2009). The policy of privatization continued with Belize privatizing its sector in 1989 but this time to British Telecom who purchased 25% of Belize Telecommunications Limited.

The new terms for the sector were concluded in licenses signed individually between C&W and governments which saw the amalgamation of international and domestic services. These granted very liberal terms to C&W, particularly in a context where countries in Latin America and elsewhere were under discussions to liberalize their communications industry (Pierre 2008; SRC 2011a, 2011b). As such, while policy developments are not unique and represent reform adopted elsewhere (e.g., Wellenius 1993), they have tended to take place a decade or two behind the developed world. Among the terms across the region were exemption from some duties and the freedom to higher expats, cross-subsidization to allow for reduced local call rates, virtual monopoly over the industry through renewable contracts in some cases lasting for 25 years, very little regulatory restraint or minimum service standard requirements, and guaranteed rate of return. In Jamaica, the terms of the arrangements were encapsulated in five licenses, namely, the All Island Telephone License of 1988, which guaranteed a 17.5%–20% return on its investments. These established dominance in telecommunications, telegraphy, wireless, and telex (Minto 2009: 40). Even so, expansion of the network was done at the government's expense with governments promising to assist the firm in securing loans for investments (e.g., Minto 2009), there in demonstrating a serious flaw in the policy toward the development of the industry. Serious flaws were further demonstrated in the fact that these conditions meant that little incentives were actually provided for the firm to develop the industry, since its profitability was essentially guaranteed under policy (Insight 2001). Dunn and Gooden (2007: 38) also note these terms to be liberal given that it would take 7–10 years for the firm to recuperate its investments.

Discussions that shaped industry policy were characterized by secrecy and bilateralism, a pattern that defined policy discussions in the communications industry up to the end of the 1990s with the regulatory and policy space being exclusive. In this case, the management of telecommunications was still absent of influence by nongovernmental groups with the operator focusing on maintaining profits as opposed to making improvements.

C&W was seen as the likely inheritor of industry in most cases, given its history in the region, the fact that it was well resourced and its close relationship with policy makers (Minto 2009; see also Pierre 2008; Wint 1996). Indeed, policy and regulation of the communications industry could be said to have been captured by C&W. This was facilitated largely by the paternalistic relationship, which the firm had built with the Caribbean through its corporate philanthropy. Here many government ministers and their relatives had benefitted in one form or the other from the Company (e.g., as former scholarship recipients or employees). Furthermore, given the importance of the firm to the countries, governments had a stake in the success of these firms (e.g., given cross-subsidization or part ownership). For instance, C&W in the 1990s was the largest corporate taxpayer in some countries and a significant employer and earner of foreign exchange (Minto 2009: 37). As such, it was not uncommon for industry policy to be geared toward the success of the operators or for the firm to direct sector policy. For example, requests for rate increases were met with little resistance (Minto 2009). Indeed, as has been argued elsewhere, the resources at the firm's disposal rivaled that of Jamaica (the largest of the English-speaking countries) and as such it was not necessarily a surprise that governments allowed C&W to play a major role in directing industry policy. Furthermore, the firm's benevolence also meant that it had wide appeal within the region.

By the mid-1990s, the firm operated in 15 English-speaking territories. It had as much as 100% ownership of nine and a low of 49% (in T&T) of telecoms in these countries, controlling international and satellite access to the region (Dunn and Gooden 2007: 37). As such, it is not far flung to assert that the history of C&W in the region is essentially the story of Caribbean communications, at least up to the end of the 1980s. Further, the story of the communications industry up to the 1990s was also mainly that of telecoms, given the low development of value-added services and ICTs more generally, across the region. The policy of the 1960s and 1970s was very much about reducing C&W's ownership. The 1980s and 1990s were more about extending C&W's ownership. While policy shifts in the 1960s were about ideology and politics, the reforms of the 1980s were more about economics.

Privatization continued across the region into the early 1990s. For instance, Guyana Telecommunication Corporation was privatized between 1990 and 1991 with the government retaining 20% and Atlantic Telecommunication Network gaining 80% (Persaud 2006). This essentially transformed the state monopoly into the private monopoly of Guyana Telephone and Telegraph limited. The policy in many cases was for governments to maintain some ownership in the private monopoly as a means of maintaining some direction over these companies, especially given the absence of independent regulators. This also allowed a route to facilitate regulation and operation in the public interest. Nonetheless, governments did little in the way of regulation or offering any restraints to these firms with monopoly guarantees resulting in little motivation toward operational efficiency.

This is not to suggest, however, that nothing happened in terms of the development of the sector with new services such as direct distance dialing and call waiting. Nevertheless, prices remained high with little guidelines for the minimum levels of service provision and little room for public participation in the policy and regulatory processes. The problems were exacerbated by difficulties in accessing telecoms for domestic services. It is not surprising then that the sector at the end of the 1990s was still fairly underdeveloped and infrastructure across the region outdated. Spiller and Sampson (1996: 75) have noted that regulatory reform and privatization provided C&W with the incentives to invest in upgrading the sector but ironically this was not the case, given the relative underdeveloped nature of the industry at the start of the twenty-first century.

Reform in the Regulation, Management, and Structure of the Communications Industry: 1995–2010

By the mid-1990s, however, a shift in the tide and fortunes of C&W was beginning to emerge across the region marking the start of the most far-reaching policy developments to date. This period witnessed the World Trade Organization taking steps toward encouraging member states to liberalize their telecommunications regimes, after it took on negotiations on services in the 1980s. This was in the form of the General Agreement on Trade and Services (GATS) (see Fredebeul-Krein and Fretag for a comprehensive review of the GATS 1997: 477–491). A Negotiating Group on Basic Telecommunications was set up in 1994 to design a framework for liberalizing telecommunications (Lodge and Stirton 2001, 2002). The result of the negotiations came into force in 1998 with six Caribbean states signing up to the GATS and pledging specific timelines on when they would liberalize their national infrastructure (Stern 2006). These were Jamaica, Dominica, Grenada, T&T, and Antigua and Barbuda.

These instructions provided opportunities for regional governments to make policy shifts under the guise of being pushed by these international organizations in a game of blame shifting (Minto 2009: 122). T&T's signing saw the establishment of a multi-sectoral Working Group on Telecommunications, a move noted as the beginning of a "formal and structured approach to telecommunications sector planning" (Mitchell 2007: 17). The group carried out its activities with the advice of an International Telecommunications Union (ITU) consultant. Among the emphases of the groups was the need to liberalize as a means of increasing exports, job creation, as well as recommendations for the establishment of a telecommunications act and an independent regulator. Barbados signed on to the GATS and saw its moves to liberalize as fulfillment of its obligations even while local imperatives acted to inform the process. For instance, developments have also been informed by a desire to shore up the services sector, thus improving job creation and the competitiveness of regional economies (Mitchell 2007; Schmid 2006).

Public awareness of issues, such as the benefits of competition, was also on the rise. New players also wanted to enter the market and saw existing policies and C&W's dominance as a hindrance. These agitated for governments to review the regulation and structure of the industry. The desire for reduced costs from consumers also fueled the desire for reform and strengthened governments' hand vis-à-vis the operator. Governments recognized the need to advance policies and regulations in order to modernize the industry and to benefit from the promised economic gains. Technological advances also challenged the rationale for maintaining monopoly control. The guiding philosophy behind transformation in policy and practice across the region was the view that competition would best serve the interests of the various stakeholders and that monopoly was not conducive to growth and modernization of confidence would increase under a deregulated and demonopolized regime.

With the coming together of these points, the telecommunications and ICT environment have seen remarkable transformation within the last two decades. The international finance and development institutions played a major role in the liberalization of the telecommunications sector in the region. The drafting of T&T's Telecommunications Act was aided by the ITU and the Commonwealth Telecommunications Union, while interestingly the Inter-American Development Bank (IDB) provided funding for the government to secure the services of a US-based law firm to bolster its negotiating position with C&W toward securing the firm's agreement to liberalize the sector. The IDB also helped with the creation of an ICT roadmap (Mitchell 2007: 17–19). Digicel's entry was important as this monopoly breaker, then went on to break C&W's control in a number of territories, using Jamaica as the point of entry.

Industry reform during this period saw phased liberalization and competition throughout the region, beginning with Jamaica from 1999. C&W lobbied most actively to control the profitable international market while competition was introduced in mobile telephony, Internet, and value-added services. Previous license arrangements between governments and the incumbent (C&W) required the latter to agree to changes before licenses could be adjusted. Failure to adhere to this requirement would have triggered compensation rights and possibly legal battles, which the cash-strapped governments across the region wanted to avoid. The preference was therefore for negotiated as opposed to forced reforms. This is not to suggest that C&W was supportive of reform given the implications for its operations (i.e., reduced power, market share, and profits). In Jamaica, this was to see the firm challenging the government in court (Minto 2009). Indeed, the agreement to have phased reform as well as the very service area liberalized at each level represented an attempt by government to adopt a conciliatory approach with the firm. The negotiations marked the end of the legal battles between the two. In countries such as Barbados, the first area to be opened was Internet services with international long distance and fixed line services being opened to competition last.

Reforms were achieved through the introduction of new legislation as well as the revision of others. For example, telecommunications and fair trading acts were introduced across the region. In the main, the legal and regulatory frameworks covered pricing, licensing, spectrum management, dominance, interconnection, access, customer service, and institutional arrangements (e.g., independent regulator or regulation by the line minister), general offences, and universal service (e.g., see Jamaica Telecommunications Act of 2001; for Guyana see Brennan 2014). Barbados's act (the Telecommunications Act 2001-36 CAP282B) passed in 2001 established an independent regulator and allowed for interconnection across networks. These upgrades represented much needed advancement in the legal framework governing the industry, given the fact that existing legislations were outdated. In the case of Jamaica, for example, regulation was facilitated by an 1893 Telegraphs Act that preceded much of the developments in technology, including value-added services (Lodge and Stirton 2002). Thus, even while the early legislation had granted monopoly over telecommunications, it was always unclear as to whether this extended to mobile and value-added services, even though C&W argued this to be the case (Minto 2009).

The license agreements between the firms and governments exist as another major layer in the regulatory and policy framework in the industry. The islands are characterized by a strong respect for property rights, and as such, arrangements have tended to be framed in contracts to prevent either party reneging on agreements. The tendency toward framing policies in contracts has also been deemed necessary given the flexibility of the legislature to change agreements at will (see e.g., Levy and Spiller 1994: 211). The Telco's and new entrants have therefore focused much attention on the phase of policy formulation and on contract negotiations given the implications for their performance.

Furthermore, whereas the regulation of the sector had been tasked to the line minister, this has since been handed over to independent regulatory authorities (IRA) in some countries. Barbados and Guyana are among those territories where regulation is carried out by a competition regulator. In the past, the minster did not always have the information or expertise to regulate the operators. With the opening up of the industry and the entry of new players, as well as the proliferation of new technologies and services, policies and regulations have become more complex, demanding more focused attention. The emphasis on fair trading and independent regulation has also contributed to the distancing between the policy making on one hand and implementation and regulatory functions. The establishment of IRAs has also helped to reduce the influence over policy previously exercised by C&W and operators, generally through their political influence (see Minto 2009). As such, policy-making functions were vested in the office of the prime minister and line ministry with regulators making recommendations to government. Where both an IRA and a competition regulator exists (as in Jamaica), there tends to be an arrangement where the sector regulator maintains main responsibilities for regulation with the competition regulator stepping in rarely and mainly on matters directly relating to competition. Along with the spectrum or national frequency management units (responsible for managing radio frequency) and licenses, laws, and sale agreements, these form the main policy and regulatory governance institutions and mechanisms governing the communications industry across the region.

The next section considers some of the major developments more closely at the level of individual states. The coverage here reflects the experiences of some of the main countries in the region and act as specific examples of some of the more general points made above. They demonstrate some of the specific issues and processes involved in formulating communications policies and regulating the sector across the region. They also demonstrate the role of international actors in bolstering the position of governments in small and developing states vis-à-vis a powerful multinational with resources to rival those of the state (Minto 2009). The review starts with the case of the regional grouping of the Organization of Eastern Caribbean States (OECS), given the uniqueness of the arrangements, regionally and globally.

Major Developments in the Policy and Management of the Communications Industry in the Organisation of Eastern Caribbean States

The development of communications and, more generally, ICT policy in the Organisation of Eastern Caribbean States (OECS), a subgrouping of nine countries within the wider CARICOM merits specific attention in this coverage.* More broadly, the experiences here suggest how small states can maximize their impact via collective action. The case also helps to indicate the level of dissatisfaction with monopolies and conditions in the industry across the region and hence the imperative for reform.

The communications landscape at the end of the 1990s was typified by high prices and characterized by a monopoly felt to be indifferent and out of touch with the vision and ambition of OECS economies, particularly the need to diversify away from agriculture into services (see Hector 2006). The focus was on economic liberalization with telecommunications reform being viewed as key.

A practical threat to the status quo came from Dominica in the 1990s when a local entrepreneur brought a case against the state for denying his company a telecommunications license. This was seen as a denial of his constitutional right to freedom of expression. This first challenge to C&W's legal monopoly paved the way for the reform of policies in the sector and was seen as a barometer for sentiments toward the monopoly. While the case was thrown out, the court nonetheless, placed the case in the context of whether a monopoly was necessary for the provision of telecommunications on the island, that is, whether this was in the public interest and requested that the High Court make a decision on the matter.

Collectively, these developments hinted at the weaknesses in the C&W monopoly and particularly in a local environment that was becoming more aware of alternatives. The impending expiration of some of the licenses with C&W also motivated a new approach with heads of states taking the decision to approach C&W, not unilaterally as in the past but jointly with other OECS states. In so doing, strengthening their hand. However, support was initially muted given the financial implications for liberalization and privatization on national budgets, particularly where governments, including that in Grenada, had shares in the national monopolies. Nevertheless, the islands moved to negotiate with C&W who requested roughly US$97 million to give up its monopoly. Both players were prepared to go to court but were able to avoid doing so with the legal framework being provided in the Telecommunications Acts of 2000 and 2001 allowing for C&W's monopoly rights to be rescinded. Interestingly, while telecommunications reform has been guided by a strong rationale for protecting the consumer, the public was not supportive of demonopolization in all cases, and, in fact, countries such as St. Lucia witnessed public demonstration against abolishing C&W's monopoly partly out of fear of job losses (Minto 2009).

The defining feature of the communications policy landscape was the formation of the Eastern Caribbean Telecommunications Authority (ECTEL) in 2000, an initiative supported by the World Bank. ECTEL was charged with the responsibility of overseeing the liberalization of the telecommunications regimes in the OECS. The Treaty creating the ECTEL, originally signed by five members of the OECS, allows for each member country to have a National Telecommunications Regulatory Commission (NTRC), which falls under the Ministry of Telecommunications, who in turn has responsibility for operational issues.

ECTEL is among the more unique organizational structures in the global regulatory landscape given its multi-country status. An interesting provision in ECTEL's Treaty is a provision for states within the OECS and the wider region to join this regulatory body. This is important since not all OECS states are members of ECTEL (e.g., Antigua and Barbuda, though they have sought ECTEL's advice in formulating policies for their own environment).

---

* Please see the following for more detailed information on the economies, regulatory reform, and competition processes in the OECS: ITU (n.d.) and Hector (2006).

More broadly, liberalization policy in the OECS has had the effect of improving access to telecommunications and related services for customers at lower prices. Investments have increased with the emergence of new areas of economic activity, including the sale of service equipment, including handsets to customers. Other achievements include the opening up of space for businesses who are now able to leverage ICTs (e.g., for marketing and e-commerce).

Policy reform has also seen states moving to introduce their own Internet Exchange Points (IXPs). For instance, Dominica introduced its IXP—Dominica National Internet Exchange Point—in February 2013. This was done in partnership with the NTRC, the three local Internet Service Providers—Marpin 2K4, Lime Dominica, and SAT Communications, along with Packet Clearing House, a US-based firm (ECTEL 2013). Again, the power of partnerships, not only at the level of government but also the private sector and international partners, in developing the local communications industry is highlighted. Such public–private partnerships are important as a response to low human and financial capacity in small and developing states. Positive results have included faster movement in Internet traffic.

Nonetheless, the bright start to the implementation of reform policies has slowed in recent years as mobile prices, while experiencing some decline still remain relatively high. Furthermore, increased investments witnessed in the early years of reform slowed in the late 2000, a feature of the global economic downturn from the end of the first decade of the twenty-first century (see SRC 2011c). While increases were once again reported in subsequent years, the cost of services such as fixed broadband remains high (ECTEL 2014). While many policy documents and consultations have emerged on number portability, this has yet to be realized, and the passing of various legislation and plans has not seen full implementation. For example, T&T has yet to establish a competition commission after the passing of its Fair Trading Act in 2006.

Major Developments in the Policy and Management of the Communications Industry in Jamaica

Jamaica has for the most part been the epicenter of policy reform in the region, acting as the forerunner and indicator of developments that were to come in the region concerning policy, and management and particularly as it regarded the C&W monopoly across the region. The Jamaican case demonstrates the ways in which small states can secure policy reforms vis-à-vis a strong culturally embedded multinational company (i.e., C&W). Namely, by mobilizing local and international support to shift the balance of power in the local policy space. It also suggests a role for personalities and the importance of experience (i.e., in the line minister) in driving policy reforms (see Minto 2009 for a detailed discussion of these points). Thus, as will be shown here, it is not just about the policies but the existence of a policy champion which determines success.*

Signs of a shift in the mood and desire to change the status quo in telecommunications came in 1993 when a letter from the prime minister promising to update the 1893 Act to grant C&W legal exclusivity over the entire industry was leaked. This was in return for the firm extending its ownership of the telecoms monopoly by buying additional shares from a cash-strapped government (Minto 2009: 46). This drew public outcry and the government's move away from modifying the law. The reaction signaled the breaking of C&W's capture of industry policy and the start of the march to liberalization.

---

* See Dunn and Minto-Coy 2012; Minto 2009; Spiller and Sampson 1996 for more detailed accounts of the policy and regulatory developments in the Jamaican communications sector.

By 1997, the government had moved to introduce an IRA, the Office of Utilities Regulation in a further bid to introduce some distance between itself and the firm. This body was to play an important role in the policy space, helping to inform industry policy and regulation. Additional government action in the form of the signing of the GATS also signaled the change. Indeed, the actual reforms undertaken reflected the content of the GATS reform agenda, with a pledge to reform the industry by 2000. This was 10 years earlier than the government had pledged with the signing of the agreement adding weight to the government's hand in negotiating with C&W. The minister also went directly to C&W's head offices in London and the British government to secure support for industry reform. These moves helped to end the court case that C&W had brought against the government of Jamaica to prevent liberalization.

In the end, C&W agreed to negotiate and concluded a heads of agreement with the government in 1999 detailing the path to phased liberalization. While signaling policy and status quo changes in the sector, the approach to policy development here was still characterized by bilateralism with some details for the negotiations remaining private. The Telecommunications Act that emerged in 2001 reflected the terms of the agreement (Minto 2008).

The line minister played a key role in directing policy in the late 1990s and early 2000s. This minister was a lawyer who had previously headed the Fair Trading Commission. He was therefore more knowledgeable of the issues involved in liberalization and aware of the benefits of competition. He was also pivotal in seeking international support for local reforms. Whereas former ministers were complicit with the firm (Spiller and Sampson 1996; Dunn and Gooden 1997), in this instance, there was a willingness to break the firm's monopoly and in so doing mobilizing international support behind local reforms.

Jamaica is now more advanced in terms of the development of policies and legislations when compared to other countries in the region. Indeed, successive policies have sought to address some of the gaps of former efforts. For instance, the rural urban divide in access and low connectivity for domestic consumers were hallmarks of the industry up to the 1990s (Dunn and Gooden 1997; Minto 2009). These were seen in the absence of universal service obligations and low requirements for service delivery. Subsequent policies have aimed at addressing these, while liberalization allowed for increased access via mobile phones. The Universal Service Fund approved in 2005 also facilitates expansion in access to broadband via the establishment of community access points, a feature that also characterizes other countries in the region. Additional policies have also sought to address cyber security, lotto scamming, data privacy, and other policy areas that have emerged from liberalization.

Moves have also been made toward the development of e-government in Jamaica. GovNet has for instance been adopted to facilitate the transfer of information across. Other governments have also moved to adopt e-government in their interface with citizens and among government ministries and departments. Positive results have included the introduction of an electronic business registration form in 2014 which helped to increase the ease in starting a business (from 6 to 4 days).

Regional Governance of the Communications Industry

Beyond the OECS, regional organizations have also featured in the policy and regulatory landscape. At the wider level is CARICOM, which has encouraged member states to increase their attention to ICTs broadly (see Dunn and Thomas 2009). Heads of governments have also been encouraged and made pledges at the CARICOM level to developing national ICTs policies. Renewed focus on ICTs has come from the CARICOM given a number of long-standing problems ranging from climate change to economic growth with telecoms and ICTs being viewed as a player in addressing these challenges. As such, ICTS have ratcheted up on regional policy agendas over the years and has been noted as the "new frontier for regional integration" (Caribbean Life 2014).

Toward this end, mainly since 2013, there has been a focusing on the development of a single ICT space by 2016 as a crucial facilitator of the regional integration envisioned in the Caribbean Single Market and Economy. This will focus on creating digital citizens, engaging the Diaspora, spectrum management, building public–private partnerships and cyber security issues, and building upon the 2011 Regional Digital Development Strategy (Guardian 2014).

Other institutions include the Caribbean Telecommunications Union (CTU) established in 1989 and tasked with implementing ICT policy objectives agreed by the heads of CARICOM. The CTU has encouraged countries to initiate their own IXPs which has seen Dominica, among others, moving to do the same. The CTU also assists countries to secure competence to inform reforms in their own landscapes, for example, helping to source expertise for the development of local IXPs as well as by organizing training workshops. The ICTs champion, tasked with driving the policy agenda across the region, has been appointed by CARICOM. The pace at which reforms have been introduced across the region since the early 2000s is, like the national level, slow and laborious with lofty desires often not being matched by actual practice and implementation.* Other regional actors include the Organisation of Caribbean Utility Regulators (OOCUR) and the Caribbean Association of National Telecoms Organisations (CANTO), representing their respective constituents (see SRC 2011: 2; Noguera 1997).

For media and broadcasting services, the Caribbean Broadcasting Union (CBU) was formed in 1970 to foster cooperation across radio and television systems across the region. The CBU represents around 34 countries including CARICOM territories and Canada, as well as territories without full independence, including the DOMS, British and Dutch territories, and their respective metropoles. Another regional institution, the Caribbean News Agency (CANA), a regional news agency, emerged in the independence period 1976 to replace the British-owned Reuters News Agency (see Brown 1995). The functioning of these bodies has been severely hampered by insufficient funding.

Overview of the Developments in Broadcasting

The effects of liberalization and privatization of the communications sector on broadcasting is also visible across the region. For example, Brown (2000) suggests a pattern of conglomeration both at the national and regional levels, as well as the entry of more players and regulations in the market. From the single publicly owned national television and radio stations of the 1960s, into 1980s, many countries across the region now experience competition and therefore choice in these areas. For instance, Jamaica was to see the Radio Jamaica Limited move to own three radio stations and a television station. The latter had increased to four by 2014. Jamaica now has around 40 cable operators and T&T has been noted as having close to 38 radio stations up to 2010 (Farrell 2010).

The policy of opening broadcasting in the 1980s to present has seen a reduction in the number of public service broadcasters; this as governments move to reduce their ownership and investments in the industry. The space has therefore opened up for the entry of private players whom have stepped in to fill the void. Nevertheless, Barbados has maintained the government in public service

---

* It is interesting to note, however, that the idea of a single ICT space had been mooted as early as 1989 without much action toward realizing this idea.

broadcasting, in what is now a duopoly in the provision of cable television services. Television stations in Guyana are also government owned and up to at least 2010, government had a monopoly in radio broadcasting.

The structural changes witnessed in the telecommunications industry were therefore to also take route in the broadcasting sector as more private operators entered the market. New operators include cable operators who themselves have also diversified their services and products by going into non-traditional areas such as telecommunications. Flow/Columbus Communications, the dominant cable operator in the region (Farrell 2010), is an epitome of the opportunities as well as the effect of convergence as the company now provides digital telephony, cable TV, and Internet services to customers across five Caribbean nations (Jamaica, Grenada, Barbados, Curacao, and T&T). The streaming of content online has also allowed for the diversification in audiences and income streams for the industry, as access is increased beyond local to the regional, international, and Diaspora markets. Persons outside the region are now more able to participate in home affairs and keep up-to-date by accessing content from national media houses online.

Government's main role in broadcasting across the region is now more one of regulation and spectrum management bodies and broadcasting commissions. The opening up of telecoms has enabled the development of broadcasting policies, though the approach is one of promoting freedom in content—the advent of television in the 1960s had seen the discussions around the need for local content. This has been a consistent observation through the years (Brown 1987, 1995; Dunn and Minto-Coy 2010, 2012). As such, like telecommunications, broadcasting largely remains an import-intensive business with opportunities for international trade and reducing balance of payments via export of locally generated content and applications being lost. Untapped potential remains in cultural and creative industries (see, for example, Nurse et al. 2007). Further, while intellectual property regimes have been established across the region, much is wanting as it relates to implementation, with lost revenue to developers of local content from practices such as piracy.

The State of the Communications Industry in 2014

Thus up to 2014, with the exception of Guyana, most of the communications sectors across the region had been liberalized. In Guyana, as in many other countries in the region, the competitor in the mobile market is Digicel. Internet services, one of the first to be liberalized officially, has also seen the entry of many players across the Caribbean. As seen in the case of Jamaica, the early legislative policy arrangements that secured liberalization and privatization have since been followed by the introduction of other policies and regulations to address emerging areas that have been activated by earlier reforms. Included here are the 2010 Cyber Security Act and the 2013 Law Reform (fraudulent transactions) Special Provision Act to address advanced fee fraud (i.e., Lotto Scamming). These include the introduction of an Electronic Transactions and a Data Protection Bill to encourage e-commerce and protect personal information in 2012 (T&T). The introduction of these pieces of legislation has gone some way to addressing perceived regulatory and legislative gaps. Among the main features of the policy agendas across the region has been the framing of reform initiatives in law through a number of Telecommunications Act. These have helped to formalize and institutionalize policy reforms across the region, also guarding against backtracking if there is a change in leadership.

International development institutions have also featured in the development of the regional communications industry. These bodies provided the motivation, guide, and in some case funding for policy developments. Their support emboldened governments across the region to transform their industries (Minto 2009: 50).

Reforms have lowered the barriers to entry resulting in an increase in operators in all areas of the communications industry, reduced prices, and improved quality and access. In most cases, competition thrives in mobile telecommunications with most markets having two operators. With the convergence of telecommunications, data, and video, emphasis has now shifted to ICTs and attention to matters such as e-commerce and e-governance. In T&T, for example, the Ministry of Public Administration and Information was created to provide more focused and harmonized development of ICT policy and management. Policy making has also become more open, with more stakeholders from within and outside government.

National development plans also speak to the direction of communications and ICTs more generally and its place in leading development in the region, including Jamaica's vision 2030. Increased emphasis has been placed on broadband access in the region in making further advancement in the sector. For example, T&T's 2007 budget gave short-term provisions such as two year tax exemptions (from VAT) for telecommunications equipment to encourage the roll out of broadband services (Mitchell 2007). T&Ts 2003–2008 NICTS helped to deliver greater e-government, but the extent of reforms envisioned had not been realized in 2010, while in spite of efforts in pushing e-commerce usage among business still remain relatively low (see Government of Trinidad and Tobago 2012: 17). This remains the case across the region. Further, while access to mobile telephony and smart devices have increased, the latter are not fully activated with a need for increased usage of these devices in transacting business. As such, the "I" in ICTs still needs to be more fully activated toward the realization of knowledge and e-economies across the region.

In line with international trends and developments, regional and national policies have also considered the role of ICTs in development, with national ICT strategies being drawn up across the region. However, to date, many of the pledges in these documents have not been realized and others such as Guyana had up to early 2014 yet to develop a comprehensive national ICT policy. The Jamaican case also demonstrates the need for sustained reforms. Thus, whereas policy reforms of 1998–2004 had seen the country improving in international ICT indicators, less attention has since been placed on the sector resulting in the country being overtaken by many of its Caribbean neighbors (Table 16.1). Access to the Internet and mobile penetration are at notable levels but still some way behind developed standards (i.e., for Internet access), while the high mobile penetration rate reflects the absence of number portability and roaming regionally (see Table 16.1).

E-Government

The following presentation also warrants a closer review of the region's performance in the area of e-government as another indicator of developments in ICTs and given the thrust to improve e-government as a means of reducing the cost of government, increasing access and inclusion. Governments have moved to establish Community Internet Access points, as well as to introduce web sites to allow for the interface between itself and citizens (Durrant 2002). Features include the payment of taxes online, registering of complaints, and ordering official documents such as birth certificates online, while citizens can gather information on government policies and so on.

Figures 16.1 and 16.2 indicate the region's performance along certain indicators. Antigua and Barbuda, Barbados, and T&T remain some of the best performers in the region and globally. The figures demonstrate a disparity in placing among the various countries and suggest a link between poverty, level of development and e-government as suggested, for instance, in a visual comparison between countries such as Haiti and Barbados.

Table 16.1　Key Indicators in Caribbean ICTs

	Mobile Subscriptions/100 Inhabitants	Internet Usage/100 Inhabitants	Fixed (Wired) Broadband Subscriptions/100 Inhabitants			
Country	2001	2012	2001	2012	2001	2012
Antigua and Barbuda	31.66	143.01	6.48	59.00	0	4.64
Bahamas	19.98	80.65	11.80	71.75	1.37	–
Barbados	19.80	122.52	11.94	73.33	0	23.09
Belize	15.97	53.21	–	25.00	0	3.08
Bermuda	21.12	139.54	47.51	91.30	0	–
Cayman Islands	39.25	171.68	0	74.13	0	33.57
Dominica	11.07	152.47	13.25	55.18	0.25	11.86
Grenada	6.30	121.35	5.13	42.09	0	13.69
Guyana	10.07	68.78	13.21	33.00	0	3.67
Haiti	1.05	59.91	0.34	9.80	0	–
Jamaica	22.95	96.27	3.86	46.50	0.12	4.32
St. Lucia	1.70	125.50	8.18	48.63	–	13.59
Trinidad and Tobago	20.13	140.84	15.38	59.52	0	13.75
Developing world	7.90	82.10	2.80	27.40	0.20	5.40
Developed world	47.10	116.00	29.40	73.10	2.20	25.70

Source: ITU, Available at: http://www.itu.int/en/ITU-D/Statistics/Pages/stat/default.aspx.

On the whole, however, the region's performance is middling in terms of global standards and matches its status as largely comprising middle income countries. As a comparison, the top leaders in the UN's world e-government development index included Korea (0.9283) and Singapore at 0.8474. Botswana stood at 0.4186 for the 2012 period with the world average being 0.4882 (UN 2012).

Ultimately, the imperative for e-government remains urgent in the region with a need for this issue to move from "window dressing" (Rubino-Hallman and Hanna 2007) to having a real and transformative effect on the quality of public governance in the region. For instance, government web sites are in some instances not interactive or are outdated. Additionally, existing legislation prevents further development of e-commerce in government. For instance, existing laws prevent the Government of Jamaica from issuing official receipts online for e-transactions. As such, efficiency gains remain inaccessible for governments and clients with the legislative environment stymieing the development of innovation within governance. Nevertheless, the performance of countries such as Barbados and improvements made by T&T do suggest that the region has the capacity to make necessary improvements in this area.

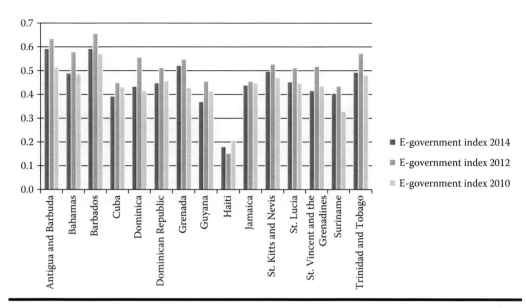

Figure 16.1 Multi-year comparison of e-government index* for select Caribbean countries. (Data from UNPAC, *UN Public Administration Country Studies*, Available at: http://unpan3.un.org/egovkb/en-us/Data/Compare-Countries, 2014.)

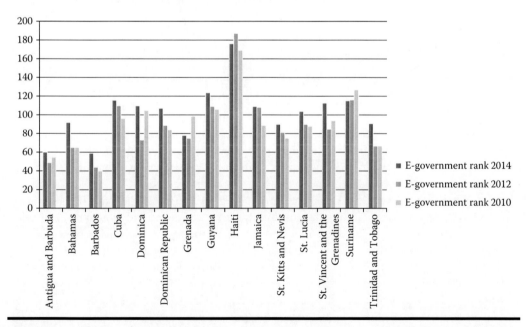

Figure 16.2 Multi-year comparison of e-government rank for various Caribbean countries.[†] (Data from UNPAC, *UN Public Administration Country Studies*, Available at: http://unpan3.un.org/egovkb/en-us/Data/Compare-Countries, 2014.)

---

* The UN's e-government development index (EGDI) measures both the willingness and capacity of governments to utilize ICTs for the delivery of inclusive, accountable, and citizen-centric public services (UN 2014: 185).

† Relative rankings of e-government development of all members states of the United Nations.

Future Developments

Thus, overall, the benefits of reforms have yet to bring the expected results on economies in the region. In spite of the growth and improvements noted above, ICT policies in the region have still not yielded the level of dynamism and improvement needed to sufficiently transform Caribbean economies.

A number of areas are prime for further action if governments are to redress some of the challenges identified. Included here is the need for action in activating the "I" in ICTs, a more vital for moving the region from digital consumers to producers. Policy is also still needed to address certain gaps and challenges including access to capital for local entrepreneurs and particularly if viable spaces are to be created for small businesses in what is now an industry dominated by large players. Opportunities have also been opened up for increased engagement and communication with the Diaspora. These include opportunities for crowd-funding and sourcing. Policy here could help to provide platforms for linking entrepreneurs at home with funders in the Diaspora. Further challenges include cyber security, need for data protection, lotto scamming, and the use of the Internet in the conduct of transnational crimes. Governments across the region need to increase the pace of their response to these emerging developmental issues which threatens the viability of the region.

Further steps also need to be taken toward reducing the cost of telecommunications and ICTs generally. Toward this end, more islands (or unitedly as a region) to establish their own IXPs to fuel indigenous innovation and growth. The possibilities for reduced prices and faster speeds are promising, likewise for distance learning and for universities and other learning institutions to integrate their multimedia content in the local IXPs (ECTEL February 2013). The focus on consumer protection also needs to be renewed. Policies also need to be more mindful of the role of ICTs as an enabler for growth and economic activity and how this can help the region participate in the digital economy more aggressively. Importantly too, formerly telecommunications focused legislation and policies need to be revisited in light of the evolution toward ICTs. Legislations passed largely since 2000 are already outdated (see Dunn and Minto-Coy 2010; Minto-Coy 2011: 137) and therefore require further updates. For instance, Jamaica is finally making precise steps to introduce a long awaited new telecommunications act by 2015. The success of policies, as demonstrated in experiences such as the OECS and Jamaica, also suggests the importance of a champion or an influential figure who has the resources and capacity to drive through policy developments, negotiate with and seek consensus among stakeholders.

The time is also relevant for consideration of a regional market in ICTs. The European Commission is already demonstrating the possibilities here with the introduction of regional rules for operators and efforts to reduce roaming charges across the region. Benefits have accrued to consumers and the economies of these countries through greater cooperation in the area of telecoms and ICT regulation and policy. Calls have been made over the years for greater levels of coordination in the Caribbean but this has been slow in coming, in spite of the gains regarding efficiency of scale and other benefits that accrue from such coordination. Talks at the national and regional levels need to be backed by tangible action among governments and other stakeholders (including local private actors). The near exhaustion in 2014 of the address pool under Internet Protocol version 4 (IPv4) in the Caribbean wider Latin American region amidst the slow pace in deploying IPv6 is also a telling sign of the slow pace in moving to the next level of reforms in the region. This is the case not only among governments who need to provide the policy direction for private entities to move forward, but also among the latter who to some degree also demonstrate a lack of responsiveness and initiative.

Two other emerging areas are worthy of direct attention here. First, the announcement at the end of 2014 and subsequent regulatory approval of the sale of Columbus Communications* to C&W is an interesting development whose end cannot be fully contemplated in this chapter. Ultimately, though, this development promises an interesting future for the policy and regulatory landscape, certainly as it relates to the potential resurgence of C&W as a dominant player, implications for competition, choice and the price reductions, and other gains made since the late 1990s. Indeed, the acquisition has already been hailed by C&W as significant to its strategy of securing greater presence, scale, and scope in the region (CWC 2014). Second, net neutrality,[†] which has more recently become an issue for the region, will be another interesting area to watch with operators such as Digicel moving at the end of 2014 to prevent over-the-top (OTT) service operators from providing such services (e.g., Internet Telephone) over its network without compensation.

Finally, the data revolution has facilitated the emergence of new technologies and concepts such as cloud government and open government. Indeed, the possibilities for citizens across the region to become more informed and empowered through greater access to government, increased accountability and transparency, and, ultimately, better government cannot be underscored. Prospects for entrepreneurship, innovation, and improved performance in business and established sectors such as agriculture and tourism are also not to be overlooked in the future development of the sector.[‡]

Conclusion

The chapter has reviewed the development of the policy and management of the communications industry in the Caribbean, focusing largely on the English-speaking region. It detailed the major developments historically ending with a review of the current state of the industry.

Government policy is particularly necessary in the Caribbean given the low development and risk-aversive nature of the private sector. As indicated from the experiences up to the mid-1990s, government policy is necessary in providing the motivation for private operators to make the necessary investments in developing the industry. Policy is also necessary in shaping the future and laying out the steps to be taken in realizing this future.

Government also has a major role to play as funder or at least in helping to identify and secure funding for developments including the role out of broadband. To this end, it must also be noted that some of the delays in implementing policies are not only about the typically slow moving public bureaucracy in the Caribbean but also the wider challenge of funding developmental programs in a developing region. To this end, governments may have to turn more fulsomely to international donors and ironically seek support from large international private firms. However, the lesson from the past is that any such public–private partnership will need to be accompanied by specifications for expected standards and improvements. Such moves would be matched by support for the involvement of local investors.

---

* Columbus International Incorporated (CII) is a privately owned telecommunications and technology firm operating in the Caribbean and Latin America. CII also owns Flow, the dominant triple play (TV, Phone, and Internet) service provider in Jamaica and other Caribbean countries.
† See Ganley and Allgrove (2006) and Kramer et al. (2013) for a more detailed discussion and definition of the term.
‡ For an indicative research in the area of agriculture see McNaughton and Soutar (2015).

References

Ahvenainen, Jorma (1996). *The History of the Caribbean Telegraphs Before the First World War*, Helsinki, Finland: Soumalainen Tiedeakatemia.

Barty-King, Hugh (1979). *Girdle Round the Earth: The Story of Cable and Wireless and Its Predecessors to Mark the Group's Jubilee 1929–1979*, London: Heinemann Ltd.

Brennan, Janis (2014). Modernization and liberalization of the telecommunications sector in Guyana: Presentation of the legal, regulatory and institutional framework, Foley & Haog.

Brown, Aggrey (1987). *TV Programming Trends in the Anglophone Caribbean: The 1980s* (CARIMAC Occasional Paper No. 2). Kingston, Jamaica: University of the West Indies.

Brown, Aggrey (1995). Towards regionalization of new communication services in the CARICOM: A technological free-for-all, *Canadian Journal of Communication*, 20(3).

Brown, Aggrey (2000). Caribbean broadcast training—A strategic perspective, *Paper Prepared for Presentation to the Regional Seminar on Challenges to Broadcasting in the Caribbean*, ACCRA Beach Hotel, Barbados, June 21–22, 2000.

Brown, Aggrey (2005). The internet, cultural networks and diversity of cultural communication: The case of the Caribbean, *Presentation to the Second World Culturelink Conference*, Zagreb, Croatia, June 11, 2005. Available at: http://www.aggreypedia.org/p/prof-browns-writings.html. Accessed on May 8, 2014.

Cable and Wireless Communications. (2010). Our history. Available at: http://www.cwc.com/live/past-present/our-history.html. Accessed on May 20, 2015.

C&W (2014). *Cable & Wireless Communications plc Proposed Acquisition of Columbus International Inc Placing of New Shares*. Available at: www.cwc.com/assets/uploads/files/IR/Transactions/CWC%20%20Columbus%20Transaction%20Announcement%206%November%202014.pdf. Accessed on April 8, 2015.

Caribbean Life (April 30, 2014). New frontier for regional integration, *Caribbean Life*. Available at: www.caribbeanlifenews.com/stories/2014_04_28_internet_governance.html. Accessed on December 15, 2015.

Dunn, Hopeton S. and Gooden, Winston S. (1996). Telecommunications in Jamaica, Virtual Institute of Information, http://www.vii.org/papers/jama.htm. Accessed on April 10, 2014.

Dunn, Hopeton S. and Gooden, Winston (1997). Telecommunications policy making in Jamaica: From state monopoly to private monopoly, in *Telecommunications in Latin America*, Eli Noam (ed.), New York: Oxford University Press, pp. 73–81.

Dunn, Hopeton S. and Minto-Coy, Indianna D. (2010). *The Communications Industry in the Caribbean: Issues, Challenges and Opportunities*. Caribbean Paper No.9. Available at: http://www.cigionline.org/publications/2010/5/communications-industry-caribbean-issues-challenges-and-opportunities. Accessed on November 3, 2014.

Dunn, Hopeton S. and Minto-Coy, Indianna D. (2012). *Ringtones of Opportunity*, Kingston, Jamaica: Ian Randle Publishers.

Dunn, Hopeton S. and Thomas, Michele (2009). Concept paper: Towards the strategic plan on telecommunication services in the CARICOM Single Market and Economy (CSME). Available at: http://www.caricom.org/jsp/single_market/services_regime/concept_paper_telecoms.pdf. Accessed on November 3, 2014.

Durrant, Fay (2002). e-Government and the internet in the Caribbean: An initial assessment, in *Proceedings of the Electronic Government: First International Conference*, Aix-en-Provence, France, September 2–6, 2002, Berlin, Germany: Springer, pp. 101–104.

ECTEL. (February 28, 2013). Dominica launches the Caribbean's newest Internet Exchange Point (IXP), *ECTEL Press Release*. Available at: http://www.ectel.int/news/PressRelease-IXP.pdf. Accessed on November 3, 2014.

ECTEL. (April 30, 2014). Sector investment recorded at $86 million, ECTEL. Available at: www.ectel.int/index.php/161-sector-investment-recorded-at-86-million. Accessed on December 15, 2014.

Farrell, Terrence W. (2010). Caribbean identity and the development of the creative audio-visual industry, *Presented to the One Caribbean Media/Caribbean Tales Symposium on the Production and Global Distribution of Caribbean Video and Film at the Best of Caribbean Tales Film Festival Barbados*. Available at: http://www.onecaribbeanmedia.net/content/45.pdf. Accessed on November 3, 2014.

Fredebeul-Krein, Markus and Freytag, Andreas (2009). Telecommunication and WTO discipline: An assessment of the WTO agreement on telecommunication services, *The WTO, Intellectual Property, E-Commerce and the Internet*, Rohan Kariyawasam (ed.), Cheltenham: Elgar.

Ganley, Paul and Allgrove, Ben (2006). Net neutrality: A user's guide, *Computer Law & Security Review*, 22(6): 454–463.

Gilmore, William (1985). Legal and institutional aspects of the organisation of eastern Caribbean states, *Review of International Studies*, 11(4): 311–328.

Glover, Bill (2010). History of the Atlantic cable and undersea communications, Available at: http://atlantic-cable.com//CableCos/CandW/WIPTC/. Accessed on May 18, 2014.

Government of Trinidad & Tobago. (2012). *T&T National ICT Plan, 2012–2016*, T&T. The National Information and Communication Technology Company Limited (iGovTT). Available at: http://cci.planning.gov.tt/sites/default/files/Trinidad%20and%20Tobago%20Final%20Draft.pdf.

Guardian (March 16, 2014). CARICOM to get single ICT space, *Guardian*. Available at: www.classifieds.guardian.co.tt/business/2014-03-16/caricom-get-single-ict-space. Accessed on November 28, 2014.

Headrick, Daniel (1991). *The Invisible Weapon: Telecommunications and International Politics 1851–1945*, New York: Oxford University Press.

Hector, Cheryl (2006). *Technological advances and competition in the telecommunications sector in the ECTEL member states*, Eastern Caribbean Telecommunications Authority/Economics Department. Available at: oocur.org/Docs/Library/2006/Cheryl%Hector_Technical%20Advances%20and%20Competition.pdf. Accessed on December 15, 2014.

IDB (July 2003). Jamaica: Privatisation and Regulation Challenges in Jamaica, *Economic and Sector Study Series*, Washington, D.C: Inter-American Development Bank.

ITU. Available at: http://www.itu.int/en/ITU-D/Statistics/Pages/stat/default.aspx. Accessed on November 20, 2014.

ITU (n.d.). *The Eastern Caribbean Telecommunications Regulatory Authority: ECTEL*. Available at: https://www.itu.int/ITU-D/treg/Events/Seminars/GSR/DSR/documents/Document17.pdf. Accessed on December 15, 2014.

Kramer, Jan, Wiewiorra, Lukas, and Weinhardt, Christof (2013). Net neutrality: A progress report, *Telecommunications Policy*, 37(9): 794–813.

Levy, Brian and Spiller, Pablo T. (1994). The institutional foundations of regulatory commitment: A comparative analysis of telecommunications regulation, *Journal of Law, Economics and Organization*, 10(2): 201–246.

Lightbourne, Robert C. (1967). *Ministry Paper No. 15: The Jamaica Telephone Company Limited*, Government of Jamaica.

Lodge, Martin and Stirton, Lindsay (2001). Regulating in the interest of the citizen: Towards a single model of regulatory accountability? *Social and Economic Studies*, 50(2): 92–108.

Lodge, Martin and Stirton, Lindsay (2002). Globalisation and regulatory autonomy in small developing states: The case of Jamaican telecommunications reform, *Centre on Regulation and Competition Working Paper Series*, Manchester: Centre on Regulation and Competition.

McCormick, Patricia K. (1993). Caribbean telecommunications: Privatisation and regulation in the information age, Paper presented at the *Caribbean Studies Association, XVIII Annual Conference*, Jamaica, May 24–30.

McNaughton, Matthew and Soutar, David (2015). Agricultural Open Data in the Caribbean, *Technical Centre for Agricultural and Rural Cooperation (CTA) Working Paper*, 15/02. Available at: www.cta.int/images/Open_Data_Carib_new_cover.pdf. Accessed on April 8, 2015.

Minto, Indianna (2009). *Incumbent Response to Telecommunications Reform: The Cases of Jamaica and Ireland, 1982–2007*. London: London School of Economics and Political Science.

Minto-Coy, Indianna (2011). Beyond remittancing: An investigation of the role of telecoms in facilitating and extending the diaspora's contribution to the Caribbean, *Canadian Foreign Policy Journal* 17(2): 129–141.

Mitchell, (2007). Multilateral organisations and Information and Communications Technology (ICT) sector planning in Caribbean economies: Example of Trinidad and Tobago, in *Proceedings of the 8th Annual Conference: Crisis, Chaos and Change: Caribbean Development Challenges in the 21st Century*, March 2007, Sir Arthur Lewis Institute of Social and Economic Research, University of the West Indies, Trinidad & Tobago Available at: http://sta.uwi.edu/conferences/salises/documents/Mitchell%20P.pdf. Accessed on August 25, 2014.

Noguera, Felipe (1997). Telecommunications in the Caribbean, in *Telecommunications in Latin America*, Eli Noam (ed.), New York: Oxford University Press.

Nurse, Keith et al. (2007). The cultural industries in CARICOM trade and development challenges, *Report prepared for the Caribbean Regional Negotiating Machinery*, November 2006. Available at: http://www.acpcultures.eu/_upload/ocr_document/CRNM_Cult%20Ind%20in%20CARICOM_2007.pdf. Accessed on November 28, 2014.

Payton, Paul (2003). Privatization in Jamaica: Success or Failure?, *Journal of Public Sector Management*, 4 (2): 99–116.

Persaud, Badrie (2006). Overview of telecommunication sector Guyana: A policy perspective, http://www.puc.org.gy/pucdocs/presentation/1_OVERVIEW%20OF%20TELECOMMUNICATION%20SECTOR.pdf. Accessed on November 3, 2014.

Pierre, Kestson H. (2008). *Telecommunications in the Caribbean: How Has Change Brought the West Indies. in the Twenty-First Century?* Dissertation, Pennsylvania, PA: The Pennsylvania State University. Available at: search.proquest.com/docview/231507654. Accessed on November 28, 2014.

Rubino-Hallman, Silvana and Hanna, Nagy K. (2007). New technologies for public sector transformation: A critical analysis of e-government initiatives in Latin America and the Caribbean, *Journal of E-Government*, 3(3): 3–39.

Schmid, Linda (2006). Barbados: Telecommunications liberalisation, *Managing the Challenges of WTO Participation: Case Study 4*. Available at: http://www.wto.org/english/res_e/booksp_e/casestudies_e/case4_e.htm#fntext6. Accessed on November 3, 2014.

Shridath Ramphal Centre (SRC) for International Trade Law, Policy and Services. (2011). *Telecommunications Services Sector*. Available at: file:///C:/Users/10016613/Downloads/CAribbean%20Telecommunications%20Policy%20(2).pdf. Accessed on December 15, 2014.

Spiller, Pablo and Sampson, Cezley (1996). Telecommunications regulation in Jamaica, in *Regulations, Institutions, and Commitment: Comparative Studies of Telecommunications*, Brian Levy and Pablo Spiller (eds.), Cambridge: Cambridge University Press, pp.36–78.

Stern, Peter (2006). Assessment of the telecommunications services sector in CARICOM: Convergence issues at the regional and international levels, Prepared for the *Caribbean Regional Negotiating Machinery*.

United Nations (UN). (2012). *United Nations E-Government Survey 2012: E-Government for the People*, New York: United Nations.

UN. (2014). *United Nations E-Government Survey 2014: E-Government for the Future We Want*. Available at http://unpan3.un.org/egovkb/Portals/egovkb/Documents/un/2014-Survey/E-Gov_Complete_Survey-2014.pdf

UNPAC. (2014). *UN Public Administration Country Studies*. Available at: http://unpan3.un.org/egovkb/en-us/Data/Compare-Countries. Accessed on November 3, 2014.

Wellenius, Bjorn (1993). *Telecommunications: World Bank Experience and Strategy*. World Bank Discussions Papers No. 192. Washington, DC: World Bank.

Winseck, Dwayne R. and Pike, Robert M. (2007). *Communication and Empire: Media, Markets and Globalisation 1860–1930*, Durham, NC: Duke University Press.

Wint, Alvin (1996). Pioneering telephone privatisation: Jamaica, *Privatising Monopolies: Lessons from the Telecommunications and Transport Sectors in Latin America*, J.Q. Wilson (ed.), Baltimore, MD: John Hopkins University.

Wint, Alvin (2005). Has the obsolescing bargain obsolesced? Negotiating with foreign investors, in *International Business and Government Relations in the 21st Century*, Robert Grosse (ed.), Cambridge: Cambridge University Press, pp. 317–338.

Chapter 17

Health Service Reform in the Caribbean: The Rise of New Mutualism

Tavis D. Jules and Landis G. Fryer

Contents

Introduction 380
Historical Aspects of Health Service Reforms 381
Historical Overview of the Aspects of Health Reforms 381
The Rise of New Managerialism as a Tool to Reform Health Systems 384
The Legal Aspects of Health Service Reform 385
The Substantive Aspects of Health Service Reform 390
Health Services Under Socialism in Cuba, Jamaica, Guyana, and Grenada 391
The Impact of HIV/AIDS 392
Health as an Enabler of the Free Movement of Skilled Labor 394
Establishment of Health and Family Life Education 396
Focus on Noncommunicable Diseases 397
The Functional Aspects of Health Service Reform: The Rise of New Mutualism 399
Conclusion 407
Bibliography 407

Abstract: This chapter is divided into four sections that discuss the historical, legal, substantive, and functional aspects of health service reforms across the Caribbean. This chapter discusses how health service reforms in the Caribbean are: forged historically by colonial and post-colonial developments; formed legally through various cooperative regional declarations commencing in 1982; developed substantively to address, among several factors, the free movement of Caribbean workers; and was operated functionally through cooperation. While this chapter discusses health reforms in the broadest sense, it also recognizes that several of the reforms grouped under these four major periods run concurrently with other national, regional, and global reforms. Additionally, this chapter provides readers with a comprehensive overview of health services as well as the regional response in dealing with communicable and noncommunicable diseases. It discusses the impact of labor mobility on national health systems and programs within the context of the Caribbean Single Market and Economy (CSME), a system designed to mitigate unforeseen social and economic changes that can devastate national systems. Overall, while the region has made slow progress in achieving the two Millennium Development Goals associated with health reform (maternal health and combating HIV/AIDS), new strategies are emerging in recognition that health service should accommodate prevention and treatment and be multi-sectoral. The chapter concludes by discussing the implications of the post-2015 development agenda or Sustainable Development Goals (SDGs), agenda on national health systems and the rise of institutional coordination and cooperation around health issues.

Introduction

Primary health service is defined as "essential health service based on practical, scientifically sound, and socially acceptable methods and technology made universally accessible to individuals and families in the community through their full participation and at a cost that the community and country can afford to maintain at every stage of their development in the spirit of self-reliance and self-determination" (World Health Organization 1978, p. 3). Therefore, in this chapter we use the terms *health service reform* and *health sector reform* interchangeably to denote significant policy shifts in primary health service at the national, regional, and international levels. Health services in the Caribbean face numerous existing challenges ranging from rising human immunodeficiency virus infection and acquired immune deficiency syndrome (HIV/AIDS) infections, mental health neglect, increased cost and access to medications, and the rise or resurgence of several diseases (such as yellow fever, malaria, heart disease, enteritis, dengue fever, and hemorrhagic fever) as well as the onset of new diseases such as the Ebola virus (in November 2014 a Cuban doctor returning from the frontlines in Sierra Leone) and chikungunya (striking in December 2013). In an effort to combat these forces, health service reform in the region has been linked to access to education, development of human capital, and the eradication of poverty and poor living conditions across the Caribbean. Current demographic trends show a new health transition is occurring as regional reform initiatives aim to enable workers to move seamlessly within a borderless region under the Caribbean Single Market and Economy (CSME) framework particularly in the English-speaking Caribbean where the Caribbean Single Economy (CSM) went into effect in 2006. The CSME, in existence in 13 of the 15 member states of the Caribbean Community (CARICOM) calls for unrestricted movement of labour, capital, services, capital and the right to establishment (ability to set up a business).

To foster this movement of labor, the Pan American Health Organization (PAHO)/World Health Organization (WHO) and Caribbean Community (CARICOM) note that Caribbean nations have made comparable advances in health reform due to their conjoined investment in clean water, sanitation, and nutrition (PAHO/WHO and CARICOM 2006). These efforts have a significant impact on the health service system, which is now demanding trained, competent, and innovative health service professionals to staff and promote local and regional initiatives. To enable these initiatives, health systems across the region use multi-sectoral, holistic, and integrated approaches to meet challenges and to finance and deliver health services. A recent example of this is the 2008 *Caribbean*

Cooperation in Health (CCH), now in its third phase. In addition to CCH, this chapter will discuss the numerous calls and accessions to several regional and subregional "declarations" in the wake of an increase in both communicable and noncommunicable diseases (NCDs): the *Declaration on Health for the Caribbean Community* (CARICOM 1982); *the Nassau Declaration on Health: The Health of the Region Is the Wealth of the Region* (CARICOM 2001); and the *Declaration of Port-of-Spain: Uniting to Stop the Epidemic of Chronic Non-Communicable Diseases* (NCDs) (CARICOM 2007a). For example, the Nassau Declaration (CARICOM 2001a) articulates, among other things, that the health of people in the region is essential to regional economic and social development since "health is a critical input into the human capital the region needs" (PAHO/WHO and CARICOM 2006, p. xiv) and the effort at health service policy reform supports such imperatives.

This chapter is divided into four sections that discuss the historical, legal, substantive, and functional aspects of health service reforms across the Caribbean: How health service reforms were (1) forged "historically" from colonial and post-colonial developments; (2) formed "legally" through various cooperative regional declarations commencing in 1982; (3) developed "substantively" to address the free movement of Caribbean workers, among several factors; and (4) operated "functionally" through cooperation. While this chapter discusses health reforms in the broadest sense, we focus on health reforms thematically (historical, legal, substantive, and functional) rather than chronologically. Therefore, we acknowledge that several reforms overlap within different time periods. The thematic framework helps situate health service reforms in the region within the context of a variety of events and circumstances including, but not limited to, vulnerabilities of size, fragility of economies, citizenry, and environmental factors—issues often associated with small and microstates (Briguglio 1995; Bune 1987; Holmes 1976; Jules 2012; Moyne et al. 2011; PAHO/WHO and CARICOM 2006). Our focus on health service reforms highlights the vulnerability of citizens in the region, and our purpose is to explain the role that health services play in a changing regional environment.

Historical Aspects of Health Service Reforms

In this section, we discuss what we see as the broad historic aspect of health service reforms in the Caribbean. We shape the discussion as a comprehensive overview of the first wave of health service reforms that took place starting in the pre-independence period up until the 1990s. This section is divided into two parts and discusses some of the historical trends in health reforms that subsequently led to the shaping of specific national reforms. First, we present a brief overview of the historical aspects of health reforms. Second, we suggest that given the ways in which health systems have developed across the region, new managerialism provided a fertile and receptive foundation for several national reforms that were undertaken at the beginning of the 1990s.

Historical Overview of the Aspects of Health Reforms

Like most former colonies, health services began as a service for colonial regiments and administrators (Gulliford 1994; Zwi and Mills 1995). As the islands' political structures developed, health services were also expanded to provide access to a wider section of the population. Given the mixture of cultural histories in the region, medical practices have often been influenced by Obeah, voodoo, and Santeria. When slavery ended in the Caribbean, many new challenges arose surrounding health services. The earliest organization to deliver health services in the Caribbean occurred in the post-slavery period and grew from concern related to high mortality rates of highly infectious diseases. To explore the concern, colonial authorities created a series of commissions to investigate conditions in the Caribbean, including *the Rockefeller Sanitary Commission* of 1901, the *Irvine Committee* of 1944, and the *Report of West India Royal Commission* (generally referred to as *The Moyne Report*) of 1945. Even though many former slaves looked to colonial governments for assistance and despite the recommendations of the commissions and committees, health service initiatives were mired by financial shortcomings. During this period, health service expenditure in the Caribbean ranged from a low of 8.9% of total expenditure in British Honduras and Montserrat to a high of 19.6% in St. Vincent. Other countries, such as Barbados, Jamaica, and Trinidad spent 11.3%, 9.8%, and 9.2% of their budgets, respectively, on health services. In time, public sector involvement increased in the latter portion of the nineteenth century as colonial governments established general hospitals in the more urban areas.

The first half of the twentieth century brought two important health service milestones to the Caribbean: the establishment of the West Indies School of Public Health to train public health nurses and inspectors, and the establishment of the University College of the West Indies (now the University of the West Indies) to train doctors. Additionally, during the early portion of the twentieth century, countries began to develop national health service systems. For example, Jamaica established its Bureau of Health Education in 1926, the School for Sanitary Inspectors in 1927, and conducted both malaria and tuberculosis surveys in 1928. Despite such early public health programs, policy and practice focused on treatment through hospitals and outpatient care instead of preventative care.

Public policy on the future of health services in the Caribbean was articulated in the 1940–1942 *Sir Frank Stockdale Report*. From this report, the Health Unit System was established in 1942. This system was based on a "health team approach," which included the creation of medical districts, and the development of health centers to provide first-line health service. In addition, this system was meant to extend the reach of health services and was intended to be multi-sectoral with links to social welfare, agriculture, and education. Since the program was designed to improve living standards in rural communities, "health units" were established in more remote, rural areas consisting of a group of health service workers who served as primary care practitioners. Also, public health nurses, nutritionists, school dental nurses and dental assistants, community health aides, and nurse practitioners later expanded the units. Functions undertaken by such units included control and prevention of endemic diseases, sanitation and hygiene, and health education.

Historically, the reforms of the 1950s and 1960s stand out for their overarching focus on malnutrition, gastroenteritis, and infections, which led to a decrease in infant mortality rates (Hagley 2005). Health reform in the early 1970s focused on eradicating tuberculosis, malaria, syphilis, and enteritis. During the late 1970s and mid-1980s, heart disease, strokes, cancer, diabetes, and injuries were primary health concerns until HIV/AIDS occupied the top position (Hospedales 2005). The 1980s saw greater strains on health systems as changing demographics led to declining social conditions and slowing economic growth. At the beginning of the 1990s, health systems were segmented, fragmented, and exclusionary, which lead to reforms focusing on social protection and health as a human right.* Broad regional reforms during the 1990s called for health services

---

* While the Declaration of Alma-Ata (World Health Organization 1978) first used the concept of health as a human right, the concept of health as a human right was not fully embraced until the late 1980s. The Declaration of Alma-Ata initially proposed clear process and strategies for primary health service that focused on using social-economic development as a curial component of health service delivery and reform. This led to the proposal in the Declaration calling for "health for all by the year 2000." The Declaration of Alma-Ata has had a tremendous impact across the Caribbean beginning with the focus on environmental health that led to the creation of the Caribbean Environmental Health Strategy and the establishment of the Pan Caribbean Disaster Prevention and Preparedness Program. The post-Alma-Ata period had given rise to research around maternal and child health services (see Ashley and McCaw 1998; McCaw-Binns 2005; Mullings and Paul 2007).

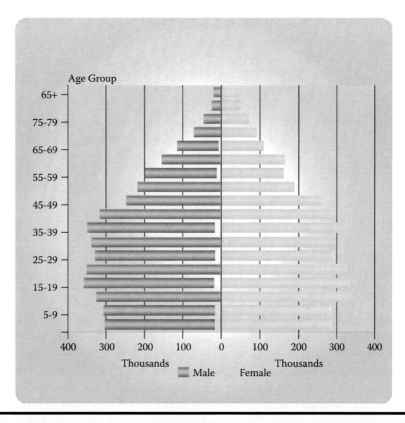

Figure 17.1 Population Pyramid for the Caribbean—2010. (Data from CAREC, 2005. *Leading Causes of Death And Mortality Rates (Counts and Rates) in Caribbean Epidemiology Centre Member Countries (CMCs): 1985 1990 1995 2000*. Port of Spain, Trinidad: Caribbean Epidemiology Centre (CAREC). Retrieved from http://carpha.net/pdf/Mortality_Final_LR%20_%20061205.pdf.)

to be more streamlined and aimed at lowering mortality rates of communicable diseases (e.g., dengue, tuberculosis, HIV/AIDS) and NCDs (e.g., cardiovascular disease, diabetes, mellitus, cancer, obesity, hypertension, hypercholesterolemia), and lifestyle-related noncommunicable risk factors (tobacco and alcohol use).

Archaeologically, health services development in the Caribbean has shown gradual improvements; first, public hospitals were developed, then attention was shifted to primary care, and now the focus is on access and improved quality. Figure 17.1 shows the current demographic trends, which indicate that Caribbean people are living longer and infant mortality has declined from 56–167 per thousand births in the 1960s to 10–48 by the mid-1990s (Alleyne 2005; Swaroop 1996). PAHO/WHO and CARICOM (2006) also note that regional investments in health services account for about 3.5% of gross domestic product (GDP) shares and in many instances often constitute, with education, the second largest share of national budgets. However, during this period we see WHO and PAHO begin to address the *Unfinished Agenda in Primary Health Services* (dating from Alma-Ata 1978). In the Caribbean, the Unfinished Agenda in Primary Health Services paid attention to the conjoining twin forces of communicable and NCDs that paralyzed health systems during the 1980s and then the semantic shift during the 1990s to NCDs (see Ault 2007).

The Rise of New Managerialism as a Tool to Reform Health Systems

Historically, health service provisions were seen as something national governments provided and allocated for within their national budgets. The implementation of structural adjustment programs during the 1980s and 1990s caused economic contraction across the Caribbean, resulting in cuts to "resources available for investment in education, health, and other social infrastructure" (Tsang et al. 2002, p. 12). As resources became limited, governments across the region became more involved in the oversight and distribution of health service funding and reform initiatives. In the 1970s, Jamaica received a World Bank loan of US$2 million for its family planning program, and beginning in the 1980s, the World Bank's Health Sector Policy Paper (World Bank 1980) firmly committed the Bank to health lending in the region. The rise of the World Bank in health spending was boosted by the publication of the *Global Strategy for Health for All by the Year 2000* (World Health Organization 1981), which calculated that the annual cost of achieving primary health care in developing countries was approximately US$30 billion. The World Bank committed to this sum, which led to an increase in loan disbursement, expanding basic health programs (such as primary care and providing technical support and training), to many developing nations. During this period of reductions in public spending on health systems, the bank was the largest funder of health service with lending in more than 30 countries (World Bank 1988). The expanded role of the World Bank had numerous policy consequences across the Caribbean. The World Bank's report on *Financing Health Services in Developing Countries: An Agenda for Reform* (1988) was very influential in calling for the reduction in governmental responsibility in paying for health services. The World Bank (1988) called attention to three main problems at that time of the public health sector: "(1) allocation—insufficient spending on cost-effective health programs; (2) internal inefficiency—wasteful public programs of poor quality; and (3) inequity—inequitable distribution of the benefits of health services" (p. 13). Since the bank stood as an alternative means to finance local health service reforms, health systems and services were susceptible to World Bank donor conditions.

Public health sector reform in the Caribbean can also be traced back to the World Bank's (1997) report entitled *The State in a Changing World*, which advocated raising state capability by reinvigorating public institutions to (1) deliver operative procedures and constraints to check peremptory state actions and rent seeking; (2) increase efficiency in state institutions by promoting more competition; (3) link incentive and higher wages to increase performance of state institutions; and (4) seek greater participation by potential users to make the state more responsive to the needs of the people. The World Bank (1997) also called for greater partnerships in health services noting existing top-down approaches at the time had failed, and despite the existence of national health plans in the majority of countries, the initiatives were rarely properly executed. The combination of these factors prompted nations in the Caribbean to embark upon new public management strategies that took the form of new managerialism in health services, designed as a broad multi-sectoral approach to make primary health systems more accountable, efficient, and accessible. Within this context and closely linked to the beginning of new managerialism to address the problems of national health systems, the proposed "financing package" of four complementary reforms suggested (1) implementing user fees; (2) providing insurance; (3) further utilizing nongovernmental resources; and (4) decentralizing health services. Jamaica became a solid example of the movement toward the World Bank's package reform initiatives when it adopted a procedure for "… exempting the poor from fees, based on eligibility for an already operating food aid program. The Ministry of Health obtained central government approval for a decentralization plan under which 50% of fees are kept by the collecting health facility and the remaining 50% go to the Ministry of Health" (World Bank 1988, p. 48).

Within the region, the World Bank (1988) suggested a shift of resources from the government to the non-governmental sector (defined as "sum of private expenditures on health service, expenditures by missions, and expenditures by Non-governmental Organizations" [see World Bank 1988, p. 13; see also Ruger 2005]) and the private sector for the funding and provision of health services. The goal of this shift was to ultimately "increase the public resources available for government provision of basic curative and referral services to the poor, who currently have only limited access to services of this nature" (Akin, Birdsall, and Ferranti 1987 p. 2). With the demand of austerity and debt servicing requirements stemming from the oil crises of the 1970s, the World Bank's prescriptive recommendations focused on "reducing public-sector wages, privatising remaining public utilities, improving cost recovery for essential services, enhancing transparency, and systematising anti-crime efforts" (Weis 2005, p. 131), which ultimately led to the implementation of user fees. As the state retreated from formerly free health service provisions, nongovernmental organizations (NGOs) came in to pick up the slack. However, since they "... are apolitical and focused on charity rather than change" (Wesi 2005, p. 132), NGOs could never be as broad in scope or in delivery as government-run programming. Countries that moved toward new managerial practices in the health sector generally had a focus on revenue generation. Indeed, several Ministries of Health within the region underwent decentralization reforms that led, in Jamaica for example, to the creation of health service boards with autonomy, quality assurance programs, trained personal in both public and private health services, and the introduction of cost sharing strategies (see King 2001). New managerialism in health reforms also shifted policies toward safeguarding and encouraging a broad tolerance for the necessity of science and technology in fostering human capital in the region and in making the sector competitive in the twenty-first century (Hall and Chuck-A-Sang 2007).

The Legal Aspects of Health Service Reform

In this section, we discuss what we see as the broad "legal aspect of health service reform." We provide a comprehensive overview of the second wave of health service reforms that took place during the immediate post-colonial period and focused on strengthening nationalism. Here, the legal aspect is used as an all-encompassing term to describe the health responsibilities of national governments and regional bodies as well as the rights and responsibilities granted under international agreements, conventions, and declarations.

Historically, the regulation, distribution, and enactment of health laws were the responsibility of colonial officials. After independence and the formation of the Caribbean Community (CARICOM) in the 1960s, CARICOM members created the Standing Committee of Ministers Responsible for Health; the coalition met for the first time in 1969 in Port of Spain, Trinidad and Tobago. The main goals of the gathered national health ministers at this initial meeting were to institute national training facilities for new doctors and to provide quality control for pharmaceuticals when purchasing in bulk (Barrow-Giles 2002). The 1977 CARICOM *Declaration on Health for the Caribbean Community* prioritized "maternal and child health food and nutrition, sexually transmitted diseases and the control of chronic diseases such as diabetes high blood pressure, heart disease and cancer" (Barrow-Giles 2002, p. 47) as the main health concerns within the region. In 1982, the Declaration on Health was revised to reflect the concerns raised in the *Global Strategy for Health for All by the Year 2000* (World Health Organization 1981). *Health for*

All encouraged a focus on disease prevention, and called for the "careful and correct diagnosis of the health situation, including the analysis of the existing health problems as well as the observable trends, the whole activity being based on adequate information system" (CARICOM 1982, p. 2). Additional objectives included (1) designing a comprehensive health service; (2) focusing on promotion, prevention, and early detection rather than relying on treatment; (3) providing adequate care for high-risk and vulnerable groups; and (4) assisting in health service reform by promoting multi-sectoral cooperation and community involvement. While this declaration was designated for the Anglophone Caribbean, it urged members outside of CARICOM to "attain the objectives ... outlined [in the *Declaration on Health*] ... Since health is inextricably linked with social and economic development" (CARICOM 1982, p. 21) for the entire region, including non-CARICOM members.

National reform challenges around health cooperation were tackled through the advancement of sectoral/thematic strategic action plans, which focused on framing health reform around regional and international declarations. In some instances, health systems were unified regionally but administered locally. For example, in 1961 all health and health service institutions in Cuba were consolidated under the *Ministerio de Salud Publica* (MINSAP), and by 1969, health facilities were consolidated under *Sistema National de Salud*. MINSAP specified that health services are the responsibility of the state and the right of people; it should be comprehensive, integrative, and preventative; free and accessible to all; coordinated; and based on popular participation (Santana 1997). Also in the case of Cuba, its 1976 Constitution established the legal foundation for health services to guarantee that everyone have access to free curative and preventive care. In other nations, reforms were part of broader World Bank reforms focused on creating neoliberal modernization projects throughout the region. For example, in Jamaica, the government decentralized their health system by transferring fiscal, administrative, and political authority for planning, management, or service delivery from the central Ministry of Health to alternate institutions or by removing these responsibilities from the government altogether (see World Bank n.d.). Similarly, other countries in the region focused on implementing new managerialism governance mechanisms, such as decentralizing health services and instituting health finance reforms.

In 1995, at a Special Meeting on Health Sector Reform in the Americas hosted by PAHO, the Inter-American Development Bank (IDB, an international organization of Latin American and Caribbean nations created to support development and regional integration), and the World Bank, countries in the Americas presented their proposals for reforming their health systems. The greatest concern for the English-speaking Caribbean, with respect to reforming its health sector, was in the area of broadening the financing options through the introduction of social insurance and an extension of user fees. This need for broadening financing options resulted from decreased government expenditure on health between 1985 and 1994. Organizational restructuring, management strengthening, and greater expenditure on curative services by Ministries of Health were the other proposed areas for reform (PAHO 1995). In support of these reforms, the then director of PAHO stated, "one of the greatest challenges at this time is the reform of the health sector that is under way in some fashion in nearly all countries" (Alleyne 1995, p. 269). He indicated regional requirements for policy reform were in the areas of strategy development, organization of health system and services, and financing the health system. Alleyne (1995) continued by stating that all players involved in health policy development, inside and outside the health sector, need to "facilitate" appropriate interventions to sustain health development. It is evident, therefore, that analysis of health reform policies is required if any intervention is to sustain the development of the health services.

As national governments began to see the impact of transnationalism upon their small economies, the local and national health service reforms witnessed a transition focusing on providing better nutrition, living standards, education, sanitation, quality services, and information. However, as Table 17.1 shows, these policy changes have led to a marginal increase in life expectancy during the last decade in the Caribbean basin. However, when Caribbean countries are compared to other Organisation for Economic Co-operation and Development (OECD) countries, there is quite a large gap in life expectancy. In the last century, infant mortality across the region has increased. The rate has gone from between 100 and 200 infants out of every 1,000 to now around a regional average of 30%, with Haiti showing rates of 80% and higher and Cuba exhibiting rates of 10% and lower (Andrus et al. 2013; Ehrenberg and Ault 2005). Exacerbated levels of malnutrition have also contributed to higher infant mortality rates. Another important health indicator is maternal mortality; recent studies have shown that "for every maternal death sixteen women become ill during pregnancy, child birth, or postpartum up to six weeks after delivery" (Ramirez and Chelala 2006, p. 62). This means that the risk of dying during childbirth continues to be high across the region. There is a growing trend among the region's poor of a rise in "neglected diseases within neglected populations"—stemming from parasitic origin, including lymphatic filariasis

Table 17.1 Life Expectancy at Birth (per thousand) for Countries in the Caribbean Basin Compared to the OECD Countries

Year	Female Life Expectancy at Birth (per thousand)		Male Life Expectancy at Birth (per thousand)		Life Expectancy at Birth in the (per thousand)	
	Caribbean Small States	OECD Members	Caribbean Small States	OECD Members	Caribbean Small States	OECD Members
2011	0.075	0.082	0.070	0.077	0.072	0.080
2010	0.075	0.082	0.069	0.077	0.072	0.079
2009	0.075	0.082	0.069	0.076	0.072	0.079
2008	0.075	0.082	0.069	0.076	0.072	0.079
2007	0.074	0.082	0.068	0.076	0.071	0.079
2006	0.074	0.081	0.068	0.076	0.071	0.079
2005	0.074	0.081	0.068	0.075	0.071	0.078
2004	0.074	0.081	0.067	0.075	0.070	0.078
2003	0.073	0.081	0.067	0.075	0.070	0.078
2002	0.073	0.080	0.067	0.075	0.070	0.077
2001	0.073	0.080	0.067	0.074	0.070	0.077
2000	0.073	0.080	0.067	0.074	0.070	0.077

Source: World Bank, Health Nutrition and Population Statistics. Retrieved from http://databank.worldbank.org/data/views/reports/tableview.aspx, 2012.

(elephantiasis),* soil-transmitted helminthiasis,† schistosomiasis,‡ onchocerciasis (river blindness or Robles' disease),§ leishmaniasis,¶ sleeping sickness (African trypanosomiasis), Chagas disease,** ectoparasitic skin infestations, and parasitic zoonoses, among others (Ehrenberg and Ault 2005, p. 13; see also Hotez et al. (2000); Mitra and Rodriguez-Fernandez (2010); PAHO 2011; WHO 2003). While there is little evidence that these neglected tropical diseases still exist across the region, they still have the potential to cause epidemiological emergencies since reliable statistics do not exist at the national level. Moreover, vulnerable populations find themselves at risk for contracting this disease. These diseases often fly under the "radar screen" since they generally affect marginalized populations. Care and treatment of these diseases are rarely covered under health insurance.

Due to changes in regional health reform, there is significant coordination in regional and national responses to new health threats (Clegg 2015). Recently, the Ebola virus and chikungunya have generated regional responses. While there have been no reported cases of Ebola in the Caribbean, Caribbean Public Health Agency (CARPHA) has designed a response system with coordinated efforts of other health organizations including PAHO/WHO and the United States Centers for Disease Control (CDC). CARPHA (2014) also provided recommendations for its member states, including for example: (1) identifying and addressing gaps in preparedness for Ebola virus disease; (2) strengthening their International Health Regulations (IHR) core capacities and health systems, particularly contact tracing, and infection prevention and control at ports of entry, isolation and health care facilities; and (3) acquiring appropriate Personal Protective Equipment (PPE). Although Ebola is a potential threat, chikungunya has made an impact within the region starting in 2013 and has spread to at least two dozen countries and territories in the Western Hemisphere (CARPHA 2015a, 2015b, 2015c). Often found in Africa and Asia, the disease first appeared in the island of St. Martin (Gillette 2014). As of February 2015, 21,733 confirmed/probable cases of chikungunya have been reported with 4,485 cases in member states and there has been one death from the disease in all 24 member states (CARPHA 2015b). Since there is no vaccine for the virus, CARPHA policies were centered on prevention through avoidance and through actively eliminating mosquito breeding grounds. These policies are similar to the fight against dengue fever, another disease spread through mosquito bites. Although the coordinated effort results have been mixed, CARPHA and CARICOM have been able to get messages to people in the region, while in Cuba, there have been great efforts to help nations where Ebola hit the hardest (Clegg 2015).

Another concern for the region is their growing elderly population. Recent estimates of the elderly, 60 years or older, project that they will comprise approximately 11.3% of the region's population by 2015 and 24.3% in 2025 (PAHO 2007). This demographic change will greatly impact

---

* Lymphatic filariasis (elephantiasis) can be found in Caribbean islands (Haiti, Dominican Republic, and Trinidad and Tobago) and coastal areas of South America (Brazil, Guyana, and Suriname).
† Of the four types of soil-transmitted helminthiasis or roundworm (*Ascaris lumbricoides*), whipworm (*Trichuris trichiura*), and the anthropophilic hookworms (*Necator americanus* and *Ancylostoma duodenale*), the lymphatic filariasis and onchocerciasis are the most common ones found in Cuba, Guyana, Haiti, St. Lucia, and Suriname.
‡ While exposure to schistosomiasis is very low in the Caribbean, Dominican Republic, Guadeloupe, Martinique, and St. Lucia have been identified as potential breeding sites for this disease.
§ Very limited data exist for the existence of onchocerciasis across the region, but the disease can be found in South America.
¶ Leishmaniasis is rare with the last known cases in the region occurring in the Dominican Republic.
** Since this chapter covers Belize, Suriname, and Guyana, Chagas disease is included since it can be found in South and Central America.

health services, since "the ageing process in the region is characterized, not just by unprecedented speed and size, but also by large potential demand for health services" (Palloni et al. 2002, p. 766). In instances where built-in cost recovery mechanisms exist across the region, this has the potential to lead to denial of access to health services and differentiated health treatment (Maharaj and Paul 2011; Palloni et al. 2002). This projected increase will also have severe consequences on national medical spending particularly in light of the 2008 financial crisis and subsequent global recession. As the population continues to age and the shift from government to nongovernmental organization for the provision of health services occurs, there was a rise in reforms aimed at affordability, sustainability, and cost-effectiveness (see Luciani and Andrus 2008). Yet, limited data exist on the current spending levels and costs of health services across the region.

Even though the level and cost of care have become difficult to calculate, particularly with estimates by PAHO (2007) noting that "circulatory system, malignant neoplasms, chronic respiratory diseases, and diabetes have become the leading causes of death, along with external causes such as accidents, homicides, and other sources of violence" (p. 1). Recent research has identified a "shift from infectious to social morbidities caused or contributed to by individual risk behaviors and environmental factors" (Halcón et al. 2003, p. 1851). For young people aged 10–24 (about 30% of the region's population), this shift, coupled with the expenses of the elderly, implies future health costs will balloon in the coming years. In a recent study, Almeida and Sarti (2013) devised methodologies to calculate the income-related inequality in health service utilization. During the last two decades, health service costs for adolescents have increased because of individual risk behavior and environmental factors. In analyzing the interwoven factors that affect adolescents, Halcón et al. (2003) report that one in five adolescents stated that their general health was poor or fair.

In recent years, the percentage of GDP spent by Caribbean countries remains higher than other developing countries as the cost of health service expenditure has increased. Several authors note that with the increase in public spending on health services, the qualitative results have been disappointing. Recent estimates posit that health expenditures have been increasing since the 1990s and have continued to increase as a percentage of GDP (Figure 17.2). For example, in 2001, estimates of national health spending placed it at 6.3% of regional GDP and ranged from 4.4% in Belize to 1.1% in Guyana (see PAHO 2007). However, PAHO (2007) estimates national health expenditures are around 7% across all Caribbean countries.

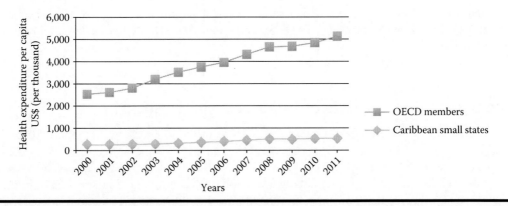

Figure 17.2 Health expenditure for Caribbean small states as compared to OECD members. (Data from World Bank, *Health Nutrition and Population Statistics*. Retrieved from http://databank .worldbank.org/data/views/reports/tableview.aspx, 2012.)

Table 17.2 Health-Related Millennium Development Goals

Health Target	Health Indicator
Goal 4: Reduce child mortality	
Reduce by two-thirds, between 1990 and 2015, the under-five mortality rate	13 Under-five mortality rate
	14 Infant mortality rate
	15 Proportion of one-year-old children immunized against measles
Goal 5: Improve maternal health	
Reduce the maternal mortality ratio by three-quarters, between 1990 and 2015	16 Maternal mortality ratio
	17 Proportion of births attended by skilled health personnel
Goal 6: Combat HIV/AIDS, malaria, and other diseases	
Have halted by 2015 and have begun to reverse the incidence of malaria and other major diseases	–a
Goal 8: Develop a global partnership for development	
Target 17: In cooperation with pharmaceutical companies, provide access to affordable essential drugs in developing countries	46 Proportion of population with access to affordable essential drugs on a sustainable basis

Source: Andrus et al., Health Affairs, 27(2), 488, 2013.

Several risk factors and social determinants to health across the region have led to a decline in health services, health standards, and health reforms. These factors conjoined with the global financial crisis of 2008 determine that much needed upgrades in technology and infrastructure have not taken place. In regard to the progress being made on achieving health-related millennium development goals (MDG), Table 17.2 shows that the region has made some progress toward child mortality (MDG4), maternal health (MDG5), and combating HIV/AIDS, malaria, and other diseases (MDG6).

The Substantive Aspects of Health Service Reform

In this section, we discuss the "substantive aspects" of health services. We begin in the 1980s and continue to the present and define this period as being substantive since it focuses on (1) providing broad-based care for all and (2) the ability of nationals to move more freely across the region under different service regimes, particularly under the Caribbean Single Market (CSM), in the Anglophone Caribbean, that came into effect in 2006 with 13 of the 15 members of CARICOM. The second part of the substantive reform agenda covers aspects of the priority areas identified in the 1990s by the Caribbean Health Research Council (CHRC) (2011) including (1) NCDs;

(2) sexually transmitted infections; (3) health promotion and other interventions; (4) sociocultural factors and health outcomes; and (5) health care delivery. The reform agenda was not fully implemented due to lack of institutional capacity at the Ministries of Health across the region. Additionally, we cover what we identify as the five broad substantive areas through which health service reform across the region occurred. These substantive aspects of health speak to independent reforms completed in conjunction with core national and regional reforms. We will discuss the role and purpose of health service systems under socialism, the impact of the HIV/AIDS epidemic upon national health service systems, health concerns surrounding the free movement of skilled labor, the reasons behind the establishment of Health and Family Life Education (HFLE), and the renewed emphasis on NCDs. We show that the various health service reforms run parallel to each other while at the same time try to address specific deficits within the health service systems.

Health Services Under Socialism in Cuba, Jamaica, Guyana, and Grenada

With the advent of self-determination in the region, health service spending bloomed. As economic nationalism became the guiding principle for many countries to enable their mixed economies to function, the social sectors benefited with greater funding. Rodney (1969) notes that growing inequality coupled with rapid population growth led to a decline in the marginal improvements on health services marked during this era. Given negligible advances in health reform and with the advent of political fragmentation/ideological pluralism (as reflected in competing socialist and capitalist ideologies), the following countries opted for different forms of egalitarianist economic reforms, particularly in Cuba (1959–present, Popular Socialism), Guyana (1971–1985, Cooperative Socialism), Grenada (1979–1983, Revolutionary Socialism), and (Jamaica 1972–1980, Democratic Socialism). In these countries under the massive nationalization of the economic commanding heights (key sectors), all hospitals became government owned and operated. The countries that experimented with socialist health systems reform focused primarily on preventive care and eradicating communicative diseases (King 2001). As Guyana, Grenada, and Jamaica began to build their nationalist health service systems, they all recruited and retained doctors from Cuba, which was and is seen as the regional leader, in the development of resources and professional training. The advent of health service nationalization saw an increase in physicians, but 75% of doctors in Guyanese hospitals were from Cuba, India, and the Philippines (Rose 2002). Nationalist health service reform in Jamaica fixated on delivering primary health services to exterminate disease-carrying insects rather than concentrating on curative reforms. Jamaica's former prime minister Manley's socialist agenda of the 1970s appealed to the poor since it promised free health services to all citizens' and infrastructural rehabilitation in the form of building clinics that offered access to medical drugs. However, the proposed reforms that seemed to mimic the Cuban model clashed with "… U.S. destabilization efforts and the exodus of the Jamaican bourgeoisie and their capital, which only exacerbated earlier problems caused by the oil embargo, the ending of the gold standard, and the deterioration of the price of raw materials (like Bauxite) on the world market" (Price 2000, p. 166). In another instance, Maurice Bishop, the former prime minister of Grenada, argued in his first national address that the Grenadian revolution was "… for work, for food, for decent housing and health services" (Rose 2002, p. 297) and allocated 22% of the 1982–1983 budget to health services and education.

The Impact of HIV/AIDS

The second substantive aspect that national and regional health reforms tackled across the Caribbean was HIV/AIDS. The regional epidemiological profile of the HIV/AIDS epidemic shows that the disease was first identified in the early 1980s in Haiti (Pape 2000) and then later in Jamaica, Trinidad and Tobago, and Bermuda (Bartholomew and Cleghorn 1989; Bartholomew et al. 1983; CAREC 2003; Narain et al. 1989). Figure 17.3 shows that by the late 1990s, the Caribbean reported the highest case of AIDS incidents in the Americas. The region has the highest adult HIV infection rate of 1% of the adult population and is second globally to sub-Saharan Africa (Joint United Nations Programme on HIV/AIDS [UNAIDS] and WHO 2009). By 2001, 48.8% of those living with AIDS in the region were women—and of that group, women of childbearing age, 15–45. Thus, the ratio of men to women with AIDS in the region has risen to about 1 to 1 compared with 4 to 1 in 1985 (see Figure 17.4). The HIV/AIDS mortality profile in the region represents high infection rates among males and females between the ages of 25 and 44. On average, 1 in 50 people in the Caribbean or 2% has AIDS or is infected with HIV, with approximately 400,000 known to be living with the disease (Hall et al. 2005).

At the national level, many country studies sought to understand the impact of the HIV/AIDS crisis in the Caribbean (CAREC and UWI 1997; Laptiste 2004; McLean 2004; Theodore 2001), while earlier studies across the region have sought to understand the impact of HIV/AIDS incidences. For example, a study in the Dominican Republic focused on the modes of transmission of HIV/AIDS by looking at the practices of the "Haitian Mystique" where Dominican men sought Haitian women because of their "cocomordon (biting vagina or a vagina capable of exerting great pleasures)" and "Masisi" where men are reared to be women, do women's work, conduct themselves as women, and at times dress like women (Kreniske 1997, pp. 43–44). Recent studies have used moderate case

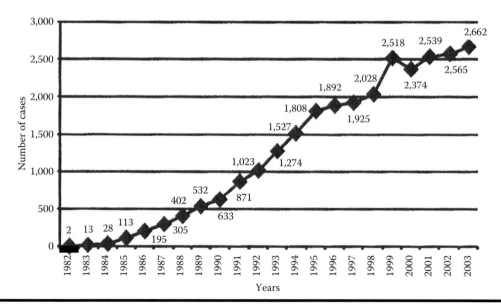

Figure 17.3 AIDS annual incidence in CAREC member countries, 1982–2003. (Data from CAREC, *HIV/AIDS Data for CAREC Member Countries, 1982–2010* [as cited in PAHO/WHO and CARICOM, 2006, p. 48]. Retrieved from http://public.tableausoftware.com/views/Tableau_HIV_AIDS_Infobase_Dec2011RegionalDashboards/Dash_RegionalAIDSbygender?:embed = yes &:toolbar = yes&:tabs = no, 2010.)

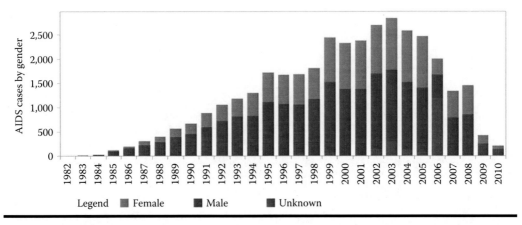

Figure 17.4 Regional AIDS CASE by gender and AIDS for 21 CAREC member countries 1982–2010.

scenarios to project the potential average increase in the total population living with HIV and AIDS in the region over the coming decade (UNAIDS and WHO 2009), and other studies have looked at the effect upon human resource development and education (Jules 2012). Today, transmission falls into what UNAIDS refers to as the "generalized epidemic" range (see Brian 2005), which has been propelled by high risk behaviors among vulnerable populations such as unemployed dependent women, men who have sex with men, persons with disabilities, commercial sex workers, bisexual men, drug and alcohol abusers, mini bus drivers, uniformed personnel, prisoners, fish-folk, and male prostitutes for tourists—"rent a dread" and "beach boys" (Jules 2012). Allen (2002) found that 55% of boys and 24% of girls in CARICOM countries state that they had sexual intercourse prior to age 10 (the last year of primary school) while an additional 23% of boys and 16% of girls reported that they had engaged in sexual activity between the ages of 11 and 12 (the first year of secondary school) (see also Andrews 1998; Government of Barbados 2008; McFarlane and Freidman 1999).

As Figure 17.5 shows that the while there has been a decrease in AIDS-related deaths across the region, currently HIV/AIDS is the leading cause of death among 25–44-year-olds. Within this context, Caribbean youth today are seen as part of the "AIDS generation" (Kiragu 2001) because of two specific indicators: (1) the high prevalence rate of HIV/AIDS in the region and (2) the youth of the Caribbean having come of age in a region plagued by the epidemic; it is an everyday fact of life for them (Jules 2012). Moreover, high incidents of HIV/AIDS and other factors (sexually transmitted infections, maternal infant morbidity and mortality, infertility, teenage pregnancy, unsafe abortions, limited fertility control, and drug abuse) continue to adversely affect reproductive health (Alleyne 2005; Frederick et al. 2005). Given the high prevalence rate of HIV/AIDS, we now see the rise of the "compartmentalization of diseases according to life cycles" (Alleyne 2005).

The profile of the disease led to several changes across national health sectors. While many countries initially developed individual national responses to HIV, the Pan Caribbean Partnership Against HIV and AIDS (PANCAP), the provision of World Bank loans, and the establishment of the Global Fund to fight AIDS heightened targeted reforms. In 2010, it was estimated that the region has received over US$1.3 billion for its HIV programs (UNAIDS and WHO, 2009). Comprehensive health sector reforms before PANCAP's existence took the form of HIV control programs for 15–20-year-olds in the Bahamas, Barbados, Bermuda, Cuba, and Jamaica (see Figueroa 2008). In the Bahamas and Barbados, other specific reforms focused on preventative programs around reducing HIV transmission from mother to child through the testing and provision of antiretroviral therapy.

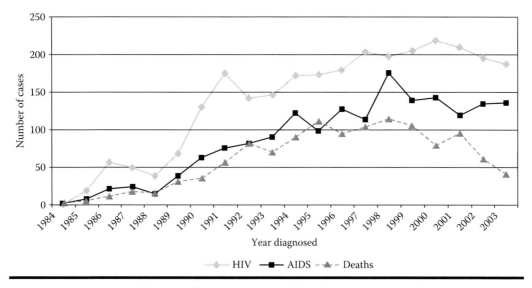

Figure 17.5 Summary of HIV and AIDS cases and deaths: 1984–2003. (Data from CAREC, *HIV/AIDS Data for CAREC Member Countries, 1982–2010*. Retrieved from http://public.tableausoftware.com/views/Tableau_HIV_AIDS_Infobase_Dec2011RegionalDashboards/Dash_RegionalAIDSbygender?:embed = yes&:toolbar = yes&:tabs = no, 2010.)

In the wake of the HIV/AIDS epidemic to human resource development in the region, the Nassau Declaration (CARICOM 2001a) called for the restructuring of health services to focus on health care access. This call was reiterated when Caribbean governments noted they were "cognizant of the critical role of health in the economic development of our people and [were] overawed by the prospect that our current health problems, especially HIV/AIDS, may impede such development through the devastation of our human capital" (CARICOM 2001b, p. 1). The economic impact of HIV/AIDS on the region led to workforce reductions and contractions in key sectors such as agriculture, manufacturing, and tourism (Hall and Chuck-A-Sang 2007; PAHO/WHO and CARICOM 2006). UNAIDS (2013) notes in Latin America and the Caribbean are six of the countries that have the highest rates of HIV/AIDS infections but these trends are changing. Recently, UNAIDS (2013) reported a 52% reduction in new HIV infections among children and a combined 33% reduction among adults and children between 2001 and 2012.

Health as an Enabler of the Free Movement of Skilled Labor

The third substantive regional health service reform focused on making national labor forces mobile and competitive. The human dimensions of the substantive aspect of health service reform within the Caribbean have been driven by the free movement of Caribbean workers, particularly in the Anglophone Caribbean and in the specific instances of Cuban nationals. The focus was to ensure that human, financial, and material resources were marshaled and overseen in order to tackle the health challenges within the region. In addition, officials examined where resources were being allocated (e.g., rural vs. urban) and used (e.g., by different socioeconomic groups) to define equity of access in the health sector (CCH 1999). The emphasis on the movement of labor was aimed at strengthening health services given the epidemiology, emerging technologies, and resource constraints that affected health service delivery at the beginning of the 1990s. While labor has been mobile across the region for decades, particularly with Cuban health professionals traveling to other countries, it was the "Vision of the Ideal Caribbean Person" (CARICOM 1998) or "neo-Caribbean citizens" (Jules, 2014) that enshrined skill mobility migration. The Vision of the Ideal Caribbean Person is seen as a regional citizen who is psychologically secure; values differences based on gender, ethnicity, religion, and other forms of diversity as sources of strength and richness; is environmentally astute; is responsible and accountable to family and community; has a strong work ethic; is ingenious and entrepreneurial; has a conversant respect for the cultural heritage; exhibits multiple literacies; is independent and thinks critically in the application of science and technology to problem solving; and embraces differences and similarities between females and males to function within the CARICOM Single Market and Economy. For young people, the Report of the CARICOM Commission on Youth (CARICOM 2010) identified that the profile of the ideal Caribbean youth should call for youth to be, among other things, sensitive to the negative consequences of poverty, HIV and AIDS, and be aware of the environment and health issues within the Caribbean. The Anglophone Caribbean gave formal recognition to portability of Ideal Caribbean Persons (and youth) to travel in 2006. One of the first skilled labor professions given recognition was professional nurses who were seen as significant for free movement within the CARICOM countries in light of regional health care needs (other skilled personal allowed to move seamlessly in the CARICOM space are university graduates, media workers, sportspersons, artists, musicians, qualified teachers, artisans with a Caribbean Vocational Qualification, and holders of associate degrees).

The rise of a transient professional labor force is significantly linked to the liberalization of health services under the World Trade Organization (WTO)—General Agreement on Trade in Services (GATS) regime. GATS differentiates the four modes of delivering services: (1) cross-border trade (movement of services from one territory to another); (2) consumption abroad (service consumers move abroad); (3) commercial presence (service suppliers create a territorial presence); (4) and the presence of natural persons (people supply services to other territory). PAHO/WHO and CARICOM (2006), in evaluating the efficacy of these modules upon health services in the region, note that while the first three GATS modules have not adversely affected the region as of yet, Module 4 (presence of natural persons) causes concern. The fulfillment of the presence of natural persons in the region means the region will encounter supply and demand issues and the shortages of nurses will give rise to a decline in the capability of health services. Several contributing push factors (low pay, poor working conditions, poor career structures, and limited employment opportunities) and pull factors (nominal wage differences, real income, standard of living, better working conditions, and opportunity to send remittances) have been identified by PAHO/WHO and CARICOM (2006) as influencing labor mobility across the region including health service workers.

Across the region, brain drain in the health sector continues to be an emerging trend, as professionals are seeking opportunities in other regional economies, such as South America and other nations. Countries like Jamaica, Cuba, and Trinidad and Tobago are strong exporters of qualified health professionals. UNPD (2011) notes that the total population in the Caribbean will increase, peaking in the year 2040 at 47,386,000 before falling again; alarming trends show that health professionals are migrating in droves. For example, between 2000 and 2010 net migration peaked at (1.1 million) with about 30% of emigrants coming annually from Latin America and the Caribbean (UNPD 2011). The Commonwealth Secretariat (2005) notes that the sustainability of Caribbean health service systems across the region are critical, due to the approximate loss of 400 nurses per annum through out-migration to Canada, the United Kingdom, and the United States. In 2010, the Regional Nursing Body established a new regional curriculum focused on quality. National reforms leading to retaining health care professionals have begun.

Establishment of Health and Family Life Education

The Caribbean Cooperation in Health II (CCH 1999) notes that improved health must include "education for healthy life choices and skills, food security, satisfactory housing, access to potable water supplies and proper disposal of waste" (p. viii). The fourth substantive reform is an educational reform to teach healthy life choices and skills. In 1994, CARICOM and the University of the West Indies (UWI) developed the HFLE initiative with five thematic areas (sexual health, health and wellness, eating and fitness, enhancing self and interpersonal relationships, and managing the environment). To streamline regional endeavors for this initiative, support was also solicited from United Nations agencies working in the Caribbean. HFLE is an example of a multi-sectoral approach, with partner agencies including the CARICOM Secretariat; the Caribbean Child Development Centre; the UWI Schools of Education; the Advanced Training and Research in Fertility Management Unit; PAHO/WHO; the United Nations Educational, Scientific and Cultural Organization (UNESCO); the United Nations International Drug Control Program (UNDCP); the United Nations Fund for Population Activities (UNFPA); the United Nations Development Programme (UNDP); the United Nations Development Fund for Women (UNIFEM); and the United Nations Children's Fund (UNICEF). In addition, the current operational mechanism for the project is a Regional Working Group, while UNICEF has been carrying out overall coordination. These partnerships allow HFLE to be positioned as a core area of instruction not only for primary schools, but for secondary and tertiary levels, as well. HFLE, a single educational initiative and reform, has had a tremendous impact on coordinating national health service by standardizing systems. As Ministries of Health are seen as integral part of HFLE, the ministries have established regional collaborative links, built national coordinating structures, and facilitated the preparation of HFLE educators. The links to national health system have been strengthened with the revision of the HLFE curricula that have moved away from a focus on "information-based skills" to "life-skills." With its dual focus on health and education, HFLE addresses issues that children and adolescents face; it is a school subject taught in many of the CARICOM member states' schools where children learns how to deal effectively with challenges found in everyday life.

HFLE reforms have undergone several iterations to keep pace with the "core areas for living which have vital implications for health" (UNICEF 2006). For example, in public schools throughout the Eastern Caribbean countries (see UNICEF 2006), HFLE reforms aim at building essential life skills: anger management, coping skills, resiliency skills, how to communicate feelings, how to handle peer pressure and grievances, and self-esteem. This skills-focused model of HFLE replaced the information-focused model in 1996 under the Council for Human and Social Development's (COHSOD) recommendations that a Regional Curriculum Framework should be developed, which could be adapted by member states to meet their specific needs. HFLE is often set as a priority for achieving national development goals, and CARICOM wants to ensure the formulation and review of national policies associated with HFLE.

A World Bank (2003) Country Study reveals that youth 10–24 years make up about 30% of the population in the Caribbean. The data for available countries indicate that the proportion of youth 10–24 years varies from as high as 34% in St. Lucia to a low of 24% in St. Kitts and Nevis. These findings also identify certain key social and environmental concerns that the regions' youths face: poverty, unemployment, high academic failure rates, family instability, fragmented communities, child abuse and neglect, violence, stress and alienation, negative influence of the media, questionable subcultures, and unavailability of physical education and recreational facilities. Health threats include such lifestyle-related conditions as diabetes, hypertension, obesity,

HIV/AIDS, sexually transmitted infections, sexual abuse, substance abuse, suicide, and teenage pregnancy. Young people across the region have historically always been "at risk." In the past, this group was more sustainable to infectious diseases. Today, however, emotional and behavioral disabilities rank high among the health conditions that affect young persons in the region. Increasingly, Caribbean youth are being adversely affected by a number of social, psychological, and physical problems. There is the perception that the traditional curricula do not ensure that children and youth achieve their full potential as citizens. In addition, increasing social pressures are impacting young persons in ways that make teaching a challenge. Teachers are noticing that young people find little relevance in schooling, which has caused the student to be more disruptive and question authority. The Caribbean youth believes that the school fails to prepare them adequately for their various life roles. The paradox is that schools are now seen as key agencies to redress some of these very issues discussed above. Within this context, HFLE, has arisen as a curriculum initiative that not only reinforces the connection between health and education, but also uses a holistic approach within a planned and coordinated framework. For example, an area of attention includes equipping students with the skills needed to reduce violence by increasing social and emotional intelligence. HFLE has, therefore, become easier, cheaper, and more effective to reach out to children overcoming severe social problems. Furthermore, HFLE prevents students from engaging in risky behaviors such as drug and substance abuse, gang entrance, and teenage pregnancy.

Focus on Noncommunicable Diseases

The fifth substantive reform focused on advocacy, care, and treatment with regard to NCDs. The Caribbean has the highest prevalence of NCDs in the Americas (Samels and Fraiser 2010). Since the 1990s, health service reforms began focusing on NCDs stemming from risk factors such as obesity, hypertension, hypercholesterolemia, and tobacco and alcohol use (e.g., cardiovascular disease [CVD], diabetes, and cancer). Research shows that since the "late 1990s, the percentage of deaths coded to the four leading causes are 35 percent for CVD, 11 percent for diabetes mellitus, five percent for cancer and three per cent for HIV" (PAHO/WHO and CARICOM 2006). Recent estimates show, for example, that "diabetes mortality in Trinidad and Tobago and in Saint Vincent and the Grenadines is 600 percent higher than in North America (United States and Canada), and cardiovascular disease mortality rates in Trinidad and Tobago, Guyana, and Suriname are 84 percent, 62 percent, and 56 percent higher, respectively, than in North America" (Samuels and Fraser 2010, p. 472). As Figure 17.6 identifies, regional trends based on a mortality analysis for the years 1985, 1990, 1995, and 2000 show that NCDs accounted for the most common cause of death (PAHO/WHO and CARICOM 2006). For example, the rise in cardiovascular diseases has been attributed to the adaption of Caribbean nationals to Western or Euro-American lifestyles causing them to abandon their ancestral diets.

This epidemiologic transition is driven by changes in lifestyles and led to a regional summit on NCDs in 2007. The summit pointed out several regional trends directly related to NCDs. For example, currently chronic diseases are the primary cause of premature mortality and account for nearly half of all deaths of persons less than 70 years old. The 2007 summit gave rise to a 15-point *Declaration of Summit of Port-of-Spain—Uniting to Stop the Epidemic of Chronic Non-Communicable Diseases* (CARICOM 2007b) that called for among other things, the strengthening of regional health institutions, the establishment of National Commissions on NCDs, the

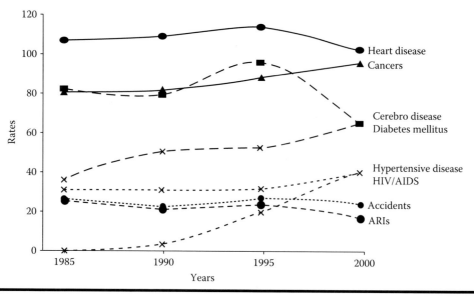

Figure 17.6 Crude Mortality Rates for select diseases by year: CAREC member countries. (Data from PAHO/WHO and CARICOM, *Report of the Caribbean Commission on Health and Development*. Kingston, Jamaica: Ian Randle Publishers, p. 2, 2006.)

ratification of the International Framework Convention on Tobacco Control, the reintroduction of physical education in schools, the elimination of trans-fats from diets, and the promotion of indigenous agricultural products and foods to combat this new threat. The summit closed by declaring that the second Saturday in September would become "Caribbean Wellness Day." In 2011, a second regional summit was held and it produced the *Strategic Plan of Action for the Prevention and Control of Chronic Non-Communicable Diseases (NCDs) in the Countries of the Caribbean Community (CARICOM) 2011–2015* (PAHO/WHO and CARICOM 2011b). This regional strategy focused on five priority actions at the national level: (1) risk factor reduction and health promotion—focusing on reducing tobacco usage, preventing alcohol abuse, and promoting healthy eating, such as reducing salt consumption, engaging in physical activity, and integrating NCD programs in the school, workplace, and faith-based setting; (2) greater disease management and patient self-management education—scaling up evidence-based treatment; (3) surveillance, monitoring, and evaluation; (4) public policy, advocacy, and communications; and (5) program management—formulating partnerships and coordinating resource mobilization, and pharmaceuticals. The renewed focus on NCDs, which include response components of several of the other reforms above, led region to spend millions of dollars on treating these diseases. As such, heads of governments called for "… Ministries of Health, in collaboration with other sectors, [to] establish by mid-2008 comprehensive plans for the screening and management of chronic diseases and risk factors so that by 2012, 80% of people with NCDs would receive quality care and have access to preventive education based on regional guidelines" (CARICOM 2007b, p. 1). Thus begun a new reform agenda that focused on "strengthening of primary health-care systems, access to essential drugs and technologies and mechanisms for aligning care with the evidence" (Samuels and Hospedales 2011, p. 388). However, subsequent reviews have shown that this call, even with its significant political support, has stalled due to a resource deficiency across the region.

The Functional Aspects of Health Service Reform: The Rise of New Mutualism

In the final section of this chapter, we discuss what we see as a functional aspect of health reform that spans both the colonial and post-colonial period. We provide a comprehensive overview of the second waves of health service reforms that took place during the immediate post-colonial period and focused to strengthen nationalism and regionalism. The Caribbean has had a long history of cooperation within the health sector through both common policies and shared visions (see Tables 17.1 and 17.3). The region has also succeeded in creating regional agencies and institutions to save on transactions costs (see Table 17.4). The current wave of the functional aspects of health reform in the Caribbean dates back to the Caribbean Cooperation in Health Initiative (CCH I) introduced in 1984 by the CARICOM Conference of Ministers Responsible for Health, which subsequently led to its launch in 1986 in collaboration with the PAHO (see Table 17.3). The CCH I (1986) gained prominence across the region, particularly in the Anglophone Caribbean, since it was argued that Caribbean countries share a similar history in

Table 17.3 Caribbean Regional Health Service Reforms

Year	Health Care Reform/Policy	Originator
1955	Standing Advisory Council (SAC) for Medical Research in the British Caribbean	United Kingdom
1956	First Council and Scientific Meeting of the SAC	United Kingdom
1977	Declaration on Health for the Caribbean Community	CARICOM
1982	Revised Declaration on Health in the Caribbean Community	CARICOM
1984	Caribbean Cooperation in Health (CCH): Phase I	
1993	Caribbean Charter for Health Promotion	CCH
1999	CCH Phase II: A New Vision for Caribbean Health	CCH
2001	Declaration of Commitment to the Pan Caribbean Partnership Against HIV/AIDS (PANCAP)	CARICOM
2001	Nassau Declaration on Health: The Health of the Region Is the Wealth of the Region	CARICOM
2002	Caribbean Regional Strategic Framework on HIV and AIDS (CRSF)	CARICOM and PANCAP
2002	Regional Strategic Plan for the Prevention and Control of Chronic Non-Communicable Diseases	CARICOM
2003	Task force arising from the 2001 Nassau Summit established as Caribbean Commission on Health and Development (CCHD)	CARICOM
2005	Caribbean Commission on Health and Development (CCHD) reported to the 26th Meeting of the CARICOM Heads of Government	CARICOM

(Continued)

Table 17.3 (*Continued*) Caribbean Regional Health Service Reforms

Year	Health Care Reform/Policy	Originator
2006	Report of the Caribbean Commission on Health and Development	PAHO
2007	Declaration of Montevideo on the New Orientations for Primary Health Care: "Designing People-centered Care Through a Primary Health-care Based System"	WHO
2007	Declaration of Port-of-Spain: "Comprehensive and Integrated Approach to the Control of CNCD"	CARICOM
2007	Declaration of Port-of-Spain: "Uniting to Stop the Epidemic of Chronic NCDs"	CARICOM
2007	Declaration of St. Ann: "Implementing Agriculture and Food Policies to Prevent Obesity and Non-Communicable Diseases (NCDs) in the Caribbean Community"	Healthy Caribbean Coalition
2007	Needham's Point Declaration	CARICOM
2008	CCH Phase III: Regional Health Framework 2010–2015	CCH
2008	Caribbean Network of Pharmacovigilance (VIGICARIB)	PAHO/WHO
2008	Revised CRSF	CARICOM and PANCAP
2011	Caribbean Pharmaceutical Policy—21st Council of Human and Social Development	CARICOM
2010	Sub-regional Cooperation Strategy for the Caribbean: 2010–2015	PAHO/WHO CPC

the development of their national health systems. Therefore, participating countries were asked to focus their objectives and resources on common health concerns identified at the regional level and utilize joint approaches and activities, in the form of technical cooperation, to support capacity building. CCH I (1986) identified six priority health areas: (1) environmental protection including vector control; (2) chronic diseases and injury prevention; (3) strengthening of health systems; (4) maternal and child health; (5) human resource development; and (6) food and nutrition. A seventh, AIDS prevention and control, was later added. CCH I (1986) was intended to address the fissures in the regional health schema through the operationalization of tactical health priorities and requirements. In 1992, CCH I (1986) was reviewed across the region, which led to its redefinition and reformulation from 1997 to 2001 including the development of CCH II for the period 1999–2005. CCH II (1999) established eight regional sectoral priorities: (1) strengthening health systems (ability to deliver effective health services); (2) human resource development (training health personnel); (3) family health (providing preventive, curative, rehabilitative, and supportive services); (4) food and nutrition (preventing malnutrition); (5) chronic NCDs (promotion of health, prevention of disease, and appropriate, quality care, including rehabilitation); (6) communicable diseases (prevention focusing on food-, water-, and vector-borne diseases, along with vaccines for preventable diseases, such as sexual transmitted

Table 17.4 Caribbean Regional Health Service Organizations

Year Established	Health Care Organization	Located In	Function
1955	Caribbean Health Research Council (CHRC) formerly known as the Commonwealth Caribbean Medical Research Council (CCMRC)	Trinidad and Tobago	Coordinates health research
1967	Caribbean Food and Nutrition Institute (CFNI) with a specialized center of the Pan American Health Organization (PAHO/WHO)	UWI, Jamaica	Improves nutritional well-being and food security
1969	1st Conference of Ministers Responsible for Health	Trinidad and Tobago	Introduces new training facilities to increase number of medical professionals
1971	CARIFTA Health Desk		
1972	Commonwealth Caribbean Medical Research Council (CCMRC)	Trinidad and Tobago	Promotes and coordinates medical research in the Caribbean and to advise the region's governments on related matters
1973	Caribbean Epidemiology Centre (CAREC)	Trinidad and Tobago	In 21 countries providing services in epidemiology and laboratory technology
1974	The Caribbean Regional Drug Testing Laboratory (CRDTL)	Jamaica	Assuring that drugs conform with appropriate standards of purity, strength, and quality
1975	Caribbean Regional Drug Testing Library (CRDTL)	Jamaica	Tests pharmaceuticals and advises pharmacy authorities
1975	Caribbean Epidemiology Centre (CAREC)	Trinidad and Tobago	Monitoring and lab tech
1979	Caribbean Environmental Health Institute (CEHI)	St. Lucia	Tech and advisory for environmental health
1986	OECS/Eastern Caribbean Drug Service	St. Lucia	Drug supply management (including selection, procurement, distribution, and use)
1995	Health Economics Unit (HEU)	UWI/ Trinidad and Tobago	Training and policy research

(*Continued*)

Table 17.4 (*Continued*) Caribbean Regional Health Service Organizations

Year Established	Health Care Organization	Located in	Function
1998	CCMRC was transformed into the Caribbean Health Research Council (CHRC)	Trinidad & Tobago	Inclusion of non-Commonwealth countries and broaden its scope to include other areas of health
2001	Council for Human and Social Development (COHSOD)	Guyana	Promotes and improves efficient and affordable health services
2001	Pan Caribbean Partnership Against HIV/AIDS (PANCAP)	Guyana	Bridges national HIV programs with international and regional organizations
Formed in 2011 launched in 2013	Caribbean Public Health Agency (CARPHA) a merger of five CARICOM Regional Health Institutions (RHIs), that is, CHRC, the Caribbean Epidemiology Centre (CAREC); Caribbean Environmental Health Institute (CEHI); Caribbean Food and Nutrition Institute (CFNI); and the Caribbean Regional Drug Testing Laboratory (CRDTL)	Trinidad and Tobago	CARPHA divisions of Research, Evaluation and Policy Development provide technical support and training in research and monitoring and evaluation, and the development of clinical guidelines

infections [STIs] and tuberculosis); (7) mental health (promotion/prevention of mental illness); and (8) environmental health (reducing health risks associated with environmental conditions through promotion of environmental health programs, including vector control).

Under CCH II (1999), the First Caribbean Conference on Health Promotion identified six regional goals: (1) formulating public policy; (2) reorienting health services; (3) empowering communities to achieve well-being; (4); creating supportive environments; (5) developing/increasing personal health skills; and (6) building alliances with a special emphasis on the media. It further noted that:

> Health promotion must build on that aspect of Caribbean culture that embraces community action and the tradition of the extended family. Communities will be provided with the information and tools to allow them to take such actions as are needed to improve health and wellbeing. Proactive community action and participation, as well as the community's involvement in determining its priorities for health promotion, must be acknowledged and facilitated by policy makers, health service providers and the media. (p. 3)

The Nassau Declaration on Health (CARICOM 2001b) under the broad theme of *The Health of the Region Is the Wealth of the Region* praised CCH II (1999) for its "emphasis on the sharing of services and an integrated approach to managing health information and health planning and programming" (p. 2). The Nassau Declaration (CARICOM 2001b) itself gave rise to the Caribbean Commission on Health and Development (CCHD) in 2003 and in its 2005 report, CCHD argued that the foremost health difficulties of the region were chronic diseases, HIV and AIDS, injuries, and violence. Therefore, public health leadership and workforce capacity, in conjunction with health information systems, were critical issues that needed to be addressed (CARICOM and PAHO/WHO 2011). CCH II (1999) fell short of its aim to "improve and sustain the health of the people of the Caribbean to add years to life and life to years for all; and guarantee increased equity within and among countries as well as universal *access* to quality care for priority problems" (as cited in Barrow-Giles 2002) since the implementation strategy for regional public goods was never addressed, and national projects were not realized due to deficits in human recourses, regional mobilization, and coordination. Thus, CCH III (2008) was launched under the theme *Investing in Health for Sustainable Development* and covers the period 2010–2015. CCH III (2008) preserved the eight regional thematic priorities identified in CCH II (1999) but focused more on "problem-solving" as a way to reverse the deficits stemming from health reform rather than on the neoliberal orthodoxy of managing health information, planning, and programming. This new strategic focus saw the Caribbean as being the first region to eliminate indigenous poliomyelitis, measles, and rubella. This plan was coordinated by PAHO/WHO through the *Regional Expanded Program on Immunizations* (EPI) which began in mid-1975 with the 21st members of the Caribbean Epidemiology Centre (CAREC). In addition to regional coordination, CCH III (2008) called for national mechanisms to "provide adequate data on monitoring indicators; ensure adequate participation of traditional and nontraditional sectors in the attainment of health and development objectives; and build capacity at national level to contribute to national and regional progress" (p. 24). With the launching of CCH III (2008), the Caribbean had applied principles and strategic approaches to regional public goods and services and national strategic directions to achieve notable gains in poliomyelitis, measles, and cholera through education, cooperation, and donor funding. The approach to health as a regional public good was addressed in the *Liliendaal Declaration on Climate Change* (CARICOM 2009), which mandated an integrated, multi-sector, and regional approach for the achievement of food and nutrition security.

It is within the movement from conceiving health as a national issue to broader regional attention to health systems that the second functional aspect of health reform arose in the region. Given the smallness of Caribbean countries, the advancements made in the functional sectors stemmed from the recognition of the role that regional institutions played alongside national institutions. Such cooperation in health at the regional level dates back to the pre-self-determination days. The first regional institution to focus solely on health systems collaboration was the CHRC (formally Standing Advisory Committee from 1955 to 1972 [SAC] and the Council Commonwealth Caribbean Medical Research Council from 1972 to 1998) located in Trinidad and Tobago (see Table 17.4). Before being subsumed into CARPHA in 2013, CHRC served 19 Caribbean territories (Table 17.5). CHRC focused on inter-territorial collaboration related to health issues within and across its members by strengthening its research capacity, coordinating and disseminating of information, monitoring and evaluating capability, and providing supplemental funding.

The Caribbean Food and Nutrition Institute (CFNI), located in Jamaica and established in 1967, was created as a specialized center for the Pan American Health Organization/World Health Organization (PAHO/WHO). CFNI focused on solving food and nutrition security challenges in the Caribbean. Before being subsumed into CARPHA in 2013, CFNI served 18 Caribbean countries with a combined population of 6 million (see Table 17.5). It was tasked with providing guidance in four broad areas (planning, promotion and dissemination, human resource development, and

Table 17.5 Caribbean Nations by Participation in Health Reform Initiatives

	HIV/AIDS Plan	CCH	EPI	CHRC	CFNI	CAREC	CEHI	PANCAP
Anguilla	×	×	×	×	×	×	×	×
Antigua and Barbuda	×	×	×	×	×	×	×	×
Aruba			×			×		
Bahamas	×	×	×	×	×	×	×	×
Barbados	×	×	×	×	×	×	×	×
Belize	×	×	×	×	×	×	×	×
Bermuda	×	×	×	×		×		×
British Virgin Islands		×	×	×	×	×	×	×
Cayman Islands		×	×	×	×	×		×
Curacao	×							
Cuba								×
Dominica	×	×	×	×	×	×	×	×
Dominican Republic	×							×
Grenada	×	×	×	×	×	×	×	×
Guadeloupe	×							
Guyana	×	×	×	×	×	×	×	×
Haiti	×							×
Jamaica	×	×	×	×	×	×	×	×
Montserrat	×	×	×	×	×	×	×	×
Netherlands Antilles			×			×		×
St. Kitts and Nevis	×	×	×	×	×	×	×	×
St. Lucia	×	×	×	×	×	×	×	×
St. Maarten	×							
St. Vincent and the Grenadines	×	×	×	×	×	×	×	×
Suriname	×	×	×	×	×	×		×
Trinidad and Tobago	×	×	×	×	×		×	×
Turks and Caicos		×	×	×	×	×	×	×
US Virgin Islands								×

surveillance and research) and also worked in collaboration with the national government to aid in the provision of services, development of education and training, dissemination of information, and coordination and research. The organization also worked in the areas of coordination and management of technical cooperation, prevention and management of obesity and NCDs, and HIV/AIDS and nutrition.

The Caribbean Epidemiology Centre (CAREC) was born out of the 1973 Caribbean Health Ministers' Conference held in Dominica and began operation in 1975 under a bilateral agreement with PAHO. Before being subsumed into CARPHA in 2013, CAREC was based in Trinidad and Tobago and it was administered on the behalf of the 21 PAHO/WHO members (see Table 17.5). It provided public health surveillance (laboratory reference) and epidemiology services inducing access and research to specialized experiments, such as an experimental mosquito colony and several epidemiological databases. CAREC also worked on HIV surveillance.

The Caribbean Environmental Health Institute (CEHI), established in 1979 by CARICOM heads of government, was a technical institute that provided technical and advisory services on sustainable development and environmental issues related to health. Before being subsumed into CARPHA in 2013, CEHI, based in St. Lucia, provided services to its 16 members on a multiplicity of health-related issues ranging from the management of human, land, and chemical resources to environmental assessment—eco-renewable energy and sustainable consumption and production (see Table 17.5).

The Caribbean Regional Drug Testing Laboratory (CRDTL), located in Jamaica and established in 1974 by CARICOM heads of government, focused on regional drug testing (see Table 17.5). Before being subsumed into CARPHA in 2013, CRDTL's mission was to ensure that drugs met the suitable benchmarks of pureness, potency, and quality. The laboratory in Jamaica focused on conducting microbiological and pharmacological tests on drugs to ensure that the drugs met nationally established standards. The administering of drug testing differs from geographic subregion to subregion. For example, Barbados, Trinidad and Tobago, Jamaica, and the Organization of Eastern Caribbean States (OECS) have independent drug standards, the Dutch Antilles is regulated by the Netherlands, and Cuba follows its own national policy. Two studies, the *Regional Assessment of Drug Regulatory and Registration Systems* (HERA 2009a) and *The Regional Assessment on Patent and Related Issues and Access to Medicines* (HERA 2009b), financed by the World Bank and PAHO/WHO, sought to understand the access to sufficient quality medicines at affordable prices in the CARICOM countries and the Dominican Republic. These two studies established the foundation of the *Caribbean Pharmaceutical Policy* (CPP), which was approved by the COHSOD VI (PAHO, WHO and CARICOM 2011a). The CPP is based on an intersectional approach (access, quality, and rational use) with seven objectives that are organized around four strategic areas: (1) pharmaceutical policy scope; (2) regulatory framework; (3) access; and (4) rational use of medicines. The premise that access to quality medicine at affordable prices is a human right for all Caribbean citizens guides the CPP. Yet, PAHO/WHO (2010) noted that 7 out of the 13* Caribbean countries involved in its report on the *Pharmaceutical Situation in the Caribbean* have national medical policies. The region faces several challenges in the quality and control of medication, including issues with counterfeit medications, inability to test all medications, and the lack of quality persons for pharmaco-vigilance to monitor adverse drug reaction.

Specialized health institutions were formed around specific health issues in addition to the regional institutions already mentioned. In 2001, the largest health institution to fight against

---

* Antigua and Barbuda, Bahamas, Barbados, Belize, Dominican Republic, Grenada, Guyana, Jamaica, St. Kitts and Nevis, St. Lucia, St. Vincent and the Grenadines, Suriname, and Trinidad and Tobago.

AIDS in the Caribbean was formed: PANCAP. PANCAP has 25 Caribbean member countries (see Table 17.5), as well as six regional institutions (CFNI, CHRC, the CAREC, the CARICOM Youth Ambassadors Programme [CYAP], the Caribbean Employers' Confederation, and the Caribbean Tourism Organisation), and works with several donor funders and NGOs. PANCAP, while seen as a specialized regional institution, is focused on providing a unified vision and direction toward mitigating the spread of HIV in the Caribbean. PANCAP oversees the coordination of all programs, activities, and resources in the region around HIV/AIDS and provides a clearinghouse for partners, as well as monitors and provides capacity building services at the regional level. In 2004, PANCAP was designated as a United Nations Programme on HIV/AIDS Best Practice. Since its development, PANCAP has developed two regional policy frameworks around the coordination of HIV/AIDS: *The Caribbean Regional Strategic Framework for HIV/AIDS 2002–2006* (CARICOM and PANCAP 2002) and *The Caribbean Regional Strategic Framework on HIV and AIDS 2008–2012* (CARICOM and PANCAP 2008). To date, 21 countries across the Caribbean region have a national strategic plan on HIV/AIDS (see Table 17.5). There has also been a rise in specialized NGOs that focus on health service provisions including the Caribbean Coalition of National AIDS Programme Coordinators, Caribbean Vulnerable Communities Coalition, and the Caribbean Regional Network of People Living with HIV/AIDS.

Caribbean countries recognized early that additional benefits in health service reforms along with the adequate implementation of national health policies would lead to the establishment of specialized regional institutions. Thus, regional institutional collaboration peaked in 2009 when CARICOM heads of government established CARPHA to integrate the function and administration of the five existing Caribbean Regional Health Institutions: the CAREC, the CFNI, the CEHI, the CRDTL, and the CHRC (see Table 17.4). CARPHA was developed since several of the five existing agencies were duplicating efforts with regard to in-country training, distance education, curriculum development and evaluation, research capacity development, and collaboration with other institutions. The new mega entity was legally created in 2011, but functionally operational in January 2013. CARPHA is able to achieve health security through cooperation and coordination and is tasked with the responsibility of addressing public health challenges, in relation to communicable diseases, such as HIV/AIDS, and NCDs, such as obesity, cancer, heart disease, and diabetes by (1) translating technical instructions in English, Dutch, French, and Spanish; (2) building capacity in research and social marketing; and (3) providing strategic planning and coordinating for the delivery of CCH III (2008). With the creating of CARPHA, a new wave of health reform has begun in line with CARPHA's new objectives given as follows:

1. Providing countries with reference and referral services as well as laboratory strengthening
2. Conducting surveillance of both communicable and NCDs
3. Providing leadership instruction to define effective public health interventions in the Caribbean
4. Producing accurate, reliable, timely, and relevant public health information to various Caribbean and international audiences
5. Coordinating effective responses to public health crises in the Caribbean
6. Enhancing national capacities to deliver public health goods and services to public health priorities in the Caribbean
7. Mobilizing resources for priority public health issues (CARICOM n.d.).

These new reforms to combat communicable diseases and NCDs are based upon "new-mutualism" (Jules 2012) that focuses on deeper cooperation and coordination through (1) a multi-sectoral approach; (2) international target setting; and (3) regional benchmarking. CARICOM (1999) notes that great collaboration and cooperation is essential to abate the challenges and increasing threats national economies are faced with through emerging and reemerging problems in the health sector. The rise of new mutualism in health systems reform uses "integrated comprehensive multi-sector measures including information and communication networks, legal and fiscal reform and healthy public policies ... in the public and private sectors of national, regional and international entities" (CCH III 2008, p. 13) to ensure regional adoption across national borders within CARICOM members.

Conclusion

The previous waves of health reform have only paid attention to prevention and treatment. The current wave of health reforms now calls for a "sustainable health systems ... to support the goal of 'Health for All'" by paying attention to the changing trends in violence, injuries, sexual behavior, and environmental management (CCH II 1990, p. 13). The WHO (2005) and global surveillance note that yellow fever and cholera pose challenges to the Caribbean Region. Despite numerous gains made in health reform, approximately 35% of the Caribbean population still lives in poverty. Moreover, as the regional focus has now moved away from reducing HIV/AIDS and toward reducing NCDs, this new shift in policy has the potential of increasing the rates of HIV infections.

As the Caribbean heads into a post-2015 sustainable development agenda, perhaps the major public administration challenge for the region is that many of the national health plans that call for broad based reforms have remained out of the public eye and instead attention is spent on quibbling for donor funding on "suggestive fundable projects." However, in a post-2008 financial crisis era with the sequestration of donor funding, we saw the rise of "new mutualism" (Jules 2012) premised upon core foundations and philosophies of CCH I (1996). While cooperation is not dead in health service, as the creation of CARPHA shows, there is residual tension between nation states as to what kinds of health service reforms are most beneficial for a viable community. So in reality, rather than having central coordination around sectoral areas, there could be a slow movement towards isolationist national health service development. Moreover, with the post-2015 development agenda shaping up around sustainability, the regional priority might shift away from health and human services altogether.

Bibliography

Allen, C. F. (2002). Gender and the transmission of HIV in the Caribbean. In S. Courtman (Ed.), *The Society for Caribbean Studies Annual Conference Papers*, Volume 3, University of Warwick, July 1–3.

Alleyne, G. (1995). Prospects and challenges for health in the Americas. *Bulletin of the Pan American Health Organization*, 29(3), 264–271.

Alleyne, G. (2005). The way forward. In O. Morgan (Ed.), *Health Issues in the Caribbean* (pp. 255–264). Kingston, Jamaica: Ian Randle Publishers.

Almeida, G., and Sarti, F. M. (2013). Measuring evolution of income-related inequalities in health and health care utilization in selected Latin American and Caribbean countries. *Revista Panamericana De Salud Pública = Pan American Journal of Public Health*, 33(2), 83–89. Retrieved from http://www.ncbi.nlm.nih.gov/pubmed/23525337.

Andrews, E. A. (1998). *Determinants of Condom Use Among Adolescents and Young Adults in Jamaica, 1989 and 1993*. Unpublished paper, The University of the West Indies Department of Sociology and Social Work, Mona, Jamaica.

Andrus, J. K., Crouch, A. A., Fitzsimmons, J., Vicari, A., and Tambini, G. (2013). Immunization and the millennium development goals: Progress and the challenges in Latin America and the Caribbean. *Health Affairs*, 27(2), 487–493. doi:10.1377/hlthaff.27.2.487.

Ashley, D., and McCaw-Binns, A. (1998). Informing maternal and child health policy through research. *West Indian Medical Journal*, 47(4), 16–19.

Ault, S. (2007). Pan American Health Organization's Regional Strategic Framework for addressing neglected diseases in neglected populations in Latin America and the Caribbean. *Memórias do Instituto Oswaldo Cruz*, 102, 99–107. Retrieved from http://www.scielo.br/scielo.php?pid=S007402762007000900016&script=sci_arttext&tlng=en.

Barbados Today. (2014). *No Chikungunya in Barbados*. Retrieved from http://www.barbadostoday.bb/2014/01/17/no-chikungunya-in-barbados/Barrow-Giles, C.

Barrow-Giles, C. (2002). *Introduction to Caribbean Politics*. Kingston, Jamaica: Ian Randle Publishers.

Bartholomew, C., and Cleghorn, F. (1989). Retroviruses in the Caribbean. *Bulletin of the Pan American Health Organization*, 23, 76–80.

Bartholomew, C., Raju, C. C., and Jankey, N. (1983). The acquired immune deficiency syndrome in Trinidad: A report of two cases. *West Indian Medical Journal*, 32, 177–180.

Brian, B. (2005). HIV/AIDS—The rude awakening stemming the tide. In O. Morgan (Ed.), *Health Issues in the Caribbean* (pp. 62–76). Kingston, Jamaica: Ian Randle Publishers.

Briguglio, L. (1995). Small island developing states and their economic vulnerabilities. *World Development*, 23, 1615–1632.

Bune, P. (1987). Vulnerability. *The Courier*, 4, 85–87.

CAREC. (2005). *Leading Causes of Death And Mortality Rates (Counts and Rates) in Caribbean Epidemiology Centre Member Countries (CMCs): 1985 1990 1995 2000*. Port of Spain, Trinidad: Caribbean Epidemiology Centre (CAREC). Retrieved from http://carpha.net/pdf/Mortality_Final_LR%20_%20061205.pdf.

CAREC. (2010). *HIV/AIDS Data for CAREC Member Countries, 1982–2010*. Retrieved from http://public.tableausoftware.com/views/Tableau_HIV_AIDS_Infobase_Dec2011RegionalDashboards/Dash_RegionalAIDSbygender?:embed=yes&:toolbar=yes&:tabs=no.

CAREC and University of the West Indies. (1997). *Modelling and Projecting HIV and Its Impact in the Caribbean: The Experience of and Tobago and Jamaica*. Mona, Jamaica: UWI-Health Economics Unit.

Caribbean Community. (1977). *Policy Declaration on Health for the Caribbean Community*. Georgetown, Guyana: CARICOM Secretariat.

Caribbean Cooperation in Health. (1993). *Caribbean Charter for Health Promotion*. Retrieved from http://www.bvsde.ops-oms.org/bvsdeps/fulltext/declarationCar.pdf.

Caribbean Epidemiology Centre. (2003). *CAREC Surveillance Report Supplement*, Volume 23 Supplement (1) October, pp. 1–16. Retrieved from: http://www.msmgf.org/files/msmgf//Caribbean/ART_EN_011003_CAR.pdf.

Caribbean Health Research Council. (2011). *Health Research Agenda for the Caribbean*. Port of Spain, Trinidad and Tobago: Caribbean Health Research Council.

CARICOM. (1982). *Declaration on Health for the Caribbean Community, 1982*. Retrieved from http://www.caricom.org/jsp/secretariat/legal_instruments/declarationonhealth.jsp?menu=secretariat.

CARICOM. (1986). *Caribbean Cooperation in Health (CCH) Initiative*. Georgetown, Guyana: The Caribbean Community (CARICOM) Secretariat.

CARICOM. (1998). Creative and productive citizens for the twenty-first century. *Paper Presented at Ninth Inter-Sessional Meeting of the Conference of Heads of Government of the Caribbean Community*. St. George's, Grenada: CARICOM. MARCH 2–3.

CARICOM. (1999). *Caribbean Cooperation in Health Phase II: A New Vision for Caribbean Health*. Georgetown, Guyana: CCH Secretariat, c/o The Caribbean Community (CARICOM) Secretariat.

CARICOM. (2001a). *Nassau Declaration on Health: The Health of the Region is the Wealth of the Region*. Retrieved from http://www.caricom.org/jsp/communications/meetings_statements/nassau_declaration_on_health.jsp?menu=communications.

CARICOM. (2001b). *The 2001 Declaration of Commitment to the Pan Caribbean Partnership Against HIV/AIDS: Provide Supportive Environment for the Collaborative Response to Fighting HIV/AIDS*. Retrieved from http://www.caricom.org/jsp/secretariat/legal_instruments/caribbean_partnership_commitment.jsp.

CARICOM. (2007a). *Declaration of Port-of-Spain: Comprehensive and Integrated Approach to the Control of CNCD*. Retrieved from http://www.caricom.org/jsp/pressreleases/pres212_07.jsp.

CARICOM. (2007b). *Declaration of Port-of-Spain: Uniting to Stop the Epidemic of Chronic NCDs Issued by the Regional Summit on Chronic Non-Communicable Diseases*. Retrieved from http://www.caricom.org/jsp/community/chronic_non_communicable_diseases/summit_chronic_non_communicable_diseases_index.jsp.

CARICOM. (2007c). *Healthy Caribbean Coalition—Declaration of St. Ann: Implementing Agriculture and Food Policies to Prevent Obesity and Non-Communicable Diseases (NCDs) in the Caribbean Community*. Retrieved from http://www.healthycaribbean.org/governments/declaration_of_st_ann.html.

CARICOM. (2007d). *Needham's Point Declaration*. Retrieved from http://www.caricom.org/jsp/pressreleases/pres167_07.jsp.

CARICOM. (2009). *Liliendaal Declaration on Climate Change and Development Issued by the Thirtieth Meeting of the Conference of Heads of Government of the Caribbean Community*. Retrieved from http://www.caricom.org/jsp/communications/meetings_statements/liliendaal_declaration_climate_change_development.jsp.

CARICOM. (2010). *The Report of the CARICOM Commission on Youth on Youth Development (CCYD)*. Retrieved from http://www.caricom.org/jsp/community_organs/cohsod_youth/eye_on_the_future_ccyd_report.pdf.

CARICOM (n.d.). *Caribbean Public Health Agency (CARPHA): Advancing Public Health in the Caribbean*. Retrieved from http://www.caricom.org/jsp/community_organs/carpha/carpha_objectives.jsp.

CARICOM and Pan American Health Organization/World Health Organization. (2011). *Strategic Plan of Action for the Prevention and Control of Chronic Non-Communicable Diseases (NCDs) for Countries of the Caribbean Community (CARICOM) 2011–2015*. Retrieved from http://www.caricom.org/jsp/community_organs/health/chronic_non_communicable_diseases/ncds_plan_of_action_2011_2015.pdf.

CARICOM and Pan Caribbean Partnership Against HIV/AIDS. (2002). *The Caribbean Regional Strategic Framework for HIV/AIDS 2002–2006*. Retrieved from http://www.caricom.org/jsp/projects/hiv-aidsstrategicframework.pdf.

CARICOM and PANCAP. (2008). *The Caribbean Regional Strategic Framework on HIV and AIDS 2008–2012*. Retrieved from http://www.caricom.org/jsp/projects/crsf-hiv-pancap.pdf.

CARICOM and Pan Caribbean Partnership against HIV/AIDS. (2011). *Caribbean Regional Strategic Framework on HIV and AIDS 2002–2006*. Retrieved from http://www.caricom.org/jsp/community_organs/health/health_main_page.jsp.

CARPHA. (2014). *CARPHA Statement on Ebola Virus Disease*. Retrieved from http://carpha.org/Portals/0/articles/documents/GeneralEbolaStatement.pdf.

CARPHA. (2015a). *CARPHA's Interim Guidelines*. Retrieved from http://carpha.org/What-We-Do/Public-Health-Activities/Chikungunya.

CARPHA. (2015b). *Chikungunya Update #53*. Retrieved from http://carpha.org/DesktopModules/Bring2mind/DMX/Download.aspx?EntryId=1452&PortalId=0&DownloadMethod=attachment.

CARPHA. (2015c). *Ebola Virus Disease*. Retrieved from http://carpha.org/What-We-Do/Public-Health-Activities/Ebola.

Carter, R. (2004). *Proceedings of the HIV/AIDS Research Symposium Report: Survey on HIV/AIDS 2001. National Expanded Response to HIV/AIDS: The Barbados Experience*. Bridgetown, Barbados.

CCH I. (1986). *Caribbean Cooperation in Health (CCH)*. Georgetown, Guyana: CCH Secretariat.

CCH II. (1999). *Caribbean Cooperation in Health Phase II: A New Vision for Caribbean Health*. Retrieved from http://www.bvsde.paho.org/bvsaia/fulltext/caribbean.pdf.

CCH III. (2008). *Caribbean Cooperation in Health Phase III: Regional Health Framework 2010–2015*. Retrieved from http://new.paho.org/ocpc/index.php?option=com_docman&task=doc_download&gid=24&Itemid=.

Clegg, P. (2015). Ebola, Chikungunya, and the Caribbean: Struggling to prepare and respond. *The Round Table* (1–3). doi:10.1080/00358533.2015.1005357.

COHSDO XXI. (2011). *Communiqué Issued at the Conclusion of the Twenty-First Meeting of the Council for Human and Social Development (COHSOD)*. Retrieved from http://www.caricom.org/jsp/communications/communiques/21cohsod_2011_communique.jsp.

Commonwealth Advisory Group. (1997). *A Future for Small States: Overcoming Vulnerability.* London: Commonwealth Secretariat.

Commonwealth Consultative Group. (1985). *Vulnerability: Small States in the Global Society.* London: Commonwealth Secretariat.

Commonwealth Secretariat. (2005). *Outcomes Document—Draft Framework of Action for a Programme of Temporary Movement of Nurses Agreed at the Caribbean Conference on Temporary Movement: Towards a Trade and Development Approach.* St. Michael, Barbados: CARICOM.

Daumerie, D., and Kindhauser, M. K. (2004). *Intensified Control of Neglected Diseases: Report of an International Workshop.* Geneva, Switzerland: World Health Organization.

Division of Youth Affairs. (2001). *Report on the National Youth Knowledge, Attitudes, Beliefs and Practices (KABP) Survey on HIV/AIDS.* St. Michael, Barbados: Government of Barbados.

Ehrenberg, J. P., and Ault, S. K. (2005). Neglected Diseases of Neglected Populations: Thinking to Reshape the Determinants of Health in Latin America and the Caribbean. *BMC Public Health*, 13, 1–13. doi:10.1186/1471-2458-5-119.

Figueroa, J. P. (2008). The HIV epidemic in the Caribbean: Meeting the challenges of achieving universal access to prevention, treatment and care. *The West Indian Medical Journal*, 57(3). Retrieved from http://www.ncbi.nlm.nih.gov/pubmed/19583117.

Frederick, J., Hakiltiom, P., Frederick. C., Wynter, S., DaCosta, V., and Wynter, H. (2005). Issues affecting reproduction health in the Caribbean. In O. Morgan (Ed.), *Health Issues in the Caribbean* (pp. 41–50). Kingston, Jamaica: Ian Randle Publishers.

Gillette, H. (2014). *Caribbean Experiences Outbreak of Chikungunya.* Retrieved from http://voxxi.com/2014/01/23/chikungunya-mosquito-illness-carribean/.

Government of Barbados. (2008). *National Strategic Plan for the Prevention and Control of HIV 2008–2013.* St. Michael, Barbados: Ministry of Health.

Government of Trinidad and Tobago. (2009). *Vision 2020 Operational Plan: Progress Report.* Retrieved from http://www.finance.gov.tt/content/pubFAFC0C.pdf.

Gulliford, M. (1994). Health and health care in the English-speaking Caribbean: A British public health physician's view of the Caribbean. *Journal of Public Health Medicine*, 16(3), 263–269.

Hagley, K. (2005). Introduction. In O. Morgan (Ed.), *Health Issues in the Caribbean* (pp. 3–4). Kingston, Jamaica: Ian Randle Publishers.

Halcón, L., Blum, R. W., Beuhring, T., Pate, E., Campbell-Forrester, S., and Venema, A. (2003). Adolescent health in the Caribbean: A regional portrait. *American Journal of Public Health*, 93(11), 456–460.

Hall, K. O., and Chuck-A-Sang, M. (2007). *The Caribbean Integration Process: A People Centered Approach.* Kingston, Jamaica: Ian Randle Publishers.

Hall, G., and Patrinos, H. A. (Eds.). (2006). *Indigenous Peoples, Poverty, and Human Development in Latin America.* New York: Palgrave Macmillan.

Health Research for Action. (2009a). *Regional Assessment on Patent and Related Issues and Access to Medicines in CARICOM Member States and the Dominican Republic.* Georgetown, Guyana: CARICOM.

Health Research for Action. (2009b). *Report on Regional Assessment of Drug Registration and Regulatory Systems of CARICOM Member States and the Dominican Republic.* Georgetown, Guyana: CARICOM.

Holmes, F. (1976). Development problems of small countries. In L. V. Castle and F. Holmes (Eds.), *Co-Operation and Development in Asia Pacific Region: Relations Between Large and Small Countries* (pp. 43–66). Tokyo, Japan: Japan Economic Research Centre.

Hospedales, J. (2005). Health status in the region—A historical overview. In O. Morgan (Ed.), *Health Issues in the Caribbean* (pp. 5–12). Kingston, Jamaica: Ian Randle Publishers.

Hotez, P. J., Bottazzi, M. E., Franco-Paredes, C., Ault, S. K., and Periago, M. R. (2008). The neglected tropical diseases of Latin America and the Caribbean: A review of disease burden and distribution and a roadmap for control and elimination. *PLoS Neglected Tropical Diseases*, 2(9), e300. doi:10.1371/journal.pntd.0000300.

Inter-American Development Bank. (2005). *The Millennium Development Goals in Latin America and the Caribbean: Progress, Priorities and IDB Support for Their Implementation.* Retrieved from http://idbdocs.iadb.org/wsdocs/getdocument.aspx?docnum=591088.

Joint United Nations Programme on HIV/AIDS and WHO. (2009). *AIDS Epidemic Update.* Geneva, Switzerland: UNAIDS. Retrieved from http://data.unaids.org/pub/report/2009/jc1700_epi_update_2009_en.pdf.

Jules, T. D. (2012). "New mutualism" in small (and micro) states: The AIDS generation and AIDS fatigue in the Caribbean Educational Policy Space. In A. Wiseman and R. Glover (Eds.), *The Impact of HIV/AIDS on Education Worldwide* (pp. 259–285). doi:10.1108/S1479-3679(2012)0000018014.

Jules, T. D. (2014). Trans-regional regimes and globalization in education: Constructing the neo-Caribbean citizen. In I. Silova and D. Hobson (Eds.), *Globalizing Minds: Rhetoric and Realities in International Schools.* (pp. 249–276). Chapel Hill, NC: Information Age Publishing.

Kiragu, K. (2001). *Youth and HIV/AIDS: Can We Avoid Catastrophe? Population Reports, Series L, No. 12. Population Information Program, Bloomberg School of Public Health.* Baltimore, MD: Johns Hopkins University Press.

King, D. (2001). The evolution of structural adjustment and stabilisation policy in Jamaica. *Social and Economic Studies*, 50(1), 1–53. Retrieved from http://www.jstor.org/stable/10.2307/27865221.

Kreniske, J. (1997). AIDS in the Dominican Republic: Anthropological reflections on the social nature of disease. In G. C. Bond, J. Kreniske, and I. Susser (Eds.), *AIDS in Africa and the Caribbean.* Boulder, CO: Westview Press.

Laptiste, C. (2004). *Estimating the Economic Impact of HIV/AIDS in Suriname.* Mona, Jamaica: UWI-Health Economics Unit.

Luciani, S., and Andrus, J. K. (2008). A Pan American Health Organization strategy for cervical cancer prevention and control in Latin America and the Caribbean. *Reproductive Health Matters*, 16(32), 59–66.

Maharaj, S. R., and Paul, T. J. (2011). Ethical issues in healthcare financing. *The West Indian Medical Journal*, 60(4), 498–501.

McCaw-Binns, A. (2005). Safe motherhood in Jamaica: From slavery to self-determination. *Paediatric and Perinatal Epidemiology*, 19(4), 254–261.

McFarlane, C. P., and Freidman, J. S. (1999). *Reproductive Health Survey, 1997, Jamaica: Final Report.* Kingston, Jamaica: National Family Planning Board.

McLean, R. (2004). *Modelling and Projecting the Economic Impact of HIV/AIDS in the Caribbean: The Case of Guyana.* Mona, Jamaica: UWI-Health Economics Unit.

Mitra, A. K., and Rodriguez-Fernandez, G. (2010). Latin America and the Caribbean: Assessment of the advances in public health for the achievement of the Millennium Development Goals. *International Journal of Environmental Research and Public Health*, 7(5), 2238–2255. doi:10.3390/ijerph7052238.

Moyne, W. E. G., West India Royal Commission, and Benn, D. (2011). *The Moyne Report.* Kingston, Jamaica: Ian Randle Publishers.

Mullings, J., and Paul, T. J. (2007). Health sector challenges and responses beyond the Alma-Ata Declaration: A Caribbean perspective. *Revista Panamericana de Salud Pública*, 21(2–3), 155–163.

Narain, J. P., Hull, B., Hospedales, C. J., Mahabir, S., and Bassett, D. C. (1989). Epidemiology of AIDS and HIV infection in the Caribbean. In *AIDS, Profile of an Epidemic*, PAHO/WHO Scientific Publication no. 514 (pp. 61–71), Washington, DC: PAHO/WHO Scientific Publication.

PAHO. (1995). *Report of Special Meeting on Health Sector Reform.* Washington, DC: The Americas PAHO.

PAHO. (2006). *Report of the Caribbean Commission on Health and Development.* Retrieved from http://www.who.int/macrohealth/action/PAHO_Report.pdf.

PAHO. (2007). *Health in the Americas 2007 (V. I & II).* Washington, DC: Pan America Health Organization.

PAHO. (2011). *Prevalence and Intensity of Infection of Soil-Transmitted Helminths in Latin America and the Caribbean Countries: Mapping at Second Administrative Level 2000–2010.* Washington, DC: Pan America Health Organization. Retrieved from http://www.paho.org/hq/index.php?option=com_docman&task=doc_view&gid=14335&Itemid=.

PAHO and WHO. (2010). *Pharmaceutical Situation in the Caribbean: Fact Book on Level I Monitoring Indicators 2007.* Retrieved from http://apps.who.int/medicinedocs/documents/s17562en/s17562en.pdf.

PAHO, WHO, and CARICOM. (2011a). *Caribbean Pharmaceutical Policy.* Washington, DC: Pan American Health Organiztion. Retrieved from http://www.paho.org/hq/index.php?option=com_docman&task=doc_view-&gid=23746&Itemid=.

PAHO/WHO and CARICOM. (2006). *Report of the Caribbean Commission on Health and Development.* Kingston, Jamaica: Ian Randle Publishers.

PAHO/WHO and CARICOM. (2011b). *Strategic Plan of Action for the Prevention and Control of Chronic Non-Communicable Diseases (NCDs) in the Countries of the Caribbean Community (CARICOM) 2011–2015.* Georgetown, Guyana: CARICOM. Retrieved from http://www.caricom.org/jsp/community_organs/health/chronic_non_communicable_diseases/ncds_plan_of_action_2011_2015.pdf.

Palloni, A., Pinto-Aguirre, G., and Pelaez, M. (2002). Demographic and health conditions of ageing in Latin America and the Caribbean. *International Journal of Epidemiology*, 31(4), 762–71.

Pan American Health Organization. (2005). *Declaration of Montevideo on the New Orientations for Primary Health Care: Designing People-Centered Care Through a Primary Healthcare Based System.* Retrieved from http://www.paho.org/English/GOV/CD/cd46-decl-e.pdf.

Pape, J. W. (2000). AIDS in Haiti, 1980–96. In G. D. Howe and A. G. Cobley (Eds.), *The Caribbean AIDS Epidemic* (pp. 226–242). Kingston, Jamaica: University of the West Indies Press.

Price, C. R. (2000). Political and radical aspects of the Rastafarian Movement in Jamaica. *Nature, Society, and Thought*, 13(2), 155–180.

Ramirez, A., and Chelala, C. (2006). A Nonmedical Paradigm for Public Health. *Viewpoint*, 21, 62–64.

Rodney, W. (1969). *The Groundings with My Brothers.* London: MacGibbon and Keen.

Rose, E.A. (2002). *Dependency and Socialism in the Modern Caribbean: Superpower Intervention in Guyana, Jamaica and Grenada, 1970–1985.* Oxford: Lexington Books.

Ruger, J. P. (2005). The changing role of the World Bank in global health. *American Journal of Public Health*, 95(1), 60–70. doi:10.2105/AJPH.2004.042002.

Samuels, T. A., and Fraser, H. (2010). Caribbean Wellness Day: Mobilizing a region for chronic noncommunicable disease prevention and control. *Revista Panamericana De Salud Pública=Pan American Journal of Public Health*, 28(6), 472–480.

Samuels, T., and Hospedales, C. (2011). From Port-of-Spain Summit to United Nations High Level Meeting: CARICOM and the global non-communicable disease agenda. *West Indian Medical Journal*, 60(4). Retrieved from http://caribbean.scielo.org/scielo.php?script=sci_arttext&pid=S0043-31442011000400006&lng=pt&nrm=iso?iframe=true.

Santana, S. (1997). AIDS prevention, treatment, and care in Cuba. In G. C. Bond, J. Kreniske, I. Susser, and J. Vincent (Eds.), *AIDS in Africa and the Caribbean.* Boulder, CO: Westview Press.

St. Martin News Network. (2013). *Mosquito Fogging to Start Thursday Throughout Country: Residents Urged to Step Up Mosquito Elimination Measures After Emergence of Chikungunya on Island.* Retrieved from http://www.smn-news.com/st-maarten-st-martin-news/14024-mosquito-fogging-to-start-thursday-throughout-country-residents-urged-to-step-up-mosquito-elimination-measures-after-emergence-of-chikungunya-on-island.html?utm_source=twitterfeed&utm_medium=twitter.

Swaroop, V. (1996). The public sector in the Caribbean: Issues and reform options. *Policy Research Working Paper 1609.* Washington, DC: World Bank.

Theodore, K. (2001). HIV/AIDS in the Caribbean: Economic issues, impact and investment response. *Commission on Macroeconomics and Health Working Paper Series, Paper No. WG 1*(1). Geneva, Switzerland: World Health Organization.

Theodore, K., and Edwards-Wescott, P. (2011). An assessment of primary health care in the Caribbean pre and post Alma-Ata Declaration and a way forward. *International Journal of Humanities and Social Science*, 1(8), 1–10.

Tsang, M. C., Fryer, M., and Arevalo, G. (2002). *Access, Equity, and Performance: Education in Barbados, Guyana, Jamaica, and Trinidad and Tobago.* Washington, DC: Inter-American Development Bank.

UNAIDS. (2013). Global report: UNAIDS report on the global AIDS epidemic 2013. http://www.unaids.org/en/media/unaids/contentassets/documents/epidemiology/2013/gr2013/UNAIDS_Global_Report_2013_en.pdf.

UNAIDS and WHO. (2009). *AIDS Epidemic Update December 2009.* Geneva, Switzerland: UNAIDS. Retrieved from http://data.unaids.org/pub/report/2009/jc1700_epi_update_2009_en.pdf. Accessed on January 21, 2012.

UNDP. (2013). *About Millennium Development Goals: What They Are.* Retrieved from http://www.unmillenniumproject.org/goals/index.htm.

UNICEF. (2006). *HFLE in Caribbean Schools, New Approaches, Prospects and Challenges.* Barbados. Retrieved from http://www.unicef.org/barbados/cao_unicefeco_hfle(1).pdf.

United Nations Development Programme. (2008). *Millennium Development Goals Report, 2008.* Retrieved from http://www.undp.org/publications/MDG_Report_2008_en.pdf.

United Nations Population Division. (2011). *World Population Prospects: The 2010 Revision, Volume I: Comprehensive Tables.* ST/ESA/SER.A/313. Retrieved from http://esa.un.org/unpd/wpp/Documentation/pdf/WPP2010_Volume-I_Comprehensive-Tables.pdf.

World Bank. (1988). *Financing Health Services in Developing Countries: An Agenda for Reform.* A World Bank policy study. Washington, DC: World Bank. Retrieved form: http://documents.worldbank.org/curated/en/1989/07/440431/financing-health-services-developing-countries-agenda-reform.

World Bank. (1997). *World Development Report 1997: The State in a Changing World.* Oxford: Oxford University Press for the World Bank.

World Bank. (2003). Caribbean Country Management Unit, Poverty Reduction and Economic Management Unit, Latin America and the Caribbean Region. *Caribbean Youth Development: Issues and Policy Directions.* Washington, DC: World Bank.

World Bank. (2012) *Health Nutrition and Population Statistics.* Retrieved from http://databank.worldbank.org/data/views/reports/tableview.aspx.

World Bank. 1980. *Health sector policy paper.* Washington, DC: World Bank. http://documents.worldbank.org/curated/en/1980/02/8609122/health-sector-policy-paper.

World Health Organization. (1978). Declaration of Alma-Ata: International Conference on Primary Health service, Alma-Ata, USSR, September 6–12, 1978. Retrieved from http://whqlibdoc.who.int/publications/9241800011.pdf.

World Health Organization. (1981). *Global Strategy for Health for All by the Year 2000.* Geneva, Switzerland: World Health Organization.

World Health Organization. (2003). *International Workshop, Intensified Control of Neglected Diseases, Summary Report.* Retrieved from http://whqlibdoc.who.int/hq/2004/WHO_CDS_CPE_CEE_2004.45.pdf.

World Health Organization. (2005). *International Health Regulations.* Retrieved from http://whqlibdoc.who.int/publications/2008/9789241580410_eng.pdf.

Weis, T. (2005). A precarious balance: Neoliberalism, crisis management, and the social implosion in Jamaica. *Capital & Class*, 29(1), 115–147. doi:10.1177/030981680508500116.

Zwi, A. B., and Mills, A. (1995). Health policy in less developed countries: Past trends and future directions. *Journal of International Development*, 7, 299–328. doi:10.1002/jid.3380070302.

Chapter 18

Gender Equality and Gender Policy-Making in the Caribbean

Patricia Mohammed

Contents

Global Geopolitics and the Measurement of Gender Equality in the Caribbean 416
Primary Areas for Gender Inequality Intervention in the Caribbean 425
External and Internal Forces Influencing the Formulation of National Gender Policies 430
    External Forces 430
    Internal Forces 432
The Impact of Gender and Development Discourses on National Policy Formulation
in the Caribbean 434
    New Gender Perspectives on Human Sexuality 435
    Female Empowerment and Gender Policies: Political Leadership in Dominica 437
    The Instrumental Role of Migrant Women in Social Reproduction 438
Conclusion: Gender as a New Ingredient in Public Policy 440
References 440

> **Abstract:** By the last decade of the twentieth century, the discourse of development had fully embraced the idea that the level of gender inequality in a society is a signifier of its lag in progress. In ratifying international conventions that support the removal of discrimination against women and reduction in all gender disabilities, Caribbean states commit themselves to policy initiatives on a national scale. This chapter examines the strategy of National Gender Policy formulation and implementation undertaken by the Caribbean small states as a partnership between the national, regional, and international imperatives to achieving gender equality goals. It draws specifically on those societies in the Caribbean that have generated National Gender Policy drafts,

including four on which the author has worked directly, those of Cayman Islands, Trinidad and Tobago, Dominica, and the British Virgin Islands (BVI). The chapter thus provides a window into the factious nature of public policy-making and the role of different actors in this process. It argues that the insertion of gender into public policy has forced the Caribbean to confront the questions and issues raised by the gender and development discourse. As with all public policy formation, this presents specific challenges in different political environments, even while some gains are being met.

Global Geopolitics and the Measurement of Gender Equality in the Caribbean

The Caribbean region is inescapably embedded into current world geopolitics, as are all known societies. By the late twentieth century and into the twenty-first century, Caribbean states are called upon to demonstrate their measure of human development, and, as an integral part of human development, how they are faring in their expressions of gender equality. Many states have responded to the demands required by a new world order of global governance which accelerated from the 1990s onward. The global concern with women and gender was first advanced through the United Nations (UN) declaration of the Decade of Women—1975 to 1985, and the continued efforts by a host of UN agencies, especially and including the United National Development Programme (UNDP) and the United Nations Development Fund for Women (UNIFEM) created in 1976, with agendas geared to the eradication of gender discrimination. One must be reminded however that these corporate global initiatives rode on the crest of second wave feminism in the last three decades of the twentieth century. Second wave feminism had already firmly signaled that the subordinate status of women and children could no longer be ignored. Second wave feminism* spread like virus throughout the world and its message of the opportunities for agency of women infected many women like myself in the Caribbean. Like all social movements, however, feminism, and its conceptual category of analysis—gender—had to find footing on local and regional soil. Although immersed in global geopolitics, gender concerns in the Caribbean are constitutive of the distinctive social and historical geography of these societies—among these are the current problems and disfigurements caused by natural disasters, and the lingering burden of colonized histories that have patterned the various configurations of ethnic, class, and gender relations.†

By the last decade of the twentieth century, "gender" had also firmly entered the field of global governance and a more appeasing "gender and development discourse" (perceived as less threatening than a "feminist movement") began to flourish. The World Wide Web and accelerated forms of communication foregrounded ideas of gender in ways that could not have occurred in the early twentieth century. Thus, concepts, ideas, and their meanings underwent rapid refinements as they began to apply to global situations and through many more voices. The concept of gender has benefitted from this mushrooming of thought. Eudine Barriteau has correctly pointed out that

---

* There are disagreements among feminist and gender scholars with the designation of a feminist movement into waves, first, second, and currently a third wave. There may be some validity to this critique, but I generally have used wave in a more metaphorical than political sense as it describes for me the upsurge of a social movement or consciousness of the strength of a movement based on socioeconomic or historical circumstances that allow for this rise. For further reading see Mohammed, *Social and Economic Studies*, pp. 5–30.
† See for example O. Nigel Bolland, *The Birth of Caribbean Civilisation: A Century of Ideas About Culture and Identity, Nation and Society* (Kingston, Jamaica, 2004).

common interpretations of gender are too casually employed without acknowledgment of the extensive scholarship and complexity that the term now implies. "At one level gender has come to stand erroneously as a trendier synonym for the biological differences and signifiers implied in the word 'sex'."* Another common interpretation of gender is the literal application of its grammatical application, that is, masculine, feminine, and neuter. While the current meaning of gender is still rooted in this genealogy, Barriteau defines gender as it is employed by feminist scholars and gender analysts "… as referring to the complex systems of personal and social relations through which women and men are socially created and maintained and through which they gain access to, or are allocated status, power and material resources within society."† In addition to its encoded reference to inequality and inequity between the sexes, gender as it is applied in this chapter foregrounds another element that dominates the current application of, and for many, the problem with the concept. By the twenty-first century, a concern with gender encodes the variations in human sexuality that are either biologically or socially rendered, the difficulties that confront these variations among individuals, and the problems that this has raised for gender policy-making where in general, the state's organization of sexual difference is based on the implicit assumption of a heterosexual norm.

The idea that gender inequality could be measured and compared across nations also began to impose pressures among states to grapple with the product of gender inequity‡ in their societies, among these are the higher levels of unemployment, a lower representation in decision making at political levels and vulnerability to sexual violence that are experienced by women and girls. As the recognition of women's invisibility grew in this new gender conscious age minted in last decades of the twentieth century, the need to integrate women into development provided a trenchant critique of programs that had previously been unaware of gender roles and its impact on the poverty status of women, especially those of the Global South. Three main theoretical approaches emerged that directly feed into the currency of thought related to gender policy-making. The first was that women had to be brought into development, the Women in Development (WID) approach. The second, quickly recognizing the error of assuming women were ever outside of development corrected this misapprehension with the women and development approach and the final one which is still relevant that of gender and development or the GAD approach. The GAD approach recognizes that biology differentiates the opportunities and possibilities for each sex, and thus acknowledges sexual difference, while examining how social roles, reproductive roles and economic roles are linked to gender inequalities experienced by both masculinity and femininity (Kabeer 1994).

The idea that gender inequality, if ignored, limited human progress was underscored in the 1995 *United Nations Human Development Report* (HDR) which expressly targeted the question of gender in human development, emphasizing that "Human Development, if not engendered, is endangered."§ This global report demonstrated that progress had been made in reducing gender disparities between nations over decades of twentieth century development strategies. The 1995 report introduced two new measures that allowed comparisons between countries, concluding that near the end of the twentieth century, the opportunities available for women had not

---

* Barriteau, *Political Economy of Gender*, p. 25.
† Barriteau, ibid, p. 26.
‡ Where gender inequality refers to an ideological commitment to end forms of discrimination inequity refers to the concrete measures that need to be put in place to achieve fairness between the sexes.
§ *UNDP Human Development Report*, 1995. http://hdr.undp.org/sites/default/files/reports/256/hdr_1995_en_complete_nostats.pdf. Overview, The Revolution for Gender Equality, United Nations Development Programme, Oxford University Press, New York, p. 1.

expanded to meet the growing capabilities of women that had emerged as a result of education and experience in the public labor market. What this report introduced for the first time was the concept of a measurement of gender equality through a global comparison of selected indicators. The two new measures of gender that were assessed as part of human development were, first, the Gender Empowerment Measure (GEM) and, second, the Gender Development Indicator (GDI).

The GDI is the Human Development Indicator (HDI) discounted for gender inequality. "The derivation of a GDI," writes Mariama Williams, "therefore follows the HDI formulation but with the introduction of an assumption of difference which introduces the notion of inequality and equality between men and women."* Williams goes on to explain that inequality is assessed through either attainment or shortfall in the areas of life expectancy, educational attainment as measured through enrollment levels and literacy rates, and male and female wage and income shares in a population. The GEM calculates an index for empowerment by examining the parliamentary representation, managerial and administrative positions, and professional and technical positions held by men and women in the society.† Both of these indicators allowed for the first time a global analysis, measure, and comparison of the value that women brought to economic and social capital in their societies. What was still missing was the lack of recognition that women received for these contributions.

The UNDP HDR 1995 report noted that "Women's achievements have increased and gender gaps have narrowed considerably in education and health since 1970. But progress in women's participation in the economic and political arenas has been much less impressive."‡ Reference to Caribbean societies demonstrated specific improvements in selected sites, for instance, Jamaica was one of three countries in the world that had higher literacy rates for women than men. Globally most societies experienced an improvement in the enrollment of secondary-school-age girls. Women's representation in national parliaments in the Caribbean with the exception of Cuba (23%) continued to remain under 10%, an unfavorable comparison with the developed countries of Finland (39%), Norway (39%), Sweden (34%), and Denmark (33%), and developing countries of Seychelles (27%), South Africa (24%), and the Democratic People's Republic of Korea (20%). Thus, by the last decade of the twentieth century, there were global improvements in some areas, especially education and literacy rates, but women had made little entry into the national legislatures of most countries. Only 21 women had been elected to positions of heads of democratic states globally throughout history, with 10 in office in early 1995. One of the most insightful findings that emerged from the gender indicators published in the 1995 HDR was that "The denial of political opportunities to women is thus more than a matter of a country's stage of development, its level of income or the education level of its women. It is bound up with many cultural and social constraints."§ This was not only a critique that applied to state politics. Women also found themselves similarly underrepresented in world forums. It was calculated that of the 185 permanent representatives to the United Nations in December 1994, only 6 were women.

Between 1970 and 1992, Caribbean countries emerge nonetheless as having a better gender equality status than Latin American countries. "Most countries of Latin America have a 10–20% drop in their GDI relative to their HDI, indicating that gender inequality in basic capabilities is still a significant problem in the region. But there is less gender inequality in the Caribbean region:

---

* Mariama Williams, The dynamics of gender relations in Jamaica, Chapter IV, *UNDP Human Development Report*, UNDP, Jamaica, 2000, p. 3.
† Mohammed, *Construction of Gender Development Indicators for Jamaica*, pp. 97–100.
‡ *UNDP Human Development Report*, 1995, p. 48.
§ Ibid, p. 52.

the Bahamas' GDI, for example, is only 7% lower, Cuba's 6% and Barbados's 2%."* This overall improvement reflected in certain countries is due to higher participation rate of women in politics and lower disparities in income between men and women as, for instance, in Barbados and Cuba. Although women still continue to remain underrepresented compared to men in political leadership, there is undeniably a history of female participation in different levels of political platforms in the region. Dame Eugenia Charles had been elected as the prime minister of Dominica in 1980. Janet Jagan, although born in Chicago, Illinois, had spent a lifetime with in politics alongside her husband Cheddi Jagan, one-time president of Guyana. After his death in 1997, she was elected president of the country. These women forged the way for others like Portia Manning and Kamla Persad Bissessar who would emerge in two of the leading economies of the region—Jamaica and Trinidad and Tobago—by the twenty-first century. Their success is only one indicator of progress. There have been other slides. Between 1970 and 1992, "Guyana had the biggest drop in rank among the 79 countries (-20). Women only marginally improved their achievement levels relative to men in education and life expectancy. Not only did the country grow slowly during this period, but women did not significantly increase their share of the labor force and of earned income."†

Table 18.1 presents a GDI ranking (the measure of inequality between men and women) through a comparison of selected countries for the years 1995 and 1998 from UNDP calculations, demonstrating the position of the Caribbean in the global scene during this period.

Table 18.1 Gender Development Indicator Ranking for Selected Countries

Country	Year 1995	Year 1998
Sweden	1	6
Norway	3	2
Canada	9	1
The United States	5	4
The United Kingdom	13	10
Barbados	11	
Bahamas	26	32
Trinidad and Tobago	36	48
Belize		60
Jamaica	52	67
Guyana	70	81
Rwanda		135

Source: UNDP HDR, 2000. United Nations Human Development Report, 2000 http://hdr.undp.org/en/content/human-development-report-2000.

---

* Ibid, p. 79.
† Ibid, p. 82.

The GEM measures the relative empowerment of women and men in the economic and political spheres. It focuses on women's opportunities rather than their capabilities. Table 18.2 shows the GEM ranking that again demonstrates the global positions held by selected Caribbean societies.

From these statistics, some Caribbean countries appear to have a fairly good standing both with respect to the GDI and the GEM. The 1995 HDR measured the GEM between 1992 and 1994 for 116 countries and suggested that some developing countries had achieved a higher ranking GEM than some richer industrial societies, due primarily to overall access of women in political, economic, and professional activities. The report calculates that Barbados, the Bahamas, Trinidad and Tobago, Cuba, Costa Rica, China, Guyana, the Philippines, and Colombia were ahead of some others. "Trinidad and Tobago has a GEM of 0.533, higher than the GEM for Switzerland, Hungary, the United Kingdom, Spain, Japan or France. France's GEM, for example, is 0.433."*

The Millennium Development Goals (MDGs) 2005 noted that there has been a steady increase in women's seats in parliament globally since the 1990s, although, even with this increase, by 2005, women held only 16% of seats worldwide. Typically, it is expected that the more developed countries, particularly the Nordic ones that are leading in HDI and GDI, will come closest to parity in ensuring that women are represented in political decision making. An interesting out-runner in this respect, however, is Rwanda. Before a civil war in 1990 and genocide in 1994, Rwandan women held less than 18% of parliamentary seats. Yet by 2003, women occupied 48.8% of seats

Table 18.2 Gender Empowerment Measure Ranking

Country	Year 1995	Year 1998
Sweden	1	3
Norway	2	1
Canada	5	8
The United States	8	13
Barbados	12	17
Bahamas	14	16
Trinidad and Tobago	15	22
Cuba	16	
The United Kingdom	19	15
Belize	55	40
Suriname	64	52
Rwanda	–	

Source: UNDP HDR, 2000.

---

* Ibid, p. 83.

in Rwanda's lower house of Parliament,* rising to 56% in 2008. This was based on an intentional advancement of women generally in the society, a recognition that without women's full participation at all levels the rebuilding of a nation suffered. While the impact of more women in these positions have yet to be fully analyzed, in the context of a gender gap that has persisted in this area, the successful rise of women in Rwanda holds lessons for other developing countries.

Tables 18.1 and 18.2 demonstrate another more insidious story for the Caribbean nonetheless. There is a noticeable decline in rank both of the GDI and GEM for all of the Caribbean societies covered here. The HDR 2000 commented that the top countries such as Norway and Sweden were not only good at strengthening the basic capabilities of women relative to men but they engineered greater opportunities for women to participate more fully in the economic and political life of their countries. Interestingly, the last decades of the twentieth century saw the rise of another relapse in the achievement of gender parity in the region. Errol Miller's *Marginalization of the Black Male* and *Men at Risk*,† coupled with declining figures of males in secondary and tertiary level education and male teachers in the education system, a phenomenon that was termed "the underachievement of boys in education," was speedily picked up by the male political elite and served as a backlash to a growing women's empowerment and to policies designed to enhance women's economic and entrepreneurial opportunities. Thus, progress is achieved or sustained by systems and processes that continue to empower, rather than promote disempowerment.

By the end of the decade of the 1990s, Caribbean societies are still, however, not being perceived as sites for crisis intervention or even major targets for development work and programs, although these vary from country to country as societies such as Haiti continued to fall into the very underdeveloped country status. Despite their attempts to provide a curve and vision for gender differences and to measure gender inequality, indicators of gender measurement being employed by the HDRs cannot tell a full story. Amartya Sen has emphasized that gender difference is one field in which inequalities are difficult to assess. Sen writes "These differences may be reflected in many subtle as well as crude ways, and in various forms they can be observed in different parts of the world—among both rich and poor countries. ... it is not easy to determine what is the best indicator of advantage in terms of which these gender inequalities are to be examined."‡ Sen points out that certain aspects of inequality are made normative in various contexts because of "the quiet and ungrumbling acceptance of women of their deprived condition."§ In other words, while income earned, educational attainment or literacy levels and political participation provide one measure of difference and inequality, these are not indicative of how men and women in the Caribbean earn their wages and what burdens of labor each perform in and outside of the home, or the resulting impact on the health and welfare of each sex. The 2000 HDR reported, for instance, that women work longer hours than men in all the countries for which data as obtained for calculating indicators.¶ Sen concludes that "the need for plurality of indicators is as strong here as in any other field."**

---

* E. Powley, *Rwanda: Women Hold Up Half the Parliament—International IDEA*. www.idea.int/publications/wip2/upload/Rwanda.pdf, p. 154.
† See Errol Miller. *Marginalization of the Black Male: Insights from the Development of the Teaching Profession* (Mona, Jamaica: Canoe Press), first published, 1986, second print. 1994; and Errol Miller. *Men at Risk* (Kingston, Jamaica: Jamaica Publishing House Ltd., 1991).
‡ Sen, *Human Development,*, p. 52.
§ Ibid, p. 52.
¶ *UNDP Human Development Report,* 1995, p. 91.
** Sen, 1989, Ibid, p. 52.

If the 1995 UNDP HDR focus on gender and development differences ushered shortfalls between the sexes into the consciousness of nations and leaders, just under two decades later the 2013 HDR shifts its attention to *The Rise of the South: Human Progress in a Diverse World*. This report looks at the currently evolving geopolitics, concentrating on emerging issues and trends, and turning to the new actors who are shaping the development landscape. The 2013 report argues "the striking transformation of a large number of developing countries into dynamic major economies with growing political influence is having a significant impact on human development progress." The question then follows: how is this also impacting on gender inequalities? Another indicator is thus devised to measure gender inequality across nations. The "Gender Inequality Index" (GII) which was included in the 2013 report is a composite measure reflecting inequality in achievements between women and men in three dimensions: reproductive health, empowerment, and the labor market. Although not comparable to the GDI and GEM in that different variables and methods were used to arrive at the former measures, the GII is again linked directly to the Human Development Index of the country. The choice of the three variables of reproductive health, empowerment, and labor which are further isolated and compared with men's status allow us another insight into understanding the realpolitik of inequality which women in Caribbean societies might be experiencing in 2013, compared to their counterparts in other countries (Table 18.3).

Of the selected Caribbean societies for which data were fully available in order to arrive at a GII, Trinidad and Tobago emerges as the lead country in this region, achieving the smallest gap between men and women, although Barbados continues to rank higher in the HDI. Of the 146 countries that were ranked in the GII, the Caribbean societies of Trinidad, Barbados, Jamaica, and Belize fall within the second and third groups of countries listed under high and medium high development with Haiti falling in the low human development group. Despite the difficulties inherent in devising precise statistical indices and establishing comparisons across such a wide spectrum of nations, the data that are emerging nonetheless suggest a consistency with what we know generally of the economic, cultural, and political performance of these societies—very high maternal mortality rates in some countries as, for instance, Jamaica, Suriname, and Haiti, high adolescent fertility rates (Belize), and below 50% of population of either sex who have not had a secondary level education.

Quite apart from the UNDP measures that are generally produced at 5-year intervals, the publication of the *Global Gender Gap* report in 2013 was another attempt to measure gender inequality between nations in the twenty-first century. "The *Global Gender Gap Index* (GGGI), introduced by the World Economic Forum in 2006, is a framework for capturing the magnitude and scope of gender-based disparities and tracking their progress. The Index benchmarks national gender gaps on economic, political, education and health criteria, and provides country rankings that allow for effective comparisons across regions and income groups, and over time. The rankings are designed to create greater awareness among a global audience of the challenges posed by gender gaps and the opportunities created by reducing them. The methodology and quantitative analysis behind the rankings are intended to serve as a basis for designing effective measures for reducing gender gaps."* Due to the lack of updated data in all countries, only 136 of 200 countries were included in the 2013 report. What this index represents is the gap between men and women in four fundamental categories—"Economic Participation and Opportunity, Educational Attainment, Health and Survival, and Political Empowerment." Thus, unlike the ranking system of the former three

---

* The Global Gender Gap Report World Economic Forum, 2013, p. 3, http://www3.weforum.org/docs/WEF_GenderGap_Report_2013.pdf.

Table 18.3 Gender Inequality Index of the HDR 2013

HDI Rank/Country	Gender Inequality Index (GII) 2012	Maternal Mortality Ratio (Deaths by 100,000 Live Births) 2010	Adolescent Fertility Rate (Births per 1,000 Women Ages 15–19) 2012	Seats in National Parliament (% Female) 2012	Population with at least Secondary Education (% Age 25 and Older) 2006–2010		Labor Force Participation Rate (% Age 15 and Older) 2011	
					Female	Male	Female	Male
1 Norway	5	7	7.4	39.6	95.6	94.7	61.7	70.1
3 The United States	42	21	27.4	17.0	94.7	94.3	57.5	70.1
38 Barbados	61	51	40.8	19.6	89.5	87.6	64.8	76.2
67 Trinidad and Tobago	50	46	31.6	27.4	59.4	59.2	54.9	78.3
85 Jamaica	87	110	69.7	15.5	74.0	71.1	56.0	71.8
96 Belize	79	53	70.8	13.3	35.2	32.8	48.3	81.8
105 Suriname	94	130	34.9	11.8	40.5	47.1	40.5	68.7
161 Haiti	127	350	41.3	4.0	22.5	36.3	60.1	70.6
167 Rwanda	76	340	35.5	51.9	7.4	8.0	86.4	85.4
186 Niger	146	590	193.6	13.3	2.5	7.6	39.9	89.9

Source: UNDP Human Development Report 2013, *The Rise of the South Human Progress in a Diverse World.* http://hdr.undp.org/en/media/HDR2013_EN_Summary.pdf.

Table 18.4 The Global Gender Gap Index 2013 Rankings: Comparisons with 2012, 2011, 2010, 2009, 2008, 2007, and 2006

Country	2013 Rank	2012 Rank	2011 Rank	2010 Rank	2009 Rank	2008 Rank	2007 Rank	2006 Rank
Iceland	1	1	1	1	1	4	4	4
Sweden	4	4	4	4	4	3	1	1
Cuba	15	19	20	24	29	25	22	..
Barbados	29	27	33	31	21	26	..	..
Trinidad and Tobago	36	43	21	21	19	19	46	45
Bahamas	40	27	22	36	28	..	..	..
Jamaica	47	51	47	44	48	44	39	25
Guyana	48	42	38	38	35	..	..	..
Belize	107	102	100	93	87	86	94	..
Suriname	110	106	104	102	78	79	56	..
Pakistan	135	134	133	132	132	127	126	112
Yemen	136	135	135	134	134	130	128	115

Note: The Global Gender Gap Index 2013 rankings: Comparisons with 2012, 2011, 2010, 2009, 2008, 2007 and 2006. Table 3a, Part 1, p. 8.: symbol indicates unavailability of data for these years. http://www3.weforum.org/docs/WEF_GenderGap_Report_2013.pdf.

measures that is linked to the level of human development, this index (Table 18.4) actively sets out to measure the existing gap between men and women.

The GGGI was designed to measure gender-based gaps in access to resources and opportunities in individual countries rather than the actual levels of the available resources and opportunities in those countries, an attempt to make the GGGI independent from the countries' levels of development. This is an important theoretical and political breakthrough as it imposes gender equality and equity as an inherent right of individuals within nations rather than as a by-product of the level of development. In this respect, the GGGI in fact shows that the selected Caribbean societies offer greater access to resources and opportunities to women than when they are ranked by the measures used to define development. How much of this is as a result of progressive social and cultural dynamics of history is useful to contemplate if one considers that the lowest gaps are found among the Nordic countries which have had extremely radical gender policies and the largest gaps among those societies such as Pakistan and Yemen where women and girls have historically had less access to education, leadership, and autonomy in decision making. Where gender equality is absorbed into the realm of different inequalities as part of a country's agenda, and driven by political will of the state, it is more likely that the gaps between men and women will be reduced, as is evident in the case of Cuba which demonstrates the lowest gender gap for the Caribbean.

Caribbean community regional bodies remain unsatisfied with the progress that has been observed. The 1994–2002 CARICOM report observed that "The gap between women and men appears to have been narrowing in several spheres over the past two decades, but there are no real gains for women. Even in the field of education, where women are cited to have exceeded men in participation, they are yet to reap the benefits associated with such achievements, for example, in employment-related indicators. The progressive trends in the past two decades are often stalled, or reversed...."* The *CARICOM Report Women and Men in the Caribbean Community* 1980–2001 emphasized the need for policy intervention as a result of the impact of global macro policies on small states. "There is a need then, for a new vision matched by proactive measures for managing education, employment and health and for ensuring gender equality and justice. These measures can only become more precise by planning and implementation drawn from evidence-based research that undergirds conviction with hard data, particularly with respect to women and youth."† This is consistent with the findings from the measurement of the GEM between 1995 and 1998 above. Where data are matched by opportunities created to sustain progress, then the gender inequality gap between men and women is reduced.

What were the specific areas of marked gender imbalance in the Caribbean that required attention by the end of twentieth century and how have these continued as gender concerns into the present? In the next section, I look at some major sites that affect the gender balance of the region.

Primary Areas for Gender Inequality Intervention in the Caribbean

To establish the distinctive differences of a gender and development discourse in the late twentieth and early twenty-first centuries, we can look back briefly at the status of women in relation to men in some of the key areas that speak to gender empowerment. To every generation, change seems too slowly incremental, yet the transformations that have been wrung from resistant societies and governance processes from the beginning to end of the twentieth century are significant. A schematic historical overview also places the current concerns in context. Are these new issues that have surfaced with changing technologies, or are have they emerged because there is now a new consciousness of gender difference and gender entitlements?

From the gradual decolonization in the early twentieth century, resulting in "independence" of the most of the territories by the 1960s, a series of initiatives clearly signal a distinctive consciousness of the uneven status of women among peoples of Caribbean societies. In 1918, Jamaica's Women's Social Service Club was formed, and by 1921, Audrey Jeffers founded the Coterie of Social Workers in Trinidad with the aim of improving the status of middle-class black and colored women. Reddock (1994)‡ has pointed out that social work was the preserve of only middle-class white women at the time. Thus, one of the "first" concerns was that of the welfare and status of women and children in society and the empowerment of black and middle-class women. The Coterie of Social Workers established social work programs focused on women and children, campaigned for women's secondary education, for increased access to white collar jobs for black

---

* CARICOM *Women and Men in the Caribbean Community*, Caribbean Community Secretariat Statistics Programme, United Nations Department of Economic and Social Affairs Statistics Division, Caribbean Community Secretariat Georgetown, Guyana, 2003, p. 3
† Ibid, p. 6
‡ Reddock, *Women, Labour and Politics*.

women, for the introduction of women police and for the Divorce Act. By 1937, the Jamaican Women's Liberal Club, the Jamaican counterpart to the Coterie of Social Workers in Trinidad was formed, with similar intent. The Coterie also hosted the first conference of women social workers in the British West Indies held in Trinidad in 1936 and formed the Association of Women Workers. Apart from their service commitment, educated women clearly began to take an interest in the employment opportunities available to women. In 1929, Una Marson became editor of Jamaica's first women's publication, *The Cosmopolitan*. As the official organ of the Jamaica Stenographers Association, the publication called for increased employment opportunities for working-class women.*

At the same time, however, a move to what Reddock calls "housewifisation"† for Caribbean black and colored women was stealthily taking place. Interestingly, this move to middle-class domesticity and respectability patterned after a Victorian ideal of womanhood prefigures and parallels the process that would take place in the United States and Britain with the post-World War II return of soldiers. Men returned to take up jobs that they had left to fight in the war, leaving women to carry out these jobs. When they returned, a battery of women now employed in every possible area, from munitions factories to secret intelligence, were also meant to return to their domesticity and their primary roles of motherhood and wifehood. "Housewifization" could be recognized, for instance, in Trinidad in the 1936 act that barred married women teachers from employment. In 1939, women were banned from night work in factories, the obvious assumption being that women as the weaker sex could not work at night, that women were nurturers and should be at home taking care of children, and that they were not the sole or major provider in their family. A similar perception of gender roles could also be recognized in the recommendations of the Moyne Commission‡ which presented the model for family stability as the archetypal male breadwinner who headed a monogamous family. In an attempt to stall "promiscuity," the Commission recommended voluntary social work for women in the middle classes, opportunities for women in the professions and civil service, generally those that required lower educational skills, advocating that the majority of women, especially working class girls should be taught domestic science to outfit them for their primary roles as housewives. Questions of equal pay for equal work or career paths toward promotion of women were absent on these agendas.§

A "second" issue that appeared in the early decades was that women, especially colored and black women, were demanding more in the way of political involvement. Jamaica had an unprecedented lead having had a limited franchise for women as early as 1919. In 1924, a deputation of women went to the governor of Trinidad to discuss votes for women. By 1936, Audrey Jeffers was the first woman elected to the Port of Spain City Council in Trinidad, and by 1935–1936, women

---

* See Chapter 6, "The Early Women's movement," Reddock, *Women, Labour and Politics,* pp. 162–181.
† Ibid, p. 32
‡ The Moyne Commission refers to the West India Royal Commission which was a comprehensive investigation of the social and economic condition of all the British territories in the Caribbean. Led by Lord Moyne, the Commission held public hearings throughout the region, and recommended sweeping reforms in everything from employment practices and social welfare, to radical political change. The full findings of the commission were not published until 1945 but an immediate start was made upon the implementation of less controversial recommendations. The British government decided to make substantial increases in the amount of money available for colonial development of all kinds and set about creating a framework for change. http://www.casbah.ac.uk/cats/archive/135/ICSA00019.htm.
§ "Campaigning and Citizenship: Women in the Caribbean from emancipation to national independence," Page created by Penny Welch, March 2011. http://pers-www.wlv.ac.uk/~le1810/4GK005w22.htm.

in Trinidad got the vote in local elections. Jamaica was the first country in the English-speaking Caribbean to successfully introduce universal adult suffrage in 1944, followed by Trinidad and Tobago in 1945, Barbados in 1950, and Dominica in 1951. The first elections under universal adult suffrage were held in 1953 in Guyana. While some societies were able to forge ahead, some were still struggling for basic rights. Women in the Cayman Islands, a dependency of the United Kingdom but under the legislated control of Jamaica in the first half of the twentieth century, began the process in 1948. Between March and April 1957, some 358 women signed another petition to Legislative Assembly of Justices and Vestry. Despite the Convention regarding the political rights of women that was adopted by the General Assembly of the United Nations at its Seventh Session in 1952, in accordance with the provisions of the Charter of the United Nations and of the Universal Declaration of Human Rights that women should be entitled to vote, up to 1952 women in dependent territories like Cayman Islands were unsuccessful in their bid. The United Kingdom government, ironically, was not able to accept the Convention because of its own non-admittance of women to the House of Lords.*

This bleak picture of futile struggling for basic political rights and to engage in civic activities no longer obtains, even while there are areas that persistently retain a gender imbalance, such as women's underrepresentation in political participation. While the GII 2013 (Table 18.3) reflects women's disadvantage in three dimensions—reproductive health, empowerment, and economic activity, new areas have surfaced for concern as globally the mechanisms for development, organization, and control of populations have become more sophisticated. Caribbean societies are no longer primarily agriculturally based; in principle and largely in practice, boys and girls have equal access to education at all levels. Self-governance has given all states a far more instrumental role in ensuring that gender and human rights are observed. The discourse in gender within Caribbean societies had also caught up and shifted approaches from women and development (WID) to gender and development (GAD), the former as Eudine Barriteau observed, implying that "... the process of development bypassed women and that national and international development policies should ensure that women were integrated into development policies and planning."†

There is agreement between the scholarship and practices of feminism and gender in the Caribbean that the state, economic entrepreneurship, and cultural signifiers such as religion have retained a patriarchal or masculinist position, unintentionally perhaps as the ideas of a natural order of gender runs deeply into the veins of every societal vessel. The primary areas for gender intervention in the region thus derive still from legacies of the past gender inequity and from new challenges to the gender hierarchy. An examination of several reports including the CARICOM report of 2003, National Gender Policies of various territories, and the Caribbean Human Development Report 2013 reveals by their recurrence, the primary issues that present as gender concerns in the region.

Education surfaces as a major concern across the region. The CARICOM report identified the education progression within the secondary school, and specifically dropout and repetition rates of boys. The Jamaican National Gender Policy noted, "despite the lack of overt institutional barriers to access to education, men are increasingly under-represented and under-performing in the national educational system. Although the 2009 male enrolment rates are more or less even with

---

* Patricia Mohammed and Marilyn Connolly, *Historical Antecedents in the Development of a Gender Consciousness in the Cayman Islands*, University of the West Indies, May 2004, unpublished paper.
† Barriteau, *Political Economy*, p. 158.

the female enrolment rates at the infant, primary and secondary levels, there is a dramatic decline in male enrolment rates at the tertiary level as indicated above."*

Closely related to this is the problem of crime, male involvement in criminal activity and the impact on women and younger boys and girls. Education, or lack of education, has been identified as a key factor that influences high-risk behaviors of youth and other age groups with respect to substance abuse. "… The majority of people in conflict with the justice system in Jamaica are male; in 2009, 98.2% of the persons arrested and charged for major crimes were male and 90.6% of the persons admitted to adult correctional institutions were male."† The Caribbean Human Development Report noted "Gender is the strongest predictor of criminal behaviour and criminal victimization. … (while) women commit fewer crimes than men and are disproportionately the victims of some types of crimes. They are more at risk and more vulnerable to some types of crime, particularly gender-based violence."‡

Gender-based violence remains a top priority of any intervention program on gender equality. The 2013 online published revised draft of the Trinidad and Tobago National Gender Policy addresses this succinctly as it affects all nations: "Gender based violence is an obstacle to national development. The physical, psychological and sexual abuse inflicted against women and girls, and also men and boys, cuts across income, age, class and cultural divides, impinging on and compromising their fundamental rights and freedoms. The fear and insecurity promulgated by gender violence, is a constraint to mobility, limits access to resources, and participation in activities. The social stigma and consequences to those who experience gender violence remain one of the most persistent problems in the society. Gender based violence comes with a high social, health and economic costs to the individual, the workplace and society."§

The Caribbean Human Development Report (2012) identifies the problem of trafficking in persons particularly in some countries in the region. While trafficking occurs in a variety of exploitative forms, forced labor, domestic servitude, and sex exploitation are believed to be the most common manifestations in the Caribbean. Sex exploitation seems to be the most predominant form.¶ Kamala Kempadoo has pointed out that the old style of power and control over black women's bodies exerted under European colonial masters has now been replaced by sex tourism and sex-oriented prostitution.** In both the Cayman Islands and the BVI (now Virgin Islands), migrant laborers, particularly those who came as domestic workers, were among the most disempowered of workers. "Many female migrant workers in the lower paid sectors were overworked and underpaid but generally did not complain because of the fear of revocation of their work permits. According to a key stakeholder, the employer (male) of a female non-belonger refused to apply for a renewal of her work permit following her complaint of sexual harassment against him. Domestic workers, especially live-in immigrant domestic workers, were singled out as being particularly

---

* Jamaican National Policy for Gender Equality, Government of Jamaica, p. 9, http://www.jcdc.gov.jm/uploads/advisories/NPGE%20BOOKLET%20web.pdf.
† Ibid, p. 9.
‡ *Caribbean Human Development Report 2012: Estimating a CARICOM Human Development Index,* p. 33–34. http://hdr-caribbean.regionalcentrelac-undp.org/images/PDF/caricom_hdi.pdf.
§ *Draft National Policy on Gender and Development of the Republic of Trinidad and Tobago,* Government of Trinidad and Tobago, 2013. http://hiv.health.gov.tt/site_media/media/filer_public/2013/01/21/draft_national_gender_and_development_policy.pdf, p. 34.
¶ *Caribbean Human Development Report 2012: Human Development and Shift to Better Citizen Security,* United Nations Development Programme, New York, p. 32.
** See Kamala Kempadoo (Ed.). *Sun, Sex and Gold-Tourism and Sex Work in the Caribbean* (Oxford: Rowman and Littlefield Publishers, 1999).

vulnerable to overwork, underpayment and sexual harassment. Victimization is prohibited under the Labour Code but they are still fearful of making complaints."* The above speaks to the problem not just of human trafficking but that of population dynamics, labor codes, legal protections available to migrants, and conditions of work and life in societies to which they have migrated. How female workers who are a large proportion of the "unskilled" labor that migrates are affected differently to male workers is certainly still not fully comprehended.

The persistent area of health, especially the differentials attached to male and female health seeking behaviors, the problems attached to sexual and reproductive health, the incidence and treatment of Human Immunodeficiency Virus/Acquired Immunodeficiency Syndrome (HIV/AIDS), increasing life expectancy of the elderly, and the types of diseases that are caused by changes in lifestyle, including cardiac diseases, diabetes, obesity, and mental disorders remain consistently as problems that a gender perspective must engage with. The Trinidad and Tobago Draft Gender Policy 2009 underscored this point that applies to all Caribbean territories, "Male resistance to prostate cancer screening is one of the serious issues of male health seeking behaviour that needs to be addressed. The high incidence of male mortality due to motor vehicle accidents, drowning and homicide establishes this area as another health risk for men."† As regards women's sexual and reproductive health, despite the advances in international instruments related to maternal mortality due to childbirths, the question of abortion remains a no-go area in many of the Caribbean territories (although this has been tackled successfully in some).

The greater employment of women in the formal workplace has created challenges to work and family life balance. The impact of this on children and family life recurs in every state, with increasing attention being paid to workplace policies that encourage men and women to combine family work and corporate/market work, to encourage employers to introduce job sharing programs and flextime as innovations toward people-led over market-driven development. How different classes or groups of women are affected must also be taken into consideration. The Caribbean Human Development Report emphasizes that "Approximately half of all households in the Caribbean are headed by women, who must therefore shoulder the responsibility for both productive and reproductive work. Women also have longer life expectancies than men. Together, these factors contribute to the feminization of poverty. Women who live in poverty experience additional vulnerabilities, such as higher infant mortality rates, higher likelihood of early pregnancy, lower school enrolment, lower employment rates, and increased likelihood of experiencing violence."‡

The legal framework for fulfilling, respecting, and promoting the human rights of women, men, and children toward the achievement of gender equality and equity remains a major area of concern for any gender intervention. Legal remedies are especially required in the areas of sexual violence, inheritance rights, matrimonial rights, equal pay for equal work, maternity and paternity rights, and sexual harassment provisions.

Finally, one area of concern that has created major tensions, as will be pursued further in the last section of this chapter, is the recognition and rights attached to persons with alternative sexualities, or different sexual orientation. Homophobia remains another area of gender that is deeply

---

* British Virgin Islands Draft National Gender Policy, Government of the British Virgin Islands, 2011, p. 49. The policy was prepared by Patricia Mohammed as lead consultant with Deborah Mc Fee, Jane Parpart, and Gaietry Pargass as associates.

† *Trinidad and Tobago Draft National Gender Policy*, Government of Trinidad and Tobago, 2006, p. 42.

‡ *Caribbean Human Development Report 2012: Estimating a CARICOM Human Development Index,* p. 33 http://hdr-caribbean.regionalcentrelac-undp.org/images/PDF/caricom_hdi.pdf.

unsettling to most societies. Strongly held religious and social beliefs that hold heterosexuality as the norm, and all other forms of sexuality as aberrant, engender serious concerns for the health, safety, and welfare of transgendered and homosexual communities.

Gender cross cuts all areas of work and life in the region. Although this section has not exhausted the extent of the concerns raised by gender inequality in every area, it has sufficed to demonstrate that gender inequities cannot be ignored in policy and program interventions as each society attempts to meet the challenges of progress alongside other nations regionally and internationally. In other words, the global development discourse had not only included gender over the last two decades but had placed the achievement of gender equality and decreasing of the gender gap as central to sustainable futures. In the following section I examine the external and internal forces that reinforced and effectively mandated that the engineering of gender equality required the public policy intervention strategies.

External and Internal Forces Influencing the Formulation of National Gender Policies

External Forces

Between 1979 and the present, in addition to the attempts to measure gender inequality and gaps, a spate of conventions and programs of actions were drawn up and accepted at various global events. Perhaps the most important of these is *The Convention on the Elimination of All Forms of Discrimination Against Women* (CEDAW), adopted in 1979 by the UN General Assembly. This convention has become so instrumental in the goal of achieving gender equality that it is often referred to as an "international bill of rights for women." Comprised of a preamble and 30 articles, the convention both defines what is considered discrimination against women, and proposes an agenda for national action to end such discrimination. The Convention defines discrimination against women as "… any distinction, exclusion or restriction made on the basis of sex which has the effect or purpose of impairing or nullifying the recognition, enjoyment or exercise by women, irrespective of their marital status, on a basis of equality of men and women, of human rights and fundamental freedoms in the political, economic, social, cultural, civil or any other field."* By accepting the Convention, states commit themselves to end discrimination against women in all forms, including the following:

- Incorporating the principle of equality of men and women in their legal system, abolish all discriminatory laws and adopt appropriate ones prohibiting discrimination against women
- Establishing tribunals and other public institutions to ensure the effective protection of women against discrimination
- Ensuring elimination of all acts of discrimination against women by persons, organizations, or enterprises†

Subsequently several other conventions have both endorsed and added to these demands made on leaders and states, once they have ratified or signed onto these conventions, to comply with baseline

---

* Overview of *The Convention on the Elimination of All Forms of Discrimination Against Women*, United Nations Entity for Gender Equality and the Empowerment of Women, published December 31, 2007 http://www.un.org/womenwatch/daw/cedaw/.
† Ibid, Overview, CEDAW Convention.

requirements for achieving gender equality. The Jamaica National Gender Policy that was piloted and passed in 2011 records those that have informed the formulation and passage of this policy.

> The GOJ is a signatory to the following regional and international agreements which make commitments to gender equality: The United Nations Decade for Women (1975–1985), The Convention on the Elimination of all Forms of Discrimination Against Women (CEDAW 1981) The Nairobi World Conference (*Third*) on the Forward Looking Strategies for the Advancement of Women (1985), The Inter-American Convention on the Prevention, Punishment and Eradication of Violence Against Women (Belem do Para Convention) (1994), The Cairo Programme of Action (ICPA) (1994). The Beijing Platform for Action (1995). The Millennium Development Goals (MDGs) (2000–2015). Ten Year Review of the Beijing Platform for Action (Beijing+10). The CARICOM Plan of Action (2005). The Commonwealth Plan of Action for Gender Equality (2005–2015).*

Between 1999 and 2011, I assisted several Caribbean governments with the formulation and development of national gender policies for equality and equity—among them Cayman Islands, Trinidad and Tobago, Dominica, and BVI. Like Jamaica, the international instruments which extended to the BVI, and which had gender policy implications, are listed by date of ratification in Table 18.5. The conventions that were to inform the policies of the Virgin Islands and the Cayman Islands, still dependencies of the United Kingdom, needed to be ratified first by the UK government before they could be invoked.

Table 18.5 International Instruments with Gender Policy Implications, Extended to by the British Virgin Islands

International Instrument	*Date of Ratification*
International Covenant on Economic, Social and Cultural Rights	Ratified by the United Kingdom on May 20, 1976, and extended to the BVI on the same date
International Covenant on Civil and Political Rights	Ratified by the United Kingdom on May 20, 1976, and extended to the BVI on the same date
Convention on the Elimination of All Forms of Discrimination Against Women, 1979	Ratified by the BVI on May 7, 1986
The Beijing Platform for Action	1995
Convention on the Rights of the Child	Ratified by United Kingdom on December 16, 1991, and extended to the BVI on September 7, 1994
European Convention on Human Rights and Fundamental Freedoms	Ratified by United Kingdom on March 8, 1951, and extended to the BVI on October 23, 1953

Source: British Virgin Islands National Gender Policy on Equality and Equity, Prepared by Mohammed, P., McFee, D., Pargass, G. and Parpart, J, Government of the British Virgin Islands, *2011.*

---

* Jamaica National Gender Policy, Government of Jamaica, p. 17.

The Beijing Platform for Action in particular has been a major external influence on top of CEDAW and UN enablers. A report on African states notes that (like the Caribbean) a "key trend is the increasing popularity of ministries or ministerial departments for women as lead institutional mechanisms. Instruments to advance gender equality such as legislative reform and gender-responsive budgeting have also become very popular amongst national machineries over the last few years. The main areas of emphasis of institutional mechanisms have been influenced by the Beijing Platform for Action, resulting in continuities and a certain homogenization in their priorities."*

As signatories to these conventions and by observing some of the protocols, UN and other nongovernment organizations (NGOs) also provided governments with resources and related support to deliver on promises to achieve indicators of gender equality. Agencies like the UNDP and UNIFEM supported the production of the gender policies and projects that gender bureaus or gender affairs departments engaged in such as eradication of gender violence and gender and HIV/AIDS intervention. For instance, in both Trinidad and Tobago and Dominica, the UNDP underwrote part of the costs related to the recruitment of consultants to the gender policy research, consultation, and formulation process. Other independent initiatives internationally such as the Commonwealth Secretariat in the United Kingdom and global/regional institutions such as the German foundation Friedrich Ebert Stiftung (Jamaica Office) and the Caribbean Policy Development Centre (Barbados) supported regional training workshops for women in political participation and women in governance. Such initiatives were geared to equip women to understand the value of public policy and thus to empower them to become confident and skilled political leaders.

The choice of priorities and how these goals of equality are achieved are more or less left up to individual states and are informed by the conventions that they have ratified. In practice, the imperatives of global governance have imposed sanctions on governments and states that do not honor their commitments to end gender discrimination. A critical ingredient for success of all initiatives, however, is the internal political will to drive the policy formulation process, the deployment of additional resources and time of individuals involved in the state machinery, and a commitment to implement policies that have been advocated.

Internal Forces

Political economy in the Caribbean emerged as a separate agenda from the gender and development discourse. One of the reasons for this apparent divergence lies in the post-colonial politics of the region itself. Diana Thorburn argues that "The shift to nationalist development policies in the 1960s was more concerned with Caribbeanness and the upliftment of Caribbean people as a whole, and little or no attention was paid to the gender dimensions of development."† Barriteau observes as late as 1990s that "State bureaucracies create and implement policies and commit resources according to the demands made by citizens and other developments in the political economy. The policy formulation process is assumed to be gender neutral."‡

---

* Recent Trends in National Mechanisms for Gender Equality, http://www.uneca.org/sites/default/files/publications/report-cwd.pdf. Executive summary p. vi.
† Thorburn, "Gender in Caribbean Development Thought and State Policies 1940–1995." dthorburn.tripod.com/genderthought.htm
‡ Baritteau *op cit* 158.

While current global conventions forced states to accept more universalistic ideas of equality and freedom at the ideological level, a "world order of gender" began centuries ago* and is not a new invention. The truth is that state politics by the end of the twentieth century came to terms with the purchasing power and professional rise of women in the workforce. The global movement provided a pressure group so that by the last decade of the twentieth century several governments in the Caribbean had committed to formulating national gender policies for equity and equality? From the first world conference in 1975, states in the Caribbean were either encouraged or forced to establish women's "desks" or women's "bureaus" or gender offices. Later, these became departments of "gender affairs." The sociolinguistic undertones of all of these in this part of the world suggested a concession of space, the recognition of a constituency, and some resources, but not an equal and mutual sense of value and worth. The political leadership of the region, largely male, could no longer ignore the central role that women had always played in bolstering parties and preserving the power of the male leaders of those parties in their bid to gain and retain office.

Exemplified in the specific cases of Jamaica and the (British) Virgin Islands above, are the external pressures to which other governments also reacted, to commission gender policies. The Governments of Trinidad and Tobago and Dominica had ratified of the CEDAW in 1990. The CEDAW defines specific directions in reporting and for the drafting of national gender policies. This was supplemented by other international demands including some Caribbean governments commitment to the United Nations Declaration of Human Rights (1978), the further stimulus of the Nairobi Forward Looking Strategies (1985) and the MDGs. In June 2000, the United Nations reiterated the need for countries to establish strong institutional machineries for gender by hosting the Beijing +5 Conference in New York. At this conference, governments were called upon once again to honor, among other things, their commitment to create or strengthen national gender machineries.

Always strategically responsive to global directives, the regional machinery kicked into motion. The 15-member Caribbean Community (CARICOM) established in 1972, comprising all of the English-speaking Caribbean, the French-speaking Haiti, Dutch-speaking Suriname, Belize, and five other associate members, and guided by the need to expand the regional Human and Social Development Strategy, developed a Plan of Action to 2005. CARICOM recognized the need to mainstream gender and provided a regional perspective on priority areas for the integration of gender in development in the areas of poverty and the economy, violence against women, women and health with a focus on HIV/AIDS, leadership and decision making, and education and institutional mechanisms for gender mainstreaming. The CARICOM model is located within a social justice/gender equity framework. The objective of this framework was to "build new structures of power sharing at the household, community, national, regional and global levels, where both men and women can participate fully in developing a system of cooperation in decision-making, as equal partners in the sustainable development of their societies."†

The gender negotiators of the process for national gender policies in the Caribbean were the women's desks, women's bureaus, and gender affairs departments in ministries, rallying around them a representative range of actors who came onto this stage from different sites and positions.

---

* The Suffragette battle for the vote in both Britain and the United States and the issues raised by women under socialist democracy in the USSR in the nineteenth and early twentieth centuries all predate the contemporary agendas.
† CARICOM *Women and Men in the Caribbean Community*, Caribbean Community Secretariat Statistics Programme, United Nations Department of Economic and Social Affairs Statistics Division, Caribbean Community Secretariat Georgetown, Guyana, 2003, p. 16.

These actors included sectoral ministries, statutory bodies, community-based organizations, and NGOs, including a network of organizations which were centered around women's or gender issues, and Church and private sector organizations including financial institutions. The internal forces were also the pressure groups from within, people who came on board on the principle of engaging in a "participatory democracy" in the formulation and ownership of "their" national gender policy. In all the societies in which national gender policies have been written including those of Cayman Islands, Trinidad and Tobago, Belize, Dominica, Jamaica, and the BVI, there was a degree of local ownership of this process, despite the coercive influences of international and regional dynamics. In addition, and most crucially, in each of the policy processes in which I was involved, there has been commitment and political will from state actors in the form of women's bureaus or gender affairs personnel, many times backed by the minister with responsibility for gender affairs. Two examples suffice, although this applies to all countries. The Dominica National Gender Policy was successfully formulated, passed, and now being implemented because of the drive of the director of the Women's Bureau, Ms. Rosie Browne aided and abetted by Mr. Eisenhower Douglas, the permanent secretary, in the Ministry under which the Bureau fell. Similarly, the Virgin Islands gender policy process was a fully engaged one due to the efforts of Ms. Patricia Hackett, coordinator of gender affairs, Minister Dancia Penn, and Permanent Secretary Petrona Davies, among other Ministry officials who were very committed to this policy.

In the next section of this chapter, I demonstrate the achievement of gender equality goals and the limits imposed within this process through the formulating national gender policies for equality and equity in selected Caribbean states.

The Impact of Gender and Development Discourses on National Policy Formulation in the Caribbean*

The national gender policies for equity and equality were conceived as a foundation for anchoring a greater gender sensitivity and understanding of the impact of gender on society, at all levels. The idea of a national gender policy was premised on the basis that evidenced driven policies could be developed from sex disaggregated data, widespread consultations and driven by the political will of the minister responsible for gender affairs to ensure that programs and actions are rationally determined and executed. It proposed additional legislative reform onto the existing legal framework.

In accepting to formulate a gender policy, states committed to the following goals:

- To assist government's policy makers in understanding and tracking the gender implications of new and existing policies and to ensure all policy and planning undertaken by government is informed by a gender perspective
- To provide government with a dynamic framework to address ongoing issues of gender the society
- To inform government on strategies in training and education to maximize the country's most important resources—its people, for the benefit of the territory
- To establish a system of gender mainstreaming in all sectors in the territory

---

* This section of the chapter draws in another study entitled "Gender Politics and Global Democracy: Insights from the Caribbean" carried out for a project on Building Global Democracy, led by Jan Aaart Scholte, University of Warwick. It is currently in publication.

- To educate and change attitudes of the public on key concepts such as gender equity, gender equality, social justice, gender roles, and responsibilities toward having them accept the importance of a national policy on gender
- To review existing legislation toward removing measures that places one sex at a disadvantage in relation to the other and to facilitate legislative change and public awareness of relevant legislation and their implications for gender-differentials in the society
- To develop new strategies and approaches toward eradicating domestic and other forms of gender-based violence in the society
- To begin training a cadre of persons in the government skilled in the applications of the tools of gender analysis, while strengthening the gender bureaus or offices to implement and monitor the recommendations of the gender policy.*

The ideals or objectives goals of the gender policy are clearly honorable in their intent. In practice, each policy process is challenged by the political, economic, social, and cultural climate that either supports or rejects gender interventions. In this section, I outline how some of these challenges surfaced or were met in different contexts. The territories of Cayman Islands, Trinidad and Tobago, Dominica, and the Virgin Islands have some similarities and parallels that may be noted. They are all geographically relatively small island territories, and apart from Cayman Islands and the Virgin Islands, achieved independent status from the British Crown in the twentieth century. Both Trinidad and Dominica have influences of the French under earlier colonization, the Cayman Islands remains decidedly British while the BVI, though still under Crown rule, at present has far more daily interaction with the nearby US Virgin Islands. All four countries inherited a form of British parliamentary democracy that promotes participation and consultation in any democratic process of decision making.

New Gender Perspectives on Human Sexuality

In the published global listing, countries who have not been systematically presenting their 4-year CEDAW reports are clearly identifiable against those who have done so. In this sense, the global has a continuous role in facilitating the local processes perhaps by shaming leaders and governments into ensuring that they measure up to other economies and societies. The exposure to global trends and changes in gender practices create other positive effects. Whether driven by changing local cultural practices of sharing of housework and childcare by both sexes, or primarily as a result of global influences, many Caribbean societies have become far more conscious of rights and privileges to be accorded to women and men in such areas as provision of both maternity and paternity leave. The Dominica Gender Policy, for example, endorsed the need for both men and women to "be allowed to pursue the fulfillment of family life and the conditions under which men might be willing to accept such responsibilities and play equal or complementary roles to women in the nurturing and parenting of children."†

Some global influences have not been successfully negotiated and there are specific issues under which the global movements have worked against the local. The areas of sexual and reproductive

---

* This information is culled from various drafts of the national gender policy documents that I have co-written with other team members.
† National Policy for Gender Equality and Equity, Government of the Commonwealth of Dominica, 2006, Consultants Patricia Mohammed and Deborah McFee, commissioned by the Government of the Commonwealth of Dominica.

rights and sexual harassment in the workplace have been two such areas in the Caribbean that have prevented gender policy interventions. In fact, the militancy from other global partners has acted against the transference of such gains locally or regionally. In the attempt to incorporate issues of sexuality and alternative sexual orientation, gender policies in the Caribbean have had to first overcome major perception hurdles: that such policies were "foreign ideas" of feminists (read lesbian) rather than homegrown concerns that were pertinent, that women in the Caribbean had all the power they could want since they were dominant as heads of households, and that homosexuality did not exist and was largely an invention of western consumer society imposed on the region by the media and a vibrant tourist industry. All of these perceptions had to be counteracted, especially among local communities rather than among professional bodies. For example in Trinidad, religious groups were adamant that the word gender was a shorthand code to make more acceptable sexual practices they deemed were unnatural to human society. It was felt that the intrusion of global ideas was destabilizing if not damaging to local customs, traditions, beliefs, and practices of gender. These ideas are surprising for the region given the openness of the society to western norms and influences of all kinds, including fashion, music and consumer goods and the consistent migrations in and out to the north. The non-passage of the gender policy through Cabinet in Trinidad and Tobago in 2007 is instructive on how selected ideas of modernity and progress present possibilities or limits to the range of policy issues that a gender policy can reach at any moment to satisfy all groups.

The Government of Trinidad and Tobago had only ratified the United Nations CEDAW in 1990. The International Committee of Experts that received the report in New York in 2000 made a number of responses. Among these, the Committee observed carefully that the proposed Equal Opportunities Act of 2000 excluded sexual orientation and thus explicitly discriminated against the homosexual population. In response to the barrage of critiques resulting from the presentation of this report in New York, the state recommitted itself to the development of a national gender policy as a key instrument to critically review existing legislation and to heighten public awareness of gender-related labor issues such as workplace discrimination.

Reference to homosexuality in the national gender policy document created utter havoc when the draft was made available for public discussion (as is the democratic custom of the policy process). The policy advocated that "The state should be proactive in initiating public debate on the discrimination suffered by persons due to sexual orientation with a view to making this a prohibited ground of discrimination under the Equal Opportunity Act and decriminalizing homosexual and lesbian acts under the Sexual Offences Act, 1986" (Government of Trinidad and Tobago 2006). Some religious groups and associate organizations led an opposition to the adoption of the document by staging prayer and fast sessions under a large white tent for 3 days on a pleasant savannah green opposite the prime minister's office in the main city of Port of Spain. One of the more vocal groups in this gathering said the document attempted to undermine the fabric of the society. Another group that had not surfaced at all during the public consultations also joined the camp. The media frenzy which they fueled against the draft policy and through their impassioned pleas, they successfully petitioned the government to withdraw the document.*

Given only snippets of the document by the state, those who had not been involved in the initial discussions which led to the policy choices were ill informed about the intent of the overall policy and viewed it primarily as a mechanism to open the door to homosexuality, same-sex marriages and to promote the legalization of abortion. While nongovernmental associations, such as

---

* Coverage in the local press was widespread during this protest and covered the range of responses that are identified here.

Network of Women's organizations, groups such as Advocates for Safe Parenthood Improving Reproductive Equity, and progressive journalists made a major bid to reinstate the policy document, fear of local political reprisal outweighed the government's commitments to international conventions. In 2009, the policy process resumed, with another draft commissioned by another minister of gender who was more vociferous and far more willing to challenge those in opposition to the issue of homosexuality. Another draft was produced by 2011, with new and younger voices emerging, among them a student support group from the University of the West Indies. Cabinet has met on this draft, and various consultations with religious bodies were again held in 2012.*
To date, the Government of Trinidad and Tobago has not officially accepted the policy document.

In the Cayman Islands, the policy was equally silent on the question of homosexuality. Like Trinidad and Tobago, Cayman Islands prided itself on being a God-fearing nation and religion plays a key role in the life of the people. As a British Overseas Territory and not a sovereign state, it cannot itself ratify the CEDAW Convention so it was not duty bound to observe the demands of this convention for reporting on the status of gender under the various categories. More importantly, without a written Bill of Rights or a Human Rights act as an Overseas UK Territory, the Cayman Islands could not undertake to draft a policy without the support of the UK government. Issues such as homosexuality were considered even more taboo if placed in the policy document for this society. The BVI policy process echoed a similar attitude to incorporating explicit issues that challenge the heterosexual norm.

The problematic areas of abortion rights, sexual orientation, and sexual identity presented some of the major stumbling blocks in the policy formulation process and are perceived as damaging to the conservatism and religious base on which small societies fashion and ensure gendered behaviors deemed acceptable.

Female Empowerment and Gender Policies: Political Leadership in Dominica

An investigation of the rate of female participation in political decision making in Dominica from 1985 to 2000 revealed that the level of female participation in the general elections of 1985 was 8% of total candidates, rising to 17% in 2000. This 110% increase emerged totally out of the candidature of a new party. The two entrenched political parties had fielded the exact number of females they did at the previous election. An exploration of the longer history of women in politics in Dominica reveals that the participation rate of women in Parliament for the period 1967–1988 was 10%. The number of women in Parliament jumped by 150% between 1975–1979 and 1980–1984.†
This coincided with the reign of the Freedom Party under the leadership of Dame Mary Eugenia Charles who was not only the first woman parliamentarian in Dominica but also the most well-known and first woman in the Caribbean to become a prime minister.

From 1980 to 1988, eight women, including the speaker of the house served in Parliament. More than half of them were directly linked to the advent of Mary Eugenia Charles as leader of the ruling Freedom Party. The three women in opposition during that period were all nominees or senators meaning they had not contested elections. Despite the apparent growth in women's

---

* In 2012, I was recruited by the minister in the Ministry of Gender, Youth and Child Development of the Government of Trinidad and Tobago, Minister Marlene Coudray, to facilitate two all day consultations with the religious groups who represented all the collective religions in the society.
† "Situational Analysis of Gender" in the National Policy for Gender Equality and Equity, Government of the Commonwealth of Dominica, 2006.

participation in parliament in the 1980s, effective female involvement in government receded, shown by the presence of only one (1) woman with Ministerial Responsibility and by extension a member of Cabinet—the then prime minister Eugenia Charles. Women were increasingly becoming involved in the electoral and leadership process of the society, yet recurrent questions surfaced in gender policy consultations in the island. Why were women still hesitant to be presented as candidates for national and local elections? What were the lingering disabilities women faced when they enter this still male dominated space? Would their presence and participation make a difference in the programs implemented by government to move the society to greater gender equity and equality since its emphasis was continuously on the erosion of poverty and the stimulation of economic growth for an island beset by economic challenges and natural disasters? Such questions were common to all four territories and continue to remain on the agenda for each state.

What was also noticeable as an improvement, however, was the rise of women to the position of permanent secretaries in the various ministries. While women did not always occupy the highest seats of power, they were responsible as permanent secretaries for major decisions in the implementation of policies and advice to ministers and thus to Cabinets. They tended to head ministries that had some affinity to household care and nurturing roles, such as Education, Housing, Culture and Health, rather than Finance or National Security. And in general, they were sympathetic and aware of the different concerns which men and women had with respect to each of these areas, for instance, the challenges of "underperformance" of young males in education compared to young women recurs as a serious one in all societies. The consultation process revealed that the effects of the local and global women's movements and efforts at gender awareness had entered the consciousness of these women in terms of the contributions that they brought to the table at this level. It is no longer possible to assume a lack of gender awareness among women and men. In both the case of the Trinidad and Tobago and the BVI, female ministers with responsibility for "gender affairs" were committed to driving the policy process and piloting it through their Cabinets. While their motives could be considered "politically expedient" to harness female supporters, it is clear that their defense of a gender policy required some personal commitment to gender equality. The lessons from Rwanda are a clear example here of the need to turn political commitment into action and to turn political will into tangible results. Where there remains room for further work in selling gender, both for practitioners and committed politicians, is in translating qualitative indicators of gender differential problems into economic gains to a society and to the relief from social destabilization in the long run.

The Instrumental Role of Migrant Women in Social Reproduction

In the Caribbean, the institution of the family has never maintained a static composition or definition and is constantly adapting to the changing occupational and economic demands on both women and men over time. Family members' relationships to each other have also shifted as expectations of gender roles change with new technologies of production and reproduction. Disruptions due to economic downturns, changing cultural messages about modernization, and a perceived growing empowerment of women in the workplace are blamed for an increase in violence and abuse in the household. In Cayman Islands, accelerated economic development from the 1960s brought economic prosperity, to some if not to all. By the end of the twentieth century with shifting modes of production, more women found gainful employment away from the home in the public sector, commerce, manufacturing industry or financial sector, and in the expanding tourism sector, along with men. This increased demand for women's time in the labor market was unaccompanied by a compatible increase in male responsibility for household tasks such as childcare or by provisions in day care by the corporate or public sector.

These employment changes transformed relationships between spouses and between members of households. Households in Cayman Islands became increasingly dependent on the labor of immigrant domestic workers. In 1970, the proportion of Caymanians to non-Caymanians (i.e., those not born in the islands) was 85%; in 1999, the proportion was 53%; and in 2008, 56%. Approximately 44% of the population who live in the Cayman Islands has non-Caymanian status. The influx of migrant domestic workers changed the demographics and composition of households and altered relations between women and men. The household as a residential unit and site for domestic activities such as food preparation, cleaning and family entertainment, the socialization of the young and cultural transmission of values and traditions, in large measure, inadvertently passed to the domestic helper in the home, while mothers could now take on jobs in the public sphere.*

The Cayman gender consultations had recognized the value and necessity of women's economic contribution to both household and economy. It pointed out that help in the home enabled women and men's participation in the paid productive sector of the Caymanian economy. The policy emphasized that the worth of women's economic contributions needed to be enhanced through support services provided by the public and private sectors and by gender-responsive immigration policies. Immigration policies, however, revealed a major contradiction in the democratic process. The existing immigration laws permitted work permits to both professional males and domestic helpers. Professional males were allowed to migrate with their families who lived with them in the Cayman Islands. Domestic workers on the other hand, primarily female, many of whom came from the nearby society of Jamaica, were not allowed to live or settle in the society with their own families. The justification for this differentiation in the residency policy provided by the immigration authorities was that domestic helpers were low-income earners and thus a drain on the country's resources if their families entered the country. Professional males were deemed to bring added value, to the economy and society. The value that domestic workers brought to the private sphere that allowed Caymanian women to work in public sector or local industry was not appreciated. The gender policy argued that domestic helpers were important to the stability and function of Caymanian homes. As caregivers they ensured environmental hygiene, family nutrition and supervision of children, the elderly and the sick in the household setting, and were to be viewed as key actors in the social reproduction of Cayman society although they were not viewed as adding to social capital in the public sphere. How societies organize the care and protection of the family and dependent members such as the elderly and infirmed is both a private and a public issue that concerns gender directly, particularly because as a sex, women have been allocated this responsibility in the division of labor. With the shift by the twenty-first century to women in many occupations and professions and when largely female migrant labor absorbs the roles of domestic caregivers and nurses, as have numerous women in Cayman and BVI, it is no longer possible to conceive of the organization of sexual difference into a rigid public versus private sphere. The gender issue that the CARICOM report identified as a vulnerable area for women has surfaced as a new dimension of gender that remains resolved and further deepening in complexity each year.

---

* National Gender Policy on Equality and Equity for the Cayman Islands, Government of the Cayman Islands, 2002.

Conclusion: Gender as a New Ingredient in Public Policy

One of the major successes of the twentieth century feminist revolution is the insertion of gender as a legitimate area both for national policy formulation and as a necessary ingredient in public policy. We can no longer ignore the presence or importance of gender, even while admittedly its gains are not sufficiently understood or appreciated by all. Gender remains the often unanalyzed dimension of all public policies, yet the importance of gender as an analytical lens for policy has become more accepted over time. This is a crucial breakthrough for gender theorists who have waged a war against the public–private dichotomy that questions of gender once represented to employers, policy makers, and the political machinery. The presentation of global development data in influential documents such as the HDRs, correlated by gender differentials and attempting to measure gender inequality across nations, is an eloquent admission of the importance of this analytical category to understanding the condition of people who comprise nations.

The adoption of national gender policies in various Caribbean islands, even where these have raised challenges, has nonetheless met with some measures of success in introducing gender in to the public policy agenda. Although the policy in Trinidad and Tobago lies dormant, the process of actively formulating and challenging the policy has created the most widespread awareness of gender across all groups and classes. The BVI policy has found approved by its Cabinet and progress is currently being made in respect of several of its recommendations, among them the Child Maintenance and Access Bill that is being drafted, and the introduction of the Status of Children Bill in the House of Assembly. The Ministry of Education and Culture has announced sweeping changes to their Technical Vocation and Education and Training (TVET) program to take effect in September, and the Labour Department has introduced several new measures to better enforce the Labour Code. A recently convened Cabinet appointed national Council on Human and Social Development is specifically tasked with monitoring the implementation of social policies, while strengthening interagency collaboration and accountability.*

The conundrum that remains in the arena of public policy-making is how not to isolate gender into areas of life marked as gendered territory but to ensure that public policies can be analyzed from the perspective of gender relations or hierarchies which they affect. Even when they appear to be neutral, all public policies engage in the promotion of more equitable gender and human relations.

References

Barriteau, Eudine. *The Political Economy of Gender in Twentieth-Century Caribbean*, International Political Economy Series, General Editor Tim Shaw, Palgrave, New York, 2001.
British Virgin Islands National Gender Policy on Equity and Equality, Prepared by Patricia Mohammed, Deborah McFee, Gaietry Pargass and Jane Parpart Government of the British Virgin Islands, 2011.
Caribbean Human Development Report: Estimating a CARICOM Human, 2012 *Development Index*. http://hdr-caribbean.regionalcentrelac-undp.org/images/PDF/caricom_hdi.pdf.
Caribbean Human Development Report: Human Development and Shift to Better Citizen Security, United Nations Development Programme, New York, 2012.
Draft National Policy on Gender and Development of the Republic of Trinidad and Tobago, Government of Trinidad and Tobago, 2013. http://hiv.health.gov.tt/site_media/media/filer_public/2013/01/21/draft_national_gender_and_development_policy.pdf.

---

* Email correspondence (January 5, 2014) with Mrs. Petrona Davies, permanent secretary in the Ministry of Health and Social Development of the BVI, the ministry with the responsibility for gender affairs.

Government of Trinidad and Tobago. *Trinidad and Tobago Draft National Gender Policy on Equity and Equality*, Consultants Centre for Gender and Development Studies, University of the West Indies, St. Augustine for the Government of Trinidad and Tobago, 2006.

Kabeer, Naila. *Reversed Realities: Gender Hierarchies in Development Thought*, Verso, London, 1994.

Mohammed, Patricia. Like sugar in coffee: Third wave feminism in the Caribbean, *Social and Economic Studies*, Volume 52, No. 3 Rhoda Reddock (Ed.), Sir Arthur Lewis Institute for Social and Economic Studies, UWI, Mona, Jamaica.

Mohammed, Patricia. *The Construction of Gender Development Indicators for Jamaica*, UNDP, Planning Institute of Jamaica and CIDA, Kingston, Jamaica, 2000.

National Gender Policy on Equality and Equity for the Cayman Islands, prepared by Consultants Patricia Mohammed and Audrey Ingram Roberts, Government of the Cayman Islands, 2002.

National Policy for Gender Equality and Equity, Government of the Commonwealth of Dominica, Consultants Patricia Mohammed and Deborah McFee, commissioned by and presented to the Government of the Commonwealth of Dominica, 2006.

Reddock, Rhoda. *Women, Labour and Politics in Trinidad and Tobago: A History*, Zed Books, London, 1994.

Sen, Amartya. Development as a capability expansion, in *Human Development in the 1980s and Beyond, Journal of Development Planning*, No 19, Department of International Economic and Social Affairs, United Nations, New York, 1989.

The Global Gender Gap Report, World Economic Forum, 2012. http://www3.weforum.org/docs/WEF_GenderGap_Report_2012.pdf.

The UNDP Human Development Report, 2013. *The Rise of the South Human Progress in a Diverse World*. http://hdr.undp.org/en/media/HDR2013_EN_Summary.pdf.

Chapter 19

Poverty in the Caribbean

Charley G. Granvorka

Contents

Introduction 444
Theories versus Empiricism 446
  Some Theories for Explaining Poverty 446
The Determinants and Characteristics of Poverty in the Caribbean 447
  The Determinants of Poverty in the Caribbean… 448
  … and Characteristics 449
  Brief Insights on Poverty in the Dominican Republic and Haiti 451
    The Haitian Case 455
Remittances and Poverty; Which Relationship? 456
Public Policies Affecting Poverty in the Caribbean 460
Conclusion 461
Bibliography 462

Abstract: The Caribbean region is composed of 34 islands ranked from middle- to high-income countries, except Haiti, which is considered as the poorest one in the hemisphere. As Small Island Developing States (SIDS), these countries have to face challenges induced by their specific characteristics and their geographical localization both at the global and domestic levels. Among these challenges, the eradication of poverty is one of them. Although consensually defined by the International Institutions, poverty definition in the Caribbean is derived from the Caribbean Development Bank (CDB) methodology applied for analyzing the extent, depth, and severity of the phenomenon. This chapter exposes the determinants and characteristics of poverty in the region based upon a set of Country Poverty Assessments (CPAs) realized in 12 countries—all Borrowing Members at CDB—between 1995 and 2009. Some theoretical concepts explain the persistence and nature of poverty in a country like Haiti, whose case is compared to the Dominican Republic, its neighbor on Hispaniola. The two countries are economically divergent and high recipient of remittances. The impact of this external financial assistance on poverty reduction in both these economies is also questioned. We conclude that in Haiti poverty is due to non-monetary causes, whereas in the rest of the Caribbean it is a multidimensional phenomenon and policies have to be redesigned to better target the real and identified causes of poverty in the area.

Introduction

Among the millennium development goals (MDGs), extreme poverty eradication and hunger is the very first objective the international community is targeting at. By extension, achieving universal primary education, reducing child mortality, improving maternal health, and combating Human Immunodeficiency Virus infection and Acquired Immune Deficiency Syndrome (HIV/AIDS), malaria, and other diseases are deeply interlocked into objective number 1 as they are the direct consequences of poverty. If poverty is pervasive in the Caribbean region, it must not be regarded as fate. Nonetheless, it features some particularities in a region mainly composed of small, open, and fragile economies largely dependent upon their external environment and largely vulnerable to natural disasters as well. Economic and environmental vulnerability, globalization and competitiveness, and poverty eradication through sustainable development are the main challenges the region must face.

The concept of poverty is, most of the time, associated with the notion of well-being. But when this latter may be considered as subjective or relative for it relates to individual appreciation in terms of life quality, poverty, as a varied, multidimensional and quantitative concept, has to be examined according to different scopes; education, growth, and labor are among them. For the International Institutions, poverty may be absolute or relative. Absolute or extreme* (United Nations) poverty reflects the situation in which one cannot cover any of its primary needs in terms of food, housing, basic health care, and clothing. That is, the very poverty that the United Nations Organization is focusing its efforts on throughout the world. The relative poverty relates to the income level that does not target the minimum required in a given country for being considered as sufficient for covering the primary needs in that very country. Could it be absolute or relative, poverty yields situations that affect the most disadvantaged social classes by sustaining among them all the weaknesses of modern societies: a high level of unemployment, weak income, no access to social and cultural life, unhealthy housing, obstacles to longlife learning, basic health care, and limited access to fundamental rights as well. In terms of secondary impacts induced by poverty, one may observe the increase or a high level of crime and violence,† illegal migrations flows, organs trafficking, sexual exploitation, and gender discrimination.

Poverty is also at the same time a concept that can be measured in its qualitative and quantitative dimensions either according to an international standard or a domestic one. At the international level, the difference in poverty between a panel of given countries will be measured according the poverty line currently estimated at least 1US$ per day and per capita or by the Gini coefficient that is the index measuring the gap between two or several units. The closer the Gini is to zero, the lower is the degree of inequality and the closer it is to 1, the higher the inequality is present. According to the World Bank in its *Poverty and Inequality* handbook (2009, p.7), "there are many different definitions and concepts of well-being." For example, "we can think of one's well-being as the command over commodities in general; people are better off if they have a

---

* United Nations definition.
† IFAD, *Regional Strategy Paper* (Chap. IV, 2002).

greater command over resources."* One may also think of the ability to obtain a specific type of consumption good (e.g., food and housing). People who have a lack of capabilities might have lower well-being (Sen 2000).† Lack of capability means inability to achieve certain "functioning" ("being and doings"), lack of well-being, and vulnerability to income and weather shocks. Thus, poverty means either lack of command over commodities in general (i.e., a severe constriction of the choice set [Watts 1968]), a specific type of consumption (e.g., too little food energy intake) deemed essential to constitute a reasonable standard of living, or lack of "ability" to function in a society. Consequently, one could say that poverty refers to what namely whether households or individuals have enough resources or abilities to meet their needs. This aspect is based on the comparison of individuals' income, consumption, education, or other attributes with some defined threshold below which they are considered as being poor in that attribute. At least, poverty may be considered as a deprivation of essential assets and opportunities to which every human being is entitled. Thus, and clearly, one can think of poverty from a nonmonetary perspective, otherwise in its multidimensional perspective. Although widely used, monetary poverty is not the exclusive paradigm for poverty measurement and nonmonetary dimensions of poverty are useful in assessing poverty components, particularly for case study research. Considering what precedes could one say that poverty is featuring special characteristics in the Caribbean?

The question of poverty in the Caribbean is a recurring concern since remote times. In fact, yet after the emancipation waves the matter has been questioned either by academics or states' agencies through many social and/or economical studies for finding out the roots of poverty and inequality in the Caribbean societies. Race and classes inequalities, heritage of colonialism, or failure of structural adjustment's program have been identified as some of the liable explicative causes of the persistence of poverty.‡ The most recent and panoramic studies to estimate the nature and characteristics of poverty in the Caribbean have been driven at the domestic level within the frame of a series of Country Poverty Assessments (CPAs) undertaken throughout the islands between 1995 and 2009 following the Caribbean's decision to target more of the benefits from its development program in the Borrowing Member Countries (BMCs)§ to the poor. Mainly funded by the Caribbean Development Bank (CDB), financial assistance for CPAs has also been provided by the Department for International Development of the United Kingdom, the Canadian International Development Agency, and the United Nations Development Program (UNDP). To date, CPAs have been conducted and completed in 12 of the 17 BMCs.¶ According to an agreed opinion,** the following definition of poverty has been retained in the CPAs: "Poverty is defined on the basis of indigence lines (based on minimum food requirements) and poverty lines (minimum food requirements plus an element of non-food expenditure)" derived according to the CDB's methodology.

The poverty gap ratio gives the depth or intensity of poverty as it shows how far away the poor are from the poverty line. For the Organization of the Eastern Caribbean States (OECS) region, the indigence line has been estimated at EC$2,000 (US$740) per adult per year as the cost of a food basket valued at EC$5.51 for an adult per day over a year (CDB 2003), and the poverty line

---

* Haughton and Khandker, 2009, for the World Bank, in "The Concept of Poverty and Well-Being," Chapter 7, p. 14.
† Social Exclusion: Concepts, Application and Scrutiny.
‡ Deere et al. (1990), Stiglitz (2002).
§ BMCs at the Inter-American Development Bank (IDB).
¶ Anguilla, Barbados, Belize, British Virgin Islands, Dominica, Grenada, Guyana, Jamaica, Nevis, St. Kitts, St. Vincent and the Grenadines, Trinidad and Tobago, Turks and Caicos Islands, Haiti.
** The definition of poverty in the Dominica Poverty Assessment Final Report Executive Summary Country Poverty Assessment—Dominica Final Report Volume 1, Man Report, Halcrow Group Limited, June 2003.

is EC$3,400 (US$1,260) per adult per year. Still according to the CDB "even if current definitions of poverty are more wide-ranging than those based on income alone they include consideration of, *inter alia,* living conditions, access to health and education, and less easily defined notions such as vulnerability, noiselessness, powerlessness, and lack of opportunity." The general concept of "well-being" has been used to bracket these non-income aspects of poverty. After investigations based upon households' surveys, the CPAs have led to the definition of National Poverty Reduction Strategy (NPRS) that have been implemented more or less successfully except in Haiti where despite huge funds granted by donors poverty remains a major challenge since and for many decades. By the way, in 2012, the country's per capita gross domestic product (GDP) was US$1,240.* Regarding the real headcount index, data vary between 72.3% and 78.5% according to the sources. For whatever reason, 80% is the most recurrent headcount found in reports and studies driven either by official Haitian institutions or international organizations. That means that 8.8 million of people were living with less than US$1 in 2012. It is recognized by the CDB that although "poverty is a complex, dynamic, multi-sectoral, multi-dimensional human phenomenon that is difficult to define, measure and eradicate" (CDB 2001), works in the region demonstrate that it is a condition where people "lack … essential assets and opportunity to improve their living conditions and to achieve a quality of life they consider acceptable."

This chapter tends to describe poverty in the Caribbean region. According to data and studies availability, the Caribbean here concerned is essentially composed of the BMCs at CDB, that is, the insular English-speaking Caribbean. Nonetheless, this poverty review is broadened to the Dominican Republic as a Spanish-speaking Caribbean country. Haiti is also questioned for the following reasons: it is the one French-speaking BMC at CDB, and on the other hand, this country is regarded as the poorest in the hemisphere. At least, due to the lack of consistent data, referred studies, or reports on the topic, the French West Indies are not included in the chapter scope. The remainder of this chapter is organized as follows. Section "Theories versus Empiricism" sets the theoretical frame. Section "The Determinants and Characteristics of Poverty in the Caribbean" exposes the determinants and characteristics of poverty in the Caribbean. Section "Remittances and Poverty; Which Relationship?" indicates whether or not remittances helped in reducing poverty in the Caribbean as the different policies implemented in that view.

Theories versus Empiricism

Some Theories for Explaining Poverty

Exploring the poverty field makes arise various poverty concepts depending upon the prism it is analyzed from. It may be regarded according to social, development, or political ones. Thus, a variety of theories will both attempt to explain poverty and justify the design of anti-poverty programs or policies. According to Bradshaw (2006), the contemporary literature has provided a multiplicity of theories for explaining poverty. These theories have been classified as either conservative according to they be based upon the individual deficiencies or liberal or progressive according to they be laid on poverty as a broader social phenomena. Aside these currents of thinking, poverty may also be analyzed according to a cultural scope; Lewis (1970)[†] defined it as a "set of beliefs and values passed from generation to generation." That is, the poverty found in subcultural

---

* www.tradingeconomics.com.
† Lewis, *Anthropological Essays.*

communities or societies. Bradshaw has identified some poverty causes linked to theories that he relates to economic, political, and social distortions. In that case, insufficient wages do not allow households/units to reach self-sufficiency (Blank 1997, Quigley, 2005). Geographical disparities may also create poverty. As Shaw (1996) said "The geography of poverty is a spatial expression of the capitalist system." In other words, and still according to Shaw, "Space is not a backdrop for capitalism, but rather is restructured by it and contributes to the system's survival." One could complete by quoting Bradshaw (2006)* who said that "Rural poverty, ghetto poverty, urban disinvestment, Southern poverty, third-world poverty, and other framings of the problem represent a spatial characterization of poverty people, institutions, and cultures where certain areas lack the objective resources needed to generate well being and income." That is what is observable in rural and urban areas where poverty is concentrated in shantytowns. At least, still following Bradshaw, poverty may also be caused by cumulative and cyclical interdependencies. This explanation finds individuals in close interdependency with their community; poverty is generated and sustained by the community itself as this latter is not able to provide resources to individuals. That is what Myrdal has called an "interlocking, circular inter-dependencies within a process of cumulative causation."[†] That means that an exogenous change will affect a locality, a community, or a country in its social interdependence and transformation on the long run. The most obvious illustration is the earthquake of January 2010 that hurt Port-au-Prince (Haiti) sending urban populations back to their rural native province, while in urban areas, new shantytowns mainly composed of broken families grew up in the aftermath of the earthquake.

The Determinants and Characteristics of Poverty in the Caribbean

The insular Caribbean is composed of 34 islands. If they are sharing the same maritime space, geography, and climate, the same history based upon slavery and colonialism, the Caribbean region is also a multilingual and differentiated political status space due to the European powers these former Caribbean colonies pertained to. By the way, French, English, Spanish, and Dutch are the different languages spoken in the area where independent, associated, autonomous, and integrated territories coexist.[‡] Since 1973, the Caribbean islands are federated into CARICOM set by the Treaty of Chaguaramas that is the eponymous regional organization for both the Caribbean Community and the Caribbean Common Market. The main objectives aim to enhance and promote development and equality throughout the region while deepening their regional integration. CARICOM which widened several times since 1973—its most expansion is July 2012 dated—gathers the More and Less Developed Caribbean Countries. The smaller islands in terms of physical size and economical development level are subgrouped into the OECS[§] created in

---

* Theories of Poverty and Anti-Poverty Programs in Community Development (2006).
† Chapter 3 in *Economic Theory and Underdeveloped Regions* (1957).
‡ Some examples: Martinique and Guadeloupe are French Overseas Departments as such they are integrated to France—Haiti is independent since 1804—Puerto Rico is associated with the United States—Sint Maarten and Curaçao are autonomous Netherlands Antilles—the Caymans Islands and the British Virgin Islands are dependent from the United Kingdom.
§ OECS: Anguilla, Antigua and Barbuda, British Virgin Islands, Commonwealth of Dominica, Grenada, Montserrat, St. Lucia, St. Kitts and Nevis, St. Vincent and the Grenadines.

1981. This organization is as well a common market with a single currency and is pursuing economic harmonization and regional integration. The islands involved in OECS, like the rest of the CARICOM's members, feature all the characteristics of small economies: economic openness, dependence to external governance centers, high degree of exposure to exogenous shocks such as natural hazards and global economic fluctuations, smallness in terms of physical size, and volatility as well. If the islands differ in their level of economic development, their main development challenges are their exposure to changes in terms of trade, tourism, and foreign investment flows, as well as impacts from natural hazards and climate change. Combined with that comes before, high debt levels and limited fiscal space also pose significant constraints on governments' ability to address development needs.

The paramount importance of the services sector contrasts with the small part of manufacturing in GDP. This sector accounts for somewhat 10% in GDP in Belize, St. Kitts and Nevis, and Suriname. Either declining agriculture still accounts fairly in GDP in some of the countries owing to some basic products as rice, sugar, or banana. Just after the services' sector, agriculture fuels GDP in Guyana, Dominica, and Belize for 30%, 16.7%, and 14.5%, respectively. In Guyana, Jamaica, and Suriname mining products are accounting for 6% as an average in GDP. In Trinidad and Tobago, the oil gas industry is of major importance, accounting for more than 40% in GDP. But the first rent driver in almost these economies is the services one that accounts for 75% as an average in GDP except in Trinidad and Tobago and Guyana. These figures highlight the dependence of the Caribbean countries on tourism activities first, while few of them as the Bahamas, Barbados, and the Caymans Islands also rely on offshore financial and nonfinancial services. Even if the GDP per capita remains rather contrasted,* from US$1,240 in Haiti against US$21,280 in the Bahamas, the countries are considered as middle income and indexed as very high or middle levels countries in terms of Human Development. According to the UNDP Human Development Report Office[†] calculations and classifications, only Barbados of all CARICOM economies belongs to the group of Very High Human Development countries. Antigua and Barbuda, Bahamas, Belize, Dominica, Grenada, Jamaica, St. Kitts and Nevis, St. Lucia, St. Vincent and the Grenadines, and Trinidad and Tobago belong to the group of High Human Development countries. Guyana and Suriname are classified among the group of Medium Human Developed countries. At least, Haiti is ranked as a Low Human Developed country. However, and despite their upper middle income country status, between 18% and 38% of the Caribbean population live in poverty in most of the countries.

The Determinants of Poverty in the Caribbean ...

The causes and origins of poverty in the Caribbean have been analyzed according to two prisms at least: "historical" and "macroeconomic." History sets poverty as a heritage of colonialism for its inequality of income distribution related to the social class's repartition. Race, social classes, and gender hierarchies of colonial domination have left a legacy of exclusion of the poor (Paquin 1983[‡]; Deere et al. 1993).[§] As an example, social classes stratification based upon economic power

---

* World Development Report 2014, The World Bank.
† The *Human Development Report* (HDR) is an annual milestone published by the Human Development Report Office of the (UNDP).
‡ *The Haitians: Class and Color Politics* (1983).
§ "In the Shadows of the Sun: Caribbean Development Alternatives and US Policy."

goes on dividing society in Haiti (Granvorka 2012).* At the macroeconomic level, various studies and theoretical concepts deemed that wrong choices in policies decision, low growth, inequality in redistribution (Wilson-Forsberg et al. 2001)† or the upkeeping of some intentional dependence from the Centre by the Periphery (Prebisch 1950)‡ could also explain the persistence of poverty and underdevelopment in the former European colonies in the Caribbean Basin. The failure of structural adjustment programs, the imperfections in the labor market related to continue stratifications, and lack of education seem liable to explain the persistence of poverty in the Caribbean. Low income could also account likewise geographical location in rural area and inner city. According to Baker (1997),§ wages tend to be lower in rural and inner city than in urban areas; high level of unemployment, seasonal works and the weakness of institutions, and infrastructure could explain the severity of poverty in the Caribbean rural areas. On the other hand, Laguerre (1990)¶ found that inner city has been the "breeding grounds for the reproduction of poverty." He explains that in the region, "the formal housing sector is unable to provide low-income social groups with adequate shelter." This conclusion has been corroborated by a study driven by ECLAC in 2000.**

... and Characteristics

In the CPAs, poverty has been estimated in terms of "depth," "incidence," and "severity." The "depth" of poverty relates to the extent to which the average expenditure falls below the poverty gap that is referred at the headcount index. This index reflects the degree of inequality among the poorest as shown by Figure 19.1 for selected Caribbean countries.

"Incidence" is the proportion of individuals or households below the specific poverty line determined by the CDB for the region, that is, EC$3,400 (US$1,260) per adult per year. The "severity" of poverty shows how income or expenditure is distributed among the poor. For that, each unit in analysis has been estimated according to its degree of deprivation. The CPAs

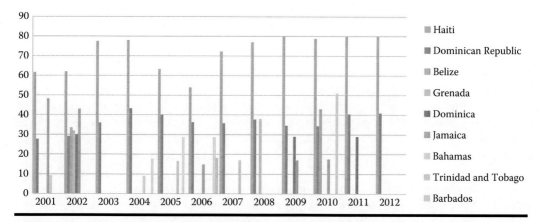

Figure 19.1 Poverty headcounts in selected Caribbean countries.

---

* "Haiti and the Dominican Republic: Two Centuries After Independence Where Do They Stand?"
† "Addressing Poverty and Inequality in Latin America and the Caribbean: A Social Primer."
‡ Prebisch (1950); Sunkel (1963); Cardoso (1969); Dos Santos (1970).
§ Poverty Reduction and Human Development in the Caribbean: A Cross-Country Study.
¶ Urban Poverty in the Caribbean: French Martinique as a Social Laboratory.
** ECLAC, *Poverty and Social Integration*.

have been dealt according to a quantitative and qualitative approach that includes five components: a review of available reports and statistics; a microeconomic and social assessment of the country; a survey of living conditions (National Survey of Living Conditions [NSLC]) within households; a participatory poverty assessment of commodities, vulnerable groups, and households; and an institutional analysis of entities involved in the fight against poverty. In this countries-panel, poverty has also integrated the "incidence" that is the proportion of people living below a targeted poverty line. According to the CDB, the objective of the CPAs was not to measure poverty, but to provide insights on the perceptions, experiences, and effects of difficult living conditions on individuals, households, groups, and resource-poor first. Second, the assessments intended as well to evaluate the effectiveness of current policies and programs in terms of their impact on the poor and vulnerable groups of the population for making recommendations for future. On the first hand, the CPAs reported that poverty exists in urban and rural areas where the conditions of poverty are more severe. One in every two households is poor. Despite access to electricity and water, poor households lack of access to wealth, education, training, and/or access to public utilities in the wealth and transportation sectors. As a result, they cannot access neither to the official labor market nor to wealth infrastructures. Subsequently, poor people suffer from malnutrition that affects children less than five first. According to a UNICEF Report for 2012, their mortality rate is neighboring 26% throughout the Caribbean. CPAs also found that the families' structure is essentially matriarchal, sustaining intergenerational connections as several generations are living together. Considering the features of poverty wherever the place, the poor people tend to be employed in basic occupations and act mainly in the "grey or informal sector"* that gives them access only to daily or partly low-paid that do not favor the human capital's accumulation. At least, this part of population being the most exposed to seasonality and breaks on the labor market due to externalities such as global costs and prices variations or scarcity in demand, stigmatization is one of the elements leading to an increase in marginalization that hampers social inclusion.

Reports indicate that poverty has decreased in some relative extent in some BMCs. However, at the regional level, one could think that the phenomenon has probably increased for the following reasons: the continued decline in the agricultural sector accompanied by a pronounced deterioration in governments' finances, tourism-based economies in recession in relation with environmental hazards consequences, and the abandon of preferential tariff trade between the Caribbean countries and the European Union within the frame of the new Economic Partnership Agreements (EPAs).† Furthermore, due to shocks related to both the international financial crisis and natural hazards in the region; sectors like tourism and agriculture have experienced little expansion. As a matter of fact, in its Annual Report (2011), the CDB stated that generally, and more specifically in the tourism-dependent states, more strategic and proactive approach has to be implanted with the view to manage risks and vulnerabilities. Accordingly, the endogenous growth remained sluggish or decreased leading to an increase in the unemployment rate in the countries yet affected by imperfections on their labor market (Figure 19.2).

In countries like Barbados or Haiti—still according to the CPAs—the proportion of poor households that were headed by females has increased, and like in most of the islands, the poor

---

* The informal economy refers to activities and income that are partially or fully outside government regulation, taxation, and observation (Workers in the Informal Economy; www.worldbank.org).
† EPAs are a form of trade partnership, required by the Cotonou Agreement, which covers economic relations between the European Union and African, Caribbean and Pacific (ACP) States. CARIFORUM, that is, CARICOM plus the Dominican Republic, is one of six ACP regional groups—http://www.tradeind.gov.tt.

Poverty in the Caribbean ■ 451

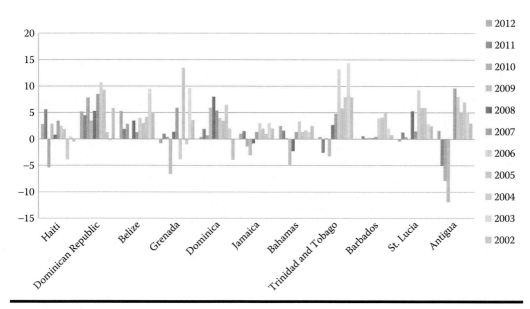

Figure 19.2   Evolution of the growth rate in selected Caribbean countries.

families greatly rely on their relatives abroad for financial supporting via remittances. Remittances are private transfers that migrants, temporary or not, return home for some variable reasons through official and informal channels. Subsequently, it is very difficult to estimate their real amount notwithstanding studies ran on the question for developed and developing countries.*

Brief Insights on Poverty in the Dominican Republic and Haiti

Haiti and the Dominican Republic are sharing the same island, Hispaniola. As a former colony of Haiti, the Dominican Republic emancipated itself from this country on February 1844. Yet after the Dominican emancipation, the initial conditions for initiating the economic development were the same in both the territories: natural endowments in production factors such as soil resources, land, manpower, and institutions. But the main macroeconomic aggregates† collected from year 1960 up to 2013‡ show that the economic divergence began since the 1960s according to Figure 19.3.

The explanation to the divergence in the economic performances has been analyzed according to several scopes: geography and environment§ and economy.¶ All of these scopes are reasonable but history has rarely been crossed with economy. The main explanation to divergence seems to be rooted in history. As a matter of fact, the absence of a political and economic project yet after the independence liable to unify the population around a strong feeling of national identity has sustained social classes' oppositions still undergoing in Haiti. Inversely, in the Dominican Republic the post-independence power reached first to gather the people around a national project funded by very attractive conditions for the Foreign Direct Investment (FDI). Second, the Dominican

---

* Carim (2013); E. Jadotte (2008); P. Acosta (2007).
† Granvorka (2013).
‡ UNStat are not available before 1960.
§ Faria and Sanchez-Fung (2009).
¶ Jamarillo and Sancak 2007.

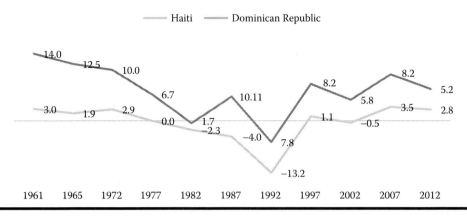

Figure 19.3 Evolution of the GDP in Haiti and the Dominican Republic.

power reached to develop a strong national identity through a feeling of supremacy of the white over the blacks in general, and from the Dominicans over the Haitians, in particular, whether the Dominicans were white or black.*

Proximity, recurrent political crisis, institutions that do not matter and underdevelopment are among the first explanations to illegal migration of the poor Haitians to the Dominican Republic. In this country, the Haitians migrants are part of the poorest of the poor who also include Dominicans concentrated alongside the Dominican–Haitian boarder.† Nonetheless, poverty is also creeping in rural and urban areas. By the way, according to the information available, poverty has been scrutinized essentially in the rural areas where it is more severe. The most recent data are those collected over the decade 2000–2011 by the World Bank.‡ The poverty line has been estimated in a twofold dimension: moderate and extreme in both the urban and rural areas. Results are expressed in Table 19.1.

Given the scarcity of data, poverty in the Dominican Republic has been estimated according to nonmonetary indicators that like elsewhere in the Caribbean are the same: lack of access to basic needs, very poor conditions of living, persistent deprivation, low school enrollment. Based upon investigations, the World Bank (January 2014) has identified four categories of poor classified as follows: "chronic poor, not-income poor but deprived, transiently poor, better off poor."§ This report also indicates that if the poor are passing from a group to another one, globally poverty remains persistent in terms of severity and population percentage affected by poverty.

To fight against poverty, the main government's plan has been launched in 2008 in a program called "Solidaridad" which goal is to provide "Eat First." This program that is essentially funded by IDB,¶ International Fund for Agricultural Development, and the European Union aside the Dominican government focuses on the social policy for allocating subsidies to the poor households for education, health, and nutrition. In his evaluation of the progresses made to reduce poverty, the government recognized in 2011 that the local implementation of the MDGs has

---

* Granvorka (2013), *General Equilibrium and Plantation Economics in the Caribbean: The Compared Case of Haiti and the Dominican Republic.*
† IFAD, Rural Poverty in the Dominican Republic.
‡ World Bank, *When Prosperity Is Not Shared: The Weak Links Between Growth and Equity in the Dominican Republic* (2014, p. 14).
§ Ibid.
¶ Inter-American Development Bank.

Table 19.1 Moderate and Extreme Poverty Rates (2000–2011) in the Dominican Republic

Poverty Line	Area	2000	2001	2002	2003	2004	2005	2006	2007	2008	2009	2010	2011
Moderate	Total	32.0	32.8	32.7	41.5	49.8	47.8	44.2	43.6	44.2	42.1	41.6	40.4
	Rural	47.3	47.5	47.2	55.4	59.9	57.0	54.0	51.8	55.2	50.8	50.4	48.4
	Urban	23.7	24.8	24.9	33.9	44.1	42.8	38.8	39.1	38.8	37.9	37.3	36.5
Extreme	Total	8.1	7.8	8.7	12.0	15.5	16.6	13.7	13.2	13.4	11.8	11.4	10.2
	Rural	14.7	13.2	16.1	19.4	22.9	23.7	19.8	18.4	20.6	17.9	16.9	15.3
	Urban	4.6	4.9	4.8	7.9	11.4	12.6	10.4	10.4	9.9	8.8	8.7	7.7

Source: World Bank, *When Prosperity Is Not Shared: The Weak Links Between Growth and Equity in the Dominican Republic*, 2014.

not taken into account the spread of the informal economy, the big number of micro, small and medium enterprises, and inequalities in access to the quality of education, health, and employment, all of which is detrimental to women, young people, and rural communities. For that very year, the government admitted also that it would be very difficult to reach the MDGs by 2015 and suggested that these would only be attained by 2020. The excuses in the official forecast point to the 2003–2004 bank crisis, and greater cutbacks in public spending are said to be needed to cope with the consequences of the crisis. The most recent MDG report (2013)* prepared by the government in collaboration with UNDP estimated that the country will not be able to achieve "MDG1-Halve, between 1990 and 2015, the proportion of people whose income is less than one dollar a day, nor MDG2—Achieving universal primary education by 2015." The number of poor households increased strongly in the mid-2000s in parallel with the decline in the level of real wages. The performance on the human development indicator is also poor; the Dominican Republic has one of the lowest indices in Latin America, ranking 24 out of 33 countries in 2011. In 2014, the World Bank (2014) stated that paradoxically and against an increase in growth poverty did not decrease. In fact, data collected show that these two curves are evolving independently. There is no real impact of growth on poverty (Figure 19.4).

This contradiction is explained by the domestic economic sensitiveness to external shocks that affect GDP. As an example, for a given decrease of GDP by 0.3 points in 2003, poverty raised up to 52% (World Bank 2014, p. 11). Moreover, in spite of a greater supply in basic services, poverty remained chronic over the decade 2000–2011 and persistent in its multidimensional characteristics.

Aside from this brief insight on poverty in the Dominican Republic, it is noteworthy to remind that if Haitians are long-standing migrants, for the poorest who are illegal migrants at the same time, the Dominican Republic is the first door. Over there, they find informal opportunities in the sugarcane plantations—bateys—the public roads construction and the informal services

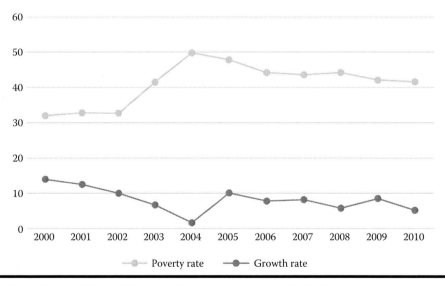

Figure 19.4 The evolution of the growth and poverty rates in Haiti.

---

* *Growth, Employment and Social Cohesion in the Dominican Republic,* ILO Background Paper (2013).

sectors as well. Due to the strong negative side effects of this illegal population, the Haitian and Dominican governments have implemented the Haitian–Dominican Bi National Commission that is in charge with the diplomatic resolution of the problems raised from the Haitian migration in the Dominican Republic. Among the negative side effects, one may cite stigmatization and marginalization, schooling problems, identity denial, violence, drug trafficking, sexual exploitation, and children work.

The Haitian Case

Haiti is regarded as one of the poorest countries in the world and the poorest in the Western Hemisphere. Most of the studies or technical papers applied to poverty driven by the international organizations agree to recognize that in Haiti monetary and abject poverty is lasting for decades.

Data collection in Haiti is very difficult. The official Statistics Office—IHSI*—has poor means and data are not subsequently collected making long time series untraceable. Consequently, and sometimes, the results of studies driven on a given topic may differ. For all these reasons, one must remain very cautious as data may not necessary reflect reality. Regarding the characteristics of poverty, the most recent reports are those of years 2007 and 2009 when it appeared necessary to identify the characteristics and determinant of poverty† before estimating the progresses made toward reduction.‡

In a joint Document,§ the International Monetary Fund (IMF) and the Government of Haiti identified the extent and characteristics of poverty over the nine departments composing the country, including the metropolitan area of Port-au-Prince. This report build upon discontinuous NSLC¶ set in 2001 that 56% of the population (4.4 million of a total population of 8.1 million) lived below the extreme poverty line (US$1 per person/per day). Approximately 7.6 of every 10 live on less than US$2 Purchasing Power Parity (PPP) per person/per day. In 2012, the situation of the poor did not improved as the GDP per capita was US$1,250, life expectation estimated at 62.5 years for the same period (World Statistics), 60% of the population is illiterate, and 80% of the whole population—10,000,000—is living under the poverty line with less than US$2 per day in rural areas, that is, 63% of the population is in very deplorable conditions. According to an IMF report (2011), 54% from these very 80% are living in abject conditions. The rest of the poor population, that is, 14% is living in urban areas. From these 14%, 9% are concentrated in Port-au-Prince where they deal with informal trade activity. By the way, gray income and "remittances" are their unique financial sources. This part of the population has no access to health care, education or training, current water, healthy housing and despite the new elected** government's declarations investment in human capital is still under the line. These persons are living in shantytowns or in sandpits where they have built temporary houses. The gap between urban and rural conditions is a major cause of Haiti's rural–urban migration and is exacerbated by the inequitable distribution of public resources that favors urban areas. As a matter of fact, if one refers to the households poverty perception, still according to the NSLC yet mentioned, in the rural areas, only 13.1% of households estimate they can meet their food

---

* Institut Haïtien pour la Statistique et l'Informatique.
† Growth and Poverty Strategy Reduction (November 2008).
‡ First Annual Report on GPSR Implementation (November 2007).
§ IMF Country Report, 2008—Government of Haiti, First Annual Report on GRSP Implementation, 2009.
¶ Surveys have been realized for years 1986–1987, 1999–2000, 2001.
** March 20, 2011.

needs, 9% assert they can meet their health needs. In the metropolitan area, 33% of the poor households can meet their food needs while 28% of them ensure to reach their health needs. Nonetheless, throughout the country, all the households that have been interviewed confess to reduce their food basket when necessary.

Haiti's poverty is reflected in its social indicators which are substantially lower than those of other countries in the region. Life expectancy is only 57 years compared with an average of 69 years in the rest of CARICOM. The total fertility rate is 4.8% compared with a regional average of 2.8%. Infant mortality is higher than 72 per 1,000 live births, almost twice the regional average. Maternal mortality, at 6 per 1,000, is among the highest in the world. Living conditions are slightly worse in rural than in urban areas. For example, under-five chronic malnutrition is 35% in rural areas, 30% in urban areas outside of Port-au-Prince, and 20% in the Port-au-Prince metropolitan area. Similarly, childhood mortality is 144 deaths per 1,000 live births in rural areas, 135 in urban areas excluding Port-au-Prince, and 131 in Port-au-Prince. In Haiti, poverty driving factors seem to be the same than in the rest of the Caribbean: vulnerable groups, gender, education, income inequality, unemployment, access to basic services, and the place of residence. As mentioned above, in Haiti poverty is monetary first and multidimensional as a consequence. By the way, Figure 19.3 shows that poverty seems to be directly linked with a poor economic growth performance lasting for decades.

Poverty reduction by horizon 2015 has been designed in 2007* through strategies liable to positively affect the growth performance. These anthropocentric strategies are based upon three pillars and they relate to agriculture, tourism, rural development, science and technology. These sectors should be framed within a modified institutional sector that would secure the citizens by improving or implementing the conditions for good governance and the expression of democracy. All conditions required for attracting the FDIs let the local business flourish and make remittances one of the engines of the endogenous growth. The January 2010 earthquake that has destroyed the country's economy has been the opportunity for revisiting the institutional framework and to redesign policies. How to recover and rebuild is contained in at least three documents. The very first one has been conceived yet after the disaster in March 2010.† Poverty is not a particular target in these plans as they all relate to the country's reconstruction and development according to the regions' specificities. Development must be balanced around pillars for growth and employment such as risk management, agriculture, tourism, and access to credit. Nonetheless, a special focus is given upon education, health, and local transportation. Four years after the earthquake, no tangible results can be observed despite new policies designed for the education sector under the state's authority.

Remittances and Poverty; Which Relationship?

Trying to estimate the impact of remittances on poverty reduction is tantamount to estimating the impact of any foreign financial assistance on the endogenous growth in the underdeveloped countries. For some, it matters‡ under certain conditions, while for some others,§ it does not. As defined

---

* Growth and Poverty Reduction Strategy Paper, Government of Haiti (2007).
† Action Plan for National Recovery and Development of Haiti, immediate keys initiative for the future, Government of Haiti, March 2010—Haïti Demain, Objectifs et Stratégies Territoriales, Mars 2010—Plan d'Aménagement du Nord-Nord-Est, Primature d'Haïti, Décembre 2012.
‡ Acemoglu, Johnson, Robinson, *Institutions as a Fundamental Cause of Long-Run Growth*.
§ Dollar 2003, Institutions, Trade and Growth.

by the IMF,* "Personal remittances are the sum of compensation of employees, personal transfers and capital transfers between households." The distribution of this additional income by the recipient-households shows that they go first to food, education's expenditure and then to health, housing, debts reimbursement and savings in line with technical reports. In this way, remittances must be regarded as a mean for survival strategies of the poor and could help in poverty reduction for they contribute to the accumulation of human capital.

For sure, the impact of remittances in addressing poverty has been questioned by both academics[†] and policy makers[‡] according to various scopes: risk management, labor supply or education among others, and channels. Does this financial assistance matter or not either at the macroeconomic or microeconomic level? The answer is controversial. The most recent study driven on the topic related to Latin America and the Caribbean is the one conducted in 2007 by Fajnzylber and Lopez.[§] In their report, the authors found that remittances slightly impacted poverty, and a report from the Multilateral Investment Fund (MIF 2013)[¶] stated that remittances steadily increased in Latin America and the Caribbean growing from US$21.9 billion in 2005 up to US$64.9 billion in 2008. Then, they fall down to US$56.5 billion in 2009 for regular growth again from US$57.6 billion in 2010 to US$61.3 billion in 2012.

Most of the literature that is dedicated to the question analyzes it either within the frame of the neoclassical migration theory** or in the frame of the New Economics of Labor Migration (NELM).[††] On the one hand, the authors thinking that remittances matter at the macroeconomic level think that remittances serve investment through the production factors. That means that the recipients' households would invest in business. On the other hand, the NELM asserts that remittances are a mean for encouraging migration and consequently dry the domestic labor market. In this regard, Thomas-Hope (1986)[‡‡] stated that the propensity to migration in the Caribbean is high and of long-standing, either for financial or social accumulation of capital. Having said that, this scope won't be considered here as it is about to try to identify whether or not remittances participated in reducing poverty in the Caribbean countries. Based upon the technical reports recently published, we will try to answer that question for selected Caribbean countries.

In accordance with a report conducted by the International Migrants Remittances Observatory (IMRO) (2013) for the Haitian government, it is stressed that the World Bank found that 55% of remittances receiving-households do not have any other income than remittances that are essentially dedicated to the cover of the primary needs first and in a lesser extent to debts reimbursement and savings. By the way, still according to AMRO, about 800,000 people receive monthly around US$125 as an average. In its bulletin no 21,[§§] the World Bank has ranked Haiti among the countries in which remittances account more than foreign exchanges reserves, that is, 126% and they equalized 21% as a ratio of GDP in 2012. The remittances from Diaspora to Haiti raised up to US$50 million in 1994, US$100 million in 1995, and US$1.8 billion in 2008. From 2007 to 2012, remittances flows evolved as shown by Figure 19.5 as a ratio of GDP.

---

* Migration and Development Brief, no. 21, October 2013, p. 4.
† Adams and Page (2005); Acosta et al. (2006, 2007).
‡ The International Monetary Fund (IMF), the World Bank, and the UNDP.
§ Close to Home. The Development Impact of Remittances in Latin America.
¶ Remittances to Latin America and the Caribbean in 2012.
** De Hass (2010).
†† Stark and Bloom (1985).
‡‡ Transients and Settlers: Varieties of Caribbean Migrants and the Socio-Economic Implications of Their Return.
§§ Migration and Remittances Flows: Recent Trends and Outlook, 2013–2016.

458 ■ *Public Administration and Policy in the Caribbean*

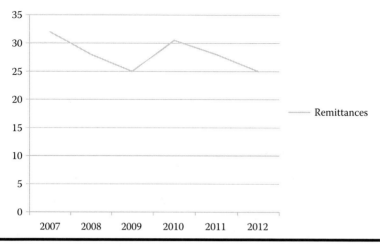

Figure 19.5 The evolution of remittances as a ratio of GDP in Haiti.

Did remittances contribute to poverty reduction in Haiti? The answer is clearly no if we refer to Figure 19.6 comparing the evolution of the poverty rate over the same period of time.

In Jamaica, the remittances flows steadily decreased from 2007 to 2009 evolving from 15.5% to 15% then 14% as a ratio of GDP. From 2010 to 2012, this ratio remained at 13%. In the meanwhile, the poverty rate went on increasing (Figure 19.7).

In the "Jamaica Country Assessment Report" (April 2012, pp. 26–28), it is recognized that it has and is still fighting against poverty through a panel of measures such as construction of communities infrastructures, development of personal skills or employment programs among others. These efforts are reputed result less at a significant level as the country suffers from a lack of coordination among the different programs. By the way, an official representative at the state level that

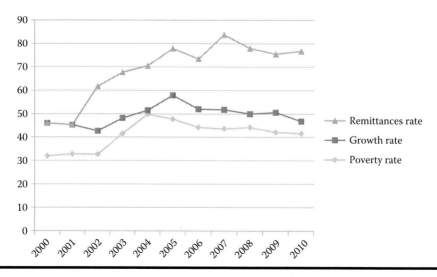

Figure 19.6 Evolution of the growth, poverty, and remittances rate in Haiti.

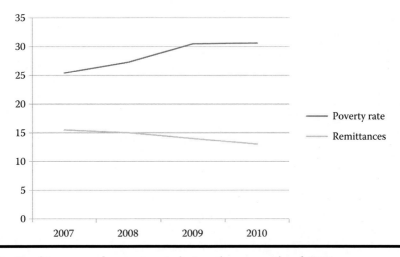

Figure 19.7 Remittances and poverty rate in Jamaica as a ratio of GDP.

would help in a better implementation and follow-up of the different initiatives is one prerequisite suggested by the Planning Institute of Jamaica (2012).*

According to Figures 19.8 and 19.9, remittances do not seem to have positively impacted the poverty rate in the Dominican Republic.

In conclusion to this section, one could say that in except in Haiti, the poverty rate has slightly decreased. This decreasing could be analyzed as a positive impact of remittances as the growth rate remained sluggish and decreasing. If one bears in mind that poverty in Haiti has been analyzed as

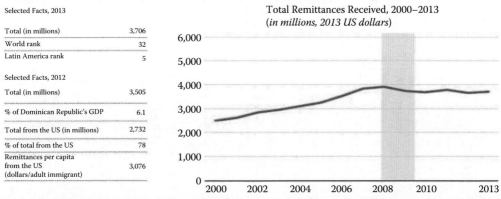

Figure 19.8 The evolution of remittances in the Dominican Republic. (Data from World Bank. Trends, 2013 total, rankings and 2012 share of GDP from 2013 Annual Remittances Data Inflows, Oct. 2013; 2012 totals, US totals and US share from 2012 Bilateral Remittance Matrix; adult immigrant population from Pew Research Center estimates based on 2012 American Community Survey. http://go.worldbank.org/092X1CHHDO.)

---

* Jamaica Country Assessment Preliminary Draft, April 2012.

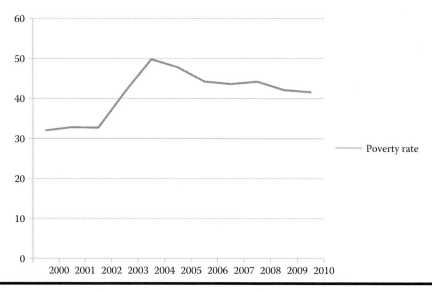

Figure 19.9 Evolution of the poverty rate in the Dominican Republic.

a nonincome poverty, one could think that this additional income to recipients' households helped them in improving their revenue. One must also know that the poor people in Haiti are mainly acting in the gray economy that is also the sector where the self-employed are the most numerous. In some extent, remittances have favored the creation of small businesses.

According to Figure 19.7 in Jamaica, remittances had no impact on the poverty rate as their amount went on steadily decreasing and poverty increased in the meanwhile. Nonetheless, one must remain cautious as for this first photography. The decline in remittances to any recipients' country is due to the global crisis; indeed, Alleyne and Williams (2009)* found that the impact of a modest reduction in remittances will affect first the severity and the gap of poverty rather that the headcount itself. They also recommend that the relation between remittances' reduction and poverty focus toward rural areas in priority.

Despite the improvement of the growth rate in the Dominican Republic, the poverty rate evolved faster than the remittances rate. That is due to the great sensitiveness of the domestic economy to the turmoil of the global environment making the redistribution of income unequal. On the other hand, poverty is concentrated rather in rural areas—more specifically on the Haitian–Dominican boarder—than in urban areas. Subsequently, remittances serve first the development of survival strategies by the recipients.

Public Policies Affecting Poverty in the Caribbean

Before the conduct of the CPAs, the question of poverty reduction was yet at the agenda of the Caribbean governments through a special trust, the Basic Needs Trust Fund (BNTF).† Incepted in 1979, the BNTF implemented programs aiming at reducing poverty at both the national and regional levels by the means of subproject scaled at communities level. From its launching up to

---

* Remittances, Poverty and the Simulation Effects of a Decline in Remittances.
† Participating Countries at BNTF are Belize, Dominica, Grenada, Guyana, Jamaica, Montserrat, St. Kitts and Nevis, St. Lucia, St. Vincent and the Grenadines, the Turks and Caicos Islands.

2013, 2,000 subprojects result-based have been implemented. They mainly relate to schooling and vocational training and health as well which first objective is to facilitate the inclusion of the vulnerable groups into society. Some of these subprojects have been implemented in Barbados, Belize, Dominica, and Montserrat.

Revealed by the NSLC, the results of the studies helped policy makers in the designing of measures targeted upon focal point: skills development, the creation of infrastructure, or the construction of retail markets for Community Markets. According to its Annual Report for 2012 (p. 24), the CDB attested that the CPAs findings informed on the meaning of poverty, the survival strategies developed by communities as the effectiveness of programs. The CPAs also made obvious poverty measurement and development planning as the gaps to be filled in the region for the future.

In the CARICOM area, Poverty Reduction Strategies are funded by the CDB owing its Special Development Fund (SDF). Contributors to the SDF are of course the different Regional Governments as Borrowing Members Countries, non-Borrowing Members,* non-Regional Members,† and the Netherlands as a nonmember. The current SDF has put emphasis on social development, poverty reduction, environmental sustainability, and good governance including programs targeted directly at the poor. According to the Bank information, "the NSRPs provided a broad framework for addressing the causes and characteristics of poverty in the Caribbean, and are consistent with the objectives of the MDGs, which emphasize poverty reduction, human development and environmental sustainability in their multi-dimensional aspects" (Caribbean Development Bank Annual Report 2012). As a consequence, three priorities have been held: "the enhancement of capabilities, the reduction of vulnerability, and good governance."

By the way, in its Annual Report 2011, CDB stressed that most of the NSLC driven in the BMCs have outlined that if the countries have difficulties in reducing poverty they could be partially explained by the weakness of the social protection systems, and inefficiency in the social services delivery. In response, the National Poverty Reduction Strategies recommended that the current social systems be reformed for going toward....

Conclusion

Poverty in the Caribbean has been analyzed according to monetary and nonmonetary criteria. In some countries like Haiti, poverty has been attributed to non-income causes first. In others, poverty has been recognized as been first a multidimensional phenomenon. Deeper insights have been given by CPAs conducted trough NSLC from 1995 to 2009 in at least 12 countries that revealed the extent, depth, and severity of poverty in the Caribbean region and also the feelings of the poor regarding poverty and their survival strategies. As a result, the CPAs led to the design of the NPRS funded by the CDB. The first results of these strategies have been estimated in 2008. Found to poor, the policies have been redesigned and scaled no longer more at the domestic level but at the locality and community levels. These strategies are developed in field such as training, personal skills development, construction of infrastructures for facilitating mobility, and access to education and health. Anyhow, before the conduct of CPAs, poverty alleviation and reduction was yet at the agenda of policy makers in the Caribbean region through the BNTF. By the way, since 1979 and up to 2013, almost 2,000 subprojects result-based have been implemented in some countries.

---

* Colombia, Mexico, and Venezuela.
† Canada, People's Republic of China, France, Germany, Italy, and the United Kingdom.

On the other hand, Caribbean people are long-standing migrants returning home financial aid known as remittances. In most of the cases, remittances represent an additional income dedicated either to survival strategies first and in some extent to the creation of self-employment. Due to the huge amounts of this external financial aid, their impact on the recipient's domestic economy has been analyzed at both the macro- and micro-levels by academics and government's agencies. In this chapter, we made the relation between remittances and poverty reduction in the three countries of Haiti, Jamaica, and the Dominican Republic. As predicted by theory, we found that sometimes it matters, like in Haiti, and sometimes it does not, like in Jamaica and the Dominican Republic. In Haiti, remittances have probably served the creation of self-employment, while in Jamaica and the Dominican Republic, they did not impact poverty. One must say that in these latter, the remittances' flows declined, correlated to the global financial crisis still impacting the countries. Thus, in these cases, remittances served first survival strategies.

At least according to the CPAs for estimating the poverty level in the Caribbean region, four main factors have been identified as its main causes: unemployment, large families and single parenting, lack of education and/or skills, and low pay (Downes 2010). For these reasons, one may say that poverty does not feature special characteristics in the Caribbean.

Bibliography

Acemoglu, D., Johnson, S., and Robinson, J. (2004). *Institutions as a fundamental cause of long-run growth.* Handbook of Economic Growth Vol. 1A, pp. 386–472.
Acosta, P., C. Calderon, P. Fajnzylber, and Lopez, H. (2006). Remittances and development in Latin America. World Economy Vol. 29, pp. 957–987.
Acosta, P.A. (2007). *The impact of remittances on poverty and human capital: Evidence from Latin American households surveys.* Policy Research Working Paper Series 4247, The World Bank.
Adams, Jr, R.H., and Page, R. (2005). Do international migration and remittance reduce poverty in developing countries? World Development Vol. 33, no. 10, pp. 1645–1669. Mars. Elsevier Ltd.
Alleyne, D., and Williams, C. (2009). *Remittances, Poverty and the Simulation Effects of a Decline in Remittances.* Presented at the Annual Review Seminar Research Department Central Bank of Barbados, July 27–30
Baker, J.L. (1997). *Poverty Reduction and Inequality in Latin America and the Caribbean: A Cross-Country Study.* World Bank discussion paper No. WDP 366, The World Bank, Washington, DC.
Blank, R.M. (1997). It takes a nation: A new agenda for fighting poverty. Princeton University Press, Princeton, NJ.
Bradshaw, T.K. (2006). *Theories of Poverty and Anti-Poverty Programs in Community Development.* Working Paper 06-05. Rural Poverty research Center, Oregon, State University.
Cardoso, F.H., and Faletto, E. (1969). *Dependencia y Desarrollo en America Latina*, Siglo XXI, Mexico.
Caribbean Development Bank. (2001). *Strategy for Poverty Reduction in the Borrowing Member Countries of the Caribbean Development Bank*, May 2001.
Caribbean Development Bank. (2003). *Government of the Commonwealth of Dominica.* Country Poverty Assessment. Final Report Volume 2 of 2: Appendices, Dominica.
Caribbean Development Bank. (2004). *Reducing Poverty in the Caribbean and Targeting the Millennium Development Goals an Issues Paper for the Replenishment.* CDB Special Development Fund (Unified).
Caribbean Development Bank. *Caribbean Development Bank Annual Report 2012.* Barbados, March 21, 2013.
Carim–East (Consortium for Applied Research on International Migration). (2013). *Development and Side-Effects of Remittances in the CIS Countries: The Case of the Republic of Moldova.* CARIM-East Report 2013/25.
Deere, C.D. (1992). In the shadows of the sun: Caribbean development alternatives and US policy. *Journal of Economic Literature* Vol. 30, no. 3, pp. 1537–1539.

Deere, C. et al. (1993). *In the Shadows of the Sun: Caribbean Development Alternatives and US Policy*. Derwin S. Munroe, Eds. *NWIG/New West Indian Guide*. Vol. 67, No. 1/2, Brill, Leiden, The Netherlands, pp. 120–132.

Dollar, D., and Kraay, A. (March 2003) *Institutions, Trade and Growth: Revisiting the Evidence*. World Bank Policy Research Working Paper Series No 3004, Washington, DC.

Dos Santos, T., Dependenci y Cambio Social (1970), *Capítulos I, II, III y IV*. Cuadernos de Estudios Socio Económicos, Universidad De Chile, Chile.

Downes, A.S. (September 8–10, 2010). Poverty and its reduction in the small developing countries of the Caribbean. *Prepared for the Conference on Ten Years of War against Poverty*. University of Manchester, UK.

Eastern Caribbean Central Bank. (November 21–22, 2002). Inequality and poverty in the Eastern Caribbean. *Prepared for the Seventh Annual Development Conference*. Mac Donald Thomas, Wint Eleanor. Basseterre, St. Kitts.

ECLAC. (September 2000). *Poverty and Social Integration in the Caribbean*. LC/CAR/G.619, Santiago, Chile.

ECLAC. (2010). *Preliminary Overview of the Economies of the Caribbean*. 2009-2010LC/CAR/252. Striving for productive diversification after the great recession.

ECLAC. (2011). *Latin America and the Caribbean on the Road to Rio+20*. LC/L.3396.

ECLAC and AFD. (December 2012). *Development Paths in the Caribbean*. ECLAC–Project Documents collection—LC/CAR/L.401, United Nations.

Eurostat. (2012). *Measuring Material Deprivation in the EU. Indicators for the Whole Population and Child-Specific Indicators*. Eurostat Methodologies and Working Papers. 2012 Edition. European Commission, Luxembourg.

De Hass, H. (2010). *Migration and Development: A Theoretical Perspective*. International Migration Institute. University of Oxford, Oxford.

Fajnzylber, P., and Lopez, H. (2007). *Close to Home/the Development Impact of Remittances in Latin America*. The World Bank, Washington, DC.

Faria, J.R, and Sanchez-Fung, J.R. (October 2009). *The Economy and the Environment in the Dominican Republic and Haiti: What Explains the Differences?* Kingston University London, UK.

Granvorka, C. (August 2012). *Haiti and the Dominican Republic Two Centuries after Independence, Where Do They Stand?* Salises Conference Uwi Mona, Jamaica.

Granvorka, C. (2013) *General Equilibrium and Plantation Economics l in the Caribbean: The Compared Case of Haiti and the Dominican Republic*.

Haughton, J., and Khandker, S.R. (2009). *Handbook on Poverty and Inequality*. The International Bank for Reconstruction and Development. The World Bank, Washington, DC. 48338.

ILO-IMF Background Paper. (January 2013). *Growth, Employment and Social Cohesion in the Dominican Republic* Geneva, Switzerland.

International Fund for Agricultural Development (IFAD). (March 2002). *IFAD Strategy for Rural Poverty Reduction in Latin American and the Caribbean*. Regional Strategy Paper, Latin America and the Caribbean Division – Programme Management Department. Rome, Italy.

International Monetary Fund. (November 2007). *First Annual Report on GPSR Implementation*, IMF, Washington, DC.

International Monetary Fund. (2008). *Haiti: Poverty Strategy Reduction Paper*. IMF Country Report 08/115, IMF, Washington, DC.

International Monetary Fund. (May 13, 2011). *World Economic and Financial Surveys*. Regional Economic Outlook. Western Hemisphere Time to Rebuilt Policy Space, IMF, Washington, DC.

International Monetary Fund. (2012). *Haiti: Poverty Reduction Strategy Paper—Progress Report*; Country Report No. 12/75, IMF, Washington, DC.

Jadotte, E. (2009). *International Migration, Remittances and Labour Supply: The Case of the Republic of Haiti*. Working Paper no 2009/28. May. UNU-WIDER.

Jamarillo, L., and Sancak, C. (2007) *Why Has the Grass Been Greener on One Side of Hispaniola*. IMF Working Paper No 07/63, Washington, DC.

Laguerre, M.S. (1990). *Urban Poverty in the Caribbean: French Martinique as a Social Laboratory*. Ed. Palgrave Macmillan, Basingstoke.

Lewis, O. (1970). *Anthropological Essays*. Ed. Random House, New York.
Mercado, L. (2012). *Caribbean Human Development Report 2012: Estimating a CARICOM Human Development Index*, UNDP, New York.
Multilateral Investment Fund. (2013). *2012 Remittances to Latin America and the Caribbean*. Washington, DC.
Myrdal, G. (1957). The drift towards inequality in regions, in *Economic Theory and Underdeveloped Regions*. Chapter 3. Transaction Publishers, New Brunswick, NJ.
Paquin, L. (December 1983). *The Haitians: Class and Color Politics*. Lyonel Paquin Publisher, Brooklyn.
Prebisch, R. (1950). *The Economic Development of Latin America and Its Principal Problems* (E/CN.12/89/Rev.1), Lake Success, NY, United Nations. United Nations publication, Sales No. 50.II.G.2.
Prebisch, R. (1951). La Teoría de la Dependencia, CEPAL, Chile.
Quigley, W.P. (2005). Ending poverty as we know it: Guaranteeing a right to a job at a living wage. *Labor Studies Journal* Vol. 29, no. 4, pp. 118–119.
Sen, A. (2000). *Social Exclusion: Concept, Application and Scrutiny*. Social Development Papers no 1. Asian Development Bank, Manila, Philippines.
Shaw, W. (1996). *The Geography of United States Poverty: Patterns of Deprivation 1980–1990*. Taylor & Francis Publisher, Taylor & Francis Publisher, London, UK.
Stark, O., and Bloom, D.E. (May 1985). *The New Economics of Labor Migration in AEA Papers and Proceedings*. pp. 173–178, Pittsburgh, PA.
Stiglitz, J.E. (2002). Gobalization and its discontents. W.W. Norton, New York.
Sunkel, O. (1963). El fracaso de las politicas de estabilización en el contexto del proceso de desarrollo latinoamericano. *El Trimestre Economico* Vol. 30, pp. 62–40.
Thomas-Hope, E. (1986). Transients and settlers: Varieties of Caribbean migrants and the socio economic implications of their return. *International Migration* Vol. 24, pp. 559–570.
UNDP. (2004). *Regional Report on the Achievement of the Millennium Goals in the Caribbean Community*. New York.
United Nations Inter-Agency Group for Child Mortality Estimation. (2012). *Levels and Trends in Child Mortality*. UN Inter-Agency Group for Child Mortality Estimation, New York.
Watts, H.W. (1968). An economic definition of poverty. In D.P. Moynihan (Ed.), *On Understanding Poverty* (pp. 316–329). New York: Basic Book.
Wilson-Forsberg, S., Schönwälder, G., and Robinson, N. (2001). *Addressing Poverty and Inequality in Latin America and the Caribbean: A Social Primer*. Policy Paper. Canadian Foundation for the Americas, Ottawa, Canada.
World Bank. (1995). *Assessing Poverty in the Dominican Republic*. Report no. 13619-DO. Available at: www.caribank.org for all the Country Poverty Assessment of the Caribbean countries.
World Bank. (1998). *Haiti the Challenges of Poverty Reduction*. Volume II: Technical Papers. Report No. 17242-HA, World Bank, Washington, DC.
World Bank. (October 2013). Migration and remittances flows: Recent trends and outlook 2013–2016, in *Migration and Development Brief 21*, World Bank, Washington, DC.
World Bank. (January 2014). *When Prosperity Is Not Shared; The Weak Links between Growth and Equity in the Dominican Republic*, World Bank, Washington, DC.

Index

Note: Locators "*f*" and "*t*" denote figures and tables in the text

A

Acquired immune deficiency syndrome (AIDS), 380
    annual incidence in CAREC member countries (1982–2003), 392*f*
    CAREC member countries, 393*f*
    case by gender, 393*f*
    crude mortality rates, 398*f*
    impact of, 392–394
    prevention and control, 400
Act of Parliament, 186
Administrative Managers, guidelines for, 198
Administrative reform programs, 128–129
Administrative sabotage, 47
Administrivia, 204
African, Caribbean, and Pacific (ACP) community, 173
Afro-Trinidadian, 117
Air Jamaica Acquisition Group (AJAG), 218, 346
Alliance of Small Island States (AOSIS), 239
Allianza Bolivariana para los Pueblos de Nuestra America (ALBA), 174–175
The Anarchical Society, 236
Anglophone Caribbean issues, 231
    lack of developmental and organizational goals, 214
    political directorate and civil service, 214
    small size of Caribbean island, 214
    time perspectives, 214
Anglo-Saxon countries, 180
Antigua and Barbuda
    comparison of e-government index, 373*f*
    disaster office arrangements and resourcing, 325*t*
    e-government rank, 373*f*
    exposure to specific natural hazards, 315*t*
    government expenditures, revenues, and debt, 123*t*
    institutional affiliations and donors, 250*t*
    key indicators, 372*t*
    participation in health reform initiatives, 404*t*
    policy census of national educational reforms, 259*t*
    public service size, 122*t*
    status of national public procurement legislative reforms, 165*t*
Antilliaanse Luchtvaart Maatschappij (ALM) airline, 86
Assimilationist policies, 72

B

Bad budgeting, 148
Bahamas
    comparison of e-government index, 373*f*
    corruption perception index (2013), 18
    disaster office arrangements and resourcing, 325*t*
    e-government rank, 373*f*
    exposure to specific natural hazards, 315*t*
    gender development indicator ranking, 419*t*
    global gender gap index ranking, 424*t*
    government expenditures, revenues, and debt, 123*t*
    institutional affiliations and donors, 250*t*
    key indicators, 372*t*
    participation in health reform initiatives, 404*t*
    policy census of national educational reforms, 259*t*–260*t*
    public service size, 122*t*
    status of national public procurement legislative reforms, 165*t*
Barbados
    affects economy, 189
    corruption perception index (2013), 18
    disaster office arrangements and resourcing, 325*t*
    e-government index, 373*f*
    exposure to specific natural hazards, 315*t*
    gender development indicator ranking, 419*t*
    global gender gap index ranking, 424*t*
    government expenditures, revenues, and debt, 123*t*
    IMP balance of payments support, 188*t*
    institutional affiliations and donors, 251*t*
    key indicators, 372*t*

Barbados (*Continued*)
  National Oil Company, 190
  National Productivity Act, 186
  participation in health reform initiatives, 404*t*
  performance management, 132
  policy census of national educational reforms, 260*t*
  public service size, 122*t*
  social partnership, 135
  status of national public procurement legislative reforms, 165*t*
Barbados National Productivity Act, 186
Barbados Programme of Action, 322
Barbados Shipping and Trading Company Limited (BS&T), 190
Basic Needs Trust Fund (BNTF), 460
Bedrijfsmatige OverheidsNota (BON), 87
Beijing Platform for Action, 432
Belize
  corruption perception index (2013), 18
  disaster office arrangements and resourcing, 325*t*
  exposure to specific natural hazards, 315*t*
  gender development indicator ranking, 419*t*
  government expenditures, revenues, and debt, 123*t*
  IMP balance of payments support, 188*t*
  institutional affiliations and donors, 251*t*
  key indicators, 372*t*
  participation in health reform initiatives, 404*t*
  policy census of national educational reforms, 259*t*, 262*t*
  public service size, 122*t*
  status of national public procurement legislative reforms, 165*t*
Bellerive, Jean-Max, 171
Bissol, Léopold, 64
Black empowerment, 54
Bolsa Familia, 305
Borrowing Member Countries (BMCs), 324, 445
Bowen, Martin, 152
British Caribbean Act (1956), 42
British colonial civil service, 114
British Overseas Territories (BOTs), 3, 35
British political model, 183
British Privy Council, 117
British Virgin Islands (BVI), 150
  policy process, 437
Budgetary Funding System, 98
Budgeting, Caribbean governments and, 298–300
  first-past-the-post or winner-takes-all electoral system, 299
  issues in fiscal capacity of, 298
  pork barrel programmes, 299
  Premchand's identified deficiencies, 299
  public spending, 300

C

Canada Caribbean Disaster Risk Management (CCDRM) Fund, 324
Canada-CARICOM Trade Agreement, 237
Canadian International Development Agency (CIDA), 54, 136
Capacity-building programs, 138
Caquetios Indians, 77
Cardiovascular disease (CVD), 397
Caribbean, 2
  Anglophone, 181
  civil services, 216
  in health reform initiatives, 404*t*
  population pyramid for, 383*f*
  public procurement policy in, 159–177
  regional health service organizations, 401*t*–402*t*
  regional health service reforms, 399*t*–400*t*
Caribbean Catastrophe Risk Insurance Facility (CCRIF)
  donor contributions disaster risk management, 333, 334*t*
  estimated fiscal deficit and payout of, 333, 333*t*
  role of, 332–334
  weakness in policy packages by, 333
Caribbean Centre for Development Administration (CARICAD), 54, 136, 211
Caribbean Commission on Health and Development (CCHD), 403
Caribbean Common Market, 447
Caribbean Community (CARICOM), 22–23, 54, 202, 313, 380, 385, 433, 439, 447
  1994–2002 report, 424–425
  Caribbean islands federated into, 447
  development of member states, 322
  economies of, 176
  established CDERA (1990), 322
  establishment of, 172
  Poverty Reduction Strategies funded by CDB, 461
  report on education, 427–428
  status of national public procurement legislative reforms, 165*t*–166*t*
Caribbean Cooperation in Health (CCH), 23, 380–381, 396
Caribbean Development Bank (CDB), 145, 449
  BMC's at, 324
  methodology, 443, 445
Caribbean Disaster Emergency Management Agency (CDEMA), 322
  governance of, 323
  main functions of, 323
  management and technical advisory committees, 323
Caribbean Disaster Emergency Response Agency (CDERA), 322
  established by CARICOM (1990), 322
  intermediate results (IRs), 322
  leads its PS and regional stakeholders, 322

Caribbean Disaster Management (CADM), 331
Caribbean Electrical Utility Association (CARILEC), 324
Caribbean Environmental Health Institute (CEHI), 405
Caribbean Epidemiology Centre (CAREC), 403, 405
Caribbean Food and Nutrition Institute (CFNI), 403
Caribbean Forum (CARIFORUM), 172–174
Caribbean Group for Cooperation in Economic Development (CGCED) countries, 112
Caribbean Health Research Council (CHRC), 390
Caribbean Hotel Association (CHA), 324
Caribbean Human Development Report, 428–429
Caribbean island
    Caribbean Common Market, 313
    Caribbean Community, 313
    chain, 314
    DRM framework and strategies in, 322–329
        national and donor efforts, 324–329
        regional efforts, 322–324
    eastern boundary of, 314
    economic loss from Hurricane Ivan, 314
    factors contributing to vulnerability of Caribbean states, 319, 320t–321t, 322
    FAO fund for regional project, 324
    federated in CARICOM, 313
    GDP since 1970, 314
    Hurricane Alley, 314
    ITCZ exposes, 313
    mountainous volcanic islands of Eastern, 314
    natural hazards in, 313–322
    risk challenges and successes in, 329–331
        in Barbados, success on pilot site led to replicability, 331
        in Dominican republic, community is aware of risk, 330
        inclusive and proactive approach in Jamaica, 330–331
    SIDS, 313
    topography, 314
Caribbean Leadership Program, 136
Caribbean Pharmaceutical Policy (CPP), 24, 405
Caribbean Policy Research Institute (CaPRI), 220
Caribbean Public Health Agency (CARPHA), 24, 388
Caribbean Regional Drug Testing Laboratory (CRDTL), 23, 405
Caribbean Regional Negotiating Machinery (CRNM), 234
Caribbean Regional Technical Assistance Centre (CARTAC), 151, 157
Caribbean Risk Catastrophe Insurance Fund, 332
Caribbean Single Market and Economy (CSME), 171, 234, 380
CARICAD (Caribbean Centre for Development Administration), 54, 136, 211
CARICOM (Caribbean Community), 22–23, 54, 202, 313, 380, 385, 433, 439, 447
Castro, Raul, 107

Cayman Islands, 15, 38, 122, 150, 157
    economic development from 1960, 438
    gender consultations, 439
    on homosexuality, 437
    households in, 439
    institutional affiliations and donors, 252t
    key indicators, 372t
    migrant laborers, 428
    participation in health reform initiatives, 404t
    population, 439
    women in, 427
Centralized planning, 307
Central treasury management with single treasury account (CTMS/TSA), 154
Centre for Ethnic Studies, 207
CEPEP Company Ltd, 168
Césaire, Aimé, 64–66
Charles, Dame Eugenia, 419
China
    corruption, 304
    economies of, 303
    model of political control, 304
Chinese Academy of Social Sciences, 304
Chirac, Jacques, 66
Chumaceiro, Abraham Mendes, 82
Civil service performance
    colonial legacy, 114–115
    future outlook, 137–138
    leadership, 135–137
    organizational culture and performance, 133–135
    public service commission, 118–121
    public service evolution, 115–118
    recruitment and selection, 126–130
    size of public service, 121–126
    supervisory practices, 130–133
Civil service reform, 193–196, 194t–195t
Clinton, Bill, 170, 171
Code Corporate Governance, 91
Collectivité d'outre-mer (COM), 73
Colonial Life Insurance Company (CLICO), 112
Colonial model, 203
Colonial-Transactional sector, Caribbean expressions of, 206t
Commissie National Herstelplan (Committee on National Recovery), 87
Commissions of Enquiries, 182
Commonwealth Caribbean, 3–5, 35
    colonial period, 35–36
        organization of colonies, 36–38
        slavery and its abolition, 38–40
    current public administration and management issues, 34, 48
        impact of size, 55–56
        migration and public administration, 52–53
        public financial management, 51–52
        public sector reform, 48–51

Commonwealth Caribbean (*Continued*)
    public services, 53–54
        regional and international influences on public administration, 54–55
    societies, 203, 208, 210, 221
Community-based Environmental Protection and Enhancement Programme (CEPEP), 168
Community Disaster Risk Reduction (CDRR) Fund, 329
Comprehensive Disaster Management (CDM), 322
Contemporary *problématique*, 231
Contextual complexity, 205
Contingency, Caribbean expressions of, 206*t*
Convention on the Elimination of All Forms of Discrimination Against Women (CEDAW), 430, 433, 435
Corruption, 17–19
    in China, 304
    perception index (2013), 18
    and public ethics, 45–47
Coterie of Social Workers in Trinidad, 425
Council for Human and Social Development (COHSOD), 22–23, 396
Country Poverty Assessments (CPAs), 445, 449
    components of quantitative and qualitative approach, 450
    objective of, 450
    poverty retained in, 445
Crown Colony system, 40–41, 44
Cuba, 10–11
    acute economic crisis, 102, 105, 107
    comparison of e-government index, 373*f*
    Cuban businesses, 101
    Cuban Management and Planning System, 101
    Cuban Model of Economic Management and Planning, 10, 100
    development challenges, 95
    disaster office arrangements and resourcing, 326*t*
    e-government rank, 373*f*
    exposure to specific natural hazards, 315*t*
    first Congress of Cuba Communist Party, 100
    global gender gap index ranking, 424*t*
    participation in health reform initiatives, 404*t*
    public policy and administrative system, 95
        in pre-revolution period, 96–97
        in socialist period, 97–106
    U.S. dollar use, 104
Cultural complexity, 205
Curaçao, 7, 81
    action group, 88
    civil servants, 88, 90
    Code Corporate Governance, 91
    and dependencies, 82
    encomienda (settlement), 79
    Financial Supervision Authority, 91
    Heeren X, 81
    industrialization policy, 85
    New Public Management Program, 87
    participation in health reform initiatives, 404*t*
    population of, 82–83
    tourism phase, 78, 85
    unemployment, 87
    unproductive civil servants, 8
    West India Company and, 77–79
Cyber Crime Act, 21
Cyber Security Strategy, 21

D

Democracy, good governance, and participation, 215–216
Democratic party (DP), 84
De novo by European imperialism, 231
Départements d'outre mer (DOMs), 6–7, 62
Départements et Régions d'outre-mer (DROMs), 73
De Toekomstconferentie (Futures Conference), 88
Developmental interventions in Caribbean, desirable, 305–309
    capacity to manage change, 309
    centralized planning, 307
    complementarity between public/private goals, 306
    day-to-day management, 307
    effective policies, 305
    embedded autonomy, 306
    issues related to structure of Caribbean economies, 307
    long-term goal, 307
    political patronage, 309
    promoting social development, 305–306
    system of accountability, 307
    technocracies, 308
    use of resources, 309
Developmental state (DS), 19, 295
Developmental state model, reassessing, 300–304
    characteristics, 302
    China's model, 304
    corporatist nature of, 301
    corruption in China, 304
    East Asian developmental state model, 301, 303
    economic bureaucracies, 301
    economic policy objectives, 301
    economies of East Asia, 303
    fundamental tension, 303
    long-term development plan, 300
    Malaysia's policy, 303
    meritocratic systems, 301
    pilot agencies of strategic economics, 300
    political and economic institutions, 302
    public–private cooperation, 301–302
    relative autonomy, 302
    state intervention, 300
    strategic industrial policy, 300–301
    successful developmental states, 300, 302
        characteristics, 302
        planned market augmentation, 300

Western countries, 303
Western-model political system, 304
Disaster Mitigation Facility for the Caribbean (DMFC), 324
Disaster procurement (Haiti), 169–171
Disaster risk management (DRM), 313
    framework and strategies in Caribbean, 322–329
        national and donor efforts, 324–329
        national disaster office arrangements and resourcing, 324, 325*t*–328*t*
        regional efforts, 322–324
    new approach to, 322–323
Disaster risk reduction (DRR) projects, 324
    medium-size grant mechanism, 329
    small-grant mechanism, 324–325, 329
Dispute settlement mechanism (DSM), 238
Dominica
    comparison of e-government index, 373*f*
    corruption perception index (2013), 18
    disaster office arrangements and resourcing, 326*t*
    e-government rank, 373*f*
    exposure to specific natural hazards, 315*t*
    government expenditures, revenues, and debt, 123*t*
    IMP balance of payments support, 188*t*
    institutional affiliations and donors, 253*t*
    key indicators, 372*t*
    participation in health reform initiatives, 404*t*
    policy census of national educational reforms, 263*t*
    political leadership, female empowerment and gender policies, 437–438
    public service size, 122*t*
    status of national public procurement legislative reforms, 165*t*
Dominican Association for Disaster Management, 330
Dominica National Gender Policy, 434–435
Dominican Republic
    estimation of poverty in, 452, 453*t*
    evolution of
        GDP in Haiti and, 451, 452*f*
        poverty rate in, 459, 460*f*
        remittances in, 459, 459*f*
    MDG report (2013), 452
    risk awareness, 330
    Solidaridad program (2008), 452
DRR/CCA (disaster risk reduction and climate change adaptation) projects, 329
Dutch–British company (Shell), 78, 83
Dutch Caribbean, 7–9
    early colonial era
        first period (1634–1688), 79–80
        second period (1648–1791), 80–81
        third period (1795–1914), 81–82
    Indians, 78
    oil era and industrialization (1915–1960), 83–84
    pre-colonial era, 78–79
    slave trade, 80

Dutch East India Company, 80, 155
Dutch Gold Coast, 81
Dutch West India Company, 81

E

East Asian developmental state model, 301, 303
Eastern Caribbean Currency Union (ECCU), 145
Eastern Caribbean Telecommunications Authority, 192–193
Ebola virus, 380, 388
Economic Calculation, 98
Economic Partnership Agreement (EPA), 16, 160, 233, 238, 450
Economic Record System, 98
Economic Recovery Program, 125
Economy and development
    communications, e-government, and cyber policy, 20–21
    developmental interventions, 19
    environmental risk management, 21–22
    tourism policy and management, 20
E-government, 20–21
Electronic public procurement system (e-PPS), 167
El Nino/Southern Oscillation (ENSO), 313
Emergency Operations Centre (EOC), 322, 330
Employee Assistance Programmes, 198
Environmental work areas (EWAs), 168
Equal Opportunities Act of 2000, 436
European Union (EU), 233
Evolution of growth rate in selected countries, 450, 451*f*
Experiences and narratives of public sector leadership, 213–215

F

Financial management and finance ministries, 154–157
First Congress of Cuba Communist Party, 100
First-past-the-post electoral system, 299–300
Fiscal capacity of states, 298
Food and Agricultural Organization (FAO), 324
Foreign Direct Investment (FDI), 451, 456
Fort Amsterdam, 79, 81
Fourth Anglo-Dutch War (1780–1784), 81
French Caribbean, 5–7
    administrative standards, 63
    change in paradigm, 70–75
    crisis in Guadeloupe (2008), 73
    Crown, 62
    Départements d'outre mer (DOMs), 6–7, 62
    departmentalization
        attempts of adaptation and marginal adjustments, 67–69
        centralization and calls for autonomy, 66–67
        key role for French state, 69–70
    first abolition of slavery, 65
    islands into French departments, 69–70

French Caribbean (*Continued*)
  laboratories of institutional engineering, 74–75
  mono-departmental regions, 69
  politico-administrative system, 64–65
  thematic of diversity and turning point of 2003, 70–74
French continental model of governance, 72
French Overseas Programme Law (LOPOM), 70

G

Gender and development (GAD) approach, 417, 427
Gender Development Indicator (GDI), 418
  ranking for selected countries, 419, 419*t*
Gender Empowerment Measure (GEM), 418
  ranking, 420, 420*t*
Gender Inequality Index (GII)
  Caribbean societies in, 422
  of HDR (2013), 422, 423*t*
  reflects women's disadvantage (2013), 427
Gender policies, Caribbean
  gender negotiators for national, 433
  global geopolitics and measurement of gender equality in, 416–425
    measures of gender of human development, 418
    Millennium Development Goals (MDGs), 420
    theoretical approaches to, 417
  goals of, 434–435
  impact of gender and development discourses on national policy formulation, 434–439
    female empowerment and gender policies, 437–438
    homosexuality in, 436
    instrumental role of migrant women in social reproduction, 438–439
    new gender perspectives on human sexuality, 435–437
  influencing formulation of national
    external forces, 430–432, 431*t*
    internal forces, 432–434
  political economy in, 432
  primary areas for gender inequality intervention in, 425–430
    female workers, 429
    sex exploitation, 428–429
General Agreement on Trade in Services (GATS), 238, 395
General chief information officers (GCIO), 221–222
General Consumption Tax, 299
Global climate politics, 230, 239–240
Global environmental politics, 239–240
Global financial crisis, 125
Global Gender Gap Index (GGGI), 26, 422
  2013 rankings, 424, 424*t*
Global geopolitics and measurement of gender equality in, 416–425
  measures of gender of human development, 418
  Millennium Development Goals (MDGs), 420
  theoretical approaches to gender policy-making, 417
Globalization, 186–187, 215
  against for, 297
  typifying includes, 186
Global trade politics, 237–239
The Golden Rock, 81
Government expenditures, revenues, and debt, 123*t*
Government policy, challenges for, 297
Government Procurement Agreement (GPA), 163
Governments and budgeting, 298–300
  first-past-the-post or winner-takes-all electoral system, 299
  issues in fiscal capacity of, 298
  pork barrel programmes, 299
  Premchand's identified deficiencies, 299
  public spending, 300
Grand design (*Groot Desseyn*), 80
Green room politics, 232
Grenada
  comparison of e-government index, 373*f*
  corruption perception index (2013), 18
  disaster office arrangements and resourcing, 326*t*
  e-government rank, 373*f*
  exposure to specific natural hazards, 315*t*
  government expenditures, revenues, and debt, 123*t*
  IMP balance of payments support, 188*t*
  institutional affiliations and donors, 253*t*
  key indicators, 372*t*
  participation in health reform initiatives, 404*t*
  policy census of national educational reforms, 263*t*
  public service size, 122*t*
  revolution, 41, 43
  status of national public procurement legislative reforms, 165*t*
Gross domestic product (GDP), 11, 51, 104, 122, 144, 170, 187, 217, 232, 273, 276, 312, 340, 383
  in 2012, 446
  Bahamas, 313
  of Caribbean since 1970, 314
  Haiti, 313
    and the Dominican Republic, evolution in, 451, 452*f*
    evolution of remittances as ratio in, 457, 458*f*
  remittances and poverty rate in Jamaica, 458, 459*f*
  of St. Vincent and Grenadines (2011), 319
Group of 20 (G20), 232–233
Growth rate in selected countries, evolution of, 450, 451*f*
Guyana
  comparison of e-government index, 373*f*
  cooperative socialist education in, 277
  corruption perception index (2013), 18
  disaster office arrangements and resourcing, 326*t*
  e-government rank, 373*f*
  exposure to specific natural hazards, 315*t*
  gender development indicator ranking, 419*t*
  global gender gap index ranking, 424*t*
  government expenditures, revenues, and debt, 123*t*
  health service organizations, 402*t*
  IMP balance of payments support, 188*t*

institutional affiliations and donors, 250*t*
key indicators, 372*t*
participation in health reform initiatives, 404*t*
policy census of national educational reforms, 263*t*
public service size, 122*t*
public service union, 121
status of national public procurement legislative reforms, 165*t*

H

Haiti, 9–10
    comparison of e-government index, 373*f*
    corruption perception index (2013), 18
    data collection in, 455
    disaster office arrangements and resourcing, 326*t*
    disaster procurement, 169–171
    e-government rank, 373*f*
    evolution of
        GDP in the Dominican Republic and, 451, 452*f*
        growth and poverty rates in, 454, 454*f*
        growth, poverty, and remittances rate in, 458, 458*f*
        remittances as ratio of GDP in, 457, 458*f*
    exposure to specific natural hazards, 315*t*
    government expenditures, revenues, and debt, 123*t*
    IMF report (2011), 455
    IMRO report (2013), 457
    key indicators, 372*t*
    mortality, 456
    participation in health reform initiatives, 404*t*
    policy census of national educational reforms, 263*t*
    poverty, 455–456
    prime minister of, 171
    public service size, 122*t*
    status of national public procurement legislative reforms, 165*t*
Hawkins, John, 39
Health and Family Life Education (HFLE), 391
    establishment of, 396–397
Health expenditure for, 389*f*
Health-related millennium development goals, 390*t*
Health service organizations, 401*t*–402*t*
Health service reforms
    Caribbean regional, 379–407, 399*t*–400*t*
    historical aspects, 381–383
    legal aspects of, 385–390
    reform initiatives, Caribbean nations participation in, 404*t*
    substantive aspects of, 390–391
Health Unit System, 382
Hispaniola island, 330, 451
Hu Jintao, 304
Human Development Indicator (HDI), 418
Human immunodeficiency virus (HIV) infection, 380
    in Caribbean, 406
    crude mortality rates, 398*f*
    Impact of, 392–394

Human resource management (HRM) approach, 126–127, 132
Hurricane Emily (2005), Grenada, 232
Hurricane Georges (1998), Dominican Republic, 330
Hurricane Ivan (2004), Grenada, 232
Hybridization process, 208
Hybrid models, 208

I

IMP balance of payments support, 188*t*
Indo-Trinidadian, 117
Influencing formulation of national gender policies
    external forces, 430–432, 431*t*
    internal forces, 432–434
Information and communication technology (ICT), 13, 49, 193, 214
Institutional complexity, profile of, 209*t*
Instituto Nacional de Reforma Agraria (INRA), 98
Integrated financial management systems (IFMIS), 153
Inter-American Development Bank (IADB), 145, 331, 386
Interim Haiti Recovery Commission (IHRC), 170
International Conference on Improving Public Management and Performance, 112
International environment, 297
International Financial Institutions (IFIs), 145, 160
International Health Regulations (IHRs), 388
International Migrants Remittances Observatory (IMRO), 457
International Monetary Fund (IMF), 8, 49, 87, 125, 145, 187, 212, 217, 455, 457
    Jamaica agreements, 232
International relations (IRs), 230
International Technical Bureaucracies (ITBs), 220
International Whaling Commission, 232
Inter-tropical Convergence Zone (ITCZ), 313

J

Jagan, Cheddi, 419
Jagan, Janet, 419
Jamaica, 48–49, 180, 303
    2008 global economic crisis, 217
    Act of Parliament, 186
    Administrative Reform Programme, 52
    Air Jamaica, 218
    Central Information Technology Office, 221
    civil service reform, 194*t*–195*t*
    commissions established (1960s–1980s), 184*t*
    Commodities Trading Corporation, 190
    comparison of e-government index, 373*f*
    corruption perception index (2013), 18
    creation of executive agencies, 216
    Cyber Crime Act in 2010, 21
    debt increased, 217
    democratic socialist education, 278
    early 1970s strongest economy, 303

Jamaica (*Continued*)
  exposure to specific natural hazards, 315*t*
  gender development indicator ranking, 419*t*
  gender inequality index of HRD (2013), 423*t*
  global gender gap index ranking, 424*t*
  government expenditures, revenues, and debt, 123*t*
  growth rate evolution, 451*f*
  health service organizations, 401*t*
  higher literacy rates for women, 418
  IMF agreements, 232
  IMP balance of payments support, 188*t*
  inclusive and proactive approach, 330–331
  JAMAL foundation, 278
  National Commercial Bank (NCB), 190–191
  national disaster office arrangements and resourcing, 327*t*
  nationalist health service reform, 391*f*
  new IMF agreement, 198
  NPM-style reforms, 13–14
  participation in health reform initiatives, 404*t*
  policy
    census of national educational reforms, 263*t*–264*t*
    and management of communications industry, 367–368
  poverty headcounts, 449*f*
  privatization program, 191, 191*t*
  public service size, 122*t*
  public service wage bill, 124*t*
  Registrar General's Department (RGD), 46
  remittances and poverty rate, 458, 459*f*
  status of national public procurement legislative reforms, 165*t*
  Urban Transport Company, 198
  Women's Liberal Club, 426
  Women's Social Service Club, 425
Jamaica Country Assessment Report, 458
Jamaica National Gender Policy (2011), 431
Jamaican law, 220
Jamaican Movement for the Advancement of Literacy (JAMAL) Foundation, 278
Japan
  corporatist nature of, 301
  economic dynamism as competition, 301
  economies of, 303
  technostructures, 308
Jeffers, Audrey, 425–427
Judicial and legal service commissions (JLSCs), 118–119, 126

K

Korean War (1950–1952), 96

L

Lago company, 78, 83, 86
Laissez-faire approach, 20, 38, 204

Landsverordening Overheidsorganisatie Land Netherlandse Antillen (LOL), 88
Leadership
  Air Jamaica, 218
  Caribbean problems, 210
  in civil service performance, 135–137
  context-specific leadership skills and orientations, 217*t*
  definition, 202
  development programs, 212
  in Dominica, political, 437–438
  emerging culture, 211
  and management development programs, 135
  problems
    collaborative/collective/networked governance styles, 210
    delivery of public goods, 210
    experience, 210–212
    regional, 210
    weak competencies, 210
  public sector domain, 202
  public sector transformation, 212
  requirements for good, 219
  strengthening capabilities, 211–212
  systems, 211
  twenty-first century, challenges, 216–222
    capabilities/competencies, building, 222
    industrial relations, 219–220
    policy framework, 221–222
    process of transformation agenda, 220–221
    scarcity and demanding clientele, 217–219
    strengthening leadership capabilities, 211–212
  World Leadership Survey, 222
Leeward Islands, 36, 77, 80
Lewis, Arthur, 121
Life expectancy, 387*t*
Limited state capacity, 231, 233
Liquefied natural gas (LNG), 167
Lyannj Kont Pwofitayon (LKP), 73

M

Malaysia's policy, 303
Management Institute for National Development (MIND), 219
Manley, Michael, 43
Marginalization of the Black Male (Book), 421
Marson, Una, 426
Martinique, 73–75
Medium Term Expenditure Framework, 152
Men at Risk (Book), 421
Meritocratic systems, Singapore, 301
Micro, small and medium enterprises (MSMEs), 168
Middle-class administrative leadership, 207
Migration management, 53
Ministerio de Salud Publica (MINSAP), 386
Ministries of finance, 154–156

Mixed economy model, 296
Modern treasury management, 151
Monnerville, Gaston, 64
Montserrat
    institutional affiliations and donors, 250*t*
    participation in health reform initiatives, 404*t*
    policy census of national educational reforms, 264*t*
    status of national public procurement legislative reforms, 165*t*
Morne Rouge, 67
Moyne Commission, 42
Multilateral Investment Fund (MIF), 457

N

National Institute of Agrarian Reform, 98
National mission, 309
National policy formulation, impact of gender and development discourses on, 434–439
    female empowerment and gender policies, 437–438
    homosexuality in, 436
    instrumental role of migrant women in social reproduction, 438–439
    new gender perspectives on human sexuality, 435–437
National policy system, 203–204
National Poverty Reduction Strategy (NPRS), 446
National Social Development Programme (NSDP), 168
Natural hazards
    analysis of country-level exposure to specific, 314, 315*t*–316*t*
    in Caribbean islands, 313–322
    insurance payouts since CCRIF inception (2007), 332–333
    St. Vincent and the Grenadines
        incidents reported in Vincentian Newspaper, 318, 318*t*–319*t*
        storm damage in five sectors of, 314, 317*f*
Neo-colonialism, 189
Neo-feudal system, 80
Netherlands, 9
    patroonship, 80
    Peace of Munster, 80
    solidarity fund (*Solidariteitsfonds*), 86
Networked governance, 203, 210
New Economics of Labor Migration (NELM), 457
New Public Administration movement, 204
New public leadership (NPL), 203
New public management (NPM), 49, 112
    movement, 216
    program, 87
    reforms, 197
New West India Company, 81
Noncommunicable diseases (NCDs), 381
    chronic, 400
    focus on, 397–398
    new-mutualism, 406

Nongovernmental organizations (NGOs), 170, 385
Northcote Trevelyan Report (1854), 114

O

Office of the Contractor General (OCG), 45
Oil era
    after, 84–87
        crisis and consultation (1990s), 87–89
        radicalization (2000s), 89–90
        rebellion (1960s), 84–85
        rebuilding (1970s), 85
        restructuring (1980s), 85–87
    and industrialization (1915–1960), 83–84
Organisational foolishness, 202
Organisation for Economic Co-operation and Development (OECD) countries, 296, 387
Organizational logics, 208
Organization and Management Division, 186
Organization of Eastern Caribbean States (OECS), 118–120, 160, 166–167, 234–235, 405, 447
    ECTEL's Treaty, 366
    GDP, 123
    ICT policy, 365
    islands involved in, 448
    member countries, 121
    poverty gap ratio, 445–446
    telecommunications liberalization, 192–193
Organization of petroleum exporting countries (OPEC), 187
Orientation law for the overseas department (LOOM), 70

P

Pan American Health Organization (PAHO), 380, 403
Pan-Caribbean Disaster Preparedness and Prevention Project, 322
Paradigm change (French Caribbean), 70–75
Patroonship, 80
Peace of Munster, 80
People's National Movement, 192
Performance Review and Development System, 132
Personal Protective Equipment (PPE), 388
Personnel Department and Service Commissions Department, 133
Petroleum Company of Trinidad and Tobago Ltd. (PETROTRIN), 192
Planned market augmentation, 300
Police service commissions (PolSCs), 118, 126
Policy formulation process, 432
Policy of Antillianization (*Antillianisering*), 85
Political economy in, 432
Political leadership, 137
Political terrorism, 47
Politico-administrative leaders, 56
Politico-administrative model, 63
Politico-administrative nexus, 47–48

Population pyramid for Caribbean (2010), 383f
Pork barrel programmes, 299
Post-Bureaucratic and Networked sector, Caribbean expressions of, 206t–207t
Post-Keynesians economics, 296–297
Post-modern administrative models, 205
Post-war period, 296, 306
Poverty
   in Caribbean
      determinants and characteristics of, 447–456
      estimation, 452
      Haitian case, 455–456
      headcounts, 449, 449f
      insights in Dominican Republic and Haiti, 451–455
      public policies affecting, 460–461
      remittances and, 456–460
      UNICEF report (2012), 450
   theories for explaining, 446–447
Primary areas for gender inequality intervention, 425–430
   female workers, 429
   sex exploitation, 428–429
Primary health service, 380
Privatization experience, 189–193
Proactive state policy, 309
Public administration
   and governance, 2
      in Commonwealth Caribbean, 3–5
      in Dutch Caribbean, 7–9
      in French Caribbean, 5–7
      ongoing and emerging challenges, 56
      in other parts of Caribbean, 9–11
      post-independence period, 43–44
      pre-independence period, 40–43
   model, 204
   system, 203, 213
Public finance programs, 298
Public financial management (PFM), 6, 51–52, 146–148
   Browne's coverage, 15
   common challenges, 148–150
   decision makers and, 148–149
   donor support, 149
   installing automation, 148–149
   and procurement policy, 14–17
   resources to fund, 148
   staged approach
      financial discipline, 150–152
      gaining operational efficiency, 153–154
      improving effectiveness of fund allocations, 152–153
   strategy, 155
   tools of budget, 143–144, 147
Public health sector reform, 384
Public institutions and national strategic plans, 113
Public management reforms, 197
Public–private partnerships, 213

Public Procurement & Disposal of Property (PP&DP) Act, 169
Public sector leadership, 203
Public sector organizations (PSOs), 134–135
Public sector reform (PSR), 12–14, 48, 114
   1960s–1980s, 181–186
   1980s–2000, 186–189
   2000–2013, 198–199
Public Service Act 2007, 127
Public service commissions (PSCs), 114, 183, 207
Public service modernization (PSM), 114
Public service size, 122t
Public service wage bill, 124t
Purchasing Power Parity (PPP), 455

R

Rajan, Raghuram, 296
Regional community
   benchmarking best, 223
   new patterns of leadership formation and habits, 223
   paper qualifications, 224
   talent management, 223
Registrar General's Department (RGD), 46
Remittance income, 146
Results-informed budget, 152
Revised Treaty of Chaguaramas, 234

S

Second Chartered West India Company, 81
Sen, Amartya, 421
Settler's spirit, 12
Singapore, meritocratic systems, 301
Sistema de Dirección y Planificación de la Economía (SDPE), 100
Sistema National de Salud, 386
Slavery and its abolition, 38–40
Slaves for freedom, 82
Slave trade, 80
Small island developing states (SIDS), 231–232, 313
Social capitalist model, 296
Social development, 305
Social policies
   education, 22–23
   health, 23–24
   migration and diasporas, 24–25
   race, class, and gender, 25–26
Social programs, 305
Solidaridad program (2008), 452
Solidarity fund (*Solidariteitsfonds*), 86
South Korea
   corporatist nature of, 301
   extreme disparity, 303
Special Development Fund (SDF), 461
State structures, 305

Status of national public procurement legislative reforms, 165t
Statutory board service commission (SBSC), 118
St. Kitts & Nevis
  comparison of e-government index, 373f
  disaster office arrangements and resourcing, 327t
  e-government rank, 373f
  exposure to specific natural hazards, 315t
  participation in health reform initiatives, 404t
  policy census of national educational reforms, 265t
  status of national public procurement legislative reforms, 165t
St. Lucia
  comparison of e-government index, 373f
  corruption perception index (2013), 18
  disaster office arrangements and resourcing, 327t
  e-government rank, 373f
  exposure to specific natural hazards, 315t
  government expenditures, revenues, and debt, 123t
  health service organizations, 401t
  institutional affiliations and donors, 250t
  key indicators, 372t
  participation in health reform initiatives, 404t
  policy census of national educational reforms, 265t
  public service size, 122t
  status of national public procurement legislative reforms, 165t
Strategic human resource management, 308–309
Strategic industrial policy, 300–301
Structural Adjustment Program (SAP), 8, 49, 78, 87, 124, 187, 190
Stuyvesant, Peter, 80
St. Vincent and the Grenadines, 186, 192–193, 196, 198
  comparison of e-government index, 373f
  corruption perception index (2013), 18
  disaster office arrangements and resourcing, 327t
  e-government rank, 373f
  exposure to specific natural hazards, 316t
  GDP in 2011, 319
  government expenditures, revenues, and debt, 123t
  institutional affiliations and donors, 250t
  natural hazard incidents in Vincentian Newspaper, 318, 318t–319t
  participation in health reform initiatives, 404t
  policy census of national educational reforms, 265t
  public service size, 122t
  status of national public procurement legislative reforms, 165t
  storm damage in five sectors of, 314, 317f
Suriname
  comparison of e-government index, 373f
  disaster office arrangements and resourcing, 327t
  e-government rank, 373f
  exposure to specific natural hazards, 316t
  global gender gap index ranking, 424t
  participation in health reform initiatives, 404t
Sustainable Development Goals (SDGs), 380

T

Talent management, 217t, 219
Tax collection, 51
Teaching service commissions (TSCs), 118, 126
Technical and Vocational Education and Training (TVET), 23
Terres Australes et Antarctiques Françaisees (TAFF), 73
Territoires d'outre-mer (TOMs), 73
Transformational sector, Caribbean expressions of, 206t
Transparency International's Corruption Perception Index (2013), 17, 18f
Treasury single account (TSA), 153
Trinidad and Tobago (T&T), 207, 233
  back agenda, 197
  comparison of e-government index, 373f
  corruption perception index (2013), 18
  disaster office arrangements and resourcing, 327t
  e-government rank, 373f
  exposure to specific natural hazards, 316t
  gender development indicator ranking, 419t
  global gender gap index ranking, 424t
  government expenditures, revenues, and debt, 123t
  health service organizations, 401t–402t
  HRM system, 132
  IMP balance of payments support, 188t
  institutional affiliations and donors, 250t
  key indicators, 372t
  oil-producing economy, 187
  participation in health reform initiatives, 404t
  Petroleum Company of Trinidad and Tobago Ltd. (PETROTRIN), 192
  policy census of national educational reforms, 266t
  public services association, 121
  public service size, 122t
  status of national public procurement legislative reforms, 165t
  TELCO, 192
  unemployment rate, 187
Twenty-first century leadership challenges
  industrial relations, 219–220
  policy framework, 221–222
  process of transformation agenda, 220–221
  scarcity and demanding clientele, 217–219
  strengthening leadership capabilities, 211–212

U

Unemployment Relief Programme (URP), 168
Unidades Básicas de Producción Cooperativas (UBPC), 105
United Kingdom, 360
  Commonwealth Caribbean with, 3–4, 35
  gender development indicator ranking, 419t
  gender empowerment measure ranking, 420t

United Kingdom (*Continued*)
  neoclassical economic reforms, 273
  NPM movement, 216
  public administrations in post-independence period, 43
  welfare programs in, 305–306
  WW system, 44
United Nations Children's Fund (UNICEF), 396
United Nations Convention against Corruption, 18
United Nations Development Fund for Women (UNIFEM), 396, 416
United Nations Development Programme (UNDP), 396, 416
United Nations Educational, Scientific and Cultural Organization (UNESCO), 396
United Nations Fund for Population Activities (UNFPA), 396
United Nations (UN) General Assembly, 232
United Nations Human Development Report (HDR), 417–418
  2000, 421
  2013, 422
United Nations International Drug Control Program (UNDCP), 396
United States Agency for International Development (USAID), 54
University of the West Indies (UWI) system, 23

V

Venezuelan oil loans, 146
Vereenigde Oost-Indische Compagnie (VOC), 80
Voluntary Separation Employment Program (VSEP), 126

W

Weberian-type principles, 203
Western-model political system, 304
West India Company (WIC), 79–81
West Indies Federation, 234
West Indies School of Public Health, 382
Westminster model, 231
West Minster–White Hall model, 181
Westminster-Whitehall (WW) system, 4–5, 34, 44–45, 115
Wiels, Helmin, 92
Winner-takes-all electoral system, 299–300
Women in Development (WID) approach, 417, 427
World Bank, 384–386
World economy, 296
World Health Organization (WHO), 380
World Leadership Survey, 222
World Trade Organization (WTO), 160, 232, 395
World Trade Organization's Agreement on Government Procurement (WTO-GPA) rules, 16